The Holy Quran
English Meanings

Translated by

Emily Assami, Amatullah Bantley & Mary Kennedy

Saheeh International

موسوعة القرآن الكريم

The Noble Quran Encyclopedia

The Noble Quran Encyclopedia
2021 CE – 1443 AH

The Noble Quran Encyclopedia is an effort towards providing reliable translations and Exegesis of the Quran in various Languages. The project is managed and run by IslamHouse a subsidiary of the Islamic Dawah Office in Rabwah, Riyadh, KSA.

The Project currently hosts multiple translations in various widely spoken languages including English, French, Spanish, German, Turkish, Bosnian, Vietnamese, Uzbek, Tajik, Amharic, Hausa, Hindi, Urdu among others. Several other languages are currently being translated including Chinese, Bulgarian, Russian and Korean.

Contents

Surah Al-Fatihah

(1) In the name of Allāh,[1] the Entirely Merciful, the Especially Merciful.[2]

(2) [All] praise is [due] to Allāh, Lord[3] of the worlds -

(3) The Entirely Merciful, the Especially Merciful,

(4) Sovereign of the Day of Recompense.[4]

(5) It is You we worship and You we ask for help.

(6) Guide us to the straight path -

(7) The path of those upon whom You have bestowed favor, not of those who have earned [Your] anger or of those who are astray.

---

[1] "Allāh is a proper name belonging only to the one Almighty God, Creator and Sustainer of the heavens and the earth and all that is within them, the Eternal and Absolute, to whom alone all worship is due.

[2] Ar-Raḥmān and ar-Raḥeem are two names of Allāh derived from the word ""raḥmah"" (mercy). In Arabic grammar both are intensive forms of ""merciful"" (i.e., extremely merciful). A complimentary and comprehensive meaning is intended by using both together. Raḥmān is used only to describe Allāh, while raḥeem might be used to describe a person as well. The Prophet (ﷺ) was described in the Qur'ān as raḥeem. Raḥmān is above the human level (i.e., intensely merciful). Since one usually understands intensity to be something of short duration, Allāh describes Himself also as raḥeem (i.e., continually merciful). Raḥmān also carries a wider meaning - merciful to all creation. Justice is a part of this mercy. Raḥeem includes the concept of speciality - especially and specifically merciful to the believers. Forgiveness is a part of this mercy. In addition, Raḥmān is adjectival, referring to an attribute of Allāh and is part of His essence. Raḥeem is verbal, indicating what He does: i.e., bestowing and implementing mercy."

[3] When referring to Allāh (subḥānahu wa ta'ālā) , the Arabic term "rabb" (translated as "Lord") includes all of the following meanings: "owner, master, ruler, controller, sustainer, provider, guardian and caretaker."

[4] i.e., repayment and compensation for whatever was earned of good or evil during life on this earth.

Surah Al-Baqarah

(1) Alif, Lām, Meem.[5]

(2) This is the Book about which there is no doubt, a guidance for those conscious of Allāh[6] -

(3) Who believe in the unseen, establish prayer,[7] and spend out of what We[8] have provided for them,

(4) And who believe in what has been revealed to you, [O Muḥammad], and what was revealed before you, and of the Hereafter they are certain [in faith].

(5) Those are upon [right] guidance from their Lord, and it is those who are the successful.

(6) Indeed, those who disbelieve[9] - it is all the same for them whether you warn them or do not warn them - they will not believe.

(7) Allāh has set a seal upon their hearts and upon their hearing, and over their vision is a veil.[10] And for them is a great punishment.

(8) And of the people are some who say, "We believe in Allāh and the Last Day," but they are not believers.

(9) They [think to] deceive Allāh and those who believe, but they deceive not except themselves and perceive [it] not.

---

[5] These are among the fourteen opening letters which occur in various combinations at the beginning of twenty-nine sūrahs in the Qur'ān. Although there has been much speculation as to their meaning, it was not, in fact, revealed by Allāh to anyone and is known only to Him.

[6] Literally, "those who have taqwā," i.e., who have piety, righteousness, fear and love of Allāh, and who take great care to avoid His displeasure.

[7] "At its proper times and according to its specified conditions.

[8] It is to be noted that the reference of Allāh (Subḥānahu wa ta'ālā) to Himself as "We" in many Qur'ānic verses is necessarily understood in the Arabic language to denote grandeur and power, as opposed to the more intimate singular form "I" used in specific instances."

[9] Literally, "cover" or "conceal" (faith or truth).

[10] A covering preventing them from discerning guidance. This condition is a direct result of their arrogance and persistence in sin.

(10) In their hearts is disease, so Allāh has increased their disease;[11] and for them is a painful punishment because they [habitually] used to lie.

(11) And when it is said to them, "Do not cause corruption on the earth," they say, "We are but reformers."

(12) Unquestionably, it is they who are the corrupters, but they perceive [it] not.

(13) And when it is said to them, "Believe as the people have believed," they say, "Should we believe as the foolish have believed?" Unquestionably, it is they who are the foolish, but they know [it] not.

(14) And when they meet those who believe, they say, "We believe"; but when they are alone with their evil ones, they say, "Indeed, we are with you; we were only mockers."

(15) [But] Allāh mocks them and prolongs them in their transgression [while] they wander blindly.

(16) Those are the ones who have purchased error [in exchange] for guidance, so their transaction has brought no profit, nor were they guided.

(17) Their example is that of one who kindled a fire, but when it illuminated what was around him, Allāh took away their light and left them in darkness [so] they could not see.

(18) Deaf, dumb and blind - so they will not return [to the right path].

(19) Or [it is] like a rainstorm from the sky within which is darkness, thunder and lightning. They put their fingers in their ears against the thunderclaps in dread of death. But Allāh is encompassing[12] of the disbelievers.

(20) The lightning almost snatches away their sight. Every time it lights [the way] for them, they walk therein; but when darkness comes over them, they stand [still].

---

[11] The "disease" mentioned here includes doubt, hypocrisy, arrogance and disbelief.

[12] Allāh states in the Qur'ān that He has certain attributes such as hearing, sight, hands, face, mercy, anger, coming, encompassing, being above the Throne, etc. Yet, He has disassociated Himself from the limitations of human attributes or human imagination. Correct Islāmic belief requires faith in the existence of these attributes as Allāh has described them without applying to them any allegorical meanings or attempting to explain how a certain quality could be (while this is known only to Allāh) and without comparing them to creation or denying that He (subḥānahu wa ta'ālā) would have such a quality. His attributes are befitting to Him alone, and "There is nothing like unto Him." (42:11)

And if Allāh had willed, He could have taken away their hearing and their sight. Indeed, Allāh is over all things competent.

(21) O mankind, worship your Lord, who created you and those before you, that you may become righteous -

(22) [He] who made for you the earth a bed [spread out] and the sky a ceiling and sent down from the sky, rain and brought forth thereby fruits as provision for you. So do not attribute to Allāh equals while you know [that there is nothing similar to Him].

(23) And if you are in doubt about what We have sent down [i.e., the Qur'ān] upon Our Servant [i.e., Prophet Muḥammad (ﷺ)], then produce a sūrah the like thereof and call upon your witnesses [i.e., supporters] other than Allāh, if you should be truthful.

(24) But if you do not - and you will never be able to - then fear the Fire, whose fuel is people and stones, prepared for the disbelievers.

(25) And give good tidings to those who believe and do righteous deeds that they will have gardens [in Paradise] beneath which rivers flow. Whenever they are provided with a provision of fruit therefrom, they will say, "This is what we were provided with before." And it is given to them in likeness. And they will have therein purified spouses, and they will abide therein eternally.

(26) Indeed, Allāh is not timid to present an example - that of a mosquito or what is smaller[13] than it. And those who have believed know that it is the truth from their Lord. But as for those who disbelieve, they say, "What did Allāh intend by this as an example?" He misleads many thereby and guides many thereby. And He misleads not except the defiantly disobedient,

(27) Who break the covenant of Allāh after contracting it and sever that which Allāh has ordered to be joined and cause corruption on earth. It is those who are the losers.

(28) How can you disbelieve in Allāh when you were lifeless and He brought you to life; then He will cause you to die, then He will bring you [back] to life, and then to Him you will be returned.

---

[13] Literally, "above it," i.e., greater in smallness.

(29) It is He who created for you all of that which is on the earth. Then He directed Himself[14] to the heaven, [His being above all creation], and made them seven heavens, and He is Knowing of all things.

(30) And [mention, O Muḥammad], when your Lord said to the angels, "Indeed, I will make upon the earth a successive authority."[15] They said, "Will You place upon it one who causes corruption therein and sheds blood, while we exalt You with praise and declare Your perfection?"[16] He [Allāh] said, "Indeed, I know that which you do not know."

(31) And He taught Adam the names - all of them. Then He showed them to the angels and said, "Inform Me of the names of these, if you are truthful."

(32) They said, "Exalted are You; we have no knowledge except what You have taught us. Indeed, it is You who is the Knowing,[17] the Wise."[18]

(33) He said, "O Adam, inform them of their names." And when he had informed them of their names, He said, "Did I not tell you that I know the unseen [aspects] of the heavens and the earth? And I know what you reveal and what you have concealed."

(34) And [mention] when We said to the angels, "Prostrate before Adam"; so they prostrated, except for Iblees.[19] He refused and was arrogant and became of the disbelievers.

(35) And We said, "O Adam, dwell, you and your wife, in Paradise and eat therefrom in [ease and] abundance from wherever you will. But do not approach this tree, lest you be among the wrongdoers."

(36) But Satan caused them to slip out of it and removed them from that [condition] in which they had been. And We said, "Go down, [all of you], as enemies to one

---

[14] See footnote to 2:19

[15] "Khalīfah: successor, or generations of man, one following another.

[16] An additional meaning is "...and we purify ourselves for You."

[17] "Whose eternal and absolute knowledge encompasses the truth and essence of all things, seen or unseen, present or absent, neither preceded by ignorance nor followed by forgetfulness.

[18] Whose wisdom includes precise and perfect knowledge of all realities and outcomes, according to which He decrees and causes various circumstances and occurrences."

[19] The proper name of Satan, who was not an angel but from the jinn, as stated in 18:50. Done in obedience to Allāh, this prostration was one of respect, not worship.

another, and you will have upon the earth a place of settlement and provision for a time."

(37) Then Adam received from his Lord [some] words,[20] and He accepted his repentance. Indeed, it is He who is the Accepting of Repentance,[21] the Merciful.

(38) We said, "Go down from it, all of you. And when guidance comes to you from Me, whoever follows My guidance - there will be no fear concerning them, nor will they grieve.

(39) And those who disbelieve and deny Our signs - those will be companions of the Fire; they will abide therein eternally."

(40) O Children of Israel, remember My favor which I have bestowed upon you and fulfill My covenant [upon you] that I will fulfill your covenant [from Me], and be afraid of [only] Me.

(41) And believe in what I have sent down confirming that which is [already] with you, and be not the first to disbelieve in it. And do not exchange My signs for a small price, and fear [only] Me.

(42) And do not mix the truth with falsehood or conceal the truth while you know [it].

(43) And establish prayer and give zakāh[22] and bow with those who bow [in worship and obedience].

(44) Do you order righteousness of the people and forget[23] yourselves while you recite the Scripture? Then will you not reason?

(45) And seek help through patience and prayer; and indeed, it is difficult except for the humbly submissive [to Allāh]

(46) Who are certain that they will meet their Lord and that they will return to Him.

(47) O Children of Israel, remember My favor that I have bestowed upon you and that I preferred you over the worlds [i.e., peoples].

---

[20] "Allāh taught Adam words of repentance that would be acceptable to Him.

[21] Literally, He who perpetually returns, i.e., reminding and enabling His servant to repent from sins and then forgiving him. Thus, He is also the constant motivator of the repentance He accepts."

[22] An annual expenditure for the benefit of the Islāmic community (see 9:60) required of those Muslims who have excess wealth. Prayer and zakāh are among the pillars of Islām.

[23] Make exceptions of.

(48) And fear a Day when no soul will suffice for another soul[24] at all, nor will intercession be accepted from it, nor will compensation be taken from it, nor will they be aided.

(49) And [recall] when We saved you [i.e., your forefathers] from the people of Pharaoh, who afflicted you with the worst torment, slaughtering your [newborn] sons and keeping your females alive. And in that was a great trial from your Lord.

(50) And [recall] when We parted the sea for you and saved you and drowned the people of Pharaoh while you were looking on.

(51) And [recall] when We made an appointment with Moses for forty nights. Then you took [for worship] the calf after him [i.e., his departure], while you were wrongdoers.

(52) Then We forgave you after that so perhaps you would be grateful.

(53) And [recall] when We gave Moses the Scripture and criterion[25] that perhaps you would be guided.

(54) And [recall] when Moses said to his people, "O my people, indeed you have wronged yourselves by your taking of the calf [for worship]. So repent to your Creator and kill yourselves [i.e., the guilty among you]. That is best for [all of] you in the sight of your Creator." Then He accepted your repentance; indeed, He is the Accepting of Repentance, the Merciful.

(55) And [recall] when you said, "O Moses, we will never believe you until we see Allāh outright"; so the thunderbolt took you while you were looking on.

(56) Then We revived you after your death that perhaps you would be grateful.

(57) And We shaded you with clouds and sent down to you manna and quails, [saying], "Eat from the good things with which We have provided you." And they wronged Us not - but they were [only] wronging themselves.

(58) And [recall] when We said, "Enter this city [i.e., Jerusalem] and eat from it wherever you will in [ease and] abundance, and enter the gate bowing humbly[26] and say, 'Relieve us of our burdens [i.e., sins].' We will [then] forgive your sins for you, and We will increase the doers of good [in goodness and reward]."

---

[24] i.e., fulfill what is due from it.

[25] Differentiating between truth and falsehood. "The Scripture and criterion" refers to the Torah.

[26] In gratitude to Allāh and admission of sin.

(59) But those who wronged changed [those words] to a statement other than that which had been said to them, so We sent down upon those who wronged a punishment [i.e., plague] from the sky because they were defiantly disobeying.

(60) And [recall] when Moses prayed for water for his people, so We said, "Strike with your staff the stone." And there gushed forth from it twelve springs, and every people [i.e., tribe] knew its watering place. "Eat and drink from the provision of Allāh, and do not commit abuse on the earth, spreading corruption."

(61) And [recall] when you said, "O Moses, we can never endure one [kind of] food. So call upon your Lord to bring forth for us from the earth its green herbs and its cucumbers and its garlic and its lentils and its onions." [Moses] said, "Would you exchange what is better for what is less? Go into [any] settlement and indeed, you will have what you have asked." And they were covered with humiliation and poverty and returned with anger from Allāh [upon them]. That was because they [repeatedly] disbelieved in the signs of Allāh and killed the prophets without right. That was because they disobeyed and were [habitually] transgressing.

(62) Indeed, those who believed and those who were Jews or Christians or Sabeans [before Prophet Muḥammad (ﷺ)] - those [among them] who believed in Allāh and the Last Day and did righteousness - will have their reward with their Lord, and no fear will there be concerning them, nor will they grieve[27].

(63) And [recall] when We took your covenant, [O Children of Israel, to abide by the Torah] and We raised over you the mount, [saying], "Take what We have given you with determination and remember what is in it that perhaps you may become righteous."

(64) Then you turned away after that. And if not for the favor of Allāh upon you and His mercy, you would have been among the losers.

(65) And you had already known about those who transgressed among you concerning the sabbath, and We said to them, "Be apes, despised."

(66) And We made it a deterrent punishment for those who were present and those who succeeded [them] and a lesson for those who fear Allāh.

(67) And [recall] when Moses said to his people, "Indeed, Allāh commands you to slaughter a cow." They said, "Do you take us in ridicule?" He said, "I seek refuge in Allāh from being among the ignorant."

---

[27] After the coming of Prophet Muḥammad (ﷺ) no religion other than Islām is acceptable to Allāh, as stated in 3:85.

(68) They said, "Call upon your Lord to make clear to us what it is." [Moses] said, "[Allāh] says, 'It is a cow which is neither old nor virgin, but median between that,' so do what you are commanded."

(69) They said, "Call upon your Lord to show us what is her color." He said, "He says, 'It is a yellow cow, bright in color - pleasing to the observers.'"

(70) They said, "Call upon your Lord to make clear to us what it is. Indeed, [all] cows look alike to us. And indeed we, if Allāh wills, will be guided."

(71) He said, "He says, 'It is a cow neither trained to plow the earth nor to irrigate the field, one free from fault with no spot upon her.'" They said, "Now you have come with the truth." So they slaughtered her, but they could hardly do it.

(72) And [recall] when you slew a man and disputed[28] over it, but Allāh was to bring out that which you were concealing.

(73) So We said, "Strike him [i.e., the slain man] with part of it."[29] Thus does Allāh bring the dead to life, and He shows you His signs that you might reason.

(74) Then your hearts became hardened after that, being like stones or even harder. For indeed, there are stones from which rivers burst forth, and there are some of them that split open and water comes out, and there are some of them that fall down for fear of Allāh. And Allāh is not unaware of what you do.

(75) Do you covet [the hope, O believers], that they would believe for you while a party of them used to hear the words of Allāh and then distort it [i.e., the Torah] after they had understood it while they were knowing?

(76) And when they meet those who believe, they say, "We have believed"; but when they are alone with one another, they say, "Do you talk to them about what Allāh has revealed to you so they can argue with you about it before your Lord?" Then will you not reason?

(77) But do they not know that Allāh knows what they conceal and what they declare?

(78) And among them are unlettered ones who do not know the Scripture except [indulgement in] wishful thinking, but they are only assuming.

---

[28] i.e., exchanged accusations and denials.

[29] i.e., the cow. Thereupon, Allāh restored life to the man, who informed them of his murderer.

(79) So woe[30] to those who write the "scripture" with their own hands, then say, "This is from Allāh," in order to exchange it for a small price. Woe to them for what their hands have written and woe to them for what they earn.

(80) And they say, "Never will the Fire touch us, except for [a few] numbered days." Say, "Have you taken a covenant with Allāh? For Allāh will never break His covenant. Or do you say about Allāh that which you do not know?"

(81) Yes, [on the contrary], whoever earns evil and his sin has encompassed him - those are the companions of the Fire; they will abide therein eternally.

(82) But they who believe and do righteous deeds - those are the companions of Paradise; they will abide therein eternally.

(83) And [recall] when We took the covenant from the Children of Israel, [enjoining upon them], "Do not worship except Allāh; and to parents do good and to relatives, orphans, and the needy. And speak to people good [words] and establish prayer and give zakāh." Then you turned away, except a few of you, and you were refusing.

(84) And [recall] when We took your covenant, [saying], "Do not shed your [i.e., each other's] blood or evict one another from your homes." Then you acknowledged [this] while you were witnessing.

(85) Then, you are those [same ones who are] killing one another and evicting a party of your people from their homes, cooperating against them in sin and aggression. And if they come to you as captives, you ransom them, although their eviction was forbidden to you. So do you believe in part of the Scripture and disbelieve in part? Then what is the recompense for those who do that among you except disgrace in worldly life; and on the Day of Resurrection they will be sent back to the severest of punishment. And Allāh is not unaware of what you do.

(86) Those are the ones who have bought the life of this world [in exchange] for the Hereafter, so the punishment will not be lightened for them, nor will they be aided.

(87) And We did certainly give Moses the Scripture [i.e., the Torah] and followed up after him with messengers. And We gave Jesus, the son of Mary, clear proofs and supported him with the Pure Spirit [i.e., the angel Gabriel]. But is it [not] that every time a messenger came to you, [O Children of Israel], with what your souls did not desire, you were arrogant? And a party [of messengers] you denied and another party you killed.

---

[30] i.e., death and destruction.

(88) And they said, "Our hearts are wrapped."[31] But, [in fact], Allāh has cursed them for their disbelief, so little is it that they believe.

(89) And when there came to them a Book [i.e., the Qur'ān] from Allāh confirming that which was with them - although before they used to pray for victory against those who disbelieved - but [then] when there came to them that which they recognized, they disbelieved in it; so the curse of Allāh will be upon the disbelievers.

(90) How wretched is that for which they sold themselves - that they would disbelieve in what Allāh has revealed through [their] outrage that Allāh would send down His favor upon whom He wills from among His servants. So they returned having [earned] wrath upon wrath. And for the disbelievers is a humiliating punishment.

(91) And when it is said to them, "Believe in what Allāh has revealed," they say, "We believe [only] in what was revealed to us." And they disbelieve in what came after it, while it is the truth confirming that which is with them. Say, "Then why did you kill the prophets of Allāh before, if you are [indeed] believers?"

(92) And Moses had certainly brought you clear proofs. Then you took the calf [in worship] after that, while you were wrongdoers.

(93) And [recall] when We took your covenant and raised over you the mount, [saying], "Take what We have given you with determination and listen." They said [instead], "We hear and disobey." And their hearts absorbed [the worship of] the calf because of their disbelief. Say, "How wretched is that which your faith enjoins upon you, if you should be believers."

(94) Say, [O Muḥammad], "If the home of the Hereafter with Allāh is for you alone and not the [other] people, then wish for death, if you should be truthful."

(95) But never will they wish for it, ever, because of what their hands have put forth. And Allāh is Knowing of the wrongdoers.

(96) And you will surely find them the most greedy of people for life - [even] more than those who associate others with Allāh. One of them wishes that he could be granted life a thousand years, but it would not remove him in the least from the [coming] punishment that he should be granted life. And Allāh is Seeing of what they do.

(97) Say, "Whoever is an enemy to Gabriel - it is [none but] he who has brought it [i.e., the Qur'ān] down upon your heart, [O Muḥammad], by permission of Allāh,

---

[31] Covered or sealed against reception of Allāh's word.

confirming that which was before it and as guidance and good tidings for the believers."

(98) Whoever is an enemy to Allāh and His angels and His messengers and Gabriel and Michael - then indeed, Allāh is an enemy to the disbelievers.

(99) And We have certainly revealed to you verses [which are] clear proofs, and no one would deny them except the defiantly disobedient.

(100) Is it not [true] that every time they took a covenant a party of them threw it away? But, [in fact], most of them do not believe.

(101) And when a messenger from Allāh came to them confirming that which was with them, a party of those who had been given the Scripture threw the Scripture of Allāh [i.e., the Torah] behind their backs as if they did not know [what it contained].

(102) And they followed [instead] what the devils had recited during the reign of Solomon. It was not Solomon who disbelieved, but the devils disbelieved, teaching people magic and that which was revealed to the two angels at Babylon, Hārūt and Mārūt. But they [i.e., the two angels] do not teach anyone unless they say, "We are a trial, so do not disbelieve [by practicing magic]."[32] And [yet] they learn from them that by which they cause separation between a man and his wife. But they do not harm anyone through it except by permission of Allāh. And they [i.e., people] learn what harms them and does not benefit them. But they [i.e., the Children of Israel] certainly knew that whoever purchased it [i.e., magic] would not have in the Hereafter any share. And wretched is that for which they sold themselves, if they only knew.

(103) And if they had believed and feared Allāh, then the reward from Allāh would have been [far] better, if they only knew.

(104) O you who have believed, say not [to Allāh's Messenger], "Rāʿinā" but say, "Unẓurnā"[33] and listen. And for the disbelievers is a painful punishment.

(105) Neither those who disbelieve from the People of the Scripture [i.e., the Jews and Christians] nor the polytheists wish that any good should be sent down to you

---

[32] They warn people against the misuse of what they have learned.

[33] The word "rāʿinā" in Arabic literally means "consider us," i.e., give us time to hear you and listen to us. The Jews used to use the same word with the meaning of an insult. Therefore, the believers were ordered to avoid this expression and use instead the word "unẓurnā," i.e., "wait for us [so that we may understand]."

from your Lord. But Allāh selects for His mercy whom He wills, and Allāh is the possessor of great bounty.

(106) We do not abrogate a verse or cause it to be forgotten except that We bring forth [one] better than it or similar to it. Do you not know that Allāh is over all things competent?

(107) Do you not know that to Allāh belongs the dominion of the heavens and the earth and [that] you have not besides Allāh any protector or any helper?

(108) Or do you intend to ask[34] your Messenger as Moses was asked before? And whoever exchanges faith for disbelief has certainly strayed from the soundness of the way.

(109) Many of the People of the Scripture wish they could turn you back to disbelief after you have believed, out of envy from themselves [even] after the truth has become clear to them. So pardon and overlook until Allāh delivers His command. Indeed, Allāh is over all things competent.

(110) And establish prayer and give zakāh, and whatever good you put forward for yourselves - you will find it with Allāh. Indeed Allāh, of what you do, is Seeing.

(111) And they say, "None will enter Paradise except one who is a Jew or a Christian." That is [merely] their wishful thinking. Say, "Produce your proof, if you should be truthful."

(112) Yes, [on the contrary], whoever submits his face [i.e., self] in Islām to Allāh while being a doer of good will have his reward with his Lord. And no fear will there be concerning them, nor will they grieve.

(113) The Jews say, "The Christians have nothing [true] to stand on," and the Christians say, "The Jews have nothing to stand on," although they [both] recite the Scripture. Thus do those who know not [i.e., the polytheists] speak the same as their words. But Allāh will judge between them on the Day of Resurrection concerning that over which they used to differ.

(114) And who are more unjust than those who prevent the name of Allāh from being mentioned [i.e., praised] in His mosques and strive toward their destruction. It is not for them to enter them except in fear. For them in this world is disgrace, and they will have in the Hereafter a great punishment.

---

[34] i.e., persistently question or, as in the case of the disbelievers, demand a miracle of the Prophet (ﷺ).

(115) And to Allāh belongs the east and the west. So wherever you [might] turn, there is the Face[35] of Allāh. Indeed, Allāh is all-Encompassing and Knowing.

(116) They say, "Allāh has taken a son." Exalted is He![36] Rather, to Him belongs whatever is in the heavens and the earth. All are devoutly obedient to Him,

(117) Originator of the heavens and the earth. When He decrees a matter, He only says to it, "Be," and it is.

(118) Those who do not know say, "Why does Allāh not speak to us or there come to us a sign?" Thus spoke those before them like their words. Their hearts resemble each other. We have shown clearly the signs to a people who are certain [in faith].

(119) Indeed, We have sent you, [O Muḥammad], with the truth as a bringer of good tidings and a warner, and you will not be asked about the companions of Hellfire.

(120) And never will the Jews and the Christians approve of you until you follow their religion. Say, "Indeed, the guidance of Allāh is the [only] guidance." If you were to follow their desires after what has come to you of knowledge, you would have against Allāh no protector or helper.

(121) Those to whom We have given the Book recite it with its true recital.[37] They [are the ones who] believe in it. And whoever disbelieves in it - it is they who are the losers.

(122) O Children of Israel, remember My favor which I have bestowed upon you and that I preferred you over the worlds.

(123) And fear a Day when no soul will suffice for another soul[38] at all, and no compensation will be accepted from it, nor will any intercession benefit it, nor will they be aided.

(124) And [mention, O Muḥammad], when Abraham was tried by his Lord with words [i.e., commands] and he fulfilled them. [Allāh] said, "Indeed, I will make you a leader for the people." [Abraham] said, "And of my descendants?" [Allāh] said, "My covenant does not include the wrongdoers."

(125) And [mention] when We made the House [i.e., the Ka'bah] a place of return for the people and [a place of] security. And take, [O believers], from the standing place of Abraham a place of prayer. And We charged Abraham and Ishmael,

---

[35] See footnote to 2:19.
[36] Subḥānahu means "far exalted is He above all they falsely attribute to Him."
[37] i.e., applying its teachings to their lives.
[38] See footnote to 2:48.

[saying], "Purify My House for those who perform ṭawāf[39] and those who are staying [there] for worship and those who bow and prostrate [in prayer]."

(126) And [mention] when Abraham said, "My Lord, make this a secure city and provide its people with fruits - whoever of them believes in Allāh and the Last Day." [Allāh] said, "And whoever disbelieves - I will grant him enjoyment for a little; then I will force him to the punishment of the Fire, and wretched is the destination."

(127) And [mention] when Abraham was raising the foundations of the House and [with him] Ishmael, [saying], "Our Lord, accept [this] from us. Indeed, You are the Hearing,[40] the Knowing.[41]

(128) Our Lord, and make us Muslims [in submission] to You and from our descendants a Muslim nation [in submission] to You. And show us our rites [of worship] and accept our repentance. Indeed, You are the Accepting of Repentance, the Merciful.

(129) Our Lord, and send among them a messenger from themselves who will recite to them Your verses and teach them the Book and wisdom and purify them. Indeed, You are the Exalted in Might,[42] the Wise."

(130) And who would be averse to the religion of Abraham except one who makes a fool of himself. And We had chosen him in this world, and indeed he, in the Hereafter, will be among the righteous.

(131) When his Lord said to him, "Submit," he said, "I have submitted [in Islām][43] to the Lord of the worlds."

(132) And Abraham instructed his sons [to do the same] and [so did] Jacob, [saying], "O my sons, indeed Allāh has chosen for you this religion, so do not die except while you are Muslims."

(133) Or were you witnesses when death approached Jacob, when he said to his sons, "What will you worship after me?" They said, "We will worship your God and

---

[39] A form of worship particular to the Ka'bah consisting of going around it in circuits.

[40] "Who hears every sound, distinguishes every voice, understands every word, and accepts and responds to supplications.

[41] Refer to footnote in 2:32."

[42] Honored for absolute power associated with wisdom and justice.

[43] The meaning of the word "Islām" is "submission to the will of Allāh." This is the way of life ordained by Allāh and taught by all of the prophets from Adam to Muḥammad (ﷺ). A Muslim is one who submits himself to Allāh.

the God of your fathers, Abraham and Ishmael and Isaac - one God.[44] And we are Muslims [in submission] to Him."

(134) That was a nation which has passed on. It will have [the consequence of] what it earned, and you will have what you have earned. And you will not be asked about what they used to do.

(135) They say, "Be Jews or Christians [so] you will be guided." Say, "Rather, [we follow] the religion of Abraham, inclining toward truth, and he was not of the polytheists."[45]

(136) Say, [O believers], "We have believed in Allāh and what has been revealed to us and what has been revealed to Abraham and Ishmael and Isaac and Jacob and the Descendants [al-Asbāṭ][46] and what was given to Moses and Jesus and what was given to the prophets from their Lord. We make no distinction between any of them, and we are Muslims [in submission] to Him."

(137) So if they believe in the same as you believe in, then they have been [rightly] guided; but if they turn away, they are only in dissension, and Allāh will be sufficient for you against them. And He is the Hearing, the Knowing.

(138) [And say, "Ours is] the religion of Allāh. And who is better than Allāh in [ordaining] religion? And we are worshippers of Him."

(139) Say, [O Muḥammad], "Do you argue with us about Allāh while He is our Lord and your Lord? For us are our deeds, and for you are your deeds. And we are sincere [in deed and intention] to Him."

(140) Or do you say that Abraham and Ishmael and Isaac and Jacob and the Descendants were Jews or Christians? Say, "Are you more knowing or is Allāh?" And who is more unjust than one who conceals a testimony[47] he has from Allāh? And Allāh is not unaware of what you do.

(141) That is a nation which has passed on. It will have [the consequence of] what it earned, and you will have what you have earned. And you will not be asked about what they used to do.

---

[44] Allāh (subḥānahu wa taʿālā) alone.

[45] Those who associate others with Allāh in worship.

[46] The twelve tribes of Israel descended from Jacob.

[47] Statements in previous scriptures attesting to the nature of Allāh's religion (Islām) and the coming of Prophet Muḥammad (ﷺ).

(142) The foolish among the people will say, "What has turned them away from their qiblah,[48] which they used to face?"[49] Say, "To Allāh belongs the east and the west. He guides whom He wills to a straight path."

(143) And thus We have made you a median [i.e., just] community that you will be witnesses over the people and the Messenger will be a witness over you. And We did not make the qiblah which you used to face except that We might make evident who would follow the Messenger from who would turn back on his heels.[50] And indeed, it is difficult except for those whom Allāh has guided. And never would Allāh have caused you to lose your faith [i.e., your previous prayers]. Indeed Allāh is, to the people, Kind and Merciful.

(144) We have certainly seen the turning of your face, [O Muḥammad], toward the heaven, and We will surely turn you to a qiblah with which you will be pleased. So turn your face [i.e., yourself] toward al-Masjid al-Ḥarām.[51] And wherever you [believers] are, turn your faces [i.e., yourselves] toward it [in prayer]. Indeed, those who have been given the Scripture [i.e., the Jews and the Christians] well know that it is the truth from their Lord. And Allāh is not unaware of what they do.

(145) And if you brought to those who were given the Scripture every sign, they would not follow your qiblah. Nor will you be a follower of their qiblah. Nor would they be followers of one another's qiblah. So if you were to follow their desires after what has come to you of knowledge, indeed, you would then be among the wrongdoers.

(146) Those to whom We gave the Scripture know him [i.e., Prophet Muḥammad (ﷺ)] as they know their own sons. But indeed, a party of them conceal the truth while they know [it].

(147) The truth is from your Lord, so never be among the doubters.

(148) For each [religious following] is a [prayer] direction toward which it faces. So race to [all that is] good. Wherever you may be, Allāh will bring you forth [for judgement] all together. Indeed, Allāh is over all things competent.

---

[48] "The direction faced in prayer.

[49] Prior to the command (in verse 144) that the Prophet (ﷺ) and his followers turn toward the Ka'bah in Makkah for prayer, they had been facing Jerusalem to the north. The implications of this change are mentioned in succeeding verses."

[50] i.e., refuse.

[51] The Sacred Mosque in Makkah containing the Ka'bah.

(149) So from wherever you go out [for prayer, O Muḥammad], turn your face toward al-Masjid al-Ḥarām, and indeed, it is the truth from your Lord. And Allāh is not unaware of what you do.

(150) And from wherever you go out [for prayer], turn your face toward al-Masjid al-Ḥarām. And wherever you [believers] may be, turn your faces toward it in order that the people will not have any argument against you, except for those of them who commit wrong; so fear them not but fear Me. And [it is] so I may complete My favor upon you and that you may be guided,

(151) Just as We have sent among you a messenger from yourselves reciting to you Our verses and purifying you and teaching you the Book and wisdom[52] and teaching you that which you did not know.

(152) So remember Me; I will remember you. And be grateful to Me and do not deny Me.

(153) O you who have believed, seek help through patience and prayer. Indeed, Allāh is with the patient.

(154) And do not say about those who are killed in the way of Allāh, "They are dead." Rather, they are alive, but you perceive [it] not.

(155) And We will surely test you with something of fear and hunger and a loss of wealth and lives and fruits, but give good tidings to the patient,

(156) Who, when disaster strikes them, say, "Indeed we belong to Allāh, and indeed to Him we will return."

(157) Those are the ones upon whom are blessings from their Lord and mercy. And it is those who are the [rightly] guided.

(158) Indeed, aṣ-Ṣafā and al-Marwah are among the symbols[53] of Allāh. So whoever makes ḥajj [pilgrimage] to the House or performs ʿumrah - there is no blame upon him for walking between them.[54] And whoever volunteers good - then indeed, Allāh is Appreciative[55] and Knowing.

---

[52] The wisdom taught by the Prophet (ﷺ) is his sunnah.
[53] "Places designated for the rites of ḥajj and ʿumrah.
[54] Some believers had previously feared that this might be a pagan practice, so Allāh confirms that saʿī is among the rites of His religion.
[55] i.e., He rewards generously."

(159) Indeed, those who conceal what We sent down of clear proofs and guidance after We made it clear for the people in the Scripture - those are cursed by Allāh and cursed by those who curse,[56]

(160) Except for those who repent and correct themselves and make evident [what they concealed]. Those - I will accept their repentance, and I am the Accepting of Repentance,[57] the Merciful.

(161) Indeed, those who disbelieve and die while they are disbelievers - upon them will be the curse of Allāh and of the angels and the people, all together,

(162) Abiding eternally therein. The punishment will not be lightened for them, nor will they be reprieved.

(163) And your god is one God. There is no deity [worthy of worship] except Him, the Entirely Merciful, the Especially Merciful.

(164) Indeed, in the creation of the heavens and the earth, and the alternation of the night and the day, and the [great] ships which sail through the sea with that which benefits people, and what Allāh has sent down from the heavens of rain, giving life thereby to the earth after its lifelessness and dispersing therein every [kind of] moving creature, and [His] directing of the winds and the clouds controlled between the heaven and earth are signs for a people who use reason.

(165) And [yet], among the people are those who take other than Allāh as equals [to Him]. They love them as they [should] love Allāh. But those who believe are stronger in love for Allāh. And if only they who have wronged would consider [that] when they see the punishment, [they will be certain] that all power belongs to Allāh and that Allāh is severe in punishment.

(166) [And they should consider that] when those who have been followed disassociate themselves from those who followed [them], and they [all] see the punishment, and cut off from them are the ties [of relationship],

(167) Those who followed will say, "If only we had another turn [at worldly life] so we could disassociate ourselves from them as they have disassociated themselves from us." Thus will Allāh show them their deeds as regrets upon them. And they are never to emerge from the Fire.

(168) O mankind, eat from whatever is on earth [that is] lawful and good and do not follow the footsteps of Satan. Indeed, he is to you a clear enemy.

---

[56] From among the angels and the believers.
[57] Refer to footnote of 2:37

(169) He only orders you to evil and immorality and to say about Allāh what you do not know.

(170) And when it is said to them, "Follow what Allāh has revealed," they say, "Rather, we will follow that which we found our fathers doing." Even though their fathers understood nothing, nor were they guided?

(171) The example of those who disbelieve is like that of one who shouts at what hears nothing but calls and cries [i.e., cattle or sheep] - deaf, dumb and blind, so they do not understand.

(172) O you who have believed, eat from the good [i.e., lawful] things which We have provided for you and be grateful to Allāh if it is [indeed] Him that you worship.

(173) He has only forbidden to you dead animals,[58] blood, the flesh of swine, and that which has been dedicated to other than Allāh. But whoever is forced [by necessity], neither desiring [it] nor transgressing [its limit], there is no sin upon him. Indeed, Allāh is Forgiving and Merciful.

(174) Indeed, they who conceal what Allāh has sent down of the Book and exchange it for a small price - those consume not into their bellies except the Fire. And Allāh will not speak to them on the Day of Resurrection, nor will He purify them. And they will have a painful punishment.

(175) Those are the ones who have exchanged guidance for error and forgiveness for punishment. How patient they are for [i.e., in pursuit of] the Fire!

(176) That is [deserved by them] because Allāh has sent down the Book in truth. And indeed, those who differ over the Book are in extreme dissension.

(177) Righteousness is not that you turn your faces toward the east or the west, but [true] righteousness is [in] one who believes in Allāh, the Last Day, the angels, the Book, and the prophets and gives wealth, in spite of love for it, to relatives, orphans, the needy, the traveler, those who ask [for help], and for freeing slaves; [and who] establishes prayer and gives zakāh; [those who] fulfill their promise when they promise; and [those who] are patient in poverty and hardship and during battle. Those are the ones who have been true, and it is those who are the righteous.

(178) O you who have believed, prescribed for you is legal retribution for those murdered - the free for the free, the slave for the slave, and the female for the

---

[58] Those not slaughtered or hunted expressly for food.

female.[59] But whoever overlooks from his brother [i.e., the killer] anything,[60] then there should be a suitable follow-up and payment to him [i.e., the deceased's heir or legal representative] with good conduct. This is an alleviation from your Lord and a mercy. But whoever transgresses after that[61] will have a painful punishment.

(179) And there is for you in legal retribution [saving of] life, O you [people] of understanding, that you may become righteous.[62]

(180) Prescribed for you when death approaches [any] one of you if he leaves wealth [is that he should make] a bequest for the parents and near relatives according to what is acceptable - a duty upon the righteous.[63]

(181) Then whoever alters it [i.e., the bequest] after he has heard it - the sin is only upon those who have altered it. Indeed, Allāh is Hearing and Knowing.

(182) But if one fears from the bequeather [some] error or sin and corrects that which is between them [i.e., the concerned parties], there is no sin upon him. Indeed, Allāh is Forgiving and Merciful.

(183) O you who have believed, decreed upon you is fasting as it was decreed upon those before you that you may become righteous -

(184) [Fasting for] a limited number of days. So whoever among you is ill or on a journey [during them] - then an equal number of other days [are to be made up]. And upon those who are able [to fast, but with hardship] - a ransom [as substitute] of feeding a poor person [each day]. And whoever volunteers good [i.e., excess] - it is better for him. But to fast is best for you, if you only knew.

(185) The month of Ramaḍān [is that] in which was revealed the Qur'ān, a guidance for the people and clear proofs of guidance and criterion. So whoever sights [the crescent of] the month,[64] let him fast it; and whoever is ill or on a journey - then an equal number of other days. Allāh intends for you ease and does not intend for you hardship and [wants] for you to complete the period and to glorify Allāh for that [to] which He has guided you; and perhaps you will be grateful.

---

[59] "No one else should be executed in place of the killer.

[60] By accepting compensation payment rather than execution.

[61] After acceptance of compensation."

[62] Or, "that you may avoid [sin]."

[63] This ruling was abrogated by the revelation in Sūrah an-Nisā' stipulating obligatory shares for parents and close relatives. Those who do not inherit by law may be remembered in a bequest. See 4:11-12.

[64] Also, "whoever is present during the month."

(186) And when My servants ask you, [O Muḥammad], concerning Me - indeed I am near. I respond to the invocation of the supplicant when he calls upon Me. So let them respond to Me [by obedience] and believe in Me that they may be [rightly] guided.

(187) It has been made permissible for you the night preceding fasting to go to your wives [for sexual relations]. They are a clothing for you and you are a clothing[65] for them. Allāh knows that you used to deceive yourselves,[66] so He accepted your repentance and forgave you. So now, have relations with them and seek that which Allāh has decreed for you [i.e., offspring]. And eat and drink until the white thread of dawn becomes distinct to you from the black thread [of night]. Then complete the fast until the night [i.e., sunset]. And do not have relations with them as long as you are staying for worship in the mosques. These are the limits [set by] Allāh, so do not approach them. Thus does Allāh make clear His verses [i.e., ordinances] to the people that they may become righteous.

(188) And do not consume one another's wealth unjustly or send it [in bribery] to the rulers in order that [they might aid] you [to] consume a portion of the wealth of the people in sin, while you know [it is unlawful].

(189) They ask you, [O Muḥammad], about the crescent moons. Say, "They are measurements of time for the people and for ḥajj [pilgrimage]." And it is not righteousness to enter houses from the back, but righteousness is [in] one who fears Allāh. And enter houses from their doors. And fear Allāh that you may succeed.

(190) Fight in the way of Allāh those who fight against you but do not transgress. Indeed, Allāh does not like transgressors.

(191) And kill them [in battle] wherever you overtake them and expel them from wherever they have expelled you, and fitnah[67] is worse than killing. And do not fight them at al-Masjid al-Ḥarām until they fight you there. But if they fight you, then kill them. Such is the recompense of the disbelievers.

(192) And if they cease, then indeed, Allāh is Forgiving and Merciful.

---

[65] "Also a source of tranquility and rest.

[66] Prior to this revelation, marital relations were unlawful during nights preceding fasting. Some were unable to refrain and secretly disobeyed, but they did not deceive Allāh."

[67] Among the meanings of fitnah are disbelief and its imposition on others, discord, dissension, civil strife, persecution, oppression, injustice, seduction, terrorism, trial and torment.

(193) Fight them until there is no [more] fitnah and [until] religion [i.e., worship] is [acknowledged to be] for Allāh. But if they cease, then there is to be no aggression [i.e., assault] except against the oppressors.

(194) [Battle in] the sacred month is for [aggression committed in] the sacred month,[68] and for [all] violations is legal retribution. So whoever has assaulted you, then assault him in the same way that he has assaulted you. And fear Allāh and know that Allāh is with those who fear Him.

(195) And spend in the way of Allāh and do not throw [yourselves] with your [own] hands into destruction [by refraining]. And do good; indeed, Allāh loves the doers of good.

(196) And complete the ḥajj and ʿumrah for Allāh. But if you are prevented, then [offer] what can be obtained with ease of sacrificial animals. And do not shave your heads until the sacrificial animal has reached its place of slaughter. And whoever among you is ill or has an ailment of the head [making shaving necessary must offer] a ransom of fasting [three days] or charity[69] or sacrifice.[70] And when you are secure,[71] then whoever performs ʿumrah [during the ḥajj months][72] followed by ḥajj [offers] what can be obtained with ease of sacrificial animals. And whoever cannot find [or afford such an animal] - then a fast of three days during ḥajj and of seven when you have returned [home]. Those are ten complete [days]. This is for those whose family is not in the area of al-Masjid al-Ḥarām. And fear Allāh and know that Allāh is severe in penalty.

(197) Ḥajj is [during] well-known months,[73] so whoever has made ḥajj obligatory upon himself therein [by entering the state of iḥrām], there is [to be for him] no sexual relations and no disobedience and no disputing during ḥajj. And whatever good you do - Allāh knows it. And take provisions, but indeed, the best provision is fear of Allāh. And fear Me, O you of understanding.

(198) There is no blame upon you for seeking bounty[74] from your Lord [during ḥajj]. But when you depart from ʿArafāt, remember Allāh at al-Mashʿar al-Ḥarām.[75] And

---

[68] The sacred months are Dhul-Qaʿdah, Dhul-Ḥijjah, Muḥarram and Rajab.

[69] "Feeding six needy persons.

[70] The slaughter of a sheep or goat.

[71] Under normal conditions, i.e., are not prevented.

[72] The months of Shawwāl, Dhul-Qaʿdah and Dhul-Ḥijjah."

[73] See previous footnote.

[74] "i.e., profit from trade or business.

[75] Which is in Muzdalifah."

remember Him, as He has guided you, for indeed, you were before that among those astray.

(199) Then depart from the place from where [all] the people depart and ask forgiveness of Allāh. Indeed, Allāh is Forgiving and Merciful.

(200) And when you have completed your rites, remember Allāh like your [previous] remembrance of your fathers or with [much] greater remembrance. And among the people is he who says, "Our Lord, give us in this world," and he will have in the Hereafter no share.

(201) But among them is he who says, "Our Lord, give us in this world [that which is] good and in the Hereafter [that which is] good and protect us from the punishment of the Fire."

(202) Those will have a share of what they have earned, and Allāh is swift in account.

(203) And remember Allāh during [specific] numbered days. Then whoever hastens [his departure] in two days - there is no sin upon him; and whoever delays [until the third] - there is no sin upon him - for him who fears Allāh. And fear Allāh and know that unto Him you will be gathered.

(204) And of the people is he whose speech pleases you in worldly life, and he calls Allāh to witness as to what is in his heart, yet he is the fiercest of opponents.

(205) And when he goes away, he strives throughout the land to cause corruption therein and destroy crops and animals. And Allāh does not like corruption.

(206) And when it is said to him, "Fear Allāh," pride in the sin takes hold of him. Sufficient for him is Hellfire, and how wretched is the resting place.

(207) And of the people is he who sells himself, seeking means to the approval of Allāh. And Allāh is Kind to [His] servants.

(208) O you who have believed, enter into Islām completely [and perfectly] and do not follow the footsteps of Satan. Indeed, he is to you a clear enemy.

(209) But if you slip [i.e., deviate] after clear proofs have come to you, then know that Allāh is Exalted in Might and Wise.

(210) Do they await but that Allāh should come to them in covers of clouds and the angels [as well] and the matter is [then] decided? And to Allāh [all] matters are returned.

(211) Ask the Children of Israel how many a sign of evidence We have given them. And whoever exchanges the favor of Allāh [for disbelief] after it has come to him - then indeed, Allāh is severe in penalty.

(212) Beautified for those who disbelieve is the life of this world, and they ridicule those who believe. But those who fear Allāh are above them on the Day of Resurrection. And Allāh gives provision to whom He wills without account.

(213) Mankind was [of] one religion [before their deviation]; then Allāh sent the prophets as bringers of good tidings and warners and sent down with them the Scripture in truth to judge between the people concerning that in which they differed. And none differed over it [i.e., the Scripture] except those who were given it - after the clear proofs came to them - out of jealous animosity among themselves. And Allāh guided those who believed to the truth concerning that over which they had differed, by His permission. And Allāh guides whom He wills to a straight path.

(214) Or do you think that you will enter Paradise while such [trial] has not yet come to you as came to those who passed on before you? They were touched by poverty and hardship and were shaken until [even their] messenger and those who believed with him said, "When is the help of Allāh?" Unquestionably, the help of Allāh is near.

(215) They ask you, [O Muḥammad], what they should spend. Say, "Whatever you spend of good is [to be] for parents and relatives and orphans and the needy and the traveler. And whatever you do of good - indeed, Allāh is Knowing of it."

(216) Battle has been enjoined upon you while it is hateful to you. But perhaps you hate a thing and it is good for you; and perhaps you love a thing and it is bad for you. And Allāh knows, while you know not.

(217) They ask you about the sacred month[76] - about fighting therein. Say, "Fighting therein is great [sin], but averting [people] from the way of Allāh and disbelief in Him and [preventing access to] al-Masjid al-Ḥarām and the expulsion of its people therefrom are greater [evil] in the sight of Allāh. And fitnah[77] is greater than killing." And they will continue to fight you until they turn you back from your religion if they are able. And whoever of you reverts from his religion [to disbelief] and dies while he is a disbeliever - for those, their deeds have become worthless in this world and the Hereafter, and those are the companions of the Fire; they will abide therein eternally.

----

[76] "See footnote to 2:194.
[77] See footnote to 2:191."

(218) Indeed, those who have believed and those who have emigrated and fought in the cause of Allāh - those expect the mercy of Allāh. And Allāh is Forgiving and Merciful.

(219) They ask you about wine[78] and gambling. Say, "In them is great sin and [yet, some] benefit for people. But their sin is greater than their benefit." And they ask you what they should spend. Say, "The excess [beyond needs]." Thus Allāh makes clear to you the verses [of revelation] that you might give thought

(220) To this world and the Hereafter. And they ask you about orphans. Say, "Improvement for them is best. And if you mix your affairs with theirs - they are your brothers. And Allāh knows the corrupter from the amender. And if Allāh had willed, He could have put you in difficulty. Indeed, Allāh is Exalted in Might and Wise."

(221) And do not marry polytheistic women until they believe.[79] And a believing slave woman is better than a polytheist, even though she might please you. And do not marry polytheistic men [to your women] until they believe. And a believing slave is better than a polytheist, even though he might please you. Those invite [you] to the Fire, but Allāh invites to Paradise and to forgiveness, by His permission. And He makes clear His verses [i.e., ordinances] to the people that perhaps they may remember.

(222) And they ask you about menstruation. Say, "It is harm, so keep away from wives[80] during menstruation. And do not approach them until they are pure. And when they have purified themselves,[81] then come to them from where Allāh has ordained for you. Indeed, Allāh loves those who are constantly repentant and loves those who purify themselves."

(223) Your wives are a place of cultivation [i.e., sowing of seed] for you, so come to your place of cultivation however you wish and put forth [righteousness] for yourselves. And fear Allāh and know that you will meet Him. And give good tidings to the believers.

(224) And do not make [your oath by] Allāh an excuse against being righteous and fearing Allāh and making peace among people. And Allāh is Hearing and Knowing.

---

[78] The word "khamr" (wine) includes all intoxicants. The final prohibition is given in 5:90-91.
[79] i.e., worship and obey Allāh alone.
[80] "i.e., refrain from sexual intercourse.
[81] By taking a complete bath (ghusl)."

(225) Allāh does not impose blame upon you for what is unintentional in your oaths, but He imposes blame upon you for what your hearts have earned. And Allāh is Forgiving and Forbearing.[82]

(226) For those who swear not to have sexual relations with their wives[83] is a waiting time of four months, but if they return [to normal relations] - then indeed, Allāh is Forgiving and Merciful.

(227) And if they decide on divorce - then indeed, Allāh is Hearing and Knowing.

(228) Divorced women remain in waiting [i.e., do not remarry] for three periods,[84] and it is not lawful for them to conceal what Allāh has created in their wombs if they believe in Allāh and the Last Day. And their husbands have more right to take them back in this [period] if they want reconciliation.[85] And due to them [i.e., the wives] is similar to what is expected of them, according to what is reasonable.[86] But the men [i.e., husbands] have a degree over them [in responsibility and authority]. And Allāh is Exalted in Might and Wise.

(229) Divorce is twice. Then [after that], either keep [her] in an acceptable manner or release [her] with good treatment. And it is not lawful for you to take anything of what you have given them unless both fear that they will not be able to keep [within] the limits of Allāh.[87] But if you fear that they will not keep [within] the limits of Allāh, then there is no blame upon either of them concerning that by which she ransoms herself. These are the limits of Allāh, so do not transgress them. And whoever transgresses the limits of Allāh - it is those who are the wrongdoers [i.e., the unjust].

(230) And if he has divorced her [for the third time], then she is not lawful to him afterward until [after] she marries a husband other than him.[88] And if he [i.e., the latter husband] divorces her [or dies], there is no blame upon them [i.e., the woman and her former husband] for returning to each other if they think that they can

---

[82] Overlooking many violations, postponing penalty and granting opportunities for repentance and rectification despite having the power to punish immediately.

[83] Without divorcing them. By such an oath the woman is deprived of her right in marriage but is not free to marry another. She may not be kept in such a condition beyond the four-month limit.

[84] "Either menstrual periods or periods of purity between menstruation. See also 65:1-7.

[85] The husband may return her to himself during the ʿiddah period of a first and second divorce without a new marriage contract.

[86] The wife has specific rights upon her husband, just as the husband has rights upon her."

[87] i.e., deal fairly with each other.

[88] With the intention of permanence, not merely in order to return to the previous husband.

keep [within] the limits of Allāh. These are the limits of Allāh, which He makes clear to a people who know [i.e.,understand].

(231) And when you divorce women and they have [nearly] fulfilled their term, either retain them according to acceptable terms or release them according to acceptable terms, and do not keep them, intending harm, to transgress [against them]. And whoever does that has certainly wronged himself. And do not take the verses of Allāh in jest. And remember the favor of Allāh upon you and what has been revealed to you of the Book [i.e., the Qur'ān] and wisdom [i.e., the Prophet's sunnah] by which He instructs you. And fear Allāh and know that Allāh is Knowing of all things.

(232) And when you divorce women[89] and they have fulfilled their term, do not prevent them from remarrying their [former] husbands if they [i.e., all parties] agree among themselves on an acceptable basis. That is instructed to whoever of you believes in Allāh and the Last Day. That is better for you and purer, and Allāh knows and you know not.

(233) Mothers may nurse [i.e., breastfeed] their children two complete years for whoever wishes to complete the nursing [period]. Upon the father is their [i.e., the mothers'] provision and their clothing according to what is acceptable. No person is charged with more than his capacity. No mother should be harmed through her child, and no father through his child. And upon the [father's] heir is [a duty] like that [of the father]. And if they both desire weaning through mutual consent from both of them and consultation, there is no blame upon either of them. And if you wish to have your children nursed by a substitute, there is no blame upon you as long as you give payment according to what is acceptable. And fear Allāh and know that Allāh is Seeing of what you do.

(234) And those who are taken in death among you and leave wives behind - they, [the wives, shall] wait four months and ten [days]. And when they have fulfilled their term, then there is no blame upon you for what they do with themselves in an acceptable manner.[90] And Allāh is [fully] Aware of what you do.

(235) There is no blame upon you for that to which you [indirectly] allude concerning a proposal to women or for what you conceal within yourselves. Allāh knows that you will have them in mind. But do not promise them secretly except for saying a proper saying. And do not determine to undertake a marriage contract until the decreed period[91] reaches its end. And know that Allāh knows what is

---

[89] For the first or second time.
[90] They may remarry if they wish.
[91] The ʿiddah (bereavement period) after the death of a husband.

within yourselves, so beware of Him. And know that Allāh is Forgiving and Forbearing.

(236) There is no blame upon you if you divorce women you have not touched[92] nor specified for them an obligation.[93] But give them [a gift of] compensation - the wealthy according to his capability and the poor according to his capability - a provision according to what is acceptable, a duty upon the doers of good.

(237) And if you divorce them before you have touched them and you have already specified for them an obligation, then [give] half of what you specified - unless they forego the right or the one in whose hand is the marriage contract foregoes it. And to forego it is nearer to righteousness. And do not forget graciousness between you. Indeed Allāh, of whatever you do, is Seeing.

(238) Maintain with care the [obligatory] prayers and [in particular] the middle [i.e., ʿaṣr] prayer and stand before Allāh, devoutly obedient.

(239) And if you fear [an enemy, then pray] on foot or riding. But when you are secure, then remember Allāh [in prayer], as He has taught you that which you did not [previously] know.

(240) And those who are taken in death among you and leave wives behind - for their wives is a bequest: maintenance for one year without turning [them] out. But if they leave [of their own accord], then there is no blame upon you for what they do with themselves in an acceptable way.[94] And Allāh is Exalted in Might and Wise.

(241) And for divorced women is a provision according to what is acceptable - a duty upon the righteous.

(242) Thus does Allāh make clear to you His verses [i.e., laws] that you might use reason.

(243) Have you not considered those who left their homes in many thousands, fearing death? Allāh said to them, "Die"; then He restored them to life. And Allāh is the possessor of bounty for the people, but most of the people do not show gratitude.

(244) And fight in the cause of Allāh and know that Allāh is Hearing and Knowing.

---

[92] "The marriage has not been consummated.
[93] Required bridal gift (mahr)."
[94] This directive was abrogated by those later revealed in 2:234 and 4:12.

(245) Who is it that would loan Allāh a goodly loan so He may multiply it for him many times over? And it is Allāh who withholds and grants abundance, and to Him you will be returned.

(246) Have you not considered the assembly of the Children of Israel after [the time of] Moses when they said to a prophet of theirs, "Send to us a king, and we will fight in the way of Allāh"? He said, "Would you perhaps refrain from fighting if battle was prescribed for you?" They said, "And why should we not fight in the cause of Allāh when we have been driven out from our homes and from our children?" But when battle was prescribed for them, they turned away, except for a few of them. And Allāh is Knowing of the wrongdoers.

(247) And their prophet said to them, "Indeed, Allāh has sent to you Saul as a king." They said, "How can he have kingship over us while we are more worthy of kingship than him and he has not been given any measure of wealth?" He said, "Indeed, Allāh has chosen him over you and has increased him abundantly in knowledge and stature. And Allāh gives His sovereignty to whom He wills. And Allāh is all-Encompassing [in favor] and Knowing."

(248) And their prophet said to them, "Indeed, a sign of his kingship is that the chest will come to you in which is assurance[95] from your Lord and a remnant of what the family of Moses and the family of Aaron had left, carried by the angels. Indeed in that is a sign for you, if you are believers."

(249) And when Saul went forth with the soldiers, he said, "Indeed, Allāh will be testing you with a river. So whoever drinks from it is not of me, and whoever does not taste it is indeed of me, excepting one who takes [from it] in the hollow of his hand." But they drank from it, except a [very] few of them. Then when he had crossed it along with those who believed with him, they said, "There is no power for us today against Goliath and his soldiers." But those who were certain that they would meet Allāh said, "How many a small company has overcome a large company by permission of Allāh. And Allāh is with the patient."

(250) And when they went forth to [face] Goliath and his soldiers, they said, "Our Lord, pour upon us patience and plant firmly our feet and give us victory over the disbelieving people."

(251) So they defeated them by permission of Allāh, and David killed Goliath, and Allāh gave him the kingship and wisdom [i.e., prophethood] and taught him from that which He willed. And if it were not for Allāh checking [some] people by means

---

[95] Signs giving reassurance.

of others, the earth would have been corrupted, but Allāh is the possessor of bounty for the worlds.

(252) These are the verses of Allāh which We recite to you, [O Muḥammad], in truth. And indeed, you are from among the messengers.

(253) Those messengers - some of them We caused to exceed others. Among them were those to whom Allāh spoke, and He raised some of them in degree. And We gave Jesus, the son of Mary, clear proofs, and We supported him with the Pure Spirit [i.e., Gabriel]. If Allāh had willed, those [generations] succeeding them would not have fought each other after the clear proofs had come to them. But they differed, and some of them believed and some of them disbelieved. And if Allāh had willed, they would not have fought each other, but Allāh does what He intends.

(254) O you who have believed, spend from that which We have provided for you before there comes a Day in which there is no exchange [i.e., ransom] and no friendship and no intercession. And the disbelievers - they are the wrongdoers.

(255) Allāh - there is no deity except Him, the Ever-Living,[96] the Self-Sustaining.[97] Neither drowsiness overtakes Him nor sleep. To Him belongs whatever is in the heavens and whatever is on the earth. Who is it that can intercede with Him except by His permission? He knows what is [presently] before them and what will be after them,[98] and they encompass not a thing of His knowledge except for what He wills. His Kursī[99] extends over the heavens and the earth, and their preservation tires Him not. And He is the Most High,[100] the Most Great.[101]

(256) There shall be no compulsion in [acceptance of] the religion. The right course has become distinct from the wrong. So whoever disbelieves in ṭāghūt[102] and believes in Allāh has grasped the most trustworthy handhold with no break in it. And Allāh is Hearing and Knowing.

---

[96] "Whose life is perfect, complete and eternal, without beginning or end, and through whom all created life originated and continues.

[97] Dependent on none for His existence while being the sustainer and administrator of all created existence.

[98] Allāh's knowledge encompasses every aspect of His creations in the past, present and future.

[99] Chair or footstool. It is not to be confused with al-ʿArsh (the Throne) , which is infinitely higher and greater than al-Kursī.

[100] Above all of His creations and superior to them in essence, rank and position.

[101] Whose greatness is unlimited, beyond description or imagination."

[102] False objects of worship, such as idols, heavenly bodies, spirits, human beings, etc.

(257) Allāh is the Ally[103] of those who believe. He brings them out from darknesses into the light. And those who disbelieve - their allies are ṭāghūt. They take them out of the light into darknesses.[104] Those are the companions of the Fire; they will abide eternally therein.

(258) Have you not considered the one who argued with Abraham about his Lord [merely] because Allāh had given him kingship? When Abraham said, "My Lord is the one who gives life and causes death," he said, "I give life and cause death." Abraham said, "Indeed, Allāh brings up the sun from the east, so bring it up from the west." So the disbeliever was overwhelmed [by astonishment], and Allāh does not guide the wrongdoing people.

(259) Or [consider such an example] as the one who passed by a township which had fallen into ruin. He said, "How will Allāh bring this to life after its death?" So Allāh caused him to die for a hundred years; then He revived him. He said, "How long have you remained?" He [the man] said, "I have remained a day or part of a day." He said, "Rather, you have remained one hundred years. Look at your food and your drink; it has not changed with time. And look at your donkey; and We will make you a sign for the people. And look at the bones [of this donkey] - how We raise them and then We cover them with flesh." And when it became clear to him, he said, "I know that Allāh is over all things competent."

(260) And [mention] when Abraham said, "My Lord, show me how You give life to the dead." [Allāh] said, "Have you not believed?" He said, "Yes, but [I ask] only that my heart may be satisfied." [Allāh] said, "Take four birds and commit them to yourself.[105] Then [after slaughtering them] put on each hill a portion of them; then call them - they will come [flying] to you in haste. And know that Allāh is Exalted in Might and Wise."

(261) The example of those who spend their wealth in the way of Allāh is like a seed [of grain] which grows seven spikes; in each spike is a hundred grains. And Allāh multiplies [His reward] for whom He wills. And Allāh is all-Encompassing and Knowing.

(262) Those who spend their wealth in the way of Allāh and then do not follow up what they have spent with reminders [of it] or [other] injury will have their reward with their Lord, and there will be no fear concerning them, nor will they grieve.

---

[103] "Including the meanings of patron, supporter, benefactor, guardian, protector, defender and caretaker.

[104] The light of truth is one, while the darknesses of disbelief, doubt and error are many."

[105] i.e., train them to come to you on command.

(263) Kind speech and forgiveness are better than charity followed by injury. And Allāh is Free of need and Forbearing.

(264) O you who have believed, do not invalidate your charities with reminders [of it] or injury as does one who spends his wealth [only] to be seen by the people and does not believe in Allāh and the Last Day. His example is like that of a [large] smooth stone upon which is dust and is hit by a downpour that leaves it bare. They are unable [to keep] anything of what they have earned. And Allāh does not guide the disbelieving people.

(265) And the example of those who spend their wealth seeking means to the approval of Allāh and assuring [reward for] themselves is like a garden on high ground which is hit by a downpour - so it yields its fruits in double. And [even] if it is not hit by a downpour, then a drizzle [is sufficient]. And Allāh, of what you do, is Seeing.

(266) Would one of you like to have a garden of palm trees and grapevines underneath which rivers flow in which he has from every fruit? But he is afflicted with old age and has weak [i.e., immature] offspring, and it is hit by a whirlwind containing fire and is burned. Thus does Allāh make clear to you [His] verses that you might give thought.

(267) O you who have believed, spend from the good things which you have earned and from that which We have produced for you from the earth. And do not aim toward the defective therefrom, spending [from that] while you would not take it [yourself] except with closed eyes. And know that Allāh is Free of need and Praiseworthy.

(268) Satan threatens you with poverty and orders you to immorality, while Allāh promises you forgiveness from Him and bounty. And Allāh is all-Encompassing and Knowing.

(269) He gives wisdom[106] to whom He wills, and whoever has been given wisdom has certainly been given much good. And none will remember except those of understanding.

(270) And whatever you spend of expenditures or make of vows - indeed, Allāh knows of it. And for the wrongdoers there are no helpers.

---

[106] The knowledge and understanding of the religion and of the Qur'ān.

(271) If you disclose your charitable expenditures, they are good; but if you conceal them and give them to the poor, it is better for you, and He will remove from you some of your misdeeds [thereby]. And Allāh, of what you do, is [fully] Aware.

(272) Not upon you, [O Muḥammad], is [responsibility for] their guidance, but Allāh guides whom He wills. And whatever good you [believers] spend is for yourselves, and you do not spend except seeking the face [i.e., approval] of Allāh. And whatever you spend of good[107] - it will be fully repaid to you, and you will not be wronged.

(273) [Charity is] for the poor who have been restricted for the cause of Allāh, unable to move about in the land. An ignorant [person] would think them self-sufficient because of their restraint, but you will know them by their [characteristic] sign. They do not ask people persistently [or at all]. And whatever you spend of good - indeed, Allāh is Knowing of it.

(274) Those who spend their wealth [in Allāh's way] by night and by day, secretly and publicly - they will have their reward with their Lord. And no fear will there be concerning them, nor will they grieve.

(275) Those who consume interest[108] cannot stand [on the Day of Resurrection] except as one stands who is being beaten by Satan into insanity. That is because they say, "Trade is [just] like interest." But Allāh has permitted trade and has forbidden interest. So whoever has received an admonition from his Lord and desists may have what is past, and his affair rests with Allāh. But whoever returns [to dealing in interest or usury] - those are the companions of the Fire; they will abide eternally therein.

(276) Allāh destroys interest and gives increase for charities. And Allāh does not like every sinning disbeliever.

(277) Indeed, those who believe and do righteous deeds and establish prayer and give zakāh will have their reward with their Lord, and there will be no fear concerning them, nor will they grieve.

(278) O you who have believed, fear Allāh and give up what remains [due to you] of interest, if you should be believers.

(279) And if you do not, then be informed of a war [against you] from Allāh and His Messenger. But if you repent, you may have your principal - [thus] you do no wrong, nor are you wronged.

---

[107] i.e., wealth, property, resources, time, effort, etc.
[108] Included is that given on commercial as well as consumer loans.

(280) And if someone is in hardship, then [let there be] postponement until [a time of] ease. But if you give [from your right as] charity, then it is better for you, if you only knew.

(281) And fear a Day when you will be returned to Allāh. Then every soul will be compensated for what it earned, and they will not be wronged [i.e., treated unjustly].

(282) O you who have believed, when you contract a debt for a specified term, write it down. And let a scribe write [it] between you in justice. Let no scribe refuse to write as Allāh has taught him. So let him write and let the one who has the obligation [i.e., the debtor] dictate. And let him fear Allāh, his Lord, and not leave anything out of it. But if the one who has the obligation is of limited understanding or weak or unable to dictate himself, then let his guardian dictate in justice. And bring to witness two witnesses from among your men. And if there are not two men [available], then a man and two women from those whom you accept as witnesses - so that if one of them [i.e., the women] errs, then the other can remind her. And let not the witnesses refuse when they are called upon. And do not be [too] weary to write it, whether it is small or large, for its [specified] term. That is more just in the sight of Allāh and stronger as evidence and more likely to prevent doubt between you, except when it is an immediate transaction which you conduct among yourselves. For [then] there is no blame upon you if you do not write it. And take witnesses when you conclude a contract. Let no scribe be harmed or any witness. For if you do so, indeed, it is [grave] disobedience in you. And fear Allāh. And Allāh teaches you. And Allāh is Knowing of all things.

(283) And if you are on a journey and cannot find a scribe, then a security deposit [should be] taken. And if one of you entrusts another, then let him who is entrusted discharge his trust [faithfully] and let him fear Allāh, his Lord. And do not conceal testimony, for whoever conceals it - his heart is indeed sinful, and Allāh is Knowing of what you do.

(284) To Allāh belongs whatever is in the heavens and whatever is in the earth. Whether you show what is within yourselves or conceal it, Allāh will bring you to account for it. Then He will forgive whom He wills and punish whom He wills, and Allāh is over all things competent.

(285) The Messenger has believed in what was revealed to him from his Lord, and [so have] the believers. All of them have believed in Allāh and His angels and His books and His messengers, [saying], "We make no distinction between any of His messengers." And they say, "We hear and we obey. [We seek] Your forgiveness, our Lord, and to You is the [final] destination."

(286) Allāh does not charge a soul except [with that within] its capacity. It will have [the consequence of] what [good] it has gained, and it will bear [the consequence of] what [evil] it has earned. "Our Lord, do not impose blame upon us if we have forgotten or erred. Our Lord, and lay not upon us a burden like that which You laid upon those before us. Our Lord, and burden us not with that which we have no ability to bear. And pardon us; and forgive us; and have mercy upon us. You are our protector, so give us victory over the disbelieving people."[109]

---

[109] Allāh (subḥānahu wa taʿālā) concludes this sūrah by directing His servants how to supplicate Him, just as He taught them in Sūrah al-Fātiḥah how to praise Him and ask for guidance.

Surah Ale Imran

(1) Alif, Lām, Meem.[110]

(2) Allāh - there is no deity except Him, the Ever-Living, the Self-Sustaining.[111]

(3) He has sent down upon you, [O Muḥammad], the Book in truth, confirming what was before it. And He revealed the Torah and the Gospel

(4) Before, as guidance for the people. And He revealed the Criterion [i.e., the Qur'ān]. Indeed, those who disbelieve in the verses of Allāh will have a severe punishment, and Allāh is Exalted in Might, the Owner of Retribution.[112]

(5) Indeed, from Allāh nothing is hidden in the earth nor in the heaven.

(6) It is He who forms you in the wombs however He wills. There is no deity except Him, the Exalted in Might, the Wise.

(7) It is He who has sent down to you, [O Muḥammad], the Book; in it are verses [that are] precise - they are the foundation of the Book - and others unspecific.[113] As for those in whose hearts is deviation [from truth], they will follow that of it which is unspecific, seeking discord and seeking an interpretation [suitable to them]. And no one knows its [true] interpretation except Allāh. But those firm in knowledge say, "We believe in it. All [of it] is from our Lord." And no one will be reminded except those of understanding.

(8) [Who say], "Our Lord, let not our hearts deviate after You have guided us and grant us from Yourself mercy. Indeed, You are the Bestower.[114]

(9) Our Lord, surely You will gather the people for a Day about which there is no doubt. Indeed, Allāh does not fail in His promise."

(10) Indeed, those who disbelieve - never will their wealth or their children avail them against Allāh at all. And it is they who are fuel for the Fire.

---

[110] See footnote to 2:1.

[111] See footnotes to 2:255.

[112] i.e., He who restores justice by punishing those who persist in wrongdoing, fail to heed warnings and are unrepentant.

[113] Those which are stated in such a way that they are open to more than one interpretation or whose meaning is known only to Allāh, such as the opening letters of certain sūrahs.

[114] Who gives and grants continually without being asked.

(11) [Theirs is] like the custom of the people of Pharaoh and those before them. They denied Our signs, so Allāh seized them for their sins. And Allāh is severe in penalty.

(12) Say to those who disbelieve, "You will be overcome and gathered together to Hell, and wretched is the resting place."

(13) Already there has been for you a sign in the two armies which met [in combat at Badr] - one fighting in the cause of Allāh and another of disbelievers. They saw them [to be] twice their [own] number by [their] eyesight.[115] But Allāh supports with His victory whom He wills. Indeed in that is a lesson for those of vision.

(14) Beautified for people is the love of that which they desire - of women and sons, heaped-up sums of gold and silver, fine branded horses, and cattle and tilled land. That is the enjoyment of worldly life, but Allāh has with Him the best return [i.e., Paradise].

(15) Say, "Shall I inform you of [something] better than that? For those who fear Allāh will be gardens in the presence of their Lord beneath which rivers flow, wherein they abide eternally, and purified spouses and approval from Allāh. And Allāh is Seeing [i.e., aware] of [His] servants -

(16) Those who say, "Our Lord, indeed we have believed, so forgive us our sins and protect us from the punishment of the Fire,"

(17) The patient, the true, the obedient, those who spend [in the way of Allāh], and those who seek forgiveness before dawn.

(18) Allāh witnesses that there is no deity except Him, and [so do] the angels and those of knowledge - [that He is] maintaining [creation] in justice. There is no deity except Him, the Exalted in Might, the Wise.

(19) Indeed, the religion in the sight of Allāh is Islām. And those who were given the Scripture did not differ except after knowledge had come to them - out of jealous animosity between themselves. And whoever disbelieves in the verses of Allāh, then indeed, Allāh is swift in [taking] account.

(20) So if they argue with you, say, "I have submitted myself to Allāh [in Islām], and [so have] those who follow me." And say to those who were given the Scripture and [to] the unlearned,[116] "Have you submitted yourselves?" And if they submit [in

---

[115] The believers saw the disbelievers to be double their own number preceding the battle of Badr, while, in fact, they were three times their number.

[116] Those who had no scripture (i.e., the pagans).

Islām], they are rightly guided; but if they turn away - then upon you is only the [duty of] notification. And Allāh is Seeing of [His] servants.

(21) Those who disbelieve in the signs of Allāh and kill the prophets without right and kill those who order justice from among the people - give them tidings of a painful punishment.

(22) They are the ones whose deeds have become worthless in this world and the Hereafter, and for them there will be no helpers.

(23) Do you not consider, [O Muḥammad], those who were given a portion of the Scripture? They are invited to the Scripture of Allāh that it should arbitrate between them;[117] then a party of them turns away, and they are refusing.

(24) That is because they say, "Never will the Fire touch us except for [a few] numbered days," and [because] they were deluded in their religion by what they were inventing.

(25) So how will it be when We assemble them for a Day about which there is no doubt? And each soul will be compensated [in full for] what it earned, and they will not be wronged.

(26) Say, "O Allāh, Owner of Sovereignty, You give sovereignty to whom You will and You take sovereignty away from whom You will. You honor whom You will and You humble whom You will. In Your hand[118] is [all] good. Indeed, You are over all things competent.

(27) You cause the night to enter the day, and You cause the day to enter the night; and You bring the living out of the dead, and You bring the dead out of the living. And You give provision to whom You will without account [i.e., limit or measure]."

(28) Let not believers take disbelievers as allies [i.e., supporters or protectors] rather than believers. And whoever [of you] does that has nothing [i.e., no association] with Allāh, except when taking precaution against them in prudence.[119] And Allāh warns you of Himself, and to Allāh is the [final] destination.

---

[117] Referring to the Jews of Madīnah who refused to implement the rulings given by Allāh in the Torah or to acknowledge the Prophet (ﷺ), whose coming was mentioned therein.

[118] See footnote to 2:19.

[119] When fearing harm from an enemy, the believer may pretend as long as his heart and intention are not affected.

(29) Say, "Whether you conceal what is in your breasts or reveal it, Allāh knows it. And He knows that which is in the heavens and that which is on the earth. And Allāh is over all things competent.

(30) The Day every soul will find what it has done of good present [before it] and what it has done of evil, it will wish that between itself and that [evil] was a great distance. And Allāh warns you of Himself, and Allāh is Kind to [His] servants."

(31) Say, [O Muḥammad], "If you should love Allāh, then follow me, [so] Allāh will love you and forgive you your sins. And Allāh is Forgiving and Merciful."

(32) Say, "Obey Allāh and the Messenger. But if you turn away - then indeed, Allāh does not like the disbelievers."

(33) Indeed, Allāh chose Adam and Noah and the family of Abraham and the family of ʿImrān over the worlds -

(34) Descendants, some of them from others. And Allāh is Hearing and Knowing.

(35) [Mention, O Muḥammad], when the wife of ʿImrān said, "My Lord, indeed I have pledged to You what is in my womb, consecrated [for Your service], so accept this from me. Indeed, You are the Hearing, the Knowing."

(36) But when she delivered her, she said, "My Lord, I have delivered a female." And Allāh was most knowing of what she delivered, and the male is not like the female. "And I have named her Mary, and I seek refuge for her in You and [for] her descendants from Satan, the expelled [from the mercy of Allāh]."

(37) So her Lord accepted her with good acceptance and caused her to grow in a good manner and put her in the care of Zechariah. Every time Zechariah entered upon her in the prayer chamber, he found with her provision. He said, "O Mary, from where is this [coming] to you?" She said, "It is from Allāh. Indeed, Allāh provides for whom He wills without account."

(38) At that, Zechariah called upon his Lord, saying, "My Lord, grant me from Yourself a good offspring. Indeed, You are the Hearer of supplication."

(39) So the angels called him while he was standing in prayer in the chamber, "Indeed, Allāh gives you good tidings of John, confirming a word[120] from Allāh and [who will be] honorable, abstaining [from women], and a prophet from among the righteous."

---

[120] Referring to the prophet Jesus (upon whom be peace) , who was conceived merely by a command from Allāh - the word "Be."

(40) He said, "My Lord, how will I have a boy when I have reached old age and my wife is barren?" He [the angel] said, "Such is Allāh; He does what He wills."

(41) He said, "My Lord, make for me a sign." He said, "Your sign is that you will not [be able to] speak to the people for three days except by gesture. And remember your Lord much and exalt [Him with praise] in the evening and the morning."

(42) And [mention] when the angels said, "O Mary, indeed Allāh has chosen you and purified you and chosen you above the women of the worlds.

(43) O Mary, be devoutly obedient to your Lord and prostrate and bow with those who bow [in prayer]."

(44) That is from the news of the unseen which We reveal to you, [O Muḥammad]. And you were not with them when they cast their pens[121] as to which of them should be responsible for Mary. Nor were you with them when they disputed.

(45) [And mention] when the angels said, "O Mary, indeed Allāh gives you good tidings of a word[122] from Him, whose name will be the Messiah, Jesus, the son of Mary - distinguished in this world and the Hereafter and among those brought near [to Allāh].

(46) He will speak to the people in the cradle and in maturity and will be of the righteous."

(47) She said, "My Lord, how will I have a child when no man has touched me?" [The angel] said, "Such is Allāh; He creates what He wills. When He decrees a matter, He only says to it, 'Be,' and it is.

(48) And He will teach him writing and wisdom[123] and the Torah and the Gospel

(49) And [make him] a messenger to the Children of Israel, [who will say], 'Indeed I have come to you with a sign from your Lord in that I design for you from clay [that which is] like the form of a bird, then I breathe into it and it becomes a bird by permission of Allāh. And I cure the blind [from birth] and the leper, and I give life to the dead - by permission of Allāh. And I inform you of what you eat and what you store in your houses. Indeed in that is a sign for you, if you are believers.

---

[121] i.e., threw lots.
[122] See footnote to 3:39.
[123] The teachings of the prophets.

(50) And [I have come] confirming what was before me of the Torah and to make lawful for you some of what was forbidden to you. And I have come to you with a sign from your Lord, so fear Allāh and obey me.

(51) Indeed, Allāh is my Lord and your Lord, so worship Him. That is the straight path.'"

(52) But when Jesus felt [persistence in] disbelief from them, he said, "Who are my supporters for [the cause of] Allāh?" The disciples said, "We are supporters for Allāh. We have believed in Allāh and testify that we are Muslims [submitting to Him].

(53) Our Lord, we have believed in what You revealed and have followed the messenger [i.e., Jesus], so register us among the witnesses [to truth]."

(54) And they [i.e., the disbelievers] planned, but Allāh planned. And Allāh is the best of planners.

(55) [Mention] when Allāh said, "O Jesus, indeed I will take you and raise you to Myself and purify [i.e., free] you from those who disbelieve and make those who follow you [in submission to Allāh alone] superior to those who disbelieve until the Day of Resurrection. Then to Me is your return, and I will judge between you concerning that in which you used to differ.

(56) And as for those who disbelieved, I will punish them with a severe punishment in this world and the Hereafter, and they will have no helpers."

(57) But as for those who believed and did righteous deeds, He will give them in full their rewards, and Allāh does not like the wrongdoers.

(58) This is what We recite to you, [O Muḥammad], of [Our] verses and the precise [and wise] message [i.e., the Qur'ān].

(59) Indeed, the example of Jesus to Allāh[124] is like that of Adam. He created him from dust; then He said to him, "Be," and he was.

(60) The truth is from your Lord, so do not be among the doubters.

(61) Then whoever argues with you about it after [this] knowledge has come to you - say, "Come, let us call our sons and your sons, our women and your women, ourselves and yourselves, then supplicate earnestly [together] and invoke the curse of Allāh upon the liars [among us]."

---

[124] i.e., regarding His creation of him.

(62) Indeed, this is the true narration. And there is no deity except Allāh. And indeed, Allāh is the Exalted in Might, the Wise.

(63) But if they turn away, then indeed - Allāh is Knowing of the corrupters.

(64) Say, "O People of the Scripture, come to a word that is equitable between us and you - that we will not worship except Allāh and not associate anything with Him and not take one another as lords instead of Allāh."[125] But if they turn away, then say, "Bear witness that we are Muslims [submitting to Him]."

(65) O People of the Scripture, why do you argue about Abraham while the Torah and the Gospel were not revealed until after him? Then will you not reason?

(66) Here you are - those who have argued about that of which you have [some] knowledge, but why do you argue about that of which you have no knowledge? And Allāh knows, while you know not.

(67) Abraham was neither a Jew nor a Christian, but he was one inclining toward truth, a Muslim [submitting to Allāh]. And he was not of the polytheists.[126]

(68) Indeed, the most worthy of Abraham among the people are those who followed him [in submission to Allāh] and this prophet [i.e., Muḥammad (ﷺ)] and those who believe [in his message]. And Allāh is the Ally[127] of the believers.

(69) A faction of the People of the Scripture wish they could mislead you. But they do not mislead except themselves, and they perceive [it] not.

(70) O People of the Scripture, why do you disbelieve in the verses of Allāh[128] while you witness [to their truth]?

(71) O People of the Scripture, why do you mix [i.e., confuse] the truth with falsehood and conceal the truth while you know [it]?

(72) And a faction of the People of the Scripture say [to each other], "Believe in that which was revealed to the believers at the beginning of the day and reject it at its end that perhaps they will return [i.e., abandon their religion],

(73) And do not trust except those who follow your religion." Say, "Indeed, the [true] guidance is the guidance of Allāh. [Do you fear] lest someone be given [knowledge] like you were given or that they would [thereby] argue with you before

---

[125] By obeying another in disobedience to Allāh.
[126] Those who associate others with Allāh.
[127] Refer to footnote in verse 2:257.
[128] i.e., deliberately reject them.

your Lord?" Say, "Indeed, [all] bounty is in the hand[129] of Allāh - He grants it to whom He wills. And Allāh is all-Encompassing and Wise."

(74) He selects for His mercy whom He wills. And Allāh is the possessor of great bounty.

(75) And among the People of the Scripture is he who, if you entrust him with a great amount [of wealth], he will return it to you. And among them is he who, if you entrust him with a [single] coin, he will not return it to you unless you are constantly standing over him [demanding it]. That is because they say, "There is no blame upon us concerning the unlearned."[130] And they speak untruth about Allāh while they know [it].

(76) But yes, whoever fulfills his commitment and fears Allāh - then indeed, Allāh loves those who fear Him.

(77) Indeed, those who exchange the covenant of Allāh and their [own] oaths for a small price will have no share in the Hereafter, and Allāh will not speak to them or look at them on the Day of Resurrection, nor will He purify them; and they will have a painful punishment.

(78) And indeed, there is among them a party who alter the Scripture with their tongues so you may think it is from the Scripture, but it is not from the Scripture. And they say, "This is from Allāh," but it is not from Allāh. And they speak untruth about Allāh while they know.

(79) It is not for a human [prophet][131] that Allāh should give him the Scripture[132] and authority and prophethood and then he would say to the people, "Be servants to me rather than Allāh," but [instead, he would say], "Be pious scholars of the Lord because of what you have taught of the Scripture and because of what you have studied."

(80) Nor could he order you to take the angels and prophets as lords. Would he order you to disbelief after you had been Muslims?

(81) And [recall, O People of the Scripture], when Allāh took the covenant of the prophets, [saying], "Whatever I give you of the Scripture and wisdom and then there comes to you a messenger confirming what is with you, you [must] believe in him and support him." [Allāh] said, "Have you acknowledged and taken upon that

---

[129] See footnote to 2:19.

[130] The Jews do not consider it a sin to cheat or lie to a gentile or a pagan.

[131] "Or any believer.

[132] Or in the case of Prophet Muḥammad (ﷺ), "the Book" (i.e., the Qur'ān)."

My commitment?"[133] They said, "We have acknowledged it." He said, "Then bear witness, and I am with you among the witnesses."

(82) And whoever turned away after that - they were the defiantly disobedient.

(83) So is it other than the religion of Allāh they desire, while to Him have submitted [all] those within the heavens and earth, willingly or by compulsion, and to Him they will be returned?

(84) Say, "We have believed in Allāh and in what was revealed to us and what was revealed to Abraham, Ishmael, Isaac, Jacob, and the Descendants [al-Asbāṭ], and in what was given to Moses and Jesus and to the prophets from their Lord. We make no distinction between any of them, and we are Muslims [submitting] to Him."

(85) And whoever desires other than Islām as religion - never will it be accepted from him, and he, in the Hereafter, will be among the losers.

(86) How shall Allāh guide a people who disbelieved after their belief and had witnessed that the Messenger is true and clear signs had come to them? And Allāh does not guide the wrongdoing people.

(87) Those - their recompense will be that upon them is the curse of Allāh and the angels and the people, all together,

(88) Abiding eternally therein. The punishment will not be lightened for them, nor will they be reprieved,

(89) Except for those who repent after that[134] and correct themselves. For indeed, Allāh is Forgiving and Merciful.

(90) Indeed, those who disbelieve [i.e., reject the message] after their belief and then increase in disbelief - never will their [claimed] repentance be accepted, and they are the ones astray.

(91) Indeed, those who disbelieve and die while they are disbelievers - never would the [whole] capacity of the earth in gold be accepted from one of them if he would [seek to] ransom himself with it. For those there will be a painful punishment, and they will have no helpers.

---

[133] i.e., Have you accepted this obligation?

[134] After their wrongdoing.

(92) Never will you attain the good [reward][135] until you spend [in the way of Allāh] from that which you love. And whatever you spend - indeed, Allāh is Knowing of it.

(93) All food was lawful to the Children of Israel except what Israel [i.e., Jacob] had made unlawful to himself before the Torah was revealed. Say, [O Muḥammad], "So bring the Torah and recite it, if you should be truthful."

(94) And whoever invents about Allāh untruth after that - then those are [truly] the wrongdoers.

(95) Say, "Allāh has told the truth. So follow the religion of Abraham, inclining toward truth; and he was not of the polytheists."[136]

(96) Indeed, the first House [of worship] established for mankind was that at Bakkah [i.e., Makkah] - blessed and a guidance for the worlds.

(97) In it are clear signs [such as] the standing place of Abraham. And whoever enters it [i.e., the Ḥaram] shall be safe. And [due] to Allāh from the people is a pilgrimage to the House - for whoever is able to find thereto a way. But whoever disbelieves [i.e., refuses] - then indeed, Allāh is free from need of the worlds.[137]

(98) Say, "O People of the Scripture, why do you disbelieve in the verses of Allāh while Allāh is Witness over what you do?"

(99) Say, "O People of the Scripture, why do you avert from the way of Allāh those who believe, seeking to make it [seem] deviant, while you are witnesses [to the truth]? And Allāh is not unaware of what you do."

(100) O you who have believed, if you obey a party of those who were given the Scripture, they would turn you back, after your belief, [to being] unbelievers.

(101) And how could you disbelieve while to you are being recited the verses of Allāh and among you is His Messenger? And whoever holds firmly to Allāh[138] has [indeed] been guided to a straight path.

(102) O you who have believed, fear Allāh as He should be feared and do not die except as Muslims [in submission to Him].

---

[135] Another meaning is "You will never attain righteousness."
[136] See footnote to 3:67.
[137] He has no need for His servants' worship; it is they who are in need of Him.
[138] i.e., adhering to His ordinances strictly, then trusting in Him and relying upon Him completely.

(103) And hold firmly to the rope[139] of Allāh all together and do not become divided. And remember the favor of Allāh upon you - when you were enemies and He brought your hearts together and you became, by His favor, brothers. And you were on the edge of a pit of the Fire, and He saved you from it. Thus does Allāh make clear to you His verses that you may be guided.

(104) And let there be [arising] from you a nation inviting to [all that is] good, enjoining what is right and forbidding what is wrong,[140] and those will be the successful.

(105) And do not be like the ones who became divided and differed after the clear proofs had come to them. And those will have a great punishment

(106) On the Day [some] faces will turn white and [some] faces will turn black. As for those whose faces turn black, [to them it will be said], "Did you disbelieve [i.e., reject faith] after your belief? Then taste the punishment for what you used to reject."

(107) But as for those whose faces turn white, [they will be] within the mercy of Allāh. They will abide therein eternally.

(108) These are the verses of Allāh. We recite them to you, [O Muḥammad], in truth; and Allāh wants no injustice to the worlds [i.e., His creatures].

(109) To Allāh belongs whatever is in the heavens and whatever is on the earth. And to Allāh will [all] matters be returned.

(110) You are the best nation produced [as an example] for mankind. You enjoin what is right and forbid what is wrong and believe in Allāh. If only the People of the Scripture had believed, it would have been better for them. Among them are believers, but most of them are defiantly disobedient.

(111) They will not harm you except for [some] annoyance. And if they fight you, they will show you their backs [i.e., retreat]; then they will not be aided.

(112) They have been put under humiliation [by Allāh] wherever they are overtaken, except for a rope [i.e., covenant] from Allāh and a rope [i.e., treaty] from the people [i.e., the Muslims].[141] And they have drawn upon themselves anger from

---

[139] Referring either to His covenant or the Qur'ān.

[140] According to the laws of Allāh.

[141] Once they have surrendered, the People of the Scripture retain their rights and honor (in spite of their refusal of Islām) through payment of the jizyah tax in place of zakāh and military service due from Muslims. They are then under the protection of the Islāmic state.

Allāh and have been put under destitution. That is because they disbelieved in [i.e., rejected] the verses of Allāh and killed the prophets without right. That is because they disobeyed and [habitually] transgressed.

(113) They are not [all] the same; among the People of the Scripture is a community[142] standing [in obedience], reciting the verses of Allāh during periods of the night and prostrating [in prayer].

(114) They believe in Allāh and the Last Day, and they enjoin what is right and forbid what is wrong and hasten to good deeds. And those are among the righteous.

(115) And whatever good they do - never will it be denied them. And Allāh is Knowing of the righteous.

(116) Indeed, those who disbelieve - never will their wealth or their children avail them against Allāh at all, and those are the companions of the Fire; they will abide therein eternally.

(117) The example of what they spend in this worldly life is like that of a wind containing frost which strikes the harvest of a people who have wronged themselves [i.e., sinned] and destroys it. And Allāh has not wronged them, but they wrong themselves.

(118) O you who have believed, do not take as intimates those other than yourselves [i.e., believers], for they will not spare you [any] ruin. They wish you would have hardship. Hatred has already appeared from their mouths, and what their breasts conceal is greater. We have certainly made clear to you the signs, if you will use reason.

(119) Here you are loving them but they are not loving you, while you believe in the Scripture - all of it.[143] And when they meet you, they say, "We believe." But when they are alone, they bite their fingertips at you in rage. Say, "Die in your rage. Indeed, Allāh is Knowing of that within the breasts."

(120) If good touches you, it distresses them; but if harm strikes you, they rejoice at it. And if you are patient and fear Allāh, their plot will not harm you at all. Indeed, Allāh is encompassing of what they do.

(121) And [remember] when you, [O Muḥammad], left your family in the morning to post the believers at their stations for the battle [of Uḥud] - and Allāh is Hearing and Knowing -

---

[142] Of people who accepted Islām.
[143] That of it revealed by Allāh, not what was subsequently altered by men.

(122) When two parties among you were about to lose courage, but Allāh was their ally; and upon Allāh the believers should rely.

(123) And already had Allāh given you victory at [the battle of] Badr while you were weak [i.e., few in number]. Then fear Allāh; perhaps you will be grateful.

(124) [Remember] when you said to the believers, "Is it not sufficient for you that your Lord should reinforce you with three thousand angels sent down?

(125) Yes, if you remain patient and conscious of Allāh and they [i.e., the enemy] come upon you [attacking] in rage, your Lord will reinforce you with five thousand angels having marks [of distinction]."

(126) And Allāh made it not except as [a sign of] good tidings for you and to reassure your hearts thereby. And victory is not except from Allāh, the Exalted in Might, the Wise -

(127) That He might cut down a section of the disbelievers or suppress them so that they turn back disappointed.

(128) Not for you, [O Muḥammad, but for Allāh], is the decision whether He should [cut them down] or forgive them or punish them, for indeed, they are wrongdoers.

(129) And to Allāh belongs whatever is in the heavens and whatever is on the earth. He forgives whom He wills and punishes whom He wills. And Allāh is Forgiving and Merciful.

(130) O you who have believed, do not consume usury, doubled and multiplied, but fear Allāh that you may be successful.

(131) And fear the Fire, which has been prepared for the disbelievers.

(132) And obey Allāh and the Messenger that you may obtain mercy.

(133) And hasten to forgiveness from your Lord and a garden [i.e., Paradise] as wide as the heavens and earth, prepared for the righteous

(134) Who spend [in the cause of Allāh] during ease and hardship and who restrain anger and who pardon the people - and Allāh loves the doers of good;

(135) And those who, when they commit an immorality or wrong themselves [by transgression], remember Allāh and seek forgiveness for their sins - and who can forgive sins except Allāh? - and [who] do not persist in what they have done while they know.

(136) Those - their reward is forgiveness from their Lord and gardens beneath which rivers flow [in Paradise], wherein they will abide eternally; and excellent is the reward of the [righteous] workers.

(137) Similar situations [as yours] have passed on before you, so proceed throughout the earth and observe how was the end of those who denied.

(138) This [Qur'ān] is a clear statement to [all] the people and a guidance and instruction for those conscious of Allāh.

(139) So do not weaken and do not grieve, and you will be superior if you are [true] believers.

(140) If a wound should touch you - there has already touched the [opposing] people a wound similar to it. And these days [of varying conditions] We alternate among the people so that Allāh may make evident those who believe and [may] take to Himself from among you martyrs - and Allāh does not like the wrongdoers -

(141) And that Allāh may purify the believers [through trials] and destroy the disbelievers.

(142) Or do you think that you will enter Paradise while Allāh has not yet made evident those of you who fight in His cause and made evident those who are steadfast?

(143) And you had certainly wished for death [i.e., martyrdom] before you encountered it, and you have [now] seen it [before you] while you were looking on.

(144) Muḥammad is not but a messenger. [Other] messengers have passed on before him. So if he was to die or be killed, would you turn back on your heels [to unbelief]? And he who turns back on his heels will never harm Allāh at all; but Allāh will reward the grateful.

(145) And it is not [possible] for one to die except by permission of Allāh at a decree determined. And whoever desires the reward of this world - We will give him thereof; and whoever desires the reward of the Hereafter - We will give him thereof. And We will reward the grateful.

(146) And how many a prophet [fought in battle and] with him fought many religious scholars. But they never lost assurance due to what afflicted them in the cause of Allāh, nor did they weaken or submit. And Allāh loves the steadfast.

(147) And their words were not but that they said, "Our Lord, forgive us our sins and the excess [committed] in our affairs and plant firmly our feet and give us victory over the disbelieving people."

(148) So Allāh gave them the reward of this world and the good reward of the Hereafter. And Allāh loves the doers of good.

(149) O you who have believed, if you obey those who disbelieve, they will turn you back on your heels, and you will [then] become losers.

(150) But Allāh is your protector, and He is the best of helpers.

(151) We will cast terror into the hearts of those who disbelieve for what they have associated with Allāh of which He had not sent down [any] authority.[144] And their refuge will be the Fire, and wretched is the residence of the wrongdoers.

(152) And Allāh had certainly fulfilled His promise to you when you were killing them [i.e., the enemy] by His permission until [the time] when you lost courage and fell to disputing about the order [given by the Prophet (ﷺ)] and disobeyed after He had shown you that which you love.[145] Among you are some who desire this world, and among you are some who desire the Hereafter. Then He turned you back from them [defeated] that He might test you. And He has already forgiven you, and Allāh is the possessor of bounty for the believers.

(153) [Remember] when you [fled and] climbed [the mountain] without looking aside at anyone while the Messenger was calling you from behind. So Allāh repaid you with distress upon distress so you would not grieve for that which had escaped you [of victory and spoils of war] or [for] that which had befallen you [of injury and death]. And Allāh is [fully] Aware of what you do.

(154) Then after distress, He sent down upon you security [in the form of] drowsiness, overcoming a faction of you, while another faction worried about themselves, thinking of Allāh other than the truth - the thought of ignorance, saying, "Is there anything for us [to have done] in this matter?" Say, "Indeed, the matter belongs completely to Allāh." They conceal within themselves what they will not reveal to you. They say, "If there was anything we could have done in the matter, we [i.e., some of us] would not have been killed right here." Say, "Even if you had been inside your houses, those decreed to be killed would have come out to their death beds." [It was] so that Allāh might test what is in your breasts and purify what is in your hearts. And Allāh is Knowing of that within the breasts.

(155) Indeed, those of you who turned back on the day the two armies met [at Uḥud] - it was Satan who caused them to slip because of some [blame] they had earned. But Allāh has already forgiven them. Indeed, Allāh is Forgiving and Forbearing.

---

[144] i.e., clear evidence.
[145] i.e., the spoils of war.

(156) O you who have believed, do not be like those who disbelieved and said about their brothers when they traveled through the land or went out to fight, "If they had been with us, they would not have died or have been killed," so Allāh makes that [misconception] a regret within their hearts. And it is Allāh who gives life and causes death, and Allāh is Seeing of what you do.

(157) And if you are killed in the cause of Allāh or die - then forgiveness from Allāh and mercy are better than whatever they accumulate [in this world].

(158) And whether you die or are killed, unto Allāh you will be gathered.

(159) So by mercy from Allāh, [O Muḥammad], you were lenient with them. And if you had been rude [in speech] and harsh in heart, they would have disbanded from about you. So pardon them and ask forgiveness for them and consult them in the matter. And when you have decided, then rely upon Allāh. Indeed, Allāh loves those who rely [upon Him].

(160) If Allāh should aid you, no one can overcome you; but if He should forsake you, who is there that can aid you after Him? And upon Allāh let the believers rely.

(161) It is not [attributable] to any prophet that he would act unfaithfully [in regard to war booty]. And whoever betrays, [taking unlawfully], will come with what he took on the Day of Resurrection. Then will every soul be [fully] compensated for what it earned, and they will not be wronged.

(162) So is one who pursues the pleasure of Allāh like one who brings upon himself the anger of Allāh and whose refuge is Hell? And wretched is the destination.

(163) They are [varying] degrees in the sight of Allāh, and Allāh is Seeing of whatever they do.

(164) Certainly did Allāh confer [great] favor upon the believers when He sent among them a Messenger from themselves, reciting to them His verses and purifying them and teaching them the Book [i.e., the Qur'ān] and wisdom,[146] although they had been before in manifest error.

(165) Why [is it that] when a [single] disaster struck you [on the day of Uḥud], although you had struck [the enemy in the battle of Badr] with one twice as great, you said, "From where is this?" Say, "It is from yourselves [i.e., due to your sin]." Indeed, Allāh is over all things competent.

---

[146] The Prophet's sunnah.

(166) And what struck you on the day the two armies met [at Uḥud] was by permission of Allāh that He might make evident the [true] believers

(167) And that He might make evident those who are hypocrites. For it was said to them, "Come, fight in the way of Allāh or [at least] defend." They said, "If we had known [there would be] battle, we would have followed you." They were nearer to disbelief that day than to faith, saying with their mouths what was not in their hearts. And Allāh is most knowing of what they conceal -

(168) Those who said about their brothers while sitting [at home], "If they had obeyed us, they would not have been killed." Say, "Then prevent death from yourselves, if you should be truthful."

(169) And never think of those who have been killed in the cause of Allāh as dead. Rather, they are alive with their Lord, receiving provision,

(170) Rejoicing in what Allāh has bestowed upon them of His bounty, and they receive good tidings about those [to be martyred] after them who have not yet joined them - that there will be no fear concerning them, nor will they grieve.

(171) They receive good tidings of favor from Allāh and bounty and [of the fact] that Allāh does not allow the reward of believers to be lost -

(172) Those [believers] who responded to Allāh and the Messenger after injury had struck them. For those who did good among them and feared Allāh is a great reward -

(173) Those to whom people [i.e., hypocrites] said, "Indeed, the people have gathered against you, so fear them." But it [merely] increased them in faith, and they said, "Sufficient for us is Allāh, and [He is] the best Disposer of affairs."[147]

(174) So they returned with favor from Allāh and bounty, no harm having touched them. And they pursued the pleasure of Allāh, and Allāh is the possessor of great bounty.

(175) That is only Satan who frightens [you] of his supporters. So fear them not, but fear Me, if you are [indeed] believers.

(176) And do not be grieved, [O Muḥammad], by those who hasten into disbelief. Indeed, they will never harm Allāh at all. Allāh intends that He should give them no share in the Hereafter, and for them is a great punishment.

---

[147] The one entrusted and relied upon; sufficient to manage all matters.

(177) Indeed, those who purchase disbelief [in exchange] for faith - never will they harm Allāh at all, and for them is a painful punishment.

(178) And let not those who disbelieve ever think that [because] We extend their time [of enjoyment] it is better for them. We only extend it for them so that they may increase in sin, and for them is a humiliating punishment.

(179) Allāh would not leave the believers in that [state] you are in [presently] until He separates the evil from the good. Nor would Allāh reveal to you the unseen. But [instead], Allāh chooses of His messengers whom He wills, so believe in Allāh and His messengers. And if you believe and fear Him, then for you is a great reward.

(180) And let not those who [greedily] withhold what Allāh has given them of His bounty ever think that it is better for them. Rather, it is worse for them. Their necks will be encircled by what they withheld on the Day of Resurrection. And to Allāh belongs the heritage of the heavens and the earth. And Allāh, of what you do, is [fully] Aware.

(181) Allāh has certainly heard the statement of those [Jews] who said, "Indeed, Allāh is poor, while we are rich." We will record what they said and their killing of the prophets without right and will say, "Taste the punishment of the Burning Fire.

(182) That is for what your hands have put forth and because Allāh is not ever unjust to [His] servants."

(183) [They are] those who said, "Indeed, Allāh has taken our promise not to believe any messenger until he brings us an offering which fire [from heaven] will consume." Say, "There have already come to you messengers before me with clear proofs and [even] that of which you speak. So why did you kill them, if you should be truthful?"

(184) Then if they deny you, [O Muḥammad] - so were messengers denied before you, who brought clear proofs and written ordinances and the enlightening Scripture.[148]

(185) Every soul will taste death, and you will only be given your [full] compensation on the Day of Resurrection. So he who is drawn away from the Fire and admitted to Paradise has attained [his desire]. And what is the life of this world except the enjoyment of delusion.

(186) You will surely be tested in your possessions and in yourselves. And you will surely hear from those who were given the Scripture before you and from those

---

[148] The unaltered, original Torah and Gospel, which were revealed by Allāh.

who associate others with Allāh much abuse. But if you are patient and fear Allāh - indeed, that is of the matters [worthy] of resolve.

(187) And [mention, O Muḥammad], when Allāh took a covenant from those who were given the Scripture, [saying], "You must make it clear [i.e., explain it] to the people and not conceal it." But they threw it away behind their backs and exchanged it for a small price. And wretched is that which they purchased.

(188) And never think that those who rejoice in what they have perpetrated and like to be praised for what they did not do - never think them [to be] in safety from the punishment, and for them is a painful punishment.

(189) And to Allāh belongs the dominion of the heavens and the earth, and Allāh is over all things competent.

(190) Indeed, in the creation of the heavens and the earth and the alternation of the night and the day are signs for those of understanding -

(191) Who remember Allāh while standing or sitting or [lying] on their sides and give thought to the creation of the heavens and the earth, [saying], "Our Lord, You did not create this aimlessly; exalted are You [above such a thing]; then protect us from the punishment of the Fire.

(192) Our Lord, indeed whoever You admit to the Fire - You have disgraced him, and for the wrongdoers there are no helpers.

(193) Our Lord, indeed we have heard a caller [i.e., Prophet Muḥammad (ﷺ)] calling to faith, [saying], 'Believe in your Lord,' and we have believed. Our Lord, so forgive us our sins and remove from us our misdeeds and cause us to die among the righteous.

(194) Our Lord, and grant us what You promised us through Your messengers and do not disgrace us on the Day of Resurrection. Indeed, You do not fail in [Your] promise."

(195) And their Lord responded to them, "Never will I allow to be lost the work of [any] worker among you, whether male or female; you are of one another. So those who emigrated or were evicted from their homes or were harmed in My cause or fought or were killed - I will surely remove from them their misdeeds, and I will surely admit them to gardens beneath which rivers flow as reward from Allāh, and Allāh has with Him the best reward."

(196) Be not deceived by the [uninhibited] movement of the disbelievers throughout the land.

(197) [It is but] a small enjoyment; then their [final] refuge is Hell, and wretched is the resting place.

(198) But those who feared their Lord will have gardens beneath which rivers flow, abiding eternally therein, as accommodation from Allāh. And that which is with Allāh is best for the righteous.

(199) And indeed, among the People of the Scripture are those who believe in Allāh and what was revealed to you and what was revealed to them, [being] humbly submissive to Allāh. They do not exchange the verses of Allāh for a small price. Those will have their reward with their Lord. Indeed, Allāh is swift in account.

(200) O you who have believed, persevere[149] and endure[150] and remain stationed[151] and fear Allāh that you may be successful.

---

[149] "In your religion and in the face of your enemies.
[150] In patience, outlasting your enemies, and against your own evil inclinations.
[151] Posted at your positions against the enemy or in the mosques, awaiting prayers."

Surah An-Nisa'

(1) O mankind, fear your Lord, who created you from one soul and created from it its mate and dispersed from both of them many men and women. And fear Allāh, through whom[152] you ask one another,[153] and the wombs.[154] Indeed Allāh is ever,[155] over you, an Observer.[156]

(2) And give to the orphans their properties and do not substitute the defective [of your own] for the good [of theirs]. And do not consume their properties into your own. Indeed, that is ever a great sin.

(3) And if you fear that you will not deal justly with the orphan girls, then marry those that please you of [other] women, two or three or four. But if you fear that you will not be just, then [marry only] one or those your right hands possess [i.e., slaves]. That is more suitable that you may not incline [to injustice].

(4) And give the women [upon marriage] their [bridal] gifts[157] graciously. But if they give up willingly to you anything of it, then take it in satisfaction and ease.[158]

(5) And do not give the weak-minded your property,[159] which Allāh has made a means of sustenance for you, but provide for them with it and clothe them and speak to them words of appropriate kindness.

(6) And test the orphans [in their abilities] until they reach marriageable age. Then if you perceive in them sound judgement, release their property to them. And do not consume it excessively and quickly, [anticipating] that they will grow up. And whoever, [when acting as guardian], is self-sufficient should refrain [from taking a fee]; and whoever is poor - let him take according to what is acceptable. Then when

---

[152] "In whose name.

[153] i.e., request favors and demand rights.

[154] i.e., fear Allāh in regard to relations of kinship.

[155] When used in conjunction with Allāh's attributes, the word "ever" (occurring repeatedly throughout this sūrah and elsewhere, such as in Sūrah al-Aḥzāb) is quite inadequate in imparting the sense of continuation expressed by the word ""kāna"" in Arabic, which indicates "always was, is, and always will be."

[156] Ever-present and taking account of everything."

[157] "The obligatory bridal gift (mahr).

[158] Knowing that it is lawful."

[159] Although it is their property, Allāh (subḥānahu wa taʿālā) refers to it in the collective sense, reminding us that all wealth is provided by Him for the maintenance of the community as well as of individual members.

you release their property to them, bring witnesses upon them. And sufficient is Allāh as Accountant.

(7) For men is a share of what the parents and close relatives leave, and for women is a share of what the parents and close relatives leave, be it little or much - an obligatory share.

(8) And when [other] relatives and orphans and the needy are present at the [time of] division, then provide for them [something] out of it [i.e., the estate] and speak to them words of appropriate kindness.

(9) And let those [executors and guardians] fear [injustice] as if they [themselves] had left weak offspring behind and feared for them. So let them fear Allāh and speak words of appropriate justice.

(10) Indeed, those who devour the property of orphans unjustly are only consuming into their bellies fire. And they will be burned in a Blaze [i.e., Hellfire].

(11) Allāh instructs you concerning your children [i.e., their portions of inheritance]: for the male, what is equal to the share of two females. But if there are [only] daughters, two or more, for them is two thirds of one's estate.[160] And if there is only one, for her is half. And for one's parents, to each one of them is a sixth of his estate if he left children. But if he had no children and the parents [alone] inherit from him, then for his mother is one third. And if he had brothers [and/or sisters], for his mother is a sixth,[161] after any bequest he [may have] made or debt.[162] Your parents or your children - you know not which of them are nearest to you in benefit. [These shares are] an obligation [imposed] by Allāh. Indeed, Allāh is ever Knowing and Wise.

(12) And for you is half of what your wives leave if they have no child. But if they have a child, for you is one fourth of what they leave, after any bequest they [may have] made or debt. And for them [i.e., the wives] is one fourth if you leave no child. But if you leave a child, then for them is an eighth of what you leave, after any bequest you [may have] made or debt. And if a man or woman leaves neither ascendants nor descendants but has a brother or a sister, then for each one of them

---

[160] "Literally, "that which he left."

[161] Although the siblings themselves do not inherit in this case.

[162] Based upon prophetic ḥadīths, scholars have ruled that debt takes precedent over a bequest, that a bequest may not include any who inherit by law, and that the total bequest may not be more than one third of one's estate. After the fulfillment of debts and bequests (if any), the remainder of the estate is to be divided according to the ordinances in this sūrah."

is a sixth. But if they are more than two, they share a third,[163] after any bequest which was made or debt, as long as there is no detriment [caused].[164] [This is] an ordinance from Allāh, and Allāh is Knowing and Forbearing.

(13) These are the limits [set by] Allāh, and whoever obeys Allāh and His Messenger will be admitted by Him to gardens [in Paradise] under which rivers flow, abiding eternally therein; and that is the great attainment.

(14) And whoever disobeys Allāh and His Messenger and transgresses His limits - He will put him into the Fire to abide eternally therein, and he will have a humiliating punishment.

(15) Those who commit immorality [i.e., unlawful sexual intercourse] of your women - bring against them four [witnesses] from among you. And if they testify,[165] confine them [i.e., the guilty women] to houses until death takes them or Allāh ordains for them [another] way.[166]

(16) And the two[167] who commit it [i.e., unlawful sexual intercourse] among you - punish [i.e., dishonor] them both. But if they repent and correct themselves, leave them alone. Indeed, Allāh is ever Accepting of Repentance and Merciful.

(17) The repentance accepted by Allāh is only for those who do wrong in ignorance [or carelessness] and then repent soon [after].[168] It is those to whom Allāh will turn in forgiveness, and Allāh is ever Knowing and Wise.

(18) But repentance is not [accepted] of those who [continue to] do evil deeds up until, when death comes to one of them, he says, "Indeed, I have repented now," or of those who die while they are disbelievers. For them We have prepared a painful punishment.

(19) O you who have believed, it is not lawful for you to inherit women by compulsion.[169] And do not make difficulties for them in order to take [back] part of

---

[163] "These shares are divided equally between males and females.

[164] This is a condition for any bequest. If it has been violated by the deceased, his bequest is not to be honored, or it may be adjusted by the executor. See 2:182."

[165] "The witnesses must swear to actually having seen the act taking place.

[166] The "other way" (i.e., penalty) was later revealed in 24:2, canceling the ruling in this verse."

[167] Scholars differ over whether "the two" refers to two of the same sex (i.e., homosexuals) or those of opposite sexes. In either case, later rulings outlined in the sunnah have replaced this one.

[168] Scholars have also interpreted "soon" to mean before death.

[169] "The deceased man's heirs have no rights of marriage or otherwise over his widow.

what you gave them[170] unless they commit a clear immorality [i.e., adultery]. And live with them in kindness. For if you dislike them - perhaps you dislike a thing and Allāh makes therein much good.

(20) But if you want to replace one wife with another and you have given one of them a great amount [in gifts], do not take [back] from it anything. Would you take it in injustice and manifest sin?

(21) And how could you take it while you have gone in unto each other and they have taken from you a solemn covenant?

(22) And do not marry those [women] whom your fathers married, except what has already occurred.[171] Indeed, it was an immorality and hateful [to Allāh] and was evil as a way.

(23) Prohibited to you [for marriage] are your mothers, your daughters, your sisters, your father's sisters, your mother's sisters, your brother's daughters, your sister's daughters, your [milk] mothers who nursed you, your sisters through nursing, your wives' mothers, and your step-daughters under your guardianship [born] of your wives unto whom you have gone in. But if you have not gone in unto them, there is no sin upon you. And [also prohibited are] the wives of your sons who are from your [own] loins, and that you take [in marriage] two sisters simultaneously, except for what has already occurred.[172] Indeed, Allāh is ever Forgiving and Merciful.

(24) And [also prohibited to you are all] married women except those your right hands possess.[173] [This is] the decree of Allāh upon you. And lawful to you are [all others] beyond these, [provided] that you seek them [in marriage] with [gifts from] your property, desiring chastity, not unlawful sexual intercourse. So for whatever you enjoy [of marriage] from them, give them their due compensation[174] as an obligation. And there is no blame upon you for what you mutually agree to beyond the obligation. Indeed, Allāh is ever Knowing and Wise.

(25) And whoever among you cannot [find] the means to marry free, believing women, then [he may marry] from those whom your right hands possess of believing slave girls. And Allāh is most knowing about your faith. You [believers]

---

[170] At the time of marriage as mahr."

[171] Before Islām. After the ruling was revealed by Allāh, men were required to release those women unlawful to them (e.g., a stepmother, one of two sisters, or any wives over the limit of four). The same obligation applies to one once he has accepted Islām.

[172] See previous footnote.

[173] "i.e., slaves or war captives who had polytheist husbands.

[174] The mahr, a specified gift to the bride required of the man upon marriage."

are of one another. So marry them with the permission of their people and give them their due compensation [i.e., mahr] according to what is acceptable. [They should be] chaste, neither [of] those who commit unlawful intercourse randomly nor those who take [secret] lovers. But once they are sheltered in marriage, if they should commit adultery, then for them is half the punishment for free [unmarried] women. This [allowance] is for him among you who fears affliction [i.e., sin], but to be patient is better for you. And Allāh is Forgiving and Merciful.

(26) Allāh wants to make clear to you [the lawful from the unlawful] and guide you to the [good] practices of those before you and to accept your repentance. And Allāh is Knowing and Wise.

(27) Allāh wants to accept your repentance, but those who follow [their] passions want you to digress [into] a great deviation.

(28) And Allāh wants to lighten for you [your difficulties]; and mankind was created weak.

(29) O you who have believed, do not consume one another's wealth unjustly[175] but only [in lawful] business by mutual consent. And do not kill yourselves [or one another]. Indeed, Allāh is to you ever Merciful.

(30) And whoever does that in aggression and injustice - then We will drive him into a Fire. And that, for Allāh, is [always] easy.

(31) If you avoid the major sins which you are forbidden, We will remove from you your lesser sins and admit you to a noble entrance [into Paradise].

(32) And do not wish for that by which Allāh has made some of you exceed others. For men is a share of what they have earned, and for women is a share of[176] what they have earned. And ask Allāh of His bounty. Indeed Allāh is ever, of all things, Knowing.

(33) And for all, We have made heirs to what is left by parents and relatives. And to those whom your oaths have bound [to you] - give them their share.[177] Indeed Allāh is ever, over all things, a Witness.

(34) Men are in charge of women[178] by [right of] what Allāh has given one over the other and what they spend [for maintenance] from their wealth. So righteous women are devoutly obedient, guarding in [the husband's] absence what Allāh

---

[175] i.e., unlawfully or under false pretense.

[176] This may refer to shares of inheritance, wages and reward in the Hereafter.

[177] By bequest, as only those relatives mentioned in verses 11 and 12 inherit fixed shares.

[178] "This applies primarily to the husband-wife relationship.

would have them guard.[179] But those [wives] from whom you fear arrogance[180] - [first] advise them; [then if they persist], forsake them in bed; and [finally], strike them [lightly].[181] But if they obey you [once more], seek no means against them. Indeed, Allāh is ever Exalted and Grand.

(35) And if you fear dissension between the two, send an arbitrator from his people and an arbitrator from her people. If they both desire reconciliation, Allāh will cause it between them. Indeed, Allāh is ever Knowing and Aware.

(36) Worship Allāh and associate nothing with Him, and to parents do good, and to relatives, orphans, the needy, the near neighbor, the neighbor farther away, the companion at your side,[182] the traveler, and those whom your right hands possess. Indeed, Allāh does not like those who are self-deluding and boastful,

(37) Who are stingy and enjoin upon [other] people stinginess and conceal what Allāh has given them of His bounty - and We have prepared for the disbelievers a humiliating punishment -

(38) And [also] those who spend of their wealth to be seen by the people and believe not in Allāh nor in the Last Day. And he to whom Satan is a companion - then evil is he as a companion.

(39) And what [harm would come] upon them if they believed in Allāh and the Last Day and spent out of what Allāh provided for them? And Allāh is ever, about them, Knowing.

(40) Indeed, Allāh does not do injustice, [even] as much as an atom's weight; while if there is a good deed, He multiplies it and gives from Himself a great reward.

(41) So how [will it be] when We bring from every nation a witness and We bring you, [O Muḥammad], against these [people] as a witness?

---

[179] i.e., their husbands' property and their own chastity.

[180] i.e., major rebellion or refusal of basic religious obligations.

[181] This final disciplinary measure is more psychological than physical. It may be resorted to only after failure of the first two measures and when it is expected to amend the situation and prevent family breakup; otherwise, it is not acceptable. The Prophet ﷺ (who never struck a woman or a servant) additionally stipulated that it must not be severe or damaging and that the face be avoided."

[182] i.e., those whose acquaintance you have made. Also interpreted as the wife.

(42) That Day, those who disbelieved and disobeyed the Messenger will wish they could be covered by the earth. And they will not conceal from Allāh a [single] statement.

(43) O you who have believed, do not approach prayer while you are intoxicated until you know what you are saying[183] or in a state of janābah,[184] except those passing through [a place of prayer], until you have washed [your whole body]. And if you are ill or on a journey or one of you comes from the place of relieving himself or you have contacted women [i.e., had sexual intercourse] and find no water, then seek clean earth and wipe over your faces and your hands [with it]. Indeed, Allāh is ever Pardoning[185] and Forgiving.

(44) Have you not seen those who were given a portion of the Scripture, purchasing error [in exchange for it] and wishing you would lose the way?

(45) And Allāh is most knowing of your enemies; and sufficient is Allāh as an ally, and sufficient is Allāh as a helper.

(46) Among the Jews are those who distort words from their [proper] places [i.e., usages] and say, "We hear and disobey" and "Hear but be not heard" and "Rā'inā,"[186] twisting their tongues and defaming the religion. And if they had said [instead], "We hear and obey" and "Wait for us [to understand]," it would have been better for them and more suitable. But Allāh has cursed them for their disbelief, so they believe not, except for a few.[187]

(47) O you who were given the Scripture, believe in what We have sent down [to Prophet Muḥammad (ﷺ)], confirming that which is with you, before We obliterate faces and turn them toward their backs or curse them as We cursed the sabbath-breakers.[188] And ever is the matter [i.e., decree] of Allāh accomplished.

(48) Indeed, Allāh does not forgive association with Him, but He forgives what is less than that for whom He wills. And he who associates others with Allāh has certainly fabricated a tremendous sin.

---

[183] "The use of intoxicants was later prohibited completely. See 5:90-91.

[184] Literally, "distance." The state of one under obligation to perform ghusl (a complete bath) due to having had sexual intercourse or ejaculation.

[185] Literally, able to erase and remove sins completely, leaving no trace of them in the record of deeds."

[186] "See footnote to 2:104.

[187] Or "except with little belief.""

[188] See 7:163-166.

(49) Have you not seen those who claim themselves to be pure? Rather, Allāh purifies whom He wills, and injustice is not done to them, [even] as much as a thread [inside a date seed].

(50) Look how they invent about Allāh untruth, and sufficient is that as a manifest sin.

(51) Have you not seen those who were given a portion of the Scripture, who believe in jibt [superstition] and ṭāghūt [false objects of worship] and say about the disbelievers, "These are better guided than the believers as to the way"?

(52) Those are the ones whom Allāh has cursed; and he whom Allāh curses - never will you find for him a helper.

(53) Or have they a share of dominion? Then [if that were so], they would not give the people [even as much as] the speck on a date seed.

(54) Or do they envy people for what Allāh has given them of His bounty? But We had already given the family of Abraham the Scripture and wisdom[189] and conferred upon them a great kingdom.

(55) And some among them believed in it,[190] and some among them were averse to it. And sufficient is Hell as a blaze.

(56) Indeed, those who disbelieve in Our verses - We will drive them into a fire. Every time their skins are roasted through, We will replace them with other skins so they may taste the punishment. Indeed, Allāh is ever Exalted in Might and Wise.

(57) But those who believe and do righteous deeds - We will admit them to gardens beneath which rivers flow, wherein they abide forever. For them therein are purified spouses, and We will admit them to deepening shade.

(58) Indeed, Allāh commands you to render trusts to whom they are due and when you judge between people to judge with justice. Excellent is that which Allāh instructs you. Indeed, Allāh is ever Hearing and Seeing.

(59) O you who have believed, obey Allāh and obey the Messenger and those in authority among you. And if you disagree over anything, refer it to Allāh and the Messenger, if you should believe in Allāh and the Last Day. That is the best [way] and best in result.

---

[189] Prophetic teachings.

[190] In what was given to them. Also interpreted as "in him," i.e., Muḥammad (ﷺ).

(60) Have you not seen those who claim to have believed in what was revealed to you, [O Muḥammad], and what was revealed before you? They wish to refer legislation to ṭāghūt,[191] while they were commanded to reject it; and Satan wishes to lead them far astray.

(61) And when it is said to them, "Come to what Allāh has revealed and to the Messenger," you see the hypocrites turning away from you in aversion.

(62) So how [will it be] when disaster strikes them because of what their hands have put forth and then they come to you swearing by Allāh, "We intended nothing but good conduct and accommodation."

(63) Those are the ones of whom Allāh knows what is in their hearts, so turn away from them[192] but admonish them and speak to them a far-reaching [i.e., effective] word.

(64) And We did not send any messenger except to be obeyed by permission of Allāh. And if, when they wronged themselves, they had come to you, [O Muḥammad], and asked forgiveness of Allāh and the Messenger had asked forgiveness for them, they would have found Allāh Accepting of Repentance and Merciful.

(65) But no, by your Lord, they will not [truly] believe until they make you, [O Muḥammad], judge concerning that over which they dispute among themselves and then find within themselves no discomfort from what you have judged and submit in [full, willing] submission.

(66) And if We had decreed upon them, "Kill yourselves" or "Leave your homes," they would not have done it, except for a few of them. But if they had done what they were instructed, it would have been better for them and a firmer position [for them in faith].

(67) And then We would have given them from Us a great reward.

(68) And We would have guided them to a straight path.

(69) And whoever obeys Allāh and the Messenger - those will be with the ones upon whom Allāh has bestowed favor of the prophets, the steadfast affirmers of truth, the martyrs and the righteous. And excellent are those as companions.

---

[191] False objects of worship or those transgressors who usurp the divine right of government.

[192] i.e., use not violence against them.

(70) That is the bounty from Allāh, and sufficient is Allāh as Knower.

(71) O you who have believed, take your precaution and [either] go forth in companies or go forth all together.

(72) And indeed, there is among you he who lingers behind; and if disaster strikes you, he says, "Allāh has favored me in that I was not present with them."

(73) But if bounty comes to you from Allāh, he will surely say, as if [i.e., showing that] there had never been between you and him any affection, "Oh, I wish I had been with them so I could have attained a great attainment."[193]

(74) So let those fight in the cause of Allāh who sell the life of this world for the Hereafter. And he who fights in the cause of Allāh and is killed or achieves victory - We will bestow upon him a great reward.

(75) And what is [the matter] with you that you fight not in the cause of Allāh and [for] the oppressed among men, women, and children who say, "Our Lord, take us out of this city of oppressive people and appoint for us from Yourself a protector and appoint for us from Yourself a helper"?

(76) Those who believe fight in the cause of Allāh, and those who disbelieve fight in the cause of ṭāghūt.[194] So fight against the allies of Satan. Indeed, the plot of Satan has ever been weak.

(77) Have you not seen those who were told, "Restrain your hands [from fighting][195] and establish prayer and give zakāh"? But then when battle was ordained for them, at once a party of them feared men as they fear Allāh or with [even] greater fear. They said, "Our Lord, why have You decreed upon us fighting? If only You had postponed [it for] us for a short time." Say, "The enjoyment of this world is little, and the Hereafter is better for he who fears Allāh. And injustice will not be done to you, [even] as much as a thread [inside a date seed]."

(78) Wherever you may be, death will overtake you, even if you should be within towers of lofty construction. But if good comes to them, they say, "This is from Allāh"; and if evil befalls them, they say,[196] "This is from you." Say, "All [things] are from Allāh." So what is [the matter] with those people that they can hardly understand any statement?

---

[193] The spoils of war. Although having pretended to befriend the believers in support of Allāh's religion, the hypocrite will not be willing to fight except for material gain.
[194] See footnote to 4:60.
[195] Before permission was given by Allāh.
[196] Addressing the Prophet (ﷺ).

(79) What comes to you of good is from Allāh, but what comes to you of evil, [O man], is from yourself.[197] And We have sent you, [O Muḥammad], to the people as a messenger, and sufficient is Allāh as Witness.[198]

(80) He who obeys the Messenger has obeyed Allāh; but those who turn away - We have not sent you over them as a guardian.

(81) And they say, "[We pledge] obedience." But when they leave you, a group of them spend the night determining to do other than what you say. But Allāh records what they plan by night. So leave them alone and rely upon Allāh. And sufficient is Allāh as Disposer of affairs.

(82) Then do they not reflect upon the Qur'ān?[199] If it had been from [any] other than Allāh, they would have found within it much contradiction.

(83) And when there comes to them something [i.e., information] about [public] security or fear, they spread it around. But if they had referred it back to the Messenger or to those of authority among them, then the ones who [can] draw correct conclusions from it would have known about it. And if not for the favor of Allāh upon you and His mercy, you would have followed Satan, except for a few.

(84) So fight, [O Muḥammad], in the cause of Allāh; you are not held responsible except for yourself. And encourage the believers [to join you] that perhaps Allāh will restrain the [military] might of those who disbelieve. And Allāh is greater in might and stronger in [exemplary] punishment.[200]

(85) Whoever intercedes for a good cause will have a share [i.e., reward] therefrom; and whoever intercedes for an evil cause will have a portion [i.e., burden] therefrom. And ever is Allāh, over all things, a Keeper.[201]

(86) And when you are greeted with a greeting, greet [in return] with one better than it or [at least] return it [in a like manner]. Indeed Allāh is ever, over all things, an Accountant.

---

[197] "As a result of your mistakes or sins.

[198] i.e., never absent, always seeing and having complete knowledge of everything within His dominion."

[199] i.e., its meanings and its objective.

[200] Allāh is able to defeat them in such a way as to deter others from attempting anything similar.

[201] Providing, protecting, witnessing, keeping precise records and capable of recompense.

(87) Allāh - there is no deity except Him. He will surely assemble you for [account on] the Day of Resurrection, about which there is no doubt. And who is more truthful than Allāh in statement.

(88) What is [the matter] with you [that you are] two groups concerning the hypocrites,[202] while Allāh has made them fall back [into error and disbelief] for what they earned.[203] Do you wish to guide those whom Allāh has sent astray? And he whom Allāh sends astray - never will you find for him a way [of guidance].[204]

(89) They wish you would disbelieve as they disbelieved so you would be alike. So do not take from among them allies until they emigrate for the cause of Allāh. But if they turn away [i.e., refuse], then seize them and kill them [for their betrayal] wherever you find them and take not from among them any ally or helper,

(90) Except for those who take refuge with a people between yourselves and whom is a treaty or those who come to you, their hearts strained at [the prospect of] fighting you or fighting their own people. And if Allāh had willed, He could have given them power over you, and they would have fought you. So if they remove themselves from you and do not fight you and offer you peace, then Allāh has not made for you a cause [for fighting] against them.

(91) You will find others who wish to obtain security from you and [to] obtain security from their people. Every time they are returned to [the influence of] disbelief, they fall back into it. So if they do not withdraw from you or offer you peace or restrain their hands, then seize them and kill them wherever you overtake them. And those - We have made for you against them a clear authorization.

(92) And never is it for a believer to kill a believer except by mistake. And whoever kills a believer by mistake - then the freeing of a believing slave and a compensation payment [diyah] presented to his [i.e., the deceased's] family [is required], unless they give [up their right as] charity. But if he [i.e., the deceased] was from a people at war with you and he was a believer - then [only] the freeing of a believing slave; and if he was from a people with whom you have a treaty - then a compensation payment presented to his family and the freeing of a believing slave. And whoever does not find [one or cannot afford to buy one] - then [instead], a fast for two

---

[202] "i.e., divided between two viewpoints - whether or not they should be fought and killed.
[203] As the result of their disobedience and disloyalty.
[204] Allāh (subḥānahu wa taʿālā) leaves or sends astray those who choose to reject His guidance."

months consecutively,[205] [seeking] acceptance of repentance from Allāh.[206] And Allāh is ever Knowing and Wise.

(93) But whoever kills a believer intentionally - his recompense is Hell, wherein he will abide eternally, and Allāh has become angry with him and has cursed him and has prepared for him a great punishment.

(94) O you who have believed, when you go forth [to fight] in the cause of Allāh, investigate; and do not say to one who gives you [a greeting of] peace, "You are not a believer,"[207] aspiring for the goods of worldly life; for with Allāh are many acquisitions. You [yourselves] were like that before; then Allāh conferred His favor [i.e., guidance] upon you, so investigate. Indeed Allāh is ever, of what you do, Aware.

(95) Not equal are those believers remaining [at home] - other than the disabled - and the mujāhideen, [who strive and fight] in the cause of Allāh with their wealth and their lives. Allāh has preferred the mujāhideen through their wealth and their lives over those who remain [behind], by degrees. And to all [i.e., both] Allāh has promised the best [reward]. But Allāh has preferred the mujāhideen over those who remain [behind] with a great reward -

(96) Degrees [of high position] from Him and forgiveness and mercy. And Allāh is ever Forgiving and Merciful.

(97) Indeed, those whom the angels take [in death] while wronging themselves[208] - [the angels] will say, "In what [condition] were you?" They will say, "We were oppressed in the land." They [the angels] will say, "Was not the earth of Allāh spacious [enough] for you to emigrate therein?" For those, their refuge is Hell - and evil it is as a destination.

(98) Except for the oppressed among men, women, and children who cannot devise a plan nor are they directed to a way[209] -

(99) For those it is expected that Allāh will pardon them, and Allāh is ever Pardoning[210] and Forgiving.

---

[205] "Uninterrupted except when there is an Islāmically valid reason, as in Ramaḍān.

[206] An accidental death usually results from some degree of negligence or error for which the believer feels the need to repent."

[207] Do not assume that he pretends Islām merely in order to save himself, for he may be sincere in faith.

[208] By preferring to remain among the disbelievers, although they have the means to emigrate, in an environment where a Muslim is unable to practice his religion freely.

[209] They are prevented by circumstances beyond their control.

[210] Refer to footnote in 4:43.

(100) And whoever emigrates for the cause of Allāh will find on the earth many [alternative] locations and abundance. And whoever leaves his home as an emigrant to Allāh and His Messenger and then death overtakes him - his reward has already become incumbent upon Allāh. And Allāh is ever Forgiving and Merciful.

(101) And when you travel throughout the land, there is no blame upon you for shortening the prayer,[211] [especially] if you fear that those who disbelieve may disrupt [or attack] you.[212] Indeed, the disbelievers are ever to you a clear enemy.

(102) And when you [i.e., the commander of an army] are among them and lead them in prayer,[213] let a group of them stand [in prayer] with you and let them carry their arms. And when they have prostrated, let them be [in position] behind you and have the other group come forward which has not [yet] prayed and let them pray with you, taking precaution and carrying their arms. Those who disbelieve wish that you would neglect your weapons and your baggage so they could come down upon you in one [single] attack. But there is no blame upon you, if you are troubled by rain or are ill, for putting down your arms, but take precaution. Indeed, Allāh has prepared for the disbelievers a humiliating punishment.

(103) And when you have completed the prayer, remember Allāh standing, sitting, or [lying] on your sides. But when you become secure, re-establish [regular] prayer. Indeed, prayer has been decreed upon the believers a decree of specified times.

(104) And do not weaken in pursuit of the enemy. If you should be suffering - so are they suffering as you are suffering, but you expect from Allāh that which they expect not. And Allāh is ever Knowing and Wise.

(105) Indeed, We have revealed to you, [O Muḥammad], the Book in truth so you may judge between the people by that which Allāh has shown you. And do not be for the deceitful an advocate.

(106) And seek forgiveness of Allāh. Indeed, Allāh is ever Forgiving and Merciful.

(107) And do not argue on behalf of those who deceive themselves. Indeed, Allāh loves not one who is a habitually sinful deceiver.

(108) They conceal [their evil intentions and deeds] from the people, but they cannot conceal [them] from Allāh, and He is with them [in His knowledge] when

---

[211] "The four rak'ah prayers are shortened to two rak'ahs.
[212] The example of the Prophet (ﷺ) and his companions illustrates that fear is not a condition for this allowance, merely travel."
[213] At times of fear on the battleground.

they spend the night in such as He does not accept of speech. And ever is Allāh, of what they do, encompassing.

(109) Here you are - those who argue on their behalf in [this] worldly life - but who will argue with Allāh for them on the Day of Resurrection, or who will [then] be their representative?

(110) And whoever does a wrong or wrongs himself but then seeks forgiveness of Allāh will find Allāh Forgiving and Merciful.

(111) And whoever earns [i.e., commits] a sin only earns it against himself. And Allāh is ever Knowing and Wise.

(112) But whoever earns an offense or a sin and then blames it on an innocent [person] has taken upon himself a slander and manifest sin.

(113) And if it was not for the favor of Allāh upon you, [O Muḥammad], and His mercy, a group of them would have determined to mislead you. But they do not mislead except themselves, and they will not harm you at all. And Allāh has revealed to you the Book and wisdom and has taught you that which you did not know. And ever has the favor of Allāh upon you been great.

(114) No good is there in much of their private conversation, except for those who enjoin charity or that which is right or conciliation between people. And whoever does that seeking means to the approval of Allāh - then We are going to give him a great reward.

(115) And whoever opposes the Messenger after guidance has become clear to him and follows other than the way of the believers - We will give him what he has taken[214] and drive him into Hell, and evil it is as a destination.

(116) Indeed, Allāh does not forgive association with Him, but He forgives what is less than that for whom He wills. And he who associates others with Allāh has certainly gone far astray.

(117) They call upon instead of Him none but female [deities], and they [actually] call upon none but a rebellious Satan,

(118) Whom Allāh has cursed. For he had said, "I will surely take from among Your servants a specific portion.

---

[214] i.e., make him responsible for his choice.

(119) And I will mislead them, and I will arouse in them [sinful] desires, and I will command them so they will slit the ears of cattle, and I will command them so they will change the creation of Allāh." And whoever takes Satan as an ally instead of Allāh has certainly sustained a clear loss.

(120) He [i.e., Satan] promises them and arouses desire in them. But Satan does not promise them except delusion.

(121) The refuge of those will be Hell, and they will not find from it an escape.

(122) But the ones who believe and do righteous deeds - We will admit them to gardens beneath which rivers flow, wherein they will abide forever. [It is] the promise of Allāh, [which is] truth, and who is more truthful than Allāh in statement.

(123) It [i.e., Paradise] is not [obtained] by your wishful thinking nor by that of the People of the Scripture. Whoever does a wrong will be recompensed for it, and he will not find besides Allāh a protector or a helper.

(124) And whoever does righteous deeds, whether male or female, while being a believer - those will enter Paradise and will not be wronged, [even as much as] the speck on a date seed.

(125) And who is better in religion than one who submits himself to Allāh while being a doer of good and follows the religion of Abraham, inclining toward truth? And Allāh took Abraham as an intimate friend.

(126) And to Allāh belongs whatever is in the heavens and whatever is on the earth. And ever is Allāh, of all things, encompassing.

(127) And they request from you, [O Muḥammad], a [legal] ruling concerning women. Say, "Allāh gives you a ruling about them and [about] what has been recited to you in the Book concerning the orphan girls to whom you do not give what is decreed for them[215] - and [yet] you desire to marry them - and concerning the oppressed among children and that you maintain for orphans [their rights] in justice." And whatever you do of good - indeed, Allāh is ever Knowing of it.

(128) And if a woman fears from her husband contempt or evasion, there is no sin upon them if they make terms of settlement between them - and settlement is best. And present in [human] souls is stinginess.[216] But if you do good and fear Allāh - then indeed Allāh is ever, of what you do, Aware.

---

[215] i.e., their rights, in general, and their mahr, specifically.
[216] i.e., holding on to self-interests.

(129) And you will never be able to be equal [in feeling] between wives, even if you should strive [to do so]. So do not incline completely [toward one] and leave another hanging.[217] And if you amend [your affairs] and fear Allāh - then indeed, Allāh is ever Forgiving and Merciful.

(130) But if they separate [by divorce], Allāh will enrich each [of them] from His abundance. And ever is Allāh Encompassing and Wise.

(131) And to Allāh belongs whatever is in the heavens and whatever is on the earth. And We have instructed those who were given the Scripture before you and yourselves to fear Allāh. But if you disbelieve - then to Allāh belongs whatever is in the heavens and whatever is on the earth. And ever is Allāh Free of need and Praiseworthy.

(132) And to Allāh belongs whatever is in the heavens and whatever is on the earth. And sufficient is Allāh as Disposer of affairs.[218]

(133) If He wills, He can do away with you, O people, and bring others [in your place]. And ever is Allāh competent to do that.

(134) Whoever desires the reward of this world - then with Allāh is the reward of this world and the Hereafter. And ever is Allāh Hearing and Seeing.

(135) O you who have believed, be persistently standing firm in justice, witnesses for Allāh, even if it be against yourselves or parents and relatives. Whether one is rich or poor, Allāh is more worthy of both.[219] So follow not [personal] inclination, lest you not be just. And if you distort [your testimony] or refuse [to give it], then indeed Allāh is ever, of what you do, Aware.

(136) O you who have believed, believe[220] in Allāh and His Messenger and the Book that He sent down upon His Messenger and the Scripture which He sent down before. And whoever disbelieves in Allāh, His angels, His books, His messengers, and the Last Day has certainly gone far astray.

(137) Indeed, those who have believed then disbelieved, then believed then disbelieved, and then increased in disbelief - never will Allāh forgive them, nor will He guide them to a way.

---

[217] Neither divorced nor enjoying the rights of marriage.

[218] Refer to footnote in 3:173.

[219] i.e., more knowledgeable of their best interests. Therefore, adhere to what He has enjoined upon you and testify honestly.

[220] i.e., renew, confirm and adhere to your belief.

(138) Give tidings to the hypocrites that there is for them a painful punishment -

(139) Those who take disbelievers as allies instead of the believers. Do they seek with them honor [through power]? But indeed, honor belongs to Allāh entirely.[221]

(140) And it has already come down to you in the Book [i.e., the Qur'ān] that when you hear the verses of Allāh [recited], they are denied [by them] and ridiculed; so do not sit with them until they enter into another conversation. Indeed, you would then be like them.[222] Indeed, Allāh will gather the hypocrites and disbelievers in Hell all together -

(141) Those who wait [and watch] you. Then if you gain a victory from Allāh, they say, "Were we not with you?" But if the disbelievers have a success, they say [to them], "Did we not gain the advantage over you, but we protected you from the believers?" Allāh will judge between [all of] you on the Day of Resurrection, and never will Allāh give the disbelievers over the believers a way [to overcome them].[223]

(142) Indeed, the hypocrites [think to] deceive Allāh, but He is deceiving them. And when they stand for prayer, they stand lazily, showing [themselves to] the people and not remembering Allāh except a little,

(143) Wavering between them, [belonging] neither to these [i.e., the believers] nor to those [i.e., the disbelievers]. And whoever Allāh sends astray - never will you find for him a way.

(144) O you who have believed, do not take the disbelievers as allies instead of the believers. Do you wish to give Allāh against yourselves a clear case?

(145) Indeed, the hypocrites will be in the lowest depths of the Fire - and never will you find for them a helper -

(146) Except for those who repent, correct themselves, hold fast to Allāh, and are sincere in their religion for Allāh, for those will be with the believers. And Allāh is going to give the believers a great reward.

---

[221] Being the source of all power and honor, Allāh grants them to whom He wills.
[222] In this world, by participation in their blasphemy, and in the next, where you will share their punishment.
[223] In the Hereafter, but possibly in this world as well.

(147) What would Allāh do with [i.e., gain from] your punishment if you are grateful and believe? And ever is Allāh Appreciative[224] and Knowing.

(148) Allāh does not like the public mention of evil except by one who has been wronged. And ever is Allāh Hearing and Knowing.

(149) If [instead] you show [some] good or conceal it or pardon an offense - indeed, Allāh is ever Pardoning and Competent.[225]

(150) Indeed, those who disbelieve in Allāh and His messengers and wish to discriminate between Allāh and His messengers and say, "We believe in some and disbelieve in others," and wish to adopt a way in between -

(151) Those are the disbelievers, truly. And We have prepared for the disbelievers a humiliating punishment.

(152) But they who believe in Allāh and His messengers and do not discriminate between any of them - to those He is going to give their rewards. And ever is Allāh Forgiving and Merciful.

(153) The People of the Scripture ask you to bring down to them a book from the heaven. But they had asked of Moses [even] greater than that and said, "Show us Allāh outright," so the thunderbolt struck them for their wrongdoing. Then they took the calf [for worship] after clear evidences had come to them, and We pardoned that. And We gave Moses a clear authority.

(154) And We raised over them the mount for [refusal of] their covenant; and We said to them, "Enter the gate bowing humbly"; and We said to them, "Do not transgress on the sabbath"; and We took from them a solemn covenant.

(155) And [We cursed them][226] for their breaking of the covenant and their disbelief in the signs of Allāh and their killing of the prophets without right and their saying, "Our hearts are wrapped" [i.e., sealed against reception]. Rather, Allāh has sealed them because of their disbelief, so they believe not, except for a few.[227]

(156) And [We cursed them] for their disbelief and their saying against Mary a great slander[228]

---

[224] Of repentance, self-discipline and good deeds, rewarding for them abundantly.

[225] Allāh is always able to exact retribution, although He pardons out of His grace.

[226] "Another interpretation is "And [We made certain good foods unlawful to them]," based upon verse 160.

[227] Or "except with little belief.""

[228] When they accused her of fornication.

(157) And [for] their saying, "Indeed, we have killed the Messiah, Jesus the son of Mary, the messenger of Allāh." And they did not kill him, nor did they crucify him; but [another] was made to resemble him to them. And indeed, those who differ over it are in doubt about it. They have no knowledge of it except the following of assumption. And they did not kill him, for certain.[229]

(158) Rather, Allāh raised him to Himself. And ever is Allāh Exalted in Might and Wise.

(159) And there is none from the People of the Scripture but that he will surely believe in him [i.e., Jesus] before his death.[230] And on the Day of Resurrection he will be against them a witness.

(160) For wrongdoing on the part of the Jews, We made unlawful for them [certain] good foods which had been lawful to them, and for their averting from the way of Allāh many [people],

(161) And [for] their taking of usury while they had been forbidden from it, and their consuming of the people's wealth unjustly. And We have prepared for the disbelievers among them a painful punishment.

(162) But those firm in knowledge among them and the believers believe in what has been revealed to you, [O Muḥammad], and what was revealed before you. And the establishers of prayer [especially] and the givers of zakāh and the believers in Allāh and the Last Day - those We will give a great reward.

(163) Indeed, We have revealed to you, [O Muḥammad], as We revealed to Noah and the prophets after him. And We revealed to Abraham, Ishmael, Isaac, Jacob, the Descendants,[231] Jesus, Job, Jonah, Aaron, and Solomon, and to David We gave the book [of Psalms].

(164) And [We sent] messengers about whom We have related [their stories] to you before and messengers about whom We have not related to you. And Allāh spoke to Moses with [direct] speech.

(165) [We sent] messengers as bringers of good tidings and warners so that mankind will have no argument against Allāh after the messengers. And ever is Allāh Exalted in Might and Wise.

---

[229] Another meaning is "And they did not kill him, being certain [of his identity]," i.e., they killed another assuming it was Jesus (upon whom be peace).
[230] One interpretation is that "his death" refers to that of Jesus after his return to earth. Or it can mean "the death of every individual from among the People of the Scripture."
[231] Al-Asbāṭ. See footnote to 2:136.

(166) But Allāh bears witness to that which He has revealed to you. He has sent it down with His knowledge, and the angels bear witness [as well]. And sufficient is Allāh as Witness.

(167) Indeed, those who disbelieve and avert [people] from the way of Allāh have certainly gone far astray.

(168) Indeed, those who disbelieve and commit wrong [or injustice] - never will Allāh forgive them, nor will He guide them to a path,

(169) Except the path of Hell; they will abide therein forever. And that, for Allāh, is [always] easy.

(170) O mankind, the Messenger has come to you with the truth from your Lord, so believe; it is better for you. But if you disbelieve - then indeed, to Allāh belongs whatever is in the heavens and earth. And ever is Allāh Knowing and Wise.

(171) O People of the Scripture, do not commit excess in your religion[232] or say about Allāh except the truth. The Messiah, Jesus the son of Mary, was but a messenger of Allāh and His word which He directed to Mary and a soul [created at a command] from Him. So believe in Allāh and His messengers. And do not say, "Three"; desist - it is better for you. Indeed, Allāh is but one God. Exalted is He above having a son. To Him belongs whatever is in the heavens and whatever is on the earth. And sufficient is Allāh as Disposer of affairs.

(172) Never would the Messiah disdain to be a servant of Allāh, nor would the angels near [to Him]. And whoever disdains His worship and is arrogant - He will gather them to Himself all together.

(173) And as for those who believed and did righteous deeds, He will give them in full their rewards and grant them extra from His bounty. But as for those who disdained and were arrogant, He will punish them with a painful punishment, and they will not find for themselves besides Allāh any protector or helper.

(174) O mankind, there has come to you a conclusive proof from your Lord, and We have sent down to you a clear light.[233]

(175) So those who believe in Allāh and hold fast to Him - He will admit them to mercy from Himself and bounty and guide them to Himself on a straight path.

---

[232] Such as attributing divine qualities to certain creations of Allāh or revering them excessively.
[233] Showing the truth (i.e., the Qur'ān).

(176) They request from you a [legal] ruling. Say, "Allāh gives you a ruling concerning one having neither descendants nor ascendants [as heirs]." If a man dies, leaving no child but [only] a sister, she will have half of what he left. And he inherits from her if she [dies and] has no child. But if there are two sisters [or more], they will have two thirds of what he left. If there are both brothers and sisters, the male will have the share of two females. Allāh makes clear to you [His law], lest you go astray. And Allāh is Knowing of all things.

Surah Al-Ma'idah

(1) O you who have believed, fulfill [all] contracts.[234] Lawful for you are the animals of grazing livestock except for that which is recited to you [in this Qur'ān] - hunting not being permitted while you are in the state of iḥrām.[235] Indeed, Allāh ordains what He intends.

(2) O you who have believed, do not violate the rites of Allāh or [the sanctity of] the sacred month or [neglect the marking of] the sacrificial animals and garlanding [them] or [violate the safety of] those coming to the Sacred House seeking bounty from their Lord and [His] approval. But when you come out of iḥrām, then [you may] hunt. And do not let the hatred of a people for having obstructed you from al-Masjid al-Ḥarām lead you to transgress. And cooperate in righteousness and piety, but do not cooperate in sin and aggression. And fear Allāh; indeed, Allāh is severe in penalty.

(3) Prohibited to you are dead animals,[236] blood, the flesh of swine, and that which has been dedicated to other than Allāh, and [those animals] killed by strangling or by a violent blow or by a head-long fall or by the goring of horns, and those from which a wild animal has eaten, except what you [are able to] slaughter [before its death], and those which are sacrificed on stone altars,[237] and [prohibited is] that you seek decision through divining arrows. That is grave disobedience. This day those who disbelieve have despaired of [defeating] your religion; so fear them not, but fear Me. This day I have perfected for you your religion and completed My favor upon you and have approved for you Islām as religion. But whoever is forced by severe hunger with no inclination to sin - then indeed, Allāh is Forgiving and Merciful.

(4) They ask you, [O Muḥammad], what has been made lawful for them. Say, "Lawful for you are [all] good foods and [game caught by] what you have trained of hunting animals[238] which you train as Allāh has taught you. So eat of what they catch for you, and mention the name of Allāh upon it, and fear Allāh." Indeed, Allāh is swift in account.

(5) This day [all] good foods have been made lawful, and the food of those who were given the Scripture is lawful for you and your food is lawful for them. And [lawful

---

[234] "Which includes promises, covenants, oaths, etc.

[235] The state of ritual consecration for ḥajj or ʿumrah."

[236] "See footnote to 2:173.

[237] In the name of anything other than Allāh."

[238] Such as dogs, falcons, etc.

in marriage are] chaste women from among the believers and chaste women from among those who were given the Scripture before you, when you have given them their due compensation,[239] desiring chastity, not unlawful sexual intercourse or taking [secret] lovers. And whoever denies the faith - his work has become worthless, and he, in the Hereafter, will be among the losers.

(6) O you who have believed, when you rise to [perform] prayer, wash your faces and your forearms to the elbows and wipe over your heads and wash your feet to the ankles. And if you are in a state of janābah,[240] then purify yourselves. But if you are ill or on a journey or one of you comes from the place of relieving himself or you have contacted women[241] and do not find water, then seek clean earth and wipe over your faces and hands with it. Allāh does not intend to make difficulty for you, but He intends to purify you and complete His favor upon you that you may be grateful.

(7) And remember the favor of Allāh upon you and His covenant with which He bound you when you said, "We hear and we obey"; and fear Allāh. Indeed, Allāh is Knowing of that within the breasts.

(8) O you who have believed, be persistently standing firm for Allāh, witnesses in justice, and do not let the hatred of a people prevent you from being just. Be just; that is nearer to righteousness. And fear Allāh; indeed, Allāh is [fully] Aware of what you do.

(9) Allāh has promised those who believe and do righteous deeds [that] for them there is forgiveness and great reward.

(10) But those who disbelieve and deny Our signs - those are the companions of Hellfire.

(11) O you who have believed, remember the favor of Allāh upon you when a people determined to extend their hands [in aggression] against you, but He withheld their hands from you; and fear Allāh. And upon Allāh let the believers rely.

(12) And Allāh had already taken a covenant from the Children of Israel, and We delegated from among them twelve leaders. And Allāh said, "I am with you. If you establish prayer and give zakāh and believe in My messengers and support them and loan Allāh a goodly loan,[242] I will surely remove from you your misdeeds and

---

[239] The specified bridal gift (mahr).
[240] "See footnote to 4:43.
[241] i.e., had sexual intercourse."
[242] By spending in the cause of Allāh, seeking His reward.

admit you to gardens beneath which rivers flow. But whoever of you disbelieves after that has certainly strayed from the soundness of the way."

(13) So for their breaking of the covenant We cursed them and made their hearts hardened. They distort words from their [proper] places [i.e., usages] and have forgotten a portion of that of which they were reminded.[243] And you will still observe deceit among them, except a few of them. But pardon them and overlook [their misdeeds]. Indeed, Allāh loves the doers of good.

(14) And from those who say, "We are Christians" We took their covenant; but they forgot a portion of that of which they were reminded.[244] So We caused among them[245] animosity and hatred until the Day of Resurrection. And Allāh is going to inform them about what they used to do.

(15) O People of the Scripture, there has come to you Our Messenger making clear to you much of what you used to conceal of the Scripture and overlooking much.[246] There has come to you from Allāh a light and a clear Book [i.e., the Qur'ān]

(16) By which Allāh guides those who pursue His pleasure to the ways of peace[247] and brings them out from darknesses into the light, by His permission, and guides them to a straight path.

(17) They have certainly disbelieved who say that Allāh is Christ, the son of Mary. Say, "Then who could prevent Allāh at all if He had intended to destroy Christ, the son of Mary, or his mother or everyone on the earth?" And to Allāh belongs the dominion of the heavens and the earth and whatever is between them. He creates what He wills, and Allāh is over all things competent.

(18) But the Jews and the Christians say, "We are the children of Allāh and His beloved." Say, "Then why does He punish you for your sins?" Rather, you are human beings from among those He has created. He forgives whom He wills, and He punishes whom He wills. And to Allāh belongs the dominion of the heavens and the earth and whatever is between them, and to Him is the [final] destination.

(19) O People of the Scripture, there has come to you Our Messenger to make clear to you [the religion] after a period [of suspension] of messengers, lest you say, "There came not to us any bringer of good tidings or a warner." But there has come

---

[243] In the Torah concerning the coming of Prophet Muḥammad (ﷺ).

[244] "In the Gospel concerning the coming of Prophet Muḥammad (ﷺ).

[245] i.e., among their various denominations or sects."

[246] Of your sin in that regard.

[247] i.e., security, well-being, integrity and escape from Hellfire. Literally, "freedom from all evil."

to you a bringer of good tidings and a warner. And Allāh is over all things competent.

(20) And [mention, O Muḥammad], when Moses said to his people, "O my people, remember the favor of Allāh upon you when He appointed among you prophets and made you possessors[248] and gave you that which He had not given anyone among the worlds.

(21) O my people, enter the blessed land [i.e., Palestine] which Allāh has assigned to you and do not turn back [from fighting in Allāh's cause] and [thus] become losers."

(22) They said, "O Moses, indeed within it is a people of tyrannical strength, and indeed, we will never enter it until they leave it; but if they leave it, then we will enter."

(23) Said two men from those who feared [to disobey] upon whom Allāh had bestowed favor, "Enter upon them through the gate, for when you have entered it, you will be predominant.[249] And upon Allāh rely, if you should be believers."

(24) They said, "O Moses, indeed we will not enter it, ever, as long as they are within it; so go, you and your Lord, and fight. Indeed, we are remaining right here."

(25) [Moses] said, "My Lord, indeed I do not possess [i.e., control] except myself and my brother, so part us[250] from the defiantly disobedient people."

(26) [Allāh] said, "Then indeed, it is forbidden to them for forty years [in which] they will wander throughout the land. So do not grieve over the defiantly disobedient people."

(27) And recite to them the story of Adam's two sons, in truth, when they both made an offering [to Allāh], and it was accepted from one of them but was not accepted from the other. Said [the latter], "I will surely kill you." Said [the former], "Indeed, Allāh only accepts from the righteous [who fear Him].

(28) If you should raise your hand toward me to kill me - I shall not raise my hand toward you to kill you. Indeed, I fear Allāh, Lord of the worlds.

(29) Indeed, I want you to obtain [thereby] my sin and your sin so you will be among the companions of the Fire. And that is the recompense of wrongdoers."

---

[248] Of all that you need - specifically, homes, wives and servants. Or "sovereigns," i.e., those of independent authority.

[249] i.e., If you obey the command of Allāh trusting in Him, He will fulfill His promise to you.

[250] Or "distinguish us" or "judge between us."

(30) And his soul permitted to him[251] the murder of his brother, so he killed him and became among the losers.

(31) Then Allāh sent a crow searching [i.e., scratching] in the ground to show him how to hide the disgrace[252] of his brother. He said, "O woe to me! Have I failed to be like this crow and hide the disgrace [i.e., body] of my brother?" And he became of the regretful.

(32) Because of that, We decreed upon the Children of Israel that whoever kills a soul unless for a soul[253] or for corruption [done] in the land[254] - it is as if he had slain mankind entirely. And whoever saves one[255] - it is as if he had saved mankind entirely. And Our messengers had certainly come to them with clear proofs. Then indeed many of them, [even] after that, throughout the land, were transgressors.[256]

(33) Indeed, the penalty[257] for those who wage war[258] against Allāh and His Messenger and strive upon earth [to cause] corruption is none but that they be killed or crucified or that their hands and feet be cut off from opposite sides or that they be exiled from the land. That is for them a disgrace in this world; and for them in the Hereafter is a great punishment,

(34) Except for those who return [repenting] before you overcome [i.e., apprehend] them. And know that Allāh is Forgiving and Merciful.

(35) O you who have believed, fear Allāh and seek the means [of nearness] to Him and strive in His cause that you may succeed.

(36) Indeed, those who disbelieve - if they should have all that is in the earth and the like of it with it by which to ransom themselves from the punishment of the Day of Resurrection, it will not be accepted from them, and for them is a painful punishment.

(37) They will wish to get out of the Fire, but never are they to emerge therefrom, and for them is an enduring punishment.

---

[251] i.e., the killer allowed himself.

[252] Referring to the dead body, evidence of his shameful deed.

[253] "i.e., in legal retribution for murder.

[254] i.e., that requiring the death penalty.

[255] Or refrains from killing.

[256] Heedless of Allāh's limits, negligent of their responsibilities."

[257] "Legal retribution.

[258] i.e., commit acts of violence and terrorism against individuals or treason and aggression against the Islāmic state."

(38) [As for] the thief, the male and the female, amputate their hands in recompense for what they earned [i.e., committed] as a deterrent [punishment] from Allāh. And Allāh is Exalted in Might and Wise.

(39) But whoever repents after his wrongdoing and reforms, indeed, Allāh will turn to him in forgiveness. Indeed, Allāh is Forgiving and Merciful.

(40) Do you not know that to Allāh belongs the dominion of the heavens and the earth? He punishes whom He wills and forgives whom He wills, and Allāh is over all things competent.

(41) O Messenger, let them not grieve you who hasten into disbelief of those who say, "We believe" with their mouths, but their hearts believe not, and from among the Jews. [They are] avid listeners to falsehood, listening to another people who have not come to you.[259] They distort words beyond their [proper] places [i.e., usages], saying, "If you are given this,[260] take it; but if you are not given it, then beware." But he for whom Allāh intends fitnah[261] - never will you possess [power to do] for him a thing against Allāh. Those are the ones for whom Allāh does not intend to purify their hearts. For them in this world is disgrace, and for them in the Hereafter is a great punishment.

(42) [They are] avid listeners to falsehood, devourers of [what is] unlawful. So if they come to you, [O Muḥammad], judge between them or turn away from them. And if you turn away from them - never will they harm you at all. And if you judge, judge between them with justice. Indeed, Allāh loves those who act justly.

(43) But how is it that they come to you for judgement while they have the Torah, in which is the judgement of Allāh? Then they turn away, [even] after that; but those are not [in fact] believers.

(44) Indeed, We sent down the Torah, in which was guidance and light. The prophets who submitted [to Allāh] judged by it for the Jews, as did the rabbis and scholars by that with which they were entrusted of the Scripture of Allāh, and they were witnesses thereto. So do not fear the people but fear Me, and do not exchange My verses for a small price [i.e., worldly gain]. And whoever does not judge by what Allāh has revealed - then it is those who are the disbelievers.

---

[259] "They had not attended the Prophet's gatherings or heard his words.
[260] The legal ruling desired by them.
[261] The meaning here is misbelief, misconception, or self-delusion as a result of one's own refusal of truth."

(45) And We ordained for them therein a life for a life, an eye for an eye, a nose for a nose, an ear for an ear, a tooth for a tooth, and for wounds is legal retribution. But whoever gives [up his right as] charity, it is an expiation for him. And whoever does not judge by what Allāh has revealed - then it is those who are the wrongdoers [i.e., the unjust].

(46) And We sent, following in their footsteps,[262] Jesus, the son of Mary, confirming that which came before him in the Torah; and We gave him the Gospel, in which was guidance and light and confirming that which preceded it of the Torah as guidance and instruction for the righteous.

(47) And let the People of the Gospel judge by what Allāh has revealed therein. And whoever does not judge by what Allāh has revealed - then it is those who are the defiantly disobedient.

(48) And We have revealed to you, [O Muḥammad], the Book [i.e., the Qur'ān] in truth, confirming that which preceded it of the Scripture and as a criterion over it. So judge between them by what Allāh has revealed and do not follow their inclinations away from what has come to you of the truth. To each of you We prescribed a law and a method.[263] Had Allāh willed, He would have made you one nation [united in religion], but [He intended] to test you in what He has given you; so race to [all that is] good.[264] To Allāh is your return all together, and He will [then] inform you concerning that over which you used to differ.

(49) And judge, [O Muḥammad], between them by what Allāh has revealed and do not follow their inclinations and beware of them, lest they tempt you away from some of what Allāh has revealed to you. And if they turn away - then know that Allāh only intends to afflict them with some of their [own] sins. And indeed, many among the people are defiantly disobedient.

(50) Then is it the judgement of [the time of] ignorance they desire? But who is better than Allāh in judgement for a people who are certain [in faith].

(51) O you who have believed, do not take the Jews and the Christians as allies. They are [in fact] allies of one another. And whoever is an ally to them among you - then indeed, he is [one] of them. Indeed, Allāh guides not the wrongdoing people.

(52) So you see those in whose hearts is disease [i.e., hypocrisy] hastening into [association with] them, saying, "We are afraid a misfortune may strike us." But

---

[262] i.e., following the tradition of the prophets of the Children of Israel.

[263] "Prior to this revelation, which supersedes all previous scriptures.

[264] i.e., obedience to Allāh according to what He enjoined in the Qur'ān and through the sunnah of His Prophet (ﷺ)."

perhaps Allāh will bring conquest or a decision from Him, and they will become, over what they have been concealing within themselves, regretful.

(53) And those who believe will say,[265] "Are these the ones who swore by Allāh their strongest oaths that indeed they were with you?" Their deeds have become worthless, and they have become losers.

(54) O you who have believed, whoever of you should revert from his religion - Allāh will bring forth [in place of them] a people He will love and who will love Him [who are] humble toward the believers, strong against the disbelievers; they strive in the cause of Allāh and do not fear the blame of a critic. That is the favor of Allāh; He bestows it upon whom He wills. And Allāh is all-Encompassing and Knowing.

(55) Your ally is none but Allāh and [therefore] His Messenger and those who have believed - those who establish prayer and give zakāh, and they bow [in worship].

(56) And whoever is an ally of Allāh and His Messenger and those who have believed - indeed, the party of Allāh - they will be the predominant.

(57) O you who have believed, take not those who have taken your religion in ridicule and amusement among the ones who were given the Scripture before you nor the disbelievers as allies. And fear Allāh, if you should [truly] be believers.

(58) And when you call to prayer, they take it in ridicule and amusement. That is because they are a people who do not use reason.

(59) Say, "O People of the Scripture, do you resent us except [for the fact] that we have believed in Allāh and what was revealed to us and what was revealed before and because most of you are defiantly disobedient?"

(60) Say, "Shall I inform you of [what is] worse than that[266] as penalty from Allāh? [It is that of] those whom Allāh has cursed and with whom He became angry and made of them apes and pigs and slaves of ṭāghūt.[267] Those are worse in position and further astray from the sound way."

(61) And when they come to you, they say, "We believe." But they have entered with disbelief [in their hearts], and they have certainly left with it. And Allāh is most knowing of what they were concealing.

---

[265] About the hypocrites after their exposure.
[266] "Referring to the punishment the People of the Scripture (in their censure of the Muslims) claimed was deserved by them.
[267] See footnote to 2:256."

(62) And you see many of them hastening into sin and aggression and the devouring of [what is] unlawful. How wretched is what they have been doing.

(63) Why do the rabbis and religious scholars not forbid them from saying what is sinful and devouring what is unlawful? How wretched is what they have been practicing.

(64) And the Jews say, "The hand of Allāh is chained."[268] Chained are their hands, and cursed are they for what they say. Rather, both His hands are extended; He spends however He wills. And that which has been revealed to you from your Lord will surely increase many of them in transgression and disbelief. And We have cast among them animosity and hatred until the Day of Resurrection. Every time they kindled the fire of war [against you], Allāh extinguished it. And they strive throughout the land [causing] corruption, and Allāh does not like corrupters.

(65) And if only the People of the Scripture had believed and feared Allāh, We would have removed from them their misdeeds and admitted them to Gardens of Pleasure.

(66) And if only they had upheld [the law of] the Torah, the Gospel, and what has been revealed to them from their Lord [i.e., the Qur'ān], they would have consumed [provision] from above them and from beneath their feet.[269] Among them are a moderate [i.e., acceptable] community, but many of them - evil is that which they do.

(67) O Messenger, announce that which has been revealed to you from your Lord, and if you do not, then you have not conveyed His message. And Allāh will protect you from the people. Indeed, Allāh does not guide the disbelieving people.

(68) Say, "O People of the Scripture, you are [standing] on nothing until you uphold [the law of] the Torah, the Gospel, and what has been revealed to you from your Lord [i.e., the Qur'ān]." And that which has been revealed to you from your Lord will surely increase many of them in transgression and disbelief. So do not grieve over the disbelieving people.

(69) Indeed, those who have believed [in Prophet Muḥammad (ﷺ)] and those [before him (ﷺ)] who were Jews or Sabeans or Christians - those [among them] who believed in Allāh and the Last Day and did righteousness - no fear will there be concerning them, nor will they grieve.[270]

---

[268] Implying inability to give or stinginess.

[269] i.e., in great abundance.

[270] See footnote to 2:62.

(70) We had already taken the covenant of the Children of Israel and had sent to them messengers. Whenever there came to them a messenger with what their souls did not desire, a party [of messengers] they denied, and another party they killed.

(71) And they thought there would be no [resulting] punishment, so they became blind and deaf. Then Allāh turned to them in forgiveness; then [again] many of them became blind and deaf. And Allāh is Seeing of what they do.

(72) They have certainly disbelieved who say, "Allāh is the Messiah, the son of Mary" while the Messiah has said, "O Children of Israel, worship Allāh, my Lord and your Lord." Indeed, he who associates others with Allāh - Allāh has forbidden him Paradise, and his refuge is the Fire. And there are not for the wrongdoers any helpers.

(73) They have certainly disbelieved who say, "Allāh is the third of three."[271] And there is no god except one God. And if they do not desist from what they are saying, there will surely afflict the disbelievers among them a painful punishment.

(74) So will they not repent to Allāh and seek His forgiveness? And Allāh is Forgiving and Merciful.

(75) The Messiah, son of Mary, was not but a messenger; [other] messengers have passed on before him. And his mother was a supporter of truth. They both used to eat food.[272] Look how We make clear to them the signs; then look how they are deluded.

(76) Say, "Do you worship besides Allāh that which holds for you no [power of] harm or benefit while it is Allāh who is the Hearing, the Knowing?"

(77) Say, "O People of the Scripture, do not exceed limits in your religion beyond the truth and do not follow the inclinations of a people who had gone astray before and misled many and have strayed from the soundness of the way."

(78) Cursed were those who disbelieved among the Children of Israel by the tongue of David and of Jesus, the son of Mary. That was because they disobeyed and [habitually] transgressed.

(79) They used not to prevent one another from wrongdoing that they did. How wretched was that which they were doing.

---

[271] i.e., one part of three, referring to the Christian concept of trinity.
[272] They were in need of sustenance, proving that they were creations of Allāh, not divine beings.

(80) You see many of them becoming allies of those who disbelieved [i.e., the polytheists]. How wretched is that which they have put forth for themselves in that Allāh has become angry with them, and in the punishment they will abide eternally.

(81) And if they had believed in Allāh and the Prophet and in what was revealed to him, they would not have taken them as allies; but many of them are defiantly disobedient.

(82) You will surely find the most intense of the people in animosity toward the believers [to be] the Jews and those who associate others with Allāh; and you will find the nearest of them in affection to the believers those who say, "We are Christians." That is because among them are priests and monks and because they are not arrogant.

(83) And when they hear what has been revealed to the Messenger, you see their eyes overflowing with tears because of what they have recognized of the truth. They say, "Our Lord, we have believed, so register us among the witnesses.

(84) And why should we not believe in Allāh and what has come to us of the truth? And we aspire that our Lord will admit us [to Paradise] with the righteous people."

(85) So Allāh rewarded them for what they said[273] with gardens [in Paradise] beneath which rivers flow, wherein they abide eternally. And that is the reward of doers of good.

(86) But those who disbelieved and denied Our signs - they are the companions of Hellfire.

(87) O you who have believed, do not prohibit the good things which Allāh has made lawful to you and do not transgress. Indeed, Allāh does not like transgressors.

(88) And eat of what Allāh has provided for you [which is] lawful and good. And fear Allāh, in whom you are believers.

(89) Allāh will not impose blame upon you for what is meaningless[274] in your oaths, but He will impose blame upon you for [breaking] what you intended of oaths. So its expiation[275] is the feeding of ten needy people from the average of that which you feed your [own] families or clothing them or the freeing of a slave. But whoever

---

[273] i.e., their admission and acceptance of the truth and commitment to Allāh's religion (Islām).

[274] "i.e., what is sworn to only out of habit of speech or what one utters carelessly without true intent.
[275] i.e., that for a deliberate oath.

cannot find [or afford it] - then a fast of three days [is required]. That is the expiation for oaths when you have sworn. But guard your oaths.[276] Thus does Allāh make clear to you His verses [i.e., revealed law] that you may be grateful.

(90) O you who have believed, indeed, intoxicants, gambling, [sacrificing on] stone alters [to other than Allāh], and divining arrows are but defilement from the work of Satan, so avoid[277] it that you may be successful.

(91) Satan only wants to cause between you animosity and hatred through intoxicants and gambling and to avert you from the remembrance of Allāh and from prayer. So will you not desist?

(92) And obey Allāh and obey the Messenger and beware. And if you turn away - then know that upon Our Messenger is only [the responsibility for] clear notification.

(93) There is not upon those who believe and do righteousness [any] blame concerning what they have eaten [in the past] if they [now] fear Allāh and believe and do righteous deeds, and then fear Allāh and believe, and then fear Allāh and do good; and Allāh loves the doers of good.

(94) O you who have believed, Allāh will surely test you through something of the game that your hands and spears [can] reach, that Allāh may make evident those who fear Him unseen. And whoever transgresses after that - for him is a painful punishment.

(95) O you who have believed, do not kill game while you are in the state of iḥrām.[278] And whoever of you kills it intentionally - the penalty is an equivalent from sacrificial animals to what he killed, as judged by two just men among you as an offering [to Allāh] delivered to the Ka'bah, or an expiation: the feeding of needy people or the equivalent of that in fasting, that he may taste the consequence of his matter [i.e., deed]. Allāh has pardoned what is past; but whoever returns [to violation], then Allāh will take retribution from him. And Allāh is Exalted in Might and Owner of Retribution.[279]

---

[276] i.e., do not take oaths indiscriminately or swear to do that which is sinful, requiring expiation."

[277] The prohibition understood from the word "avoid" is stronger than if Allāh (subḥānahu wa ta'ālā) had merely said, "Abstain." The former requires distancing oneself from anything remotely related to these practices.

[278] "See footnote to 5:1.

[279] Refer to footnote for 3:5."

(96) Lawful to you is game from the sea and its food as provision for you and the travelers,[280] but forbidden to you is game from the land as long as you are in the state of iḥrām. And fear Allāh to whom you will be gathered.

(97) Allāh has made the Ka'bah, the Sacred House, standing[281] for the people and [has sanctified] the sacred months and the sacrificial animals and the garlands [by which they are identified]. That is so you may know that Allāh knows what is in the heavens and what is in the earth and that Allāh is Knowing of all things.

(98) Know that Allāh is severe in penalty and that Allāh is Forgiving and Merciful.

(99) Not upon the Messenger is [responsibility] except [for] notification. And Allāh knows whatever you reveal and whatever you conceal.

(100) Say, "Not equal are the evil and the good, although the abundance of evil might impress you." So fear Allāh, O you of understanding, that you may be successful.

(101) O you who have believed, do not ask about things which, if they are shown to you, will distress you. But if you ask about them while the Qur'ān is being revealed, they will be shown to you. Allāh has pardoned it [i.e., that which is past]; and Allāh is Forgiving and Forbearing.

(102) A people asked such [questions] before you; then they became thereby disbelievers.[282]

(103) Allāh has not appointed [such innovations as] baḥīrah or sā'ibah or waṣīlah or ḥām.[283] But those who disbelieve invent falsehood about Allāh, and most of them do not reason.

(104) And when it is said to them, "Come to what Allāh has revealed and to the Messenger," they say, "Sufficient for us is that upon which we found our fathers." Even though their fathers knew nothing, nor were they guided?

(105) O you who have believed, upon you is [responsibility for] yourselves. Those who have gone astray will not harm you when you have been guided. To Allāh is your return all together; then He will inform you of what you used to do.

---

[280] Fishing and eating whatever is caught from the sea is permitted even during iḥrām.
[281] Conspicuously as a symbol of Allāh's religion.
[282] By their unwillingness to carry out what was commanded of them.
[283] Categories of particular camels which were dedicated to the idols and set free to pasture, liberated from the service of man.

(106) O you who have believed, testimony [should be taken] among you when death approaches one of you at the time of bequest - [that of] two just men from among you or two others from outside if you are traveling through the land and the disaster of death should strike you. Detain them after the prayer and let them both swear by Allāh if you doubt [their testimony, saying], "We will not exchange it [i.e., our oath] for a price [i.e., worldly gain], even if he should be a near relative, and we will not withhold the testimony of [i.e., ordained by] Allāh. Indeed, we would then be of the sinful."

(107) But if it is found that those two were guilty of sin [i.e., perjury], let two others stand in their place [who are] foremost [in claim] from those who have a lawful right. And let them swear by Allāh, "Our testimony is truer than their testimony, and we have not transgressed. Indeed, we would then be of the wrongdoers."

(108) That is more likely that they will give testimony according to its [true] objective, or [at least] they would fear that [other] oaths might be taken after their oaths. And fear Allāh and listen [i.e., obey Him]; and Allāh does not guide the defiantly disobedient people.

(109) [Be warned of] the Day when Allāh will assemble the messengers and say, "What was the response you received?" They will say, "We have no knowledge. Indeed, it is You who is Knower of the unseen" -

(110) [The Day] when Allāh will say, "O Jesus, Son of Mary, remember My favor upon you and upon your mother when I supported you with the Pure Spirit [i.e., the angel Gabriel] and you spoke to the people in the cradle and in maturity; and [remember] when I taught you writing and wisdom and the Torah and the Gospel; and when you designed from clay [what was] like the form of a bird with My permission, then you breathed into it, and it became a bird with My permission; and you healed the blind [from birth] and the leper with My permission; and when you brought forth the dead with My permission; and when I restrained the Children of Israel from [killing] you when you came to them with clear proofs and those who disbelieved among them said, "This is not but obvious magic."

(111) And [remember] when I inspired to the disciples, "Believe in Me and in My messenger [i.e., Jesus]." They said, "We have believed, so bear witness that indeed we are Muslims [in submission to Allāh]."

(112) [And remember] when the disciples said, "O Jesus, Son of Mary, can your Lord[284] send down to us a table [spread with food] from the heaven?" [Jesus] said, "Fear Allāh, if you should be believers."

---

[284] i.e., will Allāh consent to. (His ability is undoubted)

(113) They said, "We wish to eat from it and let our hearts be reassured and know that you have been truthful to us and be among its witnesses."

(114) Said Jesus, the son of Mary, "O Allāh, our Lord, send down to us a table [spread with food] from the heaven to be for us a festival for the first of us and the last of us and a sign from You. And provide for us, and You are the best of providers."

(115) Allāh said, "Indeed, I will send it down to you, but whoever disbelieves afterwards from among you - then indeed will I punish him with a punishment by which I have not punished anyone among the worlds."

(116) And [beware the Day] when Allāh will say, "O Jesus, Son of Mary, did you say to the people, 'Take me and my mother as deities besides Allāh?'" He will say, "Exalted are You! It was not for me to say that to which I have no right. If I had said it, You would have known it. You know what is within myself, and I do not know what is within Yourself. Indeed, it is You who is Knower of the unseen.

(117) I said not to them except what You commanded me - to worship Allāh, my Lord and your Lord. And I was a witness over them as long as I was among them; but when You took me up, You were the Observer over them, and You are, over all things, Witness.

(118) If You should punish them - indeed they are Your servants; but if You forgive them - indeed it is You who is the Exalted in Might, the Wise."

(119) Allāh will say, "This is the Day when the truthful will benefit from their truthfulness." For them are gardens [in Paradise] beneath which rivers flow, wherein they will abide forever, Allāh being pleased with them, and they with Him. That is the great attainment.

(120) To Allāh belongs the dominion of the heavens and the earth and whatever is within them. And He is over all things competent.

Surah Al-An'am

(1) [All] praise is [due] to Allāh, who created the heavens and the earth and made the darkness and the light. Then those who disbelieve equate [others] with their Lord.

(2) It is He who created you from clay and then decreed a term[285] and a specified time [known] to Him;[286] then [still] you are in dispute.

(3) And He is Allāh, [the only deity] in the heavens and the earth. He knows your secret and what you make public, and He knows that which you earn.

(4) And no sign comes to them from the signs of their Lord except that they turn away therefrom.

(5) For they had denied the truth when it came to them, but there is going to reach them the news of what they used to ridicule.[287]

(6) Have they not seen how many generations We destroyed before them which We had established upon the earth as We have not established you? And We sent [rain from] the sky upon them in showers and made rivers flow beneath them; then We destroyed them for their sins and brought forth after them a generation of others.

(7) And even if We had sent down to you, [O Muḥammad], a written scripture on a page and they touched it with their hands, the disbelievers would say, "This is not but obvious magic."

(8) And they say, "Why was there not sent down to him an angel?"[288] But if We had sent down an angel, the matter would have been decided;[289] then they would not be reprieved.

(9) And if We had made him [i.e., the messenger] an angel, We would have made him [appear as] a man, and We would have covered them with that in which they cover themselves [i.e., confusion and doubt].

(10) And already were messengers ridiculed before you, but those who mocked them were enveloped by that which they used to ridicule.

---

[285] "An appointed time for death.

[286] For resurrection."

[287] They will experience the reality of what they had denied and the consequence of their denial.

[288] "In support of his prophethood (ﷺ).

[289] They would have been destroyed immediately with no chance for repentance."

(11) Say, "Travel through the land; then observe how was the end of the deniers."

(12) Say, "To whom belongs whatever is in the heavens and earth?" Say, "To Allāh." He has decreed upon Himself mercy. He will surely assemble you for the Day of Resurrection, about which there is no doubt. Those who will lose themselves [that Day] do not believe.

(13) And to Him belongs that which reposes by night and by day, and He is the Hearing, the Knowing.

(14) Say, "Is it other than Allāh I should take as a protector, Creator of the heavens and earth, while it is He who feeds and is not fed?" Say, [O Muḥammad], "Indeed, I have been commanded to be the first [among you] who submit [to Allāh] and [was commanded], 'Do not ever be of the polytheists."

(15) Say, "Indeed I fear, if I should disobey my Lord, the punishment of a tremendous Day."

(16) He from whom it is averted that Day - [Allāh] has granted him mercy. And that is the clear attainment.

(17) And if Allāh should touch you with adversity, there is no remover of it except Him. And if He touches you with good - then He is over all things competent.

(18) And He is the subjugator over His servants. And He is the Wise,[290] the Aware.[291]

(19) Say, "What thing is greatest in testimony?" Say, "Allāh is witness between me and you. And this Qur'ān was revealed to me that I may warn you thereby and whomever it reaches.[292] Do you [truly] testify that with Allāh there are other deities?" Say, "I will not testify [with you]." Say, "Indeed, He is but one God, and indeed, I am free of what you associate [with Him]."

(20) Those to whom We have given the Scripture recognize it[293] as they recognize their [own] sons. Those who will lose themselves [in the Hereafter] do not believe.

(21) And who is more unjust than one who invents about Allāh a lie or denies His verses? Indeed, the wrongdoers will not succeed.

---

[290] "Whose wisdom includes precise, perfect and absolute knowledge of all realities and outcomes, according to which He decrees and causes circumstances and occurrences.

[291] Fully acquainted and familiar with every hidden thought, intent and condition of His servants."

[292] At every time and place until the Day of Judgement.

[293] The Qur'ān. Also interpreted as "him," meaning Muḥammad (ﷺ).

(22) And [mention, O Muḥammad], the Day We will gather them all together; then We will say to those who associated others with Allāh, "Where are your 'partners' that you used to claim [with Him]?"

(23) Then there will be no [excuse upon] examination except they will say, "By Allāh, our Lord, we were not those who associated."

(24) See how they will lie about themselves. And lost from them will be what they used to invent.

(25) And among them are those who listen to you,[294] but We have placed over their hearts coverings, lest they understand it, and in their ears deafness. And if they should see every sign, they will not believe in it. Even when they come to you arguing with you, those who disbelieve say, "This is not but legends of the former peoples."

(26) And they prevent [others] from him and are [themselves] remote from him. And they do not destroy except themselves, but they perceive [it] not.

(27) If you could but see when they are made to stand before the Fire and will say, "Oh, would that we could be returned [to life on earth] and not deny the signs of our Lord and be among the believers."

(28) But what they concealed before has [now] appeared to them. And even if they were returned, they would return to that which they were forbidden; and indeed, they are liars.

(29) And they say, "There is none but our worldly life, and we will not be resurrected."

(30) If you could but see when they will be made to stand before their Lord. He will say, "Is this not the truth?" They will say, "Yes, by our Lord." He will [then] say, "So taste the punishment for what you used to deny."

(31) Those will have lost who deny the meeting with Allāh, until when the Hour [of resurrection] comes upon them unexpectedly, they will say, "Oh, [how great is] our regret over what we neglected concerning it [i.e., the Hour]," while they bear their burdens [i.e., sins] on their backs. Unquestionably, evil is that which they bear.

(32) And the worldly life is not but amusement and diversion; but the home of the Hereafter is best for those who fear Allāh, so will you not reason?

---

[294] When you recite the Qur'ān.

(33) We know that you, [O Muḥammad], are saddened by what they say. And indeed, they do not call you untruthful, but it is the verses of Allāh that the wrongdoers reject.

(34) And certainly were messengers denied before you, but they were patient over the denial, and they were harmed until Our victory came to them. And none can alter the words [i.e., decrees] of Allāh. And there has certainly come to you some information about the [previous] messengers.

(35) And if their evasion is difficult for you, then if you are able to seek a tunnel into the earth or a stairway into the sky to bring them a sign, [then do so]. But if Allāh had willed, He would have united them upon guidance. So never be of the ignorant.

(36) Only those who hear will respond. But the dead[295] - Allāh will resurrect them; then to Him they will be returned.

(37) And they say, "Why has a sign not been sent down to him from his Lord?" Say, "Indeed, Allāh is Able to send down a sign, but most of them do not know."

(38) And there is no creature on [or within] the earth or bird that flies with its wings except [that they are] communities like you. We have not neglected in the Register[296] a thing. Then unto their Lord they will be gathered.

(39) But those who deny Our verses are deaf and dumb within darknesses. Whomever Allāh wills - He sends astray; and whomever He wills - He puts him on a straight path.

(40) Say, "Have you considered:[297] if there came to you the punishment of Allāh or there came to you the Hour - is it other than Allāh you would invoke, if you should be truthful?"

(41) No, it is Him [alone] you would invoke, and He would remove that for which you invoked Him if He willed, and you would forget what you associate [with Him].

(42) And We have already sent [messengers] to nations before you, [O Muḥammad]; then We seized them with poverty and hardship that perhaps they might humble themselves [to Us].

---

[295] i.e., the dead of heart, meaning the disbelievers.
[296] The Preserved Slate (al-Lawḥ al-Maḥfūẓ), in which all things are recorded.
[297] The meaning is understood to be "Tell me..."

(43) Then why, when Our punishment came to them, did they not humble themselves? But their hearts became hardened, and Satan made attractive to them that which they were doing.

(44) So when they forgot that by which they had been reminded,[298] We opened to them the doors of every [good] thing until, when they rejoiced in that which they were given, We seized them suddenly, and they were [then] in despair.

(45) So the people that committed wrong were eliminated. And praise to Allāh, Lord of the worlds.

(46) Say, "Have you considered:[299] if Allāh should take away your hearing and your sight and set a seal upon your hearts, which deity other than Allāh could bring them [back] to you?" Look how We diversify[300] the verses; then they [still] turn away.

(47) Say, "Have you considered: if the punishment of Allāh should come to you unexpectedly or manifestly,[301] will any be destroyed but the wrongdoing people?"

(48) And We send not the messengers except as bringers of good tidings and warners. So whoever believes and reforms - there will be no fear concerning them, nor will they grieve.

(49) But those who deny Our verses - the punishment will touch[302] them for their defiant disobedience.

(50) Say, [O Muḥammad], "I do not tell you that I have the depositories [containing the provision] of Allāh or that I know the unseen, nor do I tell you that I am an angel. I only follow what is revealed to me." Say, "Is the blind equivalent to the seeing? Then will you not give thought?"

(51) And warn by it [i.e., the Qur'ān] those who fear that they will be gathered before their Lord - for them besides Him will be no protector and no intercessor - that they might become righteous.

(52) And do not send away those who call upon their Lord morning and afternoon, seeking His face [i.e., favor]. Not upon you is anything of their account and not upon

---

[298] i.e., their trial by poverty and hardship or the warnings of their prophets.
[299] "See footnote to verse 40.
[300] Repeat in various ways for emphasis and clarification."
[301] i.e., before your eyes.
[302] i.e., reach and afflict.

them is anything of your account.[303] So were you to send them away, you would [then] be of the wrongdoers.

(53) And thus We have tried some of them through others that they [i.e., the disbelievers] might say, "Is it these whom Allāh has favored among us?" Is not Allāh most knowing of those who are grateful?[304]

(54) And when those come to you who believe in Our verses, say, "Peace be upon you. Your Lord has decreed upon Himself mercy: that any of you who does wrong out of ignorance and then repents after that and corrects himself - indeed, He is Forgiving and Merciful."

(55) And thus do We detail the verses, and [thus] the way of the criminals will become evident.

(56) Say, "Indeed, I have been forbidden to worship those you invoke besides Allāh." Say, "I will not follow your desires, for I would then have gone astray, and I would not be of the [rightly] guided."

(57) Say, "Indeed, I am on clear evidence from my Lord, and you have denied it. I do not have that for which you are impatient.[305] The decision is only for Allāh. He relates the truth, and He is the best of deciders."

(58) Say, "If I had that for which you are impatient, the matter would have been decided between me and you, but Allāh is most knowing of the wrongdoers."

(59) And with Him are the keys of the unseen; none knows them except Him. And He knows what is on the land and in the sea. Not a leaf falls but that He knows it. And no grain is there within the darknesses of the earth and no moist or dry [thing] but that it is [written] in a clear record.

(60) And it is He who takes your souls by night[306] and knows what you have committed by day. Then He revives you therein [i.e., by day] that a specified term[307]

---

[303] No one is held accountable for the deeds or intentions of another. That is left to Allāh's judgement.

[304] Those referred to in verses 52-54 are the poor Muslims who were sincere believers and students of the Prophet (ﷺ). The influential leaders of Quraysh had disdained to sit with them, saying to Prophet Muḥammad (ﷺ), "Perhaps if you evicted them, we would follow you."

[305] The disbelievers would challenge the Prophet (ﷺ), telling him to bring on Allāh's punishment if he should be truthful in his warning.

[306] "i.e., when you sleep.

[307] One's decreed life span."

may be fulfilled. Then to Him will be your return; then He will inform you about what you used to do.

(61) And He is the subjugator over His servants, and He sends over you guardian-angels until, when death comes to one of you, Our messengers [i.e., angels of death] take him, and they do not fail [in their duties].

(62) Then they [i.e., His servants] are returned to Allāh, their true Lord. Unquestionably, His is the judgement, and He is the swiftest of accountants.

(63) Say, "Who rescues you from the darknesses of the land and sea [when] you call upon Him imploring [aloud] and privately, 'If He should save us from this [crisis], we will surely be among the thankful.'"

(64) Say, "It is Allāh who saves you from it and from every distress; then you [still] associate others with Him."

(65) Say, "He is the [one] Able to send upon you affliction from above you or from beneath your feet or to confuse you [so you become] sects[308] and make you taste the violence of one another." Look how We diversify the signs that they might understand.

(66) But your people have denied it while it is the truth. Say, "I am not over you a manager [i.e., authority]."

(67) For every news [i.e., happening] is a finality;[309] and you are going to know.

(68) And when you see those who engage in [offensive] discourse[310] concerning Our verses, then turn away from them until they enter into another conversation. And if Satan should cause you to forget, then do not remain after the reminder with the wrongdoing people.

(69) And those who fear Allāh are not held accountable for them [i.e., the disbelievers] at all, but [only for] a reminder - that perhaps they will fear Him.

(70) And leave those who take their religion as amusement and diversion and whom the worldly life has deluded. But remind with it [i.e., the Qur'ān], lest a soul be given up to destruction for what it earned; it will have other than Allāh no protector and no intercessor. And if it should offer every compensation, it would not be taken from it [i.e., that soul]. Those are the ones who are given to destruction for what

---

[308] Following your own inclinations rather than the truth, biased and hostile toward each other.

[309] Other shades of meaning include "a permanence," "a realization" and "a time of stability."

[310] i.e., denials or mockery.

they have earned. For them will be a drink of scalding water and a painful punishment because they used to disbelieve.

(71) Say, "Shall we invoke[311] instead of Allāh that which neither benefits us nor harms us and be turned back on our heels after Allāh has guided us? [We would then be] like one whom the devils enticed [to wander] upon the earth confused, [while] he has companions inviting him to guidance, [calling], 'Come to us.'"[312] Say, "Indeed, the guidance of Allāh is the [only] guidance; and we have been commanded to submit to the Lord of the worlds.

(72) And to establish prayer and fear Him." And it is He to whom you will be gathered.

(73) And it is He who created the heavens and earth in truth. And the day [i.e., whenever] He says, "Be," and it is, His word is the truth.[313] And His is the dominion [on] the Day the Horn is blown. [He is] Knower of the unseen[314] and the witnessed;[315] and He is the Wise, the Aware.

(74) And [mention, O Muḥammad], when Abraham said to his father Āzar, "Do you take idols as deities? Indeed, I see you and your people to be in manifest error."

(75) And thus did We show Abraham the realm of the heavens and the earth that he would be among the certain [in faith].

(76) So when the night covered him [with darkness], he saw a star. He said, "This is my lord."[316] But when it set, he said, "I like not those that set [i.e., disappear]."

---

[311] "i.e., worship.

[312] The example given is of one who has lost his way and is further confused by the evil ones who tempt him to follow various directions, all leading to destruction. Although his sincere friends call him back to the right path, he ignores them."

[313] "When interpreted as the "Day" (of resurrection), the sentence would read: "And the Day He says, 'Be,' and it is, His word will be the truth."

[314] That which is absent, invisible, or beyond the perception of the senses or of the mind and therefore is unknown to man, except for what Allāh chooses to reveal.

[315] What is present, visible and known to man. The knowledge of Allāh (subḥānahu wa taʿālā) includes the reality of all things and all occurrences, no matter how they might appear to human beings."

[316] In verses 76-79, beginning from the people's own assertions, Abraham presents a picture of his dissatisfaction as the only logical conclusion one could reach, in order to show them the futility of their false objects of worship.

(77) And when he saw the moon rising, he said, "This is my lord." But when it set, he said, "Unless my Lord guides me, I will surely be among the people gone astray."

(78) And when he saw the sun rising, he said, "This is my lord; this is greater." But when it set, he said, "O my people, indeed I am free from what you associate with Allāh.

(79) Indeed, I have turned my face [i.e., self] toward He who created the heavens and the earth, inclining toward truth, and I am not of those who associate others with Allāh."

(80) And his people argued with him. He said, "Do you argue with me concerning Allāh while He has guided me? And I fear not what you associate with Him [and will not be harmed] unless my Lord should will something. My Lord encompasses all things in knowledge; then will you not remember?

(81) And how should I fear what you associate while you do not fear that you have associated with Allāh that for which He has not sent down to you any authority? So which of the two parties has more right to security, if you should know?"

(82) They who believe and do not mix their belief with injustice[317] - those will have security, and they are [rightly] guided.

(83) And that was Our [conclusive] argument which We gave Abraham against his people. We raise by degrees whom We will. Indeed, your Lord is Wise and Knowing.

(84) And We gave to him [i.e., Abraham] Isaac and Jacob - all [of them] We guided. And Noah, We guided before; and among his descendants, David and Solomon and Job and Joseph and Moses and Aaron. Thus do We reward the doers of good.

(85) And Zechariah and John and Jesus and Elias - and all were of the righteous.

(86) And Ishmael and Elisha and Jonah and Lot - and all [of them] We preferred over the worlds.

(87) And [some] among their fathers and their descendants and their brothers - and We chose them and We guided them to a straight path.

(88) That is the guidance of Allāh by which He guides whomever He wills of His servants. But if they had associated others with Allāh, then worthless for them would be whatever they were doing.

---

[317] Specifically, the association of others in divinity with Allāh.

(89) Those are the ones to whom We gave the Scripture and authority and prophethood. But if they [i.e., the disbelievers] deny it, then We have entrusted it to a people who are not therein disbelievers.

(90) Those are the ones whom Allāh has guided, so from their guidance take an example. Say, "I ask of you for it [i.e., this message] no payment. It is not but a reminder for the worlds."

(91) And they did not appraise Allāh with true appraisal[318] when they said, "Allāh did not reveal to a human being anything." Say, "Who revealed the Scripture that Moses brought as light and guidance to the people? You [Jews] make it into pages, disclosing [some of] it and concealing much. And you[319] were taught that which you knew not - neither you nor your fathers." Say, "Allāh [revealed it]." Then leave them in their [empty] discourse, amusing themselves.

(92) And this is a Book which We have sent down, blessed and confirming what was before it, that you may warn the Mother of Cities [i.e., Makkah] and those around it.[320] Those who believe in the Hereafter believe in it, and they are maintaining their prayers.

(93) And who is more unjust than one who invents a lie about Allāh or says, "It has been inspired to me," while nothing has been inspired to him, and one who says, "I will reveal [something] like what Allāh revealed." And if you could but see when the wrongdoers are in the overwhelming pangs of death while the angels extend their hands,[321] [saying], "Discharge your souls! Today you will be awarded the punishment of [extreme] humiliation for what you used to say against Allāh other than the truth and [that] you were, toward His verses, being arrogant."

(94) [It will be said to them], "And you have certainly come to Us alone [i.e., individually] as We created you the first time, and you have left whatever We bestowed upon you behind you. And We do not see with you your 'intercessors' which you claimed that they were among you associates [of Allāh]. It has [all] been severed between you,[322] and lost from you is what you used to claim."

---

[318] "i.e., they did not appreciate the extent of His ability and wisdom.

[319] The Jews, or it may refer to the believers, who are taught by the Qur'ān."

[320] i.e., all other peoples.

[321] Striking them, as they are unwilling to give up their souls for judgement.

[322] Between yourselves and the claimed associates and intercessors.

(95) Indeed, Allāh is the cleaver of grain and date seeds.[323] He brings the living out of the dead and brings the dead out of the living. That is Allāh; so how are you deluded?

(96) [He is] the cleaver of daybreak and has made the night for rest and the sun and moon for calculation.[324] That is the determination of the Exalted in Might, the Knowing.

(97) And it is He who placed for you the stars that you may be guided by them through the darknesses of the land and sea. We have detailed the signs for a people who know.

(98) And it is He who produced you from one soul and [gave you] a place of dwelling and of storage.[325] We have detailed the signs for a people who understand.

(99) And it is He who sends down rain from the sky, and We produce thereby the growth of all things. We produce from it greenery from which We produce grains arranged in layers. And from the palm trees - of its emerging fruit are clusters hanging low. And [We produce] gardens of grapevines and olives and pomegranates, similar yet varied. Look at [each of] its fruit when it yields and [at] its ripening. Indeed in that are signs for a people who believe.

(100) But they have attributed to Allāh partners - the jinn, while He has created them - and have fabricated for Him sons and daughters without knowledge. Exalted is He and high above what they describe.

(101) [He is] Originator of the heavens and the earth. How could He have a son when He does not have a companion [i.e., wife] and He created all things? And He is, of all things, Knowing.

(102) That is Allāh, your Lord; there is no deity except Him, the Creator of all things, so worship Him. And He is Disposer of all things.

---

[323] He (subḥānahu wa ta'ālā) causes them to split and sprout.
[324] Or "according to calculation," referring to their precise movement.
[325] In the earth. See 77:25-26.

(103) Vision perceives Him not,[326] but He perceives [all] vision; and He is the Subtle,[327] the Aware.[328]

(104) There has come to you enlightenment from your Lord. So whoever will see does so for [the benefit of] his soul, and whoever is blind [does harm] against it. And [say], "I am not a guardian over you."[329]

(105) And thus do We diversify the verses so they [i.e., the disbelievers] will say, "You have studied,"[330] and so We may make it [i.e., the Qur'ān] clear for a people who know.

(106) Follow, [O Muḥammad], what has been revealed to you from your Lord - there is no deity except Him - and turn away from those who associate others with Allāh.

(107) But if Allāh had willed, they would not have associated. And We have not appointed you over them as a guardian, nor are you a manager over them.[331]

(108) And do not insult those they invoke other than Allāh, lest they insult Allāh in enmity without knowledge. Thus We have made pleasing to every community their deeds. Then to their Lord is their return, and He will inform them about what they used to do.

(109) And they swear by Allāh their strongest oaths that if a sign came to them, they would surely believe in it. Say, "The signs are only with [i.e., from] Allāh." And what will make you perceive that even if it [i.e., a sign] came, they would not believe.

(110) And We will turn away their hearts and their eyes just as they refused to believe in it [i.e., the revelation] the first time. And We will leave them in their transgression, wandering blindly.

(111) And even if We had sent down to them the angels [with the message] and the dead spoke to them [of it] and We gathered together every [created] thing in front

---

[326] "In the life of this world. The people of Paradise will be able to see Allāh in the Hereafter. See 75:22-23.

[327] Perceptive of the most precise and unapparent matters and the intricacies of all affairs. Also, He who benefits His servants in indiscernible ways.

[328] See footnote in 6:18."

[329] The Prophet (ﷺ) is directed to disassociate himself from all erroneous belief and practice.

[330] Accusing the Prophet (ﷺ) of having learned from the Jews and Christians.

[331] The Prophet's duty did not go beyond delivery of the message.

of them, they would not believe unless Allāh should will. But most of them, [of that], are ignorant.

(112) And thus We have made for every prophet an enemy - devils from mankind and jinn, inspiring to one another decorative speech in delusion. But if your Lord had willed, they would not have done it, so leave them and that which they invent.

(113) And [it is] so the hearts of those who disbelieve in the Hereafter will incline toward it [i.e., deceptive speech] and that they will be satisfied with it and that they will commit that which they are committing.

(114) [Say], "Then is it other than Allāh I should seek as judge while it is He who has revealed to you the Book [i.e., the Qur'ān] explained in detail?" And those to whom We [previously] gave the Scripture know that it is sent down from your Lord in truth, so never be among the doubters.

(115) And the word of your Lord has been fulfilled in truth and in justice. None can alter His words, and He is the Hearing, the Knowing.

(116) And if you obey most of those upon the earth, they will mislead you from the way of Allāh. They follow not except assumption, and they are not but misjudging.[332]

(117) Indeed, your Lord is most knowing of who strays from His way, and He is most knowing of the [rightly] guided.

(118) So eat of that [meat] upon which the name of Allāh has been mentioned,[333] if you are believers in His verses [i.e., revealed law].

(119) And why should you not eat of that upon which the name of Allāh has been mentioned while He has explained in detail to you what He has forbidden you, excepting that to which you are compelled.[334] And indeed do many lead [others] astray through their [own] inclinations without knowledge. Indeed, your Lord - He is most knowing of the transgressors.

(120) And leave [i.e., desist from] what is apparent of sin and what is concealed thereof. Indeed, those who earn [blame for] sin will be recompensed for that which they used to commit.

---

[332] Out of ignorance and blind imitation.

[333] At the time of slaughter.

[334] In cases of dire necessity, what is normally prohibited becomes permissible, but only to the extent of the need.

(121) And do not eat of that upon which the name of Allāh has not been mentioned, for indeed, it is grave disobedience. And indeed do the devils inspire their allies [among men] to dispute with you. And if you were to obey them, indeed, you would be associators [of others with Him].[335]

(122) And is one who was dead and We gave him life and made for him light by which to walk among the people like one who is in darkness, never to emerge therefrom? Thus it has been made pleasing to the disbelievers that which they were doing.

(123) And thus We have placed within every city the greatest of its criminals to conspire therein. But they conspire not except against themselves, and they perceive [it] not.

(124) And when a sign comes to them, they say, "Never will we believe until we are given like that which was given to the messengers of Allāh." Allāh is most knowing of where [i.e., with whom] He places His message. There will afflict those who committed crimes debasement before Allāh and severe punishment for what they used to conspire.

(125) So whoever Allāh wants to guide - He expands his breast to [contain] Islām; and whoever He wants to send astray[336] - He makes his breast tight and constricted as though he were climbing into the sky. Thus does Allāh place defilement upon those who do not believe.

(126) And this is the path of your Lord, [leading] straight. We have detailed the verses for a people who remember.

(127) For them will be the Home of Peace [i.e., Paradise] with their Lord. And He will be their protecting friend because of what they used to do.

(128) And [mention, O Muḥammad], the Day when He will gather them together [and say], "O company of jinn, you have [misled] many of mankind." And their allies among mankind will say, "Our Lord, some of us made use of others, and we have [now] reached our term which You appointed for us." He will say, "The Fire is your residence, wherein you will abide eternally, except for what Allāh wills. Indeed, your Lord is Wise and Knowing."

---

[335] i.e., by your obedience to them - obedience being the basis of worship.
[336] As a result of the person's arrogance and persistence in sin.

(129) And thus will We make some of the wrongdoers allies of others for what they used to earn.[337]

(130) "O company of jinn and mankind,[338] did there not come to you messengers from among you, relating to you My verses and warning you of the meeting of this Day of yours?" They will say, "We bear witness against ourselves"; and the worldly life had deluded them, and they will bear witness against themselves that they were disbelievers.

(131) That is because your Lord would not destroy the cities for wrongdoing[339] while their people were unaware.

(132) And for all are degrees [i.e., positions resulting] from what they have done. And your Lord is not unaware of what they do.

(133) And your Lord is the Free of need, the possessor of mercy. If He wills, He can do away with you and give succession after you to whomever He wills, just as He produced you from the descendants of another people.

(134) Indeed, what you are promised is coming, and you will not cause failure [to Allāh].[340]

(135) Say, "O my people, work according to your position; [for] indeed, I am working. And you are going to know who will have succession in the home.[341] Indeed, the wrongdoers will not succeed."

(136) And they [i.e., the polytheists] assign to Allāh from that which He created of crops and livestock a share and say, "This is for Allāh," by their claim, "and this is for our 'partners' [associated with Him]." But what is for their "partners" does not reach Allāh, while what is for Allāh - this reaches their "partners." Evil is that which they rule.

(137) And likewise, to many of the polytheists their partners[342] have made [to seem] pleasing the killing of their children in order to bring about their destruction and

---

[337] Another interpretation pertaining to this world is "And thus do We make some of the wrongdoers allies of others for what they have been earning."
[338] They will be reproached thus at the Judgement.
[339] Or "unjustly."
[340] i.e., You will neither escape nor prevent its occurrence.

[341] i.e., in the land or in the Hereafter.
[342] Their evil associates.

to cover them with confusion in their religion. And if Allāh had willed, they would not have done so. So leave them and that which they invent.

(138) And they say, "These animals[343] and crops are forbidden; no one may eat from them except whom we will," by their claim. And there are those [camels] whose backs are forbidden [by them][344] and those upon which the name of Allāh is not mentioned[345] - [all of this] an invention of untruth about Him.[346] He will punish them for what they were inventing.

(139) And they say, "What is in the bellies of these animals[347] is exclusively for our males and forbidden to our females. But if it is [born] dead, then all of them have shares therein." He will punish them for their description.[348] Indeed, He is Wise and Knowing.

(140) They will have lost who killed their children in foolishness without knowledge and prohibited what Allāh had provided for them, inventing untruth about Allāh. They have gone astray and were not [rightly] guided.

(141) And He it is who causes gardens to grow, [both] trellised and untrellised, and palm trees and crops of different [kinds of] food and olives and pomegranates, similar and dissimilar. Eat of [each of] its fruit when it yields and give its due [zakāh] on the day of its harvest. And be not excessive.[349] Indeed, He does not like those who commit excess.

(142) And of the grazing livestock are carriers [of burdens] and those [too] small. Eat of what Allāh has provided for you and do not follow the footsteps of Satan.[350] Indeed, he is to you a clear enemy.

(143) [They are] eight mates - of the sheep, two and of the goats, two. Say, "Is it the two males He has forbidden or the two females or that which the wombs of the two females contain? Inform me with knowledge, if you should be truthful."

---

[343] "The four categories of grazing livestock called ""an'ām"" collectively.

[344] See 5:103.

[345] At the time of slaughter. Rather, they are dedicated to others among their "deities."

[346] i.e., false assertions that such practices are part of Allāh's religion."

[347] "i.e., their milk and offspring.

[348] Of what is lawful and unlawful according to their whims."

[349] In eating, as well as in all things generally.

[350] As the disbelievers have done in making their own rulings about what is permissible and what is prohibited.

(144) And of the camels, two and of the cattle, two. Say, "Is it the two males He has forbidden or the two females or that which the wombs of the two females contain? Or were you witnesses when Allāh charged you with this? Then who is more unjust than one who invents a lie about Allāh to mislead the people by [something] other than knowledge? Indeed, Allāh does not guide the wrongdoing people."

(145) Say, "I do not find within that which was revealed to me [anything] forbidden to one who would eat it unless it be a dead animal or blood spilled out or the flesh of swine - for indeed, it is impure - or it be [that slaughtered in] disobedience, dedicated to other than Allāh.[351] But whoever is forced [by necessity], neither desiring [it] nor transgressing [its limit], then indeed, your Lord is Forgiving and Merciful."

(146) And to those who are Jews We prohibited every animal of uncloven hoof; and of the cattle and the sheep We prohibited to them their fat, except what adheres to their backs or the entrails or what is joined with bone. [By] that We repaid them for their transgression. And indeed, We are truthful.

(147) So if they deny you, [O Muḥammad], say, "Your Lord is the possessor of vast mercy; but His punishment cannot be repelled from the people who are criminals."

(148) Those who associated [others] with Allāh will say, "If Allāh had willed, we would not have associated [anything] and neither would our fathers, nor would we have prohibited anything." Likewise did those before deny until they tasted Our punishment. Say, "Do you have any knowledge that you can produce for us? You follow not except assumption, and you are not but misjudging."

(149) Say, "With Allāh is the far-reaching [i.e., conclusive] argument. If He had willed, He would have guided you all."

(150) Say, [O Muḥammad], "Bring forward your witnesses who will testify that Allāh has prohibited this." And if they testify, do not testify with them. And do not follow the desires of those who deny Our verses and those who do not believe in the Hereafter, while they equate [others] with their Lord.

(151) Say, "Come, I will recite what your Lord has prohibited to you. [He commands] that you not associate anything with Him, and to parents, good treatment, and do not kill your children out of poverty; We will provide for you and them. And do not approach immoralities - what is apparent of them and what is concealed. And do not kill the soul which Allāh has forbidden [to be killed] except by [legal] right. This has He instructed you that you may use reason."

---

[351] Refer to 2:173 and 5:3.

(152) And do not approach the orphan's property except in a way that is best [i.e., intending improvement] until he reaches maturity. And give full measure and weight in justice. We do not charge any soul except [with that within] its capacity. And when you speak [i.e., testify], be just, even if [it concerns] a near relative. And the covenant of Allāh fulfill. This has He instructed you that you may remember.

(153) And, [moreover], this is My path, which is straight, so follow it; and do not follow [other] ways, for you will be separated from His way. This has He instructed you that you may become righteous.

(154) Then[352] We gave Moses the Scripture, making complete [Our favor] upon the one who did good [i.e., Moses] and as a detailed explanation of all things and as guidance and mercy that perhaps in the meeting with their Lord they would believe.

(155) And this [Qur'ān] is a Book We have revealed [which is] blessed, so follow it and fear Allāh that you may receive mercy.

(156) [We revealed it] lest you say, "The Scripture was only sent down to two groups before us, but we were of their study unaware,"

(157) Or lest you say, "If only the Scripture had been revealed to us, we would have been better guided than they." So there has [now] come to you a clear evidence from your Lord and a guidance and mercy. Then who is more unjust than one who denies the verses of Allāh and turns away from them? We will recompense those who turn away from Our verses with the worst of punishment for their having turned away.

(158) Do they [then] wait for anything except that the angels should come to them or your Lord should come or that there come some of the signs[353] of your Lord? The Day that some of the signs of your Lord will come no soul will benefit from its faith as long as it had not believed before or had earned through its faith some good. Say, "Wait. Indeed, we [also] are waiting."

(159) Indeed, those who have divided their religion and become sects - you, [O Muḥammad], are not [associated] with them in anything. Their affair is only [left] to Allāh; then He will inform them about what they used to do.

---

[352] Meaning "additionally" or "moreover," not denoting time sequence.
[353] Those denoting the approach of the Last Hour.

(160) Whoever comes [on the Day of Judgement] with a good deed will have ten times the like thereof [to his credit], and whoever comes with an evil deed will not be recompensed except the like thereof; and they will not be wronged.[354]

(161) Say, "Indeed, my Lord has guided me to a straight path - a correct religion - the way of Abraham, inclining toward truth. And he was not among those who associated others with Allāh."

(162) Say, "Indeed, my prayer, my rites of sacrifice, my living and my dying are for Allāh, Lord of the worlds.

(163) No partner has He. And this I have been commanded, and I am the first [among you] of the Muslims."[355]

(164) Say, "Is it other than Allāh I should desire as a lord while He is the Lord of all things? And every soul earns not [blame] except against itself, and no bearer of burdens will bear the burden of another. Then to your Lord is your return, and He will inform you concerning that over which you used to differ."

(165) And it is He who has made you successors upon the earth and has raised some of you above others in degrees [of rank] that He may try you through what He has given you. Indeed, your Lord is swift in penalty; but indeed, He is Forgiving and Merciful.

---

[354] i.e., treated unjustly.
[355] i.e., those who submit to the will of Allāh.

Surah Al-A'raf

(1) Alif, Lām, Meem, Ṣād.[356]

(2) [This is] a Book revealed to you, [O Muḥammad] - so let there not be in your breast distress therefrom - that you may warn thereby and as a reminder to the believers.

(3) Follow, [O mankind], what has been revealed to you from your Lord and do not follow other than Him any allies. Little do you remember.

(4) And how many cities have We destroyed, and Our punishment came to them at night or while they were sleeping at noon.

(5) And their declaration when Our punishment came to them was only that they said, "Indeed, we were wrongdoers!"

(6) Then We will surely question those to whom [a message] was sent, and We will surely question the messengers.

(7) Then We will surely relate [their deeds] to them with knowledge, and We were not [at all] absent.

(8) And the weighing [of deeds] that Day will be the truth. So those whose scales are heavy - it is they who will be the successful.

(9) And those whose scales are light - they are the ones who will lose themselves for what injustice they were doing toward Our verses.

(10) And We have certainly established you upon the earth and made for you therein ways of livelihood. Little are you grateful.

(11) And We have certainly created you, [O mankind], and given you [human] form. Then We said to the angels, "Prostrate to Adam"; so they prostrated, except for Iblees.[357] He was not of those who prostrated.

(12) [Allāh] said, "What prevented you from prostrating when I commanded you?" [Satan] said, "I am better than him. You created me from fire and created him from clay [i.e., earth]."

---

[356] See footnote to 2:1.
[357] Satan. See footnote to 2:34.

(13) [Allāh] said, "Descend from it [i.e., Paradise], for it is not for you to be arrogant therein. So get out; indeed, you are of the debased."

(14) [Satan] said, "Reprieve me until the Day they are resurrected."

(15) [Allāh] said, "Indeed, you are of those reprieved."

(16) [Satan] said, "Because You have put me in error, I will surely sit in wait for them [i.e., mankind] on Your straight path.

(17) Then I will come to them from before them and from behind them and on their right and on their left, and You will not find most of them grateful [to You]."

(18) [Allāh] said, "Depart from it [i.e., Paradise], reproached and expelled. Whoever follows you among them - I will surely fill Hell with you, all together."

(19) And "O Adam, dwell, you and your wife, in Paradise and eat from wherever you will but do not approach this tree, lest you be among the wrongdoers."

(20) But Satan whispered to them to make apparent to them that which was concealed from them of their private parts. He said, "Your Lord did not forbid you this tree except that you become angels or become of the immortal."

(21) And he swore [by Allāh] to them, "Indeed, I am to you from among the sincere advisors."

(22) So he made them fall, through deception. And when they tasted of the tree, their private parts became apparent to them, and they began to fasten together over themselves from the leaves of Paradise. And their Lord called to them, "Did I not forbid you from that tree and tell you that Satan is to you a clear enemy?"

(23) They said, "Our Lord, we have wronged ourselves, and if You do not forgive us and have mercy upon us, we will surely be among the losers."

(24) [Allāh] said, "Descend, being to one another enemies. And for you on the earth is a place of settlement and enjoyment [i.e., provision] for a time."

(25) He said, "Therein you will live, and therein you will die, and from it you will be brought forth."

(26) O children of Adam, We have bestowed upon you clothing to conceal your private parts and as adornment. But the clothing of righteousness - that is best. That is from the signs of Allāh that perhaps they will remember.

(27) O children of Adam, let not Satan tempt you as he removed your parents from Paradise, stripping them of their clothing[358] to show them their private parts. Indeed, he sees you, he and his tribe, from where you do not see them. Indeed, We have made the devils allies to those who do not believe.

(28) And when they commit an immorality, they say, "We found our fathers doing it, and Allāh has ordered us to do it." Say, "Indeed, Allāh does not order immorality. Do you say about Allāh that which you do not know?"

(29) Say, [O Muḥammad], "My Lord has ordered justice and that you direct yourselves [to the Qiblah] at every place [or time] of prostration, and invoke Him, sincere to Him in religion." Just as He originated you, you will return [to life] -

(30) A group [of you] He guided, and a group deserved [to be in] error. Indeed, they [i.e., the latter] had taken the devils as allies instead of Allāh while they thought that they were guided.

(31) O children of Adam, take your adornment [i.e., wear your clothing] at every masjid,[359] and eat and drink, but be not excessive. Indeed, He likes not those who commit excess.

(32) Say, "Who has forbidden the adornment of [i.e., from] Allāh which He has produced for His servants and the good [lawful] things of provision?" Say, "They are for those who believed during the life of this world, exclusively [for them] on the Day of Resurrection." Thus do We detail the verses for a people who know.

(33) Say, "My Lord has only forbidden immoralities - what is apparent of them and what is concealed - and sin,[360] and oppression without right, and that you associate with Allāh that for which He has not sent down authority, and that you say about Allāh that which you do not know."

(34) And for every nation is a [specified] term. So when their time has come, they will not remain behind an hour, nor will they precede [it].

(35) O children of Adam, if there come to you messengers from among you relating to you My verses [i.e., scriptures and laws], then whoever fears Allāh and reforms - there will be no fear concerning them, nor will they grieve.

---

[358] The garments of Paradise.

[359] Literally, "place of prostration," meaning any place that a Muslim prays upon the earth. The term may also refer specifically to a mosque.

[360] Any unlawful deed.

(36) But the ones who deny Our verses and are arrogant toward them - those are the companions of the Fire; they will abide therein eternally.

(37) And who is more unjust than one who invents about Allāh a lie or denies His verses? Those will attain their portion of the decree[361] until, when Our messengers [i.e., angels] come to them to take them in death, they will say, "Where are those you used to invoke besides Allāh?" They will say, "They have departed from us," and will bear witness against themselves that they were disbelievers.

(38) [Allāh] will say, "Enter among nations which had passed on before you of jinn and mankind into the Fire." Every time a nation enters, it will curse its sister[362] until, when they have all overtaken one another therein, the last of them[363] will say about the first of them,[364] "Our Lord, these had misled us, so give them a double punishment of the Fire." He will say, "For each is double, but you do not know."

(39) And the first of them will say to the last of them, "Then you had not any favor over us, so taste the punishment for what you used to earn."

(40) Indeed, those who deny Our verses and are arrogant toward them - the gates of Heaven will not be opened for them, nor will they enter Paradise until a camel enters into the eye of a needle [i.e., never]. And thus do We recompense the criminals.

(41) They will have from Hell a bed and over them coverings [of fire]. And thus do We recompense the wrongdoers.

(42) But those who believed and did righteous deeds - We charge no soul except [within] its capacity. Those are the companions of Paradise; they will abide therein eternally.

(43) And We will have removed whatever is within their breasts of resentment,[365] [while] flowing beneath them are rivers. And they will say, "Praise to Allāh, who has guided us to this; and we would never have been guided if Allāh had not guided us. Certainly the messengers of our Lord had come with the truth." And they will be called, "This is Paradise, which you have been made to inherit for what you used to do."

---

[361] What is decreed for them.
[362] "The nation preceding it.
[363] The followers of evil leaders.
[364] Their leaders."

[365] i.e., ill will or sense of injury for what was inflicted upon them during worldly life.

(44) And the companions of Paradise will call out to the companions of the Fire, "We have already found what our Lord promised us to be true. Have you found what your Lord promised to be true?" They will say, "Yes." Then an announcer will announce among them, "The curse of Allāh shall be upon the wrongdoers

(45) Who averted [people] from the way of Allāh and sought to make it [seem] deviant while they were, concerning the Hereafter, disbelievers."

(46) And between them will be a partition [i.e., wall], and on [its] elevations are men[366] who recognize all[367] by their mark. And they call out to the companions of Paradise, "Peace be upon you." They have not [yet] entered it, but they long intensely.

(47) And when their eyes are turned toward the companions of the Fire, they say, "Our Lord, do not place us with the wrongdoing people."

(48) And the companions of the Elevations will call to men [within Hell] whom they recognize by their mark, saying, "Of no avail to you was your gathering[368] and [the fact] that you were arrogant."

(49) [Allāh will say], "Are these[369] the ones whom you [inhabitants of Hell] swore that Allāh would never offer them mercy? Enter Paradise, [O people of the Elevations]. No fear will there be concerning you, nor will you grieve."

(50) And the companions of the Fire will call to the companions of Paradise, "Pour upon us some water or from whatever Allāh has provided you." They will say, "Indeed, Allāh has forbidden them both to the disbelievers

(51) Who took their religion as distraction and amusement and whom the worldly life deluded." So today We will forget them just as they forgot the meeting of this Day of theirs and for having rejected Our verses.

(52) And We had certainly brought them a Book which We detailed by knowledge - as guidance and mercy to a people who believe.

(53) Do they await except its result?[370] The Day its result comes, those who had ignored it before will say, "The messengers of our Lord had come with the truth, so

---

[366] "Those whose scales are balanced between good and evil deeds.
[367] Both the inhabitants of Paradise and those of Hell."

[368] i.e., great numbers or gathering of wealth.
[369] The humble believers who are now in Paradise. Another interpretation regards them as the people on the elevated partition.
[370] The fulfillment of what is promised in the Qur'ān.

are there [now] any intercessors to intercede for us or could we be sent back to do other than what we used to do?" They will have lost themselves, and lost from them is what they used to invent.

(54) Indeed, your Lord is Allāh, who created the heavens and earth in six days and then established Himself above the Throne.[371] He covers the night with the day, [another night] chasing it rapidly; and [He created] the sun, the moon, and the stars, subjected by His command. Unquestionably, His is the creation and the command; blessed is Allāh, Lord of the worlds.

(55) Call upon your Lord in humility and privately; indeed, He does not like transgressors.[372]

(56) And cause not corruption upon the earth after its reformation. And invoke Him in fear and aspiration. Indeed, the mercy of Allāh is near to the doers of good.

(57) And it is He who sends the winds as good tidings before His mercy [i.e., rainfall] until, when they have carried heavy rainclouds, We drive them to a dead land and We send down rain therein and bring forth thereby [some] of all the fruits. Thus will We bring forth the dead; perhaps you may be reminded.

(58) And the good land - its vegetation emerges by permission of its Lord; but that which is bad - nothing emerges except sparsely, with difficulty. Thus do We diversify the signs for a people who are grateful.

(59) We had certainly sent Noah to his people, and he said, "O my people, worship Allāh; you have no deity other than Him. Indeed, I fear for you the punishment of a tremendous Day."

(60) Said the eminent among his people, "Indeed, we see you in clear error."

---

[371] There are several linguistic meanings of the words "istawā ʿalā," among them: to settle upon, to assume ascendancy above, and to assert authority over. However, it is known that all the attributes of Allāh are eternal, i.e., they have always existed and were present before He created. Thus, it cannot be said that He "rose" above the Throne, as Allāh has always been ascendant. Because the Creator may not be compared to His creation, the Prophet's companions and early scholars refused speculation as to how His actions could be interpreted, considering any such attempt unlawful. Similarly, the true nature of the Throne is known only to Allāh, the Exalted.

[372] In supplication or otherwise.

(61) [Noah] said, "O my people, there is not error in me, but I am a messenger from the Lord of the worlds.

(62) I convey to you the messages of my Lord and advise you; and I know from Allāh what you do not know.

(63) Then do you wonder that there has come to you a reminder from your Lord through a man from among you, that he may warn you and that you may fear Allāh so you might receive mercy?"

(64) But they denied him, so We saved him and those who were with him in the ship. And We drowned those who denied Our signs. Indeed, they were a blind people.[373]

(65) And to the ʿAad [We sent] their brother Hūd. He said, "O my people, worship Allāh; you have no deity other than Him. Then will you not fear Him?"

(66) Said the eminent ones who disbelieved among his people, "Indeed, we see you in foolishness, and indeed, we think you are of the liars."

(67) [Hūd] said, "O my people, there is not foolishness in me, but I am a messenger from the Lord of the worlds.

(68) I convey to you the messages of my Lord, and I am to you a trustworthy adviser.

(69) Then do you wonder that there has come to you a reminder from your Lord through a man from among you, that he may warn you? And remember when He made you successors after the people of Noah and increased you in stature extensively. So remember the favors of Allāh that you might succeed."

(70) They said, "Have you come to us that we should worship Allāh alone and leave what our fathers have worshipped? Then bring us what you promise us,[374] if you should be of the truthful."

(71) [Hūd] said, "Already have defilement and anger fallen upon you from your Lord. Do you dispute with me concerning [mere] names you have named them,[375] you and your fathers, for which Allāh has not sent down any authority? Then wait; indeed, I am with you among those who wait."

---

[373] For a more detailed account, see 11:25-48.

[374] i.e., Allāh's punishment.
[375] The false objects of worship which you have called "gods."

(72) So We saved him and those with him by mercy from Us. And We eliminated those who denied Our signs, and they were not [at all] believers.

(73) And to the Thamūd [We sent] their brother Ṣāliḥ. He said, "O my people, worship Allāh; you have no deity other than Him. There has come to you clear evidence from your Lord. This is the she-camel of Allāh [sent] to you as a sign. So leave her to eat within Allāh's land and do not touch her with harm, lest there seize you a painful punishment.

(74) And remember when He made you successors after the ʿAad and settled you in the land, [and] you take for yourselves palaces from its plains and carve from the mountains, homes. Then remember the favors of Allāh and do not commit abuse on the earth, spreading corruption."

(75) Said the eminent ones who were arrogant among his people to those who were oppressed - to those who believed among them, "Do you [actually] know that Ṣāliḥ is sent from his Lord?" They said, "Indeed we, in that with which he was sent, are believers."

(76) Said those who were arrogant, "Indeed we, in that which you have believed, are disbelievers."

(77) So they hamstrung the she-camel and were insolent toward the command of their Lord and said, "O Ṣāliḥ, bring us what you promise us, if you should be of the messengers."

(78) So the earthquake seized them, and they became within their home [corpses] fallen prone.

(79) And he [i.e., Ṣāliḥ] turned away from them and said, "O my people, I had certainly conveyed to you the message of my Lord and advised you, but you do not like advisors."

(80) And [We had sent] Lot when he said to his people, "Do you commit such immorality as no one has preceded you with from among the worlds [i.e., peoples]?

(81) Indeed, you approach men with desire, instead of women. Rather, you are a transgressing people."

(82) But the answer of his people was only that they said, "Evict them from your city! Indeed, they are men who keep themselves pure."

(83) So We saved him and his family, except for his wife; she was of those who remained [with the evildoers].

(84) And We rained upon them a rain [of stones]. Then see how was the end of the criminals.

(85) And to [the people of] Madyan [We sent] their brother Shuʿayb. He said, "O my people, worship Allāh; you have no deity other than Him. There has come to you clear evidence from your Lord. So fulfill the measure and weight and do not deprive people of their due and cause not corruption upon the earth after its reformation. That is better for you, if you should be believers.

(86) And do not sit on every path, threatening and averting from the way of Allāh those who believe in Him, seeking to make it [seem] deviant. And remember when you were few and He increased you. And see how was the end of the corrupters.

(87) And if there should be a group among you who has believed in that with which I have been sent and a group that has not believed, then be patient until Allāh judges between us. And He is the best of judges."

(88) Said the eminent ones who were arrogant among his people, "We will surely evict you, O Shuʿayb, and those who have believed with you from our city, or you must return to our religion." He said, "Even if we were unwilling?

(89) We would have invented against Allāh a lie if we returned to your religion after Allāh had saved us from it. And it is not for us to return to it except that Allāh, our Lord, should will. Our Lord has encompassed all things in knowledge. Upon Allāh we have relied. Our Lord, decide between us and our people in truth, and You are the best of those who give decision."

(90) Said the eminent ones who disbelieved among his people, "If you should follow Shuʿayb, indeed, you would then be losers."

(91) So the earthquake seized them, and they became within their home [corpses] fallen prone.

(92) Those who denied Shuʿayb - it was as though they had never resided there. Those who denied Shuʿayb - it was they who were the losers.

(93) And he [i.e., Shuʿayb] turned away from them and said, "O my people, I had certainly conveyed to you the messages of my Lord and advised you, so how could I grieve for a disbelieving people?"

(94) And We sent to no city a prophet [who was denied] except that We seized its people with poverty and hardship that they might humble themselves [to Allāh].

(95) Then We exchanged in place of the bad [condition], good, until they increased [and prospered] and said, "Our fathers [also] were touched with hardship and ease."[376] So We seized them suddenly while they did not perceive.[377]

(96) And if only the people of the cities had believed and feared Allāh, We would have opened [i.e., bestowed] upon them blessings from the heaven and the earth; but they denied [the messengers], so We seized them for what they were earning.[378]

(97) Then, did the people of the cities feel secure from Our punishment coming to them at night while they were asleep?

(98) Or did the people of the cities feel secure from Our punishment coming to them in the morning while they were at play?[379]

(99) Then, did they feel secure from the plan of Allāh? But no one feels secure from the plan of Allāh except the losing people.

(100) Has it not become clear to those who inherited the earth after its [previous] people that if We willed, We could afflict them for their sins? But We seal over their hearts so they do not hear.[380]

(101) Those cities - We relate to you, [O Muḥammad], some of their news. And certainly did their messengers come to them with clear proofs, but they were not to believe in that which they had denied before.[381] Thus does Allāh seal over the hearts of the disbelievers.

(102) And We did not find for most of them any covenant;[382] but indeed, We found most of them defiantly disobedient.

(103) Then We sent after them Moses with Our signs to Pharaoh and his establishment, but they were unjust toward them.[383] So see how was the end of the corrupters.

(104) And Moses said, "O Pharaoh, I am a messenger from the Lord of the worlds

---

[376] "Instead of being grateful to Allāh for His blessings, they merely attributed them to the changing fortunes of time.

[377] That they had been tried and tested."

[378] Of blame for their sin.

[379] i.e., occupied with such activities that have no benefit.

[380] They do not benefit from what they hear.

[381] i.e., they persistently denied every warning given them.

[382] i.e., they were found to be unfaithful and negligent of Allāh's covenant.

[383] i.e., they rejected and opposed the signs.

(105) [Who is] obligated not to say about Allāh except the truth. I have come to you with clear evidence from your Lord, so send with me the Children of Israel."[384]

(106) [Pharaoh] said, "If you have come with a sign, then bring it forth, if you should be of the truthful."

(107) So he [i.e., Moses] threw his staff, and suddenly it was a serpent, manifest.[385]

(108) And he drew out his hand; thereupon it was white [with radiance] for the observers.

(109) Said the eminent among the people of Pharaoh, "Indeed, this is a learned magician

(110) Who wants to expel you from your land [through magic], so what do you instruct?"

(111) They said,[386] "Postpone [the matter of] him and his brother and send among the cities gatherers

(112) Who will bring you every learned magician."

(113) And the magicians came to Pharaoh. They said, "Indeed for us is a reward if we are the predominant."

(114) He said, "Yes, and, [moreover], you will be among those made near [to me]."

(115) They said, "O Moses, either you throw [your staff], or we will be the ones to throw [first]."

(116) He said, "Throw," and when they threw, they bewitched the eyes of the people and struck terror into them, and they presented a great [feat of] magic.[387]

(117) And We inspired to Moses, "Throw your staff," and at once it devoured what they were falsifying.

(118) So the truth was established, and abolished was what they were doing.

(119) And they [i.e., Pharaoh and his people] were overcome right there and became debased.

---

[384] i.e., free them from oppression and allow them to emigrate.
[385] i.e., genuine and not imagined, as a miracle from Allāh.

[386] After mutual consultation and agreement.
[387] Their staffs and ropes appeared as writhing snakes.

(120) And the magicians fell down in prostration [to Allāh].

(121) They said, "We have believed in the Lord of the worlds,

(122) The Lord of Moses and Aaron."

(123) Said Pharaoh, "You believed in him[388] before I gave you permission. Indeed, this is a conspiracy which you conspired in the city to expel therefrom its people. But you are going to know.

(124) I will surely cut off your hands and your feet on opposite sides; then I will surely crucify you all."

(125) They said, "Indeed, to our Lord we will return.

(126) And you do not resent us except because we believed in the signs of our Lord when they came to us. Our Lord, pour upon us patience[389] and let us die as Muslims [in submission to You]."

(127) And the eminent among the people of Pharaoh said, "Will you leave Moses and his people to cause corruption in the land and abandon you and your gods?" [Pharaoh] said, "We will kill their sons and keep their women alive; and indeed, we are subjugators over them."

(128) Said Moses to his people, "Seek help through Allāh and be patient. Indeed, the earth belongs to Allāh. He causes to inherit it whom He wills of His servants. And the [best] outcome is for the righteous."

(129) They said, "We have been harmed before you came to us and after you have come to us." He said, "Perhaps your Lord will destroy your enemy and grant you succession in the land and see how you will do."

(130) And We certainly seized[390] the people of Pharaoh with years of famine and a deficiency in fruits that perhaps they would be reminded.

(131) But when good [i.e., provision] came to them, they said, "This is ours [by right]." And if a bad [condition] struck them, they saw an evil omen in Moses and those with him. Unquestionably, their fortune is with Allāh, but most of them do not know.

---

[388] i.e., in Moses, avoiding the mention of Allāh (subḥānahu wa taʿālā).
[389] To endure the torture to which we will be subjected.
[390] Imposed on them by way of trial and warning.

(132) And they said, "No matter what sign you bring us with which to bewitch us, we will not be believers in you."

(133) So We sent upon them the flood and locusts and lice and frogs and blood as distinct signs, but they were arrogant and were a criminal people.

(134) And when the punishment descended upon them, they said, "O Moses, invoke for us your Lord by what He has promised you. If you [can] remove the punishment from us, we will surely believe you, and we will send with you the Children of Israel."

(135) But when We removed the punishment from them until a term which they were to reach,[391] then at once they broke their word.

(136) So We took retribution from them, and We drowned them in the sea because they denied Our signs and were heedless of them.

(137) And We caused the people who had been oppressed to inherit the eastern regions of the land and the western ones, which We had blessed. And the good word [i.e., decree] of your Lord was fulfilled for the Children of Israel because of what they had patiently endured. And We destroyed [all] that Pharaoh and his people were producing and what they had been building.

(138) And We took the Children of Israel across the sea; then they came upon a people intent in devotion to [some] idols of theirs. They [the Children of Israel] said, "O Moses, make for us a god just as they have gods." He said, "Indeed, you are a people behaving ignorantly.

(139) Indeed, those [worshippers] - destroyed is that in which they are [engaged], and worthless is whatever they were doing."

(140) He said, "Is it other than Allāh I should desire for you as a god[392] while He has preferred you over the worlds?"

(141) And [recall, O Children of Israel], when We saved you from the people of Pharaoh, [who were] afflicting you with the worst torment - killing your sons and keeping your women alive. And in that was a great trial from your Lord.

(142) And We made an appointment with Moses for thirty nights and perfected them by [the addition of] ten; so the term of his Lord was completed as forty nights.

---

[391] i.e., a specified term which would end with their reversion to disobedience and disbelief.
[392] An object of worship.

And Moses said to his brother Aaron, "Take my place among my people, do right [by them],[393] and do not follow the way of the corrupters."

(143) And when Moses arrived at Our appointed time and his Lord spoke to him, he said, "My Lord, show me [Yourself] that I may look at You." [Allāh] said, "You will not see Me,[394] but look at the mountain; if it should remain in place, then you will see Me." But when his Lord appeared to the mountain, He rendered it level,[395] and Moses fell unconscious. And when he awoke, he said, "Exalted are You! I have repented to You, and I am the first [among my people] of the believers."[396]

(144) [Allāh] said, "O Moses, I have chosen you over the people with My messages and My words [to you]. So take what I have given you and be among the grateful."

(145) And We wrote for him on the tablets [something] of all things - instruction and explanation for all things, [saying], "Take them with determination and order your people to take the best of it. I will show you the home of the defiantly disobedient."[397]

(146) I will turn away from My signs those who are arrogant upon the earth without right; and if they should see every sign, they will not believe in it. And if they see the way of consciousness,[398] they will not adopt it as a way; but if they see the way of error, they will adopt it as a way. That is because they have denied Our signs and they were heedless of them.

(147) Those who denied Our signs and the meeting of the Hereafter - their deeds have become worthless. Are they recompensed except for what they used to do?

(148) And the people of Moses made, after [his departure], from their ornaments a calf - an image having a lowing sound. Did they not see that it could neither speak to them nor guide them to a way? They took it [for worship], and they were wrongdoers.

---

[393] i.e., keep their affairs in order.
[394] "That no one can see Allāh in this life
[395] It crumbled to dust.
[396] This is a severe warning from Allāh against rebellion."

[397] This is a severe warning from Allāh against rebellion.
[398] i.e., reason and integrity.

(149) And when regret overcame them[399] and they saw that they had gone astray, they said, "If our Lord does not have mercy upon us and forgive us, we will surely be among the losers."

(150) And when Moses returned to his people, angry and grieved, he said, "How wretched is that by which you have replaced me after [my departure]. Were you impatient over the matter of your Lord?" And he threw down the tablets and seized his brother by [the hair of] his head, pulling him toward him. [Aaron] said, "O son of my mother, indeed the people overpowered me and were about to kill me, so let not the enemies rejoice over me[400] and do not place me among the wrongdoing people."

(151) [Moses] said, "My Lord, forgive me and my brother and admit us into Your mercy, for You are the most merciful of the merciful."

(152) Indeed, those who took the calf [for worship] will obtain anger from their Lord and humiliation in the life of this world, and thus do We recompense the inventors [of falsehood].

(153) But those who committed misdeeds and then repented after them and believed - indeed your Lord, thereafter, is Forgiving and Merciful.

(154) And when the anger subsided in Moses, he took up the tablets; and in their inscription was guidance and mercy for those who are fearful of their Lord.

(155) And Moses chose from his people seventy men for Our appointment.[401] And when the earthquake seized them,[402] he said, "My Lord, if You had willed, You could have destroyed them before and me [as well]. Would You destroy us for what the foolish among us have done? This is not but Your trial by which You send astray whom You will and guide whom You will. You are our Protector, so forgive us and have mercy upon us; and You are the best of forgivers.

(156) And decree for us in this world [that which is] good and [also] in the Hereafter; indeed, we have turned back to You." [Allāh] said, "My punishment - I afflict with

---

[399] Literally, "When their hands had been descended upon," i.e., bitten by them out of severe regret.

[400] i.e., over your humiliation of me.

[401] "Whereupon they were to apologize to Allāh for having worshipped the calf.

[402] Upon reaching the appointed place, they said to Moses, "We will not believe until we see Allāh outright." So the mountain convulsed, killing them."

it whom I will, but My mercy encompasses all things." So I will decree it [especially] for those who fear Me and give zakāh and those who believe in Our verses-

(157) Those who follow the Messenger, the unlettered prophet, whom they find written [i.e., described] in what they have of the Torah and the Gospel, who enjoins upon them what is right and prohibits them from what is wrong and makes lawful for them what is good and forbids them from what is evil and relieves them of their burden[403] and the shackles which were upon them.[404] So they who have believed in him, honored him, supported him and followed the light which was sent down with him - it is those who will be the successful.

(158) Say, [O Muḥammad], "O mankind, indeed I am the Messenger of Allāh to you all, [from Him] to whom belongs the dominion of the heavens and the earth. There is no deity except Him; He gives life and causes death." So believe in Allāh and His Messenger, the unlettered prophet, who believes in Allāh and His words, and follow him that you may be guided.

(159) And among the people of Moses is a community[405] which guides by truth and by it establishes justice.

(160) And We divided them into twelve descendant tribes[406] [as distinct] nations. And We inspired to Moses when his people implored him for water, "Strike with your staff the stone," and there gushed forth from it twelve springs. Every people [i.e., tribe] knew its watering place. And We shaded them with clouds and sent down upon them manna and quails, [saying], "Eat from the good things with which We have provided you." And they wronged Us not, but they were [only] wronging themselves.

(161) And [mention, O Muḥammad], when it was said to them, "Dwell in this city [i.e., Jerusalem] and eat from it wherever you will and say, 'Relieve us of our burdens [i.e., sins],' and enter the gate bowing humbly; We will [then] forgive you your sins. We will increase the doers of good [in goodness and reward]."

(162) But those who wronged among them changed [the words] to a statement other than that which had been said to them. So We sent upon them a punishment from the sky for the wrong that they were doing.

---

[403] "Difficulties in religious practice.

[404] i.e., extreme measures previously required for repentance, and retribution without recourse to compensation."

[405] Those of them who accepted and followed the final prophet, Muḥammad (ﷺ).

[406] From the twelve sons of Jacob.

(163) And ask them about the town that was by the sea - when they transgressed in [the matter of] the sabbath - when their fish came to them openly on their sabbath day, and the day they had no sabbath they did not come to them. Thus did We give them trial because they were defiantly disobedient.

(164) And when a community among them said, "Why do you advise [or warn] a people whom Allāh is [about] to destroy or to punish with a severe punishment?" they [the advisors] said, "To be absolved before your Lord and perhaps they may fear Him."

(165) And when they [i.e., those advised] forgot that by which they had been reminded, We saved those who had forbidden evil and seized those who wronged, with a wretched punishment, because they were defiantly disobeying.

(166) So when they were insolent about that which they had been forbidden, We said to them, "Be apes, despised."

(167) And [mention] when your Lord declared that He would surely [continue to] send upon them until the Day of Resurrection those who would afflict them with the worst torment. Indeed, your Lord is swift in penalty; but indeed, He is Forgiving and Merciful.

(168) And We divided them throughout the earth into nations. Of them some were righteous, and of them some were otherwise. And We tested them with good [times] and bad that perhaps they would return [to obedience].

(169) And there followed them successors who inherited the Scripture [while] taking the commodities[407] of this lower life and saying, "It will be forgiven for us." And if an offer like it[408] comes to them, they will [again] take it. Was not the covenant of the Scripture [i.e., the Torah] taken from them that they would not say about Allāh except the truth, and they studied what was in it? And the home of the Hereafter is better for those who fear Allāh, so will you not use reason?

(170) But those who hold fast to the Book [i.e., the Qur'ān] and establish prayer - indeed, We will not allow to be lost the reward of the reformers.

(171) And [mention] when We raised the mountain above them as if it was a dark cloud and they were certain that it would fall upon them,[409] [and Allāh said], "Take what We have given you with determination and remember what is in it that you might fear Allāh."

---

[407] "i.e., unlawful gains and pleasures.
[408] i.e., a similar temptation."
[409] For their rebellion and disobedience.

(172) And [mention] when your Lord took from the children of Adam - from their loins - their descendants and made them testify of themselves, [saying to them], "Am I not your Lord?" They said, "Yes, we have testified." [This] - lest you should say on the Day of Resurrection, "Indeed, we were of this unaware."

(173) Or [lest] you say, "It was only that our fathers associated [others in worship] with Allāh before, and we were but descendants after them. Then would You destroy us for what the falsifiers have done?"

(174) And thus do We [explain in] detail the verses, and perhaps they will return.[410]

(175) And recite to them, [O Muḥammad], the news of him[411] to whom We gave [knowledge of] Our signs, but he detached himself from them; so Satan pursued him, and he became of the deviators.[412]

(176) And if We had willed, We could have elevated him thereby,[413] but he adhered [instead] to the earth[414] and followed his own desire. So his example is like that of the dog: if you chase him, he pants, or if you leave him, he [still] pants. That is the example of the people who denied Our signs.[415] So relate the stories that perhaps they will give thought.

(177) How evil an example [is that of] the people who denied Our signs and used to wrong themselves.

(178) Whoever Allāh guides - he is the [rightly] guided; and whoever He sends astray[416] - it is those who are the losers.

(179) And We have certainly created for Hell many of the jinn and mankind. They have hearts with which they do not understand, they have eyes with which they do not see, and they have ears with which they do not hear. Those are like livestock; rather, they are more astray.[417] It is they who are the heedless.

---

[410] To the way of Allāh (subḥānahu wa ta'ālā), from their diversions and deviations.

[411] "A man from the Children of Israel at the time of Moses.

[412] Those who deliberately persist in error to the point of destruction."

[413] "i.e., through the revelations, signs or evidences of which he had been given knowledge.

[414] i.e., its worldly pleasures.

[415] Whether or not they have been exposed to Allāh's signs or warnings, it is all the same: they will not believe."

[416] As a result of persistence in evil and rejection of truth.

[417] The reference is to their inability (i.e., refusal) to think and reason, while blindly following (as they are accustomed).

(180) And to Allāh belong the best names, so invoke Him by them. And leave [the company of] those who practice deviation concerning His names.[418] They will be recompensed for what they have been doing.

(181) And among those We created is a community[419] which guides by truth and thereby establishes justice.

(182) But those who deny Our signs - We will progressively lead them [to destruction][420] from where they do not know.

(183) And I will give them time. Indeed, My plan is firm.

(184) Then do they not give thought? There is in their companion [i.e., Muḥammad (ﷺ)] no madness. He is not but a clear warner.

(185) Do they not look into the realm of the heavens and the earth and everything that Allāh has created and [think] that perhaps their appointed time has come near? So in what statement [i.e., message] hereafter will they believe?

(186) Whoever Allāh sends astray - there is no guide for him. And He leaves them in their transgression, wandering blindly.

(187) They ask you, [O Muḥammad], about the Hour: when is its arrival?[421] Say, "Its knowledge is only with my Lord. None will reveal its time except Him. It lays heavily[422] upon the heavens and the earth. It will not come upon you except unexpectedly." They ask you as if you are familiar with it. Say, "Its knowledge is only with Allāh, but most of the people do not know."

(188) Say, "I hold not for myself [the power of] benefit or harm, except what Allāh has willed. And if I knew the unseen, I could have acquired much wealth, and no harm would have touched me. I am not except a warner and a bringer of good tidings to a people who believe."

(189) It is He who created you from one soul and created from it its mate that he[423] might dwell in security with her. And when he [i.e., man] covers her,[424] she carries a light burden [i.e., a pregnancy] and continues therein. And when it becomes

---

[418] i.e., use them improperly or deny them.

[419] The followers of Prophet Muḥammad (ﷺ).

[420] Allāh will test them with one favor after another in spite of their disobedience, which only increases them in arrogance and sin.

[421] "Literally, "resting" or "establishment.""

[422] i.e., it is a source of concern, worry or fear."

[423] "i.e., man or every descendent of Adam.

[424] An allusion to sexual intercourse.

heavy, they both invoke Allāh, their Lord, "If You should give us a good[425] [child], we will surely be among the grateful."

(190) But when He gives them a good [child], they[426] ascribe partners to Him concerning that which He has given them. Exalted is Allāh above what they associate with Him.

(191) Do they associate with Him those who create nothing and they are [themselves] created?

(192) And they [i.e., the false deities] are unable to [give] them help, nor can they help themselves.

(193) And if you [believers] invite them to guidance, they will not follow you. It is all the same for you whether you invite them or you are silent.

(194) Indeed, those you [polytheists] call upon besides Allāh are servants [i.e., creations] like you. So call upon them and let them respond to you, if you should be truthful.

(195) Do they have feet by which they walk? Or do they have hands by which they strike? Or do they have eyes by which they see? Or do they have ears by which they hear? Say, [O Muḥammad], "Call your 'partners' and then conspire against me and give me no respite.

(196) Indeed, my protector is Allāh, who has sent down the Book; and He is an ally to the righteous.

(197) And those you call upon besides Him are unable to help you, nor can they help themselves."

(198) And if you invite them to guidance, they do not hear; and you see them looking at you while they do not see.

(199) Take what is given freely,[427] enjoin what is good, and turn away from the ignorant.

(200) And if an evil suggestion comes to you from Satan, then seek refuge in Allāh. Indeed, He is Hearing and Knowing.

---

[425] Physically sound or righteous."
[426] The ungrateful man and woman or the polytheistic man and woman.

[427] From the dispositions of men or from their wealth. In other words, be easy in dealing with them and avoid causing them difficulty.

(201) Indeed, those who fear Allāh - when an impulse touches them from Satan, they remember [Him] and at once they have insight.

(202) But their brothers[428] - they [i.e., the devils] increase them in error; then they do not stop short.

(203) And when you, [O Muḥammad], do not bring them a sign [i.e., miracle], they say, "Why have you not contrived it?" Say, "I only follow what is revealed to me from my Lord. This [Qur'ān] is enlightenment from your Lord and guidance and mercy for a people who believe."

(204) So when the Qur'ān is recited, then listen to it and pay attention that you may receive mercy.

(205) And remember your Lord within yourself in humility and in fear without being apparent in speech - in the mornings and the evenings. And do not be among the heedless.

(206) Indeed, those who are near your Lord [i.e., the angels] are not prevented by arrogance from His worship, and they exalt Him, and to Him they prostrate.

---

[428] Those among mankind who listen to the devils and obey their orders.

Surah Al-Anfal

(1) They ask you, [O Muḥammad], about the bounties [of war]. Say, "The [decision concerning] bounties is for Allāh and the Messenger." So fear Allāh and amend that which is between you and obey Allāh and His Messenger, if you should be believers.

(2) The believers are only those who, when Allāh is mentioned, their hearts become fearful, and when His verses are recited to them, it increases them in faith; and upon their Lord they rely -

(3) The ones who establish prayer, and from what We have provided them, they spend.

(4) Those are the believers, truly. For them are degrees [of high position] with their Lord and forgiveness and noble provision.

(5) [It[429] is] just as when your Lord brought you out of your home [for the battle of Badr] in truth, while indeed, a party among the believers were unwilling,

(6) Arguing with you concerning the truth after it had become clear, as if they were being driven toward death while they were looking on.

(7) [Remember, O believers], when Allāh promised you one of the two groups[430] - that it would be yours - and you wished that the unarmed one would be yours. But Allāh intended to establish the truth by His words and to eliminate the disbelievers

(8) That He should establish the truth and abolish falsehood, even if the criminals disliked it.

(9) [Remember] when you were asking help of your Lord, and He answered you, "Indeed, I will reinforce you with a thousand from the angels, following one another."

(10) And Allāh made it not but good tidings and so that your hearts would be assured thereby. And victory is not but from Allāh. Indeed, Allāh is Exalted in Might and Wise.

(11) [Remember] when He overwhelmed you with drowsiness [giving] security from Him and sent down upon you from the sky, rain by which to purify you and

---

[429] Referring to a dispute which occurred among the Muslims over distribution of war booty.
[430] i.e., either the caravan of Quraysh or their army.

remove from you the evil [suggestions] of Satan and to make steadfast your hearts and plant firmly thereby your feet.

(12) [Remember] when your Lord inspired to the angels, "I am with you, so strengthen those who have believed. I will cast terror into the hearts of those who disbelieved, so strike [them] upon the necks and strike from them every fingertip."[431]

(13) That is because they opposed Allāh and His Messenger. And whoever opposes Allāh and His Messenger - indeed, Allāh is severe in penalty.

(14) "That [is yours], so taste it." And indeed for the disbelievers is the punishment of the Fire.

(15) O you who have believed, when you meet those who disbelieve advancing [in battle], do not turn to them your backs [in flight].

(16) And whoever turns his back to them on such a day, unless swerving [as a strategy] for war or joining [another] company, has certainly returned with anger [upon him] from Allāh, and his refuge is Hell - and wretched is the destination.

(17) And you did not kill them, but it was Allāh who killed them.[432] And you threw not, [O Muḥammad], when you threw, but it was Allāh who threw[433] that He might test the believers with a good test.[434] Indeed, Allāh is Hearing and Knowing.

(18) That [is so], and [also] that Allāh will weaken the plot of the disbelievers.

(19) If you [disbelievers] seek the decision [i.e., victory] - the decision [i.e., defeat] has come to you. And if you desist [from hostilities], it is best for you; but if you return [to war], We will return, and never will you be availed by your [large] company at all, even if it should increase; and [that is] because Allāh is with the believers.

(20) O you who have believed, obey Allāh and His Messenger and do not turn from him while you hear [his order].

---

[431] By which they grasp and manipulate their weapons. Also interpreted as "all extremities," i.e., their hands and feet.

[432] "i.e., Your strength was insufficient to overcome them, but Allāh supported you and gave you victory.

[433] When the Prophet (ﷺ) threw a handful of dust into the faces of the disbelievers, Allāh caused it to fill the eyes and nose of every soldier, preventing their advance.

[434] So that they would appreciate Allāh's favor to them."

(21) And do not be like those who say, "We have heard," while they do not hear.

(22) Indeed, the worst of living creatures in the sight of Allāh are the deaf and dumb who do not use reason [i.e., the disbelievers].

(23) Had Allāh known any good in them, He would have made them hear. And if He had made them hear, they would [still] have turned away, while they were refusing.

(24) O you who have believed, respond to Allāh and to the Messenger when he calls you to that which gives you life. And know that Allāh intervenes between a man and his heart and that to Him you will be gathered.

(25) And fear a trial[435] which will not strike those who have wronged among you exclusively, and know that Allāh is severe in penalty.

(26) And remember when you were few and oppressed in the land, fearing that people might abduct you, but He sheltered you, supported you with His victory, and provided you with good things - that you might be grateful.

(27) O you who have believed, do not betray Allāh and the Messenger or betray your trusts while you know [the consequence].

(28) And know that your properties and your children are but a trial and that Allāh has with Him a great reward.

(29) O you who have believed, if you fear Allāh, He will grant you a criterion[436] and will remove from you your misdeeds and forgive you. And Allāh is the possessor of great bounty.

(30) And [remember, O Muḥammad], when those who disbelieved plotted against you to restrain you or kill you or evict you [from Makkah]. But they plan, and Allāh plans. And Allāh is the best of planners.

(31) And when Our verses are recited to them, they say, "We have heard. If we willed, we could say [something] like this. This is not but legends of the former peoples."

(32) And [remember] when they said, "O Allāh, if this should be the truth from You, then rain down upon us stones from the sky or bring us a painful punishment."

---

[435] i.e., an affliction or punishment during life upon this earth. When corruption spreads among a people, its consequences will affect everyone.
[436] By which to judge between truth and falsehood. Also interpreted as a "way out" of difficulties.

(33) But Allāh would not punish them while you, [O Muḥammad], are among them, and Allāh would not punish them while they seek forgiveness.

(34) But why should Allāh not punish them while they obstruct [people] from al-Masjid al-Ḥarām and they were not [fit to be] its guardians? Its [true] guardians are not but the righteous, but most of them do not know.

(35) And their prayer at the House [i.e., the Ka‘bah] was not except whistling and handclapping. So taste the punishment for what you disbelieved [i.e., practiced of deviations].

(36) Indeed, those who disbelieve spend their wealth to avert [people] from the way of Allāh. So they will spend it; then it will be for them a [source of] regret; then they will be overcome. And those who have disbelieved - unto Hell they will be gathered.

(37) [It is] so that Allāh may distinguish the wicked from the good and place the wicked some of them upon others and heap them all together and put them into Hell. It is those who are the losers.

(38) Say to those who have disbelieved [that] if they cease, what has previously occurred will be forgiven for them. But if they return [to hostility] - then the precedent of the former [rebellious] peoples has already taken place.[437]

(39) And fight against them until there is no fitnah[438] and [until] the religion [i.e., worship], all of it, is for Allāh.[439] And if they cease - then indeed, Allāh is Seeing of what they do.

(40) But if they turn away - then know that Allāh is your protector. Excellent is the protector, and excellent is the helper.

(41) And know that anything you obtain of war booty - then indeed, for Allāh is one fifth of it and for the Messenger[440] and for [his] near relatives[441] and the orphans, the needy, and the [stranded] traveler,[442] if you have believed in Allāh and in that which We sent down to Our Servant[443] on the day of criterion [i.e., decisive

---

[437] This is a warning that punishment is always the result of rebellion against Allāh and His messengers.
[438] "Persecution. See footnote to 2:191.
[439] i.e., until polytheism is no longer dominant."

[440] "To be spent in Allāh's cause.
[441] The tribes of Banū Hāshim and Banū Muṭṭalib, who were not eligible for zakāh.
[442] The remaining four fifths are divided among the soldiers.
[443] Prophet Muḥammad (ﷺ)."

encounter] - the day when the two armies met [at Badr]. And Allāh, over all things, is competent.

(42) [Remember] when you were on the near side of the valley, and they were on the farther side, and the caravan was lower [in position] than you. If you had made an appointment [to meet], you would have missed the appointment. But [it was] so that Allāh might accomplish a matter already destined - that those who perished [through disbelief] would perish upon evidence and those who lived [in faith] would live upon evidence; and indeed, Allāh is Hearing and Knowing.

(43) [Remember, O Muḥammad], when Allāh showed them to you in your dream as few; and if He had shown them to you as many, you [believers] would have lost courage and would have disputed in the matter [of whether to fight], but Allāh saved [you from that]. Indeed, He is Knowing of that within the breasts.

(44) And [remember] when He showed them to you, when you met, as few in your eyes, and He made you [appear] as few in their eyes so that Allāh might accomplish a matter already destined. And to Allāh are [all] matters returned.

(45) O you who have believed, when you encounter a company [from the enemy forces], stand firm and remember Allāh much that you may be successful.

(46) And obey Allāh and His Messenger, and do not dispute and [thus] lose courage and [then] your strength would depart; and be patient. Indeed, Allāh is with the patient.

(47) And do not be like those who came forth from their homes insolently and to be seen by people and avert [them] from the way of Allāh. And Allāh is encompassing[444] of what they do.

(48) And [remember] when Satan made their deeds pleasing to them and said, "No one can overcome you today from among the people, and indeed, I am your protector." But when the two armies sighted each other, he turned on his heels and said, "Indeed, I am disassociated from you. Indeed, I see what you do not see; indeed, I fear Allāh. And Allāh is severe in penalty."

(49) [Remember] when the hypocrites and those in whose hearts was disease [i.e., arrogance and disbelief] said, "Their religion has deluded those [Muslims]." But whoever relies upon Allāh - then indeed, Allāh is Exalted in Might and Wise.

---

[444] In knowledge. See footnote to 2:19.

(50) And if you could but see when the angels take the souls of those who disbelieved...[445] They are striking their faces and their backs and [saying], "Taste the punishment of the Burning Fire.

(51) That is for what your hands have put forth [of evil] and because Allāh is not ever unjust to [His] servants."

(52) [Theirs is] like the custom of the people of Pharaoh and of those before them. They disbelieved in the signs of Allāh, so Allāh seized them for their sins. Indeed, Allāh is Powerful and severe in penalty.

(53) That is because Allāh would not change a favor which He had bestowed upon a people until they change what is within themselves. And indeed, Allāh is Hearing and Knowing.

(54) [Theirs is] like the custom of the people of Pharaoh and of those before them. They denied the signs of their Lord, so We destroyed them for their sins, and We drowned the people of Pharaoh. And all [of them] were wrongdoers.

(55) Indeed, the worst of living creatures in the sight of Allāh are those who have disbelieved, and they will not [ever] believe-

(56) The ones with whom you made a treaty but then they break their pledge every time, and they do not fear Allāh.

(57) So if you, [O Muḥammad], gain dominance over them in war, disperse by [means of] them those behind them that perhaps they will be reminded.[446]

(58) If you [have reason to] fear from a people betrayal, throw [their treaty] back to them, [putting you] on equal terms.[447] Indeed, Allāh does not like traitors.

(59) And let not those who disbelieve think they will escape. Indeed, they will not cause failure [to Allāh].

(60) And prepare against them whatever you are able of power and of steeds of war[448] by which you may terrify the enemy of Allāh and your enemy and others

---

[445] This sentence is left incomplete for additional effect. Its conclusion is left to the imagination of the reader or listener and estimated as "...you would see a dreadful sight."

[446] i.e., kill them and make an example of them to discourage those who follow them.

[447] When you see signs of treachery from those with whom you have made a treaty, announce to them its dissolution so they will know exactly where they stand.

[448] Or equipment which serves the same purpose.

besides them whom you do not know [but] whom Allāh knows. And whatever you spend in the cause of Allāh will be fully repaid to you, and you will not be wronged.

(61) And if they incline to peace, then incline to it [also] and rely upon Allāh. Indeed, it is He who is the Hearing, the Knowing.

(62) But if they intend to deceive you - then sufficient for you is Allāh. It is He who supported you with His help and with the believers

(63) And brought together their hearts. If you had spent all that is in the earth, you could not have brought their hearts together; but Allāh brought them together. Indeed, He is Exalted in Might and Wise.

(64) O Prophet, sufficient for you is Allāh and for whoever follows you of the believers.

(65) O Prophet, urge the believers to battle. If there are among you twenty [who are] steadfast, they will overcome two hundred. And if there are among you one hundred [who are steadfast], they will overcome a thousand of those who have disbelieved because they are a people who do not understand.

(66) Now, Allāh has lightened [the hardship] for you, and He knows that among you is weakness. So if there are from you one hundred [who are] steadfast, they will overcome two hundred. And if there are among you a thousand, they will overcome two thousand by permission of Allāh. And Allāh is with the steadfast.

(67) It is not for a prophet to have captives [of war] until he inflicts a massacre [upon Allāh's enemies] in the land. You [i.e., some Muslims] desire the commodities of this world,[449] but Allāh desires [for you] the Hereafter. And Allāh is Exalted in Might and Wise.

(68) If not for a decree from Allāh that preceded,[450] you would have been touched for what you took by a great punishment.

(69) So consume what you have taken of war booty [as being] lawful and good, and fear Allāh. Indeed, Allāh is Forgiving and Merciful.

---

[449] i.e., material benefit, such as the ransom paid for prisoners.

[450] Three interpretations of the "decree" are given: that by which the companions of Badr were forgiven, that by which indeliberate errors in judgement by believers are not punished, and that which made lawful the spoils of war.

(70) O Prophet, say to whoever is in your hands of the captives, "If Allāh knows [any] good in your hearts, He will give you [something] better than what was taken from you, and He will forgive you; and Allāh is Forgiving and Merciful."

(71) But if they intend to betray you - then they have already betrayed Allāh before, and He empowered [you] over them. And Allāh is Knowing and Wise.

(72) Indeed, those who have believed and emigrated and fought with their wealth and lives in the cause of Allāh and those who gave shelter and aided - they are allies of one another. But those who believed and did not emigrate - for you there is no support of them until they emigrate. And if they seek help of you for the religion, then you must help, except against a people between yourselves and whom is a treaty. And Allāh is Seeing of what you do.

(73) And those who disbelieved are allies of one another. If you do not do so [i.e., ally yourselves with other believers], there will be fitnah [i.e., disbelief and oppression] on earth and great corruption.

(74) But those who have believed and emigrated and fought in the cause of Allāh and those who gave shelter and aided - it is they who are the believers, truly. For them is forgiveness and noble provision.

(75) And those who believed after [the initial emigration] and emigrated and fought with you - they are of you. But those of [blood] relationship are more entitled [to inheritance] in the decree of Allāh.[451] Indeed, Allāh is Knowing of all things.

---

[451] This applies to Muslim relatives only. Others may be given by bequest. See 4:11.

Surah At-Tawbah

(1) [This is a declaration of] disassociation, from Allāh and His Messenger, to those with whom you had made a treaty among the polytheists.[452]

(2) So travel freely, [O disbelievers], throughout the land [during] four months but know that you cannot cause failure to Allāh and that Allāh will disgrace the disbelievers.

(3) And [it is] an announcement from Allāh and His Messenger to the people on the day of the greater pilgrimage[453] that Allāh is disassociated from the disbelievers, and [so is] His Messenger. So if you repent, that is best for you; but if you turn away - then know that you will not cause failure to Allāh.[454] And give tidings to those who disbelieve of a painful punishment.

(4) Excepted are those with whom you made a treaty among the polytheists and then they have not been deficient toward you in anything or supported anyone against you; so complete for them their treaty until their term [has ended]. Indeed, Allāh loves the righteous [who fear Him].

(5) And when the inviolable months[455] have passed, then kill the polytheists wherever you find them and capture them and besiege them and sit in wait for them at every place of ambush. But if they should repent, establish prayer, and give zakāh, let them [go] on their way. Indeed, Allāh is Forgiving and Merciful.

(6) And if any one of the polytheists seeks your protection, then grant him protection so that he may hear the words of Allāh [i.e., the Qur'ān]. Then deliver him to his place of safety. That is because they are a people who do not know.

(7) How can there be for the polytheists a treaty in the sight of Allāh and with His Messenger, except for those with whom you made a treaty at al-Masjid al-Ḥarām? So as long as they are upright toward you,[456] be upright toward them. Indeed, Allāh loves the righteous [who fear Him].

---

[452] But who had violated it.

[453] "Ḥajj. ʿUmrah is the lesser pilgrimage.

[454] i.e., you cannot escape His punishment."

[455] The four months mentioned in verse 2, in which the disbelievers were allowed free movement within the land. Other scholars have interpreted them as "the sacred months," i.e., Muḥarram, Rajab, Dhul-Qaʿdah and Dhul-Ḥijjah.

[456] i.e., maintain the terms of the treaty.

(8) How [can there be a treaty] while, if they gain dominance over you, they do not observe concerning you any pact of kinship or covenant of protection? They satisfy you with their mouths, but their hearts refuse [compliance], and most of them are defiantly disobedient.

(9) They have exchanged the signs of Allāh for a small price and averted [people] from His way. Indeed, it was evil that they were doing.

(10) They do not observe toward a believer any pact of kinship or covenant of protection. And it is they who are the transgressors.

(11) But if they repent, establish prayer, and give zakāh, then they are your brothers in religion; and We detail the verses for a people who know.

(12) And if they break their oaths after their treaty and defame your religion, then combat the leaders of disbelief, for indeed, there are no oaths [sacred] to them; [fight them that] they might cease.

(13) Would you not fight against a people who broke their oaths and determined to expel the Messenger, and they had begun [the attack upon] you the first time? Do you fear them? But Allāh has more right that you should fear Him, if you are [truly] believers.

(14) Fight them; Allāh will punish them by your hands and will disgrace them and give you victory over them and satisfy the breasts [i.e., desires] of a believing people

(15) And remove the fury in their [i.e., the believers'] hearts. And Allāh turns in forgiveness to whom He wills; and Allāh is Knowing and Wise.

(16) Do you think that you will be left [as you are] while Allāh has not yet made evident those among you who strive [for His cause] and do not take other than Allāh, His Messenger and the believers as intimates? And Allāh is [fully] Aware of what you do.

(17) It is not for the polytheists to maintain the mosques of Allāh [while] witnessing against themselves with disbelief. [For] those, their deeds have become worthless, and in the Fire they will abide eternally.

(18) The mosques of Allāh are only to be maintained by those who believe in Allāh and the Last Day and establish prayer and give zakāh and do not fear except Allāh, for it is expected that those will be of the [rightly] guided.

(19) Have you made the providing of water for the pilgrim and the maintenance of al-Masjid al-Ḥarām equal to [the deeds of] one who believes in Allāh and the Last

Day and strives in the cause of Allāh? They are not equal in the sight of Allāh. And Allāh does not guide the wrongdoing people.

(20) The ones who have believed, emigrated and striven in the cause of Allāh with their wealth and their lives are greater in rank in the sight of Allāh. And it is those who are the attainers [of success].

(21) Their Lord gives them good tidings of mercy from Him and approval and of gardens for them wherein is enduring pleasure.

(22) [They will be] abiding therein forever. Indeed, Allāh has with Him a great reward.

(23) O you who have believed, do not take your fathers or your brothers as allies if they have preferred disbelief over belief. And whoever does so among you - then it is those who are the wrongdoers.

(24) Say, [O Muḥammad], "If your fathers, your sons, your brothers, your wives, your relatives, wealth which you have obtained, commerce wherein you fear decline, and dwellings with which you are pleased are more beloved to you than Allāh and His Messenger and jihād [i.e., striving] in His cause, then wait until Allāh executes His command. And Allāh does not guide the defiantly disobedient people."

(25) Allāh has already given you victory in many regions and [even] on the day of Ḥunayn, when your great number pleased you, but it did not avail you at all, and the earth was confining for you with [i.e., in spite of] its vastness; then you turned back, fleeing.

(26) Then Allāh sent down His tranquility upon His Messenger and upon the believers and sent down soldiers [i.e., angels] whom you did not see and punished those who disbelieved. And that is the recompense of the disbelievers.

(27) Then Allāh will accept repentance after that for whom He wills; and Allāh is Forgiving and Merciful.

(28) O you who have believed, indeed the polytheists are unclean, so let them not approach al-Masjid al-Ḥarām after this, their [final] year. And if you fear privation, Allāh will enrich you from His bounty if He wills. Indeed, Allāh is Knowing and Wise.

(29) Fight against those who do not believe in Allāh or in the Last Day and who do not consider unlawful what Allāh and His Messenger have made unlawful and who

do not adopt the religion of truth [i.e., Islām] from those who were given the Scripture - [fight] until they give the jizyah[457] willingly while they are humbled.

(30) The Jews say, "Ezra is the son of Allāh"; and the Christians say, "The Messiah is the son of Allāh." That is their statement from their mouths; they imitate the saying of those who disbelieved before [them]. May Allāh destroy them; how are they deluded?

(31) They have taken their scholars and monks as lords besides Allāh,[458] and [also] the Messiah, the son of Mary.[459] And they were not commanded except to worship one God; there is no deity except Him. Exalted is He above whatever they associate with Him.

(32) They want to extinguish the light of Allāh with their mouths, but Allāh refuses except to perfect His light, although the disbelievers dislike it.

(33) It is He who has sent His Messenger with guidance and the religion of truth to manifest it over all religion, although they who associate others with Allāh dislike it.

(34) O you who have believed, indeed many of the scholars and the monks devour the wealth of people unjustly[460] and avert [them] from the way of Allāh. And those who hoard gold and silver and spend it not in the way of Allāh - give them tidings of a painful punishment.

(35) The Day when it[461] will be heated in the fire of Hell and seared therewith will be their foreheads, their flanks, and their backs, [it will be said], "This is what you hoarded for yourselves, so taste what you used to hoard."

(36) Indeed, the number of months with Allāh is twelve [lunar] months in the register of Allāh [from] the day He created the heavens and the earth; of these, four are sacred.[462] That is the correct religion [i.e., way], so do not wrong yourselves during them.[463] And fight against the disbelievers collectively as they fight against you collectively. And know that Allāh is with the righteous [who fear Him].

---

[457] A tax required of non-Muslims exempting them from military service and entitling them to the protection of the Islāmic state. Concurrently, zakāh is not taken from them, being an obligation only upon Muslims.

[458] "By their obedience to them rather than to what Allāh ordained.

[459] By their worship of him in conjunction with Allāh."

[460] i.e., through false pretense.

[461] The gold and silver which was hoarded, i.e., whose zakāh was not paid.

[462] "See footnote to 9:5.

[463] i.e., do not violate the sacred months or commit aggression therein."

(37) Indeed, the postponing [of restriction within sacred months] is an increase in disbelief by which those who have disbelieved are led [further] astray. They make it[464] lawful one year and unlawful another year to correspond to the number made unlawful by Allāh[465] and [thus] make lawful what Allāh has made unlawful. Made pleasing to them is the evil of their deeds; and Allāh does not guide the disbelieving people.

(38) O you who have believed, what is [the matter] with you that, when you are told to go forth in the cause of Allāh, you adhere heavily to the earth?[466] Are you satisfied with the life of this world rather than the Hereafter? But what is the enjoyment of worldly life compared to the Hereafter except a [very] little.

(39) If you do not go forth, He will punish you with a painful punishment and will replace you with another people, and you will not harm Him at all. And Allāh is over all things competent.

(40) If you do not aid him [i.e., the Prophet (ﷺ)] - Allāh has already aided him when those who disbelieved had driven him out [of Makkah] as one of two,[467] when they were in the cave and he [i.e., Muḥammad (ﷺ)] said to his companion, "Do not grieve; indeed Allāh is with us." And Allāh sent down His tranquility upon him and supported him with soldiers [i.e., angels] you did not see and made the word[468] of those who disbelieved the lowest,[469] while the word of Allāh[470] - that is the highest. And Allāh is Exalted in Might and Wise.

(41) Go forth, whether light or heavy,[471] and strive with your wealth and your lives in the cause of Allāh. That is better for you, if you only knew.

(42) Had it been a near [i.e., easy] gain and a moderate trip, they [i.e., the hypocrites] would have followed you, but distant to them was the journey. And they will swear by Allāh,[472] "If we were able, we would have gone forth with you," destroying themselves [through false oaths], and Allāh knows that indeed they are liars.

---

[464] "Fighting during a sacred month.

[465] If they found it advantageous to violate a sacred month, they would do so, designating another month in its place in which to observe the restrictions concerning fighting."

[466] i.e., inclining toward the comforts of worldly life.

[467] "The second was his companion, Abū Bakr.

[468] i.e., their claims and slogans.

[469] i.e., degraded and dishonored.

[470] "Lā ilāha ill-Allāh" ("There is no deity except Allāh")."

[471] i.e., young or old, riding or walking, in ease or in hardship - in all circumstances and conditions.

[472] When you return from the Tabūk expedition.

(43) Allāh has pardoned you, [O Muḥammad, but] why did you give them permission [to remain behind]? [You should not have] until it was evident to you who were truthful and you knew [who were] the liars.

(44) Those who believe in Allāh and the Last Day would not ask permission of you to be excused from striving [i.e., fighting] with their wealth and their lives. And Allāh is Knowing of those who fear Him.

(45) Only those would ask permission of you who do not believe in Allāh and the Last Day and whose hearts have doubted, and they, in their doubt, are hesitating.

(46) And if they had intended to go forth, they would have prepared for it [some] preparation. But Allāh disliked their being sent, so He kept them back, and they were told, "Remain [behind] with those who remain."[473]

(47) Had they gone forth with you, they would not have increased you except in confusion, and they would have been active among you, seeking [to cause] you fitnah [i.e., chaos and dissension]. And among you are avid listeners to them. And Allāh is Knowing of the wrongdoers.

(48) They had already desired dissension before and had upset matters for you[474] until the truth came and the ordinance [i.e., victory] of Allāh appeared, while they were averse.

(49) And among them is he who says, "Permit me [to remain at home] and do not put me to trial." Unquestionably, into trial they have fallen.[475] And indeed, Hell will encompass the disbelievers.

(50) If good befalls you, it distresses them; but if disaster strikes you, they say, "We took our matter [in hand] before,"[476] and turn away while they are rejoicing.

(51) Say, "Never will we be struck except by what Allāh has decreed for us; He is our protector." And upon Allāh let the believers rely.

(52) Say, "Do you await for us except one of the two best things [i.e., martyrdom or victory] while we await for you that Allāh will afflict you with punishment from Himself or at our hands? So wait; indeed we, along with you, are waiting."

---

[473] i.e., the women and children.

[474] Or "turned matters related to you over [in their minds, considering how to cause you failure]."

[475] By avoiding their obligation, they fell into destruction.

[476] The hypocrites claim to have protected themselves by remaining behind.

(53) Say, "Spend willingly or unwillingly; never will it be accepted from you. Indeed, you have been a defiantly disobedient people."

(54) And what prevents their expenditures from being accepted from them but that they have disbelieved in Allāh and in His Messenger and that they come not to prayer except while they are lazy and that they do not spend except while they are unwilling.

(55) So let not their wealth or their children impress you. Allāh only intends to punish them through them in worldly life and that their souls should depart [at death] while they are disbelievers.

(56) And they swear by Allāh that they are from among you while they are not from among you; but they are a people who are afraid.

(57) If they could find a refuge or some caves or any place to enter [and hide], they would turn to it while they run heedlessly.

(58) And among them are some who criticize you concerning the [distribution of] charities. If they are given from them, they approve; but if they are not given from them, at once they become angry.

(59) If only they had been satisfied with what Allāh and His Messenger gave them and said, "Sufficient for us is Allāh; Allāh will give us of His bounty, and [so will] His Messenger; indeed, we are desirous toward Allāh,"[477] [it would have been better for them].

(60) Zakāh expenditures are only for the poor and for the needy and for those employed for it[478] and for bringing hearts together [for Islām] and for freeing captives [or slaves] and for those in debt and for the cause of Allāh and for the [stranded] traveler - an obligation [imposed] by Allāh. And Allāh is Knowing and Wise.

(61) And among them are those who abuse the Prophet and say, "He is an ear."[479] Say, "[It is] an ear of goodness for you that believes in Allāh and believes the believers and [is] a mercy to those who believe among you." And those who abuse the Messenger of Allāh - for them is a painful punishment.

---

[477] Meaning "We desire Allāh and His grace and acceptance," or "We desire whatever Allāh wills to give us of His bounty."
[478] By the state to collect, guard and distribute the zakāh.
[479] i.e., one who believes everything he hears.

(62) They swear by Allāh to you [Muslims] to satisfy you. But Allāh and His Messenger are more worthy for them to satisfy,[480] if they were to be believers.

(63) Do they not know that whoever opposes Allāh and His Messenger - that for him is the fire of Hell, wherein he will abide eternally? That is the great disgrace.

(64) The hypocrites are apprehensive lest a sūrah be revealed about them, informing them of[481] what is in their hearts. Say, "Mock [as you wish]; indeed, Allāh will expose that which you fear."

(65) And if you ask them, they will surely say, "We were only conversing and playing." Say, "Is it Allāh and His verses and His Messenger that you were mocking?"

(66) Make no excuse; you have disbelieved [i.e., rejected faith] after your belief. If We pardon one faction of you - We will punish another faction because they were criminals.

(67) The hypocrite men and hypocrite women are of one another. They enjoin what is wrong and forbid what is right and close their hands.[482] They have forgotten Allāh, so He has forgotten them [accordingly]. Indeed, the hypocrites - it is they who are the defiantly disobedient.

(68) Allāh has promised the hypocrite men and hypocrite women and the disbelievers the fire of Hell, wherein they will abide eternally. It is sufficient for them. And Allāh has cursed them, and for them is an enduring punishment.

(69) [You disbelievers are] like those before you; they were stronger than you in power and more abundant in wealth and children. They enjoyed their portion [of worldly enjoyment], and you have enjoyed your portion as those before you enjoyed their portion, and you have engaged [in vanities] like that in which they engaged. [It is] those whose deeds have become worthless in this world and in the Hereafter, and it is they who are the losers.

(70) Has there not reached them the news of those before them - the people of Noah and [the tribes of] ʿAad and Thamūd and the people of Abraham and the companions [i.e., dwellers] of Madyan and the towns overturned?[483] Their

---

[480] Literally, "to satisfy Him," meaning that Allāh would be satisfied by obedience to the Messenger (ﷺ).

[481] i.e., exposing the truth about.

[482] i.e., refuse to spend in the way of Allāh.

[483] i.e., those to which Lot was sent and which earned for themselves Allāh's punishment. See 11:82-83.

messengers came to them with clear proofs. And Allāh would never have wronged them, but they were wronging themselves.

(71) The believing men and believing women are allies of one another. They enjoin what is right and forbid what is wrong and establish prayer and give zakāh and obey Allāh and His Messenger. Those - Allāh will have mercy upon them. Indeed, Allāh is Exalted in Might and Wise.

(72) Allāh has promised the believing men and believing women gardens beneath which rivers flow, wherein they abide eternally, and pleasant dwellings in gardens of perpetual residence; but approval from Allāh is greater. It is that which is the great attainment.

(73) O Prophet, fight against the disbelievers and the hypocrites and be harsh upon them. And their refuge is Hell, and wretched is the destination.

(74) They swear by Allāh that they did not say [anything against the Prophet (ﷺ)] while they had said the word of disbelief and disbelieved after their [pretense of] Islām and planned that which they were not to attain.[484] And they were not resentful except [for the fact] that Allāh and His Messenger had enriched them of His bounty.[485] So if they repent, it is better for them; but if they turn away, Allāh will punish them with a painful punishment in this world and the Hereafter. And there will not be for them on earth any protector or helper.

(75) And among them are those who made a covenant with Allāh, [saying], "If He should give us from His bounty, we will surely spend in charity, and we will surely be among the righteous."

(76) But when He gave them from His bounty, they were stingy with it and turned away while they refused.

(77) So He penalized them with hypocrisy in their hearts until the Day they will meet Him - because they failed Allāh in what they promised Him and because they [habitually] used to lie.

(78) Did they not know that Allāh knows their secrets and their private conversations and that Allāh is the Knower of the unseen?

(79) Those who criticize the contributors among the believers concerning [their] charities and [criticize] the ones who find nothing [to spend] except their effort, so

---

[484] "i.e., the murder of Prophet Muḥammad (ﷺ).
[485] i.e., for no reason. On the contrary, they should have been grateful."

they ridicule them - Allāh will ridicule them, and they will have a painful punishment.

(80) Ask forgiveness for them, [O Muḥammad], or do not ask forgiveness for them. If you should ask forgiveness for them seventy times - never will Allāh forgive them. That is because they disbelieved in Allāh and His Messenger, and Allāh does not guide the defiantly disobedient people.

(81) Those who remained behind[486] rejoiced in their staying [at home] after [the departure of] the Messenger of Allāh and disliked to strive with their wealth and their lives in the cause of Allāh and said, "Do not go forth in the heat." Say, "The fire of Hell is more intense in heat" - if they would but understand.

(82) So let them laugh a little and [then] weep much as recompense for what they used to earn.

(83) If Allāh should return you to a faction of them [after the expedition] and then they ask your permission to go out [to battle], say, "You will not go out with me, ever, and you will never fight with me an enemy. Indeed, you were satisfied with sitting [at home] the first time, so sit [now] with those who stay behind."

(84) And do not pray [the funeral prayer, O Muḥammad], over any of them who has died - ever - or stand at his grave. Indeed, they disbelieved in Allāh and His Messenger and died while they were defiantly disobedient.

(85) And let not their wealth and their children impress you. Allāh only intends to punish them through them in this world and that their souls should depart [at death] while they are disbelievers.

(86) And when a sūrah was revealed [enjoining them] to believe in Allāh and to fight with His Messenger, those of wealth among them asked your permission [to stay back] and said, "Leave us to be with them who sit [at home]."

(87) They were satisfied to be with those who stay behind, and their hearts were sealed over, so they do not understand.

(88) But the Messenger and those who believed with him fought with their wealth and their lives. Those will have [all that is] good and it is those who are the successful.

---

[486] Literally, "were left behind [as Allāh willed]" due to their false excuses having been accepted by the Prophet (ﷺ). While pleased with their assumed deception, in reality, Allāh had prevented their participation knowing of their hypocrisy and evil intent.

(89) Allāh has prepared for them gardens beneath which rivers flow, wherein they will abide eternally. That is the great attainment.

(90) And those with excuses among the bedouins came to be permitted [to remain], and they who had lied[487] to Allāh and His Messenger sat [at home]. There will strike those who disbelieved among them a painful punishment.

(91) There is not upon the weak or upon the ill or upon those who do not find anything to spend any discomfort [i.e., guilt] when they are sincere to Allāh and His Messenger. There is not upon the doers of good any cause [for blame]. And Allāh is Forgiving and Merciful.

(92) Nor [is there blame] upon those who, when they came to you for you to take them along, you said, "I can find nothing upon which to carry you."[488] They turned back while their eyes overflowed with tears out of grief that they could not find something to spend [for the cause of Allāh].

(93) The cause [for blame] is only upon those who ask permission of you while they are rich. They are satisfied to be with those who stay behind, and Allāh has sealed over their hearts, so they do not know.

(94) They will make excuses to you when you have returned to them. Say, "Make no excuse - never will we believe you. Allāh has already informed us of your news [i.e., affair]. And Allāh will observe your deeds, and [so will] His Messenger; then you will be taken back to the Knower of the unseen and the witnessed,[489] and He will inform you of what you used to do."

(95) They will swear by Allāh to you when you return to them that you would leave them alone. So leave them alone; indeed they are evil; and their refuge is Hell as recompense for what they had been earning.

(96) They swear to you so that you might be satisfied with them. But if you should be satisfied with them - indeed, Allāh is not satisfied with a defiantly disobedient people.

(97) The bedouins are stronger in disbelief and hypocrisy and more likely not to know the limits of what [laws] Allāh has revealed to His Messenger. And Allāh is Knowing and Wise.

---

[487] i.e., claimed faith.

[488] No mounts or even shoes were available.

[489] See footnotes to 6:73.

(98) And among the bedouins are some who consider what they spend as a loss[490] and await for you turns of misfortune. Upon them will be a misfortune of evil. And Allāh is Hearing and Knowing.

(99) But among the bedouins are some who believe in Allāh and the Last Day and consider what they spend as means of nearness to Allāh and of [obtaining] invocations of the Messenger. Unquestionably, it is a means of nearness for them. Allāh will admit them to His mercy. Indeed, Allāh is Forgiving and Merciful.

(100) And the first forerunners [in the faith] among the Muhājireen[491] and the Anṣār[492] and those who followed them with good conduct - Allāh is pleased with them and they are pleased with Him, and He has prepared for them gardens beneath which rivers flow, wherein they will abide forever. That is the great attainment.

(101) And among those around you of the bedouins are hypocrites, and [also] from the people of Madīnah. They have persisted in hypocrisy. You, [O Muḥammad], do not know them, [but] We know them. We will punish them twice [in this world]; then they will be returned to a great punishment.

(102) And [there are] others who have acknowledged their sins. They had mixed [i.e., polluted] a righteous deed with another that was bad.[493] Perhaps Allāh will turn to them in forgiveness. Indeed, Allāh is Forgiving and Merciful.

(103) Take, [O Muḥammad], from their wealth a charity by which you purify them and cause them increase, and invoke [Allāh's blessings] upon them. Indeed, your invocations are reassurance for them. And Allāh is Hearing and Knowing.

(104) Do they not know that it is Allāh who accepts repentance from His servants and receives charities and that it is Allāh who is the Accepting of Repentance,[494] the Merciful?

---

[490] i.e., a fine or penalty.

[491] "Those who emigrated from Makkah and settled in Madīnah for the cause of Islām.

[492] The inhabitants of Madīnah who had accepted Islām and assisted the Prophet (ﷺ) and other emigrants upon their arrival there."

[493] This refers to their having previously taken part in jihād but having abstained on the occasion of Tabūk.

[494] Refer to footnote in 2:37.

(105) And say, "Do [as you will], for Allāh will see your deeds, and [so will] His Messenger and the believers. And you will be returned to the Knower of the unseen and the witnessed, and He will inform you of what you used to do."

(106) And [there are] others deferred until the command of Allāh - whether He will punish them or whether He will forgive them. And Allāh is Knowing and Wise.

(107) And [there are] those [hypocrites] who took for themselves a mosque for causing harm and disbelief and division among the believers and as a station for whoever had warred against Allāh and His Messenger before. And they will surely swear, "We intended only the best." And Allāh testifies that indeed they are liars.

(108) Do not stand [for prayer] within it - ever. A mosque founded on righteousness from the first day[495] is more worthy for you to stand in. Within it are men who love to purify themselves; and Allāh loves those who purify themselves.

(109) Then is one who laid the foundation of his building on righteousness [with fear] from Allāh and [seeking] His approval better or one who laid the foundation of his building on the edge of a bank about to collapse, so it collapsed with him into the fire of Hell? And Allāh does not guide the wrongdoing people.

(110) Their building which they built will not cease to be a [cause of] skepticism in their hearts until their hearts are cut [i.e., stopped]. And Allāh is Knowing and Wise.

(111) Indeed, Allāh has purchased from the believers their lives and their properties [in exchange] for that they will have Paradise. They fight in the cause of Allāh, so they kill and are killed. [It is] a true promise [binding] upon Him in the Torah and the Gospel and the Qur'ān. And who is truer to his covenant than Allāh? So rejoice in your transaction which you have contracted. And it is that which is the great attainment.

(112) [Such believers are] the repentant, the worshippers, the praisers [of Allāh], the travelers [for His cause], those who bow and prostrate [in prayer], those who enjoin what is right and forbid what is wrong, and those who observe the limits [set by] Allāh. And give good tidings to the believers.

(113) It is not for the Prophet and those who have believed to ask forgiveness for the polytheists, even if they were relatives, after it has become clear to them that they are companions of Hellfire.

(114) And the request of forgiveness of Abraham for his father was only because of a promise he had made to him. But when it became apparent to him [i.e., Abraham]

---

[495] This description is of the Qubā' mosque.

that he [i.e., the father] was an enemy to Allāh, he disassociated himself from him. Indeed was Abraham compassionate and patient.

(115) And Allāh would not let a people stray after He has guided them until He makes clear to them what they should avoid. Indeed, Allāh is Knowing of all things.

(116) Indeed, to Allāh belongs the dominion of the heavens and the earth; He gives life and causes death. And you have not besides Allāh any protector or any helper.

(117) Allāh has already forgiven the Prophet and the Muhājireen and the Anṣār who followed him in the hour of difficulty after the hearts of a party of them had almost inclined [to doubt], and then He forgave them. Indeed, He was to them Kind and Merciful.

(118) And [He also forgave] the three who were left alone [i.e., boycotted, regretting their error] to the point that the earth closed in on them in spite of its vastness[496] and their souls confined [i.e., anguished] them and they were certain that there is no refuge from Allāh except in Him. Then He turned to them so they could repent. Indeed, Allāh is the Accepting of Repentance,[497] the Merciful.

(119) O you who have believed, fear Allāh and be with those who are true.

(120) It was not [proper] for the people of Madīnah and those surrounding them of the bedouins that they remain behind after [the departure of] the Messenger of Allāh or that they prefer themselves over his self.[498] That is because they are not afflicted by thirst or fatigue or hunger in the cause of Allāh, nor do they tread on any ground that enrages the disbelievers, nor do they inflict upon an enemy any infliction but that it is registered for them as a righteous deed. Indeed, Allāh does not allow to be lost the reward of the doers of good.

(121) Nor do they spend an expenditure, small or large, or cross a valley but that it is registered for them that Allāh may reward them for the best of what they were doing.

(122) And it is not for the believers to go forth [to battle] all at once. For there should separate from every division of them a group [remaining] to obtain understanding in the religion and warn [i.e., advise] their people when they return to them that they might be cautious.

---

[496] "Thus it seemed to them in their extreme distress.

[497] Refer to footnote in 2:37."

[498] In times of hardship. Rather, they should have been willing to endure with the Prophet (ﷺ) whatever was necessary for Islām.

(123) O you who have believed, fight against those adjacent to you of the disbelievers and let them find in you harshness. And know that Allāh is with the righteous.

(124) And whenever a sūrah is revealed, there are among them [i.e., the hypocrites] those who say, "Which of you has this increased in faith?" As for those who believed, it has increased them in faith, while they are rejoicing.

(125) But as for those in whose hearts is disease, it has [only] increased them in evil [in addition] to their evil.[499] And they will have died while they are disbelievers.

(126) Do they not see that they are tried every year once or twice but then they do not repent nor do they remember?

(127) And whenever a sūrah is revealed, they look at each other, [as if saying], "Does anyone see you?" and then they dismiss themselves. Allāh has dismissed their hearts because they are a people who do not understand.

(128) There has certainly come to you a Messenger from among yourselves. Grievous to him is what you suffer; [he is] concerned over you [i.e., your guidance] and to the believers is kind and merciful.

(129) But if they turn away, [O Muḥammad], say, "Sufficient for me is Allāh; there is no deity except Him. On Him I have relied, and He is the Lord of the Great Throne."

---

[499] Literally, "filth," i.e., disbelief and hypocrisy.

Surah Yunus

(1) Alif, Lām, Rā.[500] These are the verses of the wise[501] Book.

(2) Have the people been amazed that We revealed [revelation] to a man from among them, [saying], "Warn mankind and give good tidings to those who believe that they will have a [firm] precedence of honor[502] with their Lord"? [But] the disbelievers say, "Indeed, this is an obvious magician."

(3) Indeed, your Lord is Allāh, who created the heavens and the earth in six days and then established Himself above the Throne,[503] arranging the matter [of His creation]. There is no intercessor except after His permission. That is Allāh, your Lord, so worship Him. Then will you not remember?

(4) To Him is your return all together. [It is] the promise of Allāh [which is] truth. Indeed, He begins the [process of] creation and then repeats it that He may reward those who have believed and done righteous deeds, in justice. But those who disbelieved will have a drink of scalding water and a painful punishment for what they used to deny.

(5) It is He who made the sun a shining light and the moon a derived light and determined for it phases - that you may know the number of years and account [of time]. Allāh has not created this except in truth. He details the signs for a people who know.

(6) Indeed, in the alternation of the night and the day and [in] what Allāh has created in the heavens and the earth are signs for a people who fear Allāh.

(7) Indeed, those who do not expect the meeting with Us and are satisfied with the life of this world and feel secure therein and those who are heedless of Our signs -

(8) For those their refuge will be the Fire because of what they used to earn.

(9) Indeed, those who have believed and done righteous deeds - their Lord will guide them because of their faith. Beneath them rivers will flow in the Gardens of Pleasure.

---

[500] "See footnote to 2:1.
[501] The adjective "wise" expresses the qualities of will, purpose, discrimination and precision."
[502] i.e., a sure position due to their righteous deeds.
[503] See footnotes to 2:19 and 7:54.

(10) Their call therein will be, "Exalted are You, O Allāh," and their greeting therein will be, "Peace." And the last of their call will be, "Praise to Allāh, Lord of the worlds!"

(11) And if Allāh was to hasten for the people the evil [they invoke][504] as He hastens for them the good, their term would have been ended for them.[505] But We leave the ones who do not expect the meeting with Us, in their transgression, wandering blindly.

(12) And when affliction touches man, he calls upon Us, whether lying on his side or sitting or standing; but when We remove from him his affliction, he continues [in disobedience] as if he had never called upon Us to [remove] an affliction that touched him. Thus is made pleasing to the transgressors that which they have been doing.

(13) And We had already destroyed generations before you when they wronged, and their messengers had come to them with clear proofs, but they were not to believe. Thus do We recompense the criminal people.

(14) Then We made you successors in the land after them so that We may observe how you will do.

(15) And when Our verses are recited to them as clear evidences, those who do not expect the meeting with Us say, "Bring us a Qur'ān other than this or change it." Say, [O Muḥammad], "It is not for me to change it on my own accord. I only follow what is revealed to me. Indeed I fear, if I should disobey my Lord, the punishment of a tremendous Day."

(16) Say, "If Allāh had willed, I would not have recited it to you, nor would He have made it known to you, for I had remained among you a lifetime before it.[506] Then will you not reason?"

(17) So who is more unjust than he who invents a lie about Allāh or denies His signs? Indeed, the criminals will not succeed.

(18) And they worship other than Allāh that which neither harms them nor benefits them, and they say, "These are our intercessors with Allāh." Say, "Do you inform Allāh of something He does not know in the heavens or on the earth?" Exalted is He and high above what they associate with Him.

---

[504] "In anger or in heedlessness.

[505] i.e., Allāh would have destroyed them on account of that."

[506] The Prophet (ﷺ) lived among his people forty years before receiving any revelation.

(19) And mankind was not but one community [united in religion], but [then] they differed. And if not for a word[507] that preceded from your Lord, it would have been judged between them [immediately] concerning that over which they differ.

(20) And they say, "Why is a sign not sent down to him from his Lord?" So say, "The unseen is only for Allāh [to administer], so wait; indeed, I am with you among those who wait."

(21) And when We give the people a taste of mercy after adversity has touched them, at once they conspire against Our verses. Say, "Allāh is swifter in strategy." Indeed, Our messengers [i.e., angels] record that which you conspire.

(22) It is He who enables you to travel on land and sea until, when you are in ships and they sail with them[508] by a good wind and they rejoice therein, there comes a storm wind and the waves come upon them from every place and they expect to be engulfed, they supplicate Allāh, sincere to Him in religion, "If You should save us from this, we will surely be among the thankful."

(23) But when He saves them, at once they commit injustice[509] upon the earth without right. O mankind, your injustice is only against yourselves, [being merely] the enjoyment of worldly life. Then to Us is your return, and We will inform you of what you used to do.

(24) The example of [this] worldly life is but like rain which We have sent down from the sky that the plants of the earth absorb - [those] from which men and livestock eat - until, when the earth has taken on its adornment and is beautified and its people suppose that they have capability over it, there comes to it Our command by night or by day, and We make it as a harvest,[510] as if it had not flourished yesterday. Thus do We explain in detail the signs for a people who give thought.

(25) And Allāh invites to the Home of Peace [i.e., Paradise] and guides whom He wills to a straight path.

---

[507] Allāh's decree to allow time on earth for His creation or not to punish anyone before evidence has come to him.

[508] The change in pronoun from the second to third person shows that the following description applies specifically to the disbelievers.

[509] By oppression and disobedience or by invoking others besides Allāh.

[510] Its vegetation having been cut down or uprooted, i.e., utterly destroyed.

(26) For them who have done good is the best [reward] - and extra.[511] No darkness will cover their faces, nor humiliation. Those are companions of Paradise; they will abide therein eternally.

(27) But they who have earned [blame for] evil doings - the recompense of an evil deed is its equivalent, and humiliation will cover them. They will have from Allāh no protector. It will be as if their faces are covered with pieces of the night - so dark [are they]. Those are the companions of the Fire; they will abide therein eternally.

(28) And [mention, O Muḥammad], the Day We will gather them all together - then We will say to those who associated others with Allāh, "[Remain in] your place, you and your 'partners.'"[512] Then We will separate them,[513] and their "partners" will say, "You did not used to worship us,[514]

(29) And sufficient is Allāh as a witness between us and you that we were of your worship unaware."

(30) There, [on that Day], every soul will be put to trial for what it did previously, and they will be returned to Allāh, their master, the Truth, and lost from them is whatever they used to invent.

(31) Say, "Who provides for you from the heaven and the earth? Or who controls hearing and sight and who brings the living out of the dead and brings the dead out of the living and who arranges [every] matter?" They will say, "Allāh," so say, "Then will you not fear Him?"

(32) For that is Allāh, your Lord, the Truth. And what can be beyond truth except error? So how are you averted?

(33) Thus the word [i.e., decree] of your Lord has come into effect upon those who defiantly disobeyed - that they will not believe.

(34) Say, "Are there of your 'partners' any who begins creation and then repeats it?" Say, "Allāh begins creation and then repeats it, so how are you deluded?"

(35) Say, "Are there of your 'partners' any who guides to the truth?" Say, "Allāh guides to the truth. So is He who guides to the truth more worthy to be followed or

---

[511] In addition to the pleasures of Paradise, they will be able to see Allāh (subḥānahu wa taʿālā), as reported in an authentic ḥadīth narrated by Muslim.
[512] "Those they had associated with Allāh.
[513] From the believers.
[514] The inanimate objects, such as idols, will not have been aware of their worship of them. But those beings who consented to be worshipped will lie and deny it on the Day of Judgement."

he who guides not unless he is guided? Then what is [wrong] with you - how do you judge?"

(36) And most of them follow not except assumption. Indeed, assumption avails not against the truth at all. Indeed, Allāh is Knowing of what they do.

(37) And it was not [possible] for this Qur'ān to be produced by other than Allāh, but [it is] a confirmation of what was before it and a detailed explanation of the [former] Scripture, about which there is no doubt,[515] from the Lord of the worlds.

(38) Or do they say [about the Prophet (ﷺ)], "He invented it?" Say, "Then bring forth a sūrah like it and call upon [for assistance] whomever you can besides Allāh, if you should be truthful."

(39) Rather, they have denied that which they encompass not in knowledge and whose interpretation has not yet come to them. Thus did those before them deny. Then observe how was the end of the wrongdoers.

(40) And of them are those who believe in it, and of them are those who do not believe in it. And your Lord is most knowing of the corrupters.

(41) And if they deny you, [O Muḥammad], then say, "For me are my deeds, and for you are your deeds. You are disassociated from what I do, and I am disassociated from what you do."

(42) And among them are those who listen to you. But can you cause the deaf to hear [i.e., benefit from this hearing], although they will not use reason?

(43) And among them are those who look at you. But can you guide the blind although they will not [attempt to] see?

(44) Indeed, Allāh does not wrong the people at all, but it is the people who are wronging themselves.

(45) And on the Day when He will gather them, [it will be] as if they had not remained [in the world] but an hour of the day, [and] they will know each other. Those will have lost who denied the meeting with Allāh and were not guided.

(46) And whether We show you some of what We promise them, [O Muḥammad], or We take you in death, to Us is their return; then, [either way], Allāh is a witness concerning what they are doing.

---

[515] This phrase refers back to the Qur'ān.

(47) And for every nation is a messenger. So when their messenger comes,[516] it will be judged between them in justice, and they will not be wronged.

(48) And they say, "When is [the fulfillment of] this promise, if you should be truthful?"

(49) Say, "I possess not for myself any harm or benefit except what Allāh should will. For every nation is a [specified] term. When their time has come, then they will not remain behind an hour, nor will they precede [it]."

(50) Say, "Have you considered: if His punishment should come to you by night or by day - for which [aspect] of it would the criminals be impatient?"[517]

(51) Then is it that when it has [actually] occurred you will believe in it? Now?[518] And you were [once] for it impatient.[519]

(52) Then it will be said to those who had wronged, "Taste the punishment of eternity; are you being recompensed except for what you used to earn?"

(53) And they ask information of you, [O Muḥammad], "Is it true?" Say, "Yes, by my Lord. Indeed, it is truth; and you will not cause failure [to Allāh]."

(54) And if each soul that wronged had everything on earth, it would offer it in ransom. And they will confide regret when they see the punishment; and they will be judged in justice, and they will not be wronged.

(55) Unquestionably, to Allāh belongs whatever is in the heavens and the earth. Unquestionably, the promise of Allāh is truth, but most of them do not know.

(56) He gives life and causes death, and to Him you will be returned.

(57) O mankind, there has come to you instruction from your Lord and healing for what is in the breasts and guidance and mercy for the believers.

(58) Say, "In the bounty of Allāh and in His mercy - in that let them rejoice; it is better than what they accumulate."

---

[516] To witness on the Day of Judgement. Another meaning is "Once a messenger has come [to them in this world]..."

[517] "Impatience" refers to the disbelievers' ridicule of the Prophet (ﷺ) by telling him to produce Allāh's punishment as proof of his truthfulness.
[518] "i.e., when it is too late to benefit from belief.
[519] Challenging those who warned of it to bring it on immediately."

(59) Say, "Have you seen what Allāh has sent down to you of provision of which you have made [some] lawful and [some] unlawful?" Say, "Has Allāh permitted you [to do so], or do you invent [something] about Allāh?"

(60) And what will be the supposition of those who invent falsehood about Allāh on the Day of Resurrection?[520] Indeed, Allāh is the possessor of bounty for the people, but most of them are not grateful.

(61) And, [O Muḥammad], you are not [engaged] in any matter and do not recite any of the Qur'ān and you [people] do not do any deed except that We are witness over you when you are involved in it. And not absent from your Lord is any [part] of an atom's weight[521] within the earth or within the heaven or [anything] smaller than that or greater but that it is in a clear register.

(62) Unquestionably, [for] the allies of Allāh there will be no fear concerning them, nor will they grieve -

(63) Those who believed and were fearing Allāh.

(64) For them are good tidings in the worldly life and in the Hereafter. No change is there in the words [i.e., decrees] of Allāh. That is what is the great attainment.

(65) And let not their speech grieve you. Indeed, honor [due to power] belongs to Allāh entirely. He is the Hearing, the Knowing.

(66) Unquestionably, to Allāh belongs whoever is in the heavens and whoever is on the earth. And those who invoke other than Allāh do not [actually] follow [His] "partners." They follow not except assumption, and they are not but misjudging.

(67) It is He who made for you the night to rest therein and the day, giving sight.[522] Indeed in that are signs for a people who listen.

(68) They[523] have said, "Allāh has taken a son." Exalted is He; He is the [one] Free of need. To Him belongs whatever is in the heavens and whatever is in the earth. You have no authority[524] for this [claim]. Do you say about Allāh that which you do not know?

(69) Say, "Indeed, those who invent falsehood about Allāh will not succeed."

---

[520] i.e., what do they think He will do with them.
[521] Or "the weight of a small ant."

[522] i.e., making things visible.
[523] "The Christians and others.
[524] Or "evidence.""

(70) [For them is brief] enjoyment in this world; then to Us is their return; then We will make them taste the severe punishment because they used to disbelieve.

(71) And recite to them the news of Noah, when he said to his people, "O my people, if my residence and my reminding of the signs of Allāh has become burdensome upon you - then I have relied upon Allāh. So resolve upon your plan and [call upon] your associates. Then let not your plan be obscure to you.[525] Then carry it out upon me and do not give me respite.

(72) And if you turn away [from my advice] - then no payment have I asked of you. My reward is only from Allāh, and I have been commanded to be of the Muslims [i.e., those who submit to Allāh]."

(73) And they denied him, so We saved him and those with him in the ship and made them successors, and We drowned those who denied Our signs. Then see how was the end of those who were warned.

(74) Then We sent after him messengers to their peoples, and they came to them with clear proofs. But they were not to believe in that which they had denied before.[526] Thus We seal over the hearts of the transgressors.

(75) Then We sent after them Moses and Aaron to Pharaoh and his establishment with Our signs, but they behaved arrogantly and were a criminal people.

(76) So when there came to them the truth from Us, they said, "Indeed, this is obvious magic."

(77) Moses said, "Do you say [thus] about the truth when it has come to you? Is this magic? But magicians will not succeed."

(78) They said, "Have you come to us to turn us away from that upon which we found our fathers and so that you two may have grandeur in the land? And we are not believers in you."

(79) And Pharaoh said, "Bring to me every learned magician."

(80) So when the magicians came, Moses said to them, "Throw down whatever you will throw."

---

[525] i.e., Do not let it be a source of doubt or anxiety to you but let it be clear, open and defined.

[526] i.e., the succeeding generations were persistent in disbelief.

(81) And when they had thrown, Moses said, "What you have brought is [only] magic. Indeed, Allāh will expose its worthlessness. Indeed, Allāh does not amend the work of corrupters.

(82) And Allāh will establish the truth by His words, even if the criminals dislike it."

(83) But no one believed Moses, except [some] offspring [i.e., youths] among his people, for fear of Pharaoh and his establishment that they would persecute them. And indeed, Pharaoh was haughty within the land, and indeed, he was of the transgressors.

(84) And Moses said, "O my people, if you have believed in Allāh, then rely upon Him, if you should be Muslims [i.e., submitting to Him]."

(85) So they said, "Upon Allāh do we rely. Our Lord, make us not [objects of] trial for the wrongdoing people

(86) And save us by Your mercy from the disbelieving people."

(87) And We inspired to Moses and his brother, "Settle your people in Egypt in houses and make your houses [facing the] qiblah[527] and establish prayer and give good tidings to the believers."

(88) And Moses said, "Our Lord, indeed You have given Pharaoh and his establishment splendor and wealth in the worldly life, our Lord, that they may lead [men] astray from Your way. Our Lord, obliterate their wealth and harden their hearts so that they will not believe until they see the painful punishment."

(89) [Allāh] said, "Your supplication has been answered."[528] So remain on a right course and follow not the way of those who do not know."

(90) And We took the Children of Israel across the sea, and Pharaoh and his soldiers pursued them in tyranny and enmity until, when drowning overtook him, he said, "I believe that there is no deity except that in whom the Children of Israel believe, and I am of the Muslims."

(91) Now? And you had disobeyed [Him] before and were of the corrupters?

---

[527] In order that they might pray therein unseen by their enemy.

[528] Literally, "the supplication of both of you," i.e., that of Moses and of Aaron, who joined by saying, "Āmeen" ("O Allāh, respond").

(92) So today We will save you in body[529] that you may be to those who succeed you a sign. And indeed, many among the people, of Our signs, are heedless.

(93) And We had certainly settled the Children of Israel in an agreeable settlement and provided them with good things. And they did not differ until [after] knowledge had come to them. Indeed, your Lord will judge between them on the Day of Resurrection concerning that over which they used to differ.

(94) So if you are in doubt, [O Muḥammad], about that which We have revealed to you, then ask those who have been reading the Scripture before you. The truth has certainly come to you from your Lord, so never be among the doubters.

(95) And never be of those who deny the signs of Allāh and [thus] be among the losers.[530]

(96) Indeed, those upon whom the word [i.e., decree] of your Lord has come into effect will not believe,

(97) Even if every sign should come to them, until they see the painful punishment.

(98) Then has there not been a [single] city that believed so its faith benefited it except the people of Jonah? When they believed, We removed from them the punishment of disgrace in worldly life and gave them enjoyment [i.e., provision] for a time.

(99) And had your Lord willed, those on earth would have believed - all of them entirely. Then, [O Muḥammad], would you compel the people in order that they become believers?

(100) And it is not for a soul [i.e., anyone] to believe except by permission of Allāh, and He will place defilement[531] upon those who will not use reason.

(101) Say, "Observe what is in the heavens and the earth." But of no avail will be signs or warners to a people who do not believe.

(102) So do they wait except for like [what occurred in] the days of those who passed on before them? Say, "Then wait; indeed, I am with you among those who wait."

---

[529] i.e., his dead body will be preserved and not destroyed.

[530] Among the interpretations of the last two verses is that they were meant to stir the Prophet (ﷺ) to declare and confirm his certainty, which he did. Another is that although the words are addressed to the Prophet (ﷺ), they are directed to all people.

[531] Among its meanings are filth, wrath, punishment, disbelief, confusion and error.

(103) Then We will save Our messengers and those who have believed. Thus, it is an obligation upon Us that We save the believers.[532]

(104) Say, [O Muḥammad], "O people, if you are in doubt as to my religion - then I do not worship those which you worship besides Allāh; but I worship Allāh, who causes your death. And I have been commanded to be of the believers

(105) And [commanded], 'Direct your face [i.e., self] toward the religion, inclining to truth, and never be of those who associate others with Allāh;

(106) And do not invoke[533] besides Allāh that which neither benefits you nor harms you, for if you did, then indeed you would be of the wrongdoers.'"[534]

(107) And if Allāh should touch you with adversity, there is no remover of it except Him; and if He intends for you good, then there is no repeller of His bounty. He causes it to reach whom He wills of His servants. And He is the Forgiving, the Merciful.

(108) Say, "O mankind, the truth has come to you from your Lord, so whoever is guided is only guided for [the benefit of] his soul, and whoever goes astray only goes astray [in violation] against it. And I am not over you a manager."

(109) And follow what is revealed to you, [O Muḥammad], and be patient until Allāh will judge. And He is the best of judges.

---

[532] From Allāh's punishment.
[533] "i.e., worship.
[534] See footnote to 10:95."

Surah Hud

(1) Alif, Lām, Rā.[535] [This is] a Book whose verses are perfected and then presented in detail from [one who is] Wise and Aware[536]

(2) [Through a messenger, saying], "Do not worship except Allāh. Indeed, I am to you from Him a warner and a bringer of good tidings,"

(3) And [saying], "Seek forgiveness of your Lord and repent to Him, [and] He will let you enjoy a good provision for a specified term and give every doer of favor his favor [i.e., reward]. But if you turn away, then indeed, I fear for you the punishment of a great Day.

(4) To Allāh is your return, and He is over all things competent."

(5) Unquestionably, they [i.e., the disbelievers] turn away their breasts to hide themselves from him. Unquestionably, [even] when they cover themselves in their clothing, He [i.e., Allāh] knows what they conceal and what they declare. Indeed, He is Knowing of that within the breasts.

(6) And there is no creature on earth but that upon Allāh is its provision, and He knows its place of dwelling and place of storage.[537] All is in a clear register.

(7) And it is He who created the heavens and the earth in six days - and His Throne had been upon water - that He might test you as to which of you is best in deed. But if you say, "Indeed, you are resurrected after death," those who disbelieve will surely say, "This is not but obvious magic."

(8) And if We hold back from them the punishment for a limited time, they will surely say,[538] "What detains it?" Unquestionably, on the Day it comes to them, it will not be averted from them, and they will be enveloped by what they used to ridicule.

(9) And if We give man a taste of mercy from Us and then We withdraw it from him, indeed, he is despairing and ungrateful.

(10) But if We give him a taste of favor after hardship has touched him, he will surely say, "Bad times have left me." Indeed, he is exultant and boastful -

---

[535] "See footnote to 2:1.
[536] Refer to footnotes of 6:18."
[537] Before birth and after death.
[538] In ridicule and disbelief.

(11) Except for those who are patient and do righteous deeds; those will have forgiveness and great reward.

(12) Then would you possibly leave [out] some of what is revealed to you,[539] or is your breast constrained by it because they say, "Why has there not been sent down to him a treasure or come with him an angel?" But you are only a warner. And Allāh is Disposer of all things.

(13) Or do they say, "He invented it"? Say, "Then bring ten sūrahs like it that have been invented and call upon [for assistance] whomever you can besides Allāh, if you should be truthful."

(14) And if they do not respond to you - then know that it [i.e., the Qur'ān] was revealed with the knowledge of Allāh[540] and that there is no deity except Him. Then,[541] would you [not] be Muslims?

(15) Whoever desires the life of this world and its adornments - We fully repay them for their deeds therein,[542] and they therein will not be deprived.

(16) Those are the ones for whom there is not in the Hereafter but the Fire. And lost is what they did therein,[543] and worthless is what they used to do.

(17) So is one who [stands] upon a clear evidence from his Lord [like the aforementioned]? And a witness[544] from Him follows it,[545] and before it was the Scripture of Moses to lead and as mercy. Those [believers in the former revelations] believe in it [i.e., the Qur'ān]. But whoever disbelieves in it from the [various] factions - the Fire is his promised destination. So be not in doubt about it. Indeed, it is the truth from your Lord, but most of the people do not believe.

(18) And who is more unjust than he who invents a lie about Allāh? Those will be presented before their Lord, and the witnesses will say, "These are the ones who lied against their Lord." Unquestionably, the curse of Allāh is upon the wrongdoers.

(19) Who averted [people] from the way of Allāh and sought to make it [seem] deviant while they, concerning the Hereafter, were disbelievers.

---

[539] Knowing of the Prophet's difficulties, Allāh (subḥānahu wa ta'ālā) urges him to patience, certain that he would not fail to convey the message in its entirety.

[540] "i.e., that knowledge which no one possesses except Him (subḥānahu wa ta'ālā).

[541] After having been convinced by such evidence."

[542] i.e., during worldly life.

[543] i.e., during worldly life.

[544] "Referring to Prophet Muḥammad (ﷺ) or to the angel Gabriel.

[545] Testifying to its truth. Additionally, it can mean "recites it," i.e., the Qur'ān."

(20) Those were not causing failure [to Allāh] on earth, nor did they have besides Allāh any protectors. For them the punishment will be multiplied. They were not able to hear, nor did they see.[546]

(21) Those are the ones who will have lost themselves, and lost from them is what they used to invent.

(22) Assuredly, it is they in the Hereafter who will be the greatest losers.

(23) Indeed, they who have believed and done righteous deeds and humbled themselves to their Lord - those are the companions of Paradise; they will abide eternally therein.

(24) The example of the two parties is like the blind and deaf, and the seeing and hearing. Are they equal in comparison? Then, will you not remember?

(25) And We had certainly sent Noah to his people, [saying], "Indeed, I am to you a clear warner

(26) That you not worship except Allāh. Indeed, I fear for you the punishment of a painful day."

(27) So the eminent among those who disbelieved from his people said, "We do not see you but as a man like ourselves, and we do not see you followed except by those who are the lowest of us [and] at first suggestion.[547] And we do not see in you over us any merit; rather, we think you are liars."

(28) He said, "O my people, have you considered: if I should be upon clear evidence from my Lord while He has given me mercy from Himself but it has been made unapparent to you, should we force it upon you while you are averse to it?

(29) And O my people, I ask not of you for it any wealth. My reward is not but from Allāh. And I am not one to drive away those who have believed. Indeed, they will meet their Lord, but I see that you are a people behaving ignorantly.

(30) And O my people, who would protect me from Allāh if I drove them away? Then will you not be reminded?

(31) And I do not tell you that I have the depositories [containing the provision] of Allāh or that I know the unseen, nor do I tell you that I am an angel, nor do I say of those upon whom your eyes look down that Allāh will never grant them any good.

---

[546] They refused to listen to the truth or to perceive it.

[547] i.e., without any thought or hesitation.

Allāh is most knowing of what is within their souls. Indeed, I would then be among the wrongdoers [i.e., the unjust]."

(32) They said, "O Noah, you have disputed [i.e., opposed] us and been frequent in dispute of us. So bring us what you threaten us, if you should be of the truthful."

(33) He said, "Allāh will only bring it to you if He wills, and you will not cause [Him] failure.

(34) And my advice will not benefit you - although I wished to advise you - if Allāh should intend to put you in error. He is your Lord, and to Him you will be returned."

(35) Or do they say [about Prophet Muḥammad (ﷺ)], "He invented it"? Say, "If I have invented it, then upon me is [the consequence of] my crime; but I am innocent of what [crimes] you commit."

(36) And it was revealed to Noah that, "No one will believe from your people except those who have already believed, so do not be distressed by what they have been doing.

(37) And construct the ship under Our observation and Our inspiration and do not address Me concerning those who have wronged; indeed, they are [to be] drowned."

(38) And he constructed the ship, and whenever an assembly of the eminent of his people passed by him, they ridiculed him. He said, "If you ridicule us, then we will ridicule you just as you ridicule.

(39) And you are going to know who will get a punishment that will disgrace him [on earth] and upon whom will descend an enduring punishment [in the Hereafter]."

(40) [So it was], until when Our command came and the oven overflowed,[548] We said, "Load upon it [i.e., the ship] of each [creature] two mates and your family, except those about whom the word [i.e., decree] has preceded, and [include] whoever has believed." But none had believed with him, except a few.

(41) And [Noah] said, "Embark therein; in the name of Allāh [are] its course and its anchorage. Indeed, my Lord is Forgiving and Merciful."

---

[548] As a sign to Noah of the imminence of the flood. The tannūr is a large, rounded oven. The word can also mean the earth's lowlands.

(42) And it sailed with them through waves like mountains, and Noah called to his son who was apart [from them], "O my son, come aboard with us and be not with the disbelievers."

(43) [But] he said, "I will take refuge on a mountain to protect me from the water." [Noah] said, "There is no protector today from the decree of Allāh, except for whom He gives mercy." And the waves came between them, and he was among the drowned.

(44) And it was said, "O earth, swallow your water, and O sky, withhold [your rain]." And the water subsided, and the matter was accomplished, and it [i.e., the ship] came to rest on the [mountain of] Jūdiyy. And it was said, "Away with the wrongdoing people."

(45) And Noah called to his Lord and said, "My Lord, indeed my son is of my family; and indeed, Your promise is true; and You are the most just of judges!"

(46) He said, "O Noah, indeed he is not of your family; indeed, he is [one whose] work was other than righteous, so ask Me not for that about which you have no knowledge. Indeed, I advise you, lest you be among the ignorant."

(47) [Noah] said, "My Lord, I seek refuge in You from asking that of which I have no knowledge. And unless You forgive me and have mercy upon me, I will be among the losers."

(48) It was said, "O Noah, disembark in security from Us and blessings upon you and upon nations [descending] from those with you. But other nations [of them] We will grant enjoyment; then there will touch them from Us a painful punishment."

(49) That is from the news of the unseen which We reveal to you, [O Muḥammad]. You knew it not, neither you nor your people, before this. So be patient; indeed, the [best] outcome is for the righteous.

(50) And to ʿAad [We sent] their brother Hūd. He said, "O my people, worship Allāh; you have no deity other than Him. You are not but inventors [of falsehood].

(51) O my people, I do not ask you for it [i.e., my advice] any reward. My reward is only from the one who created me. Then will you not reason?

(52) And O my people, ask forgiveness of your Lord and then repent to Him. He will send [rain from] the sky upon you in showers and increase you in strength [added] to your strength. And do not turn away, [being] criminals."

(53) They said, "O Hūd, you have not brought us clear evidence, and we are not ones to leave our gods on your say-so. Nor are we believers in you.

(54) We only say that some of our gods have possessed you with evil [i.e., insanity]." He said, "Indeed, I call Allāh to witness, and witness [yourselves] that I am free from whatever you associate with Allāh

(55) Other than Him. So plot against me all together; then do not give me respite.

(56) Indeed, I have relied upon Allāh, my Lord and your Lord. There is no creature but that He holds it by its forelock [i.e., controls it]. Indeed, my Lord is on a path [that is] straight.

(57) But if you turn away, then I have already conveyed that with which I was sent to you. My Lord will give succession to a people other than you, and you will not harm Him at all. Indeed my Lord is, over all things, Guardian."[549]

(58) And when Our command came, We saved Hūd and those who believed with him, by mercy from Us; and We saved them from a harsh punishment.

(59) And that was ʿAad, who rejected the signs of their Lord and disobeyed His messengers and followed the order of every obstinate tyrant.

(60) And they were [therefore] followed in this world with a curse and [as well] on the Day of Resurrection. Unquestionably, ʿAad denied their Lord; then away with ʿAad, the people of Hūd.

(61) And to Thamūd [We sent] their brother Ṣāliḥ. He said, "O my people, worship Allāh; you have no deity other than Him. He has produced you from the earth and settled you in it, so ask forgiveness of Him and then repent to Him. Indeed, my Lord is near and responsive."

(62) They said, "O Ṣāliḥ, you were among us a man of promise before this. Do you forbid us to worship what our fathers worshipped? And indeed we are, about that to which you invite us, in disquieting doubt."

(63) He said, "O my people, have you considered: if I should be upon clear evidence from my Lord and He has given me mercy from Himself, who would protect me from Allāh if I disobeyed Him? So you would not increase me except in loss.

(64) And O my people, this is the she-camel of Allāh - [she is] to you a sign. So let her feed upon Allāh's earth and do not touch her with harm, or you will be taken by an impending punishment."

(65) But they hamstrung her, so he said, "Enjoy yourselves in your homes for three days. That is a promise not to be denied [i.e., unfailing]."

---

[549] Protecting and preserving the existence and attributes of His creations.

(66) So when Our command came, We saved Ṣāliḥ and those who believed with him, by mercy from Us, and [saved them] from the disgrace of that day.[550] Indeed, it is your Lord who is the Powerful, the Exalted in Might.

(67) And the shriek[551] seized those who had wronged, and they became within their homes [corpses] fallen prone

(68) As if they had never prospered therein. Unquestionably, Thamūd denied their Lord; then, away with Thamūd.

(69) And certainly did Our messengers [i.e., angels] come to Abraham with good tidings; they said, "Peace." He said, "Peace," and did not delay in bringing [them] a roasted calf.

(70) But when he saw their hands not reaching for it, he distrusted them and felt from them apprehension.[552] They said, "Fear not. We have been sent to the people of Lot."

(71) And his wife was standing, and she smiled.[553] Then We gave her good tidings of Isaac and after Isaac, Jacob.

(72) She said, "Woe to me![554] Shall I give birth while I am an old woman and this, my husband, is an old man? Indeed, this is an amazing thing!"

(73) They said, "Are you amazed at the decree of Allāh? May the mercy of Allāh and His blessings be upon you, people of the house. Indeed, He is Praiseworthy and Honorable."

(74) And when the fright had left Abraham and the good tidings had reached him, he began to argue [i.e., plead] with Us[555] concerning the people of Lot.

(75) Indeed, Abraham was forbearing, grieving[556] and [frequently] returning [to Allāh].

---

[550] The day of Thamūd's destruction.

[551] A piercing cry or blast from the sky.

[552] Traditionally, if a guest refused to eat, it meant that he harbored ill will toward the host or intended him harm.

[553] In pleasure at the news of the forthcoming punishment of the evil people who denied Prophet Lot (upon him be peace).

[554] An expression of surprise and amazement.

[555] i.e., with Our angels.

[556] i.e., sighing or moaning during supplication out of grief for people and fear of Allāh.

(76) [The angels said], "O Abraham, give up this [plea]. Indeed, the command of your Lord has come, and indeed, there will reach them a punishment that cannot be repelled."

(77) And when Our messengers, [the angels], came to Lot, he was anguished for them and felt for them great discomfort[557] and said, "This is a trying day."

(78) And his people came hastening to him, and before [this] they had been doing evil deeds.[558] He said, "O my people, these are my daughters;[559] they are purer for you. So fear Allāh and do not disgrace me concerning my guests. Is there not among you a man of reason?"

(79) They said, "You have already known that we have not concerning your daughters [i.e., women] any claim [i.e., desire], and indeed, you know what we want."

(80) He said, "If only I had against you some power or could take refuge in a strong support."

(81) They [the angels] said, "O Lot, indeed we are messengers of your Lord; [therefore], they will never reach you. So set out with your family during a portion of the night[560] and let not any among you look back - except your wife; indeed, she will be struck by that which strikes them. Indeed, their appointment is [for] the morning. Is not the morning near?"

(82) So when Our command came, We made the highest part [of the city] its lowest and rained upon them stones of layered hard clay, [which were]

(83) Marked from your Lord. And it [i.e., Allāh's punishment] is not from the wrongdoers [very] far.

(84) And to Madyan [We sent] their brother Shu'ayb. He said, "O my people, worship Allāh; you have no deity other than Him. And do not decrease from the measure and the scale. Indeed, I see you in prosperity, but indeed, I fear for you the punishment of an all-encompassing Day.

(85) And O my people, give full measure and weight in justice and do not deprive the people of their due and do not commit abuse on the earth, spreading corruption.

---

[557] Prophet Lot feared for the safety and honor of his guests.
[558] "Referring to their practice of sodomy and homosexual rape of males.
[559] i.e., the women of his community who were available for marriage."
[560] i.e., sometime before dawn.

(86) What remains [lawful] from Allāh is best for you, if you would be believers. But I am not a guardian over you."

(87) They said, "O Shuʿayb, does your prayer [i.e., religion] command you that we should leave what our fathers worship or not do with our wealth what we please? Indeed, you are the forbearing, the discerning!"[561]

(88) He said, "O my people, have you considered: if I am upon clear evidence from my Lord and He has provided me with a good provision from Him...?[562] And I do not intend to differ from you in that which I have forbidden you; I only intend reform as much as I am able. And my success is not but through Allāh. Upon Him I have relied, and to Him I return.[563]

(89) And O my people, let not [your] dissension from me cause you to be struck by that similar to what struck the people of Noah or the people of Hūd or the people of Ṣāliḥ. And the people of Lot are not from you far away.

(90) And ask forgiveness of your Lord and then repent to Him. Indeed, my Lord is Merciful and Affectionate."

(91) They said, "O Shuʿayb, we do not understand much of what you say, and indeed, we consider you among us as weak. And if not for your family, we would have stoned you [to death]; and you are not to us one respected."

(92) He said, "O my people, is my family more respected for power by you than Allāh? But you put Him behind your backs [in neglect]. Indeed, my Lord is encompassing of what you do.

(93) And O my people, work according to your position; indeed, I am working. You are going to know to whom will come a punishment that will disgrace him and who is a liar. So watch; indeed, I am with you a watcher, [awaiting the outcome]."

(94) And when Our command came, We saved Shuʿayb and those who believed with him, by mercy from Us. And the shriek seized those who had wronged, and they became within their homes [corpses] fallen prone

(95) As if they had never prospered therein. Then, away with Madyan as Thamūd was taken away.

---

[561] This is a sarcastic description implying the opposite.

[562] "The conclusion of the sentence is estimated as ""...would it not be my duty to warn you against corruption and disobedience?""

[563] i.e., I turn to Allāh frequently in supplication and repentance."

(96) And We did certainly send Moses with Our signs and a clear authority[564]

(97) To Pharaoh and his establishment, but they followed the command of Pharaoh, and the command of Pharaoh was not [at all] discerning.

(98) He will precede his people on the Day of Resurrection and lead them into the Fire; and wretched is the place to which they are led.

(99) And they were followed in this [world] with a curse and on the Day of Resurrection. And wretched is the gift[565] which is given.

(100) That is from the news of the cities, which We relate to you; of them, some are [still] standing and some are [as] a harvest [mowed down].[566]

(101) And We did not wrong them, but they wronged themselves. And they were not availed at all by their gods which they invoked other than Allāh when there came the command of your Lord. And they did not increase them in other than ruin.

(102) And thus is the seizure of your Lord when He seizes the cities while they are committing wrong. Indeed, His seizure is painful and severe.

(103) Indeed in that is a sign for those who fear the punishment of the Hereafter. That is a Day for which the people will be collected, and that is a Day [which will be] witnessed.

(104) And We do not delay it except for a limited term.

(105) The Day it comes no soul will speak except by His permission. And among them will be the wretched and the prosperous.

(106) As for those who were [destined to be] wretched, they will be in the Fire. For them therein is [violent] exhaling and inhaling.[567]

(107) [They will be] abiding therein as long as the heavens and the earth endure, except what your Lord should will. Indeed, your Lord is an effecter of what He intends.

---

[564] i.e., evidences from Allāh.

[565] i.e., the curse which follows them in both worlds.

[566] Their structures have been completely destroyed.

[567] i.e., their sighs and sobs, resembling the bray of a donkey.

(108) And as for those who were [destined to be] prosperous, they will be in Paradise, abiding therein as long as the heavens and the earth endure, except what your Lord should will - a bestowal uninterrupted.

(109) So do not be in doubt, [O Muḥammad], as to what these [polytheists] are worshipping. They worship not except as their fathers worshipped before. And indeed, We will give them their share undiminished.

(110) And We had certainly given Moses the Scripture, but it came under disagreement. And if not for a word[568] that preceded from your Lord, it would have been judged between them. And indeed they are, concerning it [i.e., the Qur'ān], in disquieting doubt.

(111) And indeed, each [of the believers and disbelievers] - your Lord will fully compensate them for their deeds. Indeed, He is Aware of what they do.

(112) So remain on a right course as you have been commanded, [you] and those who have turned back with you [to Allāh], and do not transgress. Indeed, He is Seeing of what you do.

(113) And do not incline toward those who do wrong, lest you be touched by the Fire, and you would not have other than Allāh any protectors; then you would not be helped.

(114) And establish prayer at the two ends of the day and at the approach of the night. Indeed, good deeds do away with misdeeds. That is a reminder for those who remember.

(115) And be patient, for indeed, Allāh does not allow to be lost the reward of those who do good.

(116) So why were there not[569] among the generations before you those of enduring discrimination forbidding corruption on earth - except a few of those We saved from among them? But those who wronged pursued what luxury they were given therein, and they were criminals.

(117) And your Lord would not have destroyed the cities unjustly while their people were reformers.

(118) And if your Lord had willed, He could have made mankind one community; but they will not cease to differ,

---

[568] See footnote to 10:19.
[569] Meaning "If only there had been..."

(119) Except whom your Lord has given mercy, and for that He created them. But the word of your Lord is to be fulfilled that, "I will surely fill Hell with jinn and men all together."

(120) And each [story] We relate to you from the news of the messengers is that by which We make firm your heart. And there has come to you, in this, the truth and an instruction and a reminder for the believers.

(121) And say to those who do not believe, "Work according to your position; indeed, we are working.

(122) And wait; indeed, we are waiting."

(123) And to Allāh belong the unseen [aspects] of the heavens and the earth and to Him will be returned the matter, all of it, so worship Him and rely upon Him. And your Lord is not unaware of that which you do.

Surah Yusuf

(1) Alif, Lām, Rā.[570] These are the verses of the clear Book.

(2) Indeed, We have sent it down as an Arabic Qur'ān[571] that you might understand.

(3) We relate to you, [O Muḥammad], the best of stories in what We have revealed to you of this Qur'ān although you were, before it, among the unaware.

(4) [Of these stories mention] when Joseph said to his father,[572] "O my father, indeed I have seen [in a dream] eleven stars and the sun and the moon; I saw them prostrating to me."

(5) He said, "O my son, do not relate your vision to your brothers or they will contrive against you a plan. Indeed Satan, to man, is a manifest enemy.

(6) And thus will your Lord choose you and teach you the interpretation of narratives [i.e., events or dreams] and complete His favor upon you and upon the family of Jacob, as He completed it upon your fathers before, Abraham and Isaac. Indeed, your Lord is Knowing and Wise."

(7) Certainly were there in Joseph and his brothers signs for those who ask, [such as]

(8) When they said, "Joseph and his brother[573] are more beloved to our father than we, while we are a clan. Indeed, our father is in clear error.

(9) Kill Joseph or cast him out to [another] land; the countenance [i.e., attention] of your father will [then] be only for you, and you will be after that a righteous people."[574]

(10) Said a speaker among them, "Do not kill Joseph but throw him into the bottom of the well; some travelers will pick him up - if you would do [something]."

(11) They said, "O our father, why do you not entrust us with Joseph while indeed, we are to him sincere counselors?

---

[570] See footnote to 2:1.
[571] i.e., revealed in the Arabic language.
[572] The prophet Jacob (upon whom be peace).
[573] Benjamin, who was born of the same mother as Joseph.
[574] i.e., You can repent thereafter.

(12) Send him with us tomorrow that he may eat well and play. And indeed, we will be his guardians."

(13) [Jacob] said, "Indeed, it saddens me that you should take him, and I fear that a wolf would eat him while you are of him unaware."

(14) They said, "If a wolf should eat him while we are a [strong] clan, indeed, we would then be losers."

(15) So when they took him [out] and agreed to put him into the bottom of the well...[575] But We inspired to him, "You will surely inform them [someday] about this affair of theirs while they do not perceive [your identity]."

(16) And they came to their father at night, weeping.

(17) They said, "O our father, indeed we went racing each other and left Joseph with our possessions, and a wolf ate him. But you would not believe us, even if we were truthful."

(18) And they brought upon his shirt false blood.[576] [Jacob] said, "Rather, your souls have enticed you to something, so patience is most fitting. And Allāh is the one sought for help against that which you describe."

(19) And there came a company of travelers; then they sent their water drawer, and he let down his bucket. He said, "Good news! Here is a boy." And they concealed him, [taking him] as merchandise;[577] and Allāh was Knowing of what they did.

(20) And they sold him for a reduced price - a few dirhams - and they were, concerning him, of those content with little.

(21) And the one from Egypt[578] who bought him said to his wife, "Make his residence comfortable. Perhaps he will benefit us, or we will adopt him as a son." And thus, We established Joseph in the land that We might teach him the interpretation of events [i.e., dreams]. And Allāh is predominant over His affair, but most of the people do not know.

(22) And when he [i.e., Joseph] reached maturity, We gave him judgement and knowledge. And thus We reward the doers of good.

---

[575] The conclusion of this sentence is estimated to be "...they tormented him."
[576] They had stained Joseph's shirt with the blood of a lamb but had forgotten to tear it, thereby arousing their father's suspicion.
[577] To be sold as a slave.
[578] The minister in charge of supplies, whose title was al-ʿAzeez.

(23) And she, in whose house he was, sought to seduce him. She closed the doors and said, "Come, you." He said, "[I seek] the refuge of Allāh. Indeed, he[579] is my master, who has made good my residence. Indeed, wrongdoers will not succeed."

(24) And she certainly determined [to seduce] him, and he would have inclined to her had he not seen the proof [i.e., sign] of his Lord. And thus [it was] that We should avert from him evil and immorality. Indeed, he was of Our chosen servants.

(25) And they both raced to the door, and she tore his shirt from the back, and they found her husband at the door. She said, "What is the recompense of one who intended evil for your wife but that he be imprisoned or a painful punishment?"

(26) [Joseph] said, "It was she who sought to seduce me." And a witness from her family testified, "If his shirt is torn from the front, then she has told the truth, and he is of the liars.

(27) But if his shirt is torn from the back, then she has lied, and he is of the truthful."

(28) So when he [i.e., her husband] saw his shirt torn from the back, he said, "Indeed, it is of your [i.e., women's] plan. Indeed, your plan is great [i.e., vehement].

(29) Joseph, ignore this.[580] And, [my wife], ask forgiveness for your sin. Indeed, you were of the sinful."

(30) And women in the city said, "The wife of al-ʿAzeez is seeking to seduce her slave boy; he has impassioned her with love. Indeed, we see her [to be] in clear error."

(31) So when she heard of their scheming, she sent for them and prepared for them a banquet and gave each one of them a knife and said [to Joseph], "Come out before them." And when they saw him, they greatly admired him and cut their hands[581] and said, "Perfect is Allāh![582] This is not a man; this is none but a noble angel."

(32) She said, "That is the one about whom you blamed me. And I certainly sought to seduce him, but he firmly refused; and if he will not do what I order him, he will surely be imprisoned and will be of those debased."

(33) He said, "My Lord, prison is more to my liking than that to which they invite me. And if You do not avert from me their plan, I might incline toward them and [thus] be of the ignorant."

---

[579] Her husband, al-ʿAzeez.

[580] i.e., conceal it and act as if it had not taken place.

[581] "So distracted were they at the sight of him.

[582] In His ability to create such beauty."

(34) So his Lord responded to him and averted from him their plan. Indeed, He is the Hearing, the Knowing.

(35) Then it appeared to them after they had seen the signs[583] that he [i.e., al-ʿAzeez] should surely imprison him for a time.[584]

(36) And there entered the prison with him two young men. One of them said, "Indeed, I have seen myself [in a dream] pressing [grapes for] wine." The other said, "Indeed, I have seen myself carrying upon my head [some] bread, from which the birds were eating. Inform us of its interpretation; indeed, we see you to be of those who do good."

(37) He said, "You will not receive food that is provided to you except that I will inform you of its interpretation before it comes to you. That is from what my Lord has taught me. Indeed, I have left the religion of a people who do not believe in Allāh, and they, in the Hereafter, are disbelievers.

(38) And I have followed the religion of my fathers, Abraham, Isaac and Jacob. And it was not for us to associate anything with Allāh. That is from the favor of Allāh upon us and upon the people, but most of the people are not grateful.

(39) O [my] two companions of prison, are separate lords better or Allāh, the One,[585] the Prevailing?[586]

(40) You worship not besides Him except [mere] names you have named them,[587] you and your fathers, for which Allāh has sent down no evidence. Legislation is not but for Allāh. He has commanded that you worship not except Him. That is the correct religion, but most of the people do not know.

(41) O two companions of prison, as for one of you, he will give drink to his master of wine; but as for the other, he will be crucified, and the birds will eat from his head. The matter has been decreed about which you both inquire."

(42) And he said to the one whom he knew would go free, "Mention me before your master." But Satan made him forget the mention [to] his master, and he [i.e., Joseph] remained in prison several years.

---

[583] "Proofs of his innocence.

[584] Until the scandal be forgotten."

[585] "Single, individual and unique in His attributes and His deeds.

[586] He who subdues doubts and false arguments with clear evidences and who subdues and imposes His will upon all creation."

[587] The false objects of worship which you have called "gods."

(43) And [subsequently] the king said, "Indeed, I have seen [in a dream] seven fat cows being eaten by seven [that were] lean, and seven green spikes [of grain] and others [that were] dry. O eminent ones, explain to me my vision, if you should interpret visions."

(44) They said, "[It is but] a mixture of false dreams, and we are not learned in the interpretation of dreams."

(45) But the one who was freed and remembered after a time said, "I will inform you of its interpretation, so send me forth."

(46) [He said], "Joseph, O man of truth, explain to us about seven fat cows eaten by seven [that were] lean, and seven green spikes [of grain] and others [that were] dry - that I may return to the people [i.e., the king and his court]; perhaps they will know [about you]."

(47) [Joseph] said, "You will plant for seven years consecutively; and what you harvest leave in its spikes, except a little from which you will eat.

(48) Then will come after that seven difficult [years] which will consume what you advanced [i.e., saved] for them, except a little from which you will store.

(49) Then will come after that a year in which the people will be given rain and in which they will press [olives and grapes]."

(50) And the king said, "Bring him to me." But when the messenger came to him, [Joseph] said, "Return to your master and ask him what is the case of the women who cut their hands. Indeed, my Lord is Knowing of their plan."

(51) Said [the king to the women], "What was your condition when you sought to seduce Joseph?" They said, "Perfect is Allāh![588] We know about him no evil." The wife of al-ʿAzeez said, "Now the truth has become evident. It was I who sought to seduce him, and indeed, he is of the truthful.

(52) That is so he [i.e., al-ʿAzeez] will know that I did not betray him in [his] absence and that Allāh does not guide the plan of betrayers.

---

[588] In His ability to create such purity of character.

(53) And I do not acquit myself. Indeed, the soul is a persistent enjoiner of evil, except those upon which my Lord has mercy. Indeed, my Lord is Forgiving and Merciful."[589]

(54) And the king said, "Bring him to me; I will appoint him exclusively for myself." And when he spoke to him, he said, "Indeed, you are today established [in position] and trusted."

(55) [Joseph] said, "Appoint me over the storehouses of the land. Indeed, I will be a knowing guardian."

(56) And thus We established Joseph in the land to settle therein wherever he willed. We touch with Our mercy whom We will, and We do not allow to be lost the reward of those who do good.

(57) And the reward of the Hereafter is better for those who believed and were fearing Allāh.

(58) And the brothers of Joseph came [seeking food], and they entered upon him; and he recognized them, but he was to them unknown.[590]

(59) And when he had furnished them with their supplies, he said, "Bring me a brother of yours from your father.[591] Do you not see that I give full measure and that I am the best of accommodators?

(60) But if you do not bring him to me, no measure will there be [hereafter] for you from me, nor will you approach me."

(61) They said, "We will attempt to dissuade his father from [keeping] him, and indeed, we will do [it]."

(62) And [Joseph] said to his servants, "Put their merchandise[592] into their saddlebags so they might recognize it when they have gone back to their people that perhaps they will [again] return."

---

[589] Although Ibn Katheer attributes the words of verses 52-53 to the wife of al-ʿAzeez, others have concluded that they were spoken by Joseph, thereby justifying his request for an inquiry and acknowledging Allāh's mercy to him.
[590] Due to the change in his appearance over the years.
[591] i.e., Benjamin, who had been kept at home by his father Jacob.
[592] The goods which they had brought to trade for food supplies.

(63) So when they returned to their father, they said, "O our father, [further] measure has been denied to us, so send with us our brother [that] we will be given measure. And indeed, we will be his guardians."

(64) He said, "Should I entrust you with him except [under coercion] as I entrusted you with his brother before? But Allāh is the best guardian, and He is the most merciful of the merciful."

(65) And when they opened their baggage, they found their merchandise returned to them. They said, "O our father, what [more] could we desire? This is our merchandise returned to us. And we will obtain supplies [i.e., food] for our family and protect our brother and obtain an increase of a camel's load; that is an easy measurement."[593]

(66) [Jacob] said, "Never will I send him with you until you give me a promise [i.e., oath] by Allāh that you will bring him [back] to me, unless you should be surrounded [i.e., overcome by enemies]." And when they had given their promise, he said, "Allāh, over what we say, is Entrusted."[594]

(67) And he said, "O my sons, do not enter from one gate but enter from different gates; and I cannot avail you against [the decree of] Allāh at all. The decision is only for Allāh; upon Him I have relied, and upon Him let those who would rely [indeed] rely."

(68) And when they entered from where their father had ordered them, it did not avail them against Allāh at all except [it was] a need [i.e., concern] within the soul of Jacob, which he satisfied. And indeed, he was a possessor of knowledge because of what We had taught him, but most of the people do not know.

(69) And when they entered upon Joseph, he took his brother to himself; he said, "Indeed, I am your brother, so do not despair over what they used to do [to me]."

(70) So when he had furnished them with their supplies, he put the [gold measuring] bowl into the bag of his brother. Then an announcer called out, "O caravan, indeed you are thieves."

(71) They said while approaching them, "What is it you are missing?"

(72) They said, "We are missing the measure of the king. And for he who produces it is [the reward of] a camel's load, and I am responsible for it."

---

[593] For them. Or one obtained by us with ease.
[594] i.e., sufficient to witness and deal with the matter.

(73) They said, "By Allāh, you have certainly known that we did not come to cause corruption in the land, and we have not been thieves."

(74) They [the accusers] said, "Then what would be its recompense[595] if you should be liars?"

(75) [The brothers] said, "Its recompense is that he in whose bag it is found - he [himself] will be its recompense.[596] Thus do we recompense the wrongdoers."

(76) So he began [the search] with their bags before the bag of his brother; then he extracted it from the bag of his brother. Thus did We plan for Joseph. He could not have taken his brother within the religion [i.e., law] of the king except that Allāh willed. We raise in degrees whom We will, but over every possessor of knowledge is one [more] knowing.[597]

(77) They said, "If he steals - a brother of his has stolen before." But Joseph kept it within himself and did not reveal it to them.[598] He said, "You are worse in position, and Allāh is most knowing of what you describe."

(78) They said, "O ʿAzeez,[599] indeed he has a father [who is] an old man, so take one of us in place of him. Indeed, we see you as a doer of good."

(79) He said, "[I seek] the refuge of Allāh [to prevent] that we take except him with whom we found our possession. Indeed, we would then be unjust."

(80) So when they had despaired of him, they secluded themselves in private consultation. The eldest of them said, "Do you not know that your father has taken upon you an oath by Allāh and [that] before you failed in [your duty to] Joseph? So I will never leave [this] land until my father permits me or Allāh decides for me,[600] and He is the best of judges.

(81) Return to your father and say, 'O our father, indeed your son has stolen, and we did not testify except to what we knew. And we were not witnesses of the unseen.[601]

---

[595] The punishment for theft.

[596] According to their law, a convicted thief was made a slave of the one from whom he had stolen.

[597] Ending with the ultimate knowledge of Allāh (subḥānahu wa taʿālā).

[598] He did not answer that he himself had been stolen by them from his father.

[599] Addressing Joseph, who now held the title of "al-ʿAzeez."

[600] i.e., in my favor by bringing about the release of Benjamin.

[601] i.e., We could not have known when we gave you the oath that he would steal and be apprehended.

(82) And ask the city in which we were and the caravan in which we came - and indeed, we are truthful.'"

(83) [Jacob] said, "Rather, your souls have enticed you to something, so patience is most fitting. Perhaps Allāh will bring them to me all together. Indeed, it is He who is the Knowing, the Wise."

(84) And he turned away from them and said, "Oh, my sorrow over Joseph," and his eyes became white[602] from grief, for he was [of that] a suppressor.[603]

(85) They said, "By Allāh, you will not cease remembering Joseph until you become fatally ill or become of those who perish."

(86) He said, "I only complain of my suffering and my grief to Allāh, and I know from Allāh that which you do not know.

(87) O my sons, go and find out about Joseph and his brother and despair not of relief from Allāh. Indeed, no one despairs of relief from Allāh except the disbelieving people."

(88) So when they entered upon him [i.e., Joseph], they said, "O ʿAzeez, adversity has touched us and our family, and we have come with goods poor in quality, but give us full measure and be charitable to us. Indeed, Allāh rewards the charitable."

(89) He said, "Do you know what you did with Joseph and his brother when you were ignorant?"

(90) They said, "Are you indeed Joseph?" He said, "I am Joseph, and this is my brother. Allāh has certainly favored us. Indeed, he who fears Allāh and is patient, then indeed, Allāh does not allow to be lost the reward of those who do good."

(91) They said, "By Allāh, certainly has Allāh preferred you over us, and indeed, we have been sinners."

(92) He said, "No blame will there be upon you today. May Allāh forgive you; and He is the most merciful of the merciful.

(93) Take this, my shirt, and cast it over the face of my father; he will become seeing. And bring me your family, all together."

---

[602] "i.e., he lost his sight.

[603] He did not express the extent of his grief or his anger at what he suspected his sons had done but was patient, depending only upon Allāh for help."

(94) And when the caravan departed [from Egypt], their father said,[604] "Indeed, I find the smell of Joseph [and would say that he was alive] if you did not think me weakened in mind."

(95) They said, "By Allāh, indeed you are in your [same] old error."

(96) And when the bearer of good tidings[605] arrived, he cast it over his face, and he returned [once again] seeing. He said, "Did I not tell you that I know from Allāh that which you do not know?"

(97) They said, "O our father, ask for us forgiveness of our sins; indeed, we have been sinners."

(98) He said, "I will ask forgiveness for you from my Lord. Indeed, it is He who is the Forgiving, the Merciful."

(99) And when they entered upon Joseph, he took his parents to himself [i.e., embraced them] and said, "Enter Egypt, Allāh willing, safe [and secure]."

(100) And he raised his parents upon the throne, and they bowed to him in prostration.[606] And he said, "O my father, this is the explanation of my vision of before. My Lord has made it reality. And He was certainly good to me when He took me out of prison and brought you [here] from bedouin life after Satan had induced [estrangement] between me and my brothers. Indeed, my Lord is Subtle[607] in what He wills. Indeed, it is He who is the Knowing, the Wise.

(101) My Lord, You have given me [something] of sovereignty and taught me of the interpretation of dreams. Creator of the heavens and earth, You are my protector in this world and the Hereafter. Cause me to die a Muslim and join me with the righteous."

(102) That is from the news of the unseen which We reveal, [O Muḥammad], to you. And you were not with them when they put together their plan while they conspired.

(103) And most of the people, although you strive [for it], are not believers.

---

[604] To those present with him, either some of his sons or other relatives.

[605] He who carried Joseph's shirt from among the brothers.

[606] "That of greeting and respect, which was lawful until the time of Prophet Muḥammad (ﷺ). Prostration to any person or object other than Allāh was then prohibited conclusively.

[607] Perceptive of unapparent matters within which is benefit to His servants."

(104) And you do not ask of them for it any payment. It is not except a reminder to the worlds.

(105) And how many a sign within the heavens and earth do they pass over while they, therefrom, are turning away.

(106) And most of them believe not in Allāh except while they associate others with Him.

(107) Then do they feel secure that there will not come to them an overwhelming [aspect] of the punishment of Allāh or that the Hour will not come upon them suddenly while they do not perceive?

(108) Say, "This is my way; I invite to Allāh with insight, I and those who follow me. And exalted is Allāh; and I am not of those who associate others with Him."

(109) And We sent not before you [as messengers] except men to whom We revealed from among the people of cities. So have they[608] not traveled through the earth and observed how was the end of those before them? And the home of the Hereafter is best for those who fear Allāh; then will you not reason?

(110) [They continued] until, when the messengers despaired and were certain that they had been denied, there came to them Our victory, and whoever We willed was saved. And Our punishment cannot be repelled from the people who are criminals.

(111) There was certainly in their stories a lesson for those of understanding. Never was it [i.e., the Qur'ān] a narration invented, but a confirmation of what was before it and a detailed explanation of all things and guidance and mercy for a people who believe.

---

[608] Those who deny Prophet Muḥammad (ﷺ).

Surah Ar-Ra'd

(1) Alif, Lām, Meem, Rā.[609] These are the verses of the Book; and what has been revealed to you from your Lord is the truth, but most of the people do not believe.

(2) It is Allāh who erected the heavens without pillars that you [can] see; then He established Himself above the Throne[610] and made subject[611] the sun and the moon, each running [its course] for a specified term. He arranges [each] matter; He details the signs that you may, of the meeting with your Lord, be certain.

(3) And it is He who spread the earth and placed therein firmly set mountains and rivers; and from all of the fruits He made therein two mates; He causes the night to cover the day. Indeed in that are signs for a people who give thought.

(4) And within the land are neighboring plots and gardens of grapevines and crops and palm trees, [growing] several from a root or otherwise,[612] watered with one water; but We make some of them exceed others in [quality of] fruit. Indeed in that are signs for a people who reason.

(5) And if you are astonished,[613] [O Muḥammad] - then astonishing is their saying, "When we are dust, will we indeed be [brought] into a new creation?" Those are the ones who have disbelieved in their Lord, and those will have shackles[614] upon their necks, and those are the companions of the Fire; they will abide therein eternally.

(6) They impatiently urge you to bring about evil before good,[615] while there has already occurred before them similar punishments [to what they demand]. And indeed, your Lord is the possessor of forgiveness for the people despite their wrongdoing, and indeed, your Lord is severe in penalty.

(7) And those who disbelieved say, "Why has a sign not been sent down to him from his Lord?" You are only a warner, and for every people is a guide.

---

[609] See footnote to 2:1.

[610] "See footnotes to 2:19 and 7:54.

[611] For the benefit of mankind."

[612] i.e., only one from a root.

[613] "At those who deny resurrection.

[614] Iron collars to which their hands are chained."

[615] They said, challenging the Prophet (ﷺ) in ridicule, "Bring on the punishment, if you are truthful," rather than asking for mercy and forgiveness from Allāh.

(8) Allāh knows what every female carries[616] and what the wombs lose [prematurely] or exceed.[617] And everything with Him is by due measure.

(9) [He is] Knower of the unseen and the witnessed, the Grand, the Exalted.

(10) It is the same [to Him] concerning you whether one conceals [his] speech or publicizes it and whether one is hidden by night or conspicuous [among others] by day.

(11) For him [i.e., each one] are successive [angels][618] before and behind him who protect him by the decree of Allāh.[619] Indeed, Allāh will not change the condition of a people until they change what is in themselves. And when Allāh intends for a people ill,[620] there is no repelling it. And there is not for them besides Him any patron.

(12) It is He who shows you lightning, [causing] fear and aspiration, and generates the heavy clouds.

(13) And the thunder exalts [Allāh] with praise of Him - and the angels [as well] from fear of Him - and He sends thunderbolts and strikes therewith whom He wills while they dispute about Allāh; and He is severe in assault.

(14) To Him [alone] is the supplication of truth. And those they call upon besides Him do not respond to them with a thing, except as one who stretches his hands toward water [from afar, calling it] to reach his mouth, but it will not reach it [thus].[621] And the supplication of the disbelievers is not but in error [i.e., futility].

(15) And to Allāh prostrates whoever is within the heavens and the earth, willingly or by compulsion, and their shadows [as well] in the mornings and the afternoons.

(16) Say, "Who is Lord of the heavens and earth?" Say, "Allāh." Say, "Have you then taken besides Him allies not possessing [even] for themselves any benefit or any harm?" Say, "Is the blind equivalent to the seeing? Or is darkness equivalent to light? Or have they attributed to Allāh partners who created like His creation so

---

[616] "With absolute knowledge inclusive of every aspect of the fetus' existence.

[617] Beyond their normal period of pregnancy and/or the number of fetuses therein."

[618] "Replacing each other by turn.

[619] The phrase may also be rendered "...who guard him from [everything except] the decree of Allāh."

[620] i.e., punishment or destruction because of their sins."

[621] The analogy indicates that false deities will never respond to them at all.

that the creation [of each] seemed similar to them?"[622] Say, "Allāh is the Creator of all things, and He is the One, the Prevailing."[623]

(17) He sends down from the sky, rain, and valleys flow according to their capacity, and the torrent carries a rising foam. And from that [ore] which they heat in the fire, desiring adornments and utensils, is a foam like it. Thus Allāh presents [the example of] truth and falsehood. As for the foam, it vanishes, [being] cast off; but as for that which benefits the people, it remains on the earth. Thus does Allāh present examples.

(18) For those who have responded to their Lord is the best [reward], but those who did not respond to Him - if they had all that is in the earth entirely and the like of it with it, they would [attempt to] ransom themselves thereby. Those will have the worst account, and their refuge is Hell, and wretched is the resting place.

(19) Then is he who knows that what has been revealed to you from your Lord is the truth like one who is blind? They will only be reminded who are people of understanding -

(20) Those who fulfill the covenant of Allāh and do not break the contract,

(21) And those who join that which Allāh has ordered to be joined[624] and fear their Lord and are afraid of the evil of [their] account,

(22) And those who are patient, seeking the face [i.e., acceptance] of their Lord, and establish prayer and spend from what We have provided for them secretly and publicly and prevent evil with good - those will have the good consequence of [this] home[625] -

(23) Gardens of perpetual residence; they will enter them with whoever were righteous among their forefathers, their spouses and their descendants. And the angels will enter upon them from every gate, [saying],

(24) "Peace [i.e., security] be upon you for what you patiently endured. And excellent is the final home."

---

[622] "The obvious conclusion is that the claimed partners, having no ability to create, cannot be compared to Allāh in any way.
[623] Refer to footnotes in 12:39."
[624] i.e., they uphold the ties of relationship.
[625] i.e., the world and its trials, its good consequence being Paradise.

(25) But those who break the covenant of Allāh after contracting it and sever that which Allāh has ordered to be joined and spread corruption on earth - for them is the curse, and they will have the worst home.[626]

(26) Allāh extends provision for whom He wills and restricts [it]. And they rejoice in the worldly life, while the worldly life is not, compared to the Hereafter, except [brief] enjoyment.

(27) And those who disbelieved say, "Why has a sign not been sent down to him from his Lord?" Say, [O Muḥammad], "Indeed, Allāh leaves astray whom He wills and guides to Himself whoever turns back [to Him] -

(28) Those who have believed and whose hearts are assured by the remembrance of Allāh. Unquestionably, by the remembrance of Allāh hearts are assured."

(29) Those who have believed and done righteous deeds - a good state is theirs and a good return.

(30) Thus have We sent you to a community before which [other] communities have passed on so you might recite to them that which We revealed to you, while they disbelieve in the Most Merciful. Say, "He is my Lord; there is no deity except Him. Upon Him I rely, and to Him is my return."

(31) And if there was any Qur'ān [i.e., recitation] by which the mountains would be removed or the earth would be broken apart or the dead would be made to speak,[627] [it would be this Qur'ān], but to Allāh belongs the affair entirely. Then have those who believed not accepted that had Allāh willed, He would have guided the people, all of them? And those who disbelieve do not cease to be struck, for what they have done, by calamity - or it will descend near their home - until there comes the promise of Allāh. Indeed, Allāh does not fail in [His] promise.

(32) And already were [other] messengers ridiculed before you, and I extended the time of those who disbelieved; then I seized them, and how [terrible] was My penalty.

(33) Then is He who is a maintainer of every soul, [knowing] what it has earned, [like any other]? But to Allāh they have attributed partners. Say, "Name them. Or do you inform Him of that[628] which He knows not upon the earth or of what is

---

[626] i.e., Hell. Another meaning is (in contrast to verse 22), "...and they will have the bad consequence of [this] home," also referring to Hell.
[627] As suggested by the disbelievers.

[628] "i.e., other "deities."

apparent [i.e., alleged] of speech?"[629] Rather, their [own] plan has been made attractive to those who disbelieve, and they have been averted from the way. And whomever Allāh sends astray - there will be for him no guide.

(34) For them will be punishment in the life of [this] world, and the punishment of the Hereafter is more severe. And they will not have from Allāh any protector.

(35) The example [i.e., description] of Paradise, which the righteous have been promised, is [that] beneath it rivers flow. Its fruit is lasting, and its shade. That is the consequence for the righteous, and the consequence for the disbelievers is the Fire.

(36) And [the believers among] those to whom We have given the [previous] Scripture rejoice at what has been revealed to you, [O Muḥammad], but among the [opposing] factions are those who deny part of it [i.e., the Qur'ān]. Say, "I have only been commanded to worship Allāh and not associate [anything] with Him. To Him I invite, and to Him is my return."

(37) And thus We have revealed it as an Arabic legislation.[630] And if you should follow their inclinations after what has come to you of knowledge, you would not have against Allāh any ally or any protector.

(38) And We have already sent messengers before you and assigned to them wives and descendants. And it was not for a messenger to come with a sign except by permission of Allāh. For every term is a decree.

(39) Allāh eliminates what He wills or confirms, and with Him is the Mother of the Book.[631]

(40) And whether We show you part of what We promise them or take you in death, upon you is only the [duty of] notification, and upon Us is the account.

(41) Have they not seen that We set upon the land, reducing it from its borders?[632] And Allāh decides; there is no adjuster of His decision. And He is swift in account.

---

[629] i.e., your attributing of divinity to other than Allāh."
[630] i.e., revealed in the Arabic language.

[631] The Preserved Slate (al-Lawḥ al-Maḥfūẓ), in which is inscribed the original of every scripture revealed by Allāh.
[632] Referring to the spread of Islām through Allāh's Prophet (ﷺ) and the diminishing of those areas controlled by the polytheists.

(42) And those before them had plotted, but to Allāh belongs the plan entirely. He knows what every soul earns, and the disbelievers will know for whom is the final home.

(43) And those who have disbelieved say, "You are not a messenger." Say, [O Muḥammad], "Sufficient is Allāh as Witness between me and you, and [the witness of] whoever has knowledge of the Scripture."[633]

---

[633] i.e., those who recognize the truth through their knowledge of previous scriptures.

Surah Ibraheem

(1) Alif, Lām, Rā.[634] [This is] a Book which We have revealed to you, [O Muḥammad], that you might bring mankind out of darknesses into the light by permission of their Lord - to the path of the Exalted in Might, the Praiseworthy -

(2) Allāh, to whom belongs whatever is in the heavens and whatever is on the earth. And woe [i.e., destruction] to the disbelievers from a severe punishment -

(3) The ones who prefer the worldly life over the Hereafter and avert [people] from the way of Allāh, seeking to make it [seem] deviant. Those are in extreme error.

(4) And We did not send any messenger except [speaking] in the language of his people to state clearly for them, and Allāh sends astray [thereby] whom He wills[635] and guides whom He wills. And He is the Exalted in Might, the Wise.

(5) And We certainly sent Moses with Our signs, [saying], "Bring out your people from darknesses into the light and remind them of the days[636] of Allāh." Indeed in that are signs for everyone patient and grateful.

(6) And [recall, O Children of Israel], when Moses said to his people, "Remember the favor of Allāh upon you when He saved you from the people of Pharaoh, who were afflicting you with the worst torment and were slaughtering your [newborn] sons and keeping your females alive. And in that was a great trial from your Lord.

(7) And [remember] when your Lord proclaimed, 'If you are grateful, I will surely increase you [in favor]; but if you deny, indeed, My punishment is severe.'"

(8) And Moses said, "If you should disbelieve, you and whoever is on the earth entirely - indeed, Allāh is Free of need and Praiseworthy."

(9) Has there not reached you the news of those before you - the people of Noah and ʿAad and Thamūd and those after them? No one knows them [i.e., their number] but Allāh. Their messengers brought them clear proofs, but they returned their hands to their mouths[637] and said, "Indeed, we disbelieve in that with which you

---

[634] See footnote to 2:1.

[635] i.e., those who refuse His guidance.

[636] Days of blessings bestowed upon the Children of Israel. Also interpreted as days of punishment and destruction of the former nations.

[637] Several explanations have been given as to the meaning. Based upon the conclusion of the verse, Ibn Katheer preferred that this was a gesture of denial and rejection.

have been sent, and indeed we are, about that to which you invite us, in disquieting doubt."

(10) Their messengers said, "Can there be doubt about Allāh, Creator of the heavens and earth? He invites you that He may forgive you of your sins, and He delays you [i.e., your death] for a specified term." They said, "You are not but men like us who wish to avert us from what our fathers were worshipping. So bring us a clear authority [i.e., evidence]."

(11) Their messengers said to them, "We are only men like you, but Allāh confers favor upon whom He wills of His servants. It has never been for us to bring you evidence except by permission of Allāh. And upon Allāh let the believers rely.

(12) And why should we not rely upon Allāh while He has guided us to our [good] ways. And we will surely be patient against whatever harm you should cause us. And upon Allāh let those who would rely [indeed] rely."

(13) And those who disbelieved said to their messengers, "We will surely drive you out of our land, or you must return to our religion." So their Lord inspired to them, "We will surely destroy the wrongdoers.

(14) And We will surely cause you to dwell in the land after them. That is for he who fears My position[638] and fears My threat."

(15) And they requested decision [i.e., victory from Allāh], and disappointed, [therefore], was every obstinate tyrant.

(16) Before him[639] is Hell, and he will be given a drink of purulent water.[640]

(17) He will gulp it but will hardly [be able to] swallow it. And death will come to him from everywhere, but he is not to die. And before him is a massive punishment.

(18) The example of those who disbelieve in their Lord is [that] their deeds are like ashes which the wind blows forcefully on a stormy day; they are unable [to keep] from what they earned a [single] thing. That is what is extreme error.

(19) Have you not seen [i.e., considered] that Allāh created the heavens and the earth in truth? If He wills, He can do away with you and produce a new creation.

(20) And that is not difficult for Allāh.

---

[638] An alternative meaning is "the standing [for account] before Me."
[639] "Literally, "after him [in time]," meaning ahead of him.
[640] That which oozes from the skins of Hell's inhabitants."

(21) And they will come out [for judgement] before Allāh all together, and the weak will say to those who were arrogant, "Indeed, we were your followers, so can you avail us anything against the punishment of Allāh?" They will say, "If Allāh had guided us, we would have guided you. It is all the same for us whether we show intolerance or are patient: there is for us no place of escape."

(22) And Satan will say when the matter has been concluded, "Indeed, Allāh had promised you the promise of truth. And I promised you, but I betrayed you. But I had no authority over you except that I invited you, and you responded to me. So do not blame me; but blame yourselves. I cannot be called to your aid, nor can you be called to my aid. Indeed, I deny your association of me [with Allāh] before.[641] Indeed, for the wrongdoers is a painful punishment."

(23) And those who believed and did righteous deeds will be admitted to gardens beneath which rivers flow, abiding eternally therein by permission of their Lord; and their greeting therein will be, "Peace!"

(24) Have you not considered how Allāh presents an example, [making] a good word like a good tree, whose root is firmly fixed and its branches [high] in the sky?

(25) It produces its fruit all the time, by permission of its Lord. And Allāh presents examples for the people that perhaps they will be reminded.

(26) And the example of a bad word is like a bad tree, uprooted from the surface of the earth, not having any stability.

(27) Allāh keeps firm those who believe, with the firm word,[642] in worldly life and in the Hereafter.[643] And Allāh sends astray the wrongdoers. And Allāh does what He wills.

(28) Have you not considered those who exchanged the favor of Allāh for disbelief[644] and settled their people [in] the home of ruin?

(29) [It is] Hell, which they will [enter to] burn, and wretched is the settlement.

(30) And they have attributed to Allāh equals to mislead [people] from His way. Say, "Enjoy yourselves, for indeed, your destination is the Fire."

---

[641] By your obedience to me instead of Him during life on earth.

[642] "The testimony that there is no deity except Allāh and that Muḥammad (ﷺ) is the messenger of Allāh.

[643] When questioned in their graves by the angels after death."

[644] They met Allāh's blessing with denial instead of gratitude.

(31) [O Muḥammad], tell My servants who have believed to establish prayer and spend from what We have provided them, secretly and publicly, before a Day comes in which there will be no exchange [i.e., ransom], nor any friendships.

(32) It is Allāh who created the heavens and the earth and sent down rain from the sky and produced thereby some fruits as provision for you and subjected for you[645] the ships to sail through the sea by His command and subjected for you the rivers.

(33) And He subjected for you the sun and the moon, continuous [in orbit], and subjected for you the night and the day.

(34) And He gave you from all you asked of Him.[646] And if you should count the favor [i.e., blessings] of Allāh, you could not enumerate them. Indeed, mankind is [generally] most unjust and ungrateful.[647]

(35) And [mention, O Muḥammad], when Abraham said, "My Lord, make this city [i.e., Makkah] secure and keep me and my sons away from worshipping idols.

(36) My Lord, indeed they have led astray many among the people. So whoever follows me - then he is of me;[648] and whoever disobeys me - indeed, You are [yet] Forgiving and Merciful.

(37) Our Lord, I have settled some of my descendants in an uncultivated valley near Your sacred House, our Lord, that they may establish prayer. So make hearts among the people incline toward them and provide for them from the fruits that they might be grateful.

(38) Our Lord, indeed You know what we conceal and what we declare, and nothing is hidden from Allāh on the earth or in the heaven.

(39) Praise to Allāh, who has granted to me in old age Ishmael and Isaac. Indeed, my Lord is the Hearer of supplication.

(40) My Lord, make me an establisher of prayer, and [many] from my descendants. Our Lord, and accept my supplication.

(41) Our Lord, forgive me and my parents and the believers the Day the account is established."

---

[645] i.e., made serviceable to you.

[646] "Something of what you asked and all of what you continually require, according to His wisdom.

[647] i.e., disbelieving and denying of Allāh's favor."

[648] i.e., of my religion.

(42) And never think that Allāh is unaware of what the wrongdoers do. He only delays them [i.e., their account] for a Day when eyes will stare [in horror].

(43) Racing ahead, their heads raised up, their glance does not come back to them,[649] and their hearts are void.

(44) And, [O Muḥammad], warn the people of a Day when the punishment will come to them and those who did wrong will say, "Our Lord, delay us for a short term; we will answer Your call and follow the messengers." [But it will be said], "Had you not sworn, before, that for you there would be no cessation?[650]

(45) And you lived among the dwellings of those who wronged themselves, and it had become clear to you how We dealt with them. And We presented for you [many] examples."

(46) And they had planned their plan, but with Allāh is [recorded] their plan, even if their plan had been [sufficient] to do away with the mountains.[651]

(47) So never think that Allāh will fail in His promise to His messengers. Indeed, Allāh is Exalted in Might and Owner of Retribution.[652]

(48) [It will be] on the Day the earth will be replaced by another earth, and the heavens [as well], and they [i.e., all creatures] will come out before Allāh, the One, the Prevailing,

(49) And you will see the criminals that Day bound together in irons,

(50) Their garments of liquid pitch and their faces covered by the Fire

(51) So that Allāh will recompense every soul for what it earned. Indeed, Allāh is swift in account.

(52) This [Qur'ān] is notification for the people that they may be warned thereby and that they may know that He is but one God and that those of understanding will be reminded.

---

[649] This is their state at the time of resurrection from the graves. Their heads are upraised in fixed stares of terror, unable even to glance back.

[650] Of the blessings which Allāh had bestowed upon you during life on earth.

[651] An alternative meaning is "...and their plan was not [sufficient] to do away with the mountains," i.e., it had no effect against Allāh's will.

[652] Refer to footnote for 3:(5)

Surah Al-Hijr

(1) Alif, Lām, Rā.[653] These are the verses of the Book and a clear Qur'ān [i.e., recitation].

(2) Perhaps those who disbelieve will wish[654] that they had been Muslims.

(3) Let them eat and enjoy themselves and be diverted by [false] hope, for they are going to know.

(4) And We did not destroy any city but that for it was a known decree.

(5) No nation will precede its term, nor will they remain thereafter.

(6) And they say, "O you upon whom the message has been sent down, indeed you are mad.[655]

(7) Why do you not bring us the angels, if you should be among the truthful?"

(8) We do not send down the angels except with truth;[656] and they [i.e., the disbelievers] would not then be reprieved.

(9) Indeed, it is We who sent down the message [i.e., the Qur'ān], and indeed, We will be its guardian.

(10) And We had certainly sent [messengers] before you, [O Muḥammad], among the sects of the former peoples.

(11) And no messenger would come to them except that they ridiculed him.

(12) Thus do We insert it [i.e., denial] into the hearts of the criminals.

(13) They will not believe in it, while there has already occurred the precedent of the former peoples.

(14) And [even] if We opened to them a gate from the heaven and they continued therein to ascend,

---

[653] See footnote to 2:1.

[654] On the Day of Judgement or at the time of death.

[655] Literally, "possessed by jinn."

[656] i.e., with a message or, as the conclusion of the verse suggests, to carry out a promised punishment.

(15) They would say, "Our eyes have only been dazzled. Rather, we are a people affected by magic."

(16) And We have placed within the heaven great stars and have beautified it for the observers.

(17) And We have protected it from every devil expelled [from the mercy of Allāh]

(18) Except one who steals a hearing and is pursued by a clear burning flame.

(19) And the earth - We have spread it and cast therein firmly set mountains and caused to grow therein [something] of every well-balanced thing.

(20) And We have made for you therein means of living and [for] those for whom you are not providers.[657]

(21) And there is not a thing but that with Us are its depositories, and We do not send it down except according to a known [i.e., specified] measure.

(22) And We have sent the fertilizing winds[658] and sent down water from the sky and given you drink from it. And you are not its retainers.

(23) And indeed, it is We who give life and cause death, and We are the Inheritor.[659]

(24) And We have already known the preceding [generations] among you, and We have already known the later [ones to come].

(25) And indeed, your Lord will gather them; indeed, He is Wise and Knowing.

(26) And We did certainly create man out of clay from an altered black mud.

(27) And the jinn We created before from scorching fire.

(28) And [mention, O Muḥammad], when your Lord said to the angels, "I will create a human being out of clay from an altered black mud.

(29) And when I have proportioned him and breathed into him of My [created] soul,[660] then fall down to him in prostration."

---

[657] Allāh has put at your service other men and animals for which He provides. An additional meaning is that Allāh provides means for your living and for all other creatures as well.

[658] Causing precipitation in rainclouds or carrying pollen. Another meaning is "pregnant winds," i.e., those carrying rainclouds.

[659] Allāh (subḥānahu wa taʿālā) remains after all creation has passed away.

[660] The element of life and soul which Allāh created for that body, not His own spirit or part of Himself (as some mistakenly believe).

(30) So the angels prostrated - all of them entirely,

(31) Except Iblees;[661] he refused to be with those who prostrated.

(32) [Allāh] said, "O Iblees, what is [the matter] with you that you are not with those who prostrate?"

(33) He said, "Never would I prostrate to a human whom You created out of clay from an altered black mud."

(34) [Allāh] said, "Then depart from it,[662] for indeed, you are expelled.

(35) And indeed, upon you is the curse until the Day of Recompense."

(36) He said, "My Lord, then reprieve me until the Day they are resurrected."

(37) [Allāh] said, "So indeed, you are of those reprieved

(38) Until the Day of the time well-known."

(39) [Iblees] said, "My Lord, because You have put me in error, I will surely make [disobedience] attractive to them [i.e., mankind] on earth, and I will mislead them all

(40) Except, among them, Your chosen servants."

(41) [Allāh] said, "This is a path [of return] to Me [that is] straight.

(42) Indeed, My servants - no authority will you have over them, except those who follow you of the deviators.

(43) And indeed, Hell is the promised place for them all.

(44) It has seven gates; for every gate is of them [i.e., Satan's followers] a portion designated."

(45) Indeed, the righteous will be within gardens and springs,

(46) [Having been told], "Enter it in peace, safe [and secure]."

(47) And We will remove whatever is in their breasts of resentment,[663] [so they will be] brothers, on thrones facing each other.

(48) No fatigue will touch them therein, nor from it will they [ever] be removed.

---

[661] Who was of the jinn. See 18:50.
[662] Your position in the heavens.
[663] See footnote to 7:43.

(49) [O Muḥammad], inform My servants that it is I who am the Forgiving, the Merciful,

(50) And that it is My punishment which is the painful punishment.

(51) And inform them about the guests of Abraham,

(52) When they entered upon him and said, "Peace." [Abraham] said, "Indeed, we are fearful [i.e., apprehensive] of you."

(53) [The angels] said, "Fear not. Indeed, we give you good tidings of a learned boy."

(54) He said, "Have you given me good tidings although old age has come upon me? Then of what [wonder] do you inform?"

(55) They said, "We have given you good tidings in truth, so do not be of the despairing."

(56) He said, "And who despairs of the mercy of his Lord except for those astray?"

(57) [Abraham] said, "Then what is your business [here], O messengers?"

(58) They said, "Indeed, we have been sent to a people of criminals,

(59) Except the family of Lot; indeed, we will save them all

(60) Except his wife." We [i.e., Allāh] decreed that she is of those who remain behind.[664]

(61) And when the messengers came to the family of Lot,

(62) He said, "Indeed, you are people unknown."

(63) They said, "But we have come to you with that about which they were disputing,

(64) And we have come to you with truth, and indeed, we are truthful.

(65) So set out with your family during a portion of the night and follow behind them and let not anyone among you look back and continue on to where you are commanded."

(66) And We conveyed to him [the decree] of that matter: that those [sinners] would be eliminated by early morning.

---

[664] For having collaborated with the evildoers.

(67) And the people of the city came rejoicing.[665]

(68) [Lot] said, "Indeed, these are my guests, so do not shame me.

(69) And fear Allāh and do not disgrace me."

(70) They said, "Have we not forbidden you from [protecting] people?"

(71) [Lot] said, "These are my daughters[666] - if you would be doers [of lawful marriage]."

(72) By your life, [O Muḥammad], indeed they were, in their intoxication, wandering blindly.

(73) So the shriek[667] seized them at sunrise.

(74) And We made the highest part [of the city] its lowest and rained upon them stones of hard clay.

(75) Indeed in that are signs for those who discern.

(76) And indeed, they [i.e., those cities] are [situated] on an established road.

(77) Indeed in that is a sign for the believers.

(78) And the companions of the thicket [i.e., the people of Madyan] were [also] wrongdoers,

(79) So We took retribution from them, and indeed, both [cities] are on a clear highway.

(80) And certainly did the companions of al-Ḥijr[668] [i.e., the Thamūd] deny the messengers.

(81) And We gave them Our signs, but from them they were turning away.

(82) And they used to carve from the mountains, houses, feeling secure.

(83) But the shriek seized them at early morning,

(84) So nothing availed them [from] what they used to earn.

---

[665] At the news of Lot's visitors.
[666] i.e., the women of his community who were lawful for marriage.
[667] See footnote to 11:67.
[668] The valley of stone.

(85) And We have not created the heavens and earth and that between them except in truth. And indeed, the Hour is coming; so forgive with gracious forgiveness.

(86) Indeed, your Lord - He is the Knowing Creator.

(87) And We have certainly given you, [O Muḥammad], seven of the often repeated [verses][669] and the great Qur'ān.

(88) Do not extend your eyes toward that by which We have given enjoyment to [certain] categories of them [i.e., the disbelievers], and do not grieve over them. And lower your wing [i.e., show kindness] to the believers.

(89) And say, "Indeed, I am the clear warner" -

(90) Just as We had revealed [scriptures] to the separators[670]

(91) Who have made the Qur'ān into portions.[671]

(92) So by your Lord, We will surely question them all

(93) About what they used to do.

(94) Then declare what you are commanded[672] and turn away from the polytheists.[673]

(95) Indeed, We are sufficient for you against the mockers

(96) Who make [equal] with Allāh another deity. But they are going to know.

(97) And We already know that your breast is constrained by what they say.

(98) So exalt [Allāh] with praise of your Lord and be of those who prostrate [to Him].

(99) And worship your Lord until there comes to you the certainty [i.e., death].

---

[669] Referring to Sūrah al-Fātiḥah.

[670] Those who separated from the teachings of their prophets. Another meaning is "As We sent down [punishment] on the sworn opponents [to Allāh's message]."

[671] Accepting part and rejecting part according to their own inclinations.

[672] "The implication is "Thereby you will distinguish or separate the disbelievers from the believers."

[673] Any who persist in association of others with Allāh."

Surah An-Nahl

(1) The command of Allāh is coming,[674] so be not impatient for it. Exalted is He and high above what they associate with Him.

(2) He sends down the angels, with the inspiration [i.e., revelation] of His command, upon whom He wills of His servants, [telling them], "Warn that there is no deity except Me; so fear Me."

(3) He created the heavens and earth in truth. High is He above what they associate with Him.

(4) He created man from a sperm-drop; then at once[675] he is a clear adversary.

(5) And the grazing livestock He has created for you; in them is warmth[676] and [numerous] benefits, and from them you eat.

(6) And for you in them is [the enjoyment of] beauty when you bring them in [for the evening] and when you send them out [to pasture].

(7) And they carry your loads to a land you could not have reached except with difficulty to yourselves. Indeed, your Lord is Kind and Merciful.

(8) And [He created] the horses, mules and donkeys for you to ride and [as] adornment. And He creates that which you do not know.

(9) And upon Allāh[677] is the direction of the [right] way, and among them [i.e., the various paths] are those deviating. And if He willed, He could have guided you all.

(10) It is He who sends down rain from the sky; from it is drink and from it is foliage in which you pasture [animals].

(11) He causes to grow for you thereby the crops, olives, palm trees, grapevines, and of all the fruits. Indeed in that is a sign for a people who give thought.

---

[674] Literally, "has come," indicating the certainty and nearness of the Last Hour.
[675] As soon as he becomes strong and independent.
[676] i.e., in clothing, tents, furnishings, etc.
[677] Allāh (subḥānahu wa taʿālā) has taken it upon Himself to guide man to the right path. The meaning has also been interpreted as "To Allāh..."

(12) And He has subjected for you the night and day and the sun and moon, and the stars are subjected by His command. Indeed in that are signs for a people who reason.

(13) And [He has subjected] whatever He multiplied for you on the earth of varying colors. Indeed in that is a sign for a people who remember.

(14) And it is He who subjected the sea for you to eat from it tender meat and to extract from it ornaments which you wear. And you see the ships plowing through it, and [He subjected it] that you may seek of His bounty; and perhaps you will be grateful.

(15) And He has cast into the earth firmly set mountains, lest it shift with you, and [made] rivers and roads, that you may be guided,

(16) And landmarks. And by the stars they are [also] guided.[678]

(17) Then is He who creates like one who does not create? So will you not be reminded?

(18) And if you should count the favors of Allāh, you could not enumerate them. Indeed, Allāh is Forgiving and Merciful.

(19) And Allāh knows what you conceal and what you declare.

(20) And those they invoke other than Allāh create nothing, and they [themselves] are created.

(21) They are [in fact] dead,[679] not alive, and they do not perceive when they will be resurrected.

(22) Your god is one God. But those who do not believe in the Hereafter - their hearts are disapproving, and they are arrogant.

(23) Assuredly, Allāh knows what they conceal and what they declare. Indeed, He does not like the arrogant.

(24) And when it is said to them, "What has your Lord sent down?" they say, "Legends of the former peoples,"

---

[678] Through the desert or the sea at night.
[679] i.e., inanimate or without understanding.

(25) That they may bear their own burdens [i.e., sins] in full on the Day of Resurrection and some of the burdens of those whom they misguide without [i.e., by lack of] knowledge. Unquestionably, evil is that which they bear.

(26) Those before them had already plotted, but Allāh came at [i.e., uprooted] their building from the foundations, so the roof fell upon them from above them,[680] and the punishment came to them from where they did not perceive.

(27) Then on the Day of Resurrection He will disgrace them and say, "Where are My 'partners' for whom you used to oppose [the believers]?" Those who were given knowledge will say, "Indeed disgrace, this Day, and evil are upon the disbelievers" -

(28) The ones whom the angels take in death [while] wronging themselves,[681] and [who] then offer submission, [saying], "We were not doing any evil." But, yes! Indeed, Allāh is Knowing of what you used to do.

(29) So enter the gates of Hell to abide eternally therein, and how wretched is the residence of the arrogant.

(30) And it will be said to those who feared Allāh, "What did your Lord send down?" They will say, "[That which is] good." For those who do good in this world is good; and the home of the Hereafter is better. And how excellent is the home of the righteous -

(31) Gardens of perpetual residence, which they will enter, beneath which rivers flow. They will have therein whatever they wish. Thus does Allāh reward the righteous -

(32) The ones whom the angels take in death, [being] good and pure; [the angels] will say, "Peace be upon you. Enter Paradise for what you used to do."

(33) Do they [i.e., the disbelievers] await except that the angels should come to them or there comes the command of your Lord? Thus did those do before them. And Allāh wronged them not, but they had been wronging themselves.

(34) So they were struck by the evil consequences of what they did and were enveloped by what they used to ridicule.

(35) And those who associate others with Allāh say, "If Allāh had willed, we would not have worshipped anything other than Him, neither we nor our fathers, nor would we have forbidden anything through other than Him." Thus did those do

---

[680] i.e., Allāh caused their plan to fail and exposed their plot.
[681] i.e., having made punishment due to them for their numerous sins and crimes.

before them. So is there upon the messengers except [the duty of] clear notification?

(36) And We certainly sent into every nation a messenger, [saying], "Worship Allāh and avoid ṭāghūt."[682] And among them were those whom Allāh guided, and among them were those upon whom error was [deservedly] decreed. So proceed [i.e., travel] through the earth and observe how was the end of the deniers.

(37) [Even] if you should strive for their guidance, [O Muḥammad], indeed, Allāh does not guide those He sends astray,[683] and they will have no helpers.

(38) And they swear by Allāh their strongest oaths [that] Allāh will not resurrect one who dies. But yes - [it is] a true promise [binding] upon Him, but most of the people do not know.

(39) [It is] so He will make clear to them [the truth of] that wherein they differ and so those who have disbelieved may know that they were liars.

(40) Indeed, Our word to a thing when We intend it is but that We say to it, "Be," and it is.

(41) And those who emigrated for [the cause of] Allāh after they had been wronged - We will surely settle them in this world in a good place; but the reward of the Hereafter is greater, if only they could know.

(42) [They are] those who endured patiently and upon their Lord relied.

(43) And We sent not before you except men to whom We revealed [Our message]. So ask the people of the message [i.e., former scriptures] if you do not know.

(44) [We sent them] with clear proofs and written ordinances. And We revealed to you the message [i.e., the Qur'ān] that you may make clear to the people what was sent down to them and that they might give thought.

(45) Then, do those who have planned evil deeds feel secure that Allāh will not cause the earth to swallow them or that the punishment will not come upon them from where they do not perceive?

(46) Or that He would not seize them during their [usual] activity, and they could not cause failure [i.e., escape from Him]?

---

[682] False objects of worship.

[683] As a result of their choice to reject guidance.

(47) Or that He would not seize them gradually [in a state of dread]?[684] But indeed, your Lord is Kind and Merciful.[685]

(48) Have they not considered what things Allāh has created? Their shadows incline to the right and to the left, prostrating to Allāh, while they [i.e., those creations] are humble.

(49) And to Allāh prostrates whatever is in the heavens and whatever is on the earth of creatures, and the angels [as well], and they are not arrogant.

(50) They fear their Lord above them, and they do what they are commanded.

(51) And Allāh has said, "Do not take for yourselves two[686] deities. He [i.e., Allāh] is but one God, so fear only Me."

(52) And to Him belongs whatever is in the heavens and the earth, and to Him is [due] worship constantly. Then is it other than Allāh that you fear?

(53) And whatever you have of favor - it is from Allāh. Then when adversity touches you, to Him you cry for help.

(54) Then when He removes the adversity from you, at once a party of you associates others with their Lord

(55) So they will deny what We have given them. Then enjoy yourselves, for you are going to know.

(56) And they assign to what they do not know[687] [i.e., false deities] a portion of that which We have provided them. By Allāh, you will surely be questioned about what you used to invent.

(57) And they attribute to Allāh daughters[688] - exalted is He - and for them is what they desire [i.e., sons].

(58) And when one of them is informed of [the birth of] a female, his face becomes dark, and he suppresses grief.

---

[684] "i.e., being aware of what is about to strike them after having seen those near them succumb.

[685] Postponing deserved punishment and giving opportunities for repentance."

[686] Meaning more than one.

[687] i.e., that of which they have no knowledge; rather, they have mere assumption based upon tradition or the claims of misguided men.

[688] By claiming that the angels are His daughters

(59) He hides himself from the people because of the ill of which he has been informed. Should he keep it in humiliation or bury it in the ground? Unquestionably, evil is what they decide.

(60) For those who do not believe in the Hereafter is the description [i.e., an attribute] of evil;[689] and for Allāh is the highest attribute. And He is Exalted in Might, the Wise.

(61) And if Allāh were to impose blame on the people for their wrongdoing, He would not have left upon it [i.e., the earth] any creature, but He defers them for a specified term. And when their term has come, they will not remain behind an hour, nor will they precede [it].

(62) And they attribute to Allāh that which they dislike [i.e., daughters], and their tongues assert the lie that they will have the best [from Him]. Assuredly, they will have the Fire, and they will be [therein] neglected.[690]

(63) By Allāh, We did certainly send [messengers] to nations before you, but Satan made their deeds attractive to them. And he is their [i.e., the disbelievers] ally today [as well], and they will have a painful punishment.

(64) And We have not revealed to you the Book, [O Muḥammad], except for you to make clear to them that wherein they have differed and as guidance and mercy for a people who believe.

(65) And Allāh has sent down rain from the sky and given life thereby to the earth after its lifelessness. Indeed in that is a sign for a people who listen.

(66) And indeed, for you in grazing livestock is a lesson. We give you drink from what is in their bellies - between excretion and blood - pure milk, palatable to drinkers.

(67) And from the fruits of the palm trees and grapevines you take intoxicant and good provision.[691] Indeed in that is a sign for a people who reason.

(68) And your Lord inspired to the bee, "Take for yourself among the mountains, houses [i.e., hives], and among the trees and [in] that which they construct.

---

[689] Such as that described in the previous two verses.

[690] Another meaning is "...and they will be made to precede [all others thereto]."

[691] This verse was revealed before the prohibition of intoxicants. It alludes to the fact that there are both evil and good possibilities in certain things.

(69) Then eat from all the fruits[692] and follow the ways of your Lord laid down [for you]." There emerges from their bellies a drink, varying in colors, in which there is healing for people. Indeed in that is a sign for a people who give thought.

(70) And Allāh created you; then He will take you in death. And among you is he who is reversed to the most decrepit [old] age so that he will not know, after [having had] knowledge, a thing. Indeed, Allāh is Knowing and Competent.

(71) And Allāh has favored some of you over others in provision. But those who were favored [i.e., given more] would not hand over their provision to those whom their right hands possess [i.e., slaves] so they would be equal to them therein.[693] Then is it the favor of Allāh they reject?

(72) And Allāh has made for you from yourselves mates and has made for you from your mates sons and grandchildren and has provided for you from the good things. Then in falsehood do they believe and in the favor of Allāh they disbelieve?

(73) And they worship besides Allāh that which does not possess for them [the power of] provision from the heavens and the earth at all, and [in fact], they are unable.

(74) So do not assert similarities to Allāh.[694] Indeed, Allāh knows and you do not know.

(75) Allāh presents an example: a slave [who is] owned and unable to do a thing and he to whom We have provided from Us good provision, so he spends from it secretly and publicly. Can they be equal? Praise to Allāh! But most of them do not know.

(76) And Allāh presents an example of two men, one of them dumb and unable to do a thing, while he is a burden to his guardian. Wherever he directs him, he brings no good. Is he equal to one who commands justice, while he is on a straight path?

(77) And to Allāh belongs the unseen [aspects] of the heavens and the earth. And the command for the Hour is not but as a glance of the eye or even nearer. Indeed, Allāh is over all things competent.

(78) And Allāh has extracted you from the wombs of your mothers not knowing a thing, and He made for you hearing and vision and hearts [i.e., intellect] that perhaps you would be grateful.

---

[692] i.e., delicious substances found by the bee.

[693] The argument presented in this verse is that if they cannot consider their own possessions equal to themselves, then how can they consider Allāh's creations as being equal to Him?

[694] As there is nothing comparable to Him.

(79) Do they not see the birds controlled in the atmosphere of the sky? None holds them up except Allāh. Indeed in that are signs for a people who believe.

(80) And Allāh has made for you from your homes a place of rest and made for you from the hides of the animals tents which you find light on your day of travel and your day of encampment; and from their wool, fur and hair is furnishing and enjoyment [i.e., provision] for a time.

(81) And Allāh has made for you, from that which He has created, shadows [i.e., shade] and has made for you from the mountains, shelters and has made for you garments which protect you from the heat and garments [i.e., coats of mail] which protect you from your [enemy in] battle. Thus does He complete His favor upon you that you might submit [to Him].

(82) But if they turn away, [O Muḥammad] - then only upon you is [responsibility for] clear notification.

(83) They recognize the favor of Allāh; then they deny it. And most of them are disbelievers.

(84) And [mention] the Day when We will resurrect from every nation a witness [i.e., their prophet]. Then it will not be permitted to the disbelievers [to apologize or make excuses], nor will they be asked to appease [Allāh].

(85) And when those who wronged see the punishment, it will not be lightened for them, nor will they be reprieved.

(86) And when those who associated others with Allāh see their "partners," they will say, "Our Lord, these are our partners [to You] whom we used to invoke [in worship] besides You." But they will throw at them the statement, "Indeed, you are liars."

(87) And they will impart to Allāh that Day [their] submission, and lost from them is what they used to invent.

(88) Those who disbelieved and averted [others] from the way of Allāh - We will increase them in punishment over [their] punishment for what corruption they were causing.

(89) And [mention] the Day when We will resurrect among every nation a witness over them from themselves [i.e., their prophet]. And We will bring you, [O Muḥammad], as a witness over these [i.e., your nation]. And We have sent down to

you the Book as clarification for all things and as guidance and mercy and good tidings for the Muslims.[695]

(90) Indeed, Allāh orders justice and good conduct and giving [help] to relatives and forbids immorality and bad conduct and oppression. He admonishes you that perhaps you will be reminded.

(91) And fulfill the covenant of Allāh when you have taken it, [O believers], and do not break oaths after their confirmation while you have made Allāh, over you, a security [i.e., witness]. Indeed, Allāh knows what you do.

(92) And do not be like she who untwisted her spun thread after it was strong [by] taking your oaths as [means of] deceit between you because one community is more plentiful [in number or wealth] than another community.[696] Allāh only tries you thereby. And He will surely make clear to you on the Day of Resurrection that over which you used to differ.

(93) And if Allāh had willed, He could have made you [of] one religion, but He sends astray whom He wills and guides whom He wills.[697] And you will surely be questioned about what you used to do.

(94) And do not take your oaths as [means of] deceit between you, lest a foot slip after it was [once] firm, and you would taste evil [in this world] for what [people] you diverted from the way of Allāh,[698] and you would have [in the Hereafter] a great punishment.

(95) And do not exchange the covenant of Allāh for a small price. Indeed, what is with Allāh is best for you, if only you could know.

(96) Whatever you have will end, but what Allāh has is lasting. And We will surely give those who were patient their reward according to the best of what they used to do.

(97) Whoever does righteousness, whether male or female, while he is a believer - We will surely cause him to live a good life, and We will surely give them their reward [in the Hereafter] according to the best of what they used to do.

---

[695] Those who have submitted themselves to Allāh.

[696] i.e., do not swear falsely or break a treaty or contract merely for a worldly advantage.

[697] According to His knowledge of each soul's preference.

[698] Referring to those who would be dissuaded from Islām as a result of a Muslim's deceit and treachery.

(98) So when you recite the Qur'ān, [first] seek refuge in Allāh from Satan, the expelled [from His mercy].

(99) Indeed, there is for him no authority over those who have believed and rely upon their Lord.

(100) His authority is only over those who take him as an ally and those who through him associate others with Allāh.

(101) And when We substitute a verse in place of a verse - and Allāh is most knowing of what He sends down - they say, "You, [O Muḥammad], are but an inventor [of lies]." But most of them do not know.

(102) Say, [O Muḥammad], "The Pure Spirit [i.e., Gabriel] has brought it down from your Lord in truth to make firm those who believe and as guidance and good tidings to the Muslims."

(103) And We certainly know that they say, "It is only a human being who teaches him [i.e., the Prophet (ﷺ)]." The tongue of the one they refer to is foreign,[699] and this [recitation, i.e., Qur'ān] is [in] a clear Arabic language.

(104) Indeed, those who do not believe in the verses of Allāh - Allāh will not guide them, and for them is a painful punishment.

(105) They only invent falsehood who do not believe in the verses of Allāh, and it is those who are the liars.

(106) Whoever disbelieves in [i.e., denies] Allāh after his belief...[700] except for one who is forced [to renounce his religion] while his heart is secure in faith. But those who [willingly] open their breasts to disbelief, upon them is wrath from Allāh, and for them is a great punishment;

(107) That is because they preferred the worldly life over the Hereafter and that Allāh does not guide the disbelieving people.

(108) Those are the ones over whose hearts and hearing and vision Allāh has sealed, and it is those who are the heedless.

(109) Assuredly, it is they, in the Hereafter, who will be the losers.

---

[699] Having seen the Prophet (ﷺ) speaking with a foreign man on occasion, the Quraysh accused him of repeating the man's words.

[700] Based upon the conclusion of this verse, the omitted phrase concerning the apostate is understood to be "...has earned the wrath of Allāh..."

(110) Then, indeed your Lord, to those who emigrated after they had been compelled [to say words of disbelief] and thereafter fought [for the cause of Allāh] and were patient - indeed, your Lord, after that, is Forgiving and Merciful

(111) On the Day when every soul will come disputing [i.e., pleading] for itself, and every soul will be fully compensated for what it did, and they will not be wronged [i.e., treated unjustly].

(112) And Allāh presents an example: a city [i.e., Makkah] which was safe and secure, its provision coming to it in abundance from every location, but it denied the favors of Allāh. So Allāh made it taste the envelopment of hunger and fear for what they had been doing.

(113) And there had certainly come to them a Messenger from among themselves, but they denied him; so punishment overtook them while they were wrongdoers.

(114) Then eat of what Allāh has provided for you [which is] lawful and good. And be grateful for the favor of Allāh, if it is [indeed] Him that you worship.

(115) He has only forbidden to you dead animals,[701] blood, the flesh of swine, and that which has been dedicated to other than Allāh. But whoever is forced [by necessity], neither desiring [it] nor transgressing [its limit] - then indeed, Allāh is Forgiving and Merciful.

(116) And do not say about what your tongues assert of untruth, "This is lawful and this is unlawful," to invent falsehood about Allāh. Indeed, those who invent falsehood about Allāh will not succeed.

(117) [It is but] a brief enjoyment, and they will have a painful punishment.

(118) And to those who are Jews We have prohibited that which We related to you before.[702] And We did not wrong them [thereby], but they were wronging themselves.

(119) Then, indeed your Lord, to those who have done wrong out of ignorance and then repent after that and correct themselves - indeed, your Lord, thereafter, is Forgiving and Merciful.

(120) Indeed, Abraham was a [comprehensive] leader,[703] devoutly obedient to Allāh, inclining toward truth, and he was not of those who associate others with Allāh.

---

[701] Those not slaughtered or hunted expressly for food.
[702] See 6:146.
[703] i.e., embodying all the excellent qualities which make one an example to be followed.

(121) [He was] grateful for His favors. He [i.e., Allāh] chose him and guided him to a straight path.

(122) And We gave him good in this world, and indeed, in the Hereafter he will be among the righteous.

(123) Then We revealed to you, [O Muḥammad], to follow the religion of Abraham, inclining toward truth; and he was not of those who associate with Allāh.

(124) The sabbath was only appointed for those who differed over it. And indeed, your Lord will judge between them on the Day of Resurrection concerning that over which they used to differ.

(125) Invite to the way of your Lord with wisdom and good instruction, and argue with them in a way that is best. Indeed, your Lord is most knowing of who has strayed from His way, and He is most knowing of who is [rightly] guided.

(126) And if you punish [an enemy, O believers], punish with an equivalent of that with which you were harmed.[704] But if you are patient - it is better for those who are patient.

(127) And be patient, [O Muḥammad], and your patience is not but through Allāh. And do not grieve over them and do not be in distress over what they conspire.

(128) Indeed, Allāh is with those who fear Him and those who are doers of good.

---

[704] Not exceeding it.

Surah Al-Isra

(1) Exalted[705] is He who took His Servant [i.e., Prophet Muḥammad (ﷺ)] by night from al-Masjid al-Ḥarām to al-Masjid al-Aqṣā,[706] whose surroundings We have blessed, to show him of Our signs. Indeed, He is the Hearing,[707] the Seeing.[708]

(2) And We gave Moses the Scripture and made it a guidance for the Children of Israel that you not take other than Me as Disposer of affairs,[709]

(3) O descendants of those We carried [in the ship] with Noah. Indeed, he was a grateful servant.

(4) And We conveyed[710] to the Children of Israel in the Scripture that, "You will surely cause corruption on the earth twice, and you will surely reach [a degree of] great haughtiness."

(5) So when the [time of] promise came for the first of them,[711] We sent against you servants of Ours - those of great military might, and they probed [even] into the homes,[712] and it was a promise fulfilled.

(6) Then We gave back to you a return victory over them. And We reinforced you with wealth and sons and made you more numerous in manpower.

(7) [And said], "If you do good, you do good for yourselves; and if you do evil, [you do it] to them [i.e., yourselves]." Then when the final [i.e., second] promise came, [We sent your enemies] to sadden your faces and to enter the masjid [i.e., the temple in Jerusalem], as they entered it the first time, and to destroy what they had taken over with [total] destruction.

---

[705] "Above any imperfection or failure to do as He wills.

[706] In Jerusalem.

[707] Who hears every sound, distinguishes every voice, understands every word, and accepts and responds to supplications.

[708] After Seeing add ftnt: Who sees and understands all things apparent and unapparent, visible and invisible."

[709] i.e., trust in Allāh, knowing that He (subḥānahu wa taʿālā) is responsible for every occurrence.

[710] Foretold out of divine knowledge of what they would do.

[711] "i.e., the promised punishment for the first of their two transgressions.

[712] Violating their sanctity, to kill and plunder."

(8) [Then Allāh said], "It is expected, [if you repent], that your Lord will have mercy upon you. But if you return [to sin], We will return [to punishment]. And We have made Hell, for the disbelievers, a prison-bed."

(9) Indeed, this Qur'ān guides to that which is most suitable and gives good tidings to the believers who do righteous deeds that they will have a great reward

(10) And that those who do not believe in the Hereafter - We have prepared for them a painful punishment.

(11) And man supplicates for evil [when angry] as he supplicates for good, and man is ever hasty.[713]

(12) And We have made the night and day two signs, and We erased the sign of the night and made the sign of the day visible[714] that you may seek bounty from your Lord and may know the number of years and the account [of time]. And everything We have set out in detail.

(13) And [for] every person We have imposed his fate upon his neck,[715] and We will produce for him on the Day of Resurrection a record which he will encounter spread open.

(14) [It will be said], "Read your record. Sufficient is yourself against you this Day as accountant."

(15) Whoever is guided is only guided for [the benefit of] his soul. And whoever errs only errs against it. And no bearer of burdens will bear the burden of another. And never would We punish until We sent a messenger.

(16) And when We intend to destroy a city, We command its affluent[716] but they defiantly disobey therein; so the word [i.e., deserved decree] comes into effect upon it, and We destroy it with [complete] destruction.

(17) And how many have We destroyed from the generations after Noah. And sufficient is your Lord, concerning the sins of His servants, as Aware and Seeing.

---

[713] i.e., impatient, emotional, and acting without forethought.

[714] Or "giving sight."

[715] i.e., after having instructed him, We have made him responsible for his own destiny.

[716] To obey Allāh.

(18) Whoever should desire the immediate[717] - We hasten for him from it what We will to whom We intend. Then We have made for him Hell, which he will [enter to] burn, censured and banished.

(19) But whoever desires the Hereafter and exerts the effort due to it while he is a believer - it is those whose effort is ever appreciated [by Allāh].

(20) To each [category] We extend - to these and to those - from the gift of your Lord. And never has the gift of your Lord been restricted.

(21) Look how We have favored [in provision] some of them over others. But the Hereafter is greater in degrees [of difference] and greater in distinction.

(22) Do not make [as equal] with Allāh another deity and [thereby] become censured and forsaken.

(23) And your Lord has decreed that you worship not except Him, and to parents, good treatment. Whether one or both of them reach old age [while] with you, say not to them [so much as], "uff,"[718] and do not repel them but speak to them a noble word.

(24) And lower to them the wing of humility out of mercy and say, "My Lord, have mercy upon them as they brought me up [when I was] small."

(25) Your Lord is most knowing of what is within yourselves. If you should be righteous [in intention] - then indeed He is ever, to the often returning [to Him], Forgiving.[719]

(26) And give the relative his right, and [also] the poor and the traveler, and do not spend wastefully.[720]

(27) Indeed, the wasteful are brothers of the devils, and ever has Satan been to his Lord ungrateful.

(28) And if you [must] turn away from them [i.e., the needy] awaiting mercy from your Lord which you expect,[721] then speak to them a gentle word.

---

[717] i.e., worldly gratifications.

[718] An expression of disapproval or irritation.

[719] For those who intend righteousness, hastening to repent from sins and errors committed through human weakness, Allāh (subḥānahu wa taʿālā) promises forgiveness.

[720] i.e., on that which is unlawful or in disobedience to Allāh.

[721] i.e., if you have not the means to give them at present.

(29) And do not make your hand [as] chained to your neck[722] or extend it completely[723] and [thereby] become blamed and insolvent.

(30) Indeed, your Lord extends provision for whom He wills and restricts [it]. Indeed He is ever, concerning His servants, Aware and Seeing.

(31) And do not kill your children for fear of poverty. We provide for them and for you. Indeed, their killing is ever a great sin.

(32) And do not approach unlawful sexual intercourse.[724] Indeed, it is ever an immorality and is evil as a way.

(33) And do not kill the soul [i.e., person] which Allāh has forbidden, except by right.[725] And whoever is killed unjustly - We have given his heir authority,[726] but let him not exceed limits in [the matter of] taking life. Indeed, he has been supported [by the law].

(34) And do not approach the property of an orphan, except in the way that is best,[727] until he reaches maturity. And fulfill [every] commitment. Indeed, the commitment is ever [that about which one will be] questioned.

(35) And give full measure when you measure, and weigh with an even [i.e., honest] balance. That is the best [way] and best in result.

(36) And do not pursue[728] that of which you have no knowledge. Indeed, the hearing, the sight and the heart - about all those [one] will be questioned.

(37) And do not walk upon the earth exultantly. Indeed, you will never tear the earth [apart], and you will never reach the mountains in height.[729]

(38) All that [i.e., the aforementioned] - its evil is ever, in the sight of your Lord, detested.

(39) That is from what your Lord has revealed to you, [O Muḥammad], of wisdom. And, [O mankind], do not make [as equal] with Allāh another deity, lest you be thrown into Hell, blamed and banished.

---

[722] "i.e., refusing to spend.

[723] i.e., being extravagant."

[724] i.e., avoid all situations that might possibly lead to it.

[725] "i.e., through legal justice or during jihād.

[726] Grounds for legal action."

[727] i.e., to improve or increase it.

[728] i.e., do not assume and do not say.

[729] Man, for all his arrogance, is yet a weak and small creature.

(40) Then, has your Lord chosen you for [having] sons and taken [i.e., adopted] from among the angels daughters? Indeed, you say a grave saying.

(41) And We have certainly diversified [the contents] in this Qur'ān that they [i.e., mankind] may be reminded, but it does not increase them [i.e., the disbelievers] except in aversion.

(42) Say, [O Muḥammad], "If there had been with Him [other] gods, as they say, then they [each] would have sought to the Owner of the Throne a way."[730]

(43) Exalted is He and high above what they say by great sublimity.

(44) The seven heavens and the earth and whatever is in them exalt Him. And there is not a thing except that it exalts [Allāh] by His praise, but you do not understand their [way of] exalting. Indeed, He is ever Forbearing[731] and Forgiving.

(45) And when you recite the Qur'ān, We put between you and those who do not believe in the Hereafter a concealed partition.[732]

(46) And We have placed over their hearts coverings, lest they understand it, and in their ears deafness. And when you mention your Lord alone in the Qur'ān, they turn back in aversion.

(47) We are most knowing of how they listen to it when they listen to you and [of] when they are in private conversation, when the wrongdoers say, "You follow not but a man affected by magic."

(48) Look how they strike for you comparisons;[733] but they have strayed, so they cannot [find] a way.

(49) And they say, "When we are bones and crumbled particles, will we [truly] be resurrected as a new creation?"

(50) Say, "Be you stones or iron[734]

(51) Or [any] creation of that which is great[735] within your breasts." And they will say, "Who will restore us?" Say, "He who brought you forth the first time." Then

---

[730] To please Him, recognizing His superiority. Another interpretation is "...they would seek a way" to depose Him (subḥānahu wa taʿālā) and take over His Throne.
[731] Refer to footnote in 2:225.

[732] Preventing guidance from reaching them.
[733] Describing the Prophet (ﷺ) as a poet, a madman or one under the influence of sorcery.
[734] i.e., even if you should be stones or iron
[735] "Such as the heavens and earth.

they will nod their heads toward you[736] and say, "When is that?" Say, "Perhaps it will be soon -

(52) On the Day He will call you and you will respond with praise of Him and think that you had not remained [in the world] except for a little."

(53) And tell My servants to say that which is best. Indeed, Satan induces [dissension] among them. Indeed Satan is ever, to mankind, a clear enemy.

(54) Your Lord is most knowing of you. If He wills, He will have mercy upon you; or if He wills, He will punish you. And We have not sent you, [O Muḥammad], over them as a manager.

(55) And your Lord is most knowing of whoever is in the heavens and the earth. And We have made some of the prophets exceed others [in various ways], and to David We gave the book [of Psalms].

(56) Say, "Invoke those you have claimed [as gods] besides Him, for they do not possess the [ability for] removal of adversity from you or [for its] transfer [to someone else]."

(57) Those whom they invoke[737] seek means of access to their Lord, [striving as to] which of them would be nearest, and they hope for His mercy and fear His punishment. Indeed, the punishment of your Lord is ever feared.

(58) And there is no city but that We will destroy it[738] before the Day of Resurrection or punish it with a severe punishment. That has ever been in the Register[739] inscribed.

(59) And nothing has prevented Us from sending signs [i.e., miracles] except that the former peoples denied them. And We gave Thamūd the she-camel as a visible sign, but they wronged her. And We send not the signs except as a warning.

(60) And [remember, O Muḥammad], when We told you, "Indeed, your Lord has encompassed the people."[740] And We did not make the sight which We showed you[741] except as a trial for the people, as was the accursed tree [mentioned] in the

---

[736] In disbelief and ridicule."

[737] Among the righteous of Allāh's creation, such as angels, prophets, deceased scholars, etc.

[738] "Because of the sins of its inhabitants.

[739] The Preserved Slate (al-Lawḥ al-Maḥfūẓ), which is with Allāh."

[740] "In His knowledge and power, meaning that Allāh would protect him (ﷺ) from their harm.

[741] During the miʿrāj (ascension) into the heavens."

Qur'ān. And We threaten [i.e., warn] them, but it increases them not except in great transgression.

(61) And [mention] when We said to the angels, "Prostrate to Adam," and they prostrated, except for Iblees.[742] He said, "Should I prostrate to one You created from clay?"

(62) [Iblees] said, "Do You see this one whom You have honored above me? If You delay me [i.e., my death] until the Day of Resurrection, I will surely destroy[743] his descendants, except for a few."

(63) [Allāh] said, "Go, for whoever of them follows you, indeed Hell will be the recompense of [all of] you - an ample recompense.

(64) And incite [to senselessness] whoever you can among them with your voice and assault them with your horses and foot soldiers and become a partner in their wealth and their children and promise them." But Satan does not promise them except delusion.

(65) Indeed, over My [believing] servants there is for you no authority. And sufficient is your Lord as Disposer of affairs.[744]

(66) It is your Lord who drives the ship for you through the sea that you may seek of His bounty. Indeed, He is ever, to you, Merciful.

(67) And when adversity touches you at sea, lost are [all] those you invoke except for Him. But when He delivers you to the land, you turn away [from Him]. And ever is man ungrateful.

(68) Then do you feel secure that [instead] He will not cause a part of the land to swallow you or send against you a storm of stones? Then you would not find for yourselves an advocate.

(69) Or do you feel secure that He will not send you back into it [i.e., the sea] another time and send upon you a hurricane of wind and drown you for what you denied?[745] Then you would not find for yourselves against Us an avenger.[746]

---

[742] See footnote to 2:34.
[743] By tempting them and leading them astray.
[744] Refer to footnote in 3: 173.
[745] "Or "for your disbelief."
[746] Or "someone to demand restitution."

(70) And We have certainly honored the children of Adam and carried them on the land and sea and provided for them of the good things and preferred them over much of what We have created, with [definite] preference.

(71) [Mention, O Muḥammad], the Day We will call forth every people with their record [of deeds].[747] Then whoever is given his record in his right hand - those will read their records, and injustice will not be done to them, [even] as much as a thread [inside the date seed].

(72) And whoever is blind[748] in this [life] will be blind in the Hereafter and more astray in way.

(73) And indeed, they were about to tempt you away from that which We revealed to you in order to [make] you invent about Us something else; and then they would have taken you as a friend.

(74) And if We had not strengthened you, you would have almost inclined to them a little.

(75) Then [if you had], We would have made you taste double [punishment in] life and double [after] death. Then you would not find for yourself against Us a helper.

(76) And indeed, they were about to provoke [i.e., drive] you from the land [i.e., Makkah] to evict you therefrom. And then [when they do], they will not remain [there] after you, except for a little.[749]

(77) [That is Our] established way for those We had sent before you of Our messengers; and you will not find in Our way any alteration.

(78) Establish prayer at the decline of the sun [from its meridian] until the darkness of the night[750] and [also] the Qur'ān [i.e., recitation] of dawn.[751] Indeed, the recitation of dawn is ever witnessed.

---

[747] Other meanings are "with their leader" or "with that which they had followed."
[748] i.e., refusing to see the truth.

[749] Only ten years after the Prophet's emigration, Makkah was completely cleared of his enemies.
[750] "i.e., the period which includes the ẓuhr, aṣr, maghrib, and ʿishāʾ prayers.
[751] i.e., the fajr prayer, in which the recitation of the Qurʾān is prolonged."

(79) And from [part of] the night, pray[752] with it [i.e., recitation of the Qur'ān] as additional [worship] for you; it is expected that[753] your Lord will resurrect you to a praised station.[754]

(80) And say, "My Lord, cause me to enter a sound entrance[755] and to exit a sound exit[756] and grant me from Yourself a supporting authority."

(81) And say, "Truth has come, and falsehood has departed. Indeed is falsehood, [by nature], ever bound to depart."

(82) And We send down of the Qur'ān that which is healing and mercy for the believers, but it does not increase the wrongdoers except in loss.

(83) And when We bestow favor upon man [i.e., the disbeliever], he turns away and distances himself; and when evil touches him, he is ever despairing.

(84) Say, "Each works according to his manner, but your Lord is most knowing of who is best guided in way."

(85) And they ask you, [O Muḥammad], about the soul. Say, "The soul is of the affair [i.e., concern] of my Lord. And you [i.e., mankind] have not been given of knowledge except a little."

(86) And if We willed, We could surely do away with that which We revealed to you. Then you would not find for yourself concerning it an advocate against Us.

(87) Except [We have left it with you] as a mercy from your Lord. Indeed, His favor upon you has ever been great.

(88) Say, "If mankind and the jinn gathered in order to produce the like of this Qur'ān, they could not produce the like of it, even if they were to each other assistants."

(89) And We have certainly diversified for the people in this Qur'ān from every [kind of] example, but most of the people refused except disbelief.

(90) And they say, "We will not believe you until you break open for us from the ground a spring

---

[752] "Literally, "arise from sleep for prayer."
[753] This is a promise from Allāh (subḥānahu wa taʿālā) to Prophet Muḥammad (ﷺ).
[754] The position of intercession by permission of Allāh and the highest degree in Paradise."
[755] "Into Madīnah at the time of emigration, or into the grave.
[756] From Makkah, or from the grave at the time of resurrection."

(91) Or [until] you have a garden of palm trees and grapes and make rivers gush forth within them in force [and abundance]

(92) Or you make the heaven fall upon us in fragments as you have claimed or you bring Allāh and the angels before [us]

(93) Or you have a house of ornament [i.e., gold] or you ascend into the sky. And [even then], we will not believe in your ascension until you bring down to us a book we may read." Say, "Exalted is my Lord! Was I ever but a human messenger?"

(94) And what prevented the people from believing when guidance came to them except that they said, "Has Allāh sent a human messenger?"

(95) Say, "If there were upon the earth angels walking securely,[757] We would have sent down to them from the heaven an angel [as a] messenger."

(96) Say, "Sufficient is Allāh as Witness between me and you. Indeed He is ever, concerning His servants, Aware and Seeing."

(97) And whoever Allāh guides - he is the [rightly] guided; and whoever He sends astray[758] - you will never find for them protectors besides Him, and We will gather them on the Day of Resurrection [fallen] on their faces - blind, dumb and deaf. Their refuge is Hell; every time it subsides, We increase [for] them blazing fire.

(98) That is their recompense because they disbelieved in Our verses and said, "When we are bones and crumbled particles, will we [truly] be resurrected [in] a new creation?"

(99) Do they not see that Allāh, who created the heavens and earth, is [the one] Able to create the likes of them? And He has appointed for them a term, about which there is no doubt. But the wrongdoers refuse except disbelief.

(100) Say [to them], "If you possessed the depositories of the mercy of my Lord, then you would withhold out of fear of spending." And ever has man been stingy.

(101) And We had certainly given Moses nine evident signs, so ask the Children of Israel [about] when he came to them and Pharaoh said to him, "Indeed I think, O Moses, that you are affected by magic."

---

[757] i.e., who were settled and established there, as is man.
[758] As a result of his own preference.

(102) [Moses] said, "You have already known that none has sent down these [signs] except the Lord of the heavens and the earth as evidence, and indeed I think,[759] O Pharaoh, that you are destroyed."

(103) So he intended to drive them from the land, but We drowned him and those with him all together.

(104) And We said after him [i.e., Pharaoh] to the Children of Israel, "Dwell in the land, and when there comes the promise [i.e., appointment] of the Hereafter, We will bring you forth in [one] gathering."

(105) And with the truth We have sent it [i.e., the Qur'ān] down, and with the truth it has descended. And We have not sent you, [O Muḥammad], except as a bringer of good tidings and a warner.

(106) And [it is] a Qur'ān which We have separated [by intervals] that you might recite it to the people over a prolonged period. And We have sent it down progressively.

(107) Say, "Believe in it or do not believe." Indeed, those who were given knowledge before it[760] - when it is recited to them, they fall upon their faces in prostration,

(108) And they say, "Exalted is our Lord! Indeed, the promise of our Lord has been fulfilled."

(109) And they fall upon their faces weeping, and it [i.e., the Qur'ān] increases them in humble submission.

(110) Say, "Call upon Allāh or call upon the Most Merciful [ar-Raḥmān]. Whichever [name] you call - to Him belong the best names." And do not recite [too] loudly in your prayer or [too] quietly but seek between that an [intermediate] way.

(111) And say, "Praise to Allāh, who has not taken a son and has had no partner in [His] dominion and has no [need of a] protector out of weakness; and glorify Him with [great] glorification."

---

[759] i.e., I am certain.

[760] i.e., the righteous among the People of the Scriptures who recognize the truth contained in the Qur'ān.

Surah Al-Kahf

(1) [All] praise is [due] to Allāh, who has sent down upon His Servant [Muḥammad (ﷺ)] the Book and has not made therein any deviance.[761]

(2) [He has made it] straight, to warn of severe punishment from Him and to give good tidings to the believers who do righteous deeds that they will have a good reward [i.e., Paradise].

(3) In which they will remain forever

(4) And to warn those who say, "Allāh has taken a son".

(5) They have no knowledge of it,[762] nor had their fathers. Grave is the word that comes out of their mouths; they speak not except a lie.

(6) Then perhaps you would kill yourself through grief over them, [O Muḥammad], if they do not believe in this message, [and] out of sorrow.

(7) Indeed, We have made that which is on the earth adornment for it that We may test them [as to] which of them is best in deed.

(8) And indeed, We will make that which is upon it [into] a barren ground.

(9) Or have you thought that the companions of the cave and the inscription were, among Our signs, a wonder?[763]

(10) [Mention] when the youths retreated to the cave and said, "Our Lord, grant us from Yourself mercy and prepare for us from our affair right guidance."

(11) So We cast [a cover of sleep] over their ears within the cave for a number of years.

(12) Then We awakened them that We might show which of the two factions was most precise in calculating what [extent] they had remained in time.

(13) It is We who relate to you, [O Muḥammad], their story in truth. Indeed, they were youths who believed in their Lord, and We increased them in guidance.

---

[761] From the truth or the straight path.

[762] i.e., they could not have had knowledge of something which is not true.

[763] Rather, it is only one of the many wonders of Allāh.

(14) And We bound [i.e., made firm] their hearts when they stood up and said, "Our Lord is the Lord of the heavens and the earth. Never will we invoke besides Him any deity. We would have certainly spoken, then, an excessive transgression.

(15) These, our people, have taken besides Him deities. Why do they not bring for [worship of] them a clear evidence? And who is more unjust than one who invents about Allāh a lie?"

(16) [The youths said to one another], "And when you have withdrawn from them and that which they worship other than Allāh, retreat to the cave. Your Lord will spread out for you of His mercy and will prepare for you from your affair facility."

(17) And [had you been present], you would see the sun when it rose, inclining away from their cave on the right, and when it set, passing away from them on the left, while they were [lying] within an open space thereof. That was from the signs of Allāh. He whom Allāh guides is the [rightly] guided, but he whom He sends astray - never will you find for him a protecting guide.

(18) And you would think them awake, while they were asleep. And We turned them to the right and to the left, while their dog stretched his forelegs at the entrance. If you had looked at them, you would have turned from them in flight and been filled by them with terror.

(19) And similarly,[764] We awakened them that they might question one another. Said a speaker from among them, "How long have you remained [here]?" They said, "We have remained a day or part of a day." They said, "Your Lord is most knowing of how long you remained. So send one of you with this silver coin of yours to the city and let him look to which is the best of food and bring you provision from it and let him be cautious. And let no one be aware of you.

(20) Indeed, if they come to know of you, they will stone you or return you to their religion. And never would you succeed, then - ever."

(21) And similarly, We caused them to be found that they [who found them] would know that the promise of Allāh is truth and that of the Hour there is no doubt. [That was] when they[765] disputed among themselves about their affair and [then] said, "Construct over them a structure. Their Lord is most knowing about them." Said those who prevailed in the matter, "We will surely take [for ourselves] over them a masjid."[766]

---

[764] By the will of Allāh.
[765] "The people of the city.
[766] i.e., we will make this site a place of worship."

(22) They [i.e., people] will say there were three, the fourth of them being their dog; and they will say there were five, the sixth of them being their dog - guessing at the unseen; and they will say there were seven, and the eighth of them was their dog. Say, [O Muḥammad], "My Lord is most knowing of their number. None knows them except a few. So do not argue about them except with an obvious argument[767] and do not inquire about them among [the speculators] from anyone."

(23) And never say of anything, "Indeed, I will do that tomorrow,"

(24) Except [when adding], "If Allāh wills." And remember your Lord when you forget [it] and say, "Perhaps my Lord will guide me to what is nearer than this to right conduct."

(25) And they remained in their cave for three hundred years and exceeded by nine.[768]

(26) Say, "Allāh is most knowing of how long they remained. He has [knowledge of] the unseen [aspects] of the heavens and the earth. How Seeing is He and how Hearing! They have not besides Him any protector, and He shares not His legislation with anyone."

(27) And recite, [O Muḥammad], what has been revealed to you of the Book of your Lord. There is no changer of His words, and never will you find in other than Him a refuge.

(28) And keep yourself patient [by being] with those who call upon their Lord in the morning and the evening, seeking His face [i.e., acceptance]. And let not your eyes pass beyond them, desiring adornments of the worldly life, and do not obey one whose heart We have made heedless of Our remembrance and who follows his desire and whose affair is ever [in] neglect.[769]

(29) And say, "The truth is from your Lord, so whoever wills - let him believe; and whoever wills - let him disbelieve." Indeed, We have prepared for the wrongdoers a fire whose walls will surround them. And if they call for relief, they will be relieved with water like murky oil, which scalds [their] faces. Wretched is the drink, and evil is the resting place.

(30) Indeed, those who have believed and done righteous deeds - indeed, We will not allow to be lost the reward of any who did well in deeds.

---

[767] i.e., one from the Qur'ān, which is the only sure argument.
[768] i.e., 309 lunar years.
[769] Or "in excess," exceeding the limits of Allāh.

(31) Those will have gardens of perpetual residence; beneath them rivers will flow. They will be adorned therein with bracelets of gold and will wear green garments of fine silk and brocade, reclining therein on adorned couches. Excellent is the reward, and good is the resting place.

(32) And present to them an example of two men: We granted to one of them two gardens of grapevines, and We bordered them with palm trees and placed between them [fields of] crops.

(33) Each of the two gardens produced its fruit and did not fall short thereof in anything. And We caused to gush forth within them a river.

(34) And he had fruit, so he said to his companion while he was conversing with him, "I am greater than you in wealth and mightier in [numbers of] men."

(35) And he entered his garden while he was unjust to himself.[770] He said, "I do not think that this will perish - ever.

(36) And I do not think the Hour will occur. And even if I should be brought back to my Lord, I will surely find better than this as a return."

(37) His companion said to him while he was conversing with him, "Have you disbelieved in He who created you from dust and then from a sperm-drop and then proportioned you [as] a man?

(38) But as for me, He is Allāh, my Lord, and I do not associate with my Lord anyone.

(39) And why did you, when you entered your garden, not say, 'What Allāh willed [has occurred]; there is no power except in Allāh'? Although you see me less than you in wealth and children,

(40) It may be that my Lord will give me [something] better than your garden and will send upon it a [disastrous] penalty from the sky, and it will become a smooth, dusty ground,

(41) Or its water will become sunken [into the earth], so you would never be able to seek it."

(42) And his fruits were encompassed [by ruin], so he began to turn his hands about [in dismay] over what he had spent on it, while it had collapsed upon its trellises, and said, "Oh, I wish I had not associated with my Lord anyone."[771]

---

[770] i.e., proud and ungrateful to Allāh.

[771] He attributed his prosperity to himself rather than to Allāh and disbelieved in the account of the Hereafter.

(43) And there was for him no company to aid him other than Allāh, nor could he defend himself.

(44) There[772] the authority is [completely] for Allāh, the Truth. He is best in reward and best in outcome.

(45) And present to them the example of the life of this world, [its being] like rain which We send down from the sky, and the vegetation of the earth mingles with it[773] and [then] it becomes dry remnants, scattered by the winds. And Allāh is ever, over all things, Perfect in Ability.

(46) Wealth and children are [but] adornment of the worldly life. But the enduring good deeds are better to your Lord[774] for reward and better for [one's] hope.

(47) And [warn of] the Day when We will remove the mountains and you will see the earth exposed,[775] and We will gather them and not leave behind from them anyone.

(48) And they will be presented before your Lord in rows, [and He will say], "You have certainly come to Us just as We created you the first time. But you claimed that We would never make for you an appointment."

(49) And the record [of deeds] will be placed [open], and you will see the criminals fearful of that within it, and they will say, "Oh, woe to us! What is this book that leaves nothing small or great except that it has enumerated it?" And they will find what they did present [before them]. And your Lord does injustice to no one.

(50) And [mention] when We said to the angels, "Prostrate to Adam," and they prostrated, except for Iblees. He was of the jinn and departed from [i.e., disobeyed] the command of his Lord. Then will you take him and his descendants as allies other than Me while they are enemies to you? Wretched it is for the wrongdoers as an exchange.

(51) I did not make them witness to the creation of the heavens and the earth or to the creation of themselves, and I would not have taken the misguiders as assistants.

---

[772] i.e., at such a time or on the Day of Judgement.
[773] Absorbs it, growing lush and thick.
[774] i.e., in His sight or evaluation.
[775] i.e., flattened and bare.

(52) And [warn of] the Day when He will say, "Call My 'partners' whom you claimed," and they will invoke them, but they will not respond to them. And We will put between them [a valley of] destruction.

(53) And the criminals will see the Fire and will be certain that they are to fall therein. And they will not find from it a way elsewhere.

(54) And We have certainly diversified in this Qur'ān for the people from every [kind of] example; but man has ever been, most of anything, [prone to] dispute.

(55) And nothing has prevented the people from believing when guidance came to them and from asking forgiveness of their Lord except that there [must] befall them the [accustomed] precedent of the former peoples[776] or that the punishment should come [directly] before them.

(56) And We send not the messengers except as bringers of good tidings and warners. And those who disbelieve dispute by [using] falsehood to [attempt to] invalidate thereby the truth and have taken My verses, and that of which they are warned, in ridicule.

(57) And who is more unjust than one who is reminded of the verses of his Lord but turns away from them and forgets what his hands have put forth? Indeed, We have placed over their hearts coverings, lest they understand it, and in their ears deafness. And if you invite them to guidance - they will never be guided, then - ever.

(58) And your Lord is the Forgiving, the possessor of mercy. If He were to impose blame upon them for what they earned, He would have hastened for them the punishment. Rather, for them is an appointment from which they will never find an escape.

(59) And those cities - We destroyed them when they wronged, and We made for their destruction an appointed time.

(60) And [mention] when Moses said to his boy [i.e., servant], "I will not cease [traveling] until I reach the junction of the two seas or continue for a long period."

(61) But when they reached the junction between them, they forgot their fish, and it took its course into the sea, slipping away.

(62) So when they had passed beyond it, [Moses] said to his boy, "Bring us our morning meal. We have certainly suffered in this, our journey, [much] fatigue."

---

[776] Who denied the truth brought by Allāh's messengers.

(63) He said, "Did you see when we retired to the rock? Indeed, I forgot [there] the fish. And none made me forget it except Satan - that I should mention it. And it took its course into the sea amazingly."

(64) [Moses] said, "That is what we were seeking." So they returned, following their footprints.

(65) And they found a servant from among Our servants [i.e., al-Khiḍr] to whom We had given mercy from Us and had taught him from Us a [certain] knowledge.

(66) Moses said to him, "May I follow you on [the condition] that you teach me from what you have been taught of sound judgement?"

(67) He said, "Indeed, with me you will never be able to have patience.

(68) And how can you have patience for what you do not encompass in knowledge?"

(69) [Moses] said, "You will find me, if Allāh wills, patient, and I will not disobey you in [any] order."

(70) He said, "Then if you follow me, do not ask me about anything until I make to you about it mention [i.e., explanation]."

(71) So they set out, until when they had embarked on the ship, he [i.e., al-Khiḍr] tore it open. [Moses] said, "Have you torn it open to drown its people? You have certainly done a grave thing."

(72) [Al-Khiḍr] said, "Did I not say that with me you would never be able to have patience?"

(73) [Moses] said, "Do not blame me for what I forgot and do not overwhelm me in my matter with difficulty."

(74) So they set out, until when they met a boy, he [i.e., al-Khiḍr] killed him. [Moses] said, "Have you killed a pure soul for other than [having killed] a soul? You have certainly done a deplorable thing."

(75) [Al-Khiḍr] said, "Did I not tell you that with me you would never be able to have patience?"

(76) [Moses] said, "If I should ask you about anything after this, then do not keep me as a companion. You have obtained from me an excuse."

(77) So they set out, until when they came to the people of a town, they asked its people for food, but they refused to offer them hospitality. And they found therein

a wall about to collapse, so he [i.e., al-Khiḍr] restored it. [Moses] said, "If you wished, you could have taken for it a payment."

(78) [Al-Khiḍr] said, "This is parting between me and you. I will inform you of the interpretation of that about which you could not have patience.

(79) As for the ship, it belonged to poor people working at sea. So I intended to cause defect in it as there was after them a king who seized every [good] ship by force.

(80) And as for the boy, his parents were believers, and we feared that he would overburden them by transgression and disbelief.

(81) So we intended that their Lord should substitute for them one better than him in purity and nearer to mercy.

(82) And as for the wall, it belonged to two orphan boys in the city, and there was beneath it a treasure for them, and their father had been righteous. So your Lord intended that they reach maturity and extract their treasure, as a mercy from your Lord. And I did it not of my own accord. That is the interpretation of that about which you could not have patience."

(83) And they ask you, [O Muḥammad], about Dhul-Qarnayn. Say, "I will recite to you about him a report."

(84) Indeed, We established him upon the earth, and We gave him from everything a way [i.e., means].

(85) So he followed a way

(86) Until, when he reached the setting of the sun [i.e., the west], he found it [as if] setting in a body of dark water,[777] and he found near it a people. We [i.e., Allāh] said, "O Dhul-Qarnayn, either you punish [them] or else adopt among them [a way of] goodness."

(87) He said, "As for one who wrongs,[778] we will punish him. Then he will be returned to his Lord, and He will punish him with a terrible punishment [i.e., Hellfire].

(88) But as for one who believes and does righteousness, he will have a reward of the best [i.e., Paradise], and we [i.e., Dhul-Qarnayn] will speak to him from our command with ease."

---

[777] Another meaning is "a body of hot water.
[778] Persists in disbelief and rebellion.

(89) Then he followed a way

(90) Until, when he came to the rising of the sun [i.e., the east], he found it rising on a people for whom We had not made against it any shield.

(91) Thus.[779] And We had encompassed [all] that he had in knowledge.

(92) Then he followed a way.

(93) Until, when he reached [a pass] between two mountains, he found beside them a people who could hardly understand [his] speech.

(94) They said, "O Dhul-Qarnayn, indeed Gog and Magog[780] are [great] corrupters in the land. So may we assign for you an expenditure that you might make between us and them a barrier?"

(95) He said, "That in which my Lord has established me is better [than what you offer], but assist me with strength [i.e., manpower]; I will make between you and them a dam.

(96) Bring me bars of iron" - until, when he had leveled [them] between the two mountain walls, he said, "Blow [with bellows]," until when he had made it [like] fire, he said, "Bring me, that I may pour over it molten copper."

(97) So they [i.e., Gog and Magog] were unable to pass over it, nor were they able [to effect] in it any penetration.

(98) [Dhul-Qarnayn] said, "This is a mercy from my Lord; but when the promise of my Lord[781] comes [i.e., approaches], He will make it level, and ever is the promise of my Lord true."

(99) And We will leave them that day[782] surging over each other, and [then] the Horn will be blown, and We will assemble them in [one] assembly.

(100) And We will present Hell that Day to the disbelievers, on display -

---

[779] Such was the affair of Dhul-Qarnayn.

[780] Savage tribes who had ravaged large parts of central Asia, committing every kind of atrocity.
[781] i.e., the Hour of Resurrection.
[782] The day the dam is destroyed.

(101) Those whose eyes had been within a cover [removed] from My remembrance,[783] and they were not able to hear.[784]

(102) Then do those who disbelieve think that they can take My servants instead of Me as allies? Indeed, We have prepared Hell for the disbelievers as a lodging.

(103) Say, [O Muḥammad], "Shall we [believers] inform you of the greatest losers as to [their] deeds?

(104) [They are] those whose effort is lost in worldly life, while they think that they are doing well in work."

(105) Those are the ones who disbelieve in the verses of their Lord and in [their] meeting Him, so their deeds have become worthless; and We will not assign to them on the Day of Resurrection any weight [i.e., importance].

(106) That is their recompense - Hell - for what they denied and [because] they took My signs and My messengers in ridicule.

(107) Indeed, those who have believed and done righteous deeds - they will have the Gardens of Paradise[785] as a lodging,

(108) Wherein they abide eternally. They will not desire from it any transfer.

(109) Say, "If the sea were ink for [writing] the words[786] of my Lord, the sea would be exhausted before the words of my Lord were exhausted, even if We brought the like of it in [continual] supplement."

(110) Say, "I am only a man like you, to whom has been revealed that your god is one God. So whoever would hope for the meeting with his Lord - let him do righteous work and not associate in the worship of his Lord anyone."

---

[783] "i.e., Allāh's signs or the Qur'ān.

[784] They refused to listen to the Qur'ān or to understand it.

[785] i.e., the highest part of Paradise, al-Firdaus.

[786] The words of Allāh's unlimited knowledge or words describing His attributes and His grandeur or praise of Him (subḥānahu wa taʿālā).

Surah Maryam

(1) Kāf, Hā, Yā, ʿAyn, Ṣād.[787]

(2) [This is] a mention of the mercy of your Lord to His servant Zechariah

(3) When he called to his Lord a private call [i.e., supplication].

(4) He said, "My Lord, indeed my bones have weakened, and my head has filled[788] with white, and never have I been in my supplication to You, my Lord, unhappy [i.e., disappointed].

(5) And indeed, I fear the successors[789] after me, and my wife has been barren, so give me from Yourself an heir

(6) Who will inherit me[790] and inherit from the family of Jacob. And make him, my Lord, pleasing [to You]."

(7) [He was told],[791] "O Zechariah, indeed We give you good tidings of a boy whose name will be John. We have not assigned to any before [this] name."

(8) He said, "My Lord, how will I have a boy when my wife has been barren and I have reached extreme old age?"

(9) [An angel] said, "Thus [it will be]; your Lord says, 'It is easy for Me, for I created you before, while you were nothing.'"

(10) [Zechariah] said, "My Lord, make for me a sign." He said, "Your sign is that you will not speak to the people for three nights, [being] sound."[792]

(11) So he came out to his people from the prayer chamber and signaled to them to exalt [Allāh] in the morning and afternoon.

(12) [Allāh said], "O John, take the Scripture [i.e., adhere to it] with determination." And We gave him judgement [while yet] a boy

(13) And affection from Us and purity, and he was fearing of Allāh

---

[787] See footnote to 2:1

[788] Literally, "ignited." The spread of white hair throughout the head is likened to that of fire in the bush.

[789] Those relatives from the father's side who would inherit religious authority

[790] Inherit from me religious knowledge and prophethood.

[791] By Allāh (subḥānahu wa taʿālā) through the angels.

[792] i.e., without illness or defect.

(14) And dutiful to his parents, and he was not a disobedient tyrant.

(15) And peace be upon him the day he was born and the day he dies and the day he is raised alive.

(16) And mention, [O Muḥammad], in the Book [the story of] Mary, when she withdrew from her family to a place toward the east.

(17) And she took, in seclusion from them, a screen. Then We sent to her Our Angel [i.e., Gabriel], and he represented himself to her as a well-proportioned man.

(18) She said, "Indeed, I seek refuge in the Most Merciful from you, [so leave me], if you should be fearing of Allāh."

(19) He said, "I am only the messenger of your Lord to give you [news of] a pure boy [i.e., son]."

(20) She said, "How can I have a boy while no man has touched me and I have not been unchaste?"

(21) He said, "Thus [it will be]; your Lord says, 'It is easy for Me, and We will make him a sign to the people and a mercy from Us. And it is a matter [already] decreed.'"

(22) So she conceived him, and she withdrew with him to a remote place.

(23) And the pains of childbirth drove her to the trunk of a palm tree. She said, "Oh, I wish I had died before this and was in oblivion, forgotten."

(24) But he[793] called her from below her, "Do not grieve; your Lord has provided beneath you a stream.

(25) And shake toward you the trunk of the palm tree; it will drop upon you ripe, fresh dates.

(26) So eat and drink and be contented. And if you see from among humanity anyone, say, 'Indeed, I have vowed to the Most Merciful abstention, so I will not speak today to [any] man.'"

(27) Then she brought him to her people, carrying him. They said, "O Mary, you have certainly done a thing unprecedented.

---

[793] There is a difference of opinion among scholars as to whether "he" refers to the baby or to the angel.

(28) O sister [i.e., descendant] of Aaron, your father was not a man of evil, nor was your mother unchaste."

(29) So she pointed to him. They said, "How can we speak to one who is in the cradle a child?"

(30) [Jesus] said, "Indeed, I am the servant of Allāh. He has given me the Scripture and made me a prophet.

(31) And He has made me blessed wherever I am and has enjoined upon me prayer and zakāh as long as I remain alive

(32) And [made me] dutiful to my mother, and He has not made me a wretched tyrant.

(33) And peace is on me the day I was born and the day I will die and the day I am raised alive."

(34) That is Jesus, the son of Mary - the word of truth about which they are in dispute.

(35) It is not [befitting] for Allāh to take a son; exalted is He![794] When He decrees an affair, He only says to it, "Be," and it is.

(36) [Jesus said], "And indeed, Allāh is my Lord and your Lord, so worship Him. That is a straight path."

(37) Then the factions differed [concerning Jesus] from among them, so woe to those who disbelieved - from the scene of a tremendous Day.

(38) How [clearly] they will hear and see the Day they come to Us, but the wrongdoers today are in clear error.

(39) And warn them, [O Muḥammad], of the Day of Regret, when the matter will be concluded;[795] and [yet], they are in [a state of] heedlessness, and they do not believe.

(40) Indeed, it is We who will inherit the earth and whoever is on it, and to Us they will be returned.

(41) And mention in the Book [the story of] Abraham. Indeed, he was a man of truth and a prophet.

---

[794] i.e., far removed is He from any such need.
[795] i.e., "judged" or "accomplished."

(42) [Mention] when he said to his father, "O my father, why do you worship that which does not hear and does not see and will not benefit you at all?

(43) O my father, indeed there has come to me of knowledge that which has not come to you, so follow me; I will guide you to an even path.

(44) O my father, do not worship [i.e., obey] Satan. Indeed Satan has ever been, to the Most Merciful, disobedient.

(45) O my father, indeed I fear that there will touch you a punishment from the Most Merciful so you would be to Satan a companion [in Hellfire]."

(46) [His father] said, "Have you no desire for my gods, O Abraham? If you do not desist, I will surely stone you, so avoid me a prolonged time."

(47) [Abraham] said, "Peace [i.e., safety] will be upon you.[796] I will ask forgiveness for you of my Lord. Indeed, He is ever gracious to me.

(48) And I will leave you and those you invoke other than Allāh and will invoke[797] my Lord. I expect that I will not be in invocation to my Lord unhappy [i.e., disappointed]."

(49) So when he had left them and those they worshipped other than Allāh, We gave him Isaac and Jacob, and each [of them] We made a prophet.

(50) And We gave them of Our mercy, and We made for them a mention [i.e., reputation] of high honor.

(51) And mention in the Book, Moses. Indeed, he was chosen, and he was a messenger and a prophet.[798]

(52) And We called him from the side of the mount[799] at [his] right and brought him near, confiding [to him].

(53) And We gave him out of Our mercy his brother Aaron as a prophet.

(54) And mention in the Book, Ishmael. Indeed, he was true to his promise, and he was a messenger and a prophet.

---

[796] Meaning "You are secure" or "I will not harm you."

[797] i.e., worship.

[798] A messenger (rasūl) is one who was charged by Allāh to reform society. A prophet (nabī) is one who received revelation from Allāh, the latter being more numerous than the former.

[799] Mount Sinai.

(55) And he used to enjoin on his people prayer and zakāh and was to his Lord pleasing [i.e., accepted by Him].

(56) And mention in the Book, Idrees. Indeed, he was a man of truth and a prophet.

(57) And We raised him to a high station.

(58) Those were the ones upon whom Allāh bestowed favor from among the prophets of the descendants of Adam and of those We carried [in the ship] with Noah, and of the descendants of Abraham and Israel [i.e., Jacob], and of those whom We guided and chose. When the verses of the Most Merciful were recited to them, they fell in prostration and weeping.

(59) But there came after them successors [i.e., later generations] who neglected prayer and pursued desires; so they are going to meet evil[800] -

(60) Except those who repent, believe and do righteousness; for those will enter Paradise and will not be wronged at all.

(61) [Therein are] gardens of perpetual residence which the Most Merciful has promised His servants in the unseen. Indeed, His promise has ever been eminent.[801]

(62) They will not hear therein any ill speech - only [greetings of] peace - and they will have their provision therein, morning and afternoon.

(63) That is Paradise, which We give as inheritance to those of Our servants who were fearing of Allāh.

(64) [Gabriel said],[802] "And we [angels] descend not except by the order of your Lord. To Him belongs that before us and that behind us and what is in between. And never is your Lord forgetful -

(65) Lord of the heavens and the earth and whatever is between them - so worship Him and have patience for His worship. Do you know of any similarity to Him?"

(66) And man [i.e., the disbeliever] says, "When I have died, am I going to be brought forth alive?"

(67) Does man not remember that We created him before, while he was nothing?

---

[800] Described as a valley in Hell or may be rendered "the consequence of error.
[801] Literally, "that to which all will come."

[802] In answer to the Prophet's wish that Gabriel would visit him more often

(68) So by your Lord, We will surely gather them and the devils; then We will bring them to be present around Hell upon their knees.[803]

(69) Then We will surely extract from every sect those of them who were worst against the Most Merciful in insolence.

(70) Then, surely it is We who are most knowing of those most worthy of burning therein.

(71) And there is none of you except he will come to it.[804] This is upon your Lord an inevitability decreed.

(72) Then We will save those who feared Allāh and leave the wrongdoers within it, on their knees.

(73) And when Our verses are recited to them as clear evidences, those who disbelieve say to those who believe, "Which of [our] two parties is best in position and best in association?"[805]

(74) And how many a generation have We destroyed before them who were better in possessions and [outward] appearance?

(75) Say, "Whoever is in error - let the Most Merciful extend for him an extension [in wealth and time] until, when they see that which they were promised - either punishment [in this world] or the Hour [of resurrection] - they will come to know who is worst in position and weaker in soldiers."

(76) And Allāh increases those who were guided, in guidance, and the enduring good deeds are better to your Lord[806] for reward and better for recourse.

(77) Then, have you seen he who disbelieved in Our verses and said, "I will surely be given wealth and children [in the next life]"?

(78) Has he looked into the unseen, or has he taken from the Most Merciful a promise?

(79) No! We will record what he says and extend [i.e., increase] for him from the punishment extensively.

---

[803] i.e., fallen on their knees from terror or dragged there unwillingly on their knees.
[804] i.e., be exposed to it. However, the people of Paradise will not be harmed thereby.

[805] In regard to worldly interests.
[806] i.e., in the sight or evaluation of Allāh.

(80) And We will inherit him [in] what he mentions,[807] and he will come to Us alone.

(81) And they have taken besides Allāh [false] deities that they would be for them [a source of] honor.

(82) No! They [i.e., those "gods"] will deny their worship of them and will be against them opponents [on the Day of Judgement].

(83) Do you not see that We have sent the devils upon the disbelievers, inciting them [to evil] with [constant] incitement?

(84) So be not impatient over them. We only count out [i.e., allow] to them a [limited] number.[808]

(85) On the Day We will gather the righteous to the Most Merciful as a delegation

(86) And will drive the criminals to Hell in thirst

(87) None will have [power of] intercession except he who had taken from the Most Merciful a covenant.[809]

(88) And they say, "The Most Merciful has taken [for Himself] a son."

(89) You have done an atrocious thing.

(90) The heavens almost rupture therefrom and the earth splits open and the mountains collapse in devastation

(91) That they attribute to the Most Merciful a son.

(92) And it is not appropriate for the Most Merciful that He should take a son.

(93) There is no one in the heavens and earth but that he comes to the Most Merciful as a servant.

(94) He has enumerated them and counted them a [full] counting.

(95) And all of them are coming to Him on the Day of Resurrection alone.

---

[807] Instead of giving him wealth and children in the Hereafter, Allāh will take from him those he had in worldly life at the time of his death.

[808] Of breaths, of days, or of evil deeds.
[809] Not to worship other than Him.

(96) Indeed, those who have believed and done righteous deeds - the Most Merciful will appoint for them affection.[810]

(97) So, [O Muḥammad], We have only made it [i.e., the Qur'ān] easy in your tongue [i.e., the Arabic language] that you may give good tidings thereby to the righteous and warn thereby a hostile people.

(98) And how many have We destroyed before them of generations? Do you perceive of them anyone or hear from them a sound?

---

[810] From Himself and from among each other.

Surah Ta-Ha

(1) Ṭā, Hā.[811]

(2) We have not sent down to you the Qur'ān that you be distressed

(3) But only as a reminder for those who fear [Allāh] -

(4) A revelation from He who created the earth and highest heavens,

(5) The Most Merciful [who is] above the Throne established.[812]

(6) To Him belongs what is in the heavens and what is on the earth and what is between them and what is under the soil.

(7) And if you speak aloud - then indeed, He knows the secret and what is [even] more hidden.

(8) Allāh - there is no deity except Him. To Him belong the best names.

(9) And has the story of Moses reached you? -

(10) When he saw a fire and said to his family, "Stay here; indeed, I have perceived a fire; perhaps I can bring you a torch or find at the fire some guidance."

(11) And when he came to it, he was called, "O Moses,

(12) Indeed, I am your Lord, so remove your sandals. Indeed, you are in the blessed valley of Ṭuwā.

(13) And I have chosen you, so listen to what is revealed [to you].

(14) Indeed, I am Allāh. There is no deity except Me, so worship Me and establish prayer for My remembrance.

(15) Indeed, the Hour is coming - I almost conceal it[813] - so that every soul may be recompensed according to that for which it strives.

(16) So do not let one avert you from it[814] who does not believe in it and follows his desire, for you [then] would perish.

---

[811] See footnote to 2:1

[812] i.e., having ascendancy over all creation. See footnotes to 2:19 and 7:54

[813] Meaning that Allāh (subḥānahu wa taʿālā) keeps knowledge of the Hour hidden from everyone except Himself.

[814] From preparation for the Hour or for the Hereafter.

(17) And what is that in your right hand, O Moses?"

(18) He said, "It is my staff; I lean upon it, and I bring down leaves for my sheep and I have therein other uses."

(19) [Allāh] said, "Throw it down, O Moses."

(20) So he threw it down, and thereupon it was a snake, moving swiftly.

(21) [Allāh] said, "Seize it and fear not; We will return it to its former condition.

(22) And draw in your hand to your side; it will come out white without disease - another sign,

(23) That We may show you [some] of Our greater signs.

(24) Go to Pharaoh. Indeed, he has transgressed [i.e., tyrannized]."

(25) [Moses] said, "My Lord, expand [i.e., relax] for me my breast [with assurance]

(26) And ease for me my task

(27) And untie the knot from my tongue

(28) That they may understand my speech.

(29) And appoint for me a minister [i.e., assistant] from my family -

(30) Aaron, my brother.

(31) Increase through him my strength

(32) And let him share my task

(33) That we may exalt You much

(34) And remember You much.

(35) Indeed, You are of us ever Seeing."

(36) [Allāh] said, "You have been granted your request, O Moses.

(37) And We had already conferred favor upon you another time,

(38) When We inspired to your mother what We inspired,

(39) [Saying], 'Cast him into the chest and cast it into the river, and the river will throw it onto the bank; there will take him an enemy to Me and an enemy to him.'

And I bestowed upon you love from Me[815] that you would be brought up under My eye [i.e., observation and care].

(40) [And We favored you] when your sister went and said, 'Shall I direct you to someone who will be responsible for him?' So We restored you to your mother that she might be content and not grieve. And you killed someone,[816] but We saved you from retaliation and tried you with a [severe] trial. And you remained [some] years among the people of Madyan. Then you came [here] at the decreed time, O Moses.

(41) And I produced you for Myself.[817]

(42) Go, you and your brother, with My signs and do not slacken in My remembrance.

(43) Go, both of you, to Pharaoh. Indeed, he has transgressed.

(44) And speak to him with gentle speech that perhaps he may be reminded or fear [Allāh]."

(45) They said, "Our Lord, indeed we are afraid that he will hasten [punishment] against us or that he will transgress."

(46) [Allāh] said, "Fear not. Indeed, I am with you both; I hear and I see.

(47) So go to him and say, 'Indeed, we are messengers of your Lord, so send with us the Children of Israel and do not torment them. We have come to you with a sign from your Lord. And peace[818] will be upon he who follows the guidance.

(48) Indeed, it has been revealed to us that the punishment will be upon whoever denies and turns away.'"

(49) [Pharaoh] said, "So who is the Lord of you two, O Moses?"

(50) He said, "Our Lord is He who gave each thing its form and then guided [it]."

(51) [Pharaoh] said, "Then what is the case of the former generations?"

(52) [Moses] said, "The knowledge thereof is with my Lord in a record. My Lord neither errs nor forgets."

____

[815] Allāh put love of Moses into the hearts of the people.
[816] The Copt who died after being struck by Moses.
[817] Allāh had already selected Moses and made him strong in body and character according to the requirements of his mission.
[818] i.e., safety and security from Allāh's punishment.

(53) [It is He] who has made for you the earth as a bed [spread out] and inserted therein for you roadways and sent down from the sky, rain and produced thereby categories of various plants.

(54) Eat [therefrom] and pasture your livestock. Indeed in that are signs for those of intelligence.

(55) From it [i.e., the earth] We created you, and into it We will return you, and from it We will extract you another time.

(56) And We certainly showed him [i.e., Pharaoh] Our signs - all of them - but he denied and refused.

(57) He said, "Have you come to us to drive us out of our land with your magic, O Moses?

(58) Then we will surely bring you magic like it, so make between us and you an appointment, which we will not fail to keep and neither will you, in a place assigned."[819]

(59) [Moses] said, "Your appointment is on the day of the festival when the people assemble at mid-morning."[820]

(60) So Pharaoh went away, put together his plan, and then came [to Moses].

(61) Moses said to them [i.e., the magicians summoned by Pharaoh], "Woe to you! Do not invent a lie against Allāh or He will exterminate you with a punishment; and he has failed who invents [such falsehood]."

(62) So they disputed over their affair among themselves and concealed their private conversation.

(63) They said, "Indeed, these are two magicians who want to drive you out of your land with their magic and do away with your most exemplary way [i.e., religion or tradition].

(64) So resolve upon your plan and then come [forward] in line. And he has succeeded today who overcomes."

(65) They said, "O Moses, either you throw or we will be the first to throw."

---

[819] Literally, "marked," as to be known. Another meaning is "a place midway [between us]" or "a level place."
[820] So that the signs of Allāh would be seen clearly.

(66) He said, "Rather, you throw." And suddenly their ropes and staffs seemed to him from their magic that they were moving [like snakes].

(67) And he sensed within himself apprehension, did Moses.

(68) We [i.e., Allāh] said, "Fear not. Indeed, it is you who are superior.

(69) And throw what is in your right hand; it will swallow up what they have crafted. What they have crafted is but the trick of a magician, and the magician will not succeed wherever he is."

(70) So the magicians fell down in prostration.[821] They said, "We have believed in the Lord of Aaron and Moses."

(71) [Pharaoh] said, "You believed him [i.e., Moses] before I gave you permission. Indeed, he is your leader who has taught you magic. So I will surely cut off your hands and your feet on opposite sides, and I will crucify you on the trunks of palm trees, and you will surely know which of us is more severe in [giving] punishment and more enduring."

(72) They said, "Never will we prefer you over what has come to us of clear proofs and [over] He who created us.[822] So decree whatever you are to decree. You can only decree for this worldly life.

(73) Indeed, we have believed in our Lord that He may forgive us our sins and what you compelled us [to do] of magic. And Allāh is better and more enduring."[823]

(74) Indeed, whoever comes to his Lord as a criminal - indeed, for him is Hell; he will neither die therein nor live.

(75) But whoever comes to Him as a believer having done righteous deeds - for those will be the highest degrees [in position]:

(76) Gardens of perpetual residence beneath which rivers flow, wherein they abide eternally. And that is the reward of one who purifies himself.[824]

(77) And We had inspired to Moses, "Travel by night with My servants and strike for them a dry path through the sea; you will not fear being overtaken [by Pharaoh] nor be afraid [of drowning]."

---

[821] After they had seen the miracles which Allāh had given Moses and that they were realities and not merely impressions of magic.

[822] This phrase has also been interpreted as an oath, i.e., "...by Him who created us."

[823] In reward and in punishment.

[824] From all uncleanliness, the greatest of which is worship and obedience to other than Allāh.

(78) So Pharaoh pursued them with his soldiers, and there covered them from the sea that which covered them,[825]

(79) And Pharaoh led his people astray and did not guide [them].

(80) O Children of Israel, We delivered you from your enemy, and We made an appointment with you[826] at the right side of the mount, and We sent down to you manna and quails,

(81) [Saying], "Eat from the good things with which We have provided you and do not transgress [or oppress others] therein, lest My anger should descend upon you. And he upon whom My anger descends has certainly fallen [i.e., perished]."

(82) But indeed, I am the Perpetual Forgiver of whoever repents and believes and does righteousness and then continues in guidance.

(83) [Allāh said], "And what made you hasten from your people, O Moses?"

(84) He said, "They are close upon my tracks, and I hastened to You, my Lord, that You be pleased."

(85) [Allāh] said, "But indeed, We have tried your people after you [departed], and the Sāmirī[827] has led them astray."

(86) So Moses returned to his people, angry and grieved.[828] He said, "O my people, did your Lord not make you a good promise?[829] Then, was the time [of its fulfillment] too long for you, or did you wish that wrath from your Lord descend upon you, so you broke your promise [of obedience] to me?"

(87) They said, "We did not break our promise to you by our will, but we were made to carry burdens from the ornaments of the people [of Pharaoh], so we threw them [into the fire], and thus did the Sāmirī throw."

(88) And he extracted for them [the statue of] a calf which had a lowing sound, and they said, "This is your god and the god of Moses, but he forgot."

---

[825] i.e., not only the water but that which only Allāh knows - terror, pain, regret, etc.

[826] i.e., with your prophet, to receive the scripture for you.

[827] Translated as "the Samaritan" (from Samaria), a hypocrite among them who led the Children of Israel into idol-worship.

[828] "The meaning may also be "angry and enraged."

[829] That He would send down the Torah, containing guidance for you."

(89) Did they not see that it could not return to them any speech [i.e., response] and that it did not possess for them any harm or benefit?

(90) And Aaron had already told them before [the return of Moses], "O my people, you are only being tested by it, and indeed, your Lord is the Most Merciful, so follow me and obey my order."

(91) They said, "We will never cease being devoted to it [i.e., the calf] until Moses returns to us."

(92) [Moses] said, "O Aaron, what prevented you, when you saw them going astray,

(93) From following me? Then have you disobeyed my order?"

(94) [Aaron] said, "O son of my mother, do not seize [me] by my beard or by my head. Indeed, I feared that you would say, 'You caused division among the Children of Israel, and you did not observe [or await] my word.'"

(95) [Moses] said, "And what is your case, O Sāmirī?"

(96) He said, "I saw what they did not see, so I took a handful [of dust] from the track of the messenger[830] and threw it,[831] and thus did my soul entice me."

(97) [Moses] said, "Then go. And indeed, it is [decreed] for you in [this] life to say, 'No contact.'[832] And indeed, you have an appointment [in the Hereafter] you will not fail to keep. And look at your 'god' to which you remained devoted. We will surely burn it and blow it [i.e., its ashes] into the sea with a blast.

(98) Your god is only Allāh, except for whom there is no deity. He has encompassed all things in knowledge."

(99) Thus, [O Muḥammad], We relate to you from the news of what has preceded. And We have certainly given you from Us a message [i.e., the Qur'ān].

(100) Whoever turns away from it - then indeed, he will bear on the Day of Resurrection a burden [i.e., great sin],

---

[830] "i.e., a hoof-print in the sand left by the angel Gabriel's horse.

[831] Into the fire upon the melted ornaments in order to form the calf."
[832] i.e., Do not touch me. As chastisement, he was to be completely shunned by all people.

(101) [Abiding] eternally therein,[833] and evil it is for them on the Day of Resurrection as a load -

(102) The Day the Horn will be blown. And We will gather the criminals, that Day, blue-eyed.[834]

(103) They will murmur among themselves, "You remained not but ten [days in the world]."

(104) We are most knowing of what they say when the best of them in manner [i.e., wisdom or speech] will say, "You remained not but one day."

(105) And they ask you about the mountains, so say, "My Lord will blow them away with a blast.[835]

(106) And He will leave it [i.e., the earth] a level plain;

(107) You will not see therein a depression or an elevation."

(108) That Day, they [i.e., everyone] will follow [the call of] the Caller[836] [with] no deviation therefrom, and [all] voices will be stilled before the Most Merciful, so you will not hear except a whisper [of footsteps].

(109) That Day, no intercession will benefit except [that of] one to whom the Most Merciful has given permission and has accepted his word.

(110) He [i.e., Allāh] knows what is [presently] before them and what will be after them,[837] but they do not encompass it [i.e., what He knows] in knowledge.

(111) And [all] faces will be humbled before the Ever-Living, the Self-Sustaining.[838] And he will have failed who carries injustice.[839]

(112) But he who does of righteous deeds while he is a believer - he will neither fear injustice nor deprivation.

---

[833] i.e., in the state of sin.
[834] From terror, or blinded completely.
[835] Once they have been reduced to dust.
[836] To the gathering for judgement.
[837] See footnote to 2:255.
[838] "See footnotes to 2:255.
[839] i.e., sin or wrongdoing towards Allāh or any of His creation."

(113) And thus We have sent it down as an Arabic Qur'ān[840] and have diversified therein the warnings that perhaps they will avoid [sin] or it would cause them remembrance.

(114) So high [above all] is Allāh, the Sovereign,[841] the Truth.[842] And, [O Muḥammad], do not hasten with [recitation of] the Qur'ān before its revelation is completed to you, and say, "My Lord, increase me in knowledge."

(115) And We had already taken a promise from Adam before, but he forgot; and We found not in him determination.[843]

(116) And [mention] when We said to the angels, "Prostrate to Adam," and they prostrated, except Iblees;[844] he refused.

(117) So We said, "O Adam, indeed this is an enemy to you and to your wife. Then let him not remove you from Paradise so you would suffer.

(118) Indeed, it is [promised] for you not to be hungry therein or be unclothed.

(119) And indeed, you will not be thirsty therein or be hot from the sun."

(120) Then Satan whispered to him; he said, "O Adam, shall I direct you to the tree of eternity and possession that will not deteriorate?"

(121) And they [i.e., Adam and his wife] ate of it, and their private parts became apparent to them, and they began to fasten over themselves from the leaves of Paradise. And Adam disobeyed his Lord and erred.

(122) Then his Lord chose him and turned to him in forgiveness and guided [him].

(123) [Allāh] said, "Descend from it [i.e., Paradise] - all, [your descendants] being enemies to one another. And if there should come to you guidance from Me - then whoever follows My guidance will neither go astray [in the world] nor suffer [in the Hereafter].

---

[840] i.e., revealed in the Arabic language.

[841] "And owner of everything in existence.

[842] Or "the True Reality," i.e., the real and permanent existence upon which all other existence depends."

[843] To resist temptation.

[844] See footnote to 2:34.

(124) And whoever turns away from My remembrance - indeed, he will have a depressed [i.e., difficult] life, and We will gather [i.e., raise] him on the Day of Resurrection blind."

(125) He will say, "My Lord, why have you raised me blind while I was [once] seeing?"

(126) [Allāh] will say, "Thus did Our signs come to you, and you forgot [i.e., disregarded] them; and thus will you this Day be forgotten."

(127) And thus do We recompense he who transgressed and did not believe in the signs of his Lord. And the punishment of the Hereafter is more severe and more enduring.[845]

(128) Then, has it not become clear to them how many generations We destroyed before them as they walk among their dwellings? Indeed in that are signs for those of intelligence.

(129) And if not for a word[846] that preceded from your Lord, it [i.e., punishment] would have been an obligation [due immediately],[847] and [if not for] a specified term [decreed].

(130) So be patient over what they say and exalt [Allāh] with praise of your Lord before the rising of the sun and before its setting; and during periods of the night [exalt Him] and at the ends of the day, that you may be satisfied.

(131) And do not extend your eyes toward that by which We have given enjoyment to [some] categories of them, [its being but] the splendor of worldly life by which We test them. And the provision of your Lord is better and more enduring.

(132) And enjoin prayer upon your family [and people] and be steadfast therein. We ask you not for provision; We provide for you, and the [best] outcome is for [those of] righteousness.

(133) And they say, "Why does he not bring us a sign from his Lord?" Has there not come to them evidence of what was in the former scriptures?[848]

---

[845] Than that of this world.

[846] "See footnote to 10:19.

[847] Allāh would have punished the disbelievers in this world as He did with previous peoples."

[848] Is not the Qur'ān an adequate proof of Muḥammad's prophethood and sufficient as a lasting miracle?

(134) And if We had destroyed them with a punishment before him,[849] they would have said, "Our Lord, why did You not send to us a messenger so we could have followed Your verses [i.e., teachings] before we were humiliated and disgraced?"

(135) Say, "Each [of us] is waiting;[850] so wait. For you will know who are the companions of the sound path and who is guided."

---

[849] Prophet Muḥammad (ﷺ). Also interpreted as "before it," i.e., the Qur'ān.
[850] For the outcome of this matter.

Surah Al-Anbiya'

(1) [The time of] their account has approached for the people, while they are in heedlessness turning away.

(2) No mention [i.e., revelation] comes to them anew from their Lord except that they listen to it while they are at play

(3) With their hearts distracted. And those who do wrong conceal their private conversation, [saying], "Is this [Prophet] except a human being like you? So would you approach magic while you are aware [of it]?"

(4) He [the Prophet (ﷺ)] said, "My Lord knows whatever is said throughout the heaven and earth, and He is the Hearing, the Knowing."

(5) But they say, "[The revelation is but] a mixture of false dreams; rather, he has invented it; rather, he is a poet. So let him bring us a sign just as the previous [messengers] were sent [with miracles]."

(6) Not a [single] city which We destroyed believed before them,[851] so will they believe?

(7) And We sent not before you, [O Muḥammad], except men to whom We revealed [the message], so ask the people of the message [i.e., former scriptures] if you do not know.

(8) And We did not make them [i.e., the prophets] forms not eating food,[852] nor were they immortal [on earth].

(9) Then[853] We fulfilled for them the promise, and We saved them and whom We willed and destroyed the transgressors.

(10) We have certainly sent down to you a Book [i.e., the Qur'ān] in which is your mention.[854] Then will you not reason?

---

[851] Even though they had witnessed signs and miracles.
[852] Like the angels. Rather, they were human beings with human attributes.
[853] Once they had conveyed the message.
[854] This implies the honor of having been mentioned or addressed. Another meaning is "your reminder."

(11) And how many a city which was unjust[855] have We shattered and produced after it another people.

(12) And when they [i.e., its inhabitants] perceived Our punishment, at once they fled from it.

(13) [Some angels said], "Do not flee but return to where you were given luxury and to your homes - perhaps you will be questioned."[856]

(14) They said, "O woe to us! Indeed, we were wrongdoers."

(15) And that declaration of theirs did not cease until We made them [as] a harvest [mowed down], extinguished [like a fire].

(16) And We did not create the heaven and earth and that between them in play.

(17) Had We intended to take a diversion,[857] We could have taken it from [what is] with Us - if [indeed] We were to do so.

(18) Rather, We dash the truth upon falsehood, and it destroys it,[858] and thereupon it departs. And for you is destruction from that which you describe.[859]

(19) To Him belongs whoever is in the heavens and the earth. And those near Him [i.e., the angels] are not prevented by arrogance from His worship, nor do they tire.

(20) They exalt [Him] night and day [and] do not slacken.

(21) Or have they [i.e., men] taken for themselves gods from the earth who resurrect [the dead]?

(22) Had there been within them [i.e., the heavens and earth] gods besides Allāh, they both would have been ruined. So exalted is Allāh, Lord of the Throne, above what they describe.

(23) He is not questioned about what He does, but they will be questioned.

---

[855] i.e., its inhabitants persisting in wrongdoing.

[856] About what happened to you. This is said to them in sarcasm and ridicule.

[857] Such as a wife or a child.

[858] "Literally, "strikes its brain," disabling or killing it.

[859] Of untruth concerning Allāh, particularly here, the claim that He has a son or other "partner" in divinity."

(24) Or have they taken gods besides Him? Say, [O Muḥammad], "Produce your proof. This [Qur'ān] is the message for those with me and the message of those before me."[860] But most of them do not know the truth, so they are turning away.

(25) And We sent not before you any messenger except We revealed to him that, "There is no deity except Me, so worship Me."

(26) And they say, "The Most Merciful has taken a son." Exalted is He! Rather, they[861] are [but] honored servants.

(27) They cannot precede Him in word, and they act by His command.

(28) He knows what is [presently] before them and what will be after them,[862] and they cannot intercede except on behalf of one whom He approves. And they, from fear of Him, are apprehensive.

(29) And whoever of them should say, "Indeed, I am a god besides Him" - that one We would recompense with Hell. Thus do We recompense the wrongdoers.

(30) Have those who disbelieved not considered that the heavens and the earth were a joined entity, and then We separated them and made from water every living thing? Then will they not believe?

(31) And We placed within the earth firmly set mountains, lest it should shift with them, and We made therein [mountain] passes [as] roads that they might be guided.

(32) And We made the sky a protected ceiling, but they, from its signs,[863] are turning away.

(33) And it is He who created the night and the day and the sun and the moon; all [heavenly bodies] in an orbit are swimming.

(34) And We did not grant to any man before you eternity [on earth]; so if you die - would they be eternal?

(35) Every soul will taste death. And We test you with evil and with good as trial; and to Us you will be returned.

---

[860] All previous prophets called for the worship of Allāh alone.
[861] Those they claim to be "children" of Allāh, such as the angels, Ezra, Jesus, etc.
[862] See footnote to 2:255.
[863] The signs present in the heavens.

(36) And when those who disbelieve see you, [O Muḥammad], they take you not except in ridicule, [saying], "Is this the one who mentions [i.e., insults] your gods?" And they are, at the mention of the Most Merciful, disbelievers.

(37) Man was created of haste [i.e., impatience]. I will show you My signs [i.e., vengeance], so do not impatiently urge Me.

(38) And they say, "When is this promise, if you should be truthful?"

(39) If those who disbelieved but knew the time when they will not avert the Fire from their faces or from their backs and they will not be aided...[864]

(40) Rather, it will come to them unexpectedly and bewilder them, and they will not be able to repel it, nor will they be reprieved.

(41) And already were messengers ridiculed before you, but those who mocked them were enveloped by what they used to ridicule.

(42) Say, "Who can protect you at night or by day from the Most Merciful?" But they are, from the remembrance of their Lord, turning away.

(43) Or do they have gods to defend them other than Us? They are unable [even] to help themselves, nor can they be protected from Us.

(44) But, [on the contrary], We have provided good things for these [disbelievers] and their fathers until life was prolonged for them. Then do they not see that We set upon the land, reducing it from its borders?[865] Is it they who will overcome?

(45) Say, "I only warn you by revelation." But the deaf do not hear the call when they are warned.

(46) And if [as much as] a whiff of the punishment of your Lord should touch them, they would surely say, "O woe to us! Indeed, we have been wrongdoers."

(47) And We place the scales of justice for the Day of Resurrection, so no soul will be treated unjustly at all. And if there is [even] the weight of a mustard seed,[866] We will bring it forth. And sufficient are We as accountant.

---

[864] The completion of the sentence is understood to be "...they would not be asking in disbelief and ridicule to be shown the punishment."
[865] See footnote to 13:41.
[866] i.e., anything as small or insignificant as a mustard seed.

(48) And We had already given Moses and Aaron the criterion and a light and a reminder[867] for the righteous

(49) Who fear their Lord unseen,[868] while they are of the Hour apprehensive.

(50) And this [Qur'ān] is a blessed message which We have sent down. Then are you with it unacquainted?[869]

(51) And We had certainly given Abraham his sound judgement before,[870] and We were of him well-Knowing

(52) When he said to his father and his people, "What are these statues to which you are devoted?"

(53) They said, "We found our fathers worshippers of them."

(54) He said, "You were certainly, you and your fathers, in manifest error."

(55) They said, "Have you come to us with truth, or are you of those who jest?"

(56) He said, "[No], rather, your Lord is the Lord of the heavens and the earth who created them, and I, to that, am of those who testify.

(57) And [I swear] by Allāh, I will surely plan against your idols after you have turned and gone away."

(58) So he made them into fragments, except a large one among them, that they might return to it [and question].

(59) They said, "Who has done this to our gods? Indeed, he is of the wrongdoers."

(60) They said, "We heard a young man mention them who is called Abraham."

(61) They said, "Then bring him before the eyes of the people that they may testify."[871]

(62) They said, "Have you done this to our gods, O Abraham?"

---

[867] These are three qualities of the Torah.

[868] Which can mean "Him being unseen" by them or "though they are unseen" by others.

[869] i.e., pretending ignorance, disapproving or refusing to acknowledge it?

[870] i.e., before Moses. Allāh had guided him from early youth.

[871] To what they had heard him say. It may also mean "...that they may witness [what will be done to him as punishment]."

(63) He said, "Rather, this - the largest of them - did it, so ask them, if they should [be able to] speak."

(64) So they returned to [blaming] themselves and said [to each other], "Indeed, you are the wrongdoers."

(65) Then they reversed themselves,[872] [saying], "You have already known that these do not speak!"

(66) He said, "Then do you worship instead of Allāh that which does not benefit you at all or harm you?

(67) Uff[873] to you and to what you worship instead of Allāh. Then will you not use reason?"

(68) They said, "Burn him and support your gods - if you are to act."

(69) We [i.e., Allāh] said, "O fire, be coolness and safety upon Abraham."

(70) And they intended for him a plan [i.e., harm], but We made them the greatest losers.

(71) And We delivered him and Lot to the land which We had blessed for the worlds [i.e., peoples].

(72) And We gave him Isaac and Jacob in addition, and all [of them] We made righteous.

(73) And We made them leaders guiding by Our command. And We inspired to them the doing of good deeds, establishment of prayer, and giving of zakāh; and they were worshippers of Us.

(74) And to Lot We gave judgement and knowledge, and We saved him from the city that was committing wicked deeds. Indeed, they were a people of evil, defiantly disobedient.

(75) And We admitted him into Our mercy. Indeed, he was of the righteous.

(76) And [mention] Noah, when he called [to Allāh][874] before [that time], so We responded to him and saved him and his family from the great affliction [i.e., the flood].

---

[872] After first admitting their error, they were seized by pride and obstinacy.

[873] An exclamation of anger and displeasure.

[874] i.e., supplicated against his people who had persisted in denial and animosity. See 71:26-28.

(77) And We aided [i.e., saved] him from the people who denied Our signs. Indeed, they were a people of evil, so We drowned them, all together.

(78) And [mention] David and Solomon, when they judged concerning the field - when the sheep of a people overran it [at night],[875] and We were witness to their judgement.

(79) And We gave understanding of it [i.e., the case] to Solomon, and to each [of them] We gave judgement and knowledge. And We subjected the mountains to exalt [Us], along with David and [also] the birds. And We were doing [that].[876]

(80) And We taught him the fashioning of coats of armor to protect you from your [enemy in] battle. So will you then be grateful?

(81) And to Solomon [We subjected] the wind, blowing forcefully, proceeding by his command toward the land which We had blessed. And We are ever, of all things, Knowing.

(82) And of the devils [i.e., jinn] were those who dived for him and did work other than that. And We were of them a guardian.[877]

(83) And [mention] Job, when he called to his Lord, "Indeed, adversity has touched me, and You are the most merciful of the merciful."

(84) So We responded to him and removed what afflicted him of adversity. And We gave him [back] his family and the like thereof with them as mercy from Us and a reminder for the worshippers [of Allāh].

(85) And [mention] Ishmael and Idrees and Dhul-Kifl; all were of the patient.

(86) And We admitted them into Our mercy. Indeed, they were of the righteous.

(87) And [mention] the man of the fish [i.e., Jonah], when he went off in anger[878] and thought that We would not decree [anything] upon him.[879] And he called out within the darknesses,[880] "There is no deity except You; exalted are You. Indeed, I have been of the wrongdoers."

---

[875] Eating and destroying the crops.
[876] Meaning that Allāh has always been capable of accomplishing whatever He wills.
[877] Preventing any disobedience or deviation by them from Solomon's instructions and protecting him from being harmed by them.
[878] "At the disbelief of his people.
[879] Or "would not restrict him" in the belly of the fish.
[880] That of the night, of the sea, and of the fish's interior."

(88) So We responded to him and saved him from the distress. And thus do We save the believers.

(89) And [mention] Zechariah, when he called to his Lord, "My Lord, do not leave me alone [with no heir], while You are the best of inheritors."

(90) So We responded to him, and We gave to him John, and amended for him his wife. Indeed, they used to hasten to good deeds and supplicate[881] Us in hope and fear, and they were to Us humbly submissive.

(91) And [mention] the one who guarded her chastity [i.e., Mary], so We blew into her [garment] through Our angel [i.e., Gabriel], and We made her and her son a sign for the worlds.

(92) Indeed this, your religion, is one religion,[882] and I am your Lord, so worship Me.

(93) And [yet] they divided their affair [i.e., that of their religion] among themselves,[883] [but] all to Us will return.

(94) So whoever does righteous deeds while he is a believer - no denial will there be for his effort,[884] and indeed We [i.e., Our angels], of it, are recorders.

(95) And it is prohibited to [the people of] a city which We have destroyed that they will [ever] return[885]

(96) Until when [the dam of] Gog and Magog has been opened and they, from every elevation, descend

(97) And [when] the true promise [i.e., the resurrection] has approached; then suddenly the eyes of those who disbelieved will be staring [in horror, while they say], "O woe to us; we had been unmindful of this; rather, we were wrongdoers."

(98) Indeed, you [disbelievers] and what you worship other than Allāh are the firewood of Hell. You will be coming to [enter] it.

(99) Had these [false deities] been [actual] gods, they would not have come to it, but all are eternal therein.

(100) For them therein is heavy sighing, and they therein will not hear.

---

[881] i.e., worship.

[882] i.e., a collective way of life or course of conduct followed by a community.

[883] Becoming sects and denominations.

[884] Such a person will not be deprived of his due reward.

[885] They cannot return to this world, nor can they repent to Allāh.

(101) Indeed, those for whom the best [reward] has preceded from Us - they are from it far removed.

(102) They will not hear its sound, while they are, in that which their souls desire, abiding eternally.

(103) They will not be grieved by the greatest terror,[886] and the angels will meet them, [saying], "This is your Day which you have been promised" -

(104) The Day when We will fold the heaven like the folding of a [written] sheet for the records. As We began the first creation, We will repeat it. [That is] a promise binding upon Us. Indeed, We will do it.[887]

(105) And We have already written in the book [of Psalms][888] after the [previous] mention[889] that the land [of Paradise] is inherited by My righteous servants.

(106) Indeed, in this [Qur'ān] is notification for a worshipping people.

(107) And We have not sent you, [O Muḥammad], except as a mercy to the worlds.

(108) Say, "It is only revealed to me that your god is but one God; so will you be Muslims [in submission to Him]?"

(109) But if they turn away, then say, "I have announced to [all of] you equally.[890] And I know not whether near or far is that which you are promised.

(110) Indeed, He knows what is declared of speech, and He knows what you conceal.

(111) And I know not; perhaps it[891] is a trial for you and enjoyment for a time."

(112) [The Prophet (ﷺ)] has said, "My Lord, judge [between us] in truth. And our Lord is the Most Merciful, the one whose help is sought against that which you describe."[892]

---

[886] The events of the Last Hour or of the Resurrection.

[887] More literally, "Indeed, We are ever doers" of what We will.

[888] "Az-Zabūr can also mean "scriptures" in general.

[889] i.e., the Torah. The "mention" may also refer to the original inscription with Allāh, i.e., the Preserved Slate (al-Lawḥ al-Maḥfūẓ)."

[890] The Prophet (ﷺ) made this message known to all people, not concealing any of it from anyone or preferring any group over another.

[891] The postponement of punishment.

[892] i.e., their lies and disbelief.

Surah Al-Hajj

(1) O mankind, fear your Lord. Indeed, the convulsion of the [final] Hour is a terrible thing.

(2) On the Day you see it every nursing mother will be distracted from that [child] she was nursing, and every pregnant woman will abort her pregnancy, and you will see the people [appearing] intoxicated while they are not intoxicated; but the punishment of Allāh is severe.

(3) And of the people is he who disputes about Allāh without knowledge and follows every rebellious devil.

(4) It has been decreed for him [i.e., every devil] that whoever turns to him - he will misguide him and will lead him to the punishment of the Blaze.

(5) O people, if you should be in doubt about the Resurrection, then [consider that] indeed, We created you from dust, then from a sperm-drop, then from a clinging clot, and then from a lump of flesh, formed and unformed[893] - that We may show you.[894] And We settle in the wombs whom We will for a specified term, then We bring you out as a child, and then [We develop you] that you may reach your [time of] maturity. And among you is he who is taken in [early] death, and among you is he who is returned to the most decrepit [old] age so that he knows, after [once having] knowledge, nothing. And you see the earth barren, but when We send down upon it rain, it quivers and swells and grows [something] of every beautiful kind.

(6) That is because Allāh is the True Reality and because He gives life to the dead and because He is over all things competent

(7) And [that they may know] that the Hour is coming - no doubt about it - and that Allāh will resurrect those in the graves.

(8) And of the people is he who disputes about Allāh without knowledge or guidance or an enlightening book [from Him],

(9) Twisting his neck [in arrogance] to mislead [people] from the way of Allāh. For him in the world is disgrace, and We will make him taste on the Day of Resurrection the punishment of the Burning Fire [while it is said],

---

[893] "That which is incomplete. This may include what is aborted at that stage.
[894] Our power and creative ability."

(10) "That is for what your hands have put forth and because Allāh is not ever unjust to [His] servants."

(11) And of the people is he who worships Allāh on an edge.[895] If he is touched by good, he is reassured by it; but if he is struck by trial, he turns on his face [to unbelief]. He has lost [this] world and the Hereafter. That is what is the manifest loss.

(12) He invokes instead of Allāh that which neither harms him nor benefits him. That is what is the extreme error.

(13) He invokes one whose harm is closer than his benefit - how wretched the protector and how wretched the associate.

(14) Indeed, Allāh will admit those who believe and do righteous deeds to gardens beneath which rivers flow. Indeed, Allāh does what He intends.

(15) Whoever should think that Allāh will not support him [i.e., Prophet Muḥammad (ﷺ)] in this world and the Hereafter - let him extend a rope to the ceiling, then cut off [his breath],[896] and let him see: will his effort remove that which enrages [him]?

(16) And thus have We sent it [i.e., the Qur'ān] down as verses of clear evidence and because Allāh guides whom He intends.

(17) Indeed, those who have believed and those who were Jews and the Sabeans and the Christians and the Magians and those who associated with Allāh - Allāh will judge between them on the Day of Resurrection. Indeed Allāh is, over all things, Witness.[897]

(18) Do you not see [i.e., know] that to Allāh prostrates whoever is in the heavens and whoever is on the earth and the sun, the moon, the stars, the mountains, the trees, the moving creatures and many of the people? But upon many the punishment has been justified.[898] And he whom Allāh humiliates - for him there is no bestower of honor. Indeed, Allāh does what He wills.

---

[895] At the edge of his religion, so to speak, i.e., with uncertainty, hypocrisy or heedlessness.
[896] i.e., strangle himself.
[897] See footnote of 4:79.
[898] And therefore decreed.

(19) These[899] are two adversaries who have disputed over their Lord. But those who disbelieved will have cut out for them garments of fire. Poured upon their heads will be scalding water

(20) By which is melted that within their bellies and [their] skins.

(21) And for [striking] them are maces of iron.

(22) Every time they want to get out of it [i.e., Hellfire] from anguish, they will be returned to it, and [it will be said], "Taste the punishment of the Burning Fire!"

(23) Indeed, Allāh will admit those who believe and do righteous deeds to gardens beneath which rivers flow. They will be adorned therein with bracelets of gold and pearl, and their garments therein will be silk.

(24) And they had been guided [in worldly life] to good speech, and they were guided to the path of the Praiseworthy.

(25) Indeed, those who have disbelieved and avert [people] from the way of Allāh and [from] al-Masjid al-Ḥarām, which We made for the people - equal are the resident therein and one from outside - and [also] whoever intends [a deed] therein[900] of deviation [in religion] by wrongdoing - We will make him taste of a painful punishment.

(26) And [mention, O Muḥammad], when We designated for Abraham the site of the House, [saying], "Do not associate anything with Me and purify My House for those who perform ṭawāf[901] and those who stand [in prayer] and those who bow and prostrate.

(27) And proclaim to the people the ḥajj [pilgrimage]; they will come to you on foot and on every lean camel; they will come from every distant pass -

(28) That they may witness [i.e., attend] benefits for themselves and mention the name of Allāh on known [i.e., specific] days over what He has provided for them of [sacrificial] animals.[902] So eat of them and feed the miserable and poor.

---

[899] i.e., the believers and the disbelievers.

[900] Whether inside its boundaries or intending from afar to do evil therein. The Ḥaram is unique in that the mere intention of sin therein (whether or not it is actually carried out) is sufficient to bring punishment from Allāh.

[901] See footnote to 2:125.

[902] Al-an'ām: camels, cattle, sheep and goats.

(29) Then let them end their untidiness and fulfill their vows and perform ṭawāf around the ancient House."

(30) That [has been commanded], and whoever honors the sacred ordinances of Allāh - it is best for him in the sight of his Lord. And permitted to you are the grazing livestock, except what is recited to you.[903] So avoid the uncleanliness of idols and avoid false statement,

(31) Inclining [only] to Allāh, not associating [anything] with Him. And he who associates with Allāh - it is as though he had fallen from the sky and was snatched by the birds or the wind carried him down into a remote place.

(32) That [is so]. And whoever honors the symbols [i.e., rites] of Allāh - indeed, it is from the piety of hearts.

(33) For you therein [i.e., the animals marked for sacrifice] are benefits for a specified term;[904] then their place of sacrifice is at the ancient House.[905]

(34) And for every [religious] community We have appointed a rite [of sacrifice][906] that they may mention the name of Allāh over what He has provided for them of [sacrificial] animals. For your god is one God, so to Him submit. And, [O Muḥammad], give good tidings to the humble [before their Lord]

(35) Who, when Allāh is mentioned, their hearts are fearful, and [to] the patient over what has afflicted them, and the establishers of prayer and those who spend from what We have provided them.

(36) And the camels and cattle We have appointed for you as among the symbols [i.e., rites] of Allāh; for you therein is good. So mention the name of Allāh upon them when lined up [for sacrifice]; and when they are [lifeless] on their sides, then eat from them and feed the needy [who does not seek aid] and the beggar. Thus have We subjected them to you that you may be grateful.

(37) Their meat will not reach Allāh, nor will their blood, but what reaches Him is piety from you. Thus have We subjected them to you that you may glorify Allāh for that [to] which He has guided you; and give good tidings to the doers of good.

---

[903] See 5:3.

[904] "i.e., they may be milked or ridden (in the case of camels) before the time of slaughter.

[905] i.e., within the boundaries of the Ḥaram, which includes Minā."

[906] i.e., the right of sacrifice has always been a part of Allāh's revealed religion.

(38) Indeed, Allāh defends those who have believed. Indeed, Allāh does not like everyone treacherous and ungrateful.

(39) Permission [to fight] has been given to those who are being fought,[907] because they were wronged. And indeed, Allāh is competent to give them victory.

(40) [They are] those who have been evicted from their homes without right - only because they say, "Our Lord is Allāh." And were it not that Allāh checks the people, some by means of others, there would have been demolished monasteries, churches, synagogues, and mosques in which the name of Allāh is much mentioned [i.e., praised]. And Allāh will surely support those who support Him [i.e., His cause]. Indeed, Allāh is Powerful and Exalted in Might.

(41) [And they are] those who, if We give them authority in the land, establish prayer and give zakāh and enjoin what is right and forbid what is wrong. And to Allāh belongs the outcome of [all] matters.

(42) And if they deny you, [O Muḥammad] - so, before them, did the people of Noah and ʿAad and Thamūd deny [their prophets],

(43) And the people of Abraham and the people of Lot.

(44) And the inhabitants of Madyan. And Moses was denied, so I prolonged enjoyment for the disbelievers; then I seized them, and how [terrible] was My reproach.

(45) And how many a city did We destroy while it was committing wrong - so it is [now] fallen into ruin[908] - and [how many] an abandoned well and [how many] a lofty palace.[909]

(46) So have they not traveled through the earth and have hearts by which to reason and ears by which to hear? For indeed, it is not eyes that are blinded, but blinded are the hearts which are within the breasts.

---

[907] Referring here to the Prophet's companions.

[908] "Literally, "fallen in upon its roofs," i.e., after the roofs of its buildings had caved in, the walls collapsed over them.

[909] i.e., How many wells have been left inoperative, and how many palaces have been emptied of their occupants in the past."

(47) And they urge you to hasten the punishment. But Allāh will never fail in His promise. And indeed, a day with your Lord is like a thousand years of those which you count.

(48) And for how many a city did I prolong enjoyment while it was committing wrong. Then I seized it, and to Me is the [final] destination.

(49) Say, "O people, I am only to you a clear warner."

(50) And those who have believed and done righteous deeds - for them is forgiveness and noble provision.

(51) But the ones who strove against Our verses, [seeking] to cause failure[910] - those are the companions of Hellfire.

(52) And We did not send before you any messenger or prophet except that when he spoke [or recited], Satan threw into it [some misunderstanding]. But Allāh abolishes that which Satan throws in; then Allāh makes precise His verses.[911] And Allāh is Knowing and Wise.

(53) [That is] so He may make what Satan throws in [i.e., asserts] a trial for those within whose hearts is disease[912] and those hard of heart. And indeed, the wrongdoers are in extreme dissension.

(54) And so those who were given knowledge may know that it is the truth from your Lord and [therefore] believe in it, and their hearts humbly submit to it. And indeed is Allāh the Guide of those who have believed to a straight path.

(55) But those who disbelieve will not cease to be in doubt of it until the Hour comes upon them unexpectedly or there comes to them the punishment of a barren Day.[913]

(56) [All] sovereignty that Day is for Allāh;[914] He will judge between them. So they who believed and did righteous deeds will be in the Gardens of Pleasure.

(57) And they who disbelieved and denied Our signs - for those there will be a humiliating punishment.

---

[910] i.e., trying to undermine their credibility and thereby defeat the Prophet (ﷺ).

[911] Clarifying those issues which were misunderstood to remove any doubt.

[912] See footnote to 2:10.

[913] One which will not be followed by night and therefore will not give birth to a new day, referring to the Day of Resurrection.

[914] None will compete with Him for authority at that time.

(58) And those who emigrated for the cause of Allāh and then were killed or died - Allāh will surely provide for them a good provision. And indeed, it is Allāh who is the best of providers.

(59) He will surely cause them to enter an entrance with which they will be pleased, and indeed, Allāh is Knowing and Forbearing.

(60) That [is so]. And whoever responds [to injustice] with the equivalent of that with which he was harmed and then is tyrannized - Allāh will surely aid him. Indeed, Allāh is Pardoning and Forgiving.[915]

(61) That[916] is because Allāh causes the night to enter the day and causes the day to enter the night and because Allāh is Hearing and Seeing.

(62) That is because Allāh is the True Reality, and that which they call upon other than Him is falsehood, and because Allāh is the Most High, the Grand.

(63) Do you not see that Allāh has sent down rain from the sky and the earth becomes green? Indeed, Allāh is Subtle[917] and Aware.[918]

(64) To Him belongs what is in the heavens and what is on the earth. And indeed, Allāh is the Free of need, the Praiseworthy.

(65) Do you not see that Allāh has subjected to you whatever is on the earth and the ships which run through the sea by His command? And He restrains the sky from falling upon the earth, unless by His permission. Indeed Allāh, to the people, is Kind and Merciful.

(66) And He is the one who gave you life; then He causes you to die and then will [again] give you life. Indeed, mankind is ungrateful.

(67) For every [religious] community We have appointed rites which they perform. So, [O Muḥammad], let them [i.e., the disbelievers] not contend with you over the matter but invite [them] to your Lord. Indeed, you are upon straight guidance.

(68) And if they dispute with you, then say, "Allāh is most knowing of what you do.

(69) Allāh will judge between you on the Day of Resurrection concerning that over which you used to differ."

---

[915] In spite of His ability to take vengeance. The statement contains a suggestion that the believers pardon as well.

[916] i.e., Allāh's capability to give assistance or victory to the oppressed.

[917] "Refer to footnote of 6:103.

[918] Of His creation and of the needs of His creatures."

(70) Do you not know that Allāh knows what is in the heaven and earth? Indeed, that is in a Record.[919] Indeed that, for Allāh, is easy.

(71) And they worship besides Allāh that for which He has not sent down authority and that of which they have no knowledge. And there will not be for the wrongdoers any helper.

(72) And when Our verses are recited to them as clear evidences, you recognize in the faces of those who disbelieve disapproval. They are almost on the verge of assaulting those who recite to them Our verses. Say, "Then shall I inform you of [what is] worse than that?[920] [It is] the Fire which Allāh has promised those who disbelieve, and wretched is the destination."

(73) O people, an example is presented, so listen to it. Indeed, those you invoke besides Allāh will never create [as much as] a fly, even if they gathered together for it [i.e., that purpose]. And if the fly should steal from them a [tiny] thing, they could not recover it from him. Weak are the pursuer and pursued.[921]

(74) They have not appraised Allāh with true appraisal.[922] Indeed, Allāh is Powerful and Exalted in Might.

(75) Allāh chooses from the angels messengers and from the people. Indeed, Allāh is Hearing and Seeing.

(76) He knows what is [presently] before them and what will be after them.[923] And to Allāh will be returned [all] matters.

(77) O you who have believed, bow and prostrate and worship your Lord and do good - that you may succeed.

(78) And strive for Allāh with the striving due to Him. He has chosen you and has not placed upon you in the religion any difficulty. [It is] the religion of your father, Abraham. He [i.e., Allāh] named you "Muslims" before [in former scriptures] and in this [revelation] that the Messenger may be a witness over you and you may be witnesses over the people. So establish prayer and give zakāh and hold fast to Allāh. He is your protector; and excellent is the protector, and excellent is the helper.

____

[919] The Preserved Slate (al-Lawḥ al-Maḥfūẓ), which is with Allāh.

[920] i.e., worse than the rage you feel against those who recite Allāh's verses or worse than your threats against them.

[921] A comparison is made here to the worshipper of a false deity and that which he worships.

[922] They have not assessed Him with the assessment due to Him, meaning that they did not take into account His perfect attributes.

[923] See footnote to 2:255.

Surah Al-Mu'minoon

(1) Certainly will the believers have succeeded:

(2) They who are during their prayer humbly intent

(3) And they who turn away from ill speech

(4) And they who are observant of zakāh

(5) And they who guard their private parts

(6) Except from their wives or those their right hands possess,[924] for indeed, they will not be blamed -

(7) But whoever seeks beyond that, then those are the transgressors -

(8) And they who are to their trusts and their promises attentive

(9) And they who carefully maintain their prayers -

(10) Those are the inheritors

(11) Who will inherit al-Firdaus.[925] They will abide therein eternally.

(12) And certainly did We create man from an extract of clay.

(13) Then We placed him as a sperm-drop[926] in a firm lodging [i.e., the womb].

(14) Then We made the sperm-drop into a clinging clot, and We made the clot into a lump [of flesh], and We made [from] the lump, bones, and We covered the bones with flesh; then We developed him into another creation. So blessed is Allāh, the best of creators.[927]

(15) Then indeed, after that you are to die.

(16) Then indeed you, on the Day of Resurrection, will be resurrected.

(17) And We have created above you seven layered heavens, and never have We been of [Our] creation unaware.

---

[924] Female slaves or captives under their ownership.
[925] The highest part of Paradise.
[926] Or "as a zygote."
[927] i.e., the most skillful and only true Creator.

(18) And We have sent down rain from the sky in a measured amount and settled it in the earth. And indeed, We are Able to take it away.

(19) And We brought forth for you thereby gardens of palm trees and grapevines in which for you are abundant fruits and from which you eat.

(20) And [We brought forth] a tree issuing from Mount Sinai which produces oil and food [i.e., olives] for those who eat.

(21) And indeed, for you in livestock is a lesson. We give you drink from that which is in their bellies, and for you in them are numerous benefits, and from them you eat.

(22) And upon them and on ships you are carried.

(23) And We had certainly sent Noah to his people, and he said, "O my people, worship Allāh; you have no deity other than Him; then will you not fear Him?"

(24) But the eminent among those who disbelieved from his people said, "This is not but a man like yourselves who wishes to take precedence over you; and if Allāh had willed [to send a messenger], He would have sent down angels. We have not heard of this among our forefathers.

(25) He is not but a man possessed with madness, so wait concerning him for a time."

(26) [Noah] said, "My Lord, support me because they have denied me."

(27) So We inspired to him, "Construct the ship under Our observation and Our inspiration, and when Our command comes and the oven overflows,[928] put into it [i.e., the ship] from each [creature] two mates and your family, except him for whom the decree [of destruction] has proceeded. And do not address Me concerning those who have wronged; indeed, they are to be drowned.

(28) And when you have boarded the ship, you and those with you, then say, 'Praise to Allāh who has saved us from the wrongdoing people.'

(29) And say, 'My Lord, let me land at a blessed landing place, and You are the best to accommodate [us].'"

(30) Indeed in that are signs, and indeed, We are ever testing [Our servants].

---

[928] See footnote to 11:40.

(31) Then We produced after them a generation of others.

(32) And We sent among them a messenger[929] from themselves, [saying], "Worship Allāh; you have no deity other than Him; then will you not fear Him?"

(33) And the eminent among his people who disbelieved and denied the meeting of the Hereafter while We had given them luxury in the worldly life said, "This is not but a man like yourselves. He eats of that from which you eat and drinks of what you drink.

(34) And if you should obey a man like yourselves, indeed, you would then be losers.

(35) Does he promise you that when you have died and become dust and bones that you will be brought forth [once more]?

(36) How far, how far, is that which you are promised.[930]

(37) It [i.e., life] is not but our worldly life - we die and live, but we will not be resurrected.

(38) He is not but a man who has invented a lie about Allāh, and we will not believe him."

(39) He said, "My Lord, support me because they have denied me."

(40) [Allāh] said, "After a little, they will surely become regretful."

(41) So the shriek[931] seized them in truth,[932] and We made them as [plant] stubble. Then away with the wrongdoing people.

(42) Then We produced after them other generations.

(43) No nation will precede its time [of termination], nor will they remain [thereafter].

(44) Then We sent Our messengers in succession. Every time there came to a nation its messenger, they denied him, so We made them follow one another [to

---

[929] Prophet Hūd, who was sent to the tribe of ʿAad.

[930] i.e., how distant and improbable it is.

[931] "See footnote to 11:67.

[932] i.e., by right or in justice."

destruction], and We made them narrations.[933] So away with a people who do not believe.

(45) Then We sent Moses and his brother Aaron with Our signs and a clear authority[934]

(46) To Pharaoh and his establishment, but they were arrogant and were a haughty people.

(47) They said, "Should we believe two men like ourselves while their people are for us in servitude?"

(48) So they denied them and were of those destroyed.

(49) And We certainly gave Moses the Scripture that perhaps they[935] would be guided.

(50) And We made the son of Mary and his mother a sign and sheltered them within a high ground having level [areas] and flowing water.

(51) [Allāh said], "O messengers, eat from the good foods and work righteousness. Indeed I, of what you do, am Knowing.

(52) And indeed this, your religion, is one religion,[936] and I am your Lord, so fear Me."

(53) But they [i.e., the people] divided their religion among them into portions [i.e., sects] - each faction, in what it has,[937] rejoicing.

(54) So leave them in their confusion for a time.

(55) Do they think that what We extend to them of wealth and children

(56) Is [because] We hasten for them good things? Rather, they do not perceive.[938]

---

[933] i.e., history or lessons for mankind.

[934] i.e., evidences from Allāh.

[935] The Children of Israel.

[936] See footnote to 21:92.

[937] Of beliefs, opinions, customs, etc.

[938] That the good things given to them in this world are but a trial for them.

(57) Indeed, they who are apprehensive from fear of their Lord

(58) And they who believe in the signs of their Lord

(59) And they who do not associate anything with their Lord

(60) And they who give what they give while their hearts are fearful[939] because they will be returning to their Lord -

(61) It is those who hasten to good deeds, and they outstrip [others] therein.

(62) And We charge no soul except [with that within] its capacity, and with Us is a record which speaks with truth; and they will not be wronged.

(63) But their hearts are covered with confusion over this, and they have [evil] deeds besides that [i.e., disbelief] which they are doing,

(64) Until when We seize their affluent ones with punishment,[940] at once they are crying [to Allāh] for help.

(65) Do not cry out today. Indeed, by Us you will not be helped.

(66) My verses had already been recited to you, but you were turning back on your heels.

(67) In arrogance regarding it,[941] conversing by night, speaking evil.

(68) Then have they not reflected over the word [i.e., the Qur'ān], or has there come to them that which had not come to their forefathers?

(69) Or did they not know their Messenger, so they are toward him disacknowledging?

(70) Or do they say, "In him is madness"? Rather, he brought them the truth, but most of them, to the truth, are averse.

---

[939] Lest their deeds not be acceptable.

[940] In worldly life, before the punishment of the Hereafter. Although general, the description includes specifically the punishment of the Quraysh by famine.

[941] The revelation. Or "him," i.e., the Prophet (ﷺ).

(71) But if the Truth [i.e., Allāh] had followed their inclinations, the heavens and the earth and whoever is in them would have been ruined. Rather, We have brought them their message,[942] but they, from their message, are turning away.

(72) Or do you, [O Muḥammad], ask them for payment? But the reward of your Lord is best, and He is the best of providers.

(73) And indeed, you invite them to a straight path.

(74) But indeed, those who do not believe in the Hereafter are deviating from the path.

(75) And even if We gave them mercy and removed what was upon them of affliction, they would persist in their transgression, wandering blindly.

(76) And We had gripped them with suffering [as a warning], but they did not yield to their Lord, nor did they humbly supplicate, [and will continue thus]

(77) Until when We have opened before them a door of severe punishment, immediately they will be therein in despair.

(78) And it is He who produced for you hearing and vision and hearts [i.e., intellect]; little are you grateful.

(79) And it is He who has multiplied you throughout the earth, and to Him you will be gathered.

(80) And it is He who gives life and causes death, and His is the alternation of the night and the day. Then will you not reason?

(81) Rather,[943] they say like what the former peoples said.

(82) They said, "When we have died and become dust and bones, are we indeed to be resurrected?

(83) We have been promised this, we and our forefathers, before; this is not but legends of the former peoples."

(84) Say, [O Muḥammad], "To whom belongs the earth and whoever is in it, if you should know?"

(85) They will say, "To Allāh." Say, "Then will you not remember?"

---

942 Or "reminder."

943 Instead of understanding or reasoning.

(86) Say, "Who is Lord of the seven heavens and Lord of the Great Throne?"

(87) They will say, "[They belong] to Allāh." Say, "Then will you not fear Him?"

(88) Say, "In whose hand is the realm of all things - and He protects while none can protect against Him - if you should know?"

(89) They will say, "[All belongs] to Allāh." Say, "Then how are you deluded?"

(90) Rather, We have brought them the truth, and indeed they are liars.

(91) Allāh has not taken any son, nor has there ever been with Him any deity. [If there had been], then each deity would have taken what it created, and some of them would have [sought to] overcome others. Exalted is Allāh above what they describe [concerning Him].

(92) [He is] Knower of the unseen and the witnessed, so high is He above what they associate [with Him].

(93) Say, [O Muḥammad], "My Lord, if You should show me that which they are promised,

(94) My Lord, then do not place me among the wrongdoing people."

(95) And indeed, We are Able to show you what We have promised them.

(96) Repel, by [means of] what is best, [their] evil. We are most knowing of what they describe.

(97) And say, "My Lord, I seek refuge in You from the incitements of the devils,

(98) And I seek refuge in You, my Lord, lest they be present with me."

(99) [For such is the state of the disbelievers] until, when death comes to one of them, he says, "My Lord, send me back

(100) That I might do righteousness in that which I left behind."[944] No! It is only a word he is saying; and behind them is a barrier until the Day they are resurrected.

(101) So when the Horn is blown, no relationship will there be among them that Day, nor will they ask about one another.

(102) And those whose scales are heavy [with good deeds] - it is they who are the successful.

---

[944] Or "in that which I neglected."

(103) But those whose scales are light - those are the ones who have lost their souls, [being] in Hell, abiding eternally.

(104) The Fire will sear their faces, and they therein will have taut smiles.[945]

(105) [It will be said], "Were not My verses recited to you and you used to deny them?"

(106) They will say, "Our Lord, our wretchedness overcame us, and we were a people astray.

(107) Our Lord, remove us from it, and if we were to return [to evil], we would indeed be wrongdoers."

(108) He will say, "Remain despised therein and do not speak to Me.

(109) Indeed, there was a party of My servants who said, 'Our Lord, we have believed, so forgive us and have mercy upon us, and You are the best of the merciful.'

(110) But you took them in mockery to the point that they made you forget My remembrance, and you used to laugh at them.

(111) Indeed, I have rewarded them this Day for their patient endurance - that they are the attainers [of success]."

(112) [Allāh] will say, "How long did you remain on earth in number of years?"

(113) They will say, "We remained a day or part of a day; ask those who enumerate."

(114) He will say, "You stayed not but a little - if only you had known.

(115) Then did you think that We created you uselessly and that to Us you would not be returned?"

(116) So exalted is Allāh, the Sovereign,[946] the Truth;[947] there is no deity except Him, Lord of the Noble Throne.

(117) And whoever invokes besides Allāh another deity for which he has no proof - then his account is only with his Lord. Indeed, the disbelievers will not succeed.

---

[945] Their lips having been contracted by scorching until the teeth are exposed.
[946] "And owner of everything in existence.
[947] Or "the True Reality.""

(118) And, [O Muḥammad], say, "My Lord, forgive and have mercy, and You are the best of the merciful."

Surah An-Nur

(1) [This is] a sūrah which We have sent down and made [that within it] obligatory and revealed therein verses of clear evidence that you might remember.

(2) The [unmarried] woman or [unmarried] man found guilty of sexual intercourse[948] - lash each one of them with a hundred lashes,[949] and do not be taken by pity for them in the religion [i.e., law] of Allāh,[950] if you should believe in Allāh and the Last Day. And let a group of the believers witness their punishment.

(3) The fornicator does not marry except a [female] fornicator or polytheist, and none marries her except a fornicator[951] or a polytheist, and that [i.e., marriage to such persons] has been made unlawful to the believers.

(4) And those who accuse chaste women and then do not produce four witnesses - lash them with eighty lashes and do not accept from them testimony ever after. And those are the defiantly disobedient,

(5) Except for those who repent thereafter and reform, for indeed, Allāh is Forgiving and Merciful.

(6) And those who accuse their wives [of adultery] and have no witnesses except themselves - then the witness of one of them[952] [shall be] four testimonies [swearing] by Allāh that indeed, he is of the truthful.

(7) And the fifth [oath will be] that the curse of Allāh be upon him if he should be of the liars.

---

[948] "Either by voluntary confession of the offender or the testimony of four male witnesses to having actually seen the act take place. Otherwise, there can be no conviction.

[949] The ruling in this verse is applicable to unmarried fornicators. Execution by stoning is confirmed in the sunnah for convicted adulterers.

[950] i.e., Do not let sympathy for a guilty person move you to alter anything ordained by Allāh, for in His law is protection of society as a whole."

[951] Included in this ruling is the adulterer as well. Such persons cannot be married to believers unless they have repented and reformed.

[952] The husbands who have been betrayed.

(8) But it will prevent punishment from her if she gives four testimonies [swearing] by Allāh that indeed, he is of the liars.

(9) And the fifth [oath will be] that the wrath of Allāh be upon her if he was of the truthful.

(10) And if not for the favor of Allāh upon you and His mercy...[953] and because Allāh is Accepting of Repentance and Wise.

(11) Indeed, those who came with falsehood[954] are a group among you. Do not think it bad for you; rather, it is good for you. For every person among them is what [punishment] he has earned from the sin, and he who took upon himself the greater portion thereof[955] - for him is a great punishment [i.e., Hellfire].

(12) Why, when you heard it, did not the believing men and believing women think good of themselves [i.e., one another] and say, "This is an obvious falsehood"?

(13) Why did they [who slandered] not produce for it four witnesses? And when they do not produce the witnesses, then it is they, in the sight of Allāh, who are the liars.

(14) And if it had not been for the favor of Allāh upon you and His mercy in this world and the Hereafter, you would have been touched for that [lie] in which you were involved by a great punishment

(15) When you received it with your tongues[956] and said with your mouths that of which you had no knowledge and thought it was insignificant while it was, in the sight of Allāh, tremendous.

(16) And why, when you heard it, did you not say, "It is not for us to speak of this. Exalted are You, [O Allāh]; this is a great slander"?

(17) Allāh warns you against returning to the likes of this [conduct], ever, if you should be believers.

---

[953] The phrase omitted is estimated to be "...you would have surely been punished, destroyed or scandalized," or "...you would have suffered many difficult situations."

[954] "Referring to the incident when the Prophet's wife ʿĀʾishah was falsely accused by the hypocrites.

[955] i.e., ʿAbdullāh bin ʿUbayy, leader of the hypocrites."

[956] Rather than your ears, i.e., not thinking about what you had heard but hastening to repeat it carelessly.

(18) And Allāh makes clear to you the verses [i.e., His rulings], and Allāh is Knowing and Wise.

(19) Indeed, those who like that immorality[957] should be spread [or publicized] among those who have believed will have a painful punishment in this world and the Hereafter. And Allāh knows[958] and you do not know.

(20) And if it had not been for the favor of Allāh upon you and His mercy...[959] and because Allāh is Kind and Merciful.

(21) O you who have believed, do not follow the footsteps of Satan. And whoever follows the footsteps of Satan - indeed, he enjoins immorality and wrongdoing. And if not for the favor of Allāh upon you and His mercy, not one of you would have been pure, ever, but Allāh purifies whom He wills, and Allāh is Hearing and Knowing.

(22) And let not those of virtue among you and wealth swear not to give [aid] to their relatives and the needy and the emigrants for the cause of Allāh, and let them pardon and overlook. Would you not like that Allāh should forgive you? And Allāh is Forgiving and Merciful.

(23) Indeed, those who [falsely] accuse chaste, unaware and believing women are cursed in this world and the Hereafter; and they will have a great punishment

(24) On a Day when their tongues, their hands and their feet will bear witness against them as to what they used to do.

(25) That Day, Allāh will pay them in full their true [i.e., deserved] recompense, and they will know that it is Allāh who is the manifest Truth [i.e., perfect in justice].

(26) Evil words are for evil men, and evil men are [subjected] to evil words. And good words are for good men, and good men are [an object] of good words.[960] Those [good people] are declared innocent of what they [i.e., slanderers] say. For them is forgiveness and noble provision.

---

[957] "Specifically, unlawful sexual relations.

[958] The hidden aspects of all things: what is beneficial and what is harmful."

[959] See footnote to verse 10.

[960] Another accepted interpretation is "Evil women are for evil men, and evil men are for evil women. And good women are for good men, and good men are for good women."

(27) O you who have believed, do not enter houses other than your own houses until you ascertain welcome and greet[961] their inhabitants. That is best for you; perhaps you will be reminded [i.e., advised].

(28) And if you do not find anyone therein, do not enter them until permission has been given you. And if it is said to you, "Go back,"[962] then go back; it is purer for you. And Allāh is Knowing of what you do.

(29) There is no blame upon you for entering houses not inhabited in which there is convenience[963] for you. And Allāh knows what you reveal and what you conceal.

(30) Tell the believing men to reduce [some] of their vision[964] and guard their private parts.[965] That is purer for them. Indeed, Allāh is [fully] Aware of what they do.

(31) And tell the believing women to reduce [some] of their vision[966] and guard their private parts and not expose their adornment[967] except that which [necessarily] appears thereof[968] and to wrap [a portion of] their headcovers over their chests and not expose their adornment [i.e., beauty] except to their husbands, their fathers, their husbands' fathers, their sons, their husbands' sons, their brothers, their brothers' sons, their sisters' sons, their women, that which their right hands possess [i.e., slaves], or those male attendants having no physical desire,[969] or children who are not yet aware of the private aspects of women. And let them not stamp their feet to make known what they conceal of their adornment. And turn to Allāh in repentance, all of you, O believers, that you might succeed.

(32) And marry the unmarried among you and the righteous among your male slaves and female slaves. If they should be poor, Allāh will enrich them from His bounty, and Allāh is all-Encompassing and Knowing.

---

[961] By the words "As-salāmu ʿalaykum" ("Peace be upon you").

[962] Or a similar expression showing that the occupants are not prepared to receive visitors (which should be respected).

[963] Some benefit such as rest, shelter, commodities, one's personal belongings, etc.

[964] "Looking only at what is lawful and averting their eyes from what is unlawful.

[965] From being seen and from unlawful acts."

[966] "Looking only at what is lawful and averting their eyes from what is unlawful.

[967] Both natural beauty, such as hair or body shape, and that with which a woman beautifies herself of clothing, jewelry, etc

[968] i.e., the outer garments or whatever might appear out of necessity, such as a part of the face or the hands.

[969] Referring to an abnormal condition in which a man is devoid of sexual feeling."

(33) But let them who find not [the means for] marriage abstain [from sexual relations] until Allāh enriches them from His bounty. And those who seek a contract [for eventual emancipation] from among whom your right hands possess[970] - then make a contract with them if you know there is within them goodness and give them from the wealth of Allāh which He has given you. And do not compel your slave girls to prostitution, if they desire chastity, to seek [thereby] the temporary interests of worldly life. And if someone should compel them, then indeed, Allāh is [to them], after their compulsion, Forgiving and Merciful.

(34) And We have certainly sent down to you distinct verses[971] and examples from those who passed on before you and an admonition for those who fear Allāh.

(35) Allāh is the Light[972] of the heavens and the earth. The example of His light[973] is like a niche within which is a lamp;[974] the lamp is within glass, the glass as if it were a pearly [white] star lit from [the oil of] a blessed olive tree, neither of the east nor of the west, whose oil would almost glow even if untouched by fire. Light upon light. Allāh guides to His light whom He wills. And Allāh presents examples for the people, and Allāh is Knowing of all things.

(36) [Such niches are] in houses [i.e., mosques] which Allāh has ordered to be raised and that His name be mentioned [i.e., praised] therein; exalting Him within them in the morning and the evenings[975]

(37) [Are] men whom neither commerce nor sale distracts from the remembrance of Allāh and performance of prayer and giving of zakāh. They fear a Day in which the hearts and eyes will [fearfully] turn about -

(38) That Allāh may reward them [according to] the best of what they did and increase them from His bounty. And Allāh gives provision to whom He wills without account [i.e., limit].

(39) But those who disbelieved - their deeds are like a mirage in a lowland which a thirsty one thinks is water until, when he comes to it, he finds it is nothing but finds Allāh before him, and He will pay him in full his due; and Allāh is swift in account.

---

[970] i.e., those slaves who desire to purchase their freedom from their owners for a price agreed upon by both.

[971] i.e., rulings and ordinances, in particular those in this sūrah.

[972] "i.e., the source and bestower of light and enlightenment.

[973] His guidance in the heart of a believing servant.

[974] Literally, "a burning wick," which is the essence of a lamp."

[975] The term used here can refer to either afternoon or evening.

(40) Or [they are] like darknesses within an unfathomable sea which is covered by waves, upon which are waves, over which are clouds - darknesses, some of them upon others. When one puts out his hand [therein], he can hardly see it. And he to whom Allāh has not granted light - for him there is no light.

(41) Do you not see that Allāh is exalted by whomever is within the heavens and the earth and [by] the birds with wings spread [in flight]? Each [of them] has known his [means of] prayer and exalting [Him], and Allāh is Knowing of what they do.

(42) And to Allāh belongs the dominion of the heavens and the earth, and to Allāh is the destination.

(43) Do you not see that Allāh drives clouds? Then He brings them together; then He makes them into a mass, and you see the rain emerge from within it. And He sends down from the sky, mountains [of clouds] within which is hail, and He strikes with it whom He wills and averts it from whom He wills. The flash of its lightning almost takes away the eyesight.

(44) Allāh alternates the night and the day. Indeed in that is a lesson for those who have vision.

(45) Allāh has created every [living] creature from water. And of them are those that move on their bellies, and of them are those that walk on two legs, and of them are those that walk on four. Allāh creates what He wills. Indeed, Allāh is over all things competent.

(46) We have certainly sent down distinct verses. And Allāh guides whom He wills to a straight path.

(47) But they [i.e., the hypocrites] say, "We have believed in Allāh and in the Messenger, and we obey"; then a party of them turns away after that. And those are not believers.

(48) And when they are called to [the words of] Allāh and His Messenger to judge between them, at once a party of them turns aside [in refusal].

(49) But if the right is theirs, they come to him in prompt obedience.

(50) Is there disease in their hearts? Or have they doubted? Or do they fear that Allāh will be unjust to them, or His Messenger? Rather, it is they who are the wrongdoers [i.e., the unjust].

(51) The only statement of the [true] believers when they are called to Allāh and His Messenger to judge between them is that they say, "We hear and we obey." And those are the successful.

(52) And whoever obeys Allāh and His Messenger and fears Allāh and is conscious of Him - it is those who are the attainers.

(53) And they swear by Allāh their strongest oaths that if you ordered them, they would go forth [in Allāh's cause]. Say, "Do not swear. [Such] obedience is known.[976] Indeed, Allāh is [fully] Aware of that which you do."

(54) Say, "Obey Allāh and obey the Messenger; but if you turn away - then upon him is only that [duty] with which he has been charged, and upon you is that with which you have been charged. And if you obey him, you will be [rightly] guided. And there is not upon the Messenger except the [responsibility for] clear notification."

(55) Allāh has promised those who have believed among you and done righteous deeds that He will surely grant them succession [to authority] upon the earth just as He granted it to those before them and that He will surely establish for them [therein] their religion which He has preferred for them and that He will surely substitute for them, after their fear, security, [for] they worship Me, not associating anything with Me. But whoever disbelieves[977] after that - then those are the defiantly disobedient.

(56) And establish prayer and give zakāh and obey the Messenger - that you may receive mercy.

(57) Never think that the disbelievers are causing failure [to Allāh] upon the earth. Their refuge will be the Fire - and how wretched the destination.

(58) O you who have believed, let those whom your right hands possess and those who have not [yet] reached puberty among you ask permission of you [before entering] at three times: before the dawn prayer and when you put aside your clothing [for rest] at noon and after the night prayer. [These are] three times of privacy[978] for you. There is no blame upon you nor upon them beyond these [periods], for they continually circulate among you - some of you, among others. Thus does Allāh make clear to you the verses [i.e., His ordinances]; and Allāh is Knowing and Wise.

(59) And when the children among you reach puberty, let them ask permission [at all times] as those before them have done. Thus does Allāh make clear to you His verses; and Allāh is Knowing and Wise.

---

[976] i.e., the hypocrites' pretense of obedience is known to be a lie.
[977] i.e., denies the favor of Allāh or does not live by His ordinance.
[978] Literally, "exposure" or "being uncovered."

(60) And women of post-menstrual age who have no desire for marriage - there is no blame upon them for putting aside their outer garments [but] not displaying adornment. But to modestly refrain [from that] is better for them. And Allāh is Hearing and Knowing.

(61) There is not upon the blind [any] constraint nor upon the lame constraint nor upon the ill constraint nor upon yourselves when you eat from your [own] houses or the houses of your fathers or the houses of your mothers or the houses of your brothers or the houses of your sisters or the houses of your father's brothers or the houses of your father's sisters or the houses of your mother's brothers or the houses of your mother's sisters or [from houses] whose keys you possess or [from the house] of your friend. There is no blame upon you whether you eat together or separately. But when you enter houses, give greetings of peace[979] upon each other - a greeting from Allāh, blessed and good. Thus does Allāh make clear to you the verses [of ordinance] that you may understand.

(62) The believers are only those who believe in Allāh and His Messenger and, when they are [meeting] with him for a matter of common interest, do not depart until they have asked his permission. Indeed, those who ask your permission, [O Muḥammad] - those are the ones who believe in Allāh and His Messenger. So when they ask your permission due to something of their affairs, then give permission to whom you will among them and ask forgiveness for them of Allāh. Indeed, Allāh is Forgiving and Merciful.

(63) Do not make [your] calling of the Messenger among yourselves as the call of one of you to another. Already Allāh knows those of you who slip away, concealed by others. So let those beware who dissent from his [i.e., the Prophet's] order,[980] lest fitnah[981] strike them or a painful punishment.

(64) Unquestionably, to Allāh belongs whatever is in the heavens and earth. Already He knows that upon which you [stand][982] and [knows] the Day[983] when they will be returned to Him and He will inform them of what they have done. And Allāh is Knowing of all things.

---

[979] Saying, "As-salāmu ʿalaykum" ("Peace be upon you").
[980] "Meaning also his way or his sunnah.
[981] Trials, affliction, dissension, strife, etc."
[982] "i.e., your position - the basis for your actions (whether sincere faith or hypocrisy) and the condition of your souls.
[983] The meaning can also be rendered "...and [let them beware of] the Day...""

Surah Al-Furqan

(1) Blessed is He who sent down the Criterion upon His Servant that he may be to the worlds a warner -

(2) He to whom belongs the dominion of the heavens and the earth and who has not taken a son and has not had a partner in dominion and has created each thing and determined it with [precise] determination.

(3) But they have taken besides Him gods which create nothing, while they are created, and possess not for themselves any harm or benefit and possess not [power to cause] death or life or resurrection.

(4) And those who disbelieve say, "This [Qur'ān] is not except a falsehood he invented, and another people assisted him in it." But they have committed an injustice and a lie.

(5) And they say, "Legends of the former peoples which he has written down, and they are dictated to him morning and afternoon."

(6) Say, [O Muḥammad], "It has been revealed by He who knows [every] secret within the heavens and the earth. Indeed, He is ever Forgiving and Merciful."

(7) And they say, "What is this messenger that eats food and walks in the markets? Why was there not sent down to him an angel so he would be with him a warner?

(8) Or [why is not] a treasure presented to him [from heaven], or does he [not] have a garden from which he eats?" And the wrongdoers say, "You follow not but a man affected by magic."

(9) Look how they strike for you comparisons;[984] but they have strayed, so they cannot [find] a way.

(10) Blessed is He who, if He willed, could have made for you [something] better than that - gardens beneath which rivers flow - and could make for you palaces.

(11) But they have denied the Hour, and We have prepared for those who deny the Hour a Blaze.

(12) When it [i.e., the Hellfire] sees them from a distant place, they will hear its fury and roaring.

---

[984] From their own imaginations in order to deny and discredit you.

(13) And when they are thrown into a narrow place therein bound in chains, they will cry out thereupon for destruction.

(14) [They will be told], "Do not cry this Day for one destruction but cry for much destruction."

(15) Say, "Is that better or the Garden of Eternity which is promised to the righteous? It will be for them a reward and destination.

(16) For them therein is whatever they wish, [while] abiding eternally. It is ever upon your Lord a promise [worthy to be] requested.[985]

(17) And [mention] the Day He will gather them and that which they worship besides Allāh and will say, "Did you mislead these, My servants, or did they [themselves] stray from the way?"

(18) They will say, "Exalted are You! It was not for us to take besides You any allies [i.e., protectors]. But You provided comforts for them and their fathers until they forgot the message and became a people ruined."

(19) So they will deny you, [disbelievers], in what you say,[986] and you cannot avert [punishment] or [find] help. And whoever commits injustice[987] among you - We will make him taste a great punishment.

(20) And We did not send before you, [O Muḥammad], any of the messengers except that they ate food and walked in the markets. And We have made some of you [people] as trial for others - will you have patience? And ever is your Lord, Seeing.

(21) And those who do not expect the meeting with Us say, "Why were not angels sent down to us, or [why] do we [not] see our Lord?" They have certainly become arrogant within themselves[988] and [become] insolent with great insolence.

(22) The day they see the angels[989] - no good tidings will there be that day for the criminals, and [the angels] will say, "Prevented and inaccessible."[990]

---

[985] Or "...a promise requested [for them by the angels]."

[986] "At the time of Judgement the false objects of worship will betray their worshippers and deny them.

[987] Specifically, association of others with Allāh."

[988] Additional meanings are "among themselves" and "over [the matter of] themselves."

[989] "i.e., at the time of death.

[990] Referring to any good tidings."

(23) And We will approach [i.e., regard][991] what they have done of deeds and make them as dust dispersed.

(24) The companions of Paradise, that Day, are [in] a better settlement and better resting place.

(25) And [mention] the Day when the heaven will split open with [emerging] clouds,[992] and the angels will be sent down in successive descent.

(26) True sovereignty, that Day, is for the Most Merciful. And it will be upon the disbelievers a difficult Day.

(27) And the Day the wrongdoer will bite on his hands [in regret] he will say, "Oh, I wish I had taken with the Messenger a way.[993]

(28) Oh, woe to me! I wish I had not taken that one[994] as a friend.

(29) He led me away from the remembrance[995] after it had come to me. And ever is Satan, to man, a deserter."[996]

(30) And the Messenger has said, "O my Lord, indeed my people have taken this Qur'ān as [a thing] abandoned."[997]

(31) And thus have We made for every prophet an enemy from among the criminals. But sufficient is your Lord as a guide and a helper.

(32) And those who disbelieve say, "Why was the Qur'ān not revealed to him all at once?" Thus [it is] that We may strengthen thereby your heart. And We have spaced it distinctly.[998]

(33) And they do not come to you with an example [i.e., argument] except that We bring you the truth and the best explanation.

(34) The ones who are gathered on their faces to Hell - those are the worst in position and farthest astray in [their] way.

---

[991] On the Day of Judgement.

[992] Within which are the angels.

[993] i.e., followed the Prophet (ﷺ) on a path of guidance.

[994] The person who misguided him.

[995] "i.e., the Qur'ān or the remembrance of Allāh.

[996] Forsaking him once he has led him into evil."

[997] i.e., avoiding it, not listening to or understanding it, not living by it, or preferring something else to it.

[998] Also, "recited it with distinct recitation."

(35) And We had certainly given Moses the Scripture and appointed with him his brother Aaron as an assistant.

(36) And We said, "Go both of you to the people who have denied Our signs." Then We destroyed them with [complete] destruction.

(37) And the people of Noah - when they denied the messengers,[999] We drowned them, and We made them for mankind a sign. And We have prepared for the wrongdoers a painful punishment.

(38) And [We destroyed] ʿAad and Thamūd and the companions of the well[1000] and many generations between them.

(39) And for each We presented examples [as warnings], and each We destroyed with [total] destruction.

(40) And they have already come upon the town which was showered with a rain of evil [i.e., stones]. So have they not seen it? But they are not expecting resurrection.[1001]

(41) And when they see you, [O Muḥammad], they take you not except in ridicule, [saying], "Is this the one whom Allāh has sent as a messenger?

(42) He almost would have misled us from our gods had we not been steadfast in [worship of] them." But they are going to know, when they see the punishment, who is farthest astray in [his] way.

(43) Have you seen the one who takes as his god his own desire? Then would you be responsible for him?

(44) Or do you think that most of them hear or reason? They are not except like livestock.[1002] Rather, they are [even] more astray in [their] way.

(45) Have you not considered your Lord - how He extends the shadow, and if He willed, He could have made it stationary? Then We made the sun for it an indication.[1003]

---

[999] Their denial of Noah was as if they had denied all those who brought the same message from Allāh.

[1000] Said to be a people who denied Prophet Shuʿayb or possibly those mentioned in Sūrah Yā Seen, 36:13-29.

[1001] So they do not benefit from lessons of the past.

[1002] i.e., cattle or sheep, that follow without question wherever they are led.

[1003] i.e., showing the existence of a shadow or making it apparent by contrast.

(46) Then We [retract and] hold it with Us for a brief grasp.[1004]

(47) And it is He who has made the night for you as clothing[1005] and sleep [a means for] rest and has made the day a resurrection.[1006]

(48) And it is He who sends the winds as good tidings before His mercy [i.e., rainfall], and We send down from the sky pure water

(49) That We may bring to life thereby a dead land and give it as drink to those We created of numerous livestock and men.

(50) And We have certainly distributed it among them that they might be reminded,[1007] but most of the people refuse except disbelief.

(51) And if We had willed, We could have sent into every city a warner.[1008]

(52) So do not obey the disbelievers, and strive against them with it [i.e., the Qur'ān] a great striving.

(53) And it is He who has released [simultaneously] the two seas [i.e., bodies of water], one fresh and sweet and one salty and bitter, and He placed between them a barrier and prohibiting partition.

(54) And it is He who has created from water [i.e., semen] a human being and made him [a relative by] lineage and marriage. And ever is your Lord competent [concerning creation].

(55) But they worship rather than Allāh that which does not benefit them or harm them, and the disbeliever is ever, against his Lord, an assistant [to Satan].

(56) And We have not sent you, [O Muḥammad], except as a bringer of good tidings and a warner.

(57) Say, "I do not ask of you for it any payment - only that whoever wills might take to his Lord a way."

(58) And rely upon the Ever-Living who does not die, and exalt [Allāh] with His praise. And sufficient is He to be, with the sins of His servants, [fully] Aware -

---

[1004] i.e., when the sun is overhead at noon.

[1005] "Covering you in darkness and providing rest.

[1006] For renewal of life and activity."

[1007] Of Allāh's ability to bring the dead to life.

[1008] However, Allāh willed that Prophet Muḥammad (ﷺ) be sent as the final messenger for all peoples of the earth until the Day of Resurrection.

(59) He who created the heavens and the earth and what is between them in six days and then established Himself above the Throne[1009] - the Most Merciful, so ask about Him one well informed [i.e., the Prophet (ﷺ)].

(60) And when it is said to them, "Prostrate to the Most Merciful," they say, "And what is the Most Merciful? Should we prostrate to that which you order us?" And it increases them in aversion.

(61) Blessed is He who has placed in the sky great stars and placed therein a [burning] lamp and luminous moon.

(62) And it is He who has made the night and the day in succession for whoever desires to remember or desires gratitude.

(63) And the servants of the Most Merciful are those who walk upon the earth easily,[1010] and when the ignorant address them [harshly], they say [words of] peace,[1011]

(64) And those who spend [part of] the night to their Lord prostrating and standing [in prayer]

(65) And those who say, "Our Lord, avert from us the punishment of Hell. Indeed, its punishment is ever adhering;

(66) Indeed, it is evil as a settlement and residence."

(67) And [they are] those who, when they spend, do so not excessively or sparingly but are ever, between that, [justly] moderate

(68) And those who do not invoke[1012] with Allāh another deity or kill the soul which Allāh has forbidden [to be killed], except by right, and do not commit unlawful sexual intercourse. And whoever should do that will meet a penalty.

(69) Multiplied for him is the punishment on the Day of Resurrection, and he will abide therein humiliated -

(70) Except for those who repent, believe and do righteous work. For them Allāh will replace their evil deeds with good. And ever is Allāh Forgiving and Merciful.

[1009] See footnotes to 2:19 and 7:54.
[1010] "i.e., gently, with dignity but without arrogance.
[1011] Or "safety," i.e., words free from fault or evil.
[1012] Or "worship."

(71) And he who repents and does righteousness does indeed turn to Allāh with [accepted] repentance.

(72) And [they are] those who do not testify to falsehood, and when they pass near ill speech, they pass by with dignity.

(73) And those who, when reminded of the verses of their Lord, do not fall upon them deaf and blind.

(74) And those who say, "Our Lord, grant us from among our wives and offspring comfort to our eyes[1013] and make us a leader [i.e., example] for the righteous."

(75) Those will be awarded the Chamber[1014] for what they patiently endured, and they will be received therein with greetings and [words of] peace,

(76) Abiding eternally therein. Good is the settlement and residence.

(77) Say, "What would my Lord care for you if not for your supplication?"[1015] For you [disbelievers] have denied, so it [i.e., your denial] is going to be adherent.[1016]

[1013] i.e., a source of happiness due to their righteousness.
[1014] The most elevated portion of Paradise
[1015] "i.e., faith and worship. An alternative meaning is "What would my Lord do with you..."
[1016] It will remain with them, causing punishment to be required and imperative upon them."

Surah Ash-Shu`ara'

(1) Ṭā, Seen, Meem.[1017]

(2) These are the verses of the clear Book.

(3) Perhaps, [O Muḥammad], you would kill yourself with grief that they will not be believers.

(4) If We willed, We could send down to them from the sky a sign for which their necks would remain humbled.[1018]

(5) And no mention [i.e., revelation] comes to them anew from the Most Merciful except that they turn away from it.

(6) For they have already denied, but there will come to them the news of that which they used to ridicule.

(7) Did they not look at the earth - how much We have produced therein from every noble kind?

(8) Indeed in that is a sign, but most of them were not to be believers.

(9) And indeed, your Lord - He is the Exalted in Might, the Merciful.

(10) And [mention] when your Lord called Moses, [saying], "Go to the wrongdoing people -

(11) The people of Pharaoh. Will they not fear Allāh?"

(12) He said, "My Lord, indeed I fear that they will deny me

(13) And that my breast will tighten and my tongue will not be fluent, so send for Aaron.

(14) And they have upon me a [claim due to] sin, so I fear that they will kill me."

(15) [Allāh] said, "No. Go both of you with Our signs; indeed, We are with you, listening.

(16) Go to Pharaoh and say, 'We are the messengers[1019] of the Lord of the worlds,

---

[1017] See footnote to 2:1.
[1018] i.e., they would be compelled to believe.
[1019] The singular form in Arabic indicates that both were sent with a single message.

(17) [Commanded to say], "Send with us the Children of Israel."'"

(18) [Pharaoh] said, "Did we not raise you among us as a child, and you remained among us for years of your life?

(19) And [then] you did your deed which you did,[1020] and you were of the ungrateful."

(20) [Moses] said, "I did it, then, while I was of those astray [i.e., ignorant].

(21) So I fled from you when I feared you. Then my Lord granted me judgement [i.e., wisdom and prophet hood] and appointed me [as one] of the messengers.

(22) And is this a favor of which you remind me - that you have enslaved the Children of Israel?"

(23) Said Pharaoh, "And what is the Lord of the worlds?"

(24) [Moses] said, "The Lord of the heavens and earth and that between them, if you should be convinced."

(25) [Pharaoh] said to those around him, "Do you not hear?"

(26) [Moses] said, "Your Lord and the Lord of your first forefathers."

(27) [Pharaoh] said,[1021] "Indeed, your 'messenger' who has been sent to you is mad."

(28) [Moses] said, "Lord of the east and the west and that between them, if you were to reason."

(29) [Pharaoh] said, "If you take a god other than me, I will surely place you among those imprisoned."

(30) [Moses] said, "Even if I brought you something [i.e., proof] manifest?"

(31) [Pharaoh] said, "Then bring it, if you should be of the truthful."

(32) So [Moses] threw his staff, and suddenly it was a serpent manifest.[1022]

(33) And he drew out his hand; thereupon it was white for the observers.

(34) [Pharaoh] said to the eminent ones around him, "Indeed, this is a learned magician.

[1020] i.e., striking the Copt, who died as a result.
[1021] Angrily addressing those present.
[1022] i.e., clearly genuine.

(35) He wants to drive you out of your land by his magic, so what do you advise?"

(36) They said, "Postpone [the matter of] him and his brother and send among the cities gatherers

(37) Who will bring you every learned, skilled magician."

(38) So the magicians were assembled for the appointment of a well-known day.[1023]

(39) And it was said to the people, "Will you congregate.

(40) That we might follow the magicians if they are the predominant?"

(41) And when the magicians arrived, they said to Pharaoh, "Is there indeed for us a reward if we are the predominant?"

(42) He said, "Yes, and indeed, you will then be of those near [to me]."

(43) Moses said to them, "Throw whatever you will throw."

(44) So they threw their ropes and their staffs and said, "By the might of Pharaoh, indeed it is we who are predominant."

(45) Then Moses threw his staff, and at once it devoured what they falsified.

(46) So the magicians fell down in prostration [to Allāh].

(47) They said, "We have believed in the Lord of the worlds,

(48) The Lord of Moses and Aaron."

(49) [Pharaoh] said, "You believed him [i.e., Moses] before I gave you permission. Indeed, he is your leader who has taught you magic, but you are going to know. I will surely cut off your hands and your feet on opposite sides, and I will surely crucify you all."

(50) They said, "No harm. Indeed, to our Lord we will return.

(51) Indeed, we aspire that our Lord will forgive us our sins because we were the first of the believers."

(52) And We inspired to Moses, "Travel by night with My servants; indeed, you will be pursued."

[1023] i.e., the morning of the day of festival. See 20:58-59.

(53) Then Pharaoh sent among the cities gatherers[1024]

(54) [And said], "Indeed, those are but a small band,

(55) And indeed, they are enraging us,

(56) And indeed, we are a cautious society..."

(57) So We removed them from gardens and springs

(58) And treasures and honorable station[1025] -

(59) Thus. And We caused to inherit it the Children of Israel.

(60) So they pursued them at sunrise.

(61) And when the two companies saw one another, the companions of Moses said, "Indeed, we are to be overtaken!"

(62) [Moses] said, "No! Indeed, with me is my Lord; He will guide me."

(63) Then We inspired to Moses, "Strike with your staff the sea," and it parted, and each portion was like a great towering mountain.

(64) And We advanced thereto the others [i.e., the pursuers].

(65) And We saved Moses and those with him, all together.

(66) Then We drowned the others.

(67) Indeed in that is a sign, but most of them were not to be believers.

(68) And indeed, your Lord - He is the Exalted in Might, the Merciful.

(69) And recite to them the news of Abraham,

(70) When he said to his father and his people, "What do you worship?"

(71) They said, "We worship idols and remain to them devoted."

(72) He said, "Do they hear you when you supplicate?

(73) Or do they benefit you, or do they harm?"

(74) They said, "But we found our fathers doing thus."

[1024] Recruiters of an army to prevent the emigration of the Children of Israel.
[1025] Allāh (subḥānahu wa taʿālā) caused them to abandon their wealth and property in pursuit of the Israelites.

(75) He said, "Then do you see what you have been worshipping,

(76) You and your ancient forefathers?

(77) Indeed, they are enemies to me, except the Lord of the worlds,[1026]

(78) Who created me, and He [it is who] guides me.

(79) And it is He who feeds me and gives me drink.

(80) And when I am ill, it is He who cures me

(81) And who will cause me to die and then bring me to life

(82) And who I aspire that He will forgive me my sin on the Day of Recompense."

(83) [And he said], "My Lord, grant me authority and join me with the righteous.

(84) And grant me a mention [i.e., reputation] of honor among later generations.

(85) And place me among the inheritors of the Garden of Pleasure.

(86) And forgive my father. Indeed, he has been of those astray.

(87) And do not disgrace me on the Day they are [all] resurrected -

(88) The Day when there will not benefit [anyone] wealth or children

(89) But only one who comes to Allāh with a sound heart."

(90) And Paradise will be brought near [that Day] to the righteous.

(91) And Hellfire will be brought forth for the deviators,

(92) And it will be said to them, "Where are those you used to worship

(93) Other than Allāh? Can they help you or help themselves?"

(94) So they will be overturned into it [i.e., Hellfire], they and the deviators

(95) And the soldiers of Iblees, all together.

(96) They will say while they dispute therein,

(97) "By Allāh, we were indeed in manifest error

[1026] The people worshipped idols in addition to Allāh.

(98) When we equated you with the Lord of the worlds.

(99) And no one misguided us except the criminals.

(100) So now we have no intercessors

(101) And not a devoted friend.

(102) Then if we only had a return [to the world] and could be of the believers..."[1027]

(103) Indeed in that is a sign, but most of them were not to be believers.

(104) And indeed, your Lord - He is the Exalted in Might, the Merciful.

(105) The people of Noah denied the messengers[1028]

(106) When their brother Noah said to them, "Will you not fear Allāh?

(107) Indeed, I am to you a trustworthy messenger.

(108) So fear Allāh and obey me.

(109) And I do not ask you for it any payment. My payment is only from the Lord of the worlds.

(110) So fear Allāh and obey me."

(111) They said, "Should we believe you while you are followed by the lowest [class of people]?"

(112) He said, "And what is my knowledge of what they used to do?

(113) Their account is only upon my Lord, if you [could] perceive.

(114) And I am not one to drive away the believers.

(115) I am only a clear warner."

(116) They said, "If you do not desist, O Noah, you will surely be of those who are stoned."

(117) He said, "My Lord, indeed my people have denied me.

[1027] The conclusion of this verse is estimated as "...we would do this or that."
[1028] See footnote to 25:37.

(118) Then judge between me and them with decisive judgement and save me and those with me of the believers."

(119) So We saved him and those with him in the laden ship.

(120) Then We drowned thereafter the remaining ones.

(121) Indeed in that is a sign, but most of them were not to be believers.

(122) And indeed, your Lord - He is the Exalted in Might, the Merciful.

(123) ʿAad denied the messengers

(124) When their brother Hūd said to them, "Will you not fear Allāh?

(125) Indeed, I am to you a trustworthy messenger.

(126) So fear Allāh and obey me.

(127) And I do not ask you for it any payment. My payment is only from the Lord of the worlds.

(128) Do you construct on every elevation a sign,[1029] amusing yourselves,

(129) And take for yourselves constructions [i.e., palaces and fortresses] that you might abide eternally?

(130) And when you strike, you strike as tyrants.

(131) So fear Allāh and obey me.

(132) And fear He who provided you with that which you know,

(133) Provided you with grazing livestock and children

(134) And gardens and springs.

(135) Indeed, I fear for you the punishment of a terrible day."

(136) They said, "It is all the same to us whether you advise or are not of the advisors.

(137) This is not but the custom of the former peoples,

(138) And we are not to be punished."

[1029] i.e., a symbol or indication of their wealth and power. They used to build lofty structures along the road to be seen by all who passed by.

(139) And they denied him, so We destroyed them. Indeed in that is a sign, but most of them were not to be believers.

(140) And indeed, your Lord - He is the Exalted in Might, the Merciful.

(141) Thamūd denied the messengers

(142) When their brother Ṣāliḥ said to them, "Will you not fear Allāh?

(143) Indeed, I am to you a trustworthy messenger.

(144) So fear Allāh and obey me.

(145) And I do not ask you for it any payment. My payment is only from the Lord of the worlds.

(146) Will you be left in what is here, secure [from death],

(147) Within gardens and springs

(148) And fields of crops and palm trees with softened fruit?

(149) And you carve out of the mountains, homes, with skill.

(150) So fear Allāh and obey me.

(151) And do not obey the order of the transgressors,

(152) Who cause corruption in the land and do not amend."

(153) They said, "You are only of those affected by magic.

(154) You are but a man like ourselves, so bring a sign, if you should be of the truthful."

(155) He said, "This is a she-camel.[1030] For her is a [time of] drink, and for you is a [time of] drink, [each] on a known day.

(156) And do not touch her with harm, lest you be seized by the punishment of a terrible day."

(157) But they hamstrung her and so became regretful.

(158) And the punishment seized them. Indeed in that is a sign, but most of them were not to be believers.

[1030] Miraculously sent to them as a sign by Allāh.

(159) And indeed, your Lord - He is the Exalted in Might, the Merciful.

(160) The people of Lot denied the messengers

(161) When their brother Lot said to them, "Will you not fear Allāh?

(162) Indeed, I am to you a trustworthy messenger.

(163) So fear Allāh and obey me.

(164) And I do not ask you for it any payment. My payment is only from the Lord of the worlds.

(165) Do you approach males among the worlds[1031]

(166) And leave what your Lord has created for you as mates? But you are a people transgressing."

(167) They said, "If you do not desist, O Lot, you will surely be of those evicted."

(168) He said, "Indeed, I am, toward your deed, of those who detest [it].

(169) My Lord, save me and my family from [the consequence of] what they do."

(170) So We saved him and his family, all,

(171) Except an old woman[1032] among those who remained behind.

(172) Then We destroyed the others.

(173) And We rained upon them a rain [of stones], and evil was the rain of those who were warned.

(174) Indeed in that is a sign, but most of them were not to be believers.

(175) And indeed, your Lord - He is the Exalted in Might, the Merciful.

(176) The companions of the thicket [i.e., the people of Madyan] denied the messengers

(177) When Shu'ayb said to them, "Will you not fear Allāh?

(178) Indeed, I am to you a trustworthy messenger.

[1031] i.e., Are there, out of all Allāh's creatures, any besides you who commit this unnatural act?

[1032] Lot's wife, who had collaborated with the evildoers.

(179) So fear Allāh and obey me.

(180) And I do not ask you for it any payment. My payment is only from the Lord of the worlds.

(181) Give full measure and do not be of those who cause loss.

(182) And weigh with an even [i.e., honest] balance.

(183) And do not deprive people of their due and do not commit abuse on earth, spreading corruption.

(184) And fear He who created you and the former creation."[1033]

(185) They said, "You are only of those affected by magic.

(186) You are but a man like ourselves, and indeed, we think you are among the liars.

(187) So cause to fall upon us fragments of the sky, if you should be of the truthful."

(188) He said, "My Lord is most knowing of what you do."

(189) And they denied him, so the punishment of the day of the black cloud seized them. Indeed, it was the punishment of a terrible day.

(190) Indeed in that is a sign, but most of them were not to be believers.

(191) And indeed, your Lord - He is the Exalted in Might, the Merciful.

(192) And indeed, it [i.e., the Qur'ān] is the revelation of the Lord of the worlds.

(193) The Trustworthy Spirit [i.e., Gabriel] has brought it down

(194) Upon your heart, [O Muḥammad] - that you may be of the warners -

(195) In a clear Arabic language.

(196) And indeed, it is [mentioned] in the scriptures of former peoples.

(197) And has it not been a sign to them that it is recognized by the scholars of the Children of Israel?

(198) And even if We had revealed it to one among the foreigners[1034]

[1033] i.e., previous generations.
[1034] i.e., the non-Arabs or those who are not fluent in the Arabic language.

(199) And he had recited it to them [perfectly],[1035] they would [still] not have been believers in it.

(200) Thus have We inserted it [i.e., disbelief] into the hearts of the criminals.

(201) They will not believe in it until they see the painful punishment.

(202) And it will come to them suddenly while they perceive [it] not.

(203) And they will say, "May we be reprieved?"

(204) So for Our punishment are they impatient?

(205) Then have you considered if We gave them enjoyment for years

(206) And then there came to them that which they were promised?

(207) They would not be availed by the enjoyment with which they were provided.

(208) And We did not destroy any city except that it had warners

(209) As a reminder; and never have We been unjust.

(210) And the devils have not brought it [i.e., the revelation] down.[1036]

(211) It is not allowable for them, nor would they be able.

(212) Indeed they, from [its] hearing, are removed.[1037]

(213) So do not invoke[1038] with Allāh another deity and [thus] be among the punished.

(214) And warn, [O Muḥammad], your closest kindred.

(215) And lower your wing [i.e., show kindness] to those who follow you of the believers.

(216) And if they disobey you, then say, "Indeed, I am disassociated from what you are doing."

(217) And rely upon the Exalted in Might, the Merciful,

[1035] As a miracle from Allāh.

[1036] As was asserted by the disbelievers. Rather, it was brought by Gabriel, the Trustworthy Spirit.

[1037] As mentioned in 72:9.

[1038] Or "worship."

(218) Who sees you when you arise[1039]

(219) And your movement among those who prostrate.[1040]

(220) Indeed, He is the Hearing, the Knowing.

(221) Shall I inform you upon whom the devils descend?

(222) They descend upon every sinful liar.

(223) They pass on what is heard,[1041] and most of them are liars.

(224) And the poets - [only] the deviators follow them;

(225) Do you not see that in every valley they roam[1042]

(226) And that they say what they do not do? -

(227) Except those [poets] who believe and do righteous deeds and remember Allāh often and defend [the Muslims][1043] after they were wronged. And those who have wronged are going to know to what [kind of] return they will be returned.

[1039] From your bed at night for prayer while you are alone.
[1040] i.e., among those who pray with you in congregation.
[1041] This was before they were prevented, as described in 72:8-9.
[1042] Speaking lies indiscriminately and praising and disparaging others according to whim.
[1043] By replying through poetry to the attacks of hostile poets.

Surah An-Naml

(1) Ṭā, Seen.[1044] These are the verses of the Qur'ān [i.e., recitation] and a clear Book

(2) As guidance and good tidings for the believers

(3) Who establish prayer and give zakāh, and of the Hereafter they are certain [in faith].

(4) Indeed, for those who do not believe in the Hereafter, We have made pleasing to them their deeds, so they wander blindly.

(5) Those are the ones for whom there will be the worst of punishment, and in the Hereafter they are the greatest losers.

(6) And indeed, [O Muḥammad], you receive the Qur'ān from one Wise and Knowing.

(7) [Mention] when Moses said to his family, "Indeed, I have perceived a fire. I will bring you from there information or will bring you a burning torch that you may warm yourselves."

(8) But when he came to it, he was called, "Blessed is whoever is at the fire and whoever is around it. And exalted is Allāh, Lord of the worlds.

(9) O Moses, indeed it is I - Allāh, the Exalted in Might, the Wise."

(10) And [he was told], "Throw down your staff." But when he saw it writhing as if it were a snake, he turned in flight and did not return.[1045] [Allāh said], "O Moses, fear not. Indeed, in My presence the messengers do not fear.

(11) Otherwise, he who wrongs, then substitutes good after evil - indeed, I am Forgiving and Merciful.

(12) And put your hand into the opening of your garment [at the breast]; it will come out white without disease. [These are] among the nine signs [you will take] to Pharaoh and his people. Indeed, they have been a people defiantly disobedient."

(13) But when there came to them Our visible signs, they said, "This is obvious magic."

[1044] See footnote to 2:1.
[1045] Or "did not look back."

(14) And they rejected them, while their [inner] selves were convinced thereof, out of injustice and haughtiness. So see how was the end of the corrupters.

(15) And We had certainly given to David and Solomon knowledge, and they said, "Praise [is due] to Allāh, who has favored us over many of His believing servants."

(16) And Solomon inherited David. He said, "O people, we have been taught the language of birds, and we have been given from all things. Indeed, this is evident bounty."

(17) And gathered for Solomon were his soldiers of the jinn and men and birds, and they were [marching] in rows

(18) Until, when they came upon the valley of the ants, an ant said, "O ants, enter your dwellings that you not be crushed by Solomon and his soldiers while they perceive not."

(19) So [Solomon] smiled, amused at her speech, and said, "My Lord, enable me[1046] to be grateful for Your favor which You have bestowed upon me and upon my parents and to do righteousness of which You approve. And admit me by Your mercy into [the ranks of] Your righteous servants."[1047]

(20) And he took attendance of the birds and said, "Why do I not see the hoopoe - or is he among the absent?

(21) I will surely punish him with a severe punishment or slaughter him unless he brings me clear authorization."[1048]

(22) But he [i.e., the hoopoe] stayed not long and said, "I have encompassed [in knowledge] that which you have not encompassed, and I have come to you from Sheba with certain news.

(23) Indeed, I found [there] a woman ruling them, and she has been given of all things, and she has a great throne.

(24) I found her and her people prostrating to the sun instead of Allāh, and Satan has made their deeds pleasing to them and averted them from [His] way, so they are not guided,

---

[1046] "More literally, "gather within me the utmost strength and ability."
[1047] Or "with Your righteous servants [into Paradise].""
[1048] i.e., a valid excuse.

(25) [And] so they do not prostrate to Allāh, who brings forth what is hidden within the heavens and the earth and knows what you conceal and what you declare -

(26) Allāh - there is no deity except Him, Lord of the Great Throne."

(27) [Solomon] said, "We will see whether you were truthful or were of the liars.

(28) Take this letter of mine and deliver it to them. Then leave them and see what [answer] they will return."

(29) She said, "O eminent ones, indeed, to me has been delivered a noble letter.

(30) Indeed, it is from Solomon, and indeed, it is [i.e., reads]: 'In the name of Allāh, the Entirely Merciful, the Especially Merciful,

(31) Be not haughty with me but come to me in submission [as Muslims].'"

(32) She said, "O eminent ones, advise me in my affair. I would not decide a matter until you witness [for] me."[1049]

(33) They said, "We are men of strength and of great military might, but the command is yours, so see what you will command."

(34) She said, "Indeed kings - when they enter a city, they ruin it and render the honored of its people humbled. And thus do they do.

(35) But indeed, I will send to them a gift and see with what [reply] the messengers will return."

(36) So when they came to Solomon, he said, "Do you provide me with wealth? But what Allāh has given me is better than what He has given you. Rather, it is you who rejoice in your gift.

(37) Return to them, for we will surely come to them with soldiers that they will be powerless to encounter, and we will surely expel them therefrom in humiliation, and they will be debased."

(38) [Solomon] said, "O assembly [of jinn], which of you will bring me her throne before they come to me in submission?"

(39) A powerful one from among the jinn said, "I will bring it to you before you rise from your place, and indeed, I am for this [task] strong and trustworthy."

(40) Said one who had knowledge from the Scripture, "I will bring it to you before your glance returns to you." And when [Solomon] saw it placed before him, he said,

---

[1049] i.e., are present with me or testify in my favor.

"This is from the favor of my Lord to test me whether I will be grateful or ungrateful. And whoever is grateful - his gratitude is only for [the benefit of] himself. And whoever is ungrateful - then indeed, my Lord is Free of need and Generous."

(41) He said, "Disguise for her her throne; we will see whether she will be guided [to truth] or will be of those who is not guided."

(42) So when she arrived, it was said [to her], "Is your throne like this?" She said, "[It is] as though it was it." [Solomon said], "And we were given knowledge before her, and we have been Muslims [in submission to Allāh].

(43) And that which she was worshipping other than Allāh had averted her [from submission to Him]. Indeed, she was from a disbelieving people."

(44) She was told, "Enter the palace." But when she saw it, she thought it was a body of water[1050] and uncovered her shins [to wade through]. He said, "Indeed, it is a palace [whose floor is] made smooth with glass." She said, "My Lord, indeed I have wronged myself, and I submit with Solomon to Allāh, Lord of the worlds."

(45) And We had certainly sent to Thamūd their brother Ṣāliḥ, [saying], "Worship Allāh," and at once they were two parties conflicting.

(46) He said, "O my people, why are you impatient for evil before [i.e., instead of] good?[1051] Why do you not seek forgiveness of Allāh that you may receive mercy?"

(47) They said, "We consider you a bad omen, you and those with you." He said, "Your omen [i.e., fate] is with Allāh. Rather, you are a people being tested."[1052]

(48) And there were in the city nine family heads causing corruption in the land and not amending [its affairs].

(49) They said, "Take a mutual oath by Allāh that we will kill him by night, he and his family. Then we will say to his executor,[1053] 'We did not witness the destruction of his family, and indeed, we are truthful.'"

(50) And they planned a plan, and We planned a plan, while they perceived not.

[1050] The floor was transparent, and beneath it was flowing water.
[1051] By challenging Ṣāliḥ to bring on the promised punishment rather than asking for mercy from Allāh.
[1052] Or "being tempted [by Satan]."
[1053] i.e., the one responsible for executing his will and avenging his blood.

(51) Then look how was the outcome of their plan - that We destroyed them and their people, all.

(52) So those are their houses, desolate because of the wrong they had done. Indeed in that is a sign for people who know.

(53) And We saved those who believed and used to fear Allāh.

(54) And [mention] Lot, when he said to his people, "Do you commit immorality[1054] while you are seeing?[1055]

(55) Do you indeed approach men with desire instead of women? Rather, you are a people behaving ignorantly."

(56) But the answer of his people was not except that they said, "Expel the family of Lot from your city. Indeed, they are people who keep themselves pure."

(57) So We saved him and his family, except for his wife; We destined her to be of those who remained behind.

(58) And We rained upon them a rain [of stones], and evil was the rain of those who were warned.

(59) Say, [O Muḥammad], "Praise be to Allāh, and peace upon His servants whom He has chosen. Is Allāh better or what they associate with Him?"

(60) [More precisely], is He [not best] who created the heavens and the earth and sent down for you rain from the sky, causing to grow thereby gardens of joyful beauty which you could not [otherwise] have grown the trees thereof? Is there a deity with Allāh?[1056] [No], but they are a people who ascribe equals [to Him].

(61) Is He [not best] who made the earth a stable ground and placed within it rivers and made for it firmly set mountains and placed between the two seas a barrier? Is there a deity with Allāh? [No], but most of them do not know.

(62) Is He [not best] who responds to the desperate one when he calls upon Him and removes evil and makes you inheritors of the earth?[1057] Is there a deity with Allāh? Little do you remember.

[1054] Homosexual acts.

[1055] i.e., openly. Another meaning is "...while you are aware [that it is wrong].""

[1056] Three meanings are implied: "Is there another god who did all of this with Allāh?" or "Is there any deity worthy to be worshipped along with Allāh?" or "Is there a deity to be compared with Allāh?"

[1057] Generation after generation.

(63) Is He [not best] who guides you through the darknesses of the land and sea and who sends the winds as good tidings before His mercy? Is there a deity with Allāh? High is Allāh above whatever they associate with Him.

(64) Is He [not best] who begins creation and then repeats it and who provides for you from the heaven and earth? Is there a deity with Allāh? Say, "Produce your proof, if you should be truthful."

(65) Say, "None in the heavens and earth knows the unseen except Allāh, and they do not perceive when they will be resurrected."

(66) Rather, their knowledge is arrested concerning the Hereafter. Rather, they are in doubt about it. Rather, they are, concerning it, blind.

(67) And those who disbelieve say, "When we have become dust as well as our forefathers, will we indeed be brought out [of the graves]?

(68) We have been promised this, we and our forefathers, before. This is not but legends of the former peoples."

(69) Say, [O Muḥammad], "Proceed [i.e., travel] through the land and observe how was the end of the criminals."

(70) And grieve not over them or be in distress from what they conspire.

(71) And they say, "When is [the fulfillment of] this promise, if you should be truthful?"

(72) Say, "Perhaps it is close behind you [i.e., very near] - some of that for which you are impatient.

(73) And indeed, your Lord is the possessor of bounty for the people, but most of them are not grateful."

(74) And indeed, your Lord knows what their breasts conceal and what they declare.

(75) And there is nothing concealed[1058] within the heaven and the earth except that it is in a clear Register.[1059]

(76) Indeed, this Qur'ān relates to the Children of Israel most of that over which they disagree.

[1058] "Literally, "absent [from the senses]."
[1059] The Preserved Slate (al-Lawḥ al-Maḥfūẓ), which is with Allāh (subḥānahu wa taʿālā)."

(77) And indeed, it is guidance and mercy for the believers.

(78) Indeed, your Lord will judge between them by His [wise] judgement. And He is the Exalted in Might, the Knowing.

(79) So rely upon Allāh; indeed, you are upon the clear truth.

(80) Indeed, you will not make the dead hear, nor will you make the deaf hear the call when they have turned their backs retreating.

(81) And you cannot guide the blind away from their error. You will only make hear those who believe in Our verses so they are Muslims [i.e., submitting to Allāh].

(82) And when the word [i.e., decree] befalls them,[1060] We will bring forth for them a creature from the earth speaking to them, [saying] that the people were, of Our verses, not certain [in faith].

(83) And [warn of] the Day when We will gather from every nation a company of those who deny Our signs, and they will be [driven] in rows

(84) Until, when they arrive [at the place of Judgement], He will say, "Did you deny My signs while you encompassed them not in knowledge, or what [was it that] you were doing?"

(85) And the decree will befall them[1061] for the wrong they did, and they will not [be able to] speak.

(86) Do they not see that We made the night that they may rest therein and the day giving sight? Indeed in that are signs for a people who believe.

(87) And [warn of] the Day the Horn will be blown, and whoever is in the heavens and whoever is on the earth will be terrified except whom Allāh wills. And all will come to Him humbled.

(88) And you see the mountains, thinking them motionless,[1062] while they will pass as the passing of clouds. [It is] the work of Allāh, who perfected all things. Indeed, He is Aware of that which you do.

(89) Whoever comes [at Judgement] with a good deed will have better than it, and they, from the terror of that Day, will be safe.

1060 At the approach of the Hour.
1061 Allāh's decree will come into effect upon them, and His promise will be fulfilled.
1062 Or "solid and rigid."

(90) And whoever comes with an evil deed[1063] - their faces will be overturned into the Fire, [and it will be said], "Are you recompensed except for what you used to do?"

(91) [Say, O Muḥammad], "I have only been commanded to worship the Lord of this city,[1064] who made it sacred and to whom [belongs] all things. And I am commanded to be of the Muslims [i.e., those who submit to Allāh].

(92) And to recite the Qur'ān." And whoever is guided is only guided for [the benefit of] himself; and whoever strays - say, "I am only [one] of the warners."

(93) And say, "[All] praise is [due] to Allāh. He will show you His signs, and you will recognize them. And your Lord is not unaware of what you do."

[1063] Without having repented. It may refer generally to any sin or more specifically to association of another with Allāh.

[1064] Or region, meaning Makkah and its surroundings.

Surah Al-Qasas

(1) Ṭā, Seen, Meem.[1065]

(2) These are verses of the clear Book.

(3) We recite to you from the news of Moses and Pharaoh in truth for a people who believe.

(4) Indeed, Pharaoh exalted himself in the land and made its people into factions, oppressing a sector among them, slaughtering their [newborn] sons and keeping their females alive. Indeed, he was of the corrupters.

(5) And We wanted to confer favor upon those who were oppressed in the land and make them leaders and make them inheritors

(6) And establish them in the land and show Pharaoh and [his minister] Hāmān and their soldiers through them[1066] that which they had feared.

(7) And We inspired to the mother of Moses, "Suckle him; but when you fear for him, cast him into the river and do not fear and do not grieve. Indeed, We will return him to you and will make him [one] of the messengers."

(8) And the family of Pharaoh picked him up [out of the river] so that he would become to them an enemy and a [cause of] grief. Indeed, Pharaoh and Hāmān and their soldiers were deliberate sinners.

(9) And the wife of Pharaoh said, "[He will be] a comfort of the eye [i.e., pleasure] for me and for you. Do not kill him; perhaps he may benefit us, or we may adopt him as a son." And they perceived not.[1067]

(10) And the heart of Moses' mother became empty [of all else]. She was about to disclose [the matter concerning] him had We not bound fast her heart that she would be of the believers.

(11) And she said to his sister, "Follow him"; so she watched him from a distance while they perceived not.

[1065] See footnote to 2:1.
[1066] By means of those whom they had oppressed and enslaved.
[1067] What would be the result of that.

(12) And We had prevented from him [all] wet nurses before,[1068] so she said, "Shall I direct you to a household that will be responsible for him for you while they are to him [for his upbringing] sincere?"

(13) So We restored him to his mother that she might be content and not grieve and that she would know that the promise of Allāh is true. But most of them [i.e., the people] do not know.

(14) And when he attained his full strength and was [mentally] mature, We bestowed upon him judgement and knowledge. And thus do We reward the doers of good.

(15) And he entered the city at a time of inattention by its people[1069] and found therein two men fighting: one from his faction and one from among his enemy. And the one from his faction called for help to him against the one from his enemy, so Moses struck him and [unintentionally] killed him. [Moses] said, "This is from the work of Satan. Indeed, he is a manifest, misleading enemy."

(16) He said, "My Lord, indeed I have wronged myself, so forgive me," and He forgave him. Indeed, He is the Forgiving, the Merciful.

(17) He said, "My Lord, for the favor You bestowed upon me, I will never be an assistant to the criminals."

(18) And he became inside the city fearful and anticipating [exposure], when suddenly the one who sought his help the previous day cried out to him [once again]. Moses said to him, "Indeed, you are an evident, [persistent] deviator."

(19) And when he wanted to strike the one who was an enemy to both of them, he[1070] said, "O Moses, do you intend to kill me as you killed someone yesterday? You only want to be a tyrant in the land and do not want to be of the amenders."

(20) And a man came from the farthest end of the city, running. He said, "O Moses, indeed the eminent ones are conferring over you [intending] to kill you, so leave [the city]; indeed, I am to you of the sincere advisors."

(21) So he left it, fearful and anticipating [apprehension]. He said, "My Lord, save me from the wrongdoing people."

[1068] Prior to that, Moses had refused to nurse from any other woman.

[1069] i.e., during the noon period of rest.

[1070] i.e., the Israelite, thinking that Moses meant to strike him. Some commentators have attributed the words to the Copt; however, the Israelite was the only one who knew of the previous occurrence.

(22) And when he directed himself toward Madyan, he said, "Perhaps my Lord will guide me to the sound way."

(23) And when he came to the water [i.e., well] of Madyan, he found there a crowd of people watering [their flocks], and he found aside from them two women holding back [their flocks]. He said, "What is your circumstance?" They said, "We do not water until the shepherds dispatch [their flocks]; and our father is an old man."

(24) So he watered [their flocks] for them; then he went back to the shade and said, "My Lord, indeed I am, for whatever good You would send down to me, in need."

(25) Then one of the two women came to him walking with shyness. She said, "Indeed, my father invites you that he may reward you for having watered for us." So when he came to him[1071] and related to him the story, he said, "Fear not. You have escaped from the wrongdoing people."

(26) One of the women said, "O my father, hire him. Indeed, the best one you can hire is the strong and the trustworthy."

(27) He said, "Indeed, I wish to wed you one of these, my two daughters, on [the condition] that you serve me for eight years; but if you complete ten, it will be [as a favor] from you. And I do not wish to put you in difficulty. You will find me, if Allāh wills, from among the righteous."

(28) [Moses] said, "That is [established] between me and you. Whichever of the two terms I complete - there is no injustice to me, and Allāh, over what we say, is Witness."

(29) And when Moses had completed the term and was traveling with his family, he perceived from the direction of the mount a fire. He said to his family, "Stay here; indeed, I have perceived a fire. Perhaps I will bring you from there [some] information or burning wood from the fire that you may warm yourselves."

(30) But when he came to it, he was called from the right side of the valley in a blessed spot - from the tree,[1072] "O Moses, indeed I am Allāh, Lord of the worlds."

(31) And [he was told], "Throw down your staff." But when he saw it writhing as if it was a snake, he turned in flight and did not return.[1073] [Allāh said], "O Moses, approach and fear not. Indeed, you are of the secure.

[1071] Prophet Shuʿayb, the father of the two women.
[1072] Which was within the fire.
[1073] Or "did not look back."

(32) Insert your hand into the opening of your garment; it will come out white, without disease. And draw in your arm close to you [as prevention] from fear, for those are two proofs from your Lord to Pharaoh and his establishment. Indeed, they have been a people defiantly disobedient."

(33) He said, "My Lord, indeed I killed from among them someone, and I fear they will kill me.

(34) And my brother Aaron is more fluent than me in tongue, so send him with me as support, verifying me. Indeed, I fear that they will deny me."

(35) [Allāh] said, "We will strengthen your arm through your brother and grant you both supremacy so they will not reach you. [It will be] through Our signs; you and those who follow you will be the predominant."

(36) But when Moses came to them with Our signs as clear evidences, they said, "This is not except invented magic, and we have not heard of this [religion] among our forefathers."

(37) And Moses said, "My Lord is more knowing [than we or you] of who has come with guidance from Him and to whom will be succession in the home.[1074] Indeed, wrongdoers do not succeed."

(38) And Pharaoh said, "O eminent ones, I have not known you to have a god other than me. Then ignite for me, O Hāmān, [a fire] upon the clay[1075] and make for me a tower that I may look at the God of Moses. And indeed, I do think he is among the liars."

(39) And he was arrogant, he and his soldiers, in the land, without right, and they thought that they would not be returned to Us.

(40) So We took him and his soldiers and threw them into the sea.[1076] So see how was the end of the wrongdoers.

(41) And We made them leaders[1077] inviting to the Fire, and on the Day of Resurrection they will not be helped.

[1074] i.e., in this world or in the Hereafter.
[1075] From which bricks are made.
[1076] Allāh (subḥānahu wa ta'ālā) caused them to leave all their worldly wealth behind and enter the sea in pursuit of the Children of Israel. See 26:52-66.
[1077] i.e., examples or precedents, followed by subsequent tyrants.

(42) And We caused to overtake them in this world a curse, and on the Day of Resurrection they will be of the despised.[1078]

(43) And We gave Moses the Scripture, after We had destroyed the former generations, as enlightenment for the people and guidance and mercy that they might be reminded.

(44) And you, [O Muḥammad], were not on the western side [of the mount] when We revealed to Moses the command, and you were not among the witnesses [to that].

(45) But We produced [many] generations [after Moses], and prolonged was their duration.[1079] And you were not a resident among the people of Madyan, reciting to them Our verses, but We were senders [of this message].[1080]

(46) And you were not at the side of the mount when We called [Moses] but [were sent] as a mercy from your Lord to warn a people to whom no warner had come before you that they might be reminded.

(47) And if not that a disaster should strike them for what their hands put forth [of sins] and they would say, "Our Lord, why did You not send us a messenger so we could have followed Your verses and been among the believers?"...[1081]

(48) But when the truth came to them from Us, they said, "Why was he not given like that which was given to Moses?" Did they not disbelieve in that which was given to Moses before? They said, "[They are but] two works of magic supporting each other,[1082] and indeed we are, in both, disbelievers."

(49) Say, "Then bring a scripture from Allāh which is more guiding than either of them that I may follow it, if you should be truthful."

[1078] Literally, "those made hideous," who will be far removed from all good and mercy.

[1079] "So they forgot and neglected the ordinances of Allāh.

[1080] The Prophet (ﷺ) had no way of obtaining this information except through Allāh's revelation."

[1081] The conclusion of the sentence is understood to be "...We would not have sent messengers," meaning that Allāh (subḥānahu wa taʿālā) sent messengers and sent Muḥammad (ﷺ) with the final scripture to mankind so that no one could claim that punishment was imposed unjustly without warning.

[1082] The reference is by the disbelievers of Quraysh to the Qur'ān and the Torah.

(50) But if they do not respond to you - then know that they only follow their [own] desires. And who is more astray than one who follows his desire without guidance from Allāh? Indeed, Allāh does not guide the wrongdoing people.

(51) And We have [repeatedly] conveyed to them the word [i.e., the Qur'ān] that they might be reminded.

(52) Those to whom We gave the Scripture before it - they[1083] are believers in it.

(53) And when it is recited to them, they say, "We have believed in it; indeed, it is the truth from our Lord. Indeed we were, [even] before it, Muslims [i.e., submitting to Allāh]."

(54) Those will be given their reward twice for what they patiently endured and [because] they avert evil through good, and from what We have provided them they spend.

(55) And when they hear ill speech, they turn away from it and say, "For us are our deeds, and for you are your deeds. Peace will be upon you;[1084] we seek not the ignorant."

(56) Indeed, [O Muḥammad], you do not guide whom you like, but Allāh guides whom He wills. And He is most knowing of the [rightly] guided.

(57) And they [i.e., the Quraysh] say, "If we were to follow the guidance with you, we would be swept[1085] from our land." Have We not established for them a safe sanctuary to which are brought the fruits of all things as provision from Us? But most of them do not know.

(58) And how many a city have We destroyed that was insolent in its [way of] living, and those are their dwellings which have not been inhabited after them except briefly.[1086] And it is We who were the inheritors.

(59) And never would your Lord have destroyed the cities until He had sent to their mother [i.e., principal city] a messenger reciting to them Our verses. And We would not destroy the cities except while their people were wrongdoers.

[1083] i.e., the sincere believers among them.

[1084] This is not the Islāmic greeting of "Peace be upon you." Rather, it means "You are secure from being treated in a like manner by us."

[1085] By the other Arab tribes.

[1086] By travelers seeking temporary shelter. The reference is to the ruins which were visible to the Quraysh during their journeys.

(60) And whatever thing you [people] have been given - it is [only for] the enjoyment of worldly life and its adornment. And what is with Allāh is better and more lasting; so will you not use reason?

(61) Then is he whom We have promised a good promise which he will meet [i.e., obtain] like he for whom We provided enjoyment of worldly life [but] then he is, on the Day of Resurrection, among those presented [for punishment in Hell]?

(62) And [warn of] the Day He will call them and say, "Where are My 'partners' which you used to claim?"

(63) Those upon whom the word[1087] will have come into effect will say, "Our Lord, these are the ones we led to error. We led them to error just as we were in error. We declare our disassociation [from them] to You. They did not used to worship [i.e., obey] us."[1088]

(64) And it will be said, "Invoke your 'partners,'" and they will invoke them; but they will not respond to them, and they will see the punishment. If only they had followed guidance!

(65) And [mention] the Day He will call them and say, "What did you answer the messengers?"

(66) But the information[1089] will be unapparent to them that Day, so they will not [be able to] ask one another.

(67) But as for one who had repented, believed, and done righteousness, it is expected [i.e., promised by Allāh] that he will be among the successful.

(68) And your Lord creates what He wills and chooses; not for them was the choice. Exalted is Allāh and high above what they associate with Him.

(69) And your Lord knows what their breasts conceal and what they declare.

(70) And He is Allāh; there is no deity except Him. To Him is [due all] praise in the first [life] and the Hereafter. And His is the [final] decision, and to Him you will be returned.

[1087] "The decree for their punishment.
[1088] i.e., We did not compel them, and they did not obey us; instead, they obeyed their own desires and inclinations."
[1089] By which they might invent lies or excuses.

(71) Say, "Have you considered:[1090] if Allāh should make for you the night continuous until the Day of Resurrection, what deity other than Allāh could bring you light? Then will you not hear?"

(72) Say, "Have you considered: if Allāh should make for you the day continuous until the Day of Resurrection, what deity other than Allāh could bring you a night in which you may rest? Then will you not see?"

(73) And out of His mercy He made for you the night and the day that you may rest therein and [by day] seek from His bounty and [that] perhaps you will be grateful.

(74) And [warn of] the Day He will call them and say, "Where are My 'partners' which you used to claim?"

(75) And We will extract from every nation a witness and say, "Produce your proof," and they will know that the truth belongs to Allāh, and lost from them is that which they used to invent.

(76) Indeed, Qārūn was from the people of Moses, but he tyrannized them. And We gave him of treasures whose keys would burden a band of strong men; thereupon his people said to him, "Do not exult. Indeed, Allāh does not like the exultant.

(77) But seek, through that which Allāh has given you, the home of the Hereafter; and [yet], do not forget your share of the world. And do good as Allāh has done good to you. And desire not corruption in the land. Indeed, Allāh does not like corrupters."

(78) He said, "I was only given it because of knowledge I have." Did he not know that Allāh had destroyed before him of generations those who were greater than him in power and greater in accumulation [of wealth]? But the criminals, about their sins, will not be asked.[1091]

(79) So he came out before his people in his adornment. Those who desired the worldly life said, "Oh, would that we had like what was given to Qārūn. Indeed, he is one of great fortune."

(80) But those who had been given knowledge said, "Woe to you! The reward of Allāh is better for he who believes and does righteousness. And none are granted it except the patient."

[1090] Meaning "Inform me if you really know."

[1091] There will be no need to enumerate their sins separately, as their quantity is obvious and more than sufficient to warrant punishment in Hell.

(81) And We caused the earth to swallow him and his home. And there was for him no company to aid him other than Allāh, nor was he of those who [could] defend themselves.

(82) And those who had wished for his position the previous day began to say, "Oh, how Allāh extends provision to whom He wills of His servants and restricts it! If not that Allāh had conferred favor on us, He would have caused it to swallow us. Oh, how the disbelievers do not succeed!"

(83) That home of the Hereafter We assign to those who do not desire exaltedness upon the earth or corruption. And the [best] outcome is for the righteous.

(84) Whoever comes [on the Day of Judgement] with a good deed will have better than it; and whoever comes with an evil deed - then those who did evil deeds will not be recompensed except [as much as] what they used to do.

(85) Indeed, [O Muḥammad], He who imposed upon you the Qur'ān will take you back to a place of return.[1092] Say, "My Lord is most knowing of who brings guidance and who is in clear error."

(86) And you were not expecting that the Book would be conveyed to you, but [it is] a mercy from your Lord. So do not be an assistant to the disbelievers.[1093]

(87) And never let them avert you from the verses of Allāh after they have been revealed to you. And invite [people] to your Lord. And never be of those who associate others with Allāh.

(88) And do not invoke with Allāh another deity. There is no deity except Him. Everything will be destroyed except His Face.[1094] His is the judgement, and to Him you will be returned.

[1092] Meaning to Makkah (in this life) or to Paradise (in the Hereafter).
[1093] In their religion by making any concessions to their beliefs.
[1094] i.e., except Himself.

Surah Al-`Ankabut

(1) Alif, Lām, Meem.[1095]

(2) Do the people think that they will be left to say, "We believe" and they will not be tried?

(3) But We have certainly tried those before them, and Allāh will surely make evident those who are truthful, and He will surely make evident the liars.

(4) Or do those who do evil deeds think they can outrun [i.e., escape] Us? Evil is what they judge.

(5) Whoever should hope for the meeting with Allāh - indeed, the term [decreed by] Allāh is coming. And He is the Hearing, the Knowing.

(6) And whoever strives only strives for [the benefit of] himself. Indeed, Allāh is Free from need of the worlds.

(7) And those who believe and do righteous deeds - We will surely remove from them their misdeeds and will surely reward them according to the best of what they used to do.

(8) And We have enjoined upon man goodness to parents. But if they endeavor to make you associate with Me that of which you have no knowledge,[1096] do not obey them. To Me is your return, and I will inform you about what you used to do.

(9) And those who believe and do righteous deeds - We will surely admit them among the righteous [into Paradise].

(10) And of the people are some who say, "We believe in Allāh," but when one [of them] is harmed for [the cause of] Allāh, he considers the trial [i.e., harm] of the people as [if it were] the punishment of Allāh. But if victory comes from your Lord, they say, "Indeed, We were with you." Is not Allāh most knowing of what is within the breasts of the worlds [i.e., all creatures]?

(11) And Allāh will surely make evident those who believe, and He will surely make evident the hypocrites.

[1095] See footnote to 2:1.

[1096] i.e., no knowledge of its divinity. There can be no knowledge about something which is non-existent or untrue.

(12) And those who disbelieve say to those who believe, "Follow our way, and we will carry your sins."[1097] But they will not carry anything of their sins. Indeed, they are liars.

(13) But they will surely carry their [own] burdens and [other] burdens along with their burdens,[1098] and they will surely be questioned on the Day of Resurrection about what they used to invent.

(14) And We certainly sent Noah to his people, and he remained among them a thousand years minus fifty years, and the flood seized them while they were wrongdoers.

(15) But We saved him and the companions of the ship, and We made it[1099] a sign for the worlds.

(16) And [We sent] Abraham, when he said to his people, "Worship Allāh and fear Him. That is best for you, if you should know.

(17) You only worship, besides Allāh, idols, and you produce a falsehood. Indeed, those you worship besides Allāh do not possess for you [the power of] provision. So seek from Allāh provision and worship Him and be grateful to Him. To Him you will be returned."

(18) And if you [people] deny [the message] - already nations before you have denied. And there is not upon the Messenger except [the duty of] clear notification.[1100]

(19) Have they not considered how Allāh begins creation and then repeats it? Indeed that, for Allāh, is easy.

(20) Say, [O Muḥammad], "Travel through the land and observe how He began creation. Then Allāh will produce the final creation [i.e., development]. Indeed Allāh, over all things, is competent."

[1097] The phrase may also read: "and let us carry your sins," i.e., the responsibility for your sins.

[1098] Besides their own sins, they will carry those of the people they misled, although it will not lessen the burden of the latter.

[1099] i.e., the ship, the event or the story.

[1100] Commentators have differed over this verse - whether it is a continuation of the words of Prophet Abraham or words of comfort given by Allāh to Prophet Muḥammad (ﷺ), which according to context seems more likely.

(21) He punishes whom He wills and has mercy upon whom He wills, and to Him you will be returned.

(22) And you will not cause failure [to Allāh] upon the earth or in the heaven. And you have not other than Allāh any protector or any helper.

(23) And the ones who disbelieve in the signs of Allāh and the meeting with Him - those have despaired of My mercy, and they will have a painful punishment.

(24) And the answer of his [i.e., Abraham's] people was not but that they said, "Kill him or burn him," but Allāh saved him from the fire. Indeed in that are signs for a people who believe.

(25) And [Abraham] said, "You have only taken, other than Allāh, idols as [a bond of] affection among you in worldly life. Then on the Day of Resurrection you will deny one another and curse one another, and your refuge will be the Fire, and you will not have any helpers."

(26) And Lot believed him. [Abraham] said, "Indeed, I will emigrate to [the service of] my Lord. Indeed, He is the Exalted in Might, the Wise."

(27) And We gave to him Isaac and Jacob and placed in his descendants prophethood and scripture. And We gave him his reward in this world, and indeed, he is in the Hereafter among the righteous.

(28) And [mention] Lot, when he said to his people, "Indeed, you commit such immorality as no one has preceded you with from among the worlds.

(29) Indeed, you approach men and obstruct the road[1101] and commit in your meetings [every] evil." And the answer of his people was not but that they said, "Bring us the punishment of Allāh, if you should be of the truthful."

(30) He said, "My Lord, support me against the corrupting people."

(31) And when Our messengers [i.e., angels] came to Abraham with the good tidings,[1102] they said, "Indeed, we will destroy the people of that [i.e., Lot's] city. Indeed, its people have been wrongdoers."

(32) [Abraham] said, "Indeed, within it is Lot." They said, "We are more knowing of who is within it. We will surely save him and his family, except his wife. She is to be of those who remain behind."

[1101] i.e., commit highway robbery and acts of aggression against travelers.
[1102] Of the birth of Isaac and his descendant, Jacob.

(33) And when Our messengers [i.e., angels] came to Lot, he was distressed for them and felt for them great discomfort.[1103] They said, "Fear not, nor grieve. Indeed, we will save you and your family, except your wife; she is to be of those who remain behind.

(34) Indeed, we will bring down on the people of this city punishment from the sky because they have been defiantly disobedient."

(35) And We have certainly left of it a sign as clear evidence for a people who use reason.

(36) And to Madyan [We sent] their brother Shu'ayb, and he said, "O my people, worship Allāh and expect the Last Day and do not commit abuse on the earth, spreading corruption."

(37) But they denied him, so the earthquake seized them, and they became within their home [corpses] fallen prone.

(38) And [We destroyed] 'Aad and Thamūd, and it has become clear to you from their [ruined] dwellings. And Satan had made pleasing to them their deeds and averted them from the path, and they were endowed with perception.

(39) And [We destroyed] Qārūn and Pharaoh and Hāmān. And Moses had already come to them with clear evidences, and they were arrogant in the land, but they were not outrunners [of Our punishment].

(40) So each We seized for his sin; and among them were those upon whom We sent a storm of stones, and among them were those who were seized by the blast [from the sky], and among them were those whom We caused the earth to swallow, and among them were those whom We drowned. And Allāh would not have wronged them, but it was they who were wronging themselves.

(41) The example of those who take allies other than Allāh is like that of the spider who takes [i.e., constructs] a home. And indeed, the weakest of homes is the home of the spider, if they only knew.

(42) Indeed, Allāh knows whatever thing they call upon[1104] other than Him. And He is the Exalted in Might, the Wise.

(43) And these examples We present to the people, but none will understand them except those of knowledge.

[1103] See footnote to 11:77.
[1104] In worship.

(44) Allāh created the heavens and the earth in truth. Indeed in that is a sign for the believers.

(45) Recite, [O Muḥammad], what has been revealed to you of the Book and establish prayer. Indeed, prayer prohibits immorality and wrongdoing, and the remembrance of Allāh is greater. And Allāh knows that which you do.

(46) And do not argue with the People of the Scripture except in a way that is best, except for those who commit injustice among them, and say, "We believe in that which has been revealed to us and revealed to you. And our God and your God is one; and we are Muslims [in submission] to Him."

(47) And thus We have sent down to you the Book [i.e., the Qur'ān]. And those to whom We [previously] gave the Scripture believe in it. And among these [people of Makkah] are those who believe in it. And none reject Our verses except the disbelievers.

(48) And you did not recite before it any scripture, nor did you inscribe one with your right hand. Then [i.e., otherwise] the falsifiers would have had [cause for] doubt.

(49) Rather, it [i.e., the Qur'ān] is distinct verses [preserved] within the breasts of those who have been given knowledge. And none reject Our verses except the wrongdoers.

(50) But they say, "Why are not signs sent down to him from his Lord?" Say, "The signs are only with Allāh, and I am only a clear warner."

(51) And is it not sufficient for them that We revealed to you the Book [i.e., the Qur'ān] which is recited to them? Indeed in that is a mercy and reminder for a people who believe.

(52) Say, "Sufficient is Allāh between me and you as Witness. He knows what is in the heavens and earth. And they who have believed in falsehood and disbelieved in Allāh - it is those who are the losers."

(53) And they urge you to hasten the punishment. And if not for [the decree of] a specified term, punishment would have reached them. But it will surely come to them suddenly while they perceive not.

(54) They urge you to hasten the punishment. And indeed, Hell will be encompassing of the disbelievers

(55) On the Day the punishment will cover them from above them and from below their feet and it is said, "Taste [the result of] what you used to do."

(56) O My servants who have believed, indeed My earth is spacious, so worship only Me.

(57) Every soul will taste death. Then to Us will you be returned.

(58) And those who have believed and done righteous deeds - We will surely assign to them of Paradise [elevated] chambers beneath which rivers flow, wherein they abide eternally. Excellent is the reward of the [righteous] workers

(59) Who have been patient and upon their Lord rely.

(60) And how many a creature carries not its [own] provision. Allāh provides for it and for you. And He is the Hearing, the Knowing.

(61) If you asked them, "Who created the heavens and earth and subjected the sun and the moon?" they would surely say, "Allāh." Then how are they deluded?

(62) Allāh extends provision for whom He wills of His servants and restricts for him. Indeed Allāh is, of all things, Knowing.

(63) And if you asked them, "Who sends down rain from the sky and gives life thereby to the earth after its lifelessness?" they would surely say, "Allāh." Say, "Praise to Allāh"; but most of them do not reason.

(64) And this worldly life is not but diversion and amusement. And indeed, the home of the Hereafter - that is the [eternal] life, if only they knew.

(65) And when they board a ship, they supplicate Allāh, sincere to Him in religion [i.e., faith and hope]. But when He delivers them to the land, at once they associate others with Him

(66) So that they will deny what We have granted them, and they will enjoy themselves. But they are going to know.[1105]

(67) Have they not seen that We made [Makkah] a safe sanctuary, while people are being taken away[1106] all around them? Then in falsehood do they believe, and in the favor of Allāh they disbelieve?

(68) And who is more unjust than one who invents a lie about Allāh or denies the truth when it has come to him? Is there not in Hell a [sufficient] residence for the disbelievers?

[1105] Grammatically, the verse may also be read as a threat, i.e., "So let them deny what We have granted them and let them enjoy themselves, for they are going to know."
[1106] i.e., killed and taken captive.

(69) And those who strive for Us - We will surely guide them to Our ways.[1107] And indeed, Allāh is with the doers of good.

[1107] The various ways and means to attain the acceptance and pleasure of Allāh.

Surah Ar-Rum

(1) Alif, Lām, Meem.[1108]

(2) The Byzantines have been defeated[1109]

(3) In the nearest land.[1110] But they, after their defeat, will overcome

(4) Within three to nine years. To Allāh belongs the command [i.e., decree] before and after. And that day the believers will rejoice

(5) In the victory of Allāh.[1111] He gives victory to whom He wills, and He is the Exalted in Might, the Merciful.

(6) [It is] the promise of Allāh. Allāh does not fail in His promise, but most of the people do not know.

(7) They know what is apparent of the worldly life, but they, of the Hereafter, are unaware.

(8) Do they not contemplate within themselves?[1112] Allāh has not created the heavens and the earth and what is between them except in truth and for a specified term. And indeed, many of the people, in the meeting with their Lord, are disbelievers.

(9) Have they not traveled through the earth and observed how was the end of those before them? They were greater than them in power, and they plowed [or excavated] the earth and built it up more than they [i.e., the Makkans] have built it up, and their messengers came to them with clear evidences. And Allāh would not ever have wronged them, but they were wronging themselves.

(10) Then the end of those who did evil was the worst [consequence] because they denied the signs of Allāh and used to ridicule them.

(11) Allāh begins creation; then He will repeat it; then to Him you will be returned.

(12) And the Day the Hour appears the criminals will be in despair.

[1108] See footnote to 2:1.

[1109] By the Persians.

[1110] Another meaning is "in the lowest land."

[1111] i.e., the victory given by Allāh to a people of the Scripture (Christians) over the Magians of Persia.

[1112] An additional meaning is "Do they not contemplate concerning themselves."

(13) And there will not be for them among their [alleged] partners any intercessors, and they will [then] be disbelievers in their partners.

(14) And the Day the Hour appears - that Day they will become separated.

(15) And as for those who had believed and done righteous deeds, they will be in a garden [of Paradise], delighted.

(16) But as for those who disbelieved and denied Our verses and the meeting of the Hereafter, those will be brought into the punishment [to remain].

(17) So exalted is Allāh when you reach the evening and when you reach the morning.

(18) And to Him is [due all] praise throughout the heavens and the earth. And [exalted is He] at night and when you are at noon.

(19) He brings the living out of the dead and brings the dead out of the living and brings to life the earth after its lifelessness. And thus will you be brought out.[1113]

(20) And of His signs is that He created you from dust; then, suddenly you were human beings dispersing [throughout the earth].

(21) And of His signs is that He created for you from yourselves mates that you may find tranquility in them; and He placed between you affection and mercy. Indeed in that are signs for a people who give thought.

(22) And of His signs is the creation of the heavens and the earth and the diversity of your languages and your colors. Indeed in that are signs for those of knowledge.

(23) And of His signs is your sleep by night and day and your seeking of His bounty. Indeed in that are signs for a people who listen.

(24) And of His signs is [that] He shows you the lightning [causing] fear and aspiration, and He sends down rain from the sky by which He brings to life the earth after its lifelessness. Indeed in that are signs for a people who use reason.

(25) And of His signs is that the heaven and earth stand [i.e., remain] by His command. Then when He calls you with a [single] call from the earth, immediately you will come forth.

[1113] Of the graves or out of the earth at the time of resurrection.

(26) And to Him belongs whoever is in the heavens and earth. All are to Him devoutly obedient.

(27) And it is He who begins creation; then He repeats it, and that is [even] easier for Him. To Him belongs the highest description [i.e., attribute] in the heavens and earth. And He is the Exalted in Might, the Wise.

(28) He presents to you an example from yourselves. Do you have among those whom your right hands possess [i.e., slaves] any partners in what We have provided for you so that you are equal therein [and] would fear them as your fear of one another [within a partnership]?[1114] Thus do We detail the verses for a people who use reason.

(29) But those who wrong follow their [own] desires without knowledge. Then who can guide one whom Allāh has sent astray? And for them there are no helpers.

(30) So direct your face [i.e., self] toward the religion, inclining to truth. [Adhere to] the fiṭrah[1115] of Allāh upon which He has created [all] people. No change should there be in the creation of Allāh.[1116] That is the correct religion, but most of the people do not know.

(31) [Adhere to it], turning in repentance to Him, and fear Him and establish prayer and do not be of those who associate others with Allāh

(32) [Or] of those who have divided their religion and become sects, every faction rejoicing in what it has.[1117]

(33) And when adversity touches the people, they call upon their Lord, turning in repentance to Him. Then when He lets them taste mercy from Him, at once a party of them associate others with their Lord,

(34) So that they will deny what We have granted them.[1118] Then enjoy yourselves, for you are going to know.

(35) Or have We sent down to them an authority [i.e., a proof or scripture], and it speaks of what they have been associating with Him?

[1114] See footnote to 16:71.

[1115] "The natural inborn inclination of man to worship his Creator prior to the corruption of his nature by external influences. Thus, Islamic monotheism is described as the religion of fiṭrah - that of the inherent nature of mankind.

[1116] i.e., let people remain true to their fiṭrah within the religion of Islām."

[1117] Of beliefs, opinions, customs, etc.

[1118] Or "So let them deny what We have granted them."

(36) And when We let the people taste mercy, they rejoice therein, but if evil afflicts them for what their hands have put forth, immediately they despair.

(37) Do they not see that Allāh extends provision for whom He wills and restricts [it]? Indeed in that are signs for a people who believe.

(38) So give the relative his right, as well as the needy and the traveler. That is best for those who desire the face [i.e., approval] of Allāh, and it is they who will be the successful.

(39) And whatever you give for interest [i.e., advantage] to increase within the wealth of people[1119] will not increase with Allāh. But what you give in zakāh,[1120] desiring the face [i.e., approval] of Allāh - those are the multipliers.[1121]

(40) Allāh is the one who created you, then provided for you, then will cause you to die, and then will give you life. Are there any of your "partners" who does anything of that? Exalted is He and high above what they associate with Him.

(41) Corruption has appeared throughout the land and sea by [reason of] what the hands of people have earned so He [i.e., Allāh] may let them taste part of [the consequence of] what they have done that perhaps they will return [to righteousness].

(42) Say, [O Muḥammad], "Travel through the land and observe how was the end of those before. Most of them were associators [of others with Allāh].

(43) So direct your face [i.e., self] toward the correct religion before a Day comes from Allāh of which there is no repelling. That Day, they will be divided.[1122]

(44) Whoever disbelieves - upon him is [the consequence of] his disbelief. And whoever does righteousness - they are for themselves preparing,

(45) That He may reward those who have believed and done righteous deeds out of His bounty. Indeed, He does not like the disbelievers.

(46) And of His signs is that He sends the winds as bringers of good tidings and to let you taste His mercy [i.e., rain] and so the ships may sail at His command and so you may seek of His bounty, and perhaps you will be grateful.

[1119] "The phrase includes several connotations, among them: a) that which is given as usury or interest, b) that which is given on the condition that it be repaid with interest, and c) a gift given with the intention of obtaining from the recipient greater benefit or a larger gift.

[1120] The meaning of ṣadaqah (voluntary charity) is included here.

[1121] Of their blessings on earth and their rewards in the Hereafter."

[1122] Into those destined for Paradise and those destined for Hell.

(47) And We have already sent messengers before you to their peoples, and they came to them with clear evidences; then We took retribution from those who committed crimes, and incumbent upon Us was support[1123] of the believers.

(48) It is Allāh who sends the winds, and they stir the clouds and spread them in the sky however He wills, and He makes them fragments so you see the rain emerge from within them. And when He causes it to fall upon whom He wills of His servants, immediately they rejoice

(49) Although they were, before it was sent down upon them - before that, in despair.

(50) So observe the effects of the mercy of Allāh - how He gives life to the earth after its lifelessness. Indeed, that [same one] will give life to the dead, and He is over all things competent.

(51) But if We should send a [bad] wind and they saw [their crops] turned yellow, they would remain thereafter disbelievers.[1124]

(52) So indeed, you will not make the dead hear, nor will you make the deaf hear the call when they turn their backs, retreating.

(53) And you cannot guide the blind away from their error. You will only make hear those who believe in Our verses so they are Muslims [in submission to Allāh].

(54) Allāh is the one who created you from weakness, then made after weakness strength, then made after strength weakness and white hair. He creates what He wills, and He is the Knowing, the Competent.

(55) And the Day the Hour appears the criminals will swear they had remained but an hour. Thus they were deluded.

(56) But those who were given knowledge and faith will say, "You remained the extent of Allāh's decree until the Day of Resurrection, and this is the Day of Resurrection, but you did not used to know."[1125]

(57) So that Day, their excuse will not benefit those who wronged, nor will they be asked to appease [Allāh].

[1123] i.e., aid or the bestowal of victory.
[1124] Denying and ungrateful for the previous favors of Allāh.
[1125] i.e., acknowledge the truth.

(58) And We have certainly presented to the people in this Qur'ān from every [kind of] example. But, [O Muḥammad], if you should bring them a sign, the disbelievers will surely say, "You [believers] are but falsifiers."

(59) Thus does Allāh seal the hearts of those who do not know.[1126]

(60) So be patient. Indeed, the promise of Allāh is truth. And let them not disquiet you who are not certain [in faith].

[1126] i.e., those who do not wish to know the truth and refuse it.

Surah Luqman

(1) Alif, Lām, Meem.[1127]

(2) These are verses of the wise[1128] Book,

(3) As guidance and mercy for the doers of good

(4) Who establish prayer and give zakāh, and they, of the Hereafter, are certain [in faith].

(5) Those are on [right] guidance from their Lord, and it is those who are the successful.

(6) And of the people is he who buys the amusement of speech[1129] to mislead [others] from the way of Allāh without knowledge and who takes it [i.e., His way] in ridicule. Those will have a humiliating punishment.

(7) And when Our verses are recited to him, he turns away arrogantly as if he had not heard them, as if there was in his ears deafness. So give him tidings of a painful punishment.

(8) Indeed, those who believe and do righteous deeds - for them are the Gardens of Pleasure,

(9) Wherein they abide eternally; [it is] the promise of Allāh [which is] truth. And He is the Exalted in Might, the Wise.

(10) He created the heavens without pillars that you see and has cast into the earth firmly set mountains, lest it should shift with you, and dispersed therein from every creature. And We sent down rain from the sky and made grow therein [plants] of every noble kind.

(11) This is the creation of Allāh. So show Me what those other than Him have created. Rather, the wrongdoers are in clear error.

[1127] See footnote to 2:1.

[1128] See footnote to 10:1.

[1129] i.e., that which has no benefit. Described by different ṣaḥābah as shirk (association with Allāh), misleading stories, frivolous songs, or music but includes all which distracts or diverts one from the Qur'ān and remembrance of Allāh.

(12) And We had certainly given Luqmān wisdom [and said], "Be grateful to Allāh." And whoever is grateful is grateful for [the benefit of] himself. And whoever denies [His favor] - then indeed, Allāh is Free of need and Praiseworthy.

(13) And [mention, O Muḥammad], when Luqmān said to his son while he was instructing him, "O my son, do not associate [anything] with Allāh. Indeed, association [with Him] is great injustice."

(14) And We have enjoined upon man [care] for his parents. His mother carried him, [increasing her] in weakness upon weakness, and his weaning is in two years. Be grateful to Me and to your parents; to Me is the [final] destination.

(15) But if they endeavor to make you associate with Me that of which you have no knowledge,[1130] do not obey them but accompany them in [this] world with appropriate kindness and follow the way of those who turn back to Me [in repentance]. Then to Me will be your return, and I will inform you about what you used to do.

(16) [And Luqmān said], "O my son, indeed if it [i.e., a wrong] should be the weight of a mustard seed and should be within a rock or [anywhere] in the heavens or in the earth, Allāh will bring it forth. Indeed, Allāh is Subtle[1131] and Aware.

(17) O my son, establish prayer, enjoin what is right, forbid what is wrong, and be patient over what befalls you. Indeed, [all] that is of the matters [requiring] resolve.[1132]

(18) And do not turn your cheek [in contempt] toward people[1133] and do not walk through the earth exultantly. Indeed, Allāh does not like everyone self-deluded and boastful.

(19) And be moderate in your pace and lower your voice; indeed, the most disagreeable of sounds is the voice of donkeys."

(20) Do you not see that Allāh has made subject to you whatever is in the heavens and whatever is in the earth and amply bestowed upon you His favors, [both] apparent and unapparent? But of the people is he who disputes about Allāh without knowledge or guidance or an enlightening Book [from Him].

[1130] See footnote to 29:8.

[1131] Refer to footnote of 6:103.

[1132] For the reason that they are enjoined by Allāh.

[1133] Rather, respect them by directing your face and attention to them.

(21) And when it is said to them, "Follow what Allāh has revealed," they say, "Rather, we will follow that upon which we found our fathers." Even if Satan was inviting them to the punishment of the Blaze?

(22) And whoever submits his face [i.e., self] to Allāh while he is a doer of good - then he has grasped the most trustworthy handhold. And to Allāh will be the outcome of [all] matters.

(23) And whoever has disbelieved - let not his disbelief grieve you. To Us is their return, and We will inform them of what they did. Indeed, Allāh is Knowing of that within the breasts.

(24) We grant them enjoyment for a little; then We will force them to a massive punishment.

(25) And if you asked them, "Who created the heavens and earth?" they would surely say, "Allāh." Say, "[All] praise is [due] to Allāh"; but most of them do not know.

(26) To Allāh belongs whatever is in the heavens and earth. Indeed, Allāh is the Free of need, the Praiseworthy.

(27) And if whatever trees upon the earth were pens and the sea [was ink], replenished thereafter by seven [more] seas, the words[1134] of Allāh would not be exhausted. Indeed, Allāh is Exalted in Might and Wise.

(28) Your creation and your resurrection will not be but as that of a single soul.[1135] Indeed, Allāh is Hearing and Seeing.

(29) Do you not see [i.e., know] that Allāh causes the night to enter the day and causes the day to enter the night and has subjected the sun and the moon, each running [its course] for a specified term, and that Allāh, of whatever you do, is Aware?

(30) That is because Allāh is the True Reality, and that what they call upon[1136] other than Him is falsehood, and because Allāh is the Most High, the Grand.

(31) Do you not see that ships sail through the sea by the favor of Allāh that He may show you of His signs? Indeed in that are signs for everyone patient and grateful.

[1134] See footnote to 18:109.

[1135] The re-creation and resurrection of one or of all is accomplished with equal ease by Allāh (subḥānahu wa taʿālā).

[1136] In worship.

(32) And when waves come over them like canopies, they supplicate Allāh, sincere to Him in religion [i.e., faith]. But when He delivers them to the land, there are [some] of them who are moderate [in faith]. And none rejects Our signs except everyone treacherous and ungrateful.

(33) O mankind, fear your Lord and fear a Day when no father will avail his son, nor will a son avail his father at all. Indeed, the promise of Allāh is truth, so let not the worldly life delude you and be not deceived about Allāh by the Deceiver [i.e., Satan].

(34) Indeed, Allāh [alone] has knowledge of the Hour and sends down the rain and knows what is in the wombs.[1137] And no soul perceives what it will earn tomorrow, and no soul perceives in what land it will die. Indeed, Allāh is Knowing and Aware.

[1137] i.e., every aspect of the fetus' present and future existence.

Surah As-Sajdah

(1) Alif, Lām, Meem.[1138]

(2) [This is] the revelation of the Book about which there is no doubt from the Lord of the worlds.

(3) Or do they say, "He invented it"? Rather, it is the truth from your Lord, [O Muḥammad], that you may warn a people to whom no warner has come before you [so] perhaps they will be guided.

(4) It is Allāh who created the heavens and the earth and whatever is between them in six days; then He established Himself above the Throne.[1139] You have not besides Him any protector or any intercessor; so will you not be reminded?

(5) He arranges [each] matter from the heaven to the earth; then it will ascend to Him in a Day, the extent of which is a thousand years of those which you count.

(6) That is the Knower of the unseen and the witnessed, the Exalted in Might, the Merciful,

(7) Who perfected everything which He created and began the creation of man from clay.

(8) Then He made his posterity out of the extract of a liquid disdained.

(9) Then He proportioned him and breathed into him from His [created] soul[1140] and made for you hearing and vision and hearts [i.e., intellect]; little are you grateful.

(10) And they say, "When we are lost [i.e., disintegrated] within the earth, will we indeed be [recreated] in a new creation?" Rather, they are, in the meeting with their Lord, disbelievers.

(11) Say, "The angel of death who has been entrusted with you will take you. Then to your Lord you will be returned."

(12) If you could but see when the criminals are hanging their heads before their Lord, [saying], "Our Lord, we have seen and heard, so return us [to the world]; we will work righteousness. Indeed, we are [now] certain."

[1138] See footnote to 2:1.

[1139] See footnotes to 2:19 and 7:54.

[1140] i.e., element of life. See footnote to 15:29.

(13) And if We had willed, We could have given every soul its guidance, but the word[1141] from Me will come into effect [that] "I will surely fill Hell with jinn and people all together.

(14) So taste [punishment] because you forgot the meeting of this, your Day; indeed, We have [accordingly] forgotten you. And taste the punishment of eternity for what you used to do."

(15) Only those believe in Our verses who, when they are reminded by them, fall down in prostration and exalt [Allāh] with praise of their Lord, and they are not arrogant.

(16) Their sides part [i.e., they arise] from [their] beds; they supplicate their Lord in fear and aspiration, and from what We have provided them, they spend.[1142]

(17) And no soul knows what has been hidden for them of comfort for eyes [i.e., satisfaction] as reward for what they used to do.

(18) Then is one who was a believer like one who was defiantly disobedient? They are not equal.

(19) As for those who believed and did righteous deeds, for them will be the Gardens of Refuge as accommodation for what they used to do.

(20) But as for those who defiantly disobeyed, their refuge is the Fire. Every time they wish to emerge from it, they will be returned to it while it is said to them, "Taste the punishment of the Fire which you used to deny."

(21) And We will surely let them taste the nearer punishment[1143] short of the greater punishment that perhaps they will return [i.e., repent].

(22) And who is more unjust than one who is reminded of the verses of his Lord; then he turns away from them? Indeed We, from the criminals, will take retribution.

(23) And We certainly gave Moses the Scripture, so do not be in doubt over his meeting.[1144] And We made it [i.e., the Torah] guidance for the Children of Israel.

(24) And We made from among them leaders guiding by Our command when they were patient and [when] they were certain of Our signs.

[1141] Deserved by the evildoers.
[1142] In the cause of Allāh.
[1143] i.e., the disasters and calamities of this world.
[1144] i.e., Muḥammad's meeting Moses on the night of al-Miʿrāj (ascent).

(25) Indeed, your Lord will judge between them on the Day of Resurrection concerning that over which they used to differ.

(26) Has it not become clear to them how many generations We destroyed before them, [as] they walk among their dwellings? Indeed in that are signs; then do they not hear?

(27) Have they not seen that We drive water [in clouds] to barren land and bring forth thereby crops from which their livestock eat and [they] themselves? Then do they not see?

(28) And they say, "When will be this conquest,[1145] if you should be truthful?"

(29) Say, [O Muḥammad], "On the Day of Conquest the belief of those who had disbelieved will not benefit them, nor will they be reprieved."

(30) So turn away from them and wait. Indeed, they are waiting.

[1145] Or "decision," i.e., judgement.

Surah Al-Ahzab

(1) O Prophet, fear Allāh and do not obey the disbelievers and the hypocrites. Indeed, Allāh is ever Knowing and Wise.

(2) And follow that which is revealed to you from your Lord. Indeed Allāh is ever, of what you do, Aware.

(3) And rely upon Allāh; and sufficient is Allāh as Disposer of affairs.[1146]

(4) Allāh has not made for a man two hearts in his interior. And He has not made your wives whom you declare unlawful[1147] your mothers. And He has not made your claimed [i.e., adopted] sons your [true] sons. That is [merely] your saying by your mouths, but Allāh says the truth, and He guides to the [right] way.

(5) Call them[1148] by [the names of] their fathers; it is more just in the sight of Allāh. But if you do not know their fathers - then they are [still] your brothers in religion and those entrusted to you. And there is no blame upon you for that in which you have erred but [only for] what your hearts intended. And ever is Allāh Forgiving and Merciful.

(6) The Prophet is more worthy of the believers than themselves,[1149] and his wives are [in the position of] their mothers. And those of [blood] relationship are more entitled [to inheritance] in the decree of Allāh than the [other] believers and the emigrants, except that you may do to your close associates a kindness [through bequest]. That was in the Book[1150] inscribed.

(7) And [mention, O Muḥammad], when We took from the prophets their covenant and from you and from Noah and Abraham and Moses and Jesus, the son of Mary; and We took from them a solemn covenant

---

[1146] Refer to footnote in 3:173.

[1147] By the expression "You are to me like the back of my mother." Such an oath taken against approaching one's wife was a pre-Islāmic practice declared by Allāh (subḥānahu wa taʿālā) to be a sin requiring expiation as described in 58:3-4.

[1148] Those children under your care.

[1149] "He (ﷺ) is more worthy of their obedience and loyalty and is more concerned for them than they are for one another.

[1150] The Preserved Slate (al-Lawḥ al-Maḥfūẓ)."

(8) That He may question the truthful about their truth.[1151] And He has prepared for the disbelievers a painful punishment.

(9) O you who have believed, remember the favor of Allāh upon you when armies came to [attack] you and We sent upon them a wind and armies [of angels] you did not see. And ever is Allāh, of what you do, Seeing.

(10) [Remember] when they came at you from above you and from below you, and when eyes shifted [in fear], and hearts reached the throats, and you assumed about Allāh [various] assumptions.

(11) There the believers were tested and shaken with a severe shaking.

(12) And [remember] when the hypocrites and those in whose hearts is disease said, "Allāh and His Messenger did not promise us except delusion,"

(13) And when a faction of them said, "O people of Yathrib,[1152] there is no stability for you [here], so return [home]." And a party of them asked permission of the Prophet, saying, "Indeed, our houses are exposed [i.e., unprotected]," while they were not exposed. They did not intend except to flee.

(14) And if they had been entered upon from all its [surrounding] regions and fitnah [i.e., disbelief] had been demanded of them, they would have done it and not hesitated over it except briefly.

(15) And they had already promised Allāh before not to turn their backs [i.e., flee]. And ever is the promise to Allāh [that about which one will be] questioned.

(16) Say, [O Muḥammad], "Never will fleeing benefit you if you should flee from death or killing; and then [if you did], you would not be given enjoyment [of life] except for a little."

(17) Say, "Who is it that can protect you from Allāh[1153] if He intends for you an ill or intends for you a mercy?" And they will not find for themselves besides Allāh any protector or any helper.

[1151] i.e., that He may ask the prophets what they conveyed to their people and what response they received. "The truthful" may also refer to those who believed in the message conveyed by the prophets and imparted it to others.
[1152] The name by which al-Madīnah was known before the arrival of the Prophet (ﷺ).

[1153] i.e., prevent the will of Allāh from being carried out.

(18) Already Allāh knows the hinderers[1154] among you and those [hypocrites] who say to their brothers, "Come to us,"[1155] and do not go to battle, except for a few,[1156]

(19) Indisposed[1157] toward you. And when fear comes, you see them looking at you, their eyes revolving like one being overcome by death. But when fear departs, they lash you with sharp tongues, indisposed toward [any] good. Those have not believed, so Allāh has rendered their deeds worthless, and ever is that, for Allāh, easy.

(20) They think the companies have not [yet] withdrawn.[1158] And if the companies should come [again], they would wish they were in the desert among the bedouins, inquiring [from afar] about your news. And if they should be among you, they would not fight except for a little.

(21) There has certainly been for you in the Messenger of Allāh an excellent pattern[1159] for anyone whose hope is in Allāh and the Last Day and [who] remembers Allāh often.

(22) And when the believers saw the companies, they said, "This is what Allāh and His Messenger had promised us, and Allāh and His Messenger spoke the truth." And it increased them only in faith and acceptance.

(23) Among the believers are men true to what they promised Allāh. Among them is he who has fulfilled his vow [to the death], and among them is he who awaits [his chance]. And they did not alter [the terms of their commitment] by any alteration -

(24) That Allāh may reward the truthful for their truth and punish the hypocrites if He wills or accept their repentance. Indeed, Allāh is ever Forgiving and Merciful.

(25) And Allāh repelled those who disbelieved, in their rage, not having obtained any good. And sufficient was Allāh for the believers in battle, and ever is Allāh Powerful and Exalted in Might.

(26) And He brought down those who supported them among the People of the Scripture[1160] from their fortresses and cast terror into their hearts [so that] a party

---

[1154] "Those who dissuade others from supporting the Prophet (ﷺ) in battle.

[1155] Rather than joining the Prophet (ﷺ).

[1156] Who went out of ulterior motives."

[1157] Literally, "stingy," i.e., unwilling to offer any help.

[1158] In their excessive fear the cowardly hypocrites could not believe the enemy forces had been defeated.

[1159] An example to be followed.

[1160] The Jews of Banū Qurayẓah, who had violated their treaty with the Muslims.

[i.e., their men] you killed, and you took captive a party [i.e., the women and children].

(27) And He caused you to inherit their land and their homes and their properties and a land which you have not trodden.[1161] And ever is Allāh, over all things, competent.

(28) O Prophet, say to your wives, "If you should desire the worldly life and its adornment, then come, I will provide for you and give you a gracious release.

(29) But if you should desire Allāh and His Messenger and the home of the Hereafter - then indeed, Allāh has prepared for the doers of good among you a great reward."

(30) O wives of the Prophet, whoever of you should commit a clear immorality - for her the punishment would be doubled two fold, and ever is that, for Allāh, easy.

(31) And whoever of you devoutly obeys Allāh and His Messenger and does righteousness - We will give her her reward twice; and We have prepared for her a noble provision.

(32) O wives of the Prophet, you are not like anyone among women. If you fear Allāh, then do not be soft in speech [to men],[1162] lest he in whose heart is disease should covet, but speak with appropriate speech.

(33) And abide in your houses and do not display yourselves as [was] the display of the former times of ignorance. And establish prayer and give zakāh and obey Allāh and His Messenger. Allāh intends only to remove from you the impurity [of sin], O people of the [Prophet's] household, and to purify you with [extensive] purification.

(34) And remember what is recited in your houses of the verses of Allāh and wisdom.[1163] Indeed, Allāh is ever Subtle[1164] and Aware.

(35) Indeed, the Muslim men and Muslim women, the believing men and believing women, the obedient men and obedient women, the truthful men and truthful women, the patient men and patient women, the humble men and humble women, the charitable men and charitable women, the fasting men and fasting women, the men who guard their private parts and the women who do so, and the men who

---

[1161] i.e., that taken in subsequent conquests.

[1162] The meaning has also been given as "You are not like any among women if you fear Allāh. So do not be soft in speech..."

[1163] "The teachings of the Prophet (ﷺ) or his sunnah.

[1164] Refer to footnote of 6:103."

remember Allāh often and the women who do so - for them Allāh has prepared forgiveness and a great reward.

(36) It is not for a believing man or a believing woman, when Allāh and His Messenger have decided a matter, that they should [thereafter] have any choice about their affair. And whoever disobeys Allāh and His Messenger has certainly strayed into clear error.

(37) And [remember, O Muḥammad], when you said to the one on whom Allāh bestowed favor and you bestowed favor,[1165] "Keep your wife and fear Allāh," while you concealed within yourself that which Allāh is to disclose.[1166] And you feared the people,[1167] while Allāh has more right that you fear Him.[1168] So when Zayd had no longer any need for her, We married her to you in order that there not be upon the believers any discomfort [i.e., guilt] concerning the wives of their claimed [i.e., adopted] sons when they no longer have need of them. And ever is the command [i.e., decree] of Allāh accomplished.

(38) There is not to be upon the Prophet any discomfort concerning that which Allāh has imposed upon him.[1169] [This is] the established way of Allāh with those [prophets] who have passed on before. And ever is the command of Allāh a destiny decreed.

(39) [Allāh praises] those who convey the messages of Allāh[1170] and fear Him and do not fear anyone but Allāh. And sufficient is Allāh as Accountant.

(40) Muḥammad is not the father of [any] one of your men, but [he is] the Messenger of Allāh and seal [i.e., last] of the prophets. And ever is Allāh, of all things, Knowing.

(41) O you who have believed, remember Allāh with much remembrance

(42) And exalt Him morning and afternoon.

[1165] "Referring to the Prophet's freed slave, Zayd bin Ḥārithah.

[1166] i.e., Allāh's command to the Prophet (ﷺ) to marry Zaynab after Zayd divorced her. This was to demonstrate that a man may marry a woman formerly married to his adopted son.

[1167] i.e., feared their saying that the Prophet (ﷺ) had married the (former) wife of his son (which is prohibited by Allāh in the case of a true, begotten son).

[1168] By making known His command."

[1169] Or permitted to him.

[1170] i.e., the prophets (peace be upon them all) and after them, the followers of the final prophet, Muḥammad (ﷺ), who honestly convey Allāh's message to the people.

(43) It is He who confers blessing upon you,[1171] and His angels [ask Him to do so] that He may bring you out from darknesses into the light. And ever is He, to the believers, Merciful.

(44) Their greeting the Day they meet Him will be, "Peace." And He has prepared for them a noble reward.

(45) O Prophet, indeed We have sent you as a witness and a bringer of good tidings and a warner

(46) And one who invites to Allāh, by His permission, and an illuminating lamp.

(47) And give good tidings to the believers that they will have from Allāh great bounty.

(48) And do not obey the disbelievers and the hypocrites and disregard their annoyance, and rely upon Allāh. And sufficient is Allāh as Disposer of affairs.

(49) O you who have believed, when you marry believing women and then divorce them before you have touched them [i.e., consummated the marriage], then there is not for you any waiting period to count concerning them. So provide for them and give them a gracious release.

(50) O Prophet, indeed We have made lawful to you your wives to whom you have given their due compensation[1172] and those your right hand possesses from what Allāh has returned to you [of captives] and the daughters of your paternal uncles and the daughters of your paternal aunts and the daughters of your maternal uncles and the daughters of your maternal aunts who emigrated with you and a believing woman if she gives herself to the Prophet [and] if the Prophet wishes to marry her; [this is] only for you, excluding the [other] believers. We certainly know what We have made obligatory upon them concerning their wives and those their right hands possess, [but this is for you] in order that there will be upon you no discomfort [i.e., difficulty]. And ever is Allāh Forgiving and Merciful.

(51) You, [O Muḥammad], may put aside whom you will of them[1173] or take to yourself whom you will. And any that you desire of those [wives] from whom you had [temporarily] separated - there is no blame upon you [in returning her]. That

---

[1171] i.e., Allāh (subḥānahu wa taʿālā) cares for you and covers you with His mercy. An additional meaning is that He praises you in the presence of the angels.

[1172] i.e., bridal gifts (mahr).

[1173] Those mentioned in the previous verse as being lawful to the Prophet (ﷺ) or his wives to which he was married.

is more suitable that they should be content and not grieve and that they should be satisfied with what you have given them - all of them. And Allāh knows what is in your hearts. And ever is Allāh Knowing and Forbearing.

(52) Not lawful to you, [O Muḥammad], are [any additional] women after [this], nor [is it] for you to exchange them for [other] wives, even if their beauty were to please you, except what your right hand possesses. And ever is Allāh, over all things, an Observer.[1174]

(53) O you who have believed, do not enter the houses of the Prophet except when you are permitted for a meal, without awaiting its readiness. But when you are invited, then enter; and when you have eaten, disperse without seeking to remain for conversation. Indeed, that [behavior] was troubling the Prophet, and he is shy of [dismissing] you. But Allāh is not shy of the truth. And when you ask [his wives] for something, ask them from behind a partition. That is purer for your hearts and their hearts. And it is not [conceivable or lawful] for you to harm the Messenger of Allāh or to marry his wives after him, ever. Indeed, that would be in the sight of Allāh an enormity.

(54) Whether you reveal a thing or conceal it, indeed Allāh is ever, of all things, Knowing.

(55) There is no blame upon them [i.e., women] concerning their fathers or their sons or their brothers or their brothers' sons or their sisters' sons or their women or those their right hands possess [i.e., slaves].[1175] And fear Allāh. Indeed Allāh is ever, over all things, Witness.

(56) Indeed, Allāh confers blessing upon the Prophet, and His angels [ask Him to do so]. O you who have believed, ask [Allāh to confer] blessing upon him and ask [Allāh to grant him] peace.

(57) Indeed, those who abuse Allāh and His Messenger - Allāh has cursed them in this world and the Hereafter and prepared for them a humiliating punishment.

(58) And those who harm believing men and believing women for [something] other than what they have earned [i.e., deserved] have certainly borne upon themselves a slander and manifest sin.

[1174] See footnote to verse 4:1.

[1175] It is permissible for a woman to appear before these people without complete covering and to be alone with them. The brothers of both parents (uncles) are included as "fathers" or "parents," according to ḥadīth.

(59) O Prophet, tell your wives and your daughters and the women of the believers to bring down over themselves [part] of their outer garments.[1176] That is more suitable that they will be known[1177] and not be abused. And ever is Allāh Forgiving and Merciful.[1178]

(60) If the hypocrites and those in whose hearts is disease[1179] and those who spread rumors in al-Madīnah do not cease, We will surely incite you against them; then they will not remain your neighbors therein except for a little,

(61) Accursed wherever they are found, [being] seized and massacred completely.

(62) [This is] the established way of Allāh with those who passed on before; and you will not find in the way of Allāh any change.

(63) People ask you concerning the Hour. Say, "Knowledge of it is only with Allāh. And what may make you perceive? Perhaps the Hour is near."

(64) Indeed, Allāh has cursed the disbelievers and prepared for them a Blaze.

(65) Abiding therein forever, they will not find a protector or a helper.

(66) The Day their faces will be turned about in the Fire, they will say, "How we wish we had obeyed Allāh and obeyed the Messenger."

(67) And they will say, "Our Lord, indeed we obeyed our masters and our dignitaries,[1180] and they led us astray from the [right] way.

(68) Our Lord, give them double the punishment and curse them with a great curse."

(69) O you who have believed, be not like those who abused Moses; then Allāh cleared him of what they said. And he, in the sight of Allāh, was distinguished.

(70) O you who have believed, fear Allāh and speak words of appropriate justice.

(71) He will [then] amend for you your deeds and forgive you your sins. And whoever obeys Allāh and His Messenger has certainly attained a great attainment.

[1176] "The jilbāb, which is defined as a cloak covering the head and reaching to the ground, thereby covering the woman's entire body.

[1177] As chaste believing women.

[1178] Or "and Allāh was Forgiving and Merciful" of what occurred before this injunction or before knowledge of it."

[1179] Referring here to those who commit adultery or fornication.

[1180] Also interpreted to mean "our noble ones and our elders [i.e., distinguished scholars]."

(72) Indeed, We offered the Trust[1181] to the heavens and the earth and the mountains, and they declined to bear it and feared it; but man [undertook to] bear it. Indeed, he was unjust and ignorant.[1182]

(73) [It[1183] was] so that Allāh may punish the hypocrite men and hypocrite women and the men and women who associate others with Him and that Allāh may accept repentance from the believing men and believing women. And ever is Allāh Forgiving and Merciful.

[1181] "The acceptance of obligations and obedience to Allāh.
[1182] Coveting its reward while forgetting the penalty for failure to keep his commitment.
[1183] The reason for which mankind was permitted to carry the Trust.

Surah Saba'

(1) [All] praise is [due] to Allāh, to whom belongs whatever is in the heavens and whatever is in the earth, and to Him belongs [all] praise in the Hereafter. And He is the Wise, the Aware.

(2) He knows what penetrates into the earth and what emerges from it and what descends from the heaven and what ascends therein. And He is the Merciful, the Forgiving.

(3) But those who disbelieve say, "The Hour will not come to us." Say, "Yes, by my Lord, it will surely come to you. [Allāh is] the Knower of the unseen." Not absent from Him is an atom's weight[1184] within the heavens or within the earth or [what is] smaller than that or greater, except that it is in a clear register -

(4) That He may reward those who believe and do righteous deeds. Those will have forgiveness and noble provision.

(5) But those who strive against Our verses [seeking] to cause failure[1185] - for them will be a painful punishment of foul nature.

(6) And those who have been given knowledge see that what is revealed to you from your Lord is the truth, and it guides to the path of the Exalted in Might, the Praiseworthy.

(7) But those who disbelieve say, "Shall we direct you to a man who will inform you [that] when you have disintegrated in complete disintegration, you will [then] be [recreated] in a new creation?

(8) Has he invented about Allāh a lie or is there in him madness?" Rather, they who do not believe in the Hereafter will be in the punishment and [are in] extreme error.

(9) Then, do they not look at what is before them and what is behind them of the heaven and earth? If We should will, We could cause the earth to swallow them or [could] let fall upon them fragments from the sky. Indeed in that is a sign for every servant turning back [to Allāh].

(10) And We certainly gave David from Us bounty. [We said], "O mountains, repeat [Our] praises with him, and the birds [as well]." And We made pliable for him iron,

---

[1184] Or "the weight of a small ant."
[1185] i.e., to undermine their credibility in order to defeat the Prophet (ﷺ).

(11) [Commanding him], "Make full coats of mail and calculate [precisely] the links, and work [all of you] righteousness. Indeed I, of what you do, am Seeing."

(12) And to Solomon [We subjected] the wind - its morning [journey was that of] a month - and its afternoon [journey was that of] a month, and We made flow for him a spring of [liquid] copper. And among the jinn were those who worked for him by the permission of his Lord. And whoever deviated among them from Our command - We will make him taste of the punishment of the Blaze.

(13) They made for him what he willed of elevated chambers,[1186] statues,[1187] bowls like reservoirs, and stationary kettles. [We said], "Work, O family of David, in gratitude." And few of My servants are grateful.

(14) And when We decreed for him [i.e., Solomon] death, nothing indicated to them [i.e., the jinn] his death except a creature of the earth eating his staff.[1188] But when he fell, it became clear to the jinn that if they had known the unseen, they would not have remained in humiliating punishment.[1189]

(15) There was for [the tribe of] Saba' in their dwelling place a sign: two [fields of] gardens on the right and on the left. [They were told], "Eat from the provisions of your Lord and be grateful to Him. A good land [have you], and a forgiving Lord."

(16) But they turned away [refusing], so We sent upon them the flood of the dam,[1190] and We replaced their two [fields of] gardens with gardens of bitter fruit, tamarisks and something of sparse lote trees.

(17) [By] that We repaid them because they disbelieved. And do We [thus] repay except the ungrateful?

(18) And We placed between them and the cities which We had blessed[1191] [many] visible cities. And We determined between them the [distances of] journey,[1192] [saying], "Travel between them by night or by day in safety."

[1186] "Described by commentators as palaces, dwellings, or places of prayer.

[1187] Which were not prohibited until the time of Prophet Muḥammad (ﷺ)."

[1188] "Upon which he was leaning at the time of his death. A termite continued to gnaw into the stick until it collapsed under his weight.

[1189] i.e., hard labor. This verse is evidence that the jinn do not possess knowledge of the unseen, which belongs exclusively to Allāh (subḥānahu wa taʿālā)."

[1190] i.e., caused by a break in their dam. Another meaning is "the overwhelming flood."

[1191] "In the lands of what is now southern Syria and Palestine.

[1192] i.e., We placed the intermediate settlements at calculated distances for the convenience of travelers."

(19) But [insolently] they said, "Our Lord, lengthen the distance between our journeys," and wronged themselves, so We made them narrations[1193] and dispersed them in total dispersion. Indeed in that are signs for everyone patient and grateful.

(20) And Iblees had already confirmed through them[1194] his assumption,[1195] so they followed him, except for a party of believers.

(21) And he had over them no authority except [it was decreed] that We might make evident who believes in the Hereafter from who is thereof in doubt. And your Lord, over all things, is Guardian.[1196]

(22) Say, [O Muḥammad], "Invoke those you claim [as deities] besides Allāh." They do not possess an atom's weight [of ability] in the heavens or on the earth, and they do not have therein any partnership [with Him], nor is there for Him from among them any assistant.

(23) And intercession does not benefit with Him except for one whom He permits. [And those wait] until, when terror is removed from their hearts,[1197] they will say [to one another], "What has your Lord said?" They will say, "The truth." And He is the Most High, the Grand.

(24) Say, "Who provides for you from the heavens and the earth?" Say, "Allāh. And indeed, we or you are either upon guidance or in clear error."

(25) Say, "You will not be asked about what we committed, and we will not be asked about what you do."

(26) Say, "Our Lord will bring us together; then He will judge between us in truth. And He is the Knowing Judge."[1198]

(27) Say, "Show me those whom you have attached to Him as partners. No! Rather, He [alone] is Allāh, the Exalted in Might, the Wise."

(28) And We have not sent you except comprehensively[1199] to mankind as a bringer of good tidings and a warner. But most of the people do not know.

[1193] Stories related to others as lessons or examples.

[1194] "i.e., the people of Saba' or mankind in general.

[1195] That mankind could readily be misled by him.

[1196] Protecting and preserving the existence and attributes of His creations.

[1197] i.e., the hearts of the angels who will be permitted to intercede

[1198] Literally, "Opener," i.e., He who decides and lays open all matters in truth and justice and who opens the way to victory, success, relief, knowledge and understanding.

[1199] Literally, "inclusively, without exception."

(29) And they say, "When is this promise, if you should be truthful?"

(30) Say, "For you is the appointment of a Day [when] you will not remain thereafter an hour, nor will you precede [it]."

(31) And those who disbelieve say, "We will never believe in this Qur'ān nor in that before it." But if you could see when the wrongdoers are made to stand before their Lord, refuting each others' words...[1200] Those who were oppressed will say to those who were arrogant, "If not for you, we would have been believers."

(32) Those who were arrogant will say to those who were oppressed, "Did we avert you from guidance after it had come to you? Rather, you were criminals."

(33) Those who were oppressed will say to those who were arrogant, "Rather, [it was your] conspiracy of night and day when you were ordering us to disbelieve in Allāh and attribute to Him equals." But they will [all] confide regret when they see the punishment; and We will put shackles on the necks of those who disbelieved. Will they be recompensed except for what they used to do?

(34) And We did not send into a city any warner except that its affluent said, "Indeed we, in that with which you were sent, are disbelievers."

(35) And they[1201] said, "We are more [than the believers] in wealth and children, and we are not to be punished."

(36) Say, "Indeed, my Lord extends provision for whom He wills and restricts [it], but most of the people do not know."

(37) And it is not your wealth or your children that bring you nearer to Us in position, but it is [by being] one who has believed and done righteousness. For them there will be the double reward for what they did, and they will be in the upper chambers [of Paradise], safe [and secure].

(38) And the ones who strive against Our verses to cause [them] failure[1202] - those will be brought into the punishment [to remain].

[1200] Having been left to the imagination, the conclusion of this sentence is estimated to be "...you would see a dreadful sight."

[1201] The affluent ones in general or the people of Makkah specifically.

[1202] See footnote to 34:5.

(39) Say, "Indeed, my Lord extends provision for whom He wills of His servants and restricts [it] for him. But whatever thing you spend [in His cause] - He will compensate it; and He is the best of providers."

(40) And [mention] the Day when He will gather them all and then say to the angels, "Did these [people] used to worship you?"

(41) They will say, "Exalted are You! You, [O Allāh], are our benefactor excluding [i.e., not] them. Rather, they used to worship the jinn; most of them were believers in them."

(42) But today [i.e., the Day of Judgement] you do not hold for one another [the power of] benefit or harm, and We will say to those who wronged, "Taste the punishment of the Fire, which you used to deny."

(43) And when Our verses are recited to them as clear evidences, they say, "This is not but a man who wishes to avert you from that which your fathers were worshipping." And they say, "This is not except a lie invented." And those who disbelieve say of the truth when it has come to them, "This is not but obvious magic."

(44) And We had not given them any scriptures which they could study, and We had not sent to them before you, [O Muḥammad], any warner.

(45) And those before them denied, and they [i.e., the people of Makkah] have not attained a tenth of what We had given them. But they [i.e., the former peoples] denied My messengers, so how [terrible] was My reproach.

(46) Say, "I only advise you of one [thing] - that you stand for Allāh, [seeking truth] in pairs and individually, and then give thought." There is not in your companion any madness. He is only a warner to you before a severe punishment.

(47) Say, "Whatever payment I might have asked of you - it is yours. My payment is only from Allāh, and He is, over all things, Witness."

(48) Say, "Indeed, my Lord projects the truth, Knower of the unseen."

(49) Say, "The truth has come, and falsehood can neither begin [anything] nor repeat [it]."[1203]

(50) Say, "If I should err, I would only err against myself. But if I am guided, it is by what my Lord reveals to me. Indeed, He is Hearing and near."

[1203] This expression alludes to complete inability, meaning that falsehood was abolished.

(51) And if you could see[1204] when they are terrified but there is no escape, and they will be seized from a place nearby.

(52) And they will [then] say, "We believe in it!" But how for them will be the taking[1205] [of faith] from a place far away?[1206]

(53) And they had already disbelieved in it before and would assault[1207] the unseen from a place far away.[1208]

(54) And prevention will be placed between them and what they desire,[1209] as was done with their kind before. Indeed, they were in disquieting doubt [i.e., denial].

[1204] i.e., have a glimpse of the Hereafter.
[1205] "Literally, "taking of something within easy reach," in other words, "How can they expect to obtain faith at this point?"
[1206] i.e., their former life on earth, wherein they had every opportunity but which is now gone, never to return."
[1207] "Verbally, by conjecture and denial.
[1208] i.e., a position far from truth."
[1209] Meaning the attainment of faith and its benefits or entrance into Paradise.

Surah Fatir

(1) [All] praise is [due] to Allāh, Creator of the heavens and the earth, [who] made the angels messengers having wings, two or three or four. He increases in creation what He wills. Indeed, Allāh is over all things competent.

(2) Whatever Allāh grants to people of mercy - none can withhold it; and whatever He withholds - none can release it thereafter. And He is the Exalted in Might, the Wise.

(3) O mankind, remember the favor of Allāh upon you. Is there any creator other than Allāh who provides for you from the heaven and earth? There is no deity except Him, so how are you deluded?

(4) And if they deny you, [O Muḥammad] - already were messengers denied before you. And to Allāh are returned [all] matters.

(5) O mankind, indeed the promise of Allāh is truth, so let not the worldly life delude you and be not deceived about Allāh by the Deceiver [i.e., Satan].

(6) Indeed, Satan is an enemy to you; so take him as an enemy. He only invites his party to be among the companions of the Blaze.

(7) Those who disbelieve will have a severe punishment, and those who believe and do righteous deeds will have forgiveness and great reward.

(8) Then is one to whom the evil of his deed has been made attractive so he considers it good [like one rightly guided]? For indeed, Allāh sends astray whom He wills and guides whom He wills. So do not let yourself perish over them in regret. Indeed, Allāh is Knowing of what they do.

(9) And it is Allāh who sends the winds, and they stir the clouds, and We drive them to a dead land and give life thereby to the earth after its lifelessness. Thus is the resurrection.

(10) Whoever desires honor [through power] - then to Allāh belongs all honor.[1210] To Him ascends good speech, and righteous work raises it.[1211] But they who plot evil deeds will have a severe punishment, and the plotting of those - it will perish.

[1210] "See footnote to 4:139.

[1211] For acceptance by Allāh, meaning that righteous deeds are confirmation and proof of what is uttered by the tongue."

(11) And Allāh created you from dust, then from a sperm-drop; then He made you mates. And no female conceives nor does she give birth except with His knowledge. And no aged person is granted [additional] life nor is his lifespan lessened but that it is in a register. Indeed, that for Allāh is easy.

(12) And not alike are the two seas [i.e., bodies of water]. One is fresh and sweet, palatable for drinking, and one is salty and bitter. And from each you eat tender meat and extract ornaments which you wear, and you see the ships plowing through [them] that you might seek of His bounty; and perhaps you will be grateful.

(13) He causes the night to enter the day, and He causes the day to enter the night and has subjected the sun and the moon - each running [its course] for a specified term. That is Allāh, your Lord; to Him belongs sovereignty. And those whom you invoke other than Him do not possess [as much as] the membrane of a date seed.

(14) If you invoke them, they do not hear your supplication; and if they heard, they would not respond to you. And on the Day of Resurrection they will deny your association.[1212] And none can inform you like [one] Aware [of all matters].

(15) O mankind, you are those in need of Allāh, while Allāh is the Free of need, the Praiseworthy.

(16) If He wills, He can do away with you and bring forth a new creation.

(17) And that is for Allāh not difficult.

(18) And no bearer of burdens will bear the burden of another. And if a heavily laden soul calls [another] to [carry some of] its load, nothing of it will be carried, even if he should be a close relative. You can only warn those who fear their Lord unseen and have established prayer. And whoever purifies himself only purifies himself for [the benefit of] his soul. And to Allāh is the [final] destination.

(19) Not equal are the blind and the seeing,

(20) Nor are the darknesses and the light,

(21) Nor are the shade and the heat,[1213]

[1212] Of them with Allāh or your worship of them.

[1213] Of the sun or of a scorching wind.

(22) And not equal are the living and the dead. Indeed, Allāh causes to hear whom He wills, but you cannot make hear those in the graves.[1214]

(23) You, [O Muḥammad], are not but a warner.

(24) Indeed, We have sent you with the truth as a bringer of good tidings and a warner. And there was no nation but that there had passed within it a warner.

(25) And if they deny you - then already have those before them denied. Their messengers came to them with clear proofs and written ordinances and with the enlightening Scripture.

(26) Then I seized the ones who disbelieved, and how [terrible] was My reproach.

(27) Do you not see that Allāh sends down rain from the sky, and We produce thereby fruits of varying colors? And in the mountains are tracts, white and red of varying shades and [some] extremely black.

(28) And among people and moving creatures and grazing livestock are various colors similarly. Only those fear Allāh, from among His servants, who have knowledge. Indeed, Allāh is Exalted in Might and Forgiving.

(29) Indeed, those who recite the Book of Allāh and establish prayer and spend [in His cause] out of what We have provided them, secretly and publicly, [can] expect a transaction [i.e., profit] that will never perish -

(30) That He may give them in full their rewards and increase for them of His bounty. Indeed, He is Forgiving and Appreciative.[1215]

(31) And that which We have revealed to you, [O Muḥammad], of the Book is the truth, confirming what was before it. Indeed Allāh, of His servants, is Aware and Seeing.

(32) Then We caused to inherit the Book those We have chosen of Our servants;[1216] and among them is he who wrongs himself [i.e., sins], and among them is he who is moderate, and among them is he who is foremost in good deeds by permission of Allāh. That [inheritance] is what is the great bounty.

[1214] The four comparisons given by Allāh (subḥānahu wa ta‘ālā) in verses 19-22 are those of the believer and unbeliever, various kinds of misbelief and (true) belief, Paradise and Hellfire, and those receptive to guidance and those unreceptive.
[1215] i.e., He gives much in return for little and multiplies rewards.
[1216] The followers of Prophet Muḥammad (ﷺ).

(33) [For them are] gardens of perpetual residence which they will enter. They will be adorned therein with bracelets of gold and pearls, and their garments therein will be silk.

(34) And they will say, "Praise to Allāh, who has removed from us [all] sorrow. Indeed, our Lord is Forgiving and Appreciative -

(35) He who has settled us in the home of duration [i.e., Paradise] out of His bounty. There touches us not in it any fatigue, and there touches us not in it weariness [of mind]."

(36) And for those who disbelieve will be the fire of Hell. [Death] is not decreed for them[1217] so they may die, nor will its torment be lightened for them. Thus do We recompense every ungrateful one.

(37) And they will cry out therein, "Our Lord, remove us;[1218] we will do righteousness - other than what we were doing!" But did We not grant you life enough for whoever would remember therein to remember, and the warner had come to you? So taste [the punishment], for there is not for the wrongdoers any helper.

(38) Indeed, Allāh is Knower of the unseen [aspects] of the heavens and earth. Indeed, He is Knowing of that within the breasts.

(39) It is He who has made you successors upon the earth. And whoever disbelieves - upon him will be [the consequence of] his disbelief. And the disbelief of the disbelievers does not increase them in the sight of their Lord except in hatred; and the disbelief of the disbelievers does not increase them except in loss.

(40) Say, "Have you considered[1219] your 'partners' whom you invoke besides Allāh? Show me what they have created from the earth, or have they partnership [with Him] in the heavens? Or have We given them a book so they are [standing] on evidence therefrom? [No], rather, the wrongdoers do not promise each other except delusion."[1220]

(41) Indeed, Allāh holds the heavens and the earth, lest they cease. And if they should cease, no one could hold them [in place] after Him. Indeed, He is Forbearing[1221] and Forgiving.

[1217] Or "They are not killed."
[1218] The implication is "Return us to the previous world."
[1219] "Understood to mean "Tell me about..."
[1220] By telling their followers that the so-called deities will intercede for them with Allāh."
[1221] Refer to footnote in 2:225.

(42) And they swore by Allāh their strongest oaths that if a warner came to them, they would be more guided than [any] one of the [previous] nations. But when a warner came to them, it did not increase them except in aversion

(43) [Due to] arrogance in the land and plotting of evil; but the evil plot does not encompass except its own people. Then do they await except the way [i.e., fate] of the former peoples? But you will never find in the way [i.e., established method] of Allāh any change, and you will never find in the way of Allāh[1222] any alteration.[1223]

(44) Have they not traveled through the land and observed how was the end of those before them? And they were greater than them in power. But Allāh is not to be caused failure [i.e., prevented] by anything in the heavens or on the earth. Indeed, He is ever Knowing and Competent.

(45) And if Allāh were to impose blame on the people for what they have earned, He would not leave upon it [i.e., the earth] any creature. But He defers them for a specified term. And when their time comes, then indeed Allāh has ever been, of His servants, Seeing.

[1222] "i.e., in His punishment of those who deny the prophets.
[1223] Or "transfer" of punishment to others in place of them."

Surah Ya seen

(1) Yā, Seen.[1224]

(2) By the wise[1225] Qur'ān,

(3) Indeed you, [O Muḥammad], are from among the messengers,

(4) On a straight path.

(5) [This is] a revelation of the Exalted in Might, the Merciful,

(6) That you may warn a people whose forefathers were not warned, so they are unaware.

(7) Already the word [i.e., decree] has come into effect upon most of them, so they do not believe.

(8) Indeed, We have put shackles on their necks, and they are to their chins, so they are with heads [kept] aloft.

(9) And We have put before them a barrier and behind them a barrier and covered them, so they do not see.

(10) And it is all the same for them whether you warn them or do not warn them - they will not believe.

(11) You can only warn one who follows the message and fears the Most Merciful unseen. So give him good tidings of forgiveness and noble reward.

(12) Indeed, it is We who bring the dead to life and record what they have put forth and what they left behind, and all things We have enumerated in a clear register.

(13) And present to them an example: the people of the city, when the messengers came to it -

(14) When We sent to them two but they denied them, so We strengthened [them] with a third, and they said, "Indeed, we are messengers to you."

(15) They said, "You are not but human beings like us, and the Most Merciful has not revealed a thing. You are only telling lies."

[1224] See footnote to 2:1.
[1225] See footnote to 10:1.

(16) They said, "Our Lord knows that we are messengers to you,

(17) And we are not responsible except for clear notification."

(18) They said, "Indeed, we consider you a bad omen. If you do not desist, we will surely stone you, and there will surely touch you, from us, a painful punishment."

(19) They said, "Your omen [i.e., fate] is with yourselves. Is it[1226] because you were reminded? Rather, you are a transgressing people."

(20) And there came from the farthest end of the city a man, running. He said, "O my people, follow the messengers.

(21) Follow those who do not ask of you [any] payment, and they are [rightly] guided.

(22) And why should I not worship He who created me and to whom you will be returned?

(23) Should I take other than Him [false] deities [while], if the Most Merciful intends for me some adversity, their intercession will not avail me at all, nor can they save me?

(24) Indeed, I would then be in manifest error.

(25) Indeed, I have believed in your Lord, so listen to me."

(26) It was said, "Enter Paradise."[1227] He said, "I wish my people could know

(27) Of how my Lord has forgiven me and placed me among the honored."

(28) And We did not send down upon his people after him any soldiers from the heaven, nor would We have done so.

(29) It was not but one shout,[1228] and immediately they were extinguished.

(30) How regretful for the servants. There did not come to them any messenger except that they used to ridicule him.

(31) Have they not considered how many generations We destroyed before them - that they to them[1229] will not return?

[1226] Your threat against us.

[1227] An abrupt transfer to the Hereafter conveys the meaning that the man met a violent death at the hands of the disbelievers and so was martyred for the cause of Allāh.

[1228] From Gabriel or a blast from the sky.

[1229] i.e., to those living presently in the world.

(32) And indeed, all of them will yet be brought present before Us.

(33) And a sign for them is the dead earth. We have brought it to life and brought forth from it grain, and from it they eat.

(34) And We placed therein gardens of palm trees and grapevines and caused to burst forth therefrom some springs -

(35) That they may eat of His fruit.[1230] And their hands have not produced it,[1231] so will they not be grateful?

(36) Exalted is He who created all pairs[1232] - from what the earth grows and from themselves and from that which they do not know.

(37) And a sign for them is the night. We remove[1233] from it the [light of] day, so they are [left] in darkness.

(38) And the sun runs [on course] toward its stopping point. That is the determination of the Exalted in Might, the Knowing.

(39) And the moon - We have determined for it phases, until it returns [appearing] like the old date stalk.

(40) It is not allowable [i.e., possible] for the sun to reach the moon, nor does the night overtake the day, but each, in an orbit, is swimming.

(41) And a sign for them is that We carried their forefathers[1234] in a laden ship.

(42) And We created for them from the likes of it that which they ride.

(43) And if We should will, We could drown them; then no one responding to a cry would there be for them, nor would they be saved

(44) Except as a mercy from Us and provision for a time.

[1230] "i.e., that which Allāh has produced for them.
[1231] An alternative meaning is "And [eat from] what their hands have produced [i.e., planted and harvested]." Both are grammatically correct."
[1232] Or "all species."
[1233] Literally, "strip" or "peel." Sunlight projected onto the earth is removed from it as the earth turns and night approaches.
[1234] Usually meaning "descendants" or "offspring," the word "dhurriyyah" is used here to denote forefathers (their being the offspring of Noah), who were saved from the flood.

(45) But when it is said to them, "Beware of what is before you and what is behind you;[1235] perhaps you will receive mercy..."[1236]

(46) And no sign comes to them from the signs of their Lord except that they are from it turning away.

(47) And when it is said to them, "Spend from that which Allāh has provided for you," those who disbelieve say to those who believe, "Should we feed one whom, if Allāh had willed, He would have fed? You are not but in clear error."

(48) And they say, "When is this promise, if you should be truthful?"

(49) They do not await except one blast[1237] which will seize them while they are disputing.

(50) And they will not be able [to give] any instruction, nor to their people can they return.

(51) And the Horn will be blown;[1238] and at once from the graves to their Lord they will hasten.

(52) They will say, "O woe to us! Who has raised us up from our sleeping place?" [The reply will be], "This is what the Most Merciful had promised, and the messengers told the truth."

(53) It will not be but one blast, and at once they are all brought present before Us.

(54) So today [i.e., the Day of Judgement] no soul will be wronged at all, and you will not be recompensed except for what you used to do.

(55) Indeed the companions of Paradise, that Day, will be amused in [joyful] occupation -

(56) They and their spouses - in shade, reclining on adorned couches.

(57) For them therein is fruit, and for them is whatever they request [or wish]

(58) [And] "Peace," a word from a Merciful Lord.

[1235] "Of sins or of life in this world and the Hereafter.

[1236] The conclusion of this sentence is understood to be "...they ignored the warning.""

[1237] Literally, "cry" or "shriek," meaning the first blast of the Horn which will strike dead every living thing on the earth without warning.

[1238] For the second time, signaling the Resurrection.

(59) [Then He will say], "But stand apart today, you criminals.[1239]

(60) Did I not enjoin upon you, O children of Adam, that you not worship Satan - [for] indeed, he is to you a clear enemy -

(61) And that you worship [only] Me? This is a straight path.

(62) And he had already led astray from among you much of creation, so did you not use reason?

(63) This is the Hellfire which you were promised.

(64) [Enter to] burn therein today for what you used to deny."[1240]

(65) That Day, We will seal over their mouths, and their hands will speak to Us, and their feet will testify about what they used to earn.

(66) And if We willed, We could have obliterated their eyes, and they would race to [find] the path, and how could they see?[1241]

(67) And if We willed, We could have deformed them, [paralyzing them] in their places so they would not be able to proceed, nor could they return.[1242]

(68) And he to whom We grant long life We reverse in creation;[1243] so will they not understand?

(69) And We did not give him [i.e., Prophet Muḥammad (ﷺ)] knowledge of poetry, nor is it befitting for him. It is not but a message and a clear Qur'ān

(70) To warn whoever is alive[1244] and justify the word [i.e., decree] against the disbelievers.

(71) Do they not see that We have created for them from what Our hands[1245] have made, grazing livestock, and [then] they are their owners?

[1239] i.e., remove yourself from the ranks of the believers to be distinguished from them.

[1240] Or "because you used to disbelieve."

[1241] Allāh (subḥānahu wa taʿālā) could have left man without means of guidance in the life of this world, although in His mercy He did not.

[1242] He (subḥānahu wa taʿālā) could have prevented man from taking any action to benefit himself in this world or the Hereafter, yet He did not.

[1243] In his physical and mental capacity.

[1244] In heart and mind, i.e., the believers.

[1245] See footnote to 2:19.

(72) And We have tamed them for them, so some of them they ride, and some of them they eat.

(73) And for them therein are [other] benefits and drinks, so will they not be grateful?

(74) But they have taken besides Allāh [false] deities that perhaps they would be helped.

(75) They are not able to help them, and they [themselves] are for them soldiers in attendance.[1246]

(76) So let not their speech grieve you. Indeed, We know what they conceal and what they declare.

(77) Does man not consider that We created him from a [mere] sperm-drop - then at once[1247] he is a clear adversary?

(78) And he presents for Us an example[1248] and forgets his [own] creation. He says, "Who will give life to bones while they are disintegrated?"

(79) Say, "He will give them life who produced them the first time; and He is, of all creation, Knowing."

(80) [It is] He who made for you from the green tree, fire, and then from it you ignite.

(81) Is not He who created the heavens and the earth Able to create the likes of them? Yes, [it is so]; and He is the Knowing Creator.

(82) His command is only when He intends a thing that He says to it, "Be," and it is.

(83) So exalted is He in whose hand is the realm of all things, and to Him you will be returned.

[1246] Maintaining and protecting their "gods." Another interpretation is that they (i.e., the gods) will be soldiers set against them in Hellfire.
[1247] i.e., as soon as he becomes self-sufficient.
[1248] Attempting to establish the finality of death.

Surah As-Saffat

(1) By those [angels] lined up in rows

(2) And those who drive [the clouds]

(3) And those who recite the message,[1249]

(4) Indeed, your God is One,

(5) Lord of the heavens and the earth and that between them and Lord of the sunrises.[1250]

(6) Indeed, We have adorned the nearest heaven with an adornment of stars

(7) And as protection against every rebellious devil

(8) [So] they may not listen to the exalted assembly [of angels] and are pelted from every side,[1251]

(9) Repelled; and for them is a constant punishment,

(10) Except one who snatches [some words] by theft, but they are pursued by a burning flame, piercing [in brightness].

(11) Then inquire of them, [O Muḥammad], "Are they a stronger [or more difficult] creation or those [others] We have created?" Indeed, We created them [i.e., men] from sticky clay.

(12) But you wonder, while they mock,

(13) And when they are reminded, they remember not.

(14) And when they see a sign, they ridicule.

(15) And say, "This is not but obvious magic.

(16) When we have died and become dust and bones, are we indeed to be resurrected?

[1249] To the prophets or among themselves. Allāh (subḥānahu wa taʿālā) swears by these three kinds of angels to the fact mentioned in the following verse.
[1250] i.e., each point or place of sunrise.
[1251] By flaming meteors.

(17) And our forefathers [as well]?"

(18) Say, "Yes, and you will be [rendered] contemptible."

(19) It will be only one shout, and at once they will be observing.

(20) They will say, "O woe to us! This is the Day of Recompense."

(21) [They will be told], "This is the Day of Judgement which you used to deny."

(22) [The angels will be ordered], "Gather those who committed wrong, their kinds,[1252] and what they used to worship

(23) Other than Allāh, and guide them to the path of Hellfire

(24) And stop them; indeed, they are to be questioned."

(25) [They will be asked], "What is [wrong] with you? Why do you not help each other?"

(26) But they, that Day, are in surrender.

(27) And they will approach one another asking [i.e., blaming] each other.

(28) They will say, "Indeed, you used to come at us from the right."[1253]

(29) They [i.e., the oppressors] will say, "Rather, you [yourselves] were not believers,

(30) And we had over you no authority, but you were a transgressing people.

(31) So the word [i.e., decree] of our Lord has come into effect upon us; indeed, we will taste [punishment].

(32) And we led you to deviation; indeed, we were deviators."

(33) So indeed they, that Day, will be sharing in the punishment.

(34) Indeed, that is how We deal with the criminals.

(35) Indeed they, when it was said to them, "There is no deity but Allāh," were arrogant

---

[1252] Those similar to them in evil deeds. Another possible meaning is "their wives."
[1253] i.e., from our position of strength, oppressing us. Or from where we would have grasped the truth, preventing us.

(36) And were saying, "Are we to leave our gods for a mad poet?"

(37) Rather, he [i.e., the Prophet (ﷺ)] has come with the truth and confirmed the [previous] messengers.

(38) Indeed, you [disbelievers] will be tasters of the painful punishment,

(39) And you will not be recompensed except for what you used to do -

(40) But not the chosen servants of Allāh.

(41) Those will have a provision determined -

(42) Fruits;[1254] and they will be honored

(43) In gardens of pleasure

(44) On thrones facing one another.

(45) There will be circulated among them a cup [of wine] from a flowing spring,

(46) White and delicious to the drinkers;

(47) No bad effect is there in it, nor from it will they be intoxicated.

(48) And with them will be women limiting [their] glances,[1255] with large, [beautiful] eyes,

(49) As if they were [delicate] eggs, well-protected.

(50) And they will approach one another, inquiring of each other.

(51) A speaker among them will say, "Indeed, I had a companion [on earth].

(52) Who would say, 'Are you indeed of those who believe

(53) That when we have died and become dust and bones, we will indeed be recompensed?'"

(54) He will say,[1256] "Would you [care to] look?"

(55) And he will look and see him[1257] in the midst of the Hellfire.

[1254] Meaning everything delicious.
[1255] i.e., chaste and modest, looking only at their mates.
[1256] To his companions in Paradise.
[1257] The companion who had tried to dissuade him from belief on earth.

(56) He will say, "By Allāh, you almost ruined me.

(57) If not for the favor of my Lord, I would have been of those brought in [to Hell].

(58) Then, are we not to die

(59) Except for our first death, and we will not be punished?"

(60) Indeed, this is the great attainment.

(61) For the like of this let the workers [on earth] work.

(62) Is that [i.e., Paradise] a better accommodation or the tree of zaqqūm?

(63) Indeed, We have made it a torment for the wrongdoers.

(64) Indeed, it is a tree issuing from the bottom of the Hellfire,

(65) Its emerging fruit as if it was heads of the devils.

(66) And indeed, they will eat from it and fill with it their bellies.

(67) Then indeed, they will have after it a mixture of scalding water.

(68) Then indeed, their return will be to the Hellfire.

(69) Indeed they found their fathers astray.

(70) So they hastened [to follow] in their footsteps.

(71) And there had already strayed before them most of the former peoples,

(72) And We had already sent among them warners.

(73) Then look how was the end of those who were warned -

(74) But not the chosen servants of Allāh.

(75) And Noah had certainly called Us, and [We are] the best of responders.

(76) And We saved him and his family from the great affliction.

(77) And We made his descendants those remaining [on the earth]

(78) And left for him [favorable mention] among later generations:

(79) "Peace upon Noah among the worlds."

(80) Indeed, We thus reward the doers of good.

(81) Indeed, he was of Our believing servants.

(82) Then We drowned the others [i.e., disbelievers].

(83) And indeed, among his kind was Abraham,

(84) When he came to his Lord with a sound heart

(85) [And] when he said to his father and his people, "What do you worship?

(86) Is it falsehood [as] gods other than Allāh you desire?

(87) Then what is your thought about the Lord of the worlds?"

(88) And he cast a look at the stars.

(89) And said, "Indeed, I am [about to be] ill."

(90) So they turned away from him, departing.

(91) Then he turned to their gods and said, "Do you not eat?[1258]

(92) What is [wrong] with you that you do not speak?".

(93) And he turned upon them a blow with [his] right hand.

(94) Then they [i.e., the people] came toward him, hastening.

(95) He said, "Do you worship that which you [yourselves] carve,

(96) While Allāh created you and that which you do?"

(97) They said, "Construct for him a structure [i.e., furnace] and throw him into the burning fire."

(98) And they intended for him a plan [i.e., harm], but We made them the most debased.

(99) And [then] he said, "Indeed, I will go to [where I am ordered by] my Lord; He will guide me.

(100) My Lord, grant me [a child] from among the righteous."

(101) So We gave him good tidings of a forbearing boy.

(102) And when he reached with him [the age of] exertion,[1259] he said, "O my son, indeed I have seen in a dream that I [must] sacrifice you, so see what you think." He

---

[1258] Consume the offerings placed before them.
[1259] i.e., the ability to work and be of assistance.

said, "O my father, do as you are commanded. You will find me, if Allāh wills, of the steadfast."

(103) And when they had both submitted[1260] and he put him down upon his forehead,

(104) We called to him, "O Abraham,

(105) You have fulfilled the vision." Indeed, We thus reward the doers of good.

(106) Indeed, this was the clear trial.

(107) And We ransomed him with a great sacrifice,[1261]

(108) And We left for him [favorable mention] among later generations:

(109) "Peace upon Abraham."

(110) Indeed, We thus reward the doers of good.

(111) Indeed, he was of Our believing servants.

(112) And We gave him good tidings of Isaac, a prophet from among the righteous.[1262]

(113) And We blessed him and Isaac. But among their descendants is the doer of good and the clearly unjust to himself [i.e., sinner].

(114) And We did certainly confer favor upon Moses and Aaron.

(115) And We saved them and their people from the great affliction,

(116) And We supported them so it was they who overcame.

(117) And We gave them the explicit Scripture [i.e., the Torah],

(118) And We guided them on the straight path.

(119) And We left for them [favorable mention] among later generations:

(120) "Peace upon Moses and Aaron."

(121) Indeed, We thus reward the doers of good.

[1260] To the command of Allāh.

[1261] Allāh (subhānahu wa taʻālā) sent a huge ram to be sacrificed in place of Ishmael.

[1262] This verifies that the firstborn son who was to be sacrificed was Ishmael and not Isaac, as claimed by the Jews and Christians.

(122) Indeed, they were of Our believing servants.

(123) And indeed, Elias was from among the messengers,

(124) When he said to his people, "Will you not fear Allāh?

(125) Do you call upon Ba'l[1263] and leave the best of creators -

(126) Allāh, your Lord and the Lord of your first forefathers?"

(127) And they denied him, so indeed, they will be brought [for punishment],

(128) Except the chosen servants of Allāh.

(129) And We left for him [favorable mention] among later generations:

(130) "Peace upon Elias."[1264]

(131) Indeed, We thus reward the doers of good.

(132) Indeed, he was of Our believing servants.

(133) And indeed, Lot was among the messengers.

(134) [So mention] when We saved him and his family, all,

(135) Except an old woman [i.e., his wife] among those who remained [with the evildoers].

(136) Then We destroyed the others.

(137) And indeed, you pass by them in the morning

(138) And at night. Then will you not use reason?

(139) And indeed, Jonah was among the messengers.

(140) [Mention] when he ran away to the laden ship.

(141) And he drew lots[1265] and was among the losers.

[1263] The name of a great idol worshipped by the people and said to mean "lord."

[1264] Ilyāseen is said by some commentators to be a plural form, meaning "Elias and those who followed him."

[1265] To determine who would be cast overboard in order to save the other passengers. Having been overloaded, the ship was on the verge of sinking.

(142) Then the fish swallowed him, while he was blameworthy.[1266]

(143) And had he not been of those who exalt Allāh,

(144) He would have remained inside its belly until the Day they are resurrected.[1267]

(145) But We threw him onto the open shore while he was ill.

(146) And We caused to grow over him a gourd vine.[1268]

(147) And We sent him[1269] to [his people of] a hundred thousand or more.

(148) And they believed, so We gave them enjoyment [of life] for a time.

(149) So inquire of them, [O Muḥammad], "Does your Lord have daughters while they have sons?[1270]

(150) Or did We create the angels as females while they were witnesses?"

(151) Unquestionably, it is out of their [invented] falsehood that they say,

(152) "Allāh has begotten," and indeed, they are liars.

(153) Has He chosen daughters over sons?

(154) What is [wrong] with you? How do you make judgement?

(155) Then will you not be reminded?

(156) Or do you have a clear authority?[1271]

(157) Then produce your scripture, if you should be truthful.

(158) And they have made [i.e., claimed] between Him and the jinn a lineage, but the jinn have already known that they [who made such claims] will be brought [to punishment].

(159) Exalted is Allāh above what they describe,

[1266] For having given up hope on his people prematurely and having left them without permission from Allāh.

[1267] Meaning that the belly of the fish would have become his grave.

[1268] Which is known to give cooling shade and to be a repellent of flies.

[1269] i.e., returned him thereafter.

[1270] The people of Makkah claimed that the angels were daughters of Allāh, yet they preferred sons for themselves.

[1271] i.e., evidence.

(160) Except the chosen servants of Allāh [who do not share in that sin].

(161) So indeed, you [disbelievers] and whatever you worship,

(162) You cannot tempt [anyone] away from Him

(163) Except he who is to [enter and] burn in the Hellfire.[1272]

(164) [The angels say],[1273] "There is not among us any except that he has a known position.[1274]

(165) And indeed, we are those who line up [for prayer].

(166) And indeed, we are those who exalt Allāh."

(167) And indeed, they [i.e., the disbelievers] used to say,[1275]

(168) "If we had a message from [those of] the former peoples,

(169) We would have been the chosen servants of Allāh."

(170) But they disbelieved in it,[1276] so they are going to know.

(171) And Our word [i.e., decree] has already preceded for Our servants, the messengers,

(172) [That] indeed, they would be those given victory

(173) And [that] indeed, Our soldiers [i.e., the believers] will be those who overcome.[1277]

(174) So, [O Muḥammad], leave them for a time.

(175) And see [what will befall] them, for they are going to see.

(176) Then for Our punishment are they impatient?

(177) But when it descends in their territory, then evil is the morning of those who were warned.

[1272] Due to his disbelief and evil deeds.

[1273] "Refuting what the disbelievers had said about them.
[1274] For worship. Or "an assigned task" to perform."
[1275] Before the revelation of the Qur'ān.
[1276] i.e., in their own message, the Qur'ān.
[1277] If not in this world, then definitely in the Hereafter.

(178) And leave them for a time.

(179) And see, for they are going to see.

(180) Exalted is your Lord, the Lord of might, above what they describe.

(181) And peace upon the messengers.

(182) And praise to Allāh, Lord of the worlds.

Surah Sad

(1) Ṣād.[1278] By the Qur'ān containing reminder...[1279]

(2) But those who disbelieve are in pride and dissension.

(3) How many a generation have We destroyed before them, and they [then] called out; but it was not a time for escape.

(4) And they wonder that there has come to them a warner [i.e., Prophet Muḥammad (ﷺ)] from among themselves. And the disbelievers say, "This is a magician and a liar.

(5) Has he made the gods [only] one God? Indeed, this is a curious thing."

(6) And the eminent among them went forth, [saying], "Continue, and be patient over [the defense of] your gods. Indeed, this is a thing intended.[1280]

(7) We have not heard of this in the latest religion.[1281] This is not but a fabrication.

(8) Has the message been revealed to him out of [all of] us?" Rather, they are in doubt about My message. Rather, they have not yet tasted My punishment.

(9) Or do they have the depositories of the mercy of your Lord, the Exalted in Might, the Bestower?[1282]

(10) Or is theirs the dominion of the heavens and the earth and what is between them? Then let them ascend through [any] ways of access.[1283]

(11) [They are but] soldiers [who will be] defeated there among the companies [of disbelievers].

(12) The people of Noah denied before them, and [the tribe of] ʿAad and Pharaoh, the owner of stakes,[1284]

[1278] "See footnote to 2:1.

[1279] The completion of the oath is understood to be that the Qur'ān is inimitable and thus a miracle from Allāh."

[1280] Planned by Prophet Muḥammad (ﷺ) in order to gain influence and prestige for himself.

[1281] Referring to Christianity or possibly the pagan religion of the Quraysh.

[1282] Refer to footnote of verse 3:8.

[1283] To oversee the affairs of their dominion.

[1284] By which he tortured people.

(13) And [the tribe of] Thamūd and the people of Lot and the companions of the thicket [i.e., people of Madyan]. Those are the companies.[1285]

(14) Each of them denied the messengers, so My penalty was justified.

(15) And these [disbelievers] await not but one blast [of the Horn]; for it there will be no delay.[1286]

(16) And they say, "Our Lord, hasten for us our share [of the punishment] before the Day of Account."

(17) Be patient over what they say and remember Our servant, David, the possessor of strength; indeed, he was one who repeatedly turned back [to Allāh].

(18) Indeed, We subjected the mountains [to praise] with him, exalting [Allāh] in the [late] afternoon and [after] sunrise.

(19) And the birds were assembled, all with him repeating [praises].

(20) And We strengthened his kingdom and gave him wisdom and discernment in speech.

(21) And has there come to you the news of the adversaries, when they climbed over the wall of [his] prayer chamber -

(22) When they entered upon David and he was alarmed by them? They said, "Fear not. [We are] two adversaries, one of whom has wronged the other, so judge between us with truth and do not exceed [it] and guide us to the sound path.

(23) Indeed this, my brother, has ninety-nine ewes, and I have one ewe; so he said, 'Entrust her to me,' and he overpowered me in speech."

(24) [David] said, "He has certainly wronged you in demanding your ewe [in addition] to his ewes. And indeed, many associates oppress one another, except for those who believe and do righteous deeds - and few are they." And David became certain that We had tried him, and he asked forgiveness of his Lord[1287] and fell down bowing [in prostration] and turned in repentance [to Allāh].

[1285] That were defeated, among whom will be the disbelievers of Quraysh and others.
[1286] Or "respite." More literally, "a period between two milkings of a she-camel," which also alludes to the meanings of "return" or "repetition."
[1287] For his errors, such as fear and suspicion of the two men at the outset, any mistake in judgement he might have made, concealed feelings of partiality, etc.

(25) So We forgave him that; and indeed, for him is nearness to Us and a good place of return.

(26) [We said], "O David, indeed We have made you a successor upon the earth, so judge between the people in truth and do not follow [your own] desire, as it will lead you astray from the way of Allāh." Indeed, those who go astray from the way of Allāh will have a severe punishment for having forgotten the Day of Account.

(27) And We did not create the heaven and the earth and that between them aimlessly. That is the assumption of those who disbelieve, so woe to those who disbelieve from the Fire.

(28) Or should We treat those who believe and do righteous deeds like corrupters in the land? Or should We treat those who fear Allāh like the wicked?

(29) [This is] a blessed Book which We have revealed to you, [O Muḥammad], that they might reflect upon its verses and that those of understanding would be reminded.

(30) And to David We gave Solomon. An excellent servant, indeed he was one repeatedly turning back [to Allāh].

(31) [Mention] when there were exhibited before him in the afternoon the poised [standing] racehorses.

(32) And he said, "Indeed, I gave preference to the love of good [things] over the remembrance of my Lord until it [i.e., the sun] disappeared into the curtain [of darkness]."

(33) [He said], "Return them to me," and set about striking[1288] [their] legs and necks.

(34) And We certainly tried Solomon and placed on his throne a body;[1289] then he returned.[1290]

(35) He said, "My Lord, forgive me and grant me a kingdom such as will not belong to anyone after me. Indeed, You are the Bestower."

(36) So We subjected to him the wind blowing by his command, gently, wherever he directed,

---

[1288] With his sword as expiation. Some commentaries have also suggested the meaning of "stroking" with the hand.
[1289] "Said to be a devil or a lifeless body (one without capability), but Allāh alone knows.
[1290] To sovereignty and to Allāh in repentance."

(37) And [also] the devils [of jinn] - every builder and diver.

(38) And others bound together in irons.

(39) [We said], "This is Our gift, so grant or withhold without account."

(40) And indeed, for him is nearness to Us and a good place of return.

(41) And remember Our servant Job, when he called to his Lord, "Indeed, Satan has touched me with hardship and torment."

(42) [So he was told], "Strike [the ground] with your foot; this is a [spring for a] cool bath and drink."

(43) And We granted him his family and a like [number] with them as mercy from Us and a reminder for those of understanding.

(44) [We said], "And take in your hand a bunch [of grass] and strike with it and do not break your oath."[1291] Indeed, We found him patient, an excellent servant. Indeed, he was one repeatedly turning back [to Allāh].

(45) And remember Our servants, Abraham, Isaac and Jacob - those of strength and [religious] vision.

(46) Indeed, We chose them for an exclusive quality: remembrance of the home [of the Hereafter].

(47) And indeed they are, to Us, among the chosen and outstanding.

(48) And remember Ishmael, Elisha and Dhul-Kifl, and all are among the outstanding.

(49) This is a reminder. And indeed, for the righteous is a good place of return -

(50) Gardens of perpetual residence, whose doors will be opened to them.

(51) Reclining within them, they will call therein for abundant fruit and drink.

(52) And with them will be women limiting [their] glances[1292] and of equal age.

(53) This is what you, [the righteous], are promised for the Day of Account.

[1291] At a point during his illness, Job became angry with his wife and swore that if he recovered, he would punish her with one hundred lashes. According to Allāh's instruction, the oath was fulfilled by striking her once with one hundred blades of grass.
[1292] To their mates alone.

(54) Indeed, this is Our provision; for it there is no depletion.

(55) This [is so]. But indeed, for the transgressors is an evil place of return -

(56) Hell, which they will [enter to] burn, and wretched is the resting place.

(57) This - so let them taste it - is scalding water and [foul] purulence.

(58) And other [punishments] of its type [in various] kinds.

(59) [Its inhabitants will say], "This is a company bursting in with you. No welcome for them. Indeed, they will burn in the Fire."

(60) They will say, "Nor you! No welcome for you. You, [our leaders], brought this upon us, and wretched is the settlement."

(61) They will say, "Our Lord, whoever brought this upon us - increase for him double punishment in the Fire."

(62) And they will say, "Why do we not see men whom we used to count among the worst?[1293]

(63) Is it [because] we took them in ridicule, or has [our] vision turned away from them?"

(64) Indeed, that is truth [i.e., reality] - the quarreling of the people of the Fire.

(65) Say, [O Muḥammad], "I am only a warner, and there is not any deity except Allāh, the One, the Prevailing,[1294]

(66) Lord of the heavens and the earth and whatever is between them, the Exalted in Might,[1295] the Perpetual Forgiver."[1296]

(67) Say, "It is great news

(68) From which you turn away.

(69) I had no knowledge of the exalted assembly [of angels] when they were disputing [the creation of Adam].

(70) It has not been revealed to me except that I am a clear warner."

[1293] They are referring to the believers.
[1294] Refer to footnotes in 12:39.
[1295] "Honored for absolute power associated with wisdom and justice.
[1296] Who continually conceals sins and faults."

(71) [So mention] when your Lord said to the angels, "Indeed, I am going to create a human being from clay.

(72) So when I have proportioned him and breathed into him of My [created] soul,[1297] then fall down to him in prostration."

(73) So the angels prostrated - all of them entirely,

(74) Except Iblees;[1298] he was arrogant and became among the disbelievers.

(75) [Allāh] said, "O Iblees, what prevented you from prostrating to that which I created with My hands?[1299] Were you arrogant [then], or were you [already] among the haughty?"

(76) He said, "I am better than him. You created me from fire and created him from clay."

(77) [Allāh] said, "Then get out of it [i.e., Paradise], for indeed, you are expelled.

(78) And indeed, upon you is My curse until the Day of Recompense."

(79) He said, "My Lord, then reprieve me until the Day they are resurrected."

(80) [Allāh] said, "So indeed, you are of those reprieved

(81) Until the Day of the time well-known."

(82) [Iblees] said, "By Your might, I will surely mislead them all.

(83) Except, among them, Your chosen servants."

(84) [Allāh] said, "The truth [is My oath], and the truth I say -

(85) [That] I will surely fill Hell with you and those of them that follow you all together."

(86) Say, [O Muḥammad], "I do not ask you for it [i.e., the Qur'ān] any payment, and I am not of the pretentious.

(87) It is but a reminder to the worlds.

(88) And you will surely know [the truth of] its information after a time."

[1297] See footnote to 15:29.
[1298] See footnote to 2:34.
[1299] See footnote to 2:19.

Surah Az-Zumar

(1) The revelation of the Book [i.e., the Qur'ān] is from Allāh, the Exalted in Might, the Wise.

(2) Indeed, We have sent down to you the Book, [O Muḥammad], in truth. So worship Allāh, [being] sincere to Him in religion.

(3) Unquestionably, for Allāh is the pure religion.[1300] And those who take protectors besides Him [say], "We only worship them that they may bring us nearer to Allāh in position." Indeed, Allāh will judge between them concerning that over which they differ. Indeed, Allāh does not guide he who is a liar and [confirmed] disbeliever.

(4) If Allāh had intended to take a son, He could have chosen from what He creates whatever He willed. Exalted is He; He is Allāh, the One, the Prevailing.[1301]

(5) He created the heavens and earth in truth. He wraps the night over the day and wraps the day over the night and has subjected the sun and the moon, each running [its course] for a specified term. Unquestionably, He is the Exalted in Might, the Perpetual Forgiver.[1302]

(6) He created you from one soul. Then He made from it its mate, and He produced for you from the grazing livestock eight mates.[1303] He creates you in the wombs of your mothers, creation after creation, within three darknesses.[1304] That is Allāh, your Lord; to Him belongs dominion. There is no deity except Him, so how are you averted?

(7) If you disbelieve - indeed, Allāh is Free from need of you. And He does not approve for His servants disbelief. And if you are grateful, He approves [i.e., likes] it for you; and no bearer of burdens will bear the burden of another. Then to your Lord is your return, and He will inform you about what you used to do. Indeed, He is Knowing of that within the breasts.

(8) And when adversity touches man, he calls upon his Lord, turning to Him [alone]; then when He bestows on him a favor from Himself, he forgets Him whom he called

---

[1300] i.e., acceptable to Allāh is that none be associated with Him in worship and obedience.

[1301] Refer to footnotes in 12:39.

[1302] Refer to footnotes in 38:66.

[1303] "See 6:143-144.

[1304] i.e., the belly, the womb, and the amniotic membrane."

upon before,[1305] and he attributes to Allāh equals to mislead [people] from His way. Say, "Enjoy your disbelief for a little; indeed, you are of the companions of the Fire."

(9) Is one who is devoutly obedient during periods of the night, prostrating and standing [in prayer], fearing the Hereafter and hoping for the mercy of his Lord, [like one who does not]? Say, "Are those who know equal to those who do not know?" Only they will remember [who are] people of understanding.

(10) Say,[1306] "O My servants who have believed, fear your Lord. For those who do good in this world is good, and the earth of Allāh is spacious. Indeed, the patient will be given their reward without account [i.e., limit]."

(11) Say, [O Muḥammad], "Indeed, I have been commanded to worship Allāh, [being] sincere to Him in religion.

(12) And I have been commanded to be the first [among you] of the Muslims."

(13) Say, "Indeed I fear, if I should disobey my Lord, the punishment of a tremendous Day."

(14) Say, "Allāh [alone] do I worship, sincere to Him in my religion,

(15) So worship what you will besides Him." Say, "Indeed, the losers are the ones who will lose themselves and their families on the Day of Resurrection. Unquestionably, that is the manifest loss."

(16) They will have canopies [i.e., layers] of fire above them and below them, canopies. By that Allāh threatens [i.e., warns] His servants. O My servants, then fear Me.

(17) But those who have avoided ṭāghūt,[1307] lest they worship it, and turned back to Allāh - for them are good tidings. So give good tidings to My servants

(18) Who listen to speech and follow the best of it. Those are the ones Allāh has guided, and those are people of understanding.

(19) Then, is one who has deserved the decree of punishment [to be guided]? Then, can you save one who is in the Fire?

[1305] Or "that for which he called upon Him before."

[1306] The Prophet (ﷺ) is instructed to say on behalf of Allāh (subḥānahu wa taʿālā) to His believing servants.

[1307] i.e., Satan or any false object of worship.

(20) But those who have feared their Lord - for them are chambers,[1308] above them chambers built high, beneath which rivers flow. [This is] the promise of Allāh. Allāh does not fail in [His] promise.

(21) Do you not see that Allāh sends down rain from the sky and makes it flow as springs [and rivers] in the earth; then He produces thereby crops of varying colors; then they dry and you see them turned yellow; then He makes them [scattered] debris. Indeed in that is a reminder for those of understanding.

(22) So is one whose breast Allāh has expanded to [accept] Islām and he is upon [i.e., guided by] a light from his Lord [like one whose heart rejects it]? Then woe to those whose hearts are hardened against the remembrance of Allāh. Those are in manifest error.

(23) Allāh has sent down the best statement: a consistent Book wherein is reiteration. The skins shiver therefrom of those who fear their Lord; then their skins and their hearts relax at the remembrance [i.e., mention] of Allāh. That is the guidance of Allāh by which He guides whom He wills. And one whom Allāh sends astray - for him there is no guide.

(24) Then is he who will shield with his face[1309] the worst of the punishment on the Day of Resurrection [like one secure from it]? And it will be said to the wrongdoers, "Taste what you used to earn."

(25) Those before them denied, and punishment came upon them from where they did not perceive.

(26) So Allāh made them taste disgrace in worldly life. But the punishment of the Hereafter is greater, if they only knew.

(27) And We have certainly presented for the people in this Qur'ān from every [kind of] example - that they might remember.

(28) [It is] an Arabic Qur'ān, without any deviance[1310] that they might become righteous.[1311]

[1308] i.e., elevated rooms, dwellings or palaces.
[1309] Rather than his hands, which will be chained to his neck.
[1310] "From the truth.
[1311] Through consciousness of Allāh."

(29) Allāh presents an example: a man [i.e., slave] owned by quarreling partners and another belonging exclusively to one man - are they equal in comparison? Praise be to Allāh! But most of them do not know.

(30) Indeed, you are to die, and indeed, they are to die.

(31) Then indeed you, on the Day of Resurrection, before your Lord, will dispute.

(32) So who is more unjust than one who lies about Allāh and denies the truth when it has come to him? Is there not in Hell a residence for the disbelievers?

(33) And the one who has brought the truth [i.e., the Prophet (ﷺ)] and [they who] believed in it - those are the righteous.

(34) They will have whatever they desire with their Lord. That is the reward of the doers of good -

(35) That Allāh may remove from them the worst of what they did and reward them their due for the best of what they used to do.

(36) Is not Allāh sufficient for His Servant [i.e., Prophet Muḥammad (ﷺ)]? And [yet], they threaten you with those [they worship] other than Him. And whoever Allāh leaves astray - for him there is no guide.

(37) And whoever Allāh guides - for him there is no misleader. Is not Allāh Exalted in Might and Owner of Retribution?

(38) And if you asked them, "Who created the heavens and the earth?" they would surely say, "Allāh." Say, "Then have you considered[1312] what you invoke besides Allāh? If Allāh intended me harm, are they removers of His harm; or if He intended me mercy, are they withholders of His mercy?" Say, "Sufficient for me is Allāh; upon Him [alone] rely the [wise] reliers."

(39) Say, "O my people, work according to your position, [for] indeed, I am working; and you are going to know

(40) To whom will come a torment disgracing him and on whom will descend an enduring punishment."

(41) Indeed, We sent down to you the Book for the people in truth. So whoever is guided - it is for [the benefit of] his soul; and whoever goes astray only goes astray to its detriment. And you are not a manager [i.e., authority] over them.

[1312] i.e., "Tell me about..."

(42) Allāh takes the souls at the time of their death, and those that do not die [He takes] during their sleep. Then He keeps those for which He has decreed death and releases the others for a specified term. Indeed in that are signs for a people who give thought.

(43) Or have they taken other than Allāh as intercessors? Say, "Even though they do not possess [power over] anything, nor do they reason?"

(44) Say, "To Allāh belongs [the right to allow] intercession entirely. To Him belongs the dominion of the heavens and the earth. Then to Him you will be returned."

(45) And when Allāh is mentioned alone, the hearts of those who do not believe in the Hereafter shrink with aversion, but when those [worshipped] other than Him are mentioned, immediately they rejoice.

(46) Say, "O Allāh, Creator of the heavens and the earth, Knower of the unseen and the witnessed, You will judge between your servants concerning that over which they used to differ."

(47) And if those who did wrong had all that is in the earth entirely and the like of it with it, they would [attempt to] ransom themselves thereby from the worst of the punishment on the Day of Resurrection. And there will appear to them from Allāh that which they had not taken into account.[1313]

(48) And there will appear to them the evils they had earned, and they will be enveloped by what they used to ridicule.

(49) And when adversity touches man, he calls upon Us; then when We bestow on him a favor from Us, he says, "I have only been given it because of [my] knowledge." Rather, it is a trial, but most of them do not know.

(50) Those before them had already said it, but they were not availed by what they used to earn.

(51) And the evil consequences of what they earned struck them. And those who have wronged of these [people] will be struck [i.e., afflicted] by the evil consequences of what they earned; and they will not cause failure.[1314]

(52) Do they not know that Allāh extends provision for whom He wills and restricts [it]? Indeed in that are signs for a people who believe.

[1313] Of His anger and punishment.
[1314] i.e., prevent Allāh from what He wills or escape from the punishment.

(53) Say, "O My servants who have transgressed against themselves [by sinning], do not despair of the mercy of Allāh. Indeed, Allāh forgives all sins.[1315] Indeed, it is He who is the Forgiving, the Merciful."

(54) And return [in repentance] to your Lord and submit to Him before the punishment comes upon you; then you will not be helped.

(55) And follow the best of what was revealed to you from your Lord [i.e., the Qur'ān] before the punishment comes upon you suddenly while you do not perceive,

(56) Lest a soul should say,[1316] "Oh, [how great is] my regret over what I neglected in regard to Allāh and that I was among the mockers."

(57) Or [lest] it say, "If only Allāh had guided me, I would have been among the righteous."

(58) Or [lest] it say when it sees the punishment, "If only I had another turn[1317] so I could be among the doers of good."

(59) But yes, there had come to you My verses, but you denied them and were arrogant, and you were among the disbelievers.

(60) And on the Day of Resurrection you will see those who lied about Allāh [with] their faces blackened. Is there not in Hell a residence for the arrogant?

(61) And Allāh will save those who feared Him by their attainment;[1318] no evil will touch them, nor will they grieve.

(62) Allāh is the Creator of all things, and He is, over all things, Disposer of affairs.

(63) To Him belong the keys of the heavens and the earth. And they who disbelieve in the verses of Allāh - it is those who are the losers.

(64) Say, [O Muḥammad], "Is it other than Allāh that you order me to worship, O ignorant ones?"

(65) And it was already revealed to you and to those before you that if you should associate [anything] with Allāh, your work would surely become worthless, and you would surely be among the losers.

[1315] For those who repent and correct themselves.
[1316] On the Day of Resurrection.
[1317] At worldly life.
[1318] i.e., their success in the trials of worldly life and attainment of Paradise.

(66) Rather, worship [only] Allāh and be among the grateful.

(67) They have not appraised Allāh with true appraisal,[1319] while the earth entirely will be [within] His grip[1320] on the Day of Resurrection, and the heavens will be folded in His right hand.[1321] Exalted is He and high above what they associate with Him.

(68) And the Horn will be blown, and whoever is in the heavens and whoever is on the earth will fall dead except whom Allāh wills. Then it will be blown again, and at once they will be standing, looking on.

(69) And the earth will shine with the light of its Lord, and the record [of deeds] will be placed, and the prophets and the witnesses will be brought, and it will be judged between them in truth, and they will not be wronged.

(70) And every soul will be fully compensated [for] what it did; and He is most knowing[1322] of what they do.

(71) And those who disbelieved will be driven to Hell in groups until, when they reach it, its gates are opened and its keepers will say, "Did there not come to you messengers from yourselves, reciting to you the verses of your Lord and warning you of the meeting of this Day of yours?" They will say, "Yes, but the word [i.e., decree] of punishment has come into effect upon the disbelievers."

(72) [To them] it will be said, "Enter the gates of Hell to abide eternally therein, and wretched is the residence of the arrogant."

(73) But those who feared their Lord will be driven to Paradise in groups until, when they reach it while its gates have been opened and its keepers say, "Peace be upon you; you have become pure; so enter it to abide eternally therein," [they will enter].[1323]

(74) And they will say, "Praise to Allāh, who has fulfilled for us His promise and made us inherit the earth [so] we may settle in Paradise wherever we will. And excellent is the reward of [righteous] workers."

[1319] "i.e., appreciation of His attributes.

[1320] Literally, "no more than a handful of His."

[1321] See footnote to 2:19."

[1322] With no need for any record or witnesses, which are but means to establish proof to the soul itself in addition to its own knowledge of what it has done.

[1323] In such honor and joy that is beyond description - thus, the omission of this conclusion in the Arabic text.

(75) And you will see the angels surrounding the Throne, exalting [Allāh] with praise of their Lord. And it will be judged between them in truth, and it will be said, "[All] praise to Allāh, Lord of the worlds."

Surah Ghafir

(1) Ḥā, Meem.[1324]

(2) The revelation of the Book [i.e., the Qur'ān] is from Allāh, the Exalted in Might, the Knowing,

(3) The forgiver of sin, acceptor of repentance, severe in punishment, owner of abundance. There is no deity except Him; to Him is the destination.

(4) No one disputes concerning the signs of Allāh except those who disbelieve, so be not deceived by their [uninhibited] movement throughout the land.

(5) The people of Noah denied before them and the [disbelieving] factions after them, and every nation intended [a plot] for their messenger to seize him, and they disputed by [using] falsehood to [attempt to] invalidate thereby the truth. So I seized them, and how [terrible] was My penalty.

(6) And thus has the word [i.e., decree] of your Lord come into effect upon those who disbelieved that they are companions of the Fire.

(7) Those [angels] who carry the Throne and those around it exalt [Allāh] with praise of their Lord and believe in Him and ask forgiveness for those who have believed, [saying], "Our Lord, You have encompassed all things in mercy and knowledge, so forgive those who have repented and followed Your way and protect them from the punishment of Hellfire.

(8) Our Lord, and admit them to gardens of perpetual residence which You have promised them and whoever was righteous among their forefathers, their spouses and their offspring. Indeed, it is You who is the Exalted in Might, the Wise.

(9) And protect them from the evil consequences [of their deeds]. And he whom You protect from evil consequences that Day - You will have given him mercy. And that is the great attainment."

(10) Indeed, those who disbelieve will be addressed, "The hatred of Allāh for you was [even] greater than your hatred of yourselves [this Day in Hell] when you were invited to faith, but you disbelieved [i.e., refused]."

(11) They will say, "Our Lord, You made us lifeless twice and gave us life twice, and we have confessed our sins. So is there to an exit any way?"

[1324] See footnote to 2:1.

(12) [They will be told], "That is because, when Allāh was called upon alone, you disbelieved; but if others were associated with Him, you believed. So the judgement is with Allāh, the Most High, the Grand."

(13) It is He who shows you His signs and sends down to you from the sky, provision. But none will remember except he who turns back [in repentance].

(14) So invoke Allāh, [being] sincere to Him in religion, although the disbelievers dislike it.

(15) [He is] the Exalted above [all] degrees, Owner of the Throne; He places the inspiration of His command [i.e., revelation] upon whom He wills of His servants to warn of the Day of Meeting.

(16) The Day they come forth nothing concerning them will be concealed from Allāh. To whom belongs [all] sovereignty this Day? To Allāh, the One, the Prevailing.[1325]

(17) This Day every soul will be recompensed for what it earned. No injustice today! Indeed, Allāh is swift in account.

(18) And warn them, [O Muḥammad], of the Approaching Day, when hearts are at the throats, filled [with distress]. For the wrongdoers there will be no devoted friend and no intercessor [who is] obeyed.

(19) He knows that which deceives the eyes and what the breasts conceal.

(20) And Allāh judges with truth, while those they invoke[1326] besides Him judge not with anything. Indeed, Allāh - He is the Hearing, the Seeing.

(21) Have they not traveled through the land and observed how was the end of those who were before them? They were greater than them in strength and in impression on the land, but Allāh seized them for their sins. And they had not from Allāh any protector.

(22) That was because their messengers were coming to them with clear proofs, but they disbelieved, so Allāh seized them. Indeed, He is Powerful and severe in punishment.

(23) And We did certainly send Moses with Our signs and a clear authority[1327]

[1325] Refer to footnotes in 12:39.
[1326] In worship.
[1327] i.e., evidences from Allāh.

(24) To Pharaoh, Hāmān and Qārūn, but they said, "[He is] a magician and a liar."

(25) And when he brought them the truth from Us, they said, "Kill the sons of those who have believed with him and keep their women alive." But the plan of the disbelievers is not except in error.

(26) And Pharaoh said, "Let me kill Moses and let him call upon his Lord. Indeed, I fear that he will change your religion or that he will cause corruption[1328] in the land."

(27) But Moses said, "Indeed, I have sought refuge in my Lord and your Lord from every arrogant one who does not believe in the Day of Account."

(28) And a believing man from the family of Pharaoh who concealed his faith said, "Do you kill a man [merely] because he says, 'My Lord is Allāh' while he has brought you clear proofs from your Lord? And if he should be lying, then upon him is [the consequence of] his lie; but if he should be truthful, there will strike you some of what he promises you. Indeed, Allāh does not guide one who is a transgressor and a liar.

(29) O my people, sovereignty is yours today, [your being] dominant in the land. But who would protect us from the punishment of Allāh if it came to us?" Pharaoh said, "I do not show you except what I see, and I do not guide you except to the way of right conduct."

(30) And he who believed said, "O my people, indeed I fear for you [a fate] like the day of the companies[1329] -

(31) Like the custom of the people of Noah and of ʿAad and Thamūd and those after them. And Allāh wants no injustice for [His] servants.

(32) And O my people, indeed I fear for you the Day of Calling[1330] -

(33) The Day you will turn your backs fleeing; there is not for you from Allāh any protector. And whoever Allāh sends astray - there is not for him any guide.

[1328] i.e., dissension or civil strife.

[1329] i.e., the days on which Allāh sent His punishment upon those who rejected their prophets in former times.

[1330] i.e., the Day of Judgement, when the criminals will cry out in terror, the people will call to each other (see 7:44-51), and the angels will call out the results of each person's judgement.

(34) And Joseph had already come to you before with clear proofs, but you remained in doubt of that which he brought to you, until when he died, you said, 'Never will Allāh send a messenger after him.' Thus does Allāh leave astray he who is a transgressor and skeptic."

(35) Those who dispute concerning the signs of Allāh without an authority[1331] having come to them - great is hatred [of them] in the sight of Allāh and in the sight of those who have believed. Thus does Allāh seal over every heart [belonging to] an arrogant tyrant.

(36) And Pharaoh said, "O Hāmān, construct for me a tower that I might reach the ways[1332] -

(37) The ways into the heavens - so that I may look at the deity of Moses; but indeed, I think he is a liar." And thus was made attractive to Pharaoh the evil of his deed, and he was averted from the [right] way. And the plan of Pharaoh was not except in ruin.

(38) And he who believed said, "O my people, follow me; I will guide you to the way of right conduct.

(39) O my people, this worldly life is only [temporary] enjoyment, and indeed, the Hereafter - that is the home of [permanent] settlement.

(40) Whoever does an evil deed will not be recompensed except by the like thereof; but whoever does righteousness, whether male or female, while he is a believer - those will enter Paradise, being given provision therein without account.

(41) And O my people, how is it that I invite you to salvation while you invite me to the Fire?

(42) You invite me to disbelieve in Allāh and associate with Him that of which I have no knowledge, and I invite you to the Exalted in Might, the Perpetual Forgiver.[1333]

(43) Assuredly, that to which you invite me has no [response to a] supplication in this world or in the Hereafter; and indeed, our return is to Allāh, and indeed, the transgressors will be companions of the Fire.

[1331] i.e., evidence.

[1332] Means of ascent, pathways.

[1333] Refer to footnotes in 38:66.

(44) And you will remember what I [now] say to you, and I entrust my affair to Allāh. Indeed, Allāh is Seeing of [His] servants."

(45) So Allāh protected him from the evils they plotted, and the people of Pharaoh were enveloped by the worst of punishment -

(46) The Fire; they are exposed to it morning and evening.[1334] And the Day the Hour appears [it will be said], "Make the people of Pharaoh enter the severest punishment."

(47) And [mention] when they will argue within the Fire, and the weak will say to those who had been arrogant, "Indeed, we were [only] your followers, so will you relieve us of a share of the Fire?"

(48) Those who had been arrogant will say, "Indeed, all [of us] are in it. Indeed, Allāh has judged between the servants."

(49) And those in the Fire will say to the keepers of Hell, "Supplicate your Lord to lighten for us a day from the punishment."

(50) They will say, "Did there not come to you your messengers with clear proofs?" They will say, "Yes." They will reply, "Then supplicate [yourselves], but the supplication of the disbelievers is not except in error [i.e., futility]."

(51) Indeed, We will support Our messengers and those who believe during the life of this world and on the Day when the witnesses will stand -

(52) The Day their excuse will not benefit the wrongdoers, and they will have the curse, and they will have the worst home [i.e., Hell].

(53) And We had certainly given Moses guidance, and We caused the Children of Israel to inherit the Scripture

(54) As guidance and a reminder for those of understanding.

(55) So be patient, [O Muḥammad]. Indeed, the promise of Allāh is truth. And ask forgiveness for your sin[1335] and exalt [Allāh] with praise of your Lord in the evening and the morning.

[1334] From the time of their death until the Day of Resurrection, when they will be driven into it.

[1335] What is intended is "fault" or "error" in judgement, since all prophets were protected by Allāh from falling into sin. The implication is that all believers should seek forgiveness for their sins.

(56) Indeed, those who dispute concerning the signs of Allāh without [any] evidence having come to them - there is not within their breasts except pride, [the extent of] which they cannot reach. So seek refuge in Allāh. Indeed, it is He who is the Hearing, the Seeing.

(57) The creation of the heavens and earth is greater than the creation of mankind, but most of the people do not know.

(58) And not equal are the blind and the seeing, nor are those who believe and do righteous deeds and the evildoer. Little do you remember.

(59) Indeed, the Hour is coming - no doubt about it - but most of the people do not believe.

(60) And your Lord says, "Call upon Me; I will respond to you." Indeed, those who disdain My worship will enter Hell [rendered] contemptible.

(61) It is Allāh who made for you the night that you may rest therein and the day giving sight.[1336] Indeed, Allāh is the possessor of bounty for the people, but most of them are not grateful.

(62) That is Allāh, your Lord, Creator of all things; there is no deity except Him, so how are you deluded?

(63) Thus were those [before you] deluded who were rejecting the signs of Allāh.

(64) It is Allāh who made for you the earth a place of settlement and the sky a structure [i.e., ceiling] and formed you and perfected your forms and provided you with good things. That is Allāh, your Lord; then blessed is Allāh, Lord of the worlds.

(65) He is the Ever-Living;[1337] there is no deity except Him, so call upon Him, [being] sincere to Him in religion. [All] praise is [due] to Allāh, Lord of the worlds.

(66) Say, [O Muḥammad], "Indeed, I have been forbidden to worship those you call upon besides Allāh once the clear proofs have come to me from my Lord, and I have been commanded to submit to the Lord of the worlds."

(67) It is He who created you from dust, then from a sperm-drop, then from a clinging clot; then He brings you out as a child; then [He develops you] that you reach your [time of] maturity, then [further] that you become elders. And among

---

[1336] i.e., making things visible.
[1337] Whose life is without beginning or end, and upon whom all created life depends.

you is he who is taken in death before [that], so that you reach a specified term;[1338] and perhaps you will use reason.

(68) He it is who gives life and causes death; and when He decrees a matter, He but says to it, "Be," and it is.

(69) Do you not consider those who dispute concerning the signs of Allāh - how are they averted?

(70) Those who deny the Book [i.e., the Qur'ān] and that with which We sent Our messengers - they are going to know,

(71) When the shackles are around their necks and the chains; they will be dragged

(72) In boiling water; then in the Fire they will be filled [with flame].

(73) Then it will be said to them, "Where is that which you used to associate [with Him in worship]

(74) Other than Allāh?" They will say, "They have departed from us; rather, we did not used to invoke previously anything." Thus does Allāh put astray the disbelievers.

(75) [The angels will say], "That was because you used to exult upon the earth without right and you used to behave insolently.

(76) Enter the gates of Hell to abide eternally therein, and wretched is the residence of the arrogant."

(77) So be patient, [O Muḥammad]; indeed, the promise of Allāh is truth. And whether We show you some of what We have promised them or We take you in death, it is to Us they will be returned.

(78) And We have already sent messengers before you. Among them are those [whose stories] We have related to you, and among them are those [whose stories] We have not related to you. And it was not for any messenger to bring a sign [or verse] except by permission of Allāh. So when the command of Allāh comes, it will be concluded [i.e., judged] in truth, and the falsifiers will thereupon lose [all].

(79) It is Allāh who made for you the grazing animals upon which you ride, and some of them you eat.

1338 The time decreed for your death.

(80) And for you therein are [other] benefits and that you may realize upon them a need which is in your breasts;[1339] and upon them and upon ships you are carried.

(81) And He shows you His signs. So which of the signs of Allāh do you deny?

(82) Have they not traveled through the land and observed how was the end of those before them? They were more numerous than themselves and greater in strength and in impression on the land, but they were not availed by what they used to earn.

(83) And when their messengers came to them with clear proofs, they [merely] rejoiced in what they had of knowledge, but they were enveloped by what they used to ridicule.

(84) And when they saw Our punishment, they said, "We believe in Allāh alone and disbelieve in that which we used to associate with Him."

(85) But never did their faith benefit them once they saw Our punishment. [It is] the established way of Allāh which has preceded among His servants. And the disbelievers thereupon lost [all].

[1339] i.e., that you may use the animals to carry your loads to distant places, according to need.

Surah Fussilat

(1) Ḥā, Meem.[1340]

(2) [This is] a revelation from the Entirely Merciful, the Especially Merciful -

(3) A Book whose verses have been detailed, an Arabic Qur'ān[1341] for a people who know,

(4) As a giver of good tidings and a warner; but most of them turn away, so they do not hear.

(5) And they say, "Our hearts are within coverings [i.e., screened] from that to which you invite us, and in our ears is deafness, and between us and you is a partition, so work;[1342] indeed, we are working."

(6) Say, [O Muḥammad], "I am only a man like you to whom it has been revealed that your god is but one God; so take a straight course to Him and seek His forgiveness." And woe to those who associate others with Allāh

(7) Those who do not give zakāh, and in the Hereafter they are disbelievers.

(8) Indeed, those who believe and do righteous deeds - for them is a reward uninterrupted.

(9) Say, "Do you indeed disbelieve in He who created the earth in two days and attribute to Him equals? That is the Lord of the worlds."

(10) And He placed on it [i.e., the earth] firmly set mountains over its surface, and He blessed it and determined therein its [creatures'] sustenance in four days without distinction[1343] - for [the information of] those who ask.

(11) Then He directed Himself[1344] to the heaven while it was smoke and said to it and to the earth, "Come [into being],[1345] willingly or by compulsion." They said, "We have come willingly."

(12) And He completed them as seven heavens within two days and inspired [i.e., made known] in each heaven its command. And We adorned the nearest heaven

---

[1340] See footnote to 2:1.

[1341] i.e., revealed in the Arabic language.

[1342] For your own religion or work against us.

[1343] Also "four equal days" or "four days of completion."

[1344] "See footnote to 2:19.

[1345] Literally, "become" or "do [as commanded].""

with lamps [i.e., stars, for beauty] and as protection.[1346] That is the determination of the Exalted in Might, the Knowing.

(13) But if they turn away, then say, "I have warned you of a thunderbolt like the thunderbolt [that struck] ʿAad and Thamūd.

(14) [That occurred] when the messengers had come to them before them and after them, [saying], "Worship not except Allāh." They said, "If our Lord had willed,[1347] He would have sent down the angels, so indeed we, in that with which you have been sent, are disbelievers."

(15) As for ʿAad, they were arrogant upon the earth without right and said, "Who is greater than us in strength?" Did they not consider that Allāh who created them was greater than them in strength? But they were rejecting Our signs.

(16) So We sent upon them a screaming wind during days of misfortune to make them taste the punishment of disgrace in the worldly life; but the punishment of the Hereafter is more disgracing, and they will not be helped.

(17) And as for Thamūd, We guided them, but they preferred blindness over guidance, so the thunderbolt of humiliating punishment seized them for what they used to earn.

(18) And We saved those who believed and used to fear Allāh.

(19) And [mention, O Muḥammad], the Day when the enemies of Allāh will be gathered to the Fire while they are [driven], assembled in rows,

(20) Until, when they reach it, their hearing and their eyes and their skins will testify against them of what they used to do.

(21) And they will say to their skins, "Why have you testified against us?" They will say, "We were made to speak by Allāh, who has made everything speak; and He created you the first time, and to Him you are returned.

(22) And you were not covering [i.e., protecting] yourselves,[1348] lest your hearing testify against you or your sight or your skins, but you assumed that Allāh does not know much of what you do.

(23) And that was your assumption which you assumed about your Lord. It has brought you to ruin, and you have become among the losers."

[1346] From the devils who attempt to steal information from the angels.
[1347] To send messengers.
[1348] With righteousness or by fearing Allāh.

(24) So [even] if they are patient, the Fire is a residence for them; and if they ask to appease [Allāh], they will not be of those who are allowed to appease.

(25) And We appointed for them companions[1349] who made attractive to them what was before them and what was behind them [of sin], and the word [i.e., decree] has come into effect upon them among nations which had passed on before them of jinn and men. Indeed, they [all] were losers.

(26) And those who disbelieve say, "Do not listen to this Qur'ān and speak noisily[1350] during [the recitation of] it that perhaps you will overcome."

(27) But We will surely cause those who disbelieve to taste a severe punishment, and We will surely recompense them for the worst of what they had been doing.

(28) That is the recompense of the enemies of Allāh - the Fire. For them therein is the home of eternity as recompense for what they, of Our verses, were rejecting.

(29) And those who disbelieved will [then] say, "Our Lord, show us those who misled us of the jinn and men [so] we may put them under our feet[1351] that they will be among the lowest."

(30) Indeed, those who have said, "Our Lord is Allāh" and then remained on a right course - the angels will descend upon them, [saying], "Do not fear and do not grieve but receive good tidings of Paradise, which you were promised.

(31) We [angels] were your allies in worldly life and [are so] in the Hereafter. And you will have therein whatever your souls desire, and you will have therein whatever you request [or wish]

(32) As accommodation from a [Lord who is] Forgiving and Merciful."

(33) And who is better in speech than one who invites to Allāh and does righteousness and says, "Indeed, I am of the Muslims."

(34) And not equal are the good deed and the bad. Repel [evil] by that [deed] which is better; and thereupon, the one whom between you and him is enmity [will become] as though he was a devoted friend.

(35) But none is granted it except those who are patient, and none is granted it except one having a great portion [of good].

[1349] In this world among the evil jinn and men.
[1350] Other meanings include "speak improperly" and/or "make a clamor." The purpose of this was to prevent the hearing or understanding of the Qur'ān.
[1351] In the lowest depths of Hell. Or "that we may step on them" in revenge.

(36) And if there comes to you from Satan an evil suggestion, then seek refuge in Allāh. Indeed, He is the Hearing, the Knowing.

(37) And of His signs are the night and day and the sun and moon. Do not prostrate to the sun or to the moon, but prostrate to Allāh, who created them, if it should be Him that you worship.[1352]

(38) But if they are arrogant - then those who are near your Lord [i.e., the angels] exalt Him by night and by day, and they do not become weary.

(39) And of His signs is that you see the earth stilled, but when We send down upon it rain, it quivers and grows. Indeed, He who has given it life is the Giver of Life to the dead. Indeed, He is over all things competent.

(40) Indeed, those who inject deviation into Our verses[1353] are not concealed from Us. So, is he who is cast into the Fire better or he who comes secure on the Day of Resurrection? Do whatever you will; indeed, He is Seeing of what you do.

(41) Indeed, those who disbelieve in the message [i.e., the Qur'ān][1354] after it has come to them...[1355] And indeed, it is a mighty[1356] Book.

(42) Falsehood cannot approach it from before it or from behind it; [it is] a revelation from a [Lord who is] Wise and Praiseworthy.

(43) Nothing is said to you, [O Muḥammad], except what was already said to the messengers before you. Indeed, your Lord is a possessor of forgiveness and a possessor of painful penalty.

(44) And if We had made it a foreign [i.e., non-Arabic] Qur'ān, they would have said, "Why are its verses not explained in detail [in our language]? Is it a foreign [recitation] and an Arab [messenger]?" Say, "It is, for those who believe, a guidance and cure." And those who do not believe - in their ears is deafness, and it is upon them blindness. Those are being called from a distant place.[1357]

[1352] i.e., Do not worship Allāh through His creations but worship Him directly and exclusively.

[1353] Through deviant recitations or interpretations.
[1354] "i.e., reject it or prefer deviant interpretation.
[1355] The conclusion is understood to be "...will have earned an indescribable punishment."
[1356] Inimitable, resistant to attack, protected by Allāh."
[1357] For all practical purposes, since they neither hear nor understand.

(45) And We had already given Moses the Scripture, but it came under disagreement.[1358] And if not for a word [i.e., decree][1359] that preceded from your Lord, it would have been concluded between them. And indeed they are, concerning it [i.e., the Qur'ān], in disquieting doubt.

(46) Whoever does righteousness - it is for his [own] soul; and whoever does evil [does so] against it. And your Lord is not ever unjust to [His] servants.

(47) To Him [alone] is attributed knowledge of the Hour. And fruits emerge not from their coverings nor does a female conceive or give birth except with His knowledge. And the Day He will call to them, "Where are My 'partners'?" they will say, "We announce to You that there is [no longer] among us any witness [to that]."

(48) And lost from them will be those they were invoking before, and they will be certain that they have no place of escape.

(49) Man is not weary of supplication for good [things], but if evil touches him, he is hopeless and despairing.

(50) And if We let him taste mercy from Us after an adversity which has touched him, he will surely say, "This is [due] to me,[1360] and I do not think the Hour will occur; and [even] if I should be returned to my Lord, indeed, for me there will be with Him the best." But We will surely inform those who disbelieved about what they did, and We will surely make them taste a massive punishment.

(51) And when We bestow favor upon man, he turns away and distances himself; but when evil touches him, then he is full of extensive supplication.

(52) Say, "Have you considered: if it [i.e., the Qur'ān] is from Allāh and you disbelieved in it, who would be more astray than one who is in extreme dissension?"

(53) We will show them Our signs in the horizons and within themselves until it becomes clear to them that it is the truth.[1361] But is it not sufficient concerning your Lord that He is, over all things, a Witness?[1362]

[1358] "An alternative meaning is "he was opposed over it."
[1359] See footnote to 10:19."

[1360] Because of my effort, knowledge, excellence, etc.
[1361] "Or "that He (subḥānahu wa taʿālā) is the Truth."
[1362] See footnote of 4:79."

(54) Unquestionably, they are in doubt about the meeting with their Lord. Unquestionably He is, of all things, encompassing.

Surah Ash-Shura

(1) Ḥā, Meem.

(2) ʿAyn, Seen, Qāf.[1363]

(3) Thus has He revealed to you, [O Muḥammad], and to those before you - Allāh, the Exalted in Might, the Wise.

(4) To Him belongs whatever is in the heavens and whatever is in the earth, and He is the Most High, the Most Great.[1364]

(5) The heavens almost break from above them,[1365] and the angels exalt [Allāh] with praise of their Lord and ask forgiveness for those on earth. Unquestionably, it is Allāh who is the Forgiving, the Merciful.

(6) And those who take as allies other than Him - Allāh is [yet] Guardian over them; and you, [O Muḥammad], are not over them a manager.

(7) And thus We have revealed to you an Arabic Qurʾān that you may warn the Mother of Cities [i.e., Makkah] and those around it[1366] and warn of the Day of Assembly, about which there is no doubt. A party will be in Paradise and a party in the Blaze.

(8) And if Allāh willed, He could have made them [of] one religion, but He admits whom He wills[1367] into His mercy. And the wrongdoers have not any protector or helper.

(9) Or have they taken protectors [or allies] besides Him? But Allāh - He is the Protector, and He gives life to the dead, and He is over all things competent.

(10) And in anything over which you disagree - its ruling is [to be referred] to Allāh. [Say], "That is Allāh, my Lord; upon Him I have relied, and to Him I turn back."[1368]

[1363] See footnote to 2:1.

[1364] See footnote to 2:255.

[1365] i.e., from the grandeur of Allāh (subḥānahu wa taʿālā) above them.

[1366] i.e., all other peoples.

[1367] i.e., those who desire His guidance and His acceptance of them.

[1368] In remembrance and repentance.

(11) [He is] Creator of the heavens and the earth. He has made for you from yourselves, mates, and among the cattle, mates; He multiplies you thereby. There is nothing like unto Him,[1369] and He is the Hearing, the Seeing.[1370]

(12) To Him belong the keys of the heavens and the earth. He extends provision for whom He wills and restricts [it]. Indeed He is, of all things, Knowing.

(13) He has ordained for you of religion what He enjoined upon Noah and that which We have revealed to you, [O Muḥammad], and what We enjoined upon Abraham and Moses and Jesus - to establish the religion and not be divided therein. Difficult for those who associate others with Allāh is that to which you invite them. Allāh chooses for Himself whom He wills and guides to Himself whoever turns back [to Him].

(14) And they did not become divided until after knowledge had come to them - out of jealous animosity between themselves. And if not for a word[1371] that preceded from your Lord [postponing the penalty] until a specified time, it would have been concluded between them. And indeed, those who were granted inheritance of the Scripture after them are, concerning it, in disquieting doubt.

(15) So to that [religion of Allāh] invite, [O Muḥammad],[1372] and remain on a right course as you are commanded and do not follow their inclinations but say, "I have believed in what Allāh has revealed of scripture [i.e., the Qur'ān], and I have been commanded to do justice among you. Allāh is our Lord and your Lord. For us are our deeds, and for you your deeds.[1373] There is no [need for] argument between us and you.[1374] Allāh will bring us together, and to Him is the [final] destination."

(16) And those who argue concerning Allāh after He has been responded to[1375] - their argument is invalid with their Lord, and upon them is [His] wrath, and for them is a severe punishment.

[1369] "There is no similarity whatsoever between the Creator and His creation in essence, in attributes or in deed.

[1370] See footnotes to 17:1."

[1371] Decree. See footnote to 10:19.

[1372] "Another meaning understood from the Arabic is "So because of that [division and separation into sects], invite [them back to Allāh]..."

[1373] i.e., the consequences thereof.

[1374] Since the truth has been made clear and since those who refuse it do so only out of stubbornness or worldly interests."

[1375] i.e., after people have accepted the truth from Allāh, in an attempt to turn the believers away from His religion of Islām.

(17) It is Allāh who has sent down the Book in truth and [also] the balance [i.e., justice]. And what will make you perceive? Perhaps the Hour is near.

(18) Those who do not believe in it are impatient for it,[1376] but those who believe are fearful of it and know that it is the truth. Unquestionably, those who dispute concerning the Hour are in extreme error.

(19) Allāh is Subtle[1377] with His servants; He gives provision to whom He wills. And He is the Powerful, the Exalted in Might.

(20) Whoever desires the harvest of the Hereafter - We increase for him in his harvest [i.e., reward]. And whoever desires the harvest [i.e., benefits] of this world - We give him thereof, but there is not for him in the Hereafter any share.

(21) Or have they partners [i.e., other deities] who have ordained for them a religion to which Allāh has not consented? But if not for the decisive word,[1378] it would have been concluded between them. And indeed, the wrongdoers will have a painful punishment.

(22) You will see the wrongdoers fearful of what they have earned, and it will [certainly] befall them. And those who have believed and done righteous deeds will be in lush regions of the gardens [in Paradise] having whatever they will in the presence of their Lord. That is what is the great bounty.

(23) It is that of which Allāh gives good tidings to His servants who believe and do righteous deeds. Say, [O Muḥammad], "I do not ask you for it [i.e., this message] any payment [but] only good will through [i.e., due to] kinship." And whoever commits a good deed - We will increase for him good therein. Indeed, Allāh is Forgiving and Appreciative.[1379]

(24) Or do they say, "He has invented about Allāh a lie"? But if Allāh willed, He could seal over your heart.[1380] And Allāh eliminates falsehood and establishes the truth by His words. Indeed, He is Knowing of that within the breasts.

(25) And it is He who accepts repentance from His servants and pardons misdeeds, and He knows what you do.

[1376] They had challenged the Prophet (ﷺ) to bring it on immediately.
[1377] See footnote in 12:100.
[1378] Decree. See footnote to 10:19.
[1379] See footnote in 35:30.
[1380] i.e., He could make you forget the Qur'ān and deprive you of it.

(26) And He answers [the supplication of] those who have believed and done righteous deeds and increases [for] them from His bounty. But the disbelievers will have a severe punishment.

(27) And if Allāh had extended [excessively] provision for His servants, they would have committed tyranny throughout the earth. But He sends [it] down in an amount which He wills. Indeed He is, of His servants, Aware and Seeing.

(28) And it is He who sends down the rain after they had despaired and spreads His mercy. And He is the Protector, the Praiseworthy.

(29) And of His signs is the creation of the heavens and earth and what He has dispersed throughout them of creatures. And He, for gathering them when He wills, is competent.

(30) And whatever strikes you of disaster - it is for what your hands have earned; but He pardons much.

(31) And you will not cause failure [to Allāh][1381] upon the earth. And you have not besides Allāh any protector or helper.

(32) And of His signs are the ships in the sea, like mountains.

(33) If He willed, He could still the wind, and they would remain motionless on its surface. Indeed in that are signs for everyone patient and grateful.

(34) Or He could destroy them[1382] for what they earned; but He pardons much.

(35) And [that is so] those who dispute concerning Our signs may know that for them there is no place of escape.

(36) So whatever thing you have been given - it is but [for] enjoyment of the worldly life. But what is with Allāh is better and more lasting for those who have believed and upon their Lord rely

(37) And those who avoid the major sins and immoralities, and when they are angry, they forgive,

(38) And those who have responded to their Lord and established prayer and whose affair is [determined by] consultation among themselves, and from what We have provided them, they spend,

---

[1381] i.e., escape from Him.
[1382] Meaning that Allāh could sink the ships by means of violent winds.

(39) And those who, when tyranny strikes them, they retaliate [in a just manner].[1383]

(40) And the retribution for an evil act is an evil one like it, but whoever pardons and makes reconciliation - his reward is [due] from Allāh. Indeed, He does not like wrongdoers.

(41) And whoever retaliates after having been wronged - those have not upon them any cause [for blame].

(42) The cause is only against the ones who wrong the people and tyrannize upon the earth without right. Those will have a painful punishment.

(43) And whoever is patient and forgives - indeed, that is of the matters [worthy] of resolve.[1384]

(44) And he whom Allāh sends astray - for him there is no protector beyond Him. And you will see the wrongdoers, when they see the punishment, saying, "Is there for return [to the former world] any way?"

(45) And you will see them being exposed to it [i.e., the Fire], humbled from humiliation, looking from [behind] a covert glance. And those who had believed will say, "Indeed, the [true] losers are the ones who lost themselves and their families on the Day of Resurrection. Unquestionably, the wrongdoers are in an enduring punishment."

(46) And there will not be for them any allies to aid them other than Allāh. And whoever Allāh sends astray - for him there is no way.

(47) Respond to your Lord before a Day comes from Allāh of which there is no repelling. No refuge will you have that Day, nor for you will there be any denial.[1385]

(48) But if they turn away - then We have not sent you, [O Muḥammad], over them as a guardian; upon you is only [the duty of] notification. And indeed, when We let man taste mercy from Us, he rejoices in it; but if evil afflicts him for what his hands have put forth, then indeed, man is ungrateful.

(49) To Allāh belongs the dominion of the heavens and the earth; He creates what He wills. He gives to whom He wills female [children], and He gives to whom He wills males.

[1383] Restoring their rights and not allowing aggressors to take advantage of them out of weakness.

[1384] On the part of those seeking the reward of Allāh.
[1385] Of your sins or "disapproval" of your punishment.

(50) Or He makes them [both] males and females, and He renders whom He wills barren. Indeed, He is Knowing and Competent.

(51) And it is not for any human being that Allāh should speak to him except by revelation or from behind a partition or that He sends a messenger [i.e., angel] to reveal, by His permission, what He wills. Indeed, He is Most High and Wise.

(52) And thus We have revealed to you an inspiration of Our command [i.e., the Qur'ān]. You did not know what is the Book or [what is] faith, but We have made it a light by which We guide whom We will of Our servants. And indeed, [O Muḥammad], you guide to a straight path -

(53) The path of Allāh, to whom belongs whatever is in the heavens and whatever is on the earth. Unquestionably, to Allāh do [all] matters evolve [i.e., return].

Surah Az-Zukhruf

(1) Ḥā, Meem.[1386]

(2) By the clear Book,

(3) Indeed, We have made it an Arabic Qur'ān that you might understand.

(4) And indeed it is, in the Mother of the Book[1387] with Us, exalted and full of wisdom.[1388]

(5) Then should We turn the message away, disregarding you, because you are a transgressing people?

(6) And how many a prophet We sent among the former peoples,

(7) But there would not come to them a prophet except that they used to ridicule him.

(8) And We destroyed greater than them[1389] in [striking] power, and the example of the former peoples has preceded.

(9) And if you should ask them, "Who has created the heavens and the earth?" they would surely say, "They were created by the Exalted in Might, the Knowing,"

(10) [The one] who has made for you the earth a bed and made for you upon it roads that you might be guided

(11) And who sends down rain from the sky in measured amounts, and We revive thereby a dead land - thus will you be brought forth -

(12) And who created the species, all of them, and has made for you of ships and animals those which you mount

(13) That you may settle yourselves upon their backs and then remember the favor of your Lord when you have settled upon them and say, "Exalted is He who has subjected this to us, and we could not have [otherwise] subdued it.[1390]

(14) And indeed we, to our Lord, will [surely] return."

[1386] See footnote to 2:1.
[1387] "i.e., the Preserved Slate (al-Lawḥ al-Maḥfūẓ).
[1388] Also, "precise" or "specific.""
[1389] The disbelievers of the Quraysh, who denied Prophet Muḥammad (ﷺ).
[1390] Literally, "made it a companion" or "made it compatible."

(15) But they have attributed to Him from His servants a portion.[1391] Indeed, man is clearly ungrateful.

(16) Or has He taken, out of what He has created, daughters and chosen you for [having] sons?

(17) And when one of them is given good tidings of that which he attributes to the Most Merciful in comparison [i.e., a daughter], his face becomes dark, and he suppresses grief.

(18) So is one brought up in ornaments while being during conflict unevident[1392] [attributed to Allāh]?

(19) And they described the angels, who are servants of the Most Merciful, as females. Did they witness their creation? Their testimony will be recorded, and they will be questioned.

(20) And they said, "If the Most Merciful had willed, we would not have worshipped them." They have of that no knowledge. They are not but misjudging.

(21) Or have We given them a book before it [i.e., the Qur'ān] to which they are adhering?

(22) Rather, they say, "Indeed, we found our fathers upon a religion, and we are in their footsteps [rightly] guided."

(23) And similarly, We did not send before you any warner into a city except that its affluent said, "Indeed, we found our fathers upon a religion, and we are, in their footsteps, following."

(24) [Each warner] said, "Even if I brought you better guidance than that [religion] upon which you found your fathers?" They said, "Indeed we, in that with which you were sent, are disbelievers."

(25) So We took retribution from them; then see how was the end of the deniers.

(26) And [mention, O Muḥammad], when Abraham said to his father and his people, "Indeed, I am disassociated from that which you worship

---

[1391] By claiming that He (subḥānahu wa taʿālā) has a son or daughters, as it is said that a child is part of his parent. This concept is totally incompatible with Allāh's unity and exclusiveness.

[1392] Not "obvious" or "distinct" in an argument. Or not "seen," i.e., absent from battles. The reference is to a daughter.

(27) Except for He who created me; and indeed, He will guide me."

(28) And he made it[1393] a word remaining among his descendants that they might return [to it].

(29) However, I gave enjoyment to these [people of Makkah] and their fathers[1394] until there came to them the truth and a clear Messenger.[1395]

(30) But when the truth came to them, they said, "This is magic, and indeed we are, concerning it, disbelievers."

(31) And they said, "Why was this Qur'ān not sent down upon a great man from [one of] the two cities?"[1396]

(32) Do they distribute the mercy of your Lord? It is We who have apportioned among them their livelihood in the life of this world and have raised some of them above others in degrees [of rank] that they may make use of one another for service. But the mercy of your Lord is better than whatever they accumulate.

(33) And if it were not that the people would become one community [of disbelievers],[1397] We would have made for those who disbelieve in the Most Merciful - for their houses - ceilings and stairways of silver upon which to mount.

(34) And for their houses - doors and couches [of silver] upon which to recline

(35) And gold ornament. But all that is not but the enjoyment of worldly life. And the Hereafter with your Lord is for the righteous.

(36) And whoever is blinded from remembrance of the Most Merciful - We appoint for him a devil, and he is to him a companion.

(37) And indeed, they [i.e., the devils] avert them from the way [of guidance] while they think that they are [rightly] guided

---

[1393] i.e., his testimony that none is worthy of worship except Allāh.

[1394] "The descendants of Abraham.

[1395] i.e., one who is obvious with a clear message, meaning Muḥammad (ﷺ)."

[1396] Referring to Makkah and aṭ-Ṭā'if.

[1397] Who assumed that Allāh's generosity to them was a sign of His approval or who would hasten to disbelief in order to obtain wealth.

(38) Until, when he comes to Us [at Judgement], he says [to his companion], "How I wish there was between me and you the distance between the east and west; and what a wretched companion."

(39) And never will it benefit you that Day, when you have wronged, that you are [all] sharing in the punishment.

(40) Then will you make the deaf hear, [O Muḥammad], or guide the blind or he who is in clear error?

(41) And whether [or not] We take you away [in death], indeed, We will take retribution upon them.

(42) Or whether [or not] We show you that which We have promised them, indeed, We are Perfect in Ability.

(43) So adhere to that which is revealed to you. Indeed, you are on a straight path.

(44) And indeed, it is a remembrance[1398] for you and your people, and you [all] are going to be questioned.

(45) And ask those We sent before you of Our messengers; have We made besides the Most Merciful deities to be worshipped?

(46) And certainly did We send Moses with Our signs to Pharaoh and his establishment, and he said, "Indeed, I am the messenger of the Lord of the worlds."

(47) But when he brought them Our signs, at once they laughed at them.

(48) And We showed them not a sign except that it was greater than its sister, and We seized them with affliction that perhaps they might return [to faith].

(49) And they said [to Moses], "O magician, invoke for us your Lord by what He has promised you. Indeed, we will be guided."

(50) But when We removed from them the affliction, at once they broke their word.

(51) And Pharaoh called out among his people; he said, "O my people, does not the kingdom of Egypt belong to me, and these rivers flowing beneath me; then do you not see?

[1398] i.e., an honor. Or "a reminder."

(52) Or am I [not] better than this one [i.e., Moses] who is insignificant and hardly makes himself clear?[1399]

(53) Then why have there not been placed upon him bracelets of gold or come with him the angels in conjunction?"

(54) So he bluffed his people, and they obeyed him. Indeed, they were [themselves] a people defiantly disobedient [of Allāh].

(55) And when they angered Us, We took retribution from them and drowned them all.

(56) And We made them a precedent and an example for the later peoples.

(57) And when the son of Mary was presented as an example,[1400] immediately your people laughed aloud.

(58) And they said, "Are our gods better, or is he?"[1401] They did not present it [i.e., the comparison] except for [mere] argument. But, [in fact], they are a people prone to dispute.

(59) He [i.e., Jesus] was not but a servant upon whom We bestowed favor, and We made him an example for the Children of Israel.

(60) And if We willed, We could have made [instead] of you angels succeeding [one another][1402] on the earth.

(61) And indeed, he [i.e., Jesus] will be [a sign for] knowledge of the Hour, so be not in doubt of it, and follow Me.[1403] This is a straight path.

(62) And never let Satan avert you. Indeed, he is to you a clear enemy.

(63) And when Jesus brought clear proofs, he said, "I have come to you with wisdom [i.e., prophethood] and to make clear to you some of that over which you differ, so fear Allāh and obey me.

(64) Indeed, Allāh is my Lord and your Lord, so worship Him. This is a straight path."

[1399] That was true previous to his appointment as a prophet, at which time Allāh corrected his speech impediment.

[1400] Of a creation of Allāh which is being worshipped along with Him.
[1401] Implying that they must all be the same.
[1402] Or "succeeding [you]."
[1403] i.e., follow the guidance and instruction of Allāh.

(65) But the denominations from among them differed [and separated], so woe to those who have wronged from the punishment of a painful Day.

(66) Are they waiting except for the Hour to come upon them suddenly while they perceive not?

(67) Close friends, that Day, will be enemies to each other, except for the righteous

(68) [To whom Allāh will say], "O My servants, no fear will there be concerning you this Day, nor will you grieve,

(69) [You] who believed in Our verses and were Muslims.

(70) Enter Paradise, you and your kinds,[1404] delighted."

(71) Circulated among them will be plates and vessels of gold. And therein is whatever the souls desire and [what] delights the eyes, and you will abide therein eternally.

(72) And that is Paradise which you are made to inherit for what you used to do.

(73) For you therein is much fruit[1405] from which you will eat.

(74) Indeed, the criminals will be in the punishment of Hell, abiding eternally.

(75) It will not be allowed to subside for them, and they, therein, are in despair.

(76) And We did not wrong them, but it was they who were the wrongdoers.

(77) And they will call, "O Mālik,[1406] let your Lord put an end to us!" He will say, "Indeed, you will remain."

(78) We had certainly brought you the truth, but most of you, to the truth, were averse.

(79) Or have they devised [some] affair?[1407] But indeed, We are devising [a plan].

(80) Or do they think that We hear not their secrets and their private conversations? Yes, [We do], and Our messengers [i.e., angels] are with them recording.

[1404] i.e., those like you. Another meaning may be "your spouses," i.e., the righteous among them.
[1405] Meaning everything delicious.
[1406] Addressing the keeper of Hell.
[1407] Conspiracy against the Prophet (ﷺ). The reference here is to the disbelievers of Makkah.

(81) Say, [O Muḥammad], "If the Most Merciful had a son, then I would be the first of [his] worshippers."[1408]

(82) Exalted is the Lord of the heavens and the earth, Lord of the Throne, above what they describe.

(83) So leave them to converse vainly and amuse themselves until they meet their Day which they are promised.

(84) And it is He [i.e., Allāh] who is [the only] deity in the heaven, and on the earth [the only] deity. And He is the Wise, the Knowing.

(85) And blessed is He to whom belongs the dominion of the heavens and the earth and whatever is between them and with whom is knowledge of the Hour and to whom you will be returned.

(86) And those they invoke[1409] besides Him do not possess [power of] intercession; but only those who testify to the truth [can benefit], and they know.[1410]

(87) And if you asked them[1411] who created them, they would surely say, "Allāh." So how are they deluded?

(88) And [Allāh acknowledges] his saying,[1412] "O my Lord, indeed these are a people who do not believe."

(89) So turn aside from them and say, "Peace."[1413] But they are going to know.

[1408] Only supposing it were so, which it is not.

[1409] "i.e., worship.

[1410] That intercession is granted exclusively by permission of Allāh to those He wills.

[1411] Those who associate others with Allāh.

[1412] i.e., the complaint of Prophet Muḥammad (ﷺ) about his people.

[1413] Meaning safety or security, i.e., "I will not harm you." This was before permission was granted for armed struggle.

Surah Ad-Dukhan

(1) Ḥā, Meem.[1414]

(2) By the clear Book,

(3) Indeed, We sent it down during a blessed night.[1415] Indeed, We were to warn [mankind].

(4) Therein [i.e., on that night] is made distinct[1416] every precise matter -

(5) [Every] matter [proceeding] from Us. Indeed, We were to send [a messenger]

(6) As mercy from your Lord. Indeed, He is the Hearing, the Knowing,

(7) Lord of the heavens and the earth and that between them, if you would be certain.

(8) There is no deity except Him; He gives life and causes death. [He is] your Lord and the Lord of your first forefathers.

(9) But they are in doubt, amusing themselves.

(10) Then watch for the Day when the sky will bring a visible smoke

(11) Covering the people; this is a painful torment.

(12) [They will say], "Our Lord, remove from us the torment; indeed, we are believers."

(13) How will there be for them a reminder [at that time]? And there had come to them a clear Messenger.

(14) Then they turned away from him and said, "[He was] taught [and is] a madman."

(15) Indeed, We will remove the torment for a little. Indeed, you [disbelievers] will return [to disbelief].

[1414] See footnote to 2:1.
[1415] The Night of Decree (Qadr). See sūrah 97.
[1416] Or "is separated" or "apportioned," from what is inscribed in the Preserved Slate. The angels record and descend with whatever Allāh has decreed for the coming year.

(16) The Day We will strike with the greatest assault, indeed, We will take retribution.

(17) And We had already tried before them the people of Pharaoh, and there came to them a noble messenger [i.e., Moses],

(18) [Saying], "Render to me the servants of Allāh.[1417] Indeed, I am to you a trustworthy messenger,"

(19) And [saying], "Be not haughty with Allāh. Indeed, I have come to you with clear evidence.

(20) And indeed, I have sought refuge in my Lord and your Lord, lest you stone me.[1418]

(21) But if you do not believe me, then leave me alone."

(22) And [finally] he called to his Lord that these were a criminal people.

(23) [Allāh said], "Then set out with My servants by night. Indeed, you are to be pursued.

(24) And leave the sea in stillness.[1419] Indeed, they are an army to be drowned."

(25) How much they left behind of gardens and springs

(26) And crops and noble sites

(27) And comfort wherein they were amused.

(28) Thus. And We caused to inherit it another people.

(29) And the heaven and earth wept not for them, nor were they reprieved.

(30) And We certainly saved the Children of Israel from the humiliating torment -

(31) From Pharaoh. Indeed, he was a haughty one among the transgressors.

(32) And We certainly chose them by knowledge over [all] the worlds.

(33) And We gave them of signs that in which there was a clear trial.

[1417] i.e., the Children of Israel.

[1418] To death. Or "lest you assault me [with your tongues or harm me otherwise]."

[1419] After it has parted, in order that the soldiers of Pharaoh would follow the Children of Israel and be drowned.

(34) Indeed, these [disbelievers] are saying,

(35) "There is not but our first death, and we will not be resurrected.

(36) Then bring [back] our forefathers, if you should be truthful."

(37) Are they better or the people of Tubba'[1420] and those before them? We destroyed them, [for] indeed, they were criminals.

(38) And We did not create the heavens and earth and that between them in play.

(39) We did not create them except in truth, but most of them do not know.

(40) Indeed, the Day of Judgement is the appointed time for them all -

(41) The Day when no relation[1421] will avail a relation at all, nor will they be helped -

(42) Except those [believers] on whom Allāh has mercy. Indeed, He is the Exalted in Might, the Merciful.

(43) Indeed, the tree of zaqqūm

(44) Is food for the sinful.

(45) Like murky oil, it boils within bellies

(46) Like the boiling of scalding water.

(47) [It will be commanded], "Seize him and drag him into the midst of the Hellfire,

(48) Then pour over his head from the torment of scalding water."

(49) [It will be said], "Taste! Indeed, you are the honored, the noble![1422]

(50) Indeed, this is what you used to dispute."

(51) Indeed, the righteous will be in a secure place:

(52) Within gardens and springs,

(53) Wearing [garments of] fine silk and brocade, facing each other.

[1420] The tribe of Saba'.

[1421] i.e., patron, protector or close associate.

[1422] As he had claimed upon the earth. He is taunted with these words in Hell as a reminder and additional torment.

(54) Thus. And We will marry them to fair women with large, [beautiful] eyes.

(55) They will call therein for every [kind of] fruit - safe and secure.

(56) They will not taste death therein except the first death, and He will have protected them from the punishment of Hellfire

(57) As bounty from your Lord. That is what is the great attainment.

(58) And indeed, We have eased it [i.e., the Qur'ān] in your tongue that they might be reminded.

(59) So watch, [O Muḥammad]; indeed, they are watching [for your end].

Surah Al-Jathiyah

(1) Ḥā, Meem.[1423]

(2) The revelation of the Book is from Allāh, the Exalted in Might, the Wise.

(3) Indeed, within the heavens and earth are signs for the believers.

(4) And in the creation of yourselves and what He disperses of moving creatures are signs for people who are certain [in faith].

(5) And [in] the alternation of night and day and [in] what Allāh sends down from the sky of provision [i.e., rain] and gives life thereby to the earth after its lifelessness and [in His] directing of the winds are signs for a people who reason.

(6) These are the verses of Allāh which We recite to you in truth. Then in what statement after Allāh and His verses will they believe?

(7) Woe to every sinful liar

(8) Who hears the verses of Allāh recited to him, then persists arrogantly as if he had not heard them. So give him tidings of a painful punishment.

(9) And when he knows anything of Our verses, he takes them in ridicule. Those will have a humiliating punishment.

(10) Before them[1424] is Hell, and what they had earned will not avail them at all nor what they had taken besides Allāh as allies. And they will have a great punishment.

(11) This [Qur'ān] is guidance. And those who have disbelieved in the verses of their Lord will have a painful punishment of foul nature.

(12) It is Allāh who subjected to you the sea so that ships may sail upon it by His command and that you may seek of His bounty; and perhaps you will be grateful.

(13) And He has subjected to you whatever is in the heavens and whatever is on the earth - all from Him. Indeed in that are signs for a people who give thought.

[1423] See footnote to 2:1.
[1424] See footnote to 14:16.

(14) Say, [O Muḥammad], to those who have believed that they [should] forgive those who expect not the days of Allāh [i.e., of His retribution] so that He may recompense a people[1425] for what they used to earn.

(15) Whoever does a good deed - it is for himself; and whoever does evil - it is against it [i.e., the self or soul]. Then to your Lord you will be returned.

(16) And We did certainly give the Children of Israel the Scripture and judgement[1426] and prophethood, and We provided them with good things and preferred them over the worlds.

(17) And We gave them clear proofs of the matter [of religion]. And they did not differ except after knowledge had come to them - out of jealous animosity between themselves. Indeed, your Lord will judge between them on the Day of Resurrection concerning that over which they used to differ.

(18) Then We put you, [O Muḥammad], on an ordained way concerning the matter [of religion]; so follow it and do not follow the inclinations of those who do not know.

(19) Indeed, they will never avail you against Allāh at all. And indeed, the wrongdoers are allies of one another; but Allāh is the protector of the righteous.

(20) This [Qur'ān] is enlightenment for mankind and guidance and mercy for a people who are certain [in faith].

(21) Or do those who commit evils think We will make them like those who have believed and done righteous deeds - [make them] equal in their life and their death?[1427] Evil is that which they judge [i.e., assume].

(22) And Allāh created the heavens and earth in truth and so that every soul may be recompensed for what it has earned, and they will not be wronged.

(23) Have you seen he who has taken as his god his [own] desire, and Allāh has sent him astray due to knowledge[1428] and has set a seal upon his hearing and his heart

---

[1425] In the Hereafter, where those who forgive will be rewarded and those who earned evil will be punished. This was at the outset of da'wah (invitation to Allāh) before permission for jihād.

[1426] Understanding of the law.

[1427] Another meaning is "...[the evildoers being] equal in their life and their death," i.e., unresponsive to guidance.

[1428] This can refer to Allāh's knowledge of that person and of his preference for his own inclinations or to that person's knowledge of the truth while he refuses it.

and put over his vision a veil? So who will guide him after Allāh? Then will you not be reminded?

(24) And they say, "There is not but our worldly life; we die and live,[1429] and nothing destroys us except time." And they have of that no knowledge; they are only assuming.

(25) And when Our verses are recited to them as clear evidences, their argument is only that they say, "Bring [back] our forefathers, if you should be truthful."

(26) Say, "Allāh causes you to live, then causes you to die; then He will assemble you for the Day of Resurrection, about which there is no doubt, but most of the people do not know."

(27) And to Allāh belongs the dominion of the heavens and the earth. And the Day the Hour appears - that Day the falsifiers will lose.

(28) And you will see every nation kneeling [from fear]. Every nation will be called to its record [and told], "Today you will be recompensed for what you used to do.

(29) This, Our record, speaks about you in truth. Indeed, We were having transcribed[1430] whatever you used to do."

(30) So as for those who believed and did righteous deeds, their Lord will admit them into His mercy. That is what is the clear attainment.

(31) But as for those who disbelieved, [it will be said], "Were not Our verses recited to you, but you were arrogant and became a criminal people?

(32) And when it was said, 'Indeed, the promise of Allāh is truth and the Hour [is coming] - no doubt about it,' you said, 'We know not what is the Hour. We assume only assumption, and we are not convinced.'"

(33) And the evil consequences of what they did will appear to them, and they will be enveloped by what they used to ridicule.

(34) And it will be said, "Today We will forget you as you forgot the meeting of this Day of yours, and your refuge is the Fire, and for you there are no helpers.

(35) That is because you took the verses of Allāh in ridicule, and worldly life deluded you." So that Day they will not be removed from it, nor will they be asked to appease [Allāh].

[1429] i.e., some people die and others live, replacing them.
[1430] By recording angels.

(36) Then, to Allāh belongs [all] praise - Lord of the heavens and Lord of the earth, Lord of the worlds.

(37) And to Him belongs [all] grandeur within the heavens and the earth, and He is the Exalted in Might, the Wise.

Surah Al-Ahqaf

(1) Ḥā, Meem.[1431]

(2) The revelation of the Book is from Allāh, the Exalted in Might, the Wise.

(3) We did not create the heavens and earth and what is between them except in truth and [for] a specified term. But those who disbelieve, from that of which they are warned, are turning away.

(4) Say, [O Muḥammad], "Have you considered that which you invoke besides Allāh? Show me what they have created of the earth; or did they have partnership in [creation of] the heavens? Bring me a scripture [revealed] before this or a [remaining] trace of knowledge, if you should be truthful."

(5) And who is more astray than he who invokes besides Allāh those who will not respond to him until the Day of Resurrection [i.e., never], and they, of their invocation, are unaware.

(6) And when the people are gathered [that Day], they [who were invoked] will be enemies to them, and they will be deniers of their worship.

(7) And when Our verses are recited to them as clear evidences, those who disbelieve say of the truth when it has come to them, "This is obvious magic."

(8) Or do they say, "He has invented it"? Say, "If I have invented it, you will not possess for me [the power of protection] from Allāh at all. He is most knowing of that in which you are involved.[1432] Sufficient is He as Witness between me and you, and He is the Forgiving, the Merciful."

(9) Say, "I am not something original among the messengers,[1433] nor do I know what will be done with me or with you. I only follow that which is revealed to me, and I am not but a clear warner."

(10) Say, "Have you considered: if it [i.e., the Qur'ān] was from Allāh, and you disbelieved in it while a witness from the Children of Israel has testified to

---

[1431] See footnote to 2:1.

[1432] Of false implications and suggestions.

[1433] i.e., I am neither the first messenger to be sent, nor do I bring something different from the other messengers.

something similar[1434] and believed while you were arrogant...?"[1435] Indeed, Allāh does not guide the wrongdoing people.

(11) And those who disbelieve say of those who believe, "If it had [truly] been good, they would not have preceded us to it." And when they are not guided by it, they will say, "This is an ancient falsehood."

(12) And before it was the scripture of Moses to lead and as a mercy. And this is a confirming Book in an Arabic tongue to warn those who have wronged and as good tidings to the doers of good.

(13) Indeed, those who have said, "Our Lord is Allāh," and then remained on a right course - there will be no fear concerning them, nor will they grieve.

(14) Those are the companions of Paradise, abiding eternally therein as reward for what they used to do.

(15) And We have enjoined upon man, to his parents, good treatment. His mother carried him with hardship and gave birth to him with hardship, and his gestation and weaning [period] is thirty months. [He grows] until, when he reaches maturity and reaches [the age of] forty years, he says, "My Lord, enable me[1436] to be grateful for Your favor which You have bestowed upon me and upon my parents and to work righteousness of which You will approve and make righteous for me my offspring. Indeed, I have repented to You, and indeed, I am of the Muslims."

(16) Those are the ones from whom We will accept the best of what they did and overlook their misdeeds, [their being] among the companions of Paradise. [That is] the promise of truth which they had been promised.

(17) But one who says to his parents, "Uff[1437] to you; do you promise me that I will be brought forth [from the earth] when generations before me have already passed on [into oblivion]?" while they call to Allāh for help [and to their son], "Woe to you! Believe! Indeed, the promise of Allāh is truth." But he says, "This is not but legends of the former peoples" -

(18) Those are the ones upon whom the word [i.e., decree] has come into effect, [who will be] among nations which had passed on before them of jinn and men. Indeed, they [all] were losers.

[1434] "Based upon information from the Torah.
[1435] The conclusion is estimated to be "...would you not then be the most unjust of people?" or "...in what condition would you then be?""
[1436] Literally, "gather within me the utmost strength and ability."
[1437] An expression of distaste and irritation.

(19) And for all there are degrees [of reward and punishment] for what they have done, and [it is] so that He may fully compensate them for their deeds, and they will not be wronged.

(20) And the Day those who disbelieved are exposed to the Fire [it will be said], "You exhausted your pleasures during your worldly life and enjoyed them, so this Day you will be awarded the punishment of [extreme] humiliation because you were arrogant upon the earth without right and because you were defiantly disobedient."

(21) And mention, [O Muḥammad], the brother of ʿAad,[1438] when he warned his people in [the region of] al-Aḥqāf - and warners had already passed on before him and after him - [saying], "Do not worship except Allāh. Indeed, I fear for you the punishment of a terrible day."[1439]

(22) They said, "Have you come to delude us away from our gods? Then bring us what you promise us, if you should be of the truthful."

(23) He said, "Knowledge [of its time] is only with Allāh, and I convey to you that with which I was sent; but I see you [to be] a people behaving ignorantly."

(24) And when they saw it as a cloud approaching their valleys, they said, "This is a cloud bringing us rain!" Rather, it is that for which you were impatient:[1440] a wind, within it a painful punishment,

(25) Destroying everything by command of its Lord. And they became so that nothing was seen [of them] except their dwellings. Thus do We recompense the criminal people.

(26) And We had certainly established them in such as We have not established you, and We made for them hearing and vision and hearts [i.e., intellect]. But their hearing and vision and hearts availed them not from anything [of the punishment] when they were [continually] rejecting the signs of Allāh; and they were enveloped by what they used to ridicule.

(27) And We have already destroyed what surrounds you of [those] cities, and We have diversified the signs [or verses] that perhaps they might return [from disbelief].

[1438] "i.e., the prophet Hūd.

[1439] Upon the earth. It could also refer to "a tremendous Day," i.e., that of resurrection."

[1440] When you challenged your prophet. See verse 22 of this sūrah.

(28) Then why did those they took besides Allāh as deities by which to approach [Him][1441] not aid them? But they had strayed [i.e., departed] from them. And that was their falsehood and what they were inventing.

(29) And [mention, O Muḥammad], when We directed to you a few of the jinn, listening to the Qur’ān. And when they attended it, they said, "Listen attentively." And when it was concluded, they went back to their people as warners.

(30) They said, "O our people, indeed we have heard a [recited] Book revealed after Moses confirming what was before it which guides to the truth and to a straight path.

(31) O our people, respond to the Caller [i.e., Messenger] of Allāh[1442] and believe in him; He [i.e., Allāh] will forgive for you your sins and protect you from a painful punishment.

(32) But he who does not respond to the Caller of Allāh will not cause failure [to Him] upon earth, and he will not have besides Him any protectors. Those are in manifest error."

(33) Do they not see that Allāh, who created the heavens and earth and did not fail in their creation, is able to give life to the dead? Yes. Indeed, He is over all things competent.

(34) And the Day those who disbelieved are exposed to the Fire [it will be said], "Is this not the truth?" They will say, "Yes, by our Lord." He will say, "Then taste the punishment for what you used to deny."[1443]

(35) So be patient, [O Muḥammad], as were those of determination among the messengers and do not be impatient for them.[1444] It will be - on the Day they see that which they are promised - as though they had not remained [in the world] except an hour of a day. [This is] notification. And will [any] be destroyed except the defiantly disobedient people?

[1441] According to their claim.

[1442] Prophet Muḥammad (ﷺ).

[1443] Or "because you used to disbelieve."

[1444] i.e., for Allāh's punishment of the disbelievers.

Surah Muhammad

(1) Those who disbelieve and avert [people] from the way of Allāh - He will waste their deeds.[1445]

(2) And those who believe and do righteous deeds and believe in what has been sent down upon Muḥammad - and it is the truth from their Lord - He will remove from them their misdeeds and amend their condition.

(3) That is because those who disbelieve follow falsehood, and those who believe follow the truth from their Lord. Thus does Allāh present to the people their comparisons.[1446]

(4) So when you meet those who disbelieve [in battle], strike [their] necks until, when you have inflicted slaughter upon them, then secure [their] bonds,[1447] and either [confer] favor[1448] afterwards or ransom [them] until the war lays down its burdens.[1449] That [is the command]. And if Allāh had willed, He could have taken vengeance upon them [Himself], but [He ordered armed struggle] to test some of you by means of others. And those who are killed in the cause of Allāh - never will He waste their deeds.

(5) He will guide them and amend their condition

(6) And admit them to Paradise, which He has made known to them.

(7) O you who have believed, if you support Allāh, He will support you and plant firmly your feet.

(8) But those who disbelieve - for them is misery, and He will waste their deeds.

(9) That is because they disliked what Allāh revealed, so He rendered worthless their deeds.

(10) Have they not traveled through the land and seen how was the end of those before them? Allāh destroyed [everything] over them,[1450] and for the disbelievers is something comparable.

[1445] i.e., cause them to be lost or make them worthless, earning no reward.

[1446] So that they may know the results of their choice.

[1447] "i.e., take those remaining as captives.

[1448] i.e., release them without ransom.

[1449] i.e., its armor, machinery, etc., meaning "until the war is over.""

[1450] i.e., destroyed them and all they owned.

(11) That is because Allāh is the protector of those who have believed and because the disbelievers have no protector.

(12) Indeed, Allāh will admit those who have believed and done righteous deeds to gardens beneath which rivers flow, but those who disbelieve enjoy themselves and eat as grazing livestock eat, and the Fire will be a residence for them.

(13) And how many a city was stronger than your city [i.e., Makkah] which drove you out? We destroyed them; and there was no helper for them.

(14) So is he who is on clear evidence from his Lord like him to whom the evil of his work has been made attractive and they follow their [own] desires?

(15) Is the description of Paradise, which the righteous are promised, wherein are rivers of water unaltered,[1451] rivers of milk the taste of which never changes, rivers of wine delicious to those who drink, and rivers of purified honey, in which they will have from all [kinds of] fruits and forgiveness from their Lord... [Are its inhabitants] like those who abide eternally in the Fire and are given to drink scalding water that will sever their intestines?

(16) And among them, [O Muḥammad], are those who listen to you, until when they depart from you, they say to those who were given knowledge,[1452] "What has he said just now?" Those are the ones of whom Allāh has sealed over their hearts and who have followed their [own] desires.

(17) And those who are guided - He increases them in guidance and gives them their righteousness.[1453]

(18) Then do they await except that the Hour should come upon them unexpectedly? But already there have come [some of] its indications. Then how [i.e., what good] to them, when it has come, will be their remembrance?

(19) So know, [O Muḥammad], that there is no deity except Allāh and ask forgiveness for your sin[1454] and for the believing men and believing women. And Allāh knows of your movement and your resting place.

(20) Those who believe say, "Why has a sūrah[1455] not been sent down?" But when a precise sūrah is revealed and battle is mentioned therein, you see those in whose

---

[1451] In taste or smell, neither stagnant nor polluted.

[1452] From among the Prophet's companions.

[1453] Taqwā, meaning piety, consciousness and fear of Allāh, and care to avoid His displeasure.

[1454] See footnote to 40:55.

[1455] "i.e., one in which permission is given the believers to fight their enemies.

hearts is disease [i.e., hypocrisy] looking at you with a look of one overcome by death. And more appropriate for them[1456] [would have been]

(21) Obedience and good words. And when the matter [of fighting] was determined, if they had been true to Allāh, it would have been better for them.

(22) So would you perhaps, if you turned away,[1457] cause corruption on earth and sever your [ties of] relationship?

(23) Those [who do so] are the ones that Allāh has cursed, so He deafened them and blinded their vision.

(24) Then do they not reflect upon the Qur'ān, or are there locks upon [their] hearts?

(25) Indeed, those who reverted back [to disbelief] after guidance had become clear to them - Satan enticed them and prolonged hope for them.

(26) That is because they said to those who disliked what Allāh sent down,[1458] "We will obey you in part of the matter." And Allāh knows what they conceal.

(27) Then how [will it be] when the angels take them in death, striking their faces and their backs?

(28) That is because they followed what angered Allāh and disliked [what earns] His pleasure, so He rendered worthless their deeds.

(29) Or do those in whose hearts is disease think that Allāh would never expose their [feelings of] hatred?

(30) And if We willed, We could show them to you, and you would know them by their mark; but you will surely know them by the tone of [their] speech. And Allāh knows your deeds.

(31) And We will surely test you until We make evident those who strive among you [for the cause of Allāh] and the patient, and We will test your affairs.

[1456] The words "awlā lahum" can also be interpreted as "woe to them!" In that case, the following verse would begin, "[Better for them would have been] obedience and good words.""

[1457] From Islām or from jihād (struggling in the cause of Allāh).

[1458] i.e., the Jews of Madīnah.

(32) Indeed, those who disbelieved and averted [people] from the path of Allāh and opposed the Messenger after guidance had become clear to them - never will they harm Allāh at all, and He will render worthless their deeds.

(33) O you who have believed, obey Allāh and obey the Messenger and do not invalidate your deeds.

(34) Indeed, those who disbelieved and averted [people] from the path of Allāh and then died while they were disbelievers - never will Allāh forgive them.

(35) So do not weaken and call for peace while you are superior; and Allāh is with you and will never deprive you of [the reward of] your deeds.

(36) [This] worldly life is only amusement and diversion. And if you believe and fear Allāh, He will give you your rewards and not ask you for your properties.

(37) If He should ask you for them and press you, you would withhold, and He would expose your hatred [i.e., unwillingness].

(38) Here you are - those invited to spend in the cause of Allāh - but among you are those who withhold [out of greed]. And whoever withholds only withholds [benefit] from himself; and Allāh is the Free of need, while you are the needy. And if you turn away [i.e., refuse], He will replace you with another people; then they will not be the likes of you.

Surah Al-Fath

(1) Indeed, We have given you, [O Muḥammad], a clear conquest[1459]

(2) That Allāh may forgive for you what preceded of your sin [i.e., errors] and what will follow and complete His favor upon you and guide you to a straight path

(3) And [that] Allāh may aid you with a mighty victory.

(4) It is He who sent down tranquility into the hearts of the believers that they would increase in faith along with their [present] faith. And to Allāh belong the soldiers of the heavens and the earth, and ever is Allāh Knowing and Wise.

(5) [And] that He may admit the believing men and the believing women to gardens beneath which rivers flow to abide therein eternally and remove from them their misdeeds - and ever is that, in the sight of Allāh, a great attainment

(6) And [that] He may punish the hypocrite men and hypocrite women, and the polytheist men and polytheist women - those who assume about Allāh an assumption of evil nature. Upon them is a misfortune of evil nature; and Allāh has become angry with them and has cursed them and prepared for them Hell, and evil it is as a destination.

(7) And to Allāh belong the soldiers of the heavens and the earth. And ever is Allāh Exalted in Might and Wise.

(8) Indeed, We have sent you as a witness and a bringer of good tidings and a warner

(9) That you [people] may believe in Allāh and His Messenger and honor him and respect him [i.e., the Prophet (ﷺ)] and exalt Him [i.e., Allāh] morning and afternoon.

(10) Indeed, those who pledge allegiance to you, [O Muḥammad] - they are actually pledging allegiance to Allāh. The hand[1460] of Allāh is over their hands.[1461] So he who breaks his word only breaks it to the detriment of himself. And he who fulfills that which he has promised Allāh - He will give him a great reward.

[1459] Ibn Masʿūd said, "You [people] consider the conquest to be that of Makkah, but we consider it to be the Treaty of al-Ḥudaybiyyah." Al-Bukhārī reported a similar quotation from al-Barā' bin ʿĀzib. Although initially regarded by the companions as a setback, the treaty, in effect, served to promote the spread of Islam, which led to the conquest of Makkah two years later.

[1460] "See footnote to 2:19.
[1461] Meaning that He (subḥānahu wa taʿālā) accepted their pledge."

(11) Those who remained behind[1462] of the bedouins will say to you, "Our properties and our families occupied us, so ask forgiveness for us." They say with their tongues what is not within their hearts. Say, "Then who could prevent Allāh at all if He intended for you harm or intended for you benefit? Rather, ever is Allāh, of what you do, Aware.

(12) But you thought that the Messenger and the believers would never return to their families, ever, and that was made pleasing in your hearts. And you assumed an assumption of evil and became a people ruined."

(13) And whoever has not believed in Allāh and His Messenger - then indeed, We have prepared for the disbelievers a Blaze.

(14) And to Allāh belongs the dominion of the heavens and the earth. He forgives whom He wills and punishes whom He wills. And ever is Allāh Forgiving and Merciful.

(15) Those who remained[1463] behind will say when you set out toward the war booty to take it, "Let us follow you." They wish to change the words of Allāh. Say, "Never will you follow us. Thus did Allāh say before." So they will say, "Rather, you envy us." But [in fact] they were not understanding except a little.[1464]

(16) Say to those who remained behind of the bedouins, "You will be called to [face] a people of great military might; you may fight them, or they will submit.[1465] So if you obey, Allāh will give you a good reward; but if you turn away as you turned away before, He will punish you with a painful punishment."

(17) There is not upon the blind any guilt or upon the lame any guilt or upon the ill any guilt [for remaining behind]. And whoever obeys Allāh and His Messenger - He will admit him to gardens beneath which rivers flow; but whoever turns away - He will punish him with a painful punishment.

(18) Certainly was Allāh pleased with the believers when they pledged allegiance to you, [O Muḥammad], under the tree, and He knew what was in their hearts, so He sent down tranquility upon them and rewarded them with an imminent conquest[1466]

[1462] See footnote to 9:81.
[1463] "See footnote to 9:81.
[1464] i.e., they only understood the material aspects of life."
[1465] To Allāh in Islām.
[1466] That of Khaybar, which preceded the conquest of Makkah.

(19) And much war booty which they will take. And ever is Allāh Exalted in Might and Wise.

(20) Allāh has promised you much booty that you will take [in the future] and has hastened for you this [victory] and withheld the hands of people from you - that it may be a sign for the believers and [that] He may guide you to a straight path.

(21) And [He promises] other [victories] that you were [so far] unable to [realize] which Allāh has already encompassed.[1467] And ever is Allāh, over all things, competent.

(22) And if those [Makkans] who disbelieve had fought you, they would have turned their backs [in flight]. Then they would not find a protector or a helper.

(23) [This is] the established way of Allāh which has occurred before. And never will you find in the way of Allāh any change.

(24) And it is He who withheld their hands from you and your hands from them within [the area of] Makkah after He caused you to overcome them. And ever is Allāh, of what you do, Seeing.

(25) They are the ones who disbelieved and obstructed you from al-Masjid al-Ḥarām while the offering[1468] was prevented from reaching its place of sacrifice. And if not for believing men and believing women whom you did not know - that you might trample [i.e., kill] them and there would befall you because of them dishonor without [your] knowledge - [you would have been permitted to enter Makkah]. [This was so] that Allāh might admit to His mercy whom He willed. If they had been apart [from them], We would have punished those who disbelieved among them with painful punishment

(26) When those who disbelieved had put into their hearts chauvinism - the chauvinism of the time of ignorance. But Allāh sent down His tranquility upon His Messenger and upon the believers and imposed upon them the word of righteousness, and they were more deserving of it and worthy of it. And ever is Allāh, of all things, Knowing.

(27) Certainly has Allāh showed to His Messenger the vision [i.e., dream] in truth. You will surely enter al-Masjid al-Ḥarām, if Allāh wills, in safety, with your heads shaved and [hair] shortened,[1469] not fearing [anyone]. He knew what you did not know and has arranged before that a conquest near [at hand].

[1467] i.e., prepared for you or decreed.

[1468] i.e., seventy camels intended for sacrifice and feeding of the poor.

[1469] i.e., having completed the rites of ʿumrah.

(28) It is He who sent His Messenger with guidance and the religion of truth to manifest it over all religion. And sufficient is Allāh as Witness.

(29) Muḥammad is the Messenger of Allāh; and those with him are forceful against the disbelievers, merciful among themselves. You see them bowing and prostrating [in prayer], seeking bounty from Allāh and [His] pleasure. Their sign is in their faces from the effect of prostration [i.e., prayer]. That is their description in the Torah. And their description in the Gospel is as a plant which produces its offshoots and strengthens them so they grow firm and stand upon their stalks, delighting the sowers - so that He [i.e., Allāh] may enrage by them[1470] the disbelievers. Allāh has promised those who believe and do righteous deeds among them forgiveness and a great reward.

[1470] The given examples depict the Prophet (ﷺ) and his companions.

Surah Al-Hujurat

(1) O you who have believed, do not put [yourselves] before Allāh and His Messenger[1471] but fear Allāh. Indeed, Allāh is Hearing and Knowing.

(2) O you who have believed, do not raise your voices above the voice of the Prophet or be loud to him in speech like the loudness of some of you to others, lest your deeds become worthless while you perceive not.

(3) Indeed, those who lower their voices before the Messenger of Allāh - they are the ones whose hearts Allāh has tested for righteousness. For them is forgiveness and great reward.

(4) Indeed, those who call you, [O Muḥammad], from behind the chambers - most of them do not use reason.

(5) And if they had been patient until you [could] come out to them, it would have been better for them. But Allāh is Forgiving and Merciful.

(6) O you who have believed, if there comes to you a disobedient one with information, investigate, lest you harm a people out of ignorance and become, over what you have done, regretful.

(7) And know that among you is the Messenger of Allāh. If he were to obey you in much of the matter, you would be in difficulty, but Allāh has endeared to you the faith and has made it pleasing in your hearts and has made hateful to you disbelief, defiance and disobedience. Those are the [rightly] guided.

(8) [It is] as bounty from Allāh and favor. And Allāh is Knowing and Wise.

(9) And if two factions among the believers should fight, then make settlement between the two. But if one of them oppresses the other, then fight against the one that oppresses until it returns to the ordinance of Allāh. And if it returns, then make settlement between them in justice and act justly. Indeed, Allāh loves those who act justly.

(10) The believers are but brothers, so make settlement between your brothers. And fear Allāh that you may receive mercy.

(11) O you who have believed, let not a people ridicule [another] people; perhaps they may be better than them; nor let women ridicule [other] women; perhaps they

---

[1471] Rather, wait for instruction and follow the way of the Prophet (ﷺ).

may be better than them. And do not insult one another and do not call each other by [offensive] nicknames. Wretched is the name [i.e., mention] of disobedience after [one's] faith. And whoever does not repent - then it is those who are the wrongdoers.

(12) O you who have believed, avoid much [negative] assumption. Indeed, some assumption is sin. And do not spy or backbite each other. Would one of you like to eat the flesh of his brother when dead? You would detest it. And fear Allāh; indeed, Allāh is Accepting of Repentance and Merciful.

(13) O mankind, indeed We have created you from male and female and made you peoples and tribes that you may know one another. Indeed, the most noble of you in the sight of Allāh is the most righteous[1472] of you. Indeed, Allāh is Knowing and Aware.

(14) The bedouins say, "We have believed." Say, "You have not [yet] believed; but say [instead], 'We have submitted,' for faith has not yet entered your hearts. And if you obey Allāh and His Messenger, He will not deprive you from your deeds[1473] of anything. Indeed, Allāh is Forgiving and Merciful."

(15) The believers are only the ones who have believed in Allāh and His Messenger and then doubt not but strive with their properties and their lives in the cause of Allāh. It is those who are the truthful.

(16) Say, "Would you acquaint Allāh with your religion while Allāh knows whatever is in the heavens and whatever is on the earth, and Allāh is Knowing of all things?"

(17) They consider it a favor to you that they have accepted Islām. Say, "Do not consider your Islām a favor to me. Rather, Allāh has conferred favor upon you that He has guided you to the faith, if you should be truthful."

(18) Indeed, Allāh knows the unseen [aspects] of the heavens and the earth. And Allāh is Seeing of what you do.

[1472] Literally, "he who has the most taqwā," i.e., consciousness and fear of Allāh, piety and righteousness.
[1473] i.e., the reward thereof.

Surah Qaf

(1) Qāf.[1474] By the honored Qur'ān...[1475]

(2) But they wonder that there has come to them a warner from among themselves, and the disbelievers say, "This is an amazing thing.

(3) When we have died and have become dust, [we will return to life]? That is a distant [i.e., unlikely] return."

(4) We know what the earth diminishes [i.e., consumes] of them, and with Us is a retaining record.

(5) But they denied the truth when it came to them, so they are in a confused condition.

(6) Have they not looked at the heaven above them - how We structured it and adorned it and [how] it has no rifts?

(7) And the earth - We spread it out and cast therein firmly set mountains and made grow therein [something] of every beautiful kind,

(8) Giving insight and a reminder for every servant who turns [to Allāh].

(9) And We have sent down blessed rain from the sky and made grow thereby gardens and grain from the harvest

(10) And lofty palm trees having fruit arranged in layers -

(11) As provision for the servants, and We have given life thereby to a dead land. Thus is the emergence [i.e., resurrection].

(12) The people of Noah denied before them,[1476] and the companions of the well[1477] and Thamūd

(13) And ʿAad and Pharaoh and the brothers [i.e., people] of Lot

(14) And the companions of the thicket and the people of Tubbaʿ. All denied the messengers, so My threat was justly fulfilled.

[1474] "See footnote to 2:1.
[1475] See footnote to 38:1."
[1476] "i.e., before the disbelievers of Makkah.
[1477] See footnote to 25:38."

(15) Did We fail in the first creation? But they are in confusion over a new creation.

(16) And We have already created man and know what his soul whispers to him, and We are closer[1478] to him than [his] jugular vein.

(17) When the two receivers [i.e., recording angels] receive,[1479] seated on the right and on the left.

(18) He [i.e., man] utters no word except that with him is an observer prepared [to record].

(19) And the intoxication of death will bring the truth; that is what you were trying to avoid.

(20) And the Horn will be blown. That is the Day of [carrying out] the threat.

(21) And every soul will come, with it a driver and a witness.[1480]

(22) [It will be said], "You were certainly in unmindfulness of this, and We have removed from you your cover,[1481] so your sight, this Day, is sharp."

(23) And his companion, [the angel], will say, "This [record] is what is with me, prepared."

(24) [Allāh will say], "Throw into Hell every obstinate disbeliever,

(25) Preventer of good, aggressor, and doubter,

(26) Who made [as equal] with Allāh another deity; then throw him into the severe punishment."

(27) His [devil] companion will say, "Our Lord, I did not make him transgress, but he [himself] was in extreme error."

(28) [Allāh] will say, "Do not dispute before Me, while I had already presented to you the threat [i.e., warning].

[1478] In absolute knowledge of everything about him. "We" has also been interpreted to mean the angels who are mentioned in the following verse.
[1479] And record each word and deed.
[1480] i.e., one angel driving the soul to the Judgement and one to testify as to its deeds.
[1481] Of heedlessness, or that which had sealed your hearing, your vision and your heart from guidance.

(29) The word [i.e., decree] will not be changed with Me, and never will I be unjust to the servants."

(30) On the Day We will say to Hell, "Have you been filled?" and it will say, "Are there some more,"

(31) And Paradise will be brought near to the righteous, not far,

(32) [It will be said], "This is what you were promised - for every returner [to Allāh] and keeper [of His covenant].

(33) Who feared the Most Merciful in the unseen and came with a heart returning [in repentance].

(34) Enter it in peace. This is the Day of Eternity."

(35) They will have whatever they wish therein, and with Us is more.

(36) And how many a generation before them did We destroy who were greater than them in [striking] power and had explored throughout the lands. Is there any place of escape?

(37) Indeed in that is a reminder for whoever has a heart or who listens while he is present [in mind].

(38) And We did certainly create the heavens and earth and what is between them in six days, and there touched Us no weariness.

(39) So be patient, [O Muḥammad], over what they say and exalt [Allāh] with praise of your Lord before the rising of the sun and before its setting,

(40) And [in part] of the night exalt Him and after prostration [i.e., prayer].

(41) And listen on the Day when the Caller[1482] will call out from a place that is near -

(42) The Day they will hear the blast [of the Horn] in truth. That is the Day of Emergence [from the graves].

(43) Indeed, it is We who give life and cause death, and to Us is the destination

(44) On the Day the earth breaks away from them [and they emerge] rapidly; that is a gathering easy for Us.

[1482] An angel who will call out Allāh's command for the Resurrection.

(45) We are most knowing of what they say, and you are not over them a tyrant.[1483] But remind by the Qur'ān whoever fears My threat.

[1483] Forcing people to belief or submission.

Surah Ad-Dhariyat

(1) By the [winds] scattering [dust], dispersing [it]

(2) And the [clouds] carrying a load [of water]

(3) And the ships sailing with ease

(4) And the [angels] apportioning [each] matter,

(5) Indeed, what you are promised is true.

(6) And indeed, the recompense is to occur.

(7) By the heaven containing pathways,[1484]

(8) Indeed, you are in differing speech.[1485]

(9) Deluded away from it [i.e., the Qur'ān] is he who is deluded.

(10) Destroyed are the misinformers[1486]

(11) Who are within a flood [of confusion] and heedless.

(12) They ask, "When is the Day of Recompense?"

(13) [It is] the Day they will be tormented over the Fire.

(14) [And will be told], "Taste your torment. This is that for which you were impatient."

(15) Indeed, the righteous will be among gardens and springs,

(16) Accepting what their Lord has given them. Indeed, they were before that doers of good.

(17) They used to sleep but little of the night,[1487]

(18) And in the hours before dawn they would ask forgiveness,

---

[1484] Explained as tracks, layers or orbits.
[1485] About Prophet Muḥammad (ﷺ) and the Qur'ān.
[1486] Or "May they be destroyed" or "cursed."
[1487] i.e., spending a portion of the night in prayer and supplication.

(19) And from their properties was [given] the right of the [needy] petitioner and the deprived.

(20) And on the earth are signs for the certain [in faith]

(21) And in yourselves. Then will you not see?

(22) And in the heaven is your provision and whatever you are promised.

(23) Then by the Lord of the heaven and earth, indeed, it is truth - just as [sure as] it is that you are speaking.

(24) Has there reached you the story of the honored guests of Abraham?[1488]

(25) When they entered upon him and said, "[We greet you with] peace." He answered, "[And upon you] peace; [you are] a people unknown."

(26) Then he went to his family and came with a fat [roasted] calf.

(27) And placed it near them; he said, "Will you not eat?"

(28) And he felt from them apprehension.[1489] They said, "Fear not," and gave him good tidings of a learned boy.

(29) And his wife approached with a cry [of alarm] and struck her face and said, "[I am] a barren old woman!"

(30) They said, "Thus has said your Lord; indeed, He is the Wise, the Knowing."

(31) [Abraham] said, "Then what is your business [here], O messengers?"

(32) They said, "Indeed, we have been sent to a people of criminals[1490]

(33) To send down upon them stones of clay,

(34) Marked in the presence of your Lord for the transgressors."

(35) So We brought out whoever was in them [i.e., the cities] of the believers.

(36) And We found not within them other than a [single] house of Muslims.[1491]

(37) And We left therein a sign for those who fear the painful punishment.

[1488] Who were angels given honored positions by Allāh.
[1489] See footnote to 11:70.
[1490] i.e., those who defied Lot (upon him be peace).
[1491] i.e., Lot and his family, excepting his wife.

(38) And in Moses [was a sign], when We sent him to Pharaoh with clear authority.[1492]

(39) But he turned away with his supporters and said, "A magician or a madman."

(40) So We took him and his soldiers and cast them into the sea, and he was blameworthy.

(41) And in ʿAad [was a sign], when We sent against them the barren wind.[1493]

(42) It left nothing of what it came upon but that it made it like disintegrated ruins.

(43) And in Thamūd, when it was said to them, "Enjoy yourselves for a time."

(44) But they were insolent toward the command of their Lord, so the thunderbolt seized them while they were looking on.

(45) And they were unable to arise, nor could they defend themselves.

(46) And [We destroyed] the people of Noah before; indeed, they were a people defiantly disobedient.

(47) And the heaven We constructed with strength,[1494] and indeed, We are [its] expander.

(48) And the earth We have spread out, and excellent is the preparer.

(49) And of all things We created two mates [i.e., counterparts]; perhaps you will remember.

(50) So flee to Allāh.[1495] Indeed, I am to you from Him a clear warner.

(51) And do not make [as equal] with Allāh another deity. Indeed, I am to you from Him a clear warner.

(52) Similarly, there came not to those before them any messenger except that they said, "A magician or a madman."

[1492] i.e., evidences.

[1493] Barren of any benefit, i.e., evil.

[1494] Literally, "hands."

[1495] i.e., turn to Allāh and take refuge in Him from disbelief and sin, thereby escaping His punishment.

(53) Did they suggest it to them?[1496] Rather, they [themselves] are a transgressing people.

(54) So leave them, [O Muḥammad], for you are not to be blamed.

(55) And remind, for indeed, the reminder benefits the believers.

(56) And I did not create the jinn and mankind except to worship Me.

(57) I do not want from them any provision, nor do I want them to feed Me.

(58) Indeed, it is Allāh who is the [continual] Provider,[1497] the firm possessor of strength.

(59) And indeed, for those who have wronged is a portion [of punishment] like the portion of their companions [i.e., predecessors], so let them not impatiently urge Me.

(60) And woe to those who have disbelieved from their Day which they are promised.

[1496] i.e., Did the former disbelievers pass on these words to the Makkans so that they repeat the same expressions?

[1497] Providing everything required by His creations during their decreed existence. His provision includes guidance.

Surah At-Tur

(1) By the mount

(2) And [by] a Book inscribed[1498]

(3) In parchment spread open

(4) And [by] the frequented House[1499]

(5) And [by] the ceiling [i.e., heaven] raised high

(6) And [by] the sea set on fire,[1500]

(7) Indeed, the punishment of your Lord will occur.

(8) Of it there is no preventer.

(9) On the Day the heaven will sway with circular motion

(10) And the mountains will pass on, departing[1501] -

(11) Then woe, that Day, to the deniers,

(12) Who are in [empty] discourse amusing themselves.

(13) The Day they are thrust toward the fire of Hell with a [violent] thrust, [its angels will say],

(14) "This is the Fire which you used to deny.

(15) Then is this magic, or do you not see?

(16) [Enter to] burn therein; then be patient or impatient - it is all the same for you. You are only being recompensed [for] what you used to do."

(17) Indeed, the righteous will be in gardens and pleasure,

(18) Enjoying what their Lord has given them, and their Lord protected them from the punishment of Hellfire.

[1498] Interpreted as the Preserved Slate or possibly the Qur'ān.

[1499] The house of worship for the angels in the seventh heaven, comparable to the Ka'bah on earth.

[1500] On the Day of Resurrection. Or "the sea which has overflowed."

[1501] Becoming dust and moving as clouds.

(19) [They will be told], "Eat and drink in satisfaction for what you used to do."

(20) They will be reclining on thrones lined up, and We will marry them to fair women with large, [beautiful] eyes.

(21) And those who believed and whose descendants followed them in faith - We will join with them their descendants, and We will not deprive them of anything of their deeds.[1502] Every person, for what he earned, is retained.[1503]

(22) And We will provide them with fruit and meat from whatever they desire.

(23) They will exchange with one another a cup [of wine] wherein [results] no ill speech or commission of sin.

(24) There will circulate among them [servant] boys [especially] for them, as if they were pearls well-protected.

(25) And they will approach one another, inquiring of each other.

(26) They will say, "Indeed, we were previously among our people fearful [of displeasing Allāh].

(27) So Allāh conferred favor upon us and protected us from the punishment of the Scorching Fire.

(28) Indeed, we used to supplicate[1504] Him before. Indeed, it is He who is the Beneficent, the Merciful."

(29) So remind, [O Muḥammad], for you are not, by the favor of your Lord, a soothsayer or a madman.

(30) Or do they say [of you], "A poet for whom we await a misfortune of time"?[1505]

(31) Say, "Wait, for indeed I am, with you, among the waiters."

(32) Or do their minds[1506] command them to [say] this, or are they a transgressing people?

[1502] "i.e., the reward thereof.

[1503] i.e., subject or held responsible. Literally, "a hostage.""

[1504] i.e., worship.

[1505] i.e., some accident or inevitable death.

[1506] In this expression is also a subtle allusion to the leaders of the Quraysh, who considered themselves to be great minds.

(33) Or do they say, "He has made it up"? Rather, they do not believe.

(34) Then let them produce a statement like it, if they should be truthful.

(35) Or were they created by nothing, or were they the creators [of themselves]?

(36) Or did they create the heavens and the earth? Rather, they are not certain.

(37) Or have they the depositories [containing the provision] of your Lord? Or are they the controllers [of them]?

(38) Or have they a stairway [into the heaven] upon which they listen? Then let their listener produce a clear authority [i.e., proof].

(39) Or has He daughters while you have sons?

(40) Or do you, [O Muḥammad], ask of them a payment, so they are by debt burdened down?

(41) Or have they [knowledge of] the unseen, so they write [it] down?

(42) Or do they intend a plan? But those who disbelieve - they are the object of a plan.

(43) Or have they a deity other than Allāh? Exalted is Allāh above whatever they associate with Him.

(44) And if they were to see a fragment from the sky falling,[1507] they would say, "[It is merely] clouds heaped up."

(45) So leave them until they meet their Day in which they will be struck insensible -

(46) The Day their plan will not avail them at all, nor will they be helped.

(47) And indeed, for those who have wronged is a punishment[1508] before that, but most of them do not know.

(48) And be patient, [O Muḥammad], for the decision of your Lord, for indeed, you are in Our eyes [i.e., sight]. And exalt [Allāh] with praise of your Lord when you arise

(49) And in a part of the night exalt Him and after [the setting of] the stars.

[1507] Marking the onset of Allāh's punishment, as they had requested.
[1508] If not in this world, in the grave.

Surah An-Najm

(1) By the star when it descends,

(2) Your companion [i.e., Muḥammad] has not strayed, nor has he erred,

(3) Nor does he speak from [his own] inclination.

(4) It is not but a revelation revealed,

(5) Taught to him by one intense in strength [i.e., Gabriel] -

(6) One of soundness.[1509] And he rose to [his] true form[1510]

(7) While he was in the higher [part of the] horizon.[1511]

(8) Then he approached and descended

(9) And was at a distance of two bow lengths or nearer.

(10) And he revealed to His Servant[1512] what he revealed [i.e., conveyed].

(11) The heart[1513] did not lie [about] what it saw.

(12) So will you dispute with him over what he saw?

(13) And he certainly saw him in another descent[1514]

(14) At the Lote Tree of the Utmost Boundary -

(15) Near it is the Garden of Refuge [i.e., Paradise] -

(16) When there covered the Lote Tree that which covered [it].[1515]

(17) The sight [of the Prophet (ﷺ)] did not swerve, nor did it transgress [its limit].

[1509] "i.e., strength of body and of mind.

[1510] Gabriel appeared to Muḥammad (ﷺ) at the outset of his prophethood in the angelic form in which Allāh originally created him."

[1511] i.e., in the sky, above the eastern horizon.

[1512] i.e., to the Servant of Allāh, Prophet Muḥammad (ﷺ).

[1513] i.e., mind or perception (of the Prophet [ﷺ]).

[1514] i.e., on another occasion. During his ascent into the heavens (al-Miʿrāj), the Prophet (ﷺ) also saw Gabriel in his true form.

[1515] Then and there he (ﷺ) saw Gabriel in angelic form.

(18) He certainly saw of the greatest signs of his Lord.

(19) So have you considered al-Lāt and al-ʿUzzā?

(20) And Manāt, the third - the other one?[1516]

(21) Is the male for you and for Him the female?

(22) That, then, is an unjust division.[1517]

(23) They are not but [mere] names you have named them - you and your forefathers - for which Allāh has sent down no authority. They follow not except assumption and what [their] souls desire, and there has already come to them from their Lord guidance.

(24) Or is there for man whatever he wishes?

(25) Rather, to Allāh belongs the Hereafter and the first [life].

(26) And how many angels there are in the heavens whose intercession will not avail at all except [only] after Allāh has permitted [it] to whom He wills and approves.

(27) Indeed, those who do not believe in the Hereafter name the angels female names,

(28) And they have thereof no knowledge. They follow not except assumption, and indeed, assumption avails not against the truth at all.

(29) So turn away from whoever turns his back on Our message and desires not except the worldly life.

(30) That is their sum of knowledge. Indeed, your Lord is most knowing of who strays from His way, and He is most knowing of who is guided.

(31) And to Allāh belongs whatever is in the heavens and whatever is in the earth - that He may recompense those who do evil with [the penalty of] what they have done and recompense those who do good with the best [reward] -

(32) Those who avoid the major sins and immoralities, only [committing] slight ones. Indeed, your Lord is vast in forgiveness. He was most knowing of you when He produced you from the earth and when you were fetuses in the wombs of your

---

[1516] The three names given in this and the previous verse are those of well-known "goddesses" which were worshipped by the pagan Arabs before the spread of Islām.
[1517] According to their own standards.

mothers. So do not claim yourselves to be pure; He is most knowing of who fears Him.

(33) Have you seen the one who turned away

(34) And gave a little and [then] refrained?

(35) Does he have knowledge of the unseen, so he sees?[1518]

(36) Or has he not been informed of what was in the scriptures of Moses

(37) And [of] Abraham, who fulfilled [his obligations] -

(38) That no bearer of burdens will bear the burden of another

(39) And that there is not for man except that [good] for which he strives

(40) And that his effort is going to be seen -

(41) Then he will be recompensed for it with the fullest recompense -

(42) And that to your Lord is the finality

(43) And that it is He who makes [one] laugh and weep

(44) And that it is He who causes death and gives life

(45) And that He creates the two mates - the male and female -

(46) From a sperm-drop when it is emitted

(47) And that [incumbent] upon Him is the other [i.e., next] creation.

(48) And that it is He who enriches and suffices

(49) And that it is He who is the Lord of Sirius[1519].

(50) And that He destroyed the first [people of] ʿAad.

(51) And Thamūd - and He did not spare [them] -

(52) And the people of Noah before. Indeed, it was they who were [even] more unjust and oppressing.

[1518] Knows that his provision will be exhausted if he spends on the poor, while Allāh (subḥānahu wa taʿālā) has promised otherwise.
[1519] A star worshipped by some of the pagan Arabs.

(53) And the overturned towns[1520] He hurled down.

(54) And covered them by that which He covered.[1521]

(55) Then which of the favors of your Lord do you doubt?

(56) This [Prophet (ﷺ)] is a warner from [i.e., like] the former warners.

(57) The Approaching Day has approached.

(58) Of it, [from those] besides Allāh, there is no remover.

(59) Then at this statement do you wonder?

(60) And you laugh and do not weep

(61) While you are proudly sporting?[1522]

(62) So prostrate to Allāh and worship [Him].

[1520] Whose inhabitants defied Prophet Lot.
[1521] i.e., a rain of stones.
[1522] Additional meanings are "singing [with expanded chest]," "heedless," or "lost in vain amusements."

Surah Al-Qamar

(1) The Hour has come near, and the moon has split [in two].[1523]

(2) And if they see a sign [i.e., miracle], they turn away and say, "Passing magic."[1524]

(3) And they denied and followed their inclinations. But for every matter is a [time of] settlement.

(4) And there has already come to them of information that in which there is deterrence.

(5) Extensive wisdom - but warning does not avail [them].

(6) So leave them, [O Muḥammad]. The Day the Caller[1525] calls to something forbidding,

(7) Their eyes humbled, they will emerge from the graves as if they were locusts spreading,

(8) Racing ahead toward the Caller. The disbelievers will say, "This is a difficult Day."

(9) The people of Noah denied before them, and they denied Our servant and said, "A madman," and he was repelled.

(10) So he invoked his Lord, "Indeed, I am overpowered, so help."

(11) Then We opened the gates of the heaven with rain pouring down

(12) And caused the earth to burst with springs, and the waters met for a matter already predestined.

(13) And We carried him on a [construction of] planks and nails,

(14) Sailing under Our observation as reward for he who had been denied.

(15) And We left it as a sign, so is there any who will remember?

[1523] This was a sign given by Allāh to Prophet Muḥammad (ﷺ) when the Quraysh challenged him to show them a miracle.
[1524] Or "Continuing magic."
[1525] Said to be an angel announcing the account and judgement.

(16) And how [severe] were My punishment and warning.[1526]

(17) And We have certainly made the Qur'ān easy for remembrance, so is there any who will remember?

(18) ʿAad denied; and how [severe] were My punishment and warning.

(19) Indeed, We sent upon them a screaming wind on a day of continuous misfortune,

(20) Extracting the people[1527] as if they were trunks of palm trees uprooted.

(21) And how [severe] were My punishment and warning.

(22) And We have certainly made the Qur'ān easy for remembrance, so is there any who will remember?

(23) Thamūd denied the warning.

(24) And said, "Is it one human being[1528] among us that we should follow? Indeed, we would then be in error and madness.

(25) Has the message been sent down upon him from among us? Rather, he is an insolent liar."

(26) They will know tomorrow who is the insolent liar.

(27) Indeed, We are sending the she-camel as trial for them, so watch them and be patient.[1529]

(28) And inform them that the water is shared between them,[1530] each [day of] drink attended [by turn].

(29) But they called their companion,[1531] and he dared[1532] and hamstrung [her].

(30) And how [severe] were My punishment and warning.

(31) Indeed, We sent upon them one shriek [i.e., blast from the sky], and they became like the dry twig fragments of an [animal] pen.

[1526] To those after them, who were expected to derive a lesson from previous occurrences.
[1527] From their hiding places.
[1528] i.e., the prophet Ṣāliḥ.
[1529] This and the following verse are an address to Ṣāliḥ (upon him be peace).
[1530] i.e., between the tribe of Thamūd and the she-camel - a day for each to drink.
[1531] "i.e., the worst and most despicable among them.
[1532] Or "he took," referring to his sword or to the she-camel."

(32) And We have certainly made the Qur'ān easy for remembrance, so is there any who will remember?

(33) The people of Lot denied the warning.

(34) Indeed, We sent upon them a storm of stones, except the family of Lot - We saved them before dawn.

(35) As favor from Us. Thus do We reward he who is grateful.

(36) And he had already warned them of Our assault, but they disputed the warning.

(37) And they had demanded from him his guests, but We obliterated their eyes, [saying], "Taste My punishment and warning."

(38) And there came upon them by morning an abiding punishment.

(39) So taste My punishment and warning.

(40) And We have certainly made the Qur'ān easy for remembrance, so is there any who will remember?

(41) And there certainly came to the people of Pharaoh warning.

(42) They denied Our signs, all of them, so We seized them with a seizure of one Exalted in Might and Perfect in Ability.

(43) Are your disbelievers better than those [former ones], or have you immunity in the scriptures?

(44) Or do they say, "We are an assembly supporting [each other]"?

(45) [Their] assembly will be defeated, and they will turn their backs [in retreat].[1533]

(46) But the Hour is their appointment [for due punishment], and the Hour is more disastrous and more bitter.

(47) Indeed, the criminals are in error and madness.[1534]

(48) The Day they are dragged into the Fire on their faces [it will be said], "Taste the touch of Saqar."[1535]

(49) Indeed, all things We created with predestination.

[1533] This foretold event took place on the day of Badr.
[1534] Or "in blazing fires."
[1535] One of the proper names of Hell.

(50) And Our command is but one, like a glance of the eye.

(51) And We have already destroyed your kinds,[1536] so is there any who will remember?

(52) And everything they did is in written records.

(53) And every small and great [thing] is inscribed.

(54) Indeed, the righteous will be among gardens and rivers,

(55) In a seat of honor near a Sovereign, Perfect in Ability.[1537]

[1536] i.e., those similar to you in attitude and behavior when they rejected Allāh's messengers.
[1537] Who accomplishes whatever He wills whenever He wills.

Surah Ar-Rahman

(1) The Most Merciful

(2) Taught the Qur'ān,

(3) Created man,

(4) [And] taught him eloquence.

(5) The sun and the moon [move] by precise calculation,

(6) And the stars and trees prostrate.[1538]

(7) And the heaven He raised and imposed the balance

(8) That you not transgress within the balance.

(9) And establish weight in justice and do not make deficient the balance.

(10) And the earth He laid [out] for the creatures.

(11) Therein is fruit and palm trees having sheaths [of dates]

(12) And grain having husks and scented plants.

(13) So which of the favors of your Lord would you deny?[1539]

(14) He created man from clay like [that of] pottery.

(15) And He created the jinn from a smokeless flame of fire.

(16) So which of the favors of your Lord would you deny?

(17) [He is] Lord of the two sunrises and Lord of the two sunsets.[1540]

(18) So which of the favors of your Lord would you deny?

(19) He released the two seas,[1541] meeting [one another];

(20) Between them is a barrier so neither of them transgresses.

[1538] They submit obediently to the laws of Allāh. See 22:18. An additional meaning of "najm" is vegetation of a kind without a trunk, stalk or stem.

[1539] Literally, "you two," addressing the species of mankind and jinn.

[1540] i.e., the points of sunrise in the east and sunset in the west in both summer and winter.

[1541] Two bodies of water or two sea waters of distinct characteristics.

(21) So which of the favors of your Lord would you deny?

(22) From both of them emerge pearl and coral.

(23) So which of the favors of your Lord would you deny?

(24) And to Him belong the ships [with sails] elevated in the sea like mountains.

(25) So which of the favors of your Lord would you deny?

(26) Everyone upon it [i.e., the earth] will perish,

(27) And there will remain the Face[1542] of your Lord, Owner of Majesty and Honor.

(28) So which of the favors of your Lord would you deny?

(29) Whoever is within the heavens and earth asks Him; every day He is in [i.e., bringing about] a matter.[1543]

(30) So which of the favors of your Lord would you deny?

(31) We will attend to you, O prominent beings.[1544]

(32) So which of the favors of your Lord would you deny?

(33) O company of jinn and mankind, if you are able to pass beyond the regions of the heavens and the earth, then pass. You will not pass except by authority [from Allāh].

(34) So which of the favors of your Lord would you deny?

(35) There will be sent upon you a flame of fire and smoke,[1545] and you will not defend yourselves.

(36) So which of the favors of your Lord would you deny?

(37) And when the heaven is split open and becomes rose-colored like oil[1546]

(38) So which of the favors of your Lord would you deny? -

(39) Then on that Day none will be asked about his sin among men or jinn.[1547]

____

[1542] See footnote to 2:19.
[1543] For each of His creatures.
[1544] Specifically two: mankind and jinn.
[1545] Another possible meaning is liquefied brass or copper.
[1546] Or "like a tanned skin."
[1547] Once they have been condemned to the Fire.

(40) So which of the favors of your Lord would you deny?

(41) The criminals will be known by their marks, and they will be seized by the forelocks and the feet.

(42) So which of the favors of your Lord would you deny?

(43) This is Hell, which the criminals deny.

(44) They will circulate between it and scalding water, heated [to the utmost degree].

(45) So which of the favors of your Lord would you deny?

(46) But for he who has feared the position of his Lord[1548] are two gardens -

(47) So which of the favors of your Lord would you deny? -

(48) Having [spreading] branches.

(49) So which of the favors of your Lord would you deny?

(50) In both of them are two springs, flowing.

(51) So which of the favors of your Lord would you deny?

(52) In both of them are of every fruit, two kinds.

(53) So which of the favors of your Lord would you deny?

(54) [They are] reclining on beds whose linings are of silk brocade, and the fruit of the two gardens is hanging low.

(55) So which of the favors of your Lord would you deny?

(56) In them are women limiting [their] glances,[1549] untouched[1550] before them by man or jinnī -

(57) So which of the favors of your Lord would you deny? -

(58) As if they were rubies and coral.[1551]

(59) So which of the favors of your Lord would you deny?

[1548] An alternative meaning is "the standing [for account] before his Lord."
[1549] "To their own mates, i.e., being chaste and modest.
[1550] Literally, they have not been caused to bleed by loss of virginity."
[1551] In purity, color and beauty.

(60) Is the reward for good [anything] but good?

(61) So which of the favors of your Lord would you deny?

(62) And below them both [in excellence] are two [other] gardens -

(63) So which of the favors of your Lord would you deny? -

(64) Dark green [in color].

(65) So which of the favors of your Lord would you deny?

(66) In both of them are two springs, spouting.

(67) So which of the favors of your Lord would you deny?

(68) In both of them are fruit and palm trees and pomegranates.

(69) So which of the favors of your Lord would you deny?

(70) In them are good and beautiful women -

(71) So which of the favors of your Lord would you deny? -

(72) Fair ones reserved in pavilions -

(73) So which of the favors of your Lord would you deny? -

(74) Untouched before them by man or jinnī -

(75) So which of the favors of your Lord would you deny? -

(76) Reclining on green cushions and beautiful fine carpets.

(77) So which of the favors of your Lord would you deny?

(78) Blessed is the name of your Lord, Owner of Majesty and Honor.

Surah Al-Waqi'ah

(1) When the Occurrence occurs,

(2) There is, at its occurrence, no denial.

(3) It will bring down [some] and raise up [others].[1552]

(4) When the earth is shaken with convulsion

(5) And the mountains are broken down, crumbling

(6) And become dust dispersing,

(7) And you become [of] three kinds:

(8) Then the companions of the right - what are the companions of the right?[1553]

(9) And the companions of the left - what are companions of the left?[1554]

(10) And the forerunners, the forerunners[1555] -

(11) Those are the ones brought near [to Allāh]

(12) In the Gardens of Pleasure,

(13) A [large] company of the former peoples

(14) And a few of the later peoples,

(15) On thrones woven [with ornament],

(16) Reclining on them, facing each other.

(17) There will circulate among them young boys made eternal.

(18) With vessels, pitchers and a cup [of wine] from a flowing spring -

(19) No headache will they have therefrom, nor will they be intoxicated -

(20) And fruit of what they select

[1552] According to their deeds rather than wealth and social position, as is the case in this world.

[1553] i.e., those given their records in their right hand and who are destined for Paradise.

[1554] i.e., those given their records in their left hand and who are destined for Hell.

[1555] The words can also be understood as a complete sentence, i.e., "The forerunners [in good deeds] are the forerunners [in entering Paradise]."

(21) And the meat of fowl, from whatever they desire.

(22) And [for them are] fair women with large, [beautiful] eyes,

(23) The likenesses of pearls well-protected,

(24) As reward for what they used to do.

(25) They will not hear therein ill speech or commission of sin -

(26) Only a saying [of] peace, peace.

(27) The companions of the right - what are the companions of the right?

(28) [They will be] among lote trees with thorns removed.

(29) And [banana] trees layered [with fruit].

(30) And shade extended.

(31) And water poured out

(32) And fruit, abundant [and varied],

(33) Neither limited [to season] nor forbidden,

(34) And [upon] beds raised high.

(35) Indeed, We have produced them [i.e., the women of Paradise] in a [new] creation

(36) And made them virgins,

(37) Devoted [to their husbands] and of equal age,

(38) For the companions of the right [who are]

(39) A company of the former peoples

(40) And a company of the later peoples.

(41) And the companions of the left - what are the companions of the left?

(42) [They will be] in scorching fire and scalding water

(43) And a shade of black smoke,

(44) Neither cool nor beneficial.

(45) Indeed they were, before that, indulging in affluence,

(46) And they used to persist in the great violation,[1556]

(47) And they used to say, "When we die and become dust and bones, are we indeed to be resurrected?

(48) And our forefathers [as well]?"

(49) Say, [O Muḥammad], "Indeed, the former and later peoples

(50) Are to be gathered together for the appointment of a known Day."

(51) Then indeed you, O those astray [who are] deniers,

(52) Will be eating from trees of zaqqūm

(53) And filling with it your bellies

(54) And drinking on top of it from scalding water.

(55) And will drink as the drinking of thirsty camels.

(56) That is their accommodation on the Day of Recompense.

(57) We have created you, so why do you not believe?

(58) Have you seen that which you emit?[1557]

(59) Is it you who creates it, or are We the Creator?

(60) We have decreed death among you, and We are not to be outdone

(61) In that We will change your likenesses and produce you in that [form] which you do not know.[1558]

(62) And you have already known the first creation, so will you not remember?

(63) And have you seen that [seed] which you sow?

(64) Is it you who makes it grow, or are We the grower?

[1556] i.e., shirk (association with Allāh) or disbelief.

[1557] i.e., semen, which contains the potential for human life.

[1558] An alternative meaning has also been given: "...in that We will replace the likes of you [with others upon the earth] and create you [in the Hereafter] in that which you do not know."

(65) If We willed, We could make it [dry] debris, and you would remain in wonder,[1559]

(66) [Saying], "Indeed, we are [now] in debt;

(67) Rather, we have been deprived."

(68) And have you seen the water that you drink?

(69) Is it you who brought it down from the clouds, or is it We who bring it down?

(70) If We willed, We could make it bitter, so why are you not grateful?

(71) And have you seen the fire that you ignite?

(72) Is it you who produced its tree, or are We the producer?

(73) We have made it a reminder[1560] and provision for the travelers,[1561]

(74) So exalt the name of your Lord, the Most Great.

(75) Then I swear by the setting of the stars,[1562]

(76) And indeed, it is an oath - if you could know - [most] great.

(77) Indeed, it is a noble Qur'ān.

(78) In a Register well-protected;[1563]

(79) None touch it except the purified [i.e., the angels].

(80) [It is] a revelation from the Lord of the worlds.

(81) Then is it to this statement that you are indifferent

(82) And make [the thanks for] your provision that you deny [the Provider]?

(83) Then why, when it [i.e., the soul at death] reaches the throat

(84) And you are at that time looking on -

[1559] At what had happened or remain in a state of shock. Another meaning is "in regret".
[1560] "Of the great fire of Hell.
[1561] In the form of flints or other means by which to ignite fire. Travelers are mentioned because of the special convenience to them, although it is a provision for all people in general."
[1562] Allāh (subḥānahu wa taʿālā) confirms absolutely by oath.
[1563] The Preserved Slate (al-Lawḥ al-Maḥfūẓ), which is with Allāh (subḥānahu wa taʿālā).

(85) And We [i.e., Our angels] are nearer to him than you, but you do not see

(86) Then why do you not, if you are not to be recompensed,

(87) Bring it back,[1564] if you should be truthful?

(88) And if he [i.e., the deceased] was of those brought near [to Allāh],

(89) Then [for him is] rest and bounty and a garden of pleasure.

(90) And if he was of the companions of the right,

(91) Then [the angels will say], "Peace for you; [you are] from the companions of the right."

(92) But if he was of the deniers [who were] astray,

(93) Then [for him is] accommodation of scalding water

(94) And burning in Hellfire.

(95) Indeed, this is the true certainty,

(96) So exalt the name of your Lord, the Most Great.

[1564] i.e., return the soul to the body, meaning that just as you cannot prevent death when it is decreed, you will not escape the recompense when it is decreed.

Surah Al-Hadeed

(1) Whatever is in the heavens and earth exalts Allāh,[1565] and He is the Exalted in Might, the Wise.

(2) His is the dominion of the heavens and earth. He gives life and causes death, and He is over all things competent.

(3) He is the First[1566] and the Last,[1567] the Ascendant[1568] and the Intimate,[1569] and He is, of all things, Knowing.

(4) It is He who created the heavens and earth in six days and then established Himself above the Throne.[1570] He knows what penetrates into the earth and what emerges from it and what descends from the heaven and what ascends therein; and He is with you[1571] wherever you are. And Allāh, of what you do, is Seeing.

(5) His is the dominion of the heavens and earth. And to Allāh are returned [all] matters.

(6) He causes the night to enter the day and causes the day to enter the night, and He is Knowing of that within the breasts.

(7) Believe in Allāh and His Messenger and spend out of that in which He has made you successive inheritors. For those who have believed among you and spent,[1572] there will be a great reward.

(8) And why do you not believe in Allāh while the Messenger invites you to believe in your Lord and He has taken your covenant, if you should [truly] be believers?

(9) It is He who sends down upon His Servant [Muḥammad (ﷺ)] verses of clear evidence that He may bring you out from darknesses into the light. And indeed, Allāh is to you Kind and Merciful.

[1565] By praising Him and declaring Him far above and beyond any failure or imperfection.

[1566] "Before whom nothing existed. Also, He who is supreme, foremost or uppermost.

[1567] Enduring eternally when nothing else remains.

[1568] Nothing being above Him. Another meaning is "the Apparent," i.e., evident through His creation and revelation.

[1569] Nothing being nearer than Him by way of His knowledge. Another meaning is "the Unapparent," i.e., concealed from man's physical senses."

[1570] "See footnotes to 2:19 and 7:54.

[1571] In knowledge - observing and witnessing."

[1572] In ways pleasing to Allāh.

(10) And why do you not spend in the cause of Allāh while to Allāh belongs the heritage of the heavens and the earth? Not equal among you are those who spent before the conquest [of Makkah] and fought [and those who did so after it]. Those are greater in degree than they who spent afterwards and fought. But to all Allāh has promised the best [reward]. And Allāh, of what you do, is Aware.

(11) Who is it that would loan Allāh a goodly loan so He will multiply it for him and he will have a noble reward?

(12) On the Day you see the believing men and believing women, their light proceeding before them and on their right, [it will be said], "Your good tidings today are [of] gardens beneath which rivers flow, wherein you will abide eternally." That is what is the great attainment.

(13) On the [same] Day the hypocrite men and hypocrite women will say to those who believed, "Wait for us that we may acquire some of your light." It will be said, "Go back behind you[1573] and seek light." And a wall will be placed between them with a door, its interior containing mercy, but on the outside of it is torment.

(14) They [i.e., the hypocrites] will call to them [i.e., the believers], "Were we not with you?" They will say, "Yes, but you afflicted yourselves[1574] and awaited [misfortune for us] and doubted, and wishful thinking deluded you until there came the command of Allāh. And the Deceiver [i.e., Satan] deceived you concerning Allāh.

(15) So today no ransom will be taken from you or from those who disbelieved. Your refuge is the Fire. It is most worthy of you, and wretched is the destination."

(16) Has the time not come for those who have believed that their hearts should become humbly submissive at the remembrance of Allāh and what has come down of the truth? And let them not be like those who were given the Scripture before, and a long period passed over them, so their hearts hardened; and many of them are defiantly disobedient.

(17) Know that Allāh gives life to the earth after its lifelessness. We have made clear to you the signs; perhaps you will understand.[1575]

(18) Indeed, the men who practice charity and the women who practice charity and [they who] have loaned Allāh a goodly loan - it will be multiplied for them, and they will have a noble reward.

[1573] To where light was acquired, i.e., in the worldly life.
[1574] By hypocrisy or by falling into temptations.
[1575] That similarly, Allāh (subḥānahu wa taʿālā) can soften a heart after its hardness and guide one who had previously been astray.

(19) And those who have believed in Allāh and His messengers - those are [in the ranks of] the supporters of truth and the martyrs, with their Lord. For them is their reward and their light.[1576] But those who have disbelieved and denied Our verses - those are the companions of Hellfire.

(20) Know that the life of this world is but amusement and diversion and adornment and boasting to one another and competition in increase of wealth and children - like the example of a rain whose [resulting] plant growth pleases the tillers; then it dries and you see it turned yellow; then it becomes [scattered] debris. And in the Hereafter is severe punishment and forgiveness from Allāh and approval. And what is the worldly life except the enjoyment of delusion.

(21) Race [i.e., compete] toward forgiveness from your Lord and a Garden whose width is like the width of the heavens and earth, prepared for those who believed in Allāh and His messengers. That is the bounty of Allāh which He gives to whom He wills, and Allāh is the possessor of great bounty.

(22) No disaster strikes upon the earth or among yourselves except that it is in a register[1577] before We bring it into being - indeed that, for Allāh, is easy -

(23) In order that you not despair over what has eluded you and not exult [in pride] over what He has given you. And Allāh does not like everyone self-deluded and boastful -

(24) [Those] who are stingy and enjoin upon people stinginess. And whoever turns away[1578] - then indeed, Allāh is the Free of need, the Praiseworthy.

(25) We have already sent Our messengers with clear evidences and sent down with them the Scripture and the balance that the people may maintain [their affairs] in justice. And We sent down iron, wherein is great military might and benefits for the people, and so that Allāh may make evident those who support Him and His messengers unseen. Indeed, Allāh is Powerful and Exalted in Might.

(26) And We have already sent Noah and Abraham and placed in their descendants prophethood and scripture; and among them is he who is guided, but many of them are defiantly disobedient.

[1576] Another accepted meaning is "And those who have believed in Allāh and His messengers - they are the supporters of truth. And the martyrs, with their Lord, will have their reward and their light."

[1577] i.e., the Preserved Slate (al-Lawḥ al-Maḥfūẓ).

[1578] Refusing to spend for Allāh's cause or refusing obedience to Him.

(27) Then We sent following their footsteps [i.e., traditions] Our messengers and followed [them] with Jesus, the son of Mary, and gave him the Gospel. And We placed in the hearts of those who followed him compassion and mercy and monasticism, which they innovated; We did not prescribe it for them except [that they did so] seeking the approval of Allāh. But they did not observe it with due observance. So We gave the ones who believed among them their reward, but many of them are defiantly disobedient.

(28) O you who have believed, fear Allāh and believe in His Messenger; He will [then] give you a double portion of His mercy and make for you a light by which you will walk and forgive you; and Allāh is Forgiving and Merciful.

(29) [This is] so that the People of the Scripture may know that they are not able [to obtain] anything from the bounty of Allāh[1579] and that [all] bounty is in the hand[1580] of Allāh; He gives it to whom He wills. And Allāh is the possessor of great bounty.

[1579] "As long as they refuse to believe in the message of Allāh which was conveyed through Muḥammad (ﷺ).
[1580] See footnote to 2:19."

Surah Al-Mujadilah

(1) Certainly has Allāh heard the speech of the one who argues [i.e., pleads] with you, [O Muḥammad], concerning her husband and directs her complaint to Allāh. And Allāh hears your dialogue; indeed, Allāh is Hearing and Seeing.

(2) Those who pronounce ẓihār[1581] among you [to separate] from their wives - they are not [consequently] their mothers. Their mothers are none but those who gave birth to them. And indeed, they are saying an objectionable statement and a falsehood. But indeed, Allāh is Pardoning and Forgiving.

(3) And those who pronounce ẓihār from their wives and then [wish to] go back on what they said - then [there must be] the freeing of a slave before they touch one another. That is what you are admonished thereby; and Allāh is Aware of what you do.

(4) And he who does not find [a slave] - then a fast for two months consecutively[1582] before they touch one another; and he who is unable - then the feeding of sixty poor persons. That is for you to believe [completely] in Allāh and His Messenger; and those are the limits [set by] Allāh. And for the disbelievers is a painful punishment.

(5) Indeed, those who oppose Allāh and His Messenger are abased as those before them were abased. And We have certainly sent down verses of clear evidence. And for the disbelievers is a humiliating punishment

(6) On the Day when Allāh will resurrect them all and inform them of what they did. Allāh had enumerated it, while they forgot it; and Allāh is, over all things, Witness.[1583]

(7) Have you not considered that Allāh knows what is in the heavens and what is on the earth? There are not three in a private conversation but that He is the fourth of them,[1584] nor are there five but that He is the sixth of them - and no less than that and no more except that He is with them [in knowledge] wherever they are. Then

---

[1581] The saying by a husband to his wife, "You are to me like the back of my mother," meaning unlawful to approach. This was a type of divorce practiced by the Arabs before the prophethood of Muḥammad (ﷺ).

[1582] See footnote to 4:92.

[1583] See footnote to 4:79.

[1584] Through His knowledge of them and their secrets.

He will inform them of what they did, on the Day of Resurrection. Indeed Allāh is, of all things, Knowing.

(8) Have you not considered those who were forbidden from private conversation [i.e., ridicule and conspiracy] and then return to that which they were forbidden and converse among themselves about sin and aggression and disobedience to the Messenger? And when they come to you, they greet you with that [word] by which Allāh does not greet you[1585] and say among themselves, "Why does Allāh not punish us for what we say?" Sufficient for them is Hell, which they will [enter to] burn, and wretched is the destination.

(9) O you who have believed, when you converse privately, do not converse about sin and aggression and disobedience to the Messenger but converse about righteousness and piety. And fear Allāh, to whom you will be gathered.

(10) Private conversation is only from Satan that he may grieve those who have believed,[1586] but he will not harm them at all except by permission of Allāh. And upon Allāh let the believers rely.

(11) O you who have believed, when you are told, "Space yourselves" in assemblies, then make space; Allāh will make space for you.[1587] And when you are told, "Arise,"[1588] then arise; Allāh will raise those who have believed among you and those who were given knowledge, by degrees. And Allāh is Aware of what you do.

(12) O you who have believed, when you [wish to] privately consult the Messenger, present before your consultation a charity. That is better for you and purer. But if you find not [the means] - then indeed, Allāh is Forgiving and Merciful.

(13) Have you feared to present before your consultation charities? Then when you do not and Allāh has forgiven you, then [at least] establish prayer and give zakāh and obey Allāh and His Messenger. And Allāh is Aware of what you do.

[1585] This is in reference to the Jews who would greet the Muslims with the words "Death be upon you," rather than "Peace."

[1586] The reference may be to the sinful type of conversation, as mentioned in the previous verses, or to the practice of two persons speaking in confidence in the presence of a third, which might lead him to assume that he is the subject of their conversation. Such behavior was prohibited by the Prophet (ﷺ) in narrations of al-Bukhārī and Muslim.

[1587] "In His mercy, in Paradise, or in everything good.

[1588] To prayer, to battle, or to good deeds."

(14) Have you not considered those who make allies of a people with whom Allāh has become angry? They are neither of you nor of them, and they swear to untruth while they know [they are lying].

(15) Allāh has prepared for them a severe punishment. Indeed, it was evil that they were doing.

(16) They took their [false] oaths as a cover, so they averted [people] from the way of Allāh, and for them is a humiliating punishment.

(17) Never will their wealth or their children avail them against Allāh at all. Those are the companions of the Fire; they will abide therein eternally

(18) On the Day Allāh will resurrect them all, and they will swear to Him as they swear to you and think that they are [standing] on something.[1589] Unquestionably, it is they who are the liars.

(19) Satan has overcome them and made them forget the remembrance of Allāh. Those are the party of Satan. Unquestionably, the party of Satan - they will be the losers.

(20) Indeed, the ones who oppose Allāh and His Messenger - those will be among the most humbled.

(21) Allāh has written [i.e., decreed], "I will surely overcome, I and My messengers." Indeed, Allāh is Powerful and Exalted in Might.

(22) You will not find a people who believe in Allāh and the Last Day having affection for those who oppose Allāh and His Messenger, even if they were their fathers or their sons or their brothers or their kindred. Those - He has decreed within their hearts faith and supported them with spirit[1590] from Him. And We will admit them to gardens beneath which rivers flow, wherein they abide eternally. Allāh is pleased with them, and they are pleased with Him - those are the party of Allāh. Unquestionably, the party of Allāh - they are the successful.

[1589] They assume that their lies will be believed and that they will escape detection as they did in worldly life.

[1590] i.e., "that which gives life," explained as the guidance of the Qur'ān or victory over their opponents.

Surah Al-Hashr

(1) Whatever is in the heavens and whatever is on the earth exalts Allāh,[1591] and He is the Exalted in Might, the Wise.

(2) It is He who expelled the ones who disbelieved among the People of the Scripture[1592] from their homes at the first gathering.[1593] You did not think they would leave, and they thought that their fortresses would protect them from Allāh; but [the decree of] Allāh came upon them from where they had not expected, and He cast terror into their hearts [so] they destroyed their houses by their [own] hands and the hands of the believers. So take warning, O people of vision.

(3) And if not that Allāh had decreed for them evacuation, He would have punished them in [this] world, and for them in the Hereafter is the punishment of the Fire.

(4) That is because they opposed Allāh and His Messenger. And whoever opposes Allāh - then indeed, Allāh is severe in penalty.

(5) Whatever you have cut down of [their] palm trees or left standing on their trunks - it was by permission of Allāh and so He would disgrace the defiantly disobedient.

(6) And what Allāh restored [of property] to His Messenger from them - you did not spur for it [in an expedition] any horses or camels,[1594] but Allāh gives His messengers power over whom He wills, and Allāh is over all things competent.

(7) And what Allāh restored to His Messenger from the people of the towns - it is for Allāh and for the Messenger and for [his] near relatives[1595] and orphans and the needy and the [stranded] traveler[1596] - so that it will not be a perpetual distribution among the rich from among you. And whatever the Messenger has given you - take;

[1591] See footnote to 57:1.

[1592] "Referring to the Jews of Banun-Naḍeer, who broke their pact with the Messenger of Allāh (ﷺ).

[1593] This was the first tme they had ever been gathered and expelled."

[1594] Meaning that they went through no hardship (i.e., war) to obtain it.

[1595] "Those of Banū Hāshim and Banū Muṭṭalib, whom he (ﷺ) had prohibited from accepting zakāh.

[1596] This ruling concerning properties abandoned by an enemy without a war effort differs from that in Sūrah al-Anfāl, verse 41, which refers to spoils of war in which four fifths is distributed among those who fought in Allāh's cause."

and what he has forbidden you - refrain from. And fear Allāh; indeed, Allāh is severe in penalty.

(8) For the poor emigrants who were expelled from their homes and their properties, seeking bounty from Allāh and [His] approval and supporting [the cause of] Allāh and His Messenger, [there is also a share]. Those are the truthful.

(9) And [also for] those who were settled in the Home [i.e.,al-Madīnah] and [adopted] the faith before them.[1597] They love those who emigrated to them and find not any want in their breasts of what they [i.e., the emigrants] were given but give [them] preference over themselves, even though they are in privation. And whoever is protected from the stinginess of his soul - it is those who will be the successful.

(10) And [there is a share for] those who come after them, saying, "Our Lord, forgive us and our brothers who preceded us in faith and put not in our hearts [any] resentment toward those who have believed. Our Lord, indeed You are Kind and Merciful."

(11) Have you not considered those who practice hypocrisy, saying to their brothers [i.e., associates] who have disbelieved among the People of the Scripture, "If you are expelled, we will surely leave with you, and we will not obey, in regard to you, anyone - ever; and if you are fought, we will surely aid you." But Allāh testifies that they are liars.

(12) If they are expelled, they will not leave with them, and if they are fought, they will not aid them. And [even] if they should aid them, they will surely turn their backs; then [thereafter] they will not be aided.

(13) You [believers] are more fearful within their breasts than Allāh. That is because they are a people who do not understand.

(14) They will not fight you all except within fortified cities or from behind walls. Their violence [i.e., enmity] among themselves is severe. You think they are together, but their hearts are diverse. That is because they are a people who do not reason.

(15) [Theirs is] like the example of those shortly before them: they tasted the bad consequence of their affair, and they will have a painful punishment.

[1597] Before the settlement of the emigrants (Muhājireen) among the Anṣār, for whom a share is delegated as well.

(16) [The hypocrites are] like the example of Satan when he says to man, "Disbelieve." But when he disbelieves, he says, "Indeed, I am disassociated from you. Indeed, I fear Allāh, Lord of the worlds."

(17) So the outcome for both of them is that they will be in the Fire, abiding eternally therein. And that is the recompense of the wrongdoers.

(18) O you who have believed, fear Allāh. And let every soul look to what it has put forth for tomorrow - and fear Allāh. Indeed, Allāh is Aware of what you do.

(19) And be not like those who forgot Allāh, so He made them forget themselves. Those are the defiantly disobedient.

(20) Not equal are the companions of the Fire and the companions of Paradise. The companions of Paradise - they are the attainers [of success].

(21) If We had sent down this Qur'ān upon a mountain, you would have seen it humbled and splitting from fear of Allāh. And these examples We present to the people that perhaps they will give thought.

(22) He is Allāh, other than whom there is no deity, Knower of the unseen and the witnessed.[1598] He is the Entirely Merciful, the Especially Merciful.

(23) He is Allāh, other than whom there is no deity, the Sovereign,[1599] the Pure,[1600] the Perfection,[1601] the Grantor of Security,[1602] the Overseer,[1603] the Exalted in Might,[1604] the Compeller,[1605] the Superior.[1606] Exalted is Allāh above whatever they associate with Him.

[1598] See footnotes to 6:73.

[1599] "And owner of everything in existence.
[1600] i.e., transcendent above any aspect belonging to His creation. Also, the possessor and grantor of blessings.
[1601] Literally, "Free" from any imperfection. Also, "Peace" or "Soundness."
[1602] And safety, i.e., reassurance that His promise is always fulfilled. Also, He who bestows faith.
[1603] i.e., who observes, guards and protects. Also, "the Criterion."
[1604] Refer to footnote in 2:129.
[1605] Whose irresistible force is without limitation; the one above all things who compels the creation to be as He wills it. Also, "the Amender" or "the Rectifier" who repairs, restores, completes or sets something right once again, out of His mercy.
[1606] Supreme, complete and perfect in His essence, attributes and actions."

(24) He is Allāh, the Creator,[1607] the Producer,[1608] the Fashioner;[1609] to Him belong the best names.[1610] Whatever is in the heavens and earth is exalting Him. And He is the Exalted in Might, the Wise.[1611]

[1607] "i.e., He who destined existence for His creation.
[1608] i.e., He who brings His creation into existence.
[1609] i.e., He who gives every creation its particular form.
[1610] Refer to the final paragraphs of the "Introduction" for a brief discussion of these attributes.
[1611] Refer to footnote in 6:18."

Surah Al-Mumtahanah

(1) O you who have believed, do not take My enemies and your enemies as allies,[1612] extending to them affection while they have disbelieved in what came to you of the truth, having driven out the Prophet and yourselves [only] because you believe in Allāh, your Lord. If you have come out for jihād [i.e., fighting or striving] in My cause and seeking means to My approval, [take them not as friends]. You confide to them affection [i.e., instruction], but I am most knowing of what you have concealed and what you have declared. And whoever does it among you has certainly strayed from the soundness of the way.

(2) If they gain dominance over you, they would be [i.e., behave] to you as enemies and extend against you their hands and their tongues with evil, and they wish you would disbelieve.

(3) Never will your relatives or your children benefit you; the Day of Resurrection He will judge between you. And Allāh, of what you do, is Seeing.

(4) There has already been for you an excellent pattern[1613] in Abraham and those with him, when they said to their people, "Indeed, we are disassociated from you and from whatever you worship other than Allāh. We have denied you, and there has appeared between us and you animosity and hatred forever until you believe in Allāh alone" - except for the saying of Abraham to his father, "I will surely ask forgiveness for you, but I have not [power to do] for you anything against Allāh. Our Lord, upon You we have relied, and to You we have returned, and to You is the destination.

(5) Our Lord, make us not [objects of] torment for the disbelievers and forgive us, our Lord. Indeed, it is You who is the Exalted in Might, the Wise."

(6) There has certainly been for you in them an excellent pattern for anyone whose hope is in Allāh and the Last Day. And whoever turns away - then indeed, Allāh is the Free of need, the Praiseworthy.

(7) Perhaps Allāh will put, between you and those to whom you have been enemies among them, affection. And Allāh is competent,[1614] and Allāh is Forgiving and Merciful.

[1612] i.e., close associates and friends.
[1613] An example to be followed.
[1614] To accomplish this or whatever He should will.

(8) Allāh does not forbid you from those who do not fight you because of religion and do not expel you from your homes - from being righteous toward them and acting justly toward them. Indeed, Allāh loves those who act justly.

(9) Allāh only forbids you from those who fight you because of religion and expel you from your homes and aid in your expulsion - [forbids] that you make allies[1615] of them. And whoever makes allies of them, then it is those who are the wrongdoers.

(10) O you who have believed, when the believing women come to you as emigrants, examine [i.e., test] them. Allāh is most knowing as to their faith. And if you know them to be believers, then do not return them to the disbelievers; they are not lawful [wives] for them, nor are they lawful [husbands] for them. But give them [i.e., the disbelievers] what they have spent.[1616] And there is no blame upon you if you marry them when you have given them their due compensation [i.e., mahr]. And hold not to marriage bonds with disbelieving women, but ask for what you have spent and let them [i.e., the disbelievers] ask for what they have spent.[1617] That is the judgement of Allāh; He judges between you. And Allāh is Knowing and Wise.

(11) And if you have lost any of your wives to the disbelievers and you subsequently obtain [something],[1618] then give those whose wives have gone the equivalent of what they had spent. And fear Allāh, in whom you are believers.

(12) O Prophet, when the believing women come to you pledging to you that they will not associate anything with Allāh, nor will they steal, nor will they commit unlawful sexual intercourse, nor will they kill their children, nor will they bring forth a slander they have invented between their arms and legs,[1619] nor will they disobey you in what is right - then accept their pledge and ask forgiveness for them of Allāh. Indeed, Allāh is Forgiving and Merciful.

(13) O you who have believed, do not make allies of a people with whom Allāh has become angry. They have despaired of [reward in] the Hereafter just as the

---

[1615] See footnote to verse 1 of this sūrah.

[1616] "For marriage, i.e., compensate their loss.

[1617] When a disbelieving wife chose to join the disbelievers, a Muslim husband could demand in return the equivalent of her mahr. Likewise, the disbelievers had a similar right when a believing woman joined the Muslims. This and the following verses were revealed subsequent to the Treaty of al-Ḥudaybiyyah."

[1618] From the side of the disbelievers, i.e., war booty or a believing woman seeking refuge with the Muslims.

[1619] This is an allusion to pregnancy and childbirth, i.e., to falsely attribute a child (whether adopted or born of adultery) to a woman's husband.

disbelievers have despaired of [meeting] the companions [i.e., inhabitants] of the graves.

Surah As-Saff

(1) Whatever is in the heavens and whatever is on the earth exalts Allāh,[1620] and He is the Exalted in Might, the Wise.

(2) O you who have believed, why do you say what you do not do?

(3) Greatly hateful in the sight of Allāh is that you say what you do not do.

(4) Indeed, Allāh loves those who fight in His cause in a row as though they are a [single] structure joined firmly.

(5) And [mention, O Muḥammad], when Moses said to his people, "O my people, why do you harm me while you certainly know that I am the messenger of Allāh to you?" And when they deviated, Allāh caused their hearts to deviate. And Allāh does not guide the defiantly disobedient people.

(6) And [mention] when Jesus, the son of Mary, said, "O Children of Israel, indeed I am the messenger of Allāh to you confirming what came before me of the Torah and bringing good tidings of a messenger to come after me, whose name is Aḥmad."[1621] But when he came to them with clear evidences, they said, "This is obvious magic."[1622]

(7) And who is more unjust than one who invents about Allāh untruth while he is being invited to Islām. And Allāh does not guide the wrongdoing people.

(8) They want to extinguish the light of Allāh with their mouths, but Allāh will perfect His light, although the disbelievers dislike it.

(9) It is He who sent His Messenger with guidance and the religion of truth to manifest it over all religion, although those who associate others with Allāh dislike it.

(10) O you who have believed, shall I guide you to a transaction that will save you from a painful punishment?

(11) [It is that] you believe in Allāh and His Messenger and strive in the cause of Allāh with your wealth and your lives. That is best for you, if you only knew.

[1620] See footnote to 57:1.

[1621] "Another name of Prophet Muḥammad (ﷺ).

[1622] i.e., fraud or deception."

(12) He will forgive for you your sins and admit you to gardens beneath which rivers flow and pleasant dwellings in gardens of perpetual residence. That is the great attainment.

(13) And [you will obtain] another [favor] that you love - victory from Allāh and an imminent conquest; and give good tidings to the believers.

(14) O you who have believed, be supporters of Allāh, as when Jesus, the son of Mary, said to the disciples, "Who are my supporters for Allāh?" The disciples said, "We are supporters of Allāh." And a faction of the Children of Israel believed and a faction disbelieved. So We supported those who believed against their enemy, and they became dominant.

Surah Al-Jumu'ah

(1) Whatever is in the heavens and whatever is on the earth is exalting Allāh,[1623] the Sovereign, the Pure, the Exalted in Might, the Wise.[1624]

(2) It is He who has sent among the unlettered [Arabs] a Messenger from themselves reciting to them His verses and purifying them and teaching them the Book [i.e., the Qur'ān] and wisdom [i.e., the sunnah] - although they were before in clear error -

(3) And [to] others of them who have not yet joined them. And He is the Exalted in Might, the Wise.

(4) That is the bounty of Allāh, which He gives to whom He wills, and Allāh is the possessor of great bounty.

(5) The example of those who were entrusted with the Torah and then did not take it on[1625] is like that of a donkey who carries volumes [of books].[1626] Wretched is the example of the people who deny the signs of Allāh. And Allāh does not guide the wrongdoing people.

(6) Say, "O you who are Jews, if you claim that you are allies of Allāh, excluding the [other] people, then wish for death, if you should be truthful."

(7) But they will not wish for it, ever, because of what their hands have put forth. And Allāh is Knowing of the wrongdoers.

(8) Say, "Indeed, the death from which you flee - indeed, it will meet you. Then you will be returned to the Knower of the unseen and the witnessed, and He will inform you about what you used to do."

(9) O you who have believed, when [the adhān] is called for the prayer on the day of Jumu'ah [Friday], then proceed to the remembrance of Allāh and leave trade. That is better for you, if you only knew.

(10) And when the prayer has been concluded, disperse within the land and seek from the bounty of Allāh, and remember Allāh often that you may succeed.

[1623] "See footnote to 57:1.

[1624] Refer to footnote in 6:18."

[1625] "i.e., neglected their responsibility towards it by not putting its teachings into practice.

[1626] But does not benefit from their contents."

(11) But [on one occasion] when they saw a transaction or a diversion, [O Muḥammad], they rushed to it and left you standing. Say, "What is with Allāh is better than diversion and than a transaction, and Allāh is the best of providers."

Surah Al-Munafiqun

(1) When the hypocrites come to you, [O Muḥammad], they say, "We testify that you are the Messenger of Allāh." And Allāh knows that you are His Messenger, and Allāh testifies that the hypocrites are liars.

(2) They have taken their oaths as a cover, so they averted [people] from the way of Allāh. Indeed, it was evil that they were doing.

(3) That is because they believed, and then they disbelieved; so their hearts were sealed over, and they do not understand.

(4) And when you see them, their forms please you, and if they speak, you listen to their speech. [They are] as if they were pieces of wood propped up[1627] - they think that every shout is against them. They are the enemy, so beware of them. May Allāh destroy them; how are they deluded?

(5) And when it is said to them, "Come, the Messenger of Allāh will ask forgiveness for you," they turn their heads aside and you see them evading while they are arrogant.

(6) It is all the same for them whether you ask forgiveness for them or do not ask forgiveness for them; never will Allāh forgive them. Indeed, Allāh does not guide the defiantly disobedient people.

(7) They are the ones who say, "Do not spend on those who are with the Messenger of Allāh until they disband." And to Allāh belong the depositories of the heavens and the earth, but the hypocrites do not understand.

(8) They say, "If we return to al-Madīnah, the more honored [for power] will surely expel therefrom the more humble." And to Allāh belongs [all] honor, and to His Messenger, and to the believers, but the hypocrites do not know.

(9) O you who have believed, let not your wealth and your children divert you from the remembrance of Allāh. And whoever does that - then those are the losers.

(10) And spend [in the way of Allāh] from what We have provided you before death approaches one of you and he says, "My Lord, if only You would delay me for a brief term so I would give charity and be of the righteous."

[1627] i.e., bodies with empty minds and empty hearts.

(11) But never will Allāh delay a soul when its time has come. And Allāh is Aware of what you do.

Surah At-Taghabun

(1) Whatever is in the heavens and whatever is on the earth is exalting Allāh.[1628] To Him belongs dominion, and to Him belongs [all] praise, and He is over all things competent.

(2) It is He who created you, and among you is the disbeliever, and among you is the believer. And Allāh, of what you do, is Seeing.

(3) He created the heavens and earth in truth and formed you and perfected your forms; and to Him is the [final] destination.

(4) He knows what is within the heavens and earth and knows what you conceal and what you declare. And Allāh is Knowing of that within the breasts.

(5) Has there not come to you the news of those who disbelieved before? So they tasted the bad consequence of their affair, and they will have a painful punishment.

(6) That is because their messengers used to come to them with clear evidences, but they said, "Shall human beings guide us?" and disbelieved and turned away. And Allāh dispensed [with them]; and Allāh is Free of need and Praiseworthy.

(7) Those who disbelieve have claimed that they will never be resurrected. Say, "Yes, by my Lord, you will surely be resurrected; then you will surely be informed of what you did. And that, for Allāh, is easy."

(8) So believe in Allāh and His Messenger and the light [i.e., the Qur'ān] which We have sent down. And Allāh is Aware of what you do.

(9) The Day He will assemble you for the Day of Assembly - that is the Day of Deprivation.[1629] And whoever believes in Allāh and does righteousness - He will remove from him his misdeeds and admit him to gardens beneath which rivers flow, wherein they will abide forever. That is the great attainment.

(10) But the ones who disbelieved and denied Our verses - those are the companions of the Fire, abiding eternally therein; and wretched is the destination.

(11) No disaster strikes except by permission of Allāh. And whoever believes in Allāh - He will guide his heart. And Allāh is Knowing of all things.

[1628] See footnote to 57:1.

[1629] "At-Taghābun" suggests having been outdone by others in the acquisition of something valued. That Day, the disbelievers will suffer the loss of Paradise to the believers.

(12) And obey Allāh and obey the Messenger; but if you turn away - then upon Our Messenger is only [the duty of] clear notification.

(13) Allāh - there is no deity except Him. And upon Allāh let the believers rely.

(14) O you who have believed, indeed, among your spouses and your children are enemies to you, so beware of them. But if you pardon and overlook and forgive - then indeed, Allāh is Forgiving and Merciful.

(15) Your wealth and your children are but a trial, and Allāh has with Him a great reward.

(16) So fear Allāh as much as you are able and listen and obey and spend [in the way of Allāh]; it is better for your selves. And whoever is protected from the stinginess of his soul - it is those who will be the successful.

(17) If you loan Allāh a goodly loan, He will multiply it for you and forgive you. And Allāh is [most] Appreciative[1630] and Forbearing,[1631]

(18) Knower of the unseen and the witnessed, the Exalted in Might, the Wise.

[1630] "Who gives much in return for little.
[1631] Refer to footnote in 2:225."

Surah At-Talaq

(1) O Prophet, when you [Muslims] divorce women, divorce them for [the commencement of] their waiting period and keep count of the waiting period,[1632] and fear Allāh, your Lord. Do not turn them out of their [husbands'] houses, nor should they [themselves] leave [during that period] unless they are committing a clear immorality. And those are the limits [set by] Allāh. And whoever transgresses the limits of Allāh has certainly wronged himself. You know not; perhaps Allāh will bring about after that a [different] matter.[1633]

(2) And when they have [nearly] fulfilled their term, either retain them according to acceptable terms or part with them according to acceptable terms. And bring to witness two just men from among you and establish the testimony for [the acceptance of] Allāh. That is instructed to whoever should believe in Allāh and the Last Day. And whoever fears Allāh - He will make for him a way out[1634]

(3) And will provide for him from where he does not expect. And whoever relies upon Allāh - then He is sufficient for him. Indeed, Allāh will accomplish His purpose. Allāh has already set for everything a [decreed] extent.

(4) And those who no longer expect menstruation among your women - if you doubt, then their period is three months, and [also for] those who have not menstruated. And for those who are pregnant, their term is until they give birth.[1635] And whoever fears Allāh - He will make for him of his matter ease.

(5) That is the command of Allāh, which He has sent down to you; and whoever fears Allāh - He will remove for him his misdeeds and make great for him his reward.

(6) Lodge them[1636] [in a section] of where you dwell out of your means and do not harm them in order to oppress them.[1637] And if they should be pregnant, then spend on them until they give birth. And if they breastfeed for you, then give them their

---

[1632] "See rulings in 2:228-233. A wife should not be divorced except after the completion of her menstrual period but before sexual intercourse has occurred, or else during a confirmed pregnancy. The pronouncement of divorce begins her waiting period (ʿiddah).
[1633] Such as regret or renewed desire for the wife."
[1634] i.e., relief from distress.
[1635] The ruling concerning pregnancy applies also in the case of the husband's death.

[1636] "During their waiting period (referring to wives whose divorce has been pronounced).
[1637] So that they would be forced to leave or to ransom themselves.

payment and confer among yourselves in the acceptable way; but if you are in discord, then there may breastfeed for him [i.e., the father] another woman.[1638]

(7) Let a man of wealth spend from his wealth, and he whose provision is restricted - let him spend from what Allāh has given him. Allāh does not charge a soul except [according to] what He has given it. Allāh will bring about, after hardship, ease [i.e., relief].

(8) And how many a city was insolent toward the command of its Lord and His messengers, so We took it to severe account and punished it with a terrible punishment.

(9) And it tasted the bad consequence of its affair [i.e., rebellion], and the outcome of its affair was loss.

(10) Allāh has prepared for them a severe punishment; so fear Allāh, O you of understanding who have believed. Allāh has sent down to you a message [i.e., the Qur'ān].[1639]

(11) [He sent] a Messenger [i.e., Muḥammad (ﷺ)] reciting to you the distinct verses of Allāh that He may bring out those who believe and do righteous deeds from darknesses into the light. And whoever believes in Allāh and does righteousness - He will admit him into gardens beneath which rivers flow to abide therein forever. Allāh will have perfected for him a provision.

(12) It is Allāh who has created seven heavens and of the earth, the like of them.[1640] [His] command descends among them so you may know that Allāh is over all things competent and that Allāh has encompassed all things in knowledge.

[1638] See 2:233."

[1639] Some scholars have interpreted "dhikr" here as "a reminder," meaning the Messenger (ﷺ), since he is mentioned in the following verse.

[1640] i.e., a similar number: seven.

Surah At-Tahreem

(1) O Prophet, why do you prohibit [yourself from] what Allāh has made lawful for you, seeking the approval of your wives? And Allāh is Forgiving and Merciful.

(2) Allāh has already ordained for you [Muslims] the dissolution of your oaths.[1641] And Allāh is your protector, and He is the Knowing, the Wise.

(3) And [remember] when the Prophet confided to one of his wives a statement; and when she informed [another] of it and Allāh showed it to him, he made known part of it and ignored a part. And when he informed her about it, she said, "Who told you this?" He said, "I was informed by the Knowing, the Aware."

(4) If you two [wives] repent to Allāh, [it is best], for your hearts have deviated. But if you cooperate against him - then indeed Allāh is his protector, and Gabriel and the righteous of the believers and the angels, moreover, are [his] assistants.

(5) Perhaps his Lord, if he divorced you [all], would substitute for him wives better than you - submitting [to Allāh], believing, devoutly obedient, repentant, worshipping, and traveling[1642] - [ones] previously married and virgins.

(6) O you who have believed, protect yourselves and your families from a Fire whose fuel is people and stones, over which are [appointed] angels, harsh and severe; they do not disobey Allāh in what He commands them but do what they are commanded.

(7) O you who have disbelieved, make no excuses that Day. You will only be recompensed for what you used to do.

(8) O you who have believed, repent to Allāh with sincere repentance. Perhaps[1643] your Lord will remove from you your misdeeds and admit you into gardens beneath which rivers flow [on] the Day when Allāh will not disgrace the Prophet and those who believed with him. Their light will proceed before them and on their right; they will say, "Our Lord, perfect for us our light and forgive us. Indeed, You are over all things competent."

[1641] By means of a kaffārah (expiation). This is required when one is unable to fulfill an oath or when one has taken an oath which would not be pleasing to Allāh (subḥānahu wa taʿālā). See 5:89.

[1642] Emigrating for the cause of Allāh. Another meaning is "given to fasting."

[1643] i.e., it is expected or promised.

(9) O Prophet, strive against the disbelievers and the hypocrites and be harsh upon them. And their refuge is Hell, and wretched is the destination.

(10) Allāh presents an example of those who disbelieved: the wife of Noah and the wife of Lot. They were under two of Our righteous servants but betrayed them,[1644] so they [i.e., those prophets] did not avail them from Allāh at all, and it was said, "Enter the Fire with those who enter."

(11) And Allāh presents an example of those who believed: the wife of Pharaoh, when she said, "My Lord, build for me near You a house in Paradise and save me from Pharaoh and his deeds and save me from the wrongdoing people."

(12) And [the example of] Mary, the daughter of ʿImrān, who guarded her chastity, so We blew into [her garment] through Our angel [i.e., Gabriel], and she believed in the words of her Lord and His scriptures and was of the devoutly obedient.

[1644] In the matter of religion.

Surah Al-Mulk

(1) Blessed is He in whose hand is dominion, and He is over all things competent -

(2) [He] who created death and life to test you [as to] which of you is best in deed - and He is the Exalted in Might, the Forgiving -

(3) [And] who created seven heavens in layers.[1645] You do not see in the creation of the Most Merciful any inconsistency. So return [your] vision [to the sky]; do you see any breaks?

(4) Then return [your] vision twice again.[1646] [Your] vision will return to you humbled while it is fatigued.

(5) And We have certainly beautified the nearest heaven with lamps [i.e., stars] and have made [from] them what is thrown at the devils[1647] and have prepared for them the punishment of the Blaze.

(6) And for those who disbelieved in their Lord is the punishment of Hell, and wretched is the destination.

(7) When they are thrown into it, they hear from it a [dreadful] inhaling while it boils up.

(8) It almost bursts with rage. Every time a company is thrown into it, its keepers ask them, "Did there not come to you a warner?"

(9) They will say, "Yes, a warner had come to us, but we denied and said, 'Allāh has not sent down anything. You are not but in great error.'"

(10) And they will say, "If only we had been listening or reasoning, we would not be among the companions of the Blaze."

(11) And they will admit their sin, so [it is] alienation[1648] for the companions of the Blaze.

(12) Indeed, those who fear their Lord unseen will have forgiveness and great reward.

[1645] i.e., one covering or fitting over the other.

[1646] i.e., repeatedly.

[1647] Thereby driving them from the heavens and preventing them from eavesdropping. See 72:8-9.

[1648] From all good and from Allāh's mercy.

(13) And conceal your speech or publicize it; indeed, He is Knowing of that within the breasts.

(14) Does He who created not know,[1649] while He is the Subtle, the Aware?

(15) It is He who made the earth tame[1650] for you - so walk among its slopes and eat of His provision - and to Him is the resurrection.

(16) Do you feel secure that He who is above[1651] would not cause the earth to swallow you and suddenly it would sway?[1652]

(17) Or do you feel secure that He who is above would not send against you a storm of stones? Then you would know how [severe] was My warning.

(18) And already had those before them denied, and how [terrible] was My reproach.

(19) Do they not see the birds above them with wings outspread and [sometimes] folded in? None holds them [aloft] except the Most Merciful. Indeed He is, of all things, Seeing.

(20) Or who is it that could be an army for you to aid you other than the Most Merciful? The disbelievers are not but in delusion.

(21) Or who is it that could provide for you if He withheld His provision? But they have persisted in insolence and aversion.

(22) Then is one who walks fallen on his face better guided or one who walks erect on a straight path?

(23) Say, "It is He who has produced you and made for you hearing and vision and hearts [i.e., intellect]; little are you grateful."

(24) Say, "It is He who has multiplied you throughout the earth, and to Him you will be gathered."

(25) And they say, "When is this promise, if you should be truthful?"

(26) Say, "The knowledge is only with Allāh, and I am only a clear warner."

[1649] Another accepted meaning is "Does He not know those whom He created...?"
[1650] i.e., stable and subservient
[1651] "Literally, "in ascendancy" or "over the heaven."
[1652] In a circular motion, as in an earthquake."

(27) But when they see it[1653] approaching, the faces of those who disbelieve will be distressed, and it will be said, "This is that for which you used to call."[1654]

(28) Say, [O Muḥammad], "Have you considered:[1655] whether Allāh should cause my death and those with me or have mercy upon us, who can protect the disbelievers from a painful punishment?"

(29) Say, "He is the Most Merciful; we have believed in Him, and upon Him we have relied. And you will [come to] know who it is that is in clear error."

(30) Say, "Have you considered: if your water was to become sunken [into the earth], then who could bring you flowing water?"

[1653] "The punishment of which they were warned.
[1654] When they challenged their prophets, saying, "Bring on the punishment, if you are truthful.""
[1655] i.e., inform me.

Surah Al-Qalam

(1) Nūn.[1656] By the pen and what they inscribe,

(2) You are not, [O Muḥammad], by the favor of your Lord, a madman.

(3) And indeed, for you is a reward uninterrupted.

(4) And indeed, you are of a great moral character.

(5) So you will see and they will see.

(6) Which of you is the afflicted [by a devil].

(7) Indeed, your Lord is most knowing of who has gone astray from His way, and He is most knowing of the [rightly] guided.

(8) Then do not obey the deniers.

(9) They wish that you would soften [in your position], so they would soften [toward you].

(10) And do not obey every worthless habitual swearer

(11) [And] scorner, going about with malicious gossip -

(12) A preventer of good, transgressing and sinful,

(13) Cruel, moreover, and an illegitimate pretender.[1657]

(14) Because he is a possessor of wealth and children,

(15) When Our verses are recited to him, he says, "Legends of the former peoples."

(16) We will brand him upon the snout.[1658]

(17) Indeed, We have tried them as We tried the companions of the garden, when they swore to cut its fruit in the [early] morning

---

[1656] See footnote to 2:1.

[1657] i.e., claiming a particular lineage falsely. The description given in these verses is of al-Waleed bin al-Mugheerah (see also 74:11-25) or possibly, as asserted by Ibn Katheer, al-Akhnas bin Shurayq.

[1658] Literally, "trunk," meaning the nose of an elephant or pig.

(18) Without making exception.[1659]

(19) So there came upon it [i.e., the garden] an affliction from your Lord while they were asleep.

(20) And it became as though reaped.

(21) And they called one another at morning,

(22) [Saying], "Go early to your crop if you would cut the fruit."

(23) So they set out, while lowering their voices,

(24) [Saying], "There will surely not enter it today upon you [any] poor person."

(25) And they went early in determination, [assuming themselves] able.[1660]

(26) But when they saw it, they said, "Indeed, we are lost;

(27) Rather, we have been deprived."

(28) The most moderate of them said, "Did I not say to you, 'Why do you not exalt [Allāh]?'"[1661]

(29) They said, "Exalted is our Lord! Indeed, we were wrongdoers."

(30) Then they approached one another, blaming each other.

(31) They said, "O woe to us; indeed we were transgressors.

(32) Perhaps our Lord will substitute for us [one] better than it. Indeed, we are toward our Lord desirous."[1662]

(33) Such is the punishment [of this world]. And the punishment of the Hereafter is greater, if they only knew.

(34) Indeed, for the righteous with their Lord are the Gardens of Pleasure.

(35) Then will We treat the Muslims like the criminals?

(36) What is [the matter] with you? How do you judge?

[1659] i.e., without conceding that nothing can be accomplished unless Allāh wills, saying, "...if Allāh wills" ("in-shā'-Allāh"). See 18:23-24.

[1660] To carry out their plan, confident of their ability.

[1661] i.e., remember or mention Him by saying, "...if Allāh wills." An additional meaning is "praise" or "thank" Him for His bounty.

[1662] Of His mercy, forgiveness and bounty.

(37) Or do you have a scripture in which you learn

(38) That indeed for you is whatever you choose?

(39) Or do you have oaths [binding] upon Us, extending until the Day of Resurrection, that indeed for you is whatever you judge?

(40) Ask them which of them, for that [claim], is responsible.

(41) Or do they have partners?[1663] Then let them bring their partners, if they should be truthful.

(42) The Day the shin will be uncovered[1664] and they are invited to prostration but they [i.e., the disbelievers] will not be able,

(43) Their eyes humbled, humiliation will cover them. And they used to be invited to prostration while they were sound.[1665]

(44) So leave Me, [O Muḥammad], with [the matter of] whoever denies this statement [i.e., the Qur'ān]. We will progressively lead them [to punishment] from where they do not know.[1666]

(45) And I will give them time. Indeed, My plan is firm.

(46) Or do you ask of them a payment, so they are by debt burdened down?

(47) Or have they [knowledge of] the unseen, so they write [it] down?

(48) Then be patient for the decision of your Lord, [O Muḥammad], and be not like the companion of the fish [i.e., Jonah] when he called out while he was distressed.

(49) If not that a favor [i.e., mercy] from his Lord overtook him, he would have been thrown onto the naked shore while he was censured.[1667]

(50) And his Lord chose him and made him of the righteous.

[1663] i.e., those to whom they attribute divinity other than Allāh or partners from among themselves.

[1664] i.e., when everyone will find before him great difficulty. In accordance with authentic ḥadīths, "the shin" might also refer to that of Allāh (subḥānahu wa taʿālā), before which every believer will prostrate on the Day of Judgement. See footnote to 2:19.

[1665] During worldly life.

[1666] Allāh will increase His favors to them in this world by way of trial, whereby they will sink deeper into sin and thus into destruction.

[1667] But instead, Allāh accepted his repentance and provided means for his recovery. See 37:139-148.

(51) And indeed, those who disbelieve would almost make you slip with their eyes [i.e., looks] when they hear the message, and they say, "Indeed, he is mad."

(52) But it is not except a reminder to the worlds.

Surah Al-Haqqah

(1) The Inevitable Reality -

(2) What is the Inevitable Reality?

(3) And what can make you know what is the Inevitable Reality?

(4) Thamūd and ʿAad denied the Striking Calamity [i.e., the Resurrection].

(5) So as for Thamūd, they were destroyed by the overpowering [blast].

(6) And as for ʿAad, they were destroyed by a screaming,[1668] violent wind

(7) Which He [i.e., Allāh] imposed upon them for seven nights and eight days in succession, so you would see the people therein fallen as if they were hollow trunks of palm trees.

(8) Then do you see of them any remains?

(9) And there came Pharaoh and those before him and the overturned cities[1669] with sin.

(10) And they disobeyed the messenger of their Lord, so He seized them with a seizure exceeding [in severity].

(11) Indeed, when the water overflowed, We carried you [i.e., your ancestors] in the sailing ship[1670]

(12) That We might make it for you a reminder and [that] a conscious ear would be conscious of it.

(13) Then when the Horn is blown with one blast

(14) And the earth and the mountains are lifted and leveled with one blow [i.e., stroke] -

(15) Then on that Day, the Occurrence [i.e., Resurrection] will occur,

---

[1668] Or "cold."

[1669] Those to which Lot was sent (see 11:82-83) or generally, all cities which were destroyed due to their denial of a messenger from Allāh.

[1670] Which was constructed by Noah.

(16) And the heaven will split [open], for that Day it is infirm.[1671]

(17) And the angels are at its edges. And there will bear the Throne of your Lord above them, that Day, eight [of them].

(18) That Day, you will be exhibited [for judgement]; not hidden among you is anything concealed.[1672]

(19) So as for he who is given his record in his right hand, he will say, "Here, read my record!

(20) Indeed, I was certain that I would be meeting my account."

(21) So he will be in a pleasant life -

(22) In an elevated garden,

(23) Its [fruit] to be picked hanging near.

(24) [They will be told], "Eat and drink in satisfaction for what you put forth[1673] in the days past."

(25) But as for he who is given his record in his left hand, he will say, "Oh, I wish I had not been given my record

(26) And had not known what is my account.

(27) I wish it [i.e., my death] had been the decisive one.[1674]

(28) My wealth has not availed me.

(29) Gone from me is my authority."[1675]

(30) [Allāh will say], "Seize him and shackle him.

(31) Then into Hellfire drive him.

(32) Then into a chain whose length is seventy cubits insert him."

(33) Indeed, he did not used to believe in Allāh, the Most Great,

---

[1671] i.e., weak, enfeebled and unstable.
[1672] i.e., any person or any secret you might attempt to conceal.
[1673] Literally, "advanced" in anticipation of reward in the Hereafter.
[1674] i.e., ending life rather than being the gateway to eternal life.
[1675] i.e., I have no valid excuse to stand on.

(34) Nor did he encourage the feeding of the poor.

(35) So there is not for him here this Day any devoted friend

(36) Nor any food except from the discharge of wounds;

(37) None will eat it except the sinners.

(38) So I swear by what you see

(39) And what you do not see

(40) [That] indeed, it [i.e., the Qur'ān] is the word of a noble Messenger.

(41) And it is not the word of a poet; little do you believe.

(42) Nor the word of a soothsayer; little do you remember.

(43) [It is] a revelation from the Lord of the worlds.

(44) And if he [i.e., Muḥammad] had made up about Us some [false] sayings,

(45) We would have seized him by the right hand;[1676]

(46) Then We would have cut from him the aorta.[1677]

(47) And there is no one of you who could prevent [Us] from him.

(48) And indeed, it [i.e., the Qur'ān] is a reminder for the righteous.

(49) And indeed, We know that among you are deniers.

(50) And indeed, it will be [a cause of] regret upon the disbelievers.

(51) And indeed, it is the truth of certainty.

(52) So exalt the name of your Lord, the Most Great.

[1676] Another interpretation is "by [Our] right hand," i.e., Allāh would have exacted revenge with might and power.
[1677] Causing immediate death.

Surah Al-Ma'aarij

(1) A supplicant asked for a punishment bound to happen[1678]

(2) To the disbelievers; of it there is no preventer.

(3) [It is] from Allāh, owner of the ways of ascent.

(4) The angels and the Spirit [i.e., Gabriel] will ascend to Him during a Day the extent of which is fifty thousand years.

(5) So be patient with gracious patience.

(6) Indeed, they see it [as] distant,

(7) But We see it [as] near.

(8) On the Day the sky will be like murky oil,[1679]

(9) And the mountains will be like wool,[1680]

(10) And no friend will ask [anything of] a friend,

(11) They will be shown each other. The criminal will wish that he could be ransomed from the punishment of that Day by his children.

(12) And his wife and his brother

(13) And his nearest kindred who shelter him.

(14) And whoever is on earth entirely [so] then it could save him.

(15) No![1681] Indeed, it is the Flame [of Hell],

(16) A remover of exteriors.[1682]

(17) It invites he who turned his back [on truth] and went away [from obedience]

[1678] In the Hereafter. Disbelievers had challenged the Prophet (ﷺ) by invoking Allāh to bring on His punishment. See 8:32.
[1679] Or "molten metal."
[1680] i.e., in the process of disintegration.
[1681] An emphatic refusal meaning "It is not to be."

[1682] This refers to the skin of the head or of the body or to the body extremities - which will be burned away.

(18) And collected [wealth] and hoarded.

(19) Indeed, mankind was created anxious:

(20) When evil touches him, impatient,

(21) And when good touches him, withholding [of it],

(22) Except the observers of prayer -

(23) Those who are constant in their prayer

(24) And those within whose wealth is a known right[1683]

(25) For the petitioner and the deprived -

(26) And those who believe in the Day of Recompense

(27) And those who are fearful of the punishment of their Lord -

(28) Indeed, the punishment of their Lord is not that from which one is safe -

(29) And those who guard their private parts

(30) Except from their wives or those their right hands possess,[1684] for indeed, they are not to be blamed -

(31) But whoever seeks beyond that, then they are the transgressors -

(32) And those who are to their trusts and promises attentive.

(33) And those who are in their testimonies upright

(34) And those who [carefully] maintain their prayer:

(35) They will be in gardens,[1685] honored.

(36) So what is [the matter] with those who disbelieve, hastening [from] before you, [O Muḥammad],

(37) [To sit] on [your] right and [your] left in separate groups?[1686]

(38) Does every person among them aspire to enter a garden of pleasure?

[1683] i.e., a specified share, meaning the obligatory zakāh.

[1684] i.e., female slaves.

[1685] In Paradise.

[1686] They sat at a distance in order to oppose and mock the Prophet (ﷺ), claiming that they would enter Paradise before the believers.

(39) No! Indeed, We have created them from that which they know.[1687]

(40) So I swear by the Lord of [all] risings and settings[1688] that indeed We are able

(41) To replace them with better than them; and We are not to be outdone.

(42) So leave them to converse vainly and amuse themselves until they meet their Day which they are promised -

(43) The Day they will emerge from the graves rapidly as if they were, toward an erected idol, hastening.[1689]

(44) Their eyes humbled, humiliation will cover them. That is the Day which they had been promised.

[1687] i.e., a liquid disdained. So how can they expect to enter Paradise except by the will of their Creator?

[1688] i.e., Allāh (subḥānahu wa taʿālā), who determines the point at which the sun, moon and stars rise and set according to season and every position of observation.

[1689] i.e., just as they used to race, whenever an idol was newly appointed, to be the first of its worshippers.

Surah Nuh

(1) Indeed, We sent Noah to his people, [saying], "Warn your people before there comes to them a painful punishment."

(2) He said, "O my people, indeed I am to you a clear warner -

(3) To worship Allāh, fear Him and obey me.

(4) He [i.e., Allāh] will forgive you of your sins and delay you for a specified term. Indeed, the time [set by] Allāh, when it comes, will not be delayed, if you only knew."

(5) He said, "My Lord, indeed I invited my people [to truth] night and day.

(6) But my invitation increased them not except in flight [i.e., aversion].

(7) And indeed, every time I invited them that You may forgive them, they put their fingers in their ears, covered themselves with their garments,[1690] persisted, and were arrogant with [great] arrogance.

(8) Then I invited them publicly.

(9) Then I announced to them and [also] confided to them secretly

(10) And said, 'Ask forgiveness of your Lord. Indeed, He is ever a Perpetual Forgiver.

(11) He will send [rain from] the sky upon you in [continuing] showers

(12) And give you increase in wealth and children and provide for you gardens and provide for you rivers.

(13) What is [the matter] with you that you do not attribute to Allāh [due] grandeur

(14) While He has created you in stages?[1691]

(15) Do you not consider how Allāh has created seven heavens in layers[1692]

(16) And made the moon therein a [reflected] light and made the sun a burning lamp?

[1690] Refusing to look or listen.

[1691] i.e., in various progressive states and conditions. See also 22:5 and 23:12-14 in reference to development of the embryo.

[1692] See footnote to 67:3.

(17) And Allāh has caused you to grow from the earth a [progressive] growth.

(18) Then He will return you into it and extract you [another] extraction.

(19) And Allāh has made for you the earth an expanse

(20) That you may follow therein roads of passage.'"

(21) Noah said, "My Lord, indeed they have disobeyed me and followed him whose wealth and children will not increase him except in loss.

(22) And they conspired an immense conspiracy

(23) And said, 'Never leave your gods and never leave Wadd or Suwāʿ or Yaghūth and Yaʿūq and Nasr.'[1693]

(24) And already they have misled many. And, [my Lord], do not increase the wrongdoers except in error."

(25) Because of their sins they were drowned and put into the Fire, and they found not for themselves besides Allāh [any] helpers.

(26) And Noah said, "My Lord, do not leave upon the earth from among the disbelievers an inhabitant.

(27) Indeed, if You leave them, they will mislead Your servants and not beget except [every] wicked one and [confirmed] disbeliever.

(28) My Lord, forgive me and my parents and whoever enters my house a believer and the believing men and believing women. And do not increase the wrongdoers except in destruction."

[1693] These were the names of specific idols named after pious men of earlier generations.

Surah Al-Jinn

(1) Say, [O Muḥammad], "It has been revealed to me that a group of the jinn listened and said, 'Indeed, we have heard an amazing Qur'ān [i.e., recitation].

(2) It guides to the right course, and we have believed in it. And we will never associate with our Lord anyone.

(3) And [it teaches] that exalted is the nobleness of our Lord; He has not taken a wife or a son

(4) And that our foolish one [i.e., Iblees][1694] has been saying about Allāh an excessive transgression.

(5) And we had thought that mankind and the jinn would never speak about Allāh a lie.

(6) And there were men from mankind who sought refuge in men from the jinn, so they [only] increased them in burden [i.e., sin].

(7) And they had thought, as you thought, that Allāh would never send anyone [as a messenger].

(8) And we have sought [to reach] the heaven but found it filled with powerful guards and burning flames.

(9) And we used to sit therein in positions for hearing,[1695] but whoever listens now will find a burning flame lying in wait for him.

(10) And we do not know [therefore] whether evil is intended for those on earth or whether their Lord intends for them a right course.

(11) And among us are the righteous, and among us are [others] not so; we were [of] divided ways.[1696]

(12) And we have become certain that we will never cause failure to Allāh upon earth, nor can we escape Him by flight.

[1694] A plural form may also be understood, i.e., "the foolish ones among us."
[1695] Before the prophethood of Muḥammad (ﷺ) the jinn used to collect information by eavesdropping on the angels and then pass it on to fortunetellers and soothsayers.
[1696] In opinion, belief and religious practice.

(13) And when we heard the guidance [i.e., the Qur'ān], we believed in it. And whoever believes in his Lord will not fear deprivation or burden.[1697]

(14) And among us are Muslims [in submission to Allāh], and among us are the unjust.[1698] And whoever has become Muslim - those have sought out the right course.

(15) But as for the unjust, they will be, for Hell, firewood.'

(16) And [Allāh revealed] that if they had remained straight on the way, We would have given them abundant rain [i.e., provision].

(17) So We might test them therein. And whoever turns away from the remembrance of his Lord[1699] He will put into arduous punishment.

(18) And [He revealed] that the masjids[1700] are for Allāh, so do not invoke[1701] with Allāh anyone.

(19) And that when the Servant [i.e., Prophet] of Allāh stood up supplicating Him, they almost became about him a compacted mass."[1702]

(20) Say, [O Muḥammad], "I only invoke my Lord and do not associate with Him anyone."

(21) Say, "Indeed, I do not possess for you [the power of] harm or right direction."

(22) Say, "Indeed, there will never protect me from Allāh anyone [if I should disobey], nor will I find in other than Him a refuge.

(23) But [I have for you] only notification from Allāh, and His messages." And whoever disobeys Allāh and His Messenger - then indeed, for him is the fire of Hell; they will abide therein forever.

(24) [The disbelievers continue] until, when they see that which they are promised, then they will know who is weaker in helpers and less in number.

[1697] In regard to his account in the Hereafter. Nothing of his good will be diminished, nor will the evil of another be placed upon him.

[1698] i.e., those who deviate from the truth and act tyrannically.

[1699] i.e., refuses obedience to Him.

[1700] "The term "masjid" here includes every place of worship or the earth in general.

[1701] Or "worship.""

[1702] Crowding on top of each other in the manner of locusts in order to hear him (ﷺ). "They" may refer to the jinn or to the disbelievers among the Arabs.

(25) Say, "I do not know if what you are promised is near or if my Lord will grant for it a [long] period."

(26) [He is] Knower of the unseen, and He does not disclose His [knowledge of the] unseen to anyone

(27) Except whom He has approved of messengers, and indeed, He sends before him [i.e., each messenger] and behind him observers[1703]

(28) That he [i.e., Muhammad (ﷺ)] may know[1704] that they have conveyed the messages of their Lord; and He has encompassed whatever is with them and has enumerated all things in number.

[1703] Guardian angels to protect the messenger and the message.
[1704] This phrase may also be read: "So He [i.e., Allāh] may make evident."

Surah Al-Muzzammil

(1) O you who wraps himself [in clothing][1705]

(2) Arise [to pray] the night, except for a little -

(3) Half of it - or subtract from it a little

(4) Or add to it, and recite the Qur'ān with measured recitation.

(5) Indeed, We will cast upon you a heavy word.[1706]

(6) Indeed, the hours of the night are more effective for concurrence [of heart and tongue][1707] and more suitable for words.[1708]

(7) Indeed, for you by day is prolonged occupation.

(8) And remember the name of your Lord and devote yourself to Him with [complete] devotion.

(9) [He is] the Lord of the East and the West; there is no deity except Him, so take Him as Disposer of [your] affairs.[1709]

(10) And be patient over what they say and avoid them with gracious avoidance.

(11) And leave Me with [the matter of] the deniers, those of ease [in life], and allow them respite a little.

(12) Indeed, with Us [for them] are shackles and burning fire.

(13) And food that chokes and a painful punishment -

(14) On the Day the earth and the mountains will convulse and the mountains will become a heap of sand pouring down.

[1705] Allāh (subḥānahu wa taʿālā) addresses the Prophet (ﷺ), who was asleep, wrapped in his garments.

[1706] i.e., the revelation, which when descending on the Prophet (ﷺ) bore down upon him with a great weight. Another meaning is "important ordinances."

[1707] "Another accepted interpretation of the same words is "Indeed, arising at night is more difficult...," meaning that it will only be done by sincere believers and not others.

[1708] i.e., for recitation of the Qur'ān and for hearing and understanding it."

[1709] i.e., trust in Allāh and rely upon Him.

(15) Indeed, We have sent to you a Messenger as a witness upon you just as We sent to Pharaoh a messenger.

(16) But Pharaoh disobeyed the messenger, so We seized him with a ruinous seizure.

(17) Then how can you fear, if you disbelieve, a Day that will make the children white-haired?[1710]

(18) The heaven will break apart therefrom;[1711] ever is His promise fulfilled.

(19) Indeed, this is a reminder, so whoever wills may take to his Lord a way.

(20) Indeed, your Lord knows, [O Muḥammad], that you stand [in prayer] almost two thirds of the night or half of it or a third of it, and [so do] a group of those with you. And Allāh determines [the extent of] the night and the day. He has known that you [Muslims] will not be able to do it[1712] and has turned to you in forgiveness, so recite what is easy [for you] of the Qur'ān. He has known that there will be among you those who are ill and others traveling throughout the land seeking [something] of the bounty of Allāh and others fighting for the cause of Allāh. So recite what is easy from it and establish prayer and give zakāh and loan Allāh a goodly loan.[1713] And whatever good you put forward for yourselves - you will find it with Allāh. It is better and greater in reward. And seek forgiveness of Allāh. Indeed, Allāh is Forgiving and Merciful.

[1710] Another meaning is "How can you avoid [punishment]" on such a Day?

[1711] From the terror of that Day.

[1712] "Allāh has known that if they were to continue in such long periods of worship each night, the people would be caused much hardship.

[1713] In the form of charities and contributions to His cause."

Surah Al-Muddathir

(1) O you who covers himself [with a garment],[1714]

(2) Arise and warn.

(3) And your Lord glorify.

(4) And your clothing purify.

(5) And uncleanliness[1715] avoid.

(6) And do not confer favor to acquire more[1716].

(7) But for your Lord be patient.

(8) And when the trumpet is blown,

(9) That Day will be a difficult day

(10) For the disbelievers - not easy.

(11) Leave Me with the one I created alone[1717]

(12) And to whom I granted extensive wealth

(13) And children present [with him]

(14) And spread [everything] before him, easing [his life].

(15) Then he desires that I should add more.

(16) No! Indeed, he has been toward Our verses obstinate.

(17) I will cover him with arduous torment.

(18) Indeed, he thought and deliberated.[1718]

[1714] Referring to the Prophet (ﷺ).

[1715] Specifically, idols or generally, bad conduct and morals.

[1716] An alternative meaning is "Do not consider any favor you have conferred to be great."

[1717] i.e., without wealth or children. The reference is to al-Waleed bin al-Mugheerah, who after inclining toward the Qur'ān, denied it publicly in order to win the approval of the Quraysh.

[1718] About what he would say concerning the Qur'ān and how he might discredit the Prophet (ﷺ).

(19) So may he be destroyed [for] how he deliberated.

(20) Then may he be destroyed [for] how he deliberated.

(21) Then he considered [again];

(22) Then he frowned and scowled;

(23) Then he turned back and was arrogant

(24) And said, "This is not but magic imitated [from others].

(25) This is not but the word of a human being."

(26) I will drive him into Saqar.[1719]

(27) And what can make you know what is Saqar?

(28) It lets nothing remain and leaves nothing [unburned],

(29) Altering [i.e., blackening] the skins.

(30) Over it are nineteen [angels].

(31) And We have not made the keepers of the Fire except angels. And We have not made their number except as a trial for those who disbelieve - that those who were given the Scripture will be convinced and those who have believed will increase in faith and those who were given the Scripture and the believers will not doubt and that those in whose hearts is disease [i.e., hypocrisy] and the disbelievers will say, "What does Allāh intend by this as an example?" Thus does Allāh send astray whom He wills and guide whom He wills. And none knows the soldiers of your Lord except Him. And it [i.e., mention of the Fire] is not but a reminder to humanity.

(32) No! By the moon.

(33) And [by] the night when it departs.

(34) And [by] the morning when it brightens,

(35) Indeed, it [i.e., the Fire] is of the greatest [afflictions].

(36) As a warning to humanity -

(37) To whoever wills among you to proceed[1720] or stay behind.

[1719] One of the proper names of Hell.
[1720] To righteousness by acceptance of the warning.

(38) Every soul, for what it has earned, will be retained[1721].

(39) Except the companions of the right,[1722].

(40) [Who will be] in gardens, questioning each other

(41) About the criminals,

(42) [And asking them], "What put you into Saqar?"

(43) They will say, "We were not of those who prayed,

(44) Nor did we used to feed the poor.

(45) And we used to enter into vain discourse with those who engaged [in it],

(46) And we used to deny the Day of Recompense

(47) Until there came to us the certainty [i.e., death]."

(48) So there will not benefit them the intercession of [any] intercessors.

(49) Then what is [the matter] with them that they are, from the reminder, turning away.

(50) As if they were alarmed donkeys.

(51) Fleeing from a lion?

(52) Rather, every person among them desires that he[1723] would be given scriptures spread about.[1724]

(53) No! But they do not fear the Hereafter.

(54) No! Indeed, it [i.e., the Qur'ān] is a reminder.

(55) Then whoever wills will remember it.

(56) And they will not remember except that Allāh wills. He is worthy of fear and adequate for [granting] forgiveness.

[1721] i.e., subject or held responsible.
[1722] i.e., the righteous who receive their records in their right hands.
[1723] "Instead of Muḥammad (ﷺ).
[1724] i.e., made public. Much of their refusal of his message was due to envy and jealousy of the Prophet (ﷺ)."

Surah Al-Qiyamah

(1) I swear by the Day of Resurrection

(2) And I swear by the reproaching soul[1725] [to the certainty of resurrection].

(3) Does man think that We will not assemble his bones?

(4) Yes. [We are] Able [even] to proportion his fingertips.

(5) But man desires to continue in sin.[1726]

(6) He asks, "When is the Day of Resurrection?"

(7) So when vision is dazzled.

(8) And the moon darkens.

(9) And the sun and the moon are joined,

(10) Man will say on that Day, "Where is the [place of] escape?"

(11) No! There is no refuge.

(12) To your Lord, that Day, is the [place of] permanence.

(13) Man will be informed that Day of what he sent ahead[1727] and kept back.[1728]

(14) Rather, man, against himself, will be a witness,[1729]

(15) Even if he presents his excuses.

(16) Move not your tongue with it, [O Muḥammad], to hasten with it [i.e., recitation of the Qur'ān].

(17) Indeed, upon Us is its collection [in your heart] and [to make possible] its recitation.

(18) So when We have recited it [through Gabriel], then follow its recitation.

[1725] i.e., that of the believer, which blames him when he falls into sin or error.
[1726] Literally, "to sin ahead of him." This refers to the disbeliever, who denies the Day of Account.
[1727] "i.e., his deeds, which await him in the Hereafter.
[1728] i.e., that which he did not do or which he delayed."
[1729] As described in 36:65 and 41:20-23.

(19) Then upon Us is its clarification [to you].

(20) No! But you [i.e., mankind] love the immediate

(21) And leave [i.e., neglect] the Hereafter.

(22) [Some] faces, that Day, will be radiant,

(23) Looking at their Lord.[1730]

(24) And [some] faces, that Day, will be contorted,

(25) Expecting that there will be done to them [something] backbreaking.

(26) No! When it [i.e., the soul] has reached the collar bones[1731]

(27) And it is said, "Who will cure [him]?"

(28) And he [i.e., the dying one] is certain that it is the [time of] separation

(29) And the leg is wound about the leg,[1732]

(30) To your Lord, that Day, will be the procession.[1733]

(31) And he [i.e., the disbeliever] had not believed, nor had he prayed.

(32) But [instead], he denied and turned away.

(33) And then he went to his people, swaggering [in pride].

(34) Woe to you, and woe!

(35) Then woe to you, and woe!

(36) Does man think that he will be left neglected?[1734]

(37) Had he not been a sperm from semen emitted?

(38) Then he was a clinging clot, and [Allāh] created [his form] and proportioned [him]

[1730] The people of Paradise will actually see their Creator in the Hereafter.

[1731] At the time it is about to leave the body when one is on the verge of death.

[1732] From the difficulties the person faces at death or his sudden awareness of the realities of both this world and the Hereafter. It may also refer to his shrouding after death.

[1733] Literally, "driving" or "herding" or "the place to which one is driven."

[1734] i.e., to no end, without responsibility, or without being returned to the Creator for judgement.

(39) And made of him two mates, the male and the female.

(40) Is not that [Creator] Able to give life to the dead?

Surah Al-Insan

(1) Has there [not] come upon man a period of time when he was not a thing [even] mentioned?

(2) Indeed, We created man from a sperm-drop mixture[1735] that We may try him; and We made him hearing and seeing.

(3) Indeed, We guided him to the way, be he grateful or be he ungrateful.

(4) Indeed, We have prepared for the disbelievers chains and shackles and a blaze.

(5) Indeed, the righteous will drink from a cup [of wine] whose mixture is of Kāfūr,[1736]

(6) A spring of which the [righteous] servants of Allāh will drink; they will make it gush forth in force [and abundance].

(7) They [are those who] fulfill [their] vows and fear a Day whose evil will be widespread.

(8) And they give food in spite of love for it[1737] to the needy, the orphan, and the captive,

(9) [Saying], "We feed you only for the face [i.e., approval] of Allāh. We wish not from you reward or gratitude.

(10) Indeed, We fear from our Lord a Day austere and distressful."

(11) So Allāh will protect them from the evil of that Day and give them radiance and happiness

(12) And will reward them for what they patiently endured [with] a garden [in Paradise] and silk [garments].

(13) [They will be] reclining therein on adorned couches. They will not see therein any [burning] sun or [freezing] cold.

(14) And near above them are its shades, and its [fruit] to be picked will be lowered in compliance.

[1735] i.e., a combination of the male and female substance, within the womb.
[1736] A sweet-smelling spring in Paradise.
[1737] The meaning here may also be "out of love for Him," i.e., Allāh (subḥānahu wa ta'ālā).

(15) And there will be circulated among them vessels of silver and cups having been [created] clear [as glass],

(16) Clear glasses [made] from silver of which they have determined the measure.

(17) And they will be given to drink a cup [of wine] whose mixture is of ginger

(18) [From] a fountain within it [i.e., Paradise] named Salsabeel.

(19) There will circulate among them young boys made eternal. When you see them, you would think them [as beautiful as] scattered pearls.

(20) And when you look there [in Paradise], you will see pleasure and great dominion.

(21) Upon them [i.e., the inhabitants] will be green garments of fine silk and brocade. And they will be adorned with bracelets of silver, and their Lord will give them a purifying drink.

(22) [And it will be said], "Indeed, this is for you a reward, and your effort has been appreciated."

(23) Indeed, it is We who have sent down to you, [O Muḥammad], the Qur'ān progressively.

(24) So be patient for the decision of your Lord and do not obey from among them a sinner or ungrateful [disbeliever].

(25) And mention the name of your Lord [in prayer] morning and evening

(26) And during the night prostrate to Him and exalt [i.e., praise] Him a long [part of the] night.

(27) Indeed, these [disbelievers] love the immediate and leave behind them[1738] a grave Day.

(28) We have created them and strengthened their forms, and when We will, We can change their likenesses with [complete] alteration.

(29) Indeed, this is a reminder, so he who wills may take to his Lord a way.

(30) And you do not will except that Allāh wills. Indeed, Allāh is ever Knowing and Wise.

[1738] i.e., neglect. The meaning may also be "leave ahead of them."

(31) He admits whom He wills into His mercy; but the wrongdoers - He has prepared for them a painful punishment.

Surah Al-Mursalat

(1) By those [winds] sent forth in gusts

(2) And the winds that blow violently

(3) And [by] the winds that spread [clouds]

(4) And those [angels] who bring criterion[1739]

(5) And those [angels] who deliver a message.

(6) As justification or warning,

(7) Indeed, what you are promised is to occur.

(8) So when the stars are obliterated

(9) And when the heaven is opened

(10) And when the mountains are blown away

(11) And when the messengers' time has come...[1740]

(12) For what Day was it postponed?[1741]

(13) For the Day of Judgement.

(14) And what can make you know what is the Day of Judgement?

(15) Woe,[1742] that Day, to the deniers.

(16) Did We not destroy the former peoples?

(17) Then We will follow them with the later ones.

(18) Thus do We deal with the criminals.

(19) Woe, that Day, to the deniers.

(20) Did We not create you from a liquid disdained?

[1739] To Allāh's human messengers.

[1740] i.e., when they are gathered to witness concerning their nations. The sentence's conclusion is understood to be "...the promised judgement will then take place."

[1741] "It" may refer to either the aforementioned occurrences collectively or to the testimony of the messengers.

[1742] i.e., death and destruction.

(21) And We placed it in a firm lodging [i.e., the womb]

(22) For a known extent.

(23) And We determined [it], and excellent [are We] to determine.

(24) Woe, that Day, to the deniers.

(25) Have We not made the earth a container

(26) Of the living and the dead?

(27) And We placed therein lofty, firmly set mountains and have given you to drink sweet water.

(28) Woe, that Day, to the deniers.

(29) [They will be told], "Proceed to that which you used to deny.

(30) Proceed to a shadow [of smoke] having three columns.

(31) [But having] no cool shade and availing not against the flame."

(32) Indeed, it throws sparks [as huge] as a fortress,

(33) As if they were yellowish [black] camels.

(34) Woe, that Day, to the deniers.

(35) This is a Day they will not speak,

(36) Nor will it be permitted for them to make an excuse.

(37) Woe, that Day, to the deniers.

(38) This is the Day of Judgement; We will have assembled you and the former peoples.

(39) So if you have a plan, then plan against Me.

(40) Woe, that Day, to the deniers.

(41) Indeed, the righteous will be among shades and springs

(42) And fruits from whatever they desire,

(43) [Being told], "Eat and drink in satisfaction for what you used to do."

(44) Indeed, We thus reward the doers of good.

(45) Woe, that Day, to the deniers.

(46) [O disbelievers], eat and enjoy yourselves a little; indeed, you are criminals.

(47) Woe, that Day, to the deniers.

(48) And when it is said to them, "Bow [in prayer]," they do not bow.

(49) Woe, that Day, to the deniers.

(50) Then in what statement after it [i.e., the Qur'ān] will they believe?

Surah An-Naba'

(1) About what are they asking one another?

(2) About the great news[1743] -

(3) That over which they are in disagreement.

(4) No! They are going to know.

(5) Then, no! They are going to know.

(6) Have We not made the earth a resting place?

(7) And the mountains as stakes?[1744]

(8) And We created you in pairs.

(9) And made your sleep [a means for] rest

(10) And made the night as clothing[1745].

(11) And made the day for livelihood.

(12) And constructed above you seven strong [heavens].

(13) And made [therein] a burning lamp

(14) And sent down, from the rain clouds, pouring water.

(15) That We may bring forth thereby grain and vegetation.

(16) And gardens of entwined growth.

(17) Indeed, the Day of Judgement is an appointed time -

(18) The Day the Horn is blown and you will come forth in multitudes

(19) And the heaven is opened and will become gateways.

(20) And the mountains are removed and will be [but] a mirage.

(21) Indeed, Hell has been lying in wait

[1743] i.e., the Resurrection.
[1744] To stabilize the land and balance the earth.
[1745] Covering you in darkness and providing rest.

(22) For the transgressors, a place of return,

(23) In which they will remain for ages [unending].

(24) They will not taste therein [any] coolness or drink.

(25) Except scalding water and [foul] purulence -

(26) An appropriate recompense.[1746]

(27) Indeed, they were not expecting an account

(28) And denied Our verses with [emphatic] denial.

(29) But all things We have enumerated in writing.

(30) "So taste [the penalty], and never will We increase you except in torment."[1747]

(31) Indeed, for the righteous is attainment[1748] -

(32) Gardens and grapevines.

(33) And full-breasted [companions] of equal age.

(34) And a full cup.[1749]

(35) No ill speech will they hear therein or any falsehood -

(36) [As] reward from your Lord, [a generous] gift [made due by] account,[1750]

(37) [From] the Lord of the heavens and the earth and whatever is between them, the Most Merciful. They possess not from Him [authority for] speech.[1751]

(38) The Day that the Spirit [i.e., Gabriel] and the angels will stand in rows, they will not speak except for one whom the Most Merciful permits, and he will say what is correct.

[1746] In proportion to and comparable with their crimes.
[1747] This announcement will be made to the companions of Hell.
[1748] Of security, success and reward, including escape and safety from Hell.
[1749] Of wine which is delicious and does not intoxicate.
[1750] i.e., as a result of both their own righteous deeds and the limitless generosity of Allāh (subḥānahu wa taʿālā) . Another meaning is "a gift calculated [to be adequate]."

[1751] None of Allāh's creatures can plead with Him on the Day of Judgement except by His permission.

(39) That is the True [i.e., certain] Day; so he who wills may take to his Lord a [way of] return.[1752]

(40) Indeed, We have warned you of an impending punishment on the Day when a man will observe what his hands have put forth[1753] and the disbeliever will say, "Oh, I wish that I were dust!"

1752 i.e., a direct route through correct beliefs and righteous deeds.
1753 i.e., the deeds he did in this world, which await him in the Hereafter.

Surah An-Nazi'at

(1) By those [angels] who extract with violence[1754]

(2) And [by] those who remove with ease[1755]

(3) And [by] those who glide [as if] swimming[1756]

(4) And those who race each other in a race[1757]

(5) And those who arrange [each] matter,[1758]

(6) On the Day the blast [of the Horn] will convulse [creation],

(7) There will follow it the subsequent [one].

(8) Hearts,[1759] that Day, will tremble,

(9) Their eyes[1760] humbled.

(10) They are [presently] saying, "Will we indeed be returned to [our] former state [of life]?

(11) Even if we should be decayed bones?"[1761]

(12) They say, "That, then, would be a losing return."[1762]

(13) Indeed, it will be but one shout,

(14) And suddenly they will be [alert] upon the earth's surface.

(15) Has there reached you the story of Moses? -

(16) When his Lord called to him in the sacred valley of Ṭuwā,

(17) "Go to Pharaoh. Indeed, he has transgressed.

[1754] i.e., those who tear out the souls of those destined for Hell.

[1755] i.e., those angels who ease out the souls of those destined for Paradise.

[1756] Speeding to execute Allāh's commands.

[1757] Racing to deliver the souls of the believers to Paradise.

[1758] According to Allāh's decree.

[1759] Those of the disbelievers who denied the Resurrection.

[1760] Those of the disbelievers.

[1761] The disbelievers say this in ridicule of the warning.

[1762] i.e., "If that were so, we would not be able to escape punishment."

(18) And say to him, 'Would you [be willing to] purify yourself

(19) And let me guide you to your Lord so you would fear [Him]?'"

(20) And he showed him the greatest sign,[1763]

(21) But he [i.e., Pharaoh] denied and disobeyed.

(22) Then he turned his back, striving [i.e., plotting].[1764]

(23) And he gathered [his people] and called out.

(24) And said, "I am your most exalted lord."

(25) So Allāh seized him in exemplary punishment for the last and the first [transgression].[1765]

(26) Indeed in that is a lesson [i.e., warning] for whoever would fear [Allāh].

(27) Are you a more difficult creation or is the heaven? He [i.e., Allāh] constructed it.

(28) He raised its ceiling and proportioned it.

(29) And He darkened its night and extracted its brightness.[1766]

(30) And after that He spread the earth.

(31) He extracted from it its water and its pasture,

(32) And the mountains He set firmly

(33) As enjoyment [i.e., provision] for you and your grazing livestock.

(34) But when there comes the greatest Overwhelming Calamity[1767] -

(35) The Day when man will remember that for which he strove,

(36) And Hellfire will be exposed for [all] those who see -

[1763] i.e., the miracle of his staff becoming a great snake.
[1764] An alternative meaning is "running [from the snake]."
[1765] i.e., for Pharaoh's setting himself up as a deity and for his previous oppression of the people and denial of Moses.
[1766] i.e., created the day from within the surrounding darkness.

[1767] i.e., the Day of Resurrection.

(37) So as for he who transgressed

(38) And preferred the life of the world,

(39) Then indeed, Hellfire will be [his] refuge.

(40) But as for he who feared the position of his Lord[1768] and prevented the soul from [unlawful] inclination,

(41) Then indeed, Paradise will be [his] refuge.

(42) They ask you, [O Muḥammad], about the Hour: when is its arrival?[1769]

(43) In what [position] are you that you should mention it?[1770]

(44) To your Lord is its finality.[1771]

(45) You are only a warner for those who fear it.

(46) It will be, on the Day they see it,[1772] as though they had not remained [in the world] except for an afternoon or a morning thereof.

[1768] See footnote to 55:46
[1769] Literally, "resting" or "establishment."
[1770] Meaning that Muḥammad (ﷺ) had no knowledge of it, so how could he inform them?
[1771] i.e., its destination and termination. And to Him belongs ultimate knowledge of it.
[1772] i.e., the Hour, the Resurrection.

Surah `Abasa

(1) He [i.e., the Prophet (ﷺ)] frowned and turned away

(2) Because there came to him the blind man,[1773] [interrupting].

(3) But what would make you perceive, [O Muḥammad], that perhaps he might be purified[1774]

(4) Or be reminded and the remembrance would benefit him?

(5) As for he who thinks himself without need,[1775]

(6) To him you give attention.

(7) And not upon you [is any blame] if he will not be purified.[1776]

(8) But as for he who came to you striving [for knowledge]

(9) While he fears [Allāh],

(10) From him you are distracted.

(11) No! Indeed, they [i.e., these verses] are a reminder;

(12) So whoever wills may remember it.[1777]

(13) [It is recorded] in honored sheets,

(14) Exalted and purified,

(15) [Carried] by the hands of messenger-angels,

(16) Noble and dutiful.

(17) Destroyed [i.e., cursed] is man;[1778] how disbelieving is he.

[1773] `Abdullāh, the son of Umm Maktūm.

[1774] As a result of what he learns from you.

[1775] i.e., without need of faith or need of Allāh (subḥānahu wa ta‘ālā) . Here it is in reference to a certain influential member of the Quraysh whom the Prophet (ﷺ) had hoped to bring to Islām.

[1776] The Prophet (ﷺ) was responsible only for conveying the message, not for ultimate guidance.

[1777] The revelation. Or "Him," i.e., Allāh (subḥānahu wa ta‘ālā).

[1778] i.e., those who deny Allāh's message.

(18) From what thing [i.e., substance] did He create him?

(19) From a sperm-drop He created him and destined for him;[1779]

(20) Then He eased the way for him;[1780]

(21) Then He causes his death and provides a grave for him.[1781]

(22) Then when He wills, He will resurrect him.

(23) No! He [i.e., man] has not yet accomplished what He commanded him.

(24) Then let mankind look at his food -

(25) How We poured down water in torrents,

(26) Then We broke open the earth, splitting [it with sprouts],

(27) And caused to grow within it grain

(28) And grapes and herbage

(29) And olive and palm trees

(30) And gardens of dense shrubbery

(31) And fruit and grass -

(32) [As] enjoyment [i.e., provision] for you and your grazing livestock.

(33) But when there comes the Deafening Blast[1782]

(34) On the Day a man will flee from his brother

(35) And his mother and his father

(36) And his wife and his children,

(37) For every man, that Day, will be a matter adequate for him.[1783]

(38) [Some] faces, that Day, will be bright -

[1779] His proportions, provisions, life span, etc.

[1780] Into this world (i.e., his birth) . It may also refer to life itself, which has been made easier by Allāh's guidance.

[1781] To conceal his decaying body.

[1782] The piercing blast of the Horn which signals resurrection. Aṣ-Ṣākhkhah is also a name for the Day of Resurrection.

[1783] i.e., to occupy him. He will be concerned only with himself, thus forgetting all others.

(39) Laughing, rejoicing at good news.

(40) And [other] faces, that Day, will have upon them dust.

(41) Blackness will cover them.

(42) Those are the disbelievers, the wicked ones.

Surah At-Takweer

(1) When the sun is wrapped up [in darkness]

(2) And when the stars fall, dispersing,

(3) And when the mountains are removed

(4) And when full-term she-camels[1784] are neglected

(5) And when the wild beasts are gathered

(6) And when the seas are filled with flame[1785]

(7) And when the souls are paired[1786]

(8) And when the girl [who was] buried alive is asked

(9) For what sin she was killed

(10) And when the pages[1787] are spread [i.e., made public]

(11) And when the sky is stripped away

(12) And when Hellfire is set ablaze

(13) And when Paradise is brought near,

(14) A soul will [then] know what it has brought [with it].[1788]

(15) So I swear by the retreating stars -

(16) Those that run [their courses] and disappear [i.e., set]

(17) And by the night as it closes in[1789]

(18) And by the dawn when it breathes [i.e., stirs]

[1784] Those ten months pregnant and nearing delivery. This verse alludes to distraction from the most valued of possessions.

[1785] Or "when the seas have overflowed [into each other]."

[1786] With another like soul. It can also mean "joined" (with their groups or sects).

[1787] On which are recorded the deeds of all people.

[1788] i.e., all of one's deeds from worldly life, which have accompanied the soul to the Hereafter.

[1789] An alternative meaning is "as it departs."

(19) [That] indeed, it [i.e., the Qur'ān] is a word [conveyed by] a noble messenger [i.e., Gabriel]

(20) [Who is] possessed of power and with the Owner of the Throne, secure [in position],

(21) Obeyed there [in the heavens] and trustworthy.

(22) And your companion [i.e., Prophet Muḥammad (☺)] is not [at all] mad.[1790]

(23) And he has already seen him [i.e., Gabriel] in the clear horizon.[1791]

(24) And he [i.e., Muḥammad (☺)] is not a withholder of [knowledge of] the unseen.[1792]

(25) And it [i.e., the Qur'ān] is not the word of a devil, expelled [from the heavens].

(26) So where are you going?[1793]

(27) It is not except a reminder to the worlds

(28) For whoever wills among you to take a right course.

(29) And you do not will except that Allāh wills - Lord of the worlds.

[1790] Literally, "possessed by jinn."

[1791] i.e., the eastern horizon, where the sun rises. See footnote to 53:6

[1792] Prophet Muḥammad (☺) did not withhold that knowledge of the unseen which Allāh had revealed to him in the Qur'ān.

[1793] In your denial of the Qur'ān and in your accusations against the Prophet (☺) . The meaning is essentially "Surely, you have strayed far from Allāh's path."

Surah Al-Infitar

(1) When the sky breaks apart

(2) And when the stars fall, scattering,

(3) And when the seas are erupted

(4) And when the [contents of] graves are scattered [i.e., exposed],

(5) A soul will [then] know what it has put forth and kept back.

(6) O mankind, what has deceived you concerning your Lord, the Generous,

(7) Who created you, proportioned you, and balanced you?

(8) In whatever form He willed has He assembled you.

(9) No! But you deny the Recompense.

(10) And indeed, [appointed] over you are keepers,[1794]

(11) Noble and recording;

(12) They know whatever you do.

(13) Indeed, the righteous will be in pleasure,

(14) And indeed, the wicked will be in Hellfire.

(15) They will [enter to] burn therein on the Day of Recompense,

(16) And never therefrom will they be absent.

(17) And what can make you know what is the Day of Recompense?

(18) Then, what can make you know what is the Day of Recompense?

(19) It is the Day when a soul will not possess for another soul [power to do] a thing; and the command, that Day, is [entirely] with Allāh.

[1794] Angels who preserve the deeds of men in records.

Surah Al-Mutaffifeen

(1) Woe to those who give less [than due],[1795]

(2) Who, when they take a measure from people, take in full.

(3) But if they give by measure or by weight to them, they cause loss.

(4) Do they not think that they will be resurrected

(5) For a tremendous Day -

(6) The Day when mankind will stand before the Lord of the worlds?

(7) No! Indeed, the record of the wicked is in sijjeen.

(8) And what can make you know what is sijjeen?

(9) It is [their destination[1796] recorded in] a register inscribed.

(10) Woe, that Day, to the deniers,

(11) Who deny the Day of Recompense.

(12) And none deny it except every sinful transgressor.

(13) When Our verses are recited to him, he says, "Legends of the former peoples."

(14) No! Rather, the stain has covered their hearts of that which they were earning.[1797]

(15) No! Indeed, from their Lord, that Day, they will be partitioned.[1798]

(16) Then indeed, they will [enter and] burn in Hellfire.

(17) Then it will be said [to them], "This is what you used to deny."

(18) No! Indeed, the record of the righteous is in ʿilliyyūn.

(19) And what can make you know what is ʿilliyyūn?

[1795] i.e., those who cheat people by giving them less than what they paid for when weighing or measuring - an amount so little as to hardly be noticed.
[1796] The lowest depths of Hell.
[1797] i.e., their sins.
[1798] i.e., they will not be able to see Him.

(20) It is [their destination[1799] recorded in] a register inscribed

(21) Which is witnessed by those brought near [to Allāh].

(22) Indeed, the righteous will be in pleasure

(23) On adorned couches, observing.

(24) You will recognize in their faces the radiance of pleasure.

(25) They will be given to drink [pure] wine[1800] [which was] sealed.

(26) The last of it[1801] is musk. So for this let the competitors compete.

(27) And its mixture is of Tasneem,[1802]

(28) A spring from which those near [to Allāh] drink.

(29) Indeed, those who committed crimes used to laugh at those who believed.

(30) And when they passed by them, they would exchange derisive glances.

(31) And when they returned to their people, they would return jesting.

(32) And when they saw them, they would say, "Indeed, those are truly lost."

(33) But they had not been sent as guardians over them.

(34) So Today[1803] those who believed are laughing at the disbelievers,

(35) On adorned couches, observing.

(36) Have the disbelievers [not] been rewarded [this Day] for what they used to do?

[1799] The highest elevations of Paradise.
[1800] Which is delicious and does not intoxicate.
[1801] i.e., its lingering odor.
[1802] The highest spring in Paradise and the most favored drink of its inhabitants.
[1803] On the Day of Judgement.

Surah Al-Inshiqaq

(1) When the sky has split [open]

(2) And has listened [i.e., responded]¹⁸⁰⁴ to its Lord and was obligated [to do so]

(3) And when the earth has been extended¹⁸⁰⁵

(4) And has cast out that within it¹⁸⁰⁶ and relinquished [it].

(5) And has listened [i.e., responded] to its Lord and was obligated [to do so] -

(6) O mankind, indeed you are laboring toward your Lord with [great] exertion¹⁸⁰⁷ and will meet it.¹⁸⁰⁸

(7) Then as for he who is given his record in his right hand,

(8) He will be judged with an easy account

(9) And return to his people in happiness.

(10) But as for he who is given his record behind his back,

(11) He will cry out for destruction

(12) And [enter to] burn in a Blaze.

(13) Indeed, he had [once] been among his people in happiness;

(14) Indeed, he had thought he would never return [to Allāh].

(15) But yes! Indeed, his Lord was ever, of him, Seeing.

(16) So I swear by the twilight glow

(17) And [by] the night and what it envelops

[1804] It will have heard Allāh's command and will have inclined immediately to compliance and willing obedience.
[1805] i.e., stretched flat and spread out.
[1806] Of the dead and all else buried therein.
[1807] "i.e., striving throughout your life until you meet your Lord, hastening toward death.
[1808] i.e., you will find all that you intended and accomplished awaiting you in the Hereafter. Another meaning is "And will meet Him [i.e., your Lord]" and be recompensed in full by Him."

(18) And [by] the moon when it becomes full

(19) [That] you will surely embark upon [i.e., experience] state after state.[1809]

(20) So what is [the matter] with them [that] they do not believe,

(21) And when the Qur'ān is recited to them, they do not prostrate [to Allāh]?

(22) But those who have disbelieved deny,

(23) And Allāh is most knowing of what they keep within themselves.

(24) So give them tidings of a painful punishment,

(25) Except for those who believe and do righteous deeds. For them is a reward uninterrupted.

[1809] i.e., various stages, both in this life and in the Hereafter.

Surah Al-Burooj

(1) By the sky containing great stars

(2) And [by] the promised Day

(3) And [by] the witness and what is witnessed,

(4) Destroyed [i.e., cursed] were the companions of the trench[1810]

(5) [Containing] the fire full of fuel,

(6) When they were sitting near it.

(7) And they, to what they were doing against the believers, were witnesses.[1811]

(8) And they resented them not except because they believed in Allāh, the Exalted in Might, the Praiseworthy,

(9) To whom belongs the dominion of the heavens and the earth. And Allāh, over all things, is Witness.[1812]

(10) Indeed, those who have tortured[1813] the believing men and believing women and then have not repented will have the punishment of Hell, and they will have the punishment of the Burning Fire.

(11) Indeed, those who have believed and done righteous deeds will have gardens beneath which rivers flow. That is the great attainment.

(12) Indeed, the assault [i.e., vengeance] of your Lord is severe.

(13) Indeed, it is He who originates [creation] and repeats.

(14) And He is the Forgiving, the Affectionate,

(15) Honorable Owner of the Throne,

[1810] Or "May they be destroyed" or "cursed." The "companions of the trench" (or ditch) were agents of a tyrannical king who refused to allow his people to believe in Allāh. Their evil deed in obedience to their ruler earned for them the curse of Allāh (subḥānahu wa taʿālā).

[1811] After casting the believers into a trench filled with fire, they sat at its edge, watching them burn to death. This event occurred before the time of Prophet Muḥammad (ﷺ).

[1812] See footnote to 4:79

[1813] Or, in this instance, the literal meaning of "burned" is also appropriate.

(16) Effecter of what He intends.

(17) Has there reached you the story of the soldiers -

(18) [Those of] Pharaoh and Thamūd?

(19) But they who disbelieve are in [persistent] denial,

(20) While Allāh encompasses them from behind.[1814]

(21) But this is an honored Qur'ān

(22) [Inscribed] in a Preserved Slate.

[1814] See footnote to 2:19

Surah At-Tariq

(1) By the sky and the night comer

(2) And what can make you know what is the night comer?

(3) It is the piercing star[1815]

(4) There is no soul but that it has over it a protector.

(5) So let man observe from what he was created.

(6) He was created from a fluid, ejected,

(7) Emerging from between the backbone and the ribs.

(8) Indeed, He [i.e., Allāh], to return him [to life], is Able.

(9) The Day when secrets will be put on trial,[1816]

(10) Then he [i.e., man] will have no power or any helper.

(11) By the sky which sends back[1817]

(12) And [by] the earth which splits,[1818]

(13) Indeed, it [i.e., the Qur'ān] is a decisive statement,

(14) And it is not amusement.

(15) Indeed, they are planning a plan,

(16) But I am planning a plan.

(17) So allow time for the disbelievers. Leave them awhile.[1819]

[1815] Whose light pierces through the darkness.
[1816] i.e., exposed, examined and judged.
[1817] Rain, heat, sound waves, etc.
[1818] With plant growth or from geological rifts.
[1819] i.e., Do not be in haste for revenge, for you will see what will become of them.

Surah Al-A'la

(1) Exalt the name of your Lord, the Most High,

(2) Who created and proportioned

(3) And who destined and [then] guided

(4) And who brings out the pasture

(5) And [then] makes it black stubble.

(6) We will make you recite, [O Muḥammad], and you will not forget,

(7) Except what Allāh should will. Indeed, He knows what is declared and what is hidden.

(8) And We will ease you toward ease.[1820]

(9) So remind, if the reminder should benefit;[1821]

(10) He who fears [Allāh] will be reminded.

(11) But the wretched one will avoid it

(12) [He] who will [enter and] burn in the greatest Fire,

(13) Neither dying therein nor living.

(14) He has certainly succeeded who purifies himself

(15) And mentions the name of his Lord and prays.

(16) But you prefer the worldly life,

(17) While the Hereafter is better and more enduring.

(18) Indeed, this is in the former scriptures,

(19) The scriptures of Abraham and Moses.

[1820] To the path of Allāh's religion, which is easy and natural, or toward Paradise, by giving opportunities for righteous deeds.
[1821] i.e., wherever it will be heard and understood.

Surah Al-Ghashiyah

(1) Has there reached you the report of the Overwhelming [event]?

(2) [Some] faces, that Day, will be humbled,

(3) Working [hard] and exhausted.[1822]

(4) They will [enter to] burn in an intensely hot Fire.

(5) They will be given drink from a boiling spring.

(6) For them there will be no food except from a poisonous, thorny plant

(7) Which neither nourishes nor avails against hunger.

(8) [Other] faces, that Day, will show pleasure.

(9) With their effort [they are] satisfied

(10) In an elevated garden,

(11) Wherein they will hear no unsuitable speech.[1823]

(12) Within it is a flowing spring.

(13) Within it are couches raised high

(14) And cups put in place

(15) And cushions lined up

(16) And carpets spread around.

(17) Then do they not look at the camels - how they are created?

(18) And at the sky - how it is raised?

(19) And at the mountains - how they are erected?

(20) And at the earth - how it is spread out?

(21) So remind, [O Muḥammad]; you are only a reminder.

[1822] Another accepted meaning is "They were working hard and exhausted," i.e., doing deeds during worldly life which did not benefit them since they were not accompanied by faith or done for the acceptance of Allāh (subḥānahu wa taʿālā).

[1823] i.e., any insult, falsehood, immorality, idle or vain talk, etc.

(22) You are not over them a controller.

(23) However, he who turns away and disbelieves

(24) Then Allāh will punish him with the greatest punishment.

(25) Indeed, to Us is their return.

(26) Then indeed, upon Us is their account.

Surah Al-Fajr

(1) By the dawn

(2) And [by] ten nights[1824]

(3) And [by] the even [number] and the odd

(4) And [by] the night when it passes,

(5) Is there [not] in [all] that an oath [sufficient] for one of perception?[1825]

(6) Have you not considered how your Lord dealt with ʿAad -

(7) [With] Iram[1826] - who had lofty pillars,[1827]

(8) The likes of whom had never been created in the land?

(9) And [with] Thamūd, who carved out the rocks in the valley?

(10) And [with] Pharaoh, owner of the stakes?[1828]

(11) [All of] whom oppressed within the lands

(12) And increased therein the corruption.

(13) So your Lord poured upon them a scourge of punishment.

(14) Indeed, your Lord is in observation.

(15) And as for man, when his Lord tries him and [thus] is generous to him and favors him, he says, "My Lord has honored me."[1829]

(16) But when He tries him and restricts his provision, he says, "My Lord has humiliated me."

[1824] Usually interpreted as the first ten nights of the month of Dhul-Ḥijjah.
[1825] Based upon the following verses, what has been sworn to by Allāh is that He will certainly punish the disbelievers.
[1826] "Another name for the first people of ʿAad, to whom Prophet Hūd was sent.
[1827] Supporting their tents or buildings."
[1828] By which he tortured people.
[1829] He is proud rather than grateful, attributing the favor to his own merit.

(17) No![1830] But you do not honor the orphan

(18) And you do not encourage one another to feed the poor.

(19) And you consume inheritance, devouring [it] altogether,[1831]

(20) And you love wealth with immense love.

(21) No! When the earth has been leveled - pounded and crushed

(22) And your Lord has come[1832] and the angels, rank upon rank,

(23) And brought [within view], that Day, is Hell - that Day, man will remember, but how [i.e., what good] to him will be the remembrance?

(24) He will say, "Oh, I wish I had sent ahead [some good] for my life."[1833]

(25) So on that Day, none will punish [as severely] as His punishment,

(26) And none will bind [as severely] as His binding [of the evildoers].

(27) [To the righteous it will be said], "O reassured soul,

(28) Return to your Lord, well-pleased and pleasing [to Him],

(29) And enter among My [righteous] servants

(30) And enter My Paradise."

[1830] It is not like you imagine. Rather, Allāh tries people through prosperity and hardship and rewards both gratitude and patience with honor in the Hereafter.
[1831] Not caring whether it is lawful or unlawful.
[1832] To pass judgement. See footnote to 2:19
[1833] The everlasting life of the Hereafter.

Surah Al-Balad

(1) I swear by this city [i.e., Makkah]

(2) And you, [O Muḥammad], are free of restriction in this city

(3) And [by] the father[1834] and that which was born [of him],

(4) We have certainly created man into hardship.

(5) Does he think that never will anyone overcome him?

(6) He says, "I have spent wealth in abundance."

(7) Does he think that no one has seen him?

(8) Have We not made for him two eyes?

(9) And a tongue and two lips?

(10) And have shown him the two ways?[1835]

(11) But he has not broken through the difficult pass.[1836]

(12) And what can make you know what is [breaking through] the difficult pass?

(13) It is the freeing of a slave

(14) Or feeding on a day of severe hunger

(15) An orphan of near relationship

(16) Or a needy person in misery

(17) And then being among those who believed and advised one another to patience and advised one another to compassion.

(18) Those are the companions of the right.[1837]

[1834] Said to be Adam (upon him be peace).

[1835] Of good and evil.

[1836] i.e., the steep incline or obstacle. In other words, he has not spent in the cause of Allāh but only boasts of spending in front of others.

[1837] Or "the companions of good fortune," i.e., those who receive their records in their right hands and proceed to Paradise.

(19) But they who disbelieved in Our signs - those are the companions of the left.[1838]

(20) Over them will be fire closed in.[1839]

[1838] Or "the companions of ill fortune," i.e., those who receive their records in their left hands and proceed to Hell.
[1839] The cover over Hell will be sealed and locked, containing its fire and its inhabitants.

Surah Ash-Shams

(1) By the sun and its brightness

(2) And [by] the moon when it follows it

(3) And [by] the day when it displays it[1840]

(4) And [by] the night when it covers [i.e., conceals] it

(5) And [by] the sky and He who constructed it

(6) And [by] the earth and He who spread it

(7) And [by] the soul and He who proportioned it[1841]

(8) And inspired it [with discernment of] its wickedness and its righteousness,

(9) He has succeeded who purifies it,

(10) And he has failed who instills it [with corruption].

(11) Thamūd denied [their prophet] by reason of their transgression,

(12) When the most wretched of them was sent forth.[1842]

(13) And the messenger of Allāh [i.e., Ṣāliḥ] said to them, "[Do not harm] the she-camel of Allāh or [prevent her from] her drink."

(14) But they denied him and hamstrung[1843] her. So their Lord brought down upon them destruction for their sin and made it equal [upon all of them].

(15) And He does not fear the consequence thereof.[1844]

[1840] The earth. Also interpreted as the sun. The same applies to the following verse.
[1841] i.e., balanced and refined it, creating in it sound tendencies and consciousness.
[1842] To hamstring the she-camel which had been sent by Allāh as a sign to them.
[1843] And then killed.
[1844] Allāh is not asked about what He does, but His servants will be asked. See 21:23

Surah Al-Lail

(1) By the night when it covers[1845]

(2) And [by] the day when it appears

(3) And [by] He who created the male and female,

(4) Indeed, your efforts are diverse.

(5) As for he who gives and fears Allāh

(6) And believes in the best [reward],

(7) We will ease him toward ease.

(8) But as for he who withholds and considers himself free of need

(9) And denies the best [reward],

(10) We will ease him toward difficulty.

(11) And what will his wealth avail him when he falls?[1846]

(12) Indeed, [incumbent] upon Us is guidance.

(13) And indeed, to us belongs the Hereafter and the first [life].

(14) So I have warned you of a Fire which is blazing.

(15) None will [enter to] burn therein except the most wretched one

(16) Who had denied and turned away.

(17) But the righteous one will avoid it

(18) [He] who gives [from] his wealth to purify himself

(19) And not [giving] for anyone who has [done him] a favor to be rewarded[1847]

(20) But only seeking the face [i.e., acceptance] of his Lord, Most High.

(21) And he is going to be satisfied.

[1845] With darkness.

[1846] i.e., when he dies or is destroyed. It can also mean when he falls into the Hellfire.

[1847] i.e., without intending reciprocation for some benefit to himself.

Surah Ad-Dhuha

(1) By the morning brightness

(2) And [by] the night when it covers with darkness, [1848]

(3) Your Lord has not taken leave of you, [O Muḥammad], nor has He detested [you].

(4) And the Hereafter is better for you than the first [life].

(5) And your Lord is going to give you, and you will be satisfied.

(6) Did He not find you an orphan and give [you] refuge?

(7) And He found you lost and guided [you],

(8) And He found you poor and made [you] self-sufficient.

(9) So as for the orphan, do not oppress [him].

(10) And as for the petitioner, [1849] do not repel [him].

(11) But as for the favor of your Lord, report [it].

[1848] And becomes still.
[1849] Anyone who seeks aid or knowledge.

Surah Al-Inshirah

(1) Did We not expand for you, [O Muḥammad], your breast?[1850]

(2) And We removed from you your burden[1851]

(3) Which had weighed upon your back

(4) And raised high for you your repute.

(5) For indeed, with hardship [will be] ease [i.e., relief].

(6) Indeed, with hardship [will be] ease.

(7) So when you have finished [your duties], then stand up [for worship].

(8) And to your Lord direct [your] longing.

[1850] i.e., enlighten, assure and gladden your heart with guidance.

[1851] By forgiving any errors which you may have committed previously or might commit consequently. "Burden" can also refer to the anxiety experienced by the Prophet (ﷺ) at the beginning of his mission.

Surah At-Teen

(1) By the fig and the olive[1852]

(2) And [by] Mount Sinai

(3) And [by] this secure city [i.e., Makkah],

(4) We have certainly created man in the best of stature;[1853]

(5) Then We return him to the lowest of the low,[1854]

(6) Except for those who believe and do righteous deeds, for they will have a reward uninterrupted.

(7) So what yet causes you to deny the Recompense?[1855]

(8) Is not Allāh the most just of judges?

[1852] Referring to the places known for their production, i.e., Damascus and Jerusalem, respectively. It could also refer to the fig and olive trees or to the fruits themselves.
[1853] i.e., upright, symmetrical, and balanced in form and nature.
[1854] This can refer to the depths of Hell, to decrepit old age or to immorality.
[1855] More literally, "What makes you lie concerning it?"

Surah Al-`Alaq

(1) Recite in the name of your Lord who created

(2) Created man from a clinging substance.

(3) Recite, and your Lord is the most Generous -

(4) Who taught by the pen

(5) Taught man that which he knew not.

(6) No! [But] indeed, man transgresses

(7) Because he sees himself self-sufficient.

(8) Indeed, to your Lord is the return.

(9) Have you seen the one who forbids

(10) A servant when he prays?

(11) Have you seen if he is upon guidance

(12) Or enjoins righteousness?

(13) Have you seen if he denies and turns away -

(14) Does he not know that Allāh sees?

(15) No! If he does not desist, We will surely drag him by the forelock[1856]

(16) A lying, sinning forelock.

(17) Then let him call his associates;

(18) We will call the angels of Hell.[1857]

(19) No! Do not obey him. But prostrate and draw near [to Allāh].

[1856] It may also mean "slap him" or "blacken his face at the forelock."
[1857] Those who push the wicked into the Fire.

Surah Al-Qadr

(1) Indeed, We sent it [i.e., the Qur'ān] down during the Night of Decree.

(2) And what can make you know what is the Night of Decree?

(3) The Night of Decree is better than a thousand months.

(4) The angels and the Spirit [i.e., Gabriel] descend therein by permission of their Lord for every matter.[1858]

(5) Peace it is[1859] until the emergence of dawn.

[1858] Bringing the exact measures apportioned for everything by Allāh in the course of the coming year.
[1859] Upon the believers.

Surah Al-Bayyinah

(1) Those who disbelieved among the People of the Scripture and the polytheists were not to be parted [from misbelief][1860] until there came to them clear evidence

(2) A Messenger from Allāh, reciting purified[1861] scriptures

(3) Within which are correct writings [i.e., rulings and laws].

(4) Nor did those who were given the Scripture become divided[1862] until after there had come to them clear evidence.

(5) And they were not commanded except to worship Allāh, [being] sincere to Him in religion, inclining to truth, and to establish prayer and to give zakāh. And that is the correct religion.

(6) Indeed, they who disbelieved among the People of the Scripture and the polytheists will be in the fire of Hell, abiding eternally therein. Those are the worst of creatures.

(7) Indeed, they who have believed and done righteous deeds - those are the best of creatures.

(8) Their reward with their Lord will be gardens of perpetual residence beneath which rivers flow, wherein they will abide forever, Allāh being pleased with them and they with Him. That is for whoever has feared his Lord.

[1860] i.e., from their erroneous beliefs and superstitions.
[1861] i.e., containing no falsehood.
[1862] Into sects and denominations.

Surah Az-Zalzala

(1) When the earth is shaken with its [final] earthquake

(2) And the earth discharges its burdens[1863]

(3) And man says,[1864] "What is [wrong] with it?" -

(4) That Day, it will report its news

(5) Because your Lord has inspired [i.e., commanded] it.

(6) That Day, the people will depart[1865] separated [into categories] to be shown [the result of] their deeds.

(7) So whoever does an atom's weight[1866] of good will see it,

(8) And whoever does an atom's weight of evil will see it.

[1863] See verse 84:4

[1864] In terror and amazement.

[1865] From the place of Judgement to their final abode. Another interpretation is "emerge separately" (from the graves).

[1866] Or "the weight of a small ant."

Surah Al-Adiyat

(1) By the racers, panting,[1867]

(2) And the producers of sparks [when] striking[1868]

(3) And the chargers at dawn,[1869]

(4) Stirring up thereby [clouds of] dust,

(5) Arriving thereby in the center[1870] collectively,

(6) Indeed mankind, to his Lord, is ungrateful.

(7) And indeed, he is to that a witness.[1871]

(8) And indeed he is, in love of wealth, intense.

(9) But does he not know that when the contents of the graves are scattered

(10) And that within the breasts is obtained,[1872]

(11) Indeed, their Lord with them, that Day, is [fully] Aware.[1873]

[1867] i.e., the horses of those fighting for Allāh's cause as they race to attack the enemy.

[1868] Their hoofs while galloping over rocky terrain.

[1869] While the enemy is unaware.

[1870] i.e., penetrating into the enemy ranks during a surprise attack.

[1871] Through his speech and his actions.

[1872] i.e., when all secrets are made known.

[1873] Fully acquainted and familiar with everything about each one of them.

Surah al-Qari`ah

(1) The Striking Calamity -

(2) What is the Striking Calamity?

(3) And what can make you know what is the Striking Calamity?

(4) It is the Day when people will be like moths, dispersed,[1874]

(5) And the mountains will be like wool, fluffed up.[1875]

(6) Then as for one whose scales are heavy [with good deeds],

(7) He will be in a pleasant life.

(8) But as for one whose scales are light,

(9) His refuge[1876] will be an abyss.[1877]

(10) And what can make you know what that is?

(11) It is a Fire, intensely hot.

[1874] The people will be as such after having been expelled from their graves.
[1875] i.e., beginning to disintegrate.
[1876] "Literally, "mother" (a man's original refuge), which will envelop him as in an embrace.
[1877] i.e., the pit of Hellfire."

Surah At-Takathur

(1) Competition in [worldly] increase diverts you

(2) Until you visit the graveyards.[1878]

(3) No! You are going to know.

(4) Then, no! You are going to know.

(5) No! If you only knew with knowledge of certainty...[1879]

(6) You will surely see the Hellfire.

(7) Then you will surely see it with the eye of certainty.[1880]

(8) Then you will surely be asked that Day about pleasure.[1881]

Surah Al-Asr

(1) By time,[1882]

(2) Indeed, mankind is in loss,

(3) Except for those who have believed and done righteous deeds and advised each other to truth and advised each other to patience.

[1878] i.e., remain in them temporarily, meaning until the Day of Resurrection.
[1879] The conclusion of this verse is estimated to be "...you would not have been distracted from preparing for the Hereafter."
[1880] i.e., with actual eyesight.
[1881] i.e., the comforts of worldly life and whether you were grateful to Allāh for His blessings.
[1882] An oath in which Allāh swears by time throughout the ages.

Surah Al-Humazah

(1) Woe to every scorner and mocker

(2) Who collects wealth and [continuously] counts it.[1883]

(3) He thinks that his wealth will make him immortal.

(4) No! He will surely be thrown into the Crusher.[1884]

(5) And what can make you know what is the Crusher?

(6) It is the fire of Allāh, [eternally] fueled,

(7) Which mounts directed at the hearts.[1885]

(8) Indeed, it [i.e., Hellfire] will be closed down upon them

(9) In extended columns.[1886]

Surah Al-Feel

(1) Have you not considered, [O Muḥammad], how your Lord dealt with the companions of the elephant?[1887]

(2) Did He not make their plan into misguidance?[1888]

(3) And He sent against them birds in flocks,

(4) Striking them with stones of hard clay,

(5) And He made them like eaten straw.[1889]

[1883] Rather than spending in the way of Allāh.
[1884] i.e., Hellfire, which crushes and destroys all that enters it.
[1885] Covering them and penetrating them.
[1886] Interpreted to be either columns of fire or columns of iron to which are chained the inmates of Hell.
[1887] i.e., the army under the command of Abrahah al-Ashram which was accompanied by a huge elephant and came with the intention of destroying the Ka‘bah at Makkah.
[1888] Causing them to perish.
[1889] i.e., husks which have been chewed by cattle. This event took place in the year of the Prophet's birth.

Surah Al-Quraish

(1) For the accustomed security of the Quraysh[1890] -

(2) Their accustomed security [in] the caravan of winter and summer[1891] -

(3) Let them worship the Lord of this House,[1892]

(4) Who has fed them, [saving them] from hunger and made them safe, [saving them] from fear.

Surah Al-Maa'oun

(1) Have you seen the one who denies the Recompense?

(2) For that is the one who drives away the orphan

(3) And does not encourage the feeding of the poor.

(4) So woe to those who pray

(5) [But] who are heedless of their prayer[1893] -

(6) Those who make show [of their deeds]

(7) And withhold [simple] assistance.

[1890] i.e., the honor and reputation Allāh had given them as guardians of the Holy Ka'bah, which allowed them to travel without fear of being harmed.

[1891] i.e., the trading caravans that traveled south in winter and north in summer.

[1892] i.e., the Ka'bah.

[1893] i.e., the hypocrites who are unconcerned if they miss prayers when no one sees them.

Surah Al-Kawthar

(1) Indeed, We have granted you, [O Muḥammad], al-Kawthar.

(2) So pray to your Lord and offer sacrifice [to Him alone].

(3) Indeed, your enemy is the one cut off.[1894]

Surah Al-Kafiroun

(1) Say, "O disbelievers,

(2) I do not worship what you worship.

(3) Nor are you worshippers of what I worship.

(4) Nor will I be a worshipper of what you worship.

(5) Nor will you be worshippers of what I worship.

(6) For you is your religion, and for me is my religion."

[1894] From all good in this world and the Hereafter.

<h1 style="text-align:center">Surah An-Nasr</h1>

(1) When the victory of Allāh has come and the conquest,[1895]

(2) And you see the people entering into the religion of Allāh in multitudes,

(3) Then exalt [Him] with praise of your Lord and ask forgiveness of Him. Indeed, He is ever Accepting of Repentance.[1896]

<h1 style="text-align:center">Surah Al-Masad</h1>

(1) May the hands of Abū Lahab be ruined, and ruined is he.[1897]

(2) His wealth will not avail him or that which he gained.

(3) He will [enter to] burn in a Fire of [blazing] flame

(4) And his wife [as well] - the carrier of firewood.[1898]

(5) Around her neck is a rope of [twisted] fiber.

[1895] The conquest of Makkah.

[1896] Refer to footnote of 2:37

[1897] Abū Lahab (the Prophet's uncle), who was an enemy of Islām.

[1898] She used to put thorns in the Prophet's path and slander him (ﷺ). The word "firewood" was used by the Arabs to allude to slander and backbiting.

Surah Al-Ikhlas

(1) Say, "He is Allāh, [who is] One,[1899]

(2) Allāh, the Eternal Refuge.[1900]

(3) He neither begets nor is born,

(4) Nor is there to Him any equivalent."

Surah Al-Falaq

(1) Say, "I seek refuge in the Lord of daybreak

(2) From the evil of that which He created

(3) And from the evil of darkness when it settles

(4) And from the evil of the blowers in knots[1901]

(5) And from the evil of an envier when he envies."

[1899] Alone, without another, indivisible with absolute and permanent unity and distinct from all else. The one and only true deity, unique in His essence, attributes and deeds.

[1900] He who is absolute, perfect, complete, essential, self-sufficient and sufficient to meet the needs of all creation; the one eternally and constantly required and sought, depended upon by all existence and to whom all matters will ultimately return.

[1901] i.e., those who practice magic.

Surah An-Nas

(1) Say, "I seek refuge in the Lord of mankind,

(2) The Sovereign of mankind,

(3) The God of mankind,

(4) From the evil of the retreating whisperer[1902] -

(5) Who whispers [evil] into the breasts of mankind -

(6) From among the jinn and mankind".[1903]

[1902] i.e., a devil who makes evil suggestions to man but disappears when one remembers Allāh.

[1903] Evil prompters may be from men as well as from jinn.